Central and Eastern Europe

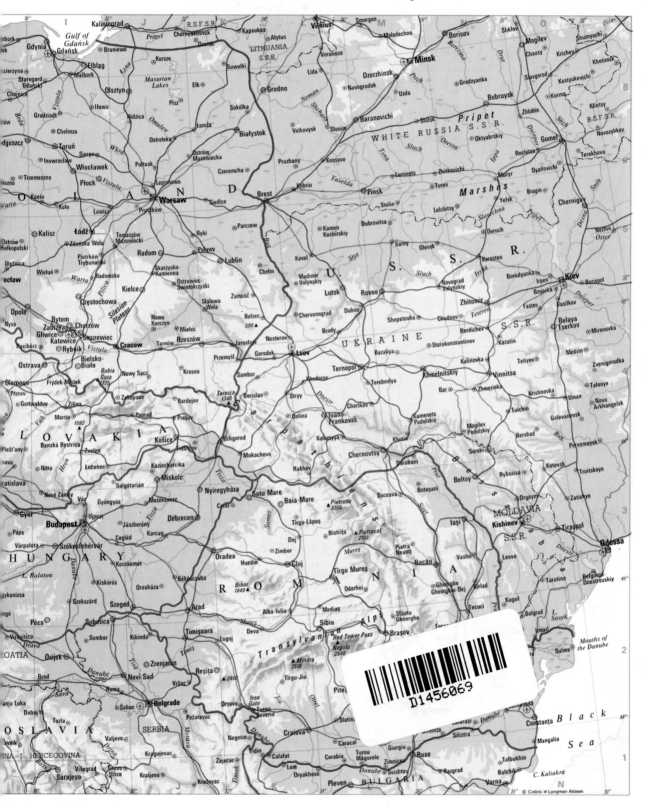

© Collins • Longman Atlases

The Balkans

Scale 1:5 250 000

0   50   100   150   200 km

Conic Projection

© Collins ◇ Longman Atlases

POLITICAL AND ECONOMIC ENCYCLOPAEDIA
OF THE SOVIET UNION AND EASTERN EUROPE

POLITICAL AND ECONOMIC ENCYCLOPAEDIA OF THE SOVIET UNION AND EASTERN EUROPE

Edited by
STEPHEN WHITE

With contributions by the following:

**Patrick Artesian (PA), Judy Batt (JB), Mary Buckley (MB),
Peter Duncan (PJSD), David Dyker (DAD), Raymond Hutchings (RH),
Paul G. Lewis (PGL), Jonathan Osmond (JO), James W. Riordan (JWR),
David Scrivener (DS), Mildred Turnbull (MT), Stephen White (SLW),
Gordon Wightman (GW), Robert Whitford (RW)**

ST. JAMES PRESS
CHICAGO AND LONDON

POLITICAL AND ECONOMIC ENCYCLOPAEDIA OF THE SOVIET UNION AND EASTERN
EUROPE

Published by Longman Group UK Limited, Westgate House,
The High, Harlow Essex, CM20 1YR, United Kingdom.
Telephone (0279) 442601
Telex 81491 Padlog
Facsimile (0279) 444501

DPA
DIRECTORY PUBLISHERS
ASSOCIATION

Published in the USA and Canada by St James Press,
233 East Ontario Street, Chicago 60611, Illinois, USA

ISBN 0-582-06036-2   (Longman)

1-55862-070-2 (St James)

British Library Cataloguing in Publication Data
Political and economic encyclopaedia of the Soviet Union and
    Eastern Europe.
    1. Eastern Europe. Social conditions
    I. White, Stephen, 1945–
    947
    ISBN 0-582-06036-2

INTRODUCTION

In contrast with the preceding publication in this series, whose subject area was the diverse Pacific region, the present volume deals with the countries of the USSR and Eastern Europe which have a remarkable unity. They are all European powers (in the case of the USSR, an Asiatic power as well). They are predominantly Slavic in their culture and their languages. They are again overwhelmingly Christian in their religious adherences. And perhaps most obviously, they constitute—or at any rate, constituted until recently—a coherent "family" of political systems, all of them based to varying degrees on Marxism-Leninism. Reflecting, particularly, the last of these circumstances, the USSR and all of the East European countries apart from Yugoslavia concluded a military alliance at Warsaw in 1955, extended in 1975 and again for 20 years in 1985, which formed the basis of the Warsaw Treaty Organization. The same countries were members of the Council for Mutual Economic Assistance (CMEA) or Comecon, established in 1949, whose objective was, according to its Charter, to "promote, by uniting and co-ordinating the efforts of the member countries, the further extension and improvement of co-operation and the development of socialist economic integration". The states concerned were defined, in official jargon, as the "socialist community"; the larger network of Communist-ruled states, including Cuba, China, Vietnam and Laos, was the "world socialist system".

A system of this kind was a relatively recent development in world politics. When World War I broke out there were no states under Communist rule; for many years after the Russian revolution there were only three, the USSR itself and the Asian outposts of Mongolia and Tuva (which was absorbed into the USSR in 1944); and at the end of World War II there were only five such states, Communists having come to power in Albania and Yugoslavia. By the 1960s, however, there were 14 states under Communist rule, and by the late 1970s there were 16, including Laos and Kampuchea in South-East Asia. These states shared a number of important similarities. They were based, first of all, on an official ideology, Marxism-Leninism, which justified their rulers' claim to exercise authority and could not legitimately be challenged. The states concerned also shared a largely publicly-owned economy and a system of central planning. They were ruled by a Communist or workers' party, within which power was highly centralized. And finally, all the parties concerned claimed to exercise a "leading role" within their respective societies, directing the arts, the media, sport and recreation just as much as they directed political life and the economy.

The Russian revolution of 1917 had been carried through on the assumption that these principles would swiftly extend to the developed capitalist countries, not simply the relatively backward countries of Eastern Europe and Asia. During the years immediately after World War I this did not seem to be an entirely unrealistic assumption, as Soviet republics were briefly established in Bavaria and Hungary and as factories were occupied in Italy and other countries. The Soviet republics, however, soon collapsed, right-wing governments came to power in much of Eastern Europe, and the USSR was left as an almost entirely isolated outpost of world socialism throughout the 1920s and 1930s. As World War II ended, with great loss of life on all sides but particularly in the USSR, the Soviet leaders had every reason to seek to construct a security zone in Eastern Europe made up of regimes in which they had a dominant influence. The post-war settlement, particularly at the Yalta conference in 1945, allowed them to do so.

The Communist takeover in Eastern Europe took a variety of forms. In some cases the Communists had little domestic support and the new administration was simply installed by the Red Army: this was the case in the GDR, Poland and Romania. In Bulgaria the Communist party had enjoyed a considerable degree of popular support, but the country had taken the Axis side during the war and it was occupied by the Red Army in 1944, with whose support a Communist government came to power two years later. In Czechoslovakia and Hungary, on the other hand, the Communist party did enjoy a substantial degree of popular support and the Red Army was seen by many as the agency that had liberated them from the Nazis. In Czechoslovakia the Communists secured 38 per cent of the vote, the largest for any single party, in the relatively free elections of 1946, while in Hungary the Communists became the largest single party after the rather less free elections of 1947. In both cases coalition governments were established in which Communists soon assumed a dominant position. In Yugoslavia and Albania a third route was followed: in these countries the Communists came to power at the head of an anti-Nazi guerrilla movement, and they accordingly enjoyed a greater degree of popular support than the governments that had been imported "in the baggage train of the Red Army".

Relations between the Communist states, over the decades, have been rather less amicable than a common dedication to working-class interests would have suggested. The first split occurred as early as 1948 when Yugoslavia was denounced by the Soviet Union and by Cominform (the Communist Information Bureau, established in 1947) for supposedly giving too much favour to the peasants at the expense of the working class and for indecisive leadership. In fact there seems no doubt that Stalin simply resented the independence the Yugoslav leaders were displaying and believed they could be brought to heel like national Communist leaders had been elsewhere in Eastern Europe. If so, he miscalculated badly; the Yugoslavs arrested Soviet supporters within the League of Communists, placed Soviet representatives in Yugoslavia under the surveillance of the secret police and weathered the storm with a largely united people behind them. In 1955 Khrushchev and Bulganin visited Belgrade and the following year a joint communiqué was signed which brought the dispute to an end on a basis that suited the Yugoslavs. In the same year there were serious disturbances in Poland and in Hungary, where an experiment in "liberal Communism" was brought to an end by the intervention of the Red Army. Some years later, in 1968, an attempt to establish "socialism with a human face" in Czechoslovakia was brought to an end by a Soviet-led invasion; and intervention also seemed likely in Poland in 1980–81, as Communist authority was challenged by the Solidarity trade union.

These developments notwithstanding, there could have been few who could have predicted the wave of political change that swept through the Soviet Union and Eastern Europe in the late 1980s, sweeping many of the countries concerned outside the Communist world entirely. The exercise of "people's power" began in Poland, where the crisis of authority between the Communist authorities and Solidarity had led to the imposition of martial law in December 1981. Although martial law had been suspended a year later, Solidarity was still, in January 1989, an outlawed organization. Round-table talks between government and opposition representatives, however, led to an agreement in April which provided (among other things) that Solidarity would be allowed to contest new and at least partly competitive elections. Under the arrangements, elections to the upper house of the Polish Parliament, the Senate, were to be entirely unrestricted, while in the lower house, the *Sejm*, only 35 per cent of the seats were to be freely chosen, the others being reserved for the Polish United Workers' (or Communist) Party, its two allied parties and several official Catholic organizations. In this way, it was thought, a Communist-dominated administration would be preserved.

In the event, the tactic badly misfired. In the elections, which took place in June 1989, Solidarity candidates won all of the 161 seats available to them in the *Sejm* and 99 of the 100 Senate seats. There was still further embarrassment for the authorities in that all but two of the candidates on a separate non-competitive list of national politicians failed to secure the 50 per cent vote that was necessary for their election. The former Communist leader, Wojciech Jaruzelski, was elected by a single vote to the newly created executive presidency, but attempts to form a Communist-led administration were unsuccessful and a coalition headed by Tadeusz Mazowiecki, the former editor of Solidarity's weekly paper who had been imprisoned under martial law, was eventually approved in September 1989. Mazowiecki was Eastern Europe's first non-Communist prime minister in 40 years; remarkably and perhaps decisively, the change appeared to occasion no particular concern in Moscow, where official spokesmen congratulated the new prime minister on his appointment and simply noted his willingness to respect Poland's international alliances. At the end of 1989 a parliamentary vote removed the "leading role" of the Communist party from the Polish constitution, and changed the name of the country from a "People's Republic" to the "Republic of Poland". The Polish party, demoralized and declining in membership, duly renamed itself the "Social Democracy of the Republic of Poland" in January 1990.

In Hungary the ruling Socialist Workers' Party had in fact been the first in Eastern Europe to renounce its leading role, early in 1989. At a party congress the following October the party formally dissolved itself and took the name of the Hungarian Socialist Party, under the mildly reformist leadership of Rezső Nyers. More radical reformist ideas emanated from Imre Pozsgay, a former minister of culture who became head of the Patriotic People's Front (a party-dominated umbrella organization) in the early 1980s and then minister of state responsible, in effect, for social and political reform. Poszgay openly embraced the idea of pluralist politics, including competitive elections and a governmental role for the variety of informal groups that were beginning to emerge in the late 1980s, the most important of which was the Hungarian Democratic Forum. Despite the more accommodating position adopted by the party authorities popular discontent continued to grow, focusing particularly on the treatment of the Hungarian minority in Romania and the environmental consequences of a planned dam on the Danube as well as on economic difficulties of a kind that were familiar elsewhere in the Communist world.

In January 1989 the National Assembly adopted a new law on associations which legalized political groups of various kinds, including (it appeared) independent political parties. In February the Hungarian Socialist Workers' Party went still further and committed itself to the reintroduction of multiparty politics. Discussions between the party authorities, the trade unions and the main informal groupings began in June 1989 with a view to agreeing the constitutional changes that would be necessary to convert Hungary into a functioning democracy. By the end of the year it had been agreed that there would be a new executive presidency, elected directly by the National Assembly, and that in advance of this there would be open elections in which all political forces would be able to compete. It was also agreed that Hungary should be simply a "Republic", not a "Socialist Republic", and a constitutional commitment was made to an "independent, democratic, legal state in which the values of bourgeois democracy and democratic socialism prevail in equal measure." In the elections, which took place in March 1990, the centre-right Hungarian Democratic Forum topped the poll; the liberal Alliance of Free Democrats came a close second, leaving the former Communist in fourth place with about one voter in ten.

The process of political change took still more dramatic forms in East Germany, Romania, Czechoslovakia and Bulgaria. The collapse of Communist rule in the GDR followed an astonishing mass exodus of East Germans, many of them young professionals and skilled workers, to West Germany through Hungary. In May 1989 the Hungarians had begun to demolish their section of the Iron Curtain along the border with Austria. First a few, and then thousands of East Germans took the opportunity to travel to Hungary, and thence to Austria and West Germany, where they enjoyed the automatic right of citizenship. The Hungarians, despite considerable pressure from the East German authorities, announced in September 1989 that for humanitarian reasons the border would remain open. Some 12,000 East Germans passed through in the first three days. Pressures for change in East Germany itself began to mount, encouraged by the Lutheran Church and by opposition groups which had formed a pressure group for change, New Forum. Attempts to restrict the flow of emigrants led to a rising tide of popular resistance during October 1989, culminating in the resignation of Erich Honecker, party leader since 1971, and his replacement by the long-standing "crown prince", Egon Krenz. Honecker was later placed under house arrest amid relevations of the corruption with which the former party leadership had been associated.

The demonstrations continued — in Leipzig, for instance, half a million protestors took to the streets — and a series of rapid concessions, including the reopening of the border with Czechoslovakia, proved insufficient to halt the movement for change. In November 1989, in an act with enormous symbolic significance for Eastern Europe as a whole, the Berlin Wall began to be demolished, allowing direct movement between the two Germanys for the first time since 1962. Despite these concessions Krenz was unable to establish his authority and a rising tide of discontent within and against the ruling Socialist Unity Party led to an emergency congress in December 1989 at which a new leader, Gregor Gysi, was chosen and the party changed its name to include the words "the Party of Democratic Socialism". Gysi was a lawyer of liberal credentials who had previously sought to legalize New Forum; another reform-minded Communist, the Dresden party secretary Hans Modrow, became prime minister. As elsewhere, the new leadership announced that competitive, multi-party elections would take place in 1990. At those elections, which took place in March, the conservative Christian Democratic Union was the clear winner with 41 per cent of the vote; the former Communists came third with just 16 per cent. The vote was in effect a mandate for the rapid reunification of the two Germanys, possibly within the framework of NATO.

The process of change in Czechoslovakia was also largely peaceful, although it began with police attacks on huge public demonstrations in November 1989. The demonstrations, the largest for 20 years, were led initially by students and increasingly involved the population as a whole. Just a week after the demonstrations had started, on Nov. 24, the Communist leader Miloš Jakeš and the whole of the Politburo resigned; four days later a parliamentary vote removed the party's leading role from the Czech constitution. The Czech government resigned on Dec. 7, and on Dec. 10 a largely non-Communist administration was formed, the first of its kind for 40 years. At the end of the month Alexander Dubček, leader of the 1968 reform movement, was elected chairman of the Czech parliament; the following day the popular playwright, Václav Havel, was sworn in as President. Havel's work had been banned for 20 years and the playwright himself, a leader of the oppositional Civic Forum group, had been arrested earlier in the year. There were, as elsewhere, to be competitive elections in 1990 at which all organized groupings would be free to compete; the Communist party, it was clear, would secure a very small minority of seats. Once again these changes appeared to be acceptable to the USSR, unlike the attempt to promote much more limited changes that had been suppressed in 1968.

Very few of the Communist-ruled nations, in fact, escaped the wave of political reform. In November 1989 there were mass demonstrations in Bulgaria led by an oppositional group, Eco-Glasnost, which led to the resignation of Todor Zhivkov, party leader since 1954. His successor, Petŭr Mladenov, renounced the Communist monopoly of power and promised to hold free, multi-party elections in 1990. As in most of the other countries, a variety of factors contributed to the change of regime: mistreatment of the Turkish minority within Bulgaria, economic difficulties, and increasing public concern with environmental issues. The Yugoslav party, the League of Communists, agreed at an emergency congress in January 1990 to renounce its constitutionally guaranteed leading role and to prepare the way for multi-party politics. The Albanian leader, Ramiz Alia, addressing his party's Central Committee in January 1990, ruled out the abandonment of socialist principles but accepted the need for some decentralization of economic management and a limited degree of electoral choice.

Most spectacular of all, however, was the overthrow of Nicolae Ceauşescu, party leader and virtual dictator of Romania since 1965. The fall of the regime began with demonstrations in the western (largely Hungarian) city of Timişoara on Dec. 17, which were crushed with exceptional ferocity; an estimated 4,000 may have died. The protest, nonetheless, spread to other towns and cities and to the capital Bucharest, where Ceauşescu, addressing a public rally on Dec. 21, found himself shouted down and almost entirely without public support. The following day Ceauşescu fled the capital but was arrested and brought to trial after fierce fighting had claimed many more lives. On Dec. 25 Ceauşescu and his wife were sentenced to death and executed; reports began to circulate at the same time of the extraordinary opulence in which the former dictator had lived, including a house crammed with art treatures and featuring a nuclear bunker lined with marble. The functions of government were performed by the National Salvation Council, a loose coalition within which there appeared to be a substantial Communist influence. Judicial processes continued against remaining members of the Ceauşescu family and governing circle; arrangements were also made for competitive elections in 1990 which, as elsewhere, would determine the future shape of the political system.

Developments of this kind were possible, to a very large extent, because the Soviet leadership under Mikhail Gorbachev appeared willing to replace the "Brezhnev doctrine" of limited sovereignty by what was humorously called the "Sinatra doctrine", meaning that individual East European states would be free to construct their political future in their own way. The Soviet leadership, indeed, appeared to regard the process of change in a broadly positive light, as corresponding with their own policies of *glasnost'* (openness) and *perestroika* (restructuring). Gorbachev, on his election as party leader in 1985, had pledged himself to continue the strategy of his predecessors, which he defined as "acceleration of socio-economic development and the perfection of all aspects of Soviet life". These relatively limited objectives soon gave way to a much more broadly conceived process of reform, embracing the political system and the economy as well as history, social life, the Soviet federation and international affairs. The early emphasis was upon economic reform, normally the first concern of Soviet and other Communist leaders. A strategy was mapped out at Central Committee meetings in 1986 and 1987 involving "radical reform" of the economy, including some decentralization of management decisions, a variety of forms of ownership and moves towards a "socialist market". At the same time the media, and cultural life generally, began to experience a greater degree of openness in the treatment of social issues such as drugs and prostitution as well as in the discussion of the Soviet past and the crimes of the Stalin period.

Political reform more particularly was launched at a Central Committee meeting in January 1987 at which the slogan of "democratization" was officially adopted. The electoral system, first of all, was reformed so as to permit a choice of candidates. Local elections, in 1987, saw a limited experiment along these lines, and then national elections, in 1989, saw three-quarters of all the seats available being competed for by party and non-party candidates. A working parliament was established, elected by a new national representative body, the Congress of People's Deputies; and in March 1990 a powerful new executive presidency was instituted.

The Communist Party held an extraordinary Conference in the summer of 1988 at which it agreed to democratize its own operations, including secret and competitive ballots for leading positions, which were themselves to be held for a limited period of time. More broadly, a vision began to be developed of a model of socialism that would be democratic and humanist, which would avoid the excesses of the past and allow the creative energies of ordinary people to express themselves much more freely than ever before. This would, it emerged, be a form of socialism that drew upon the experience of other nations, including capitalist ones, in its forms of political organization and economic life; and it would seek a solution to global issues through joint action with other members of the world community. This was certainly a distinctive vision, although it was far from clear, by the end of the 1980s, that it was a workable one. Its success or otherwise was in turn likely to determine whether the political changes that were taking place in the Communist world led back to capitalism or to a society that advanced on it by combining social equality with economic efficiency and political democracy.

The issues that are raised by the changes in the USSR and Eastern Europe can hardly be exhausted within the confines of a single volume; it is, in any case, still much too early to determine their larger significance. The contributors to this volume, a group of specialists with a close knowledge of the countries concerned, have nonetheless attempted to provide at least a large part of the economic and political background against which any judgements of this kind will have to be made. There are substantial articles on each of the countries of the USSR and Eastern Europe, covering their political and economic development with particular reference to the most recent period; and there are further entries covering a whole host of topics — parties and personalities, churches and political concepts, geographical units and the concerns of women, arms control and sport. In order to cover as much as possible of the rapid sequence of change in these countries we have covered developments up to March 31, 1990, and exceptionally beyond that date.

The main entries are in alphabetical sequence, with cross-references to other entries picked out in bold on their first occurrence within each entry; there is a detailed chronology of events, and an index of entries which also facilitates cross-referencing within each country. It remains only to thank Dr John Harper of Longman, for his constructive interest in all stages of the production of this book, and Nicola Greenwood, for her careful attention to the final manuscript.

Stephen White

The Publishers would like to thank Collins Longman Atlases for permission to reproduce the maps on the endpapers of this book, and CARPRESS International Press Agency for the maps of the Soviet Union, the Baltic Republics and the autonomous region of Nagorno-Karabakh, USSR, on p. x.

The USSR, showing the Republics

The Baltic Republics of the USSR

The autonomous region of Nagorno-Karabakh, USSR

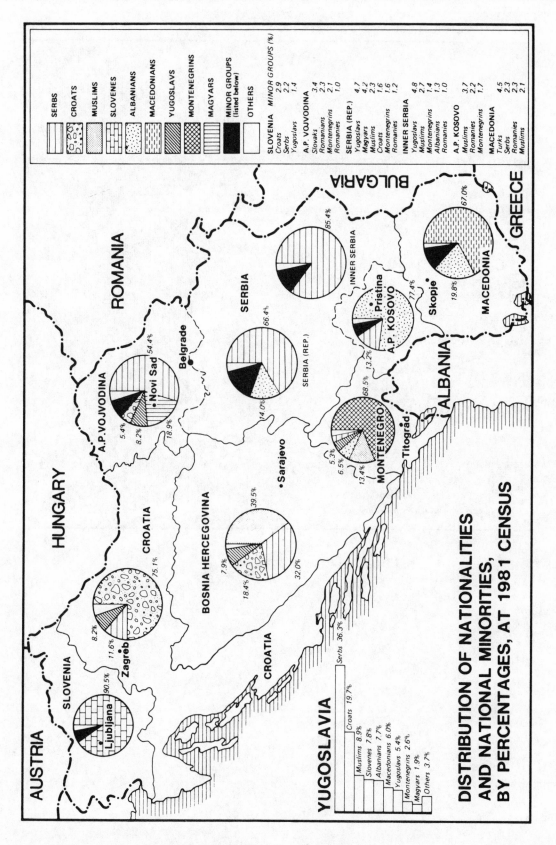

DISTRIBUTION OF NATIONALITIES AND NATIONAL MINORITIES, BY PERCENTAGES, AT 1981 CENSUS

Territorial changes in Eastern Europe following World War II

German territory annexed by USSR
German territory annexed by Poland
Polish territory annexed by USSR
Czechoslovakian territory annexed by USSR

CHRONOLOGICAL TABLE 1945–1990

1945

February	Yalta Conference
April	Death of Roosevelt; Truman becomes president
May	German Act of surrender
June	United Nations Charter signed
July – August	Potsdam Conference
August	Atomic bomb dropped on Hiroshima (Aug. 6)
	Atomic bomb dropped on Nagasaki (Aug. 9)
	Japanese surrender (Aug. 15)
September	Democratic Republic of Vietnam proclaimed by Ho Chi Minh
November	Communists win Bulgarian elections

1946

February	Kennan's Long Telegram
March	Churchill's Iron Curtain speech
	Soviet Union agrees to withdraw from Azerbaidzhan (withdrawal complete May 6)
April	Forced merger of Social Democratic Party with Communists in Soviet zone of Germany
May	Communists win 114 out of 300 seats in Czechoslovak parliamentary elections
July	Beginning of Civil War in China
July – October	21-nation Peace Conference in Paris
September	Burnes' Stuttgart speech on Germans having responsibility for running their own affairs and American troops in Germany
November	War in Indo-China begins

1947

January	United States and Britain establish Bizonia in Germany
	Communist-controlled elections in Poland
February	Peace Treaties signed with Italy, Romania, Bulgaria, Finland and Hungary
March	Truman Doctrine
May	Communists expelled from governments in France and Italy
June	Marshall's speech at Harvard opens prospect of Marshall Aid
June – July	Meeting in Paris of British, French and Soviet Foreign Ministers to consider Marshall Plan; Molotov walks out (July 2)
July	Conference of 16 European States in Paris to plan Marshall Aid; Committee on European Economic Co-operation set up
	Kennan's "Mr X" article published in *Foreign Affairs*
August	Defeat for Smallholders' Party in Hungarian elections
September	Petkov executed in Bulgaria
	Cominform established
October	Peasant Party dissolved in Romania
	Mikolaczyk flees Poland

December	King Michael of Romania abdicates

1948

February	Communist takeover in Czechoslovakia
	Social Democrats fused with Communists in Romania
March	Death of Jan Masaryk
	Soviet withdrawal from Allied Control Council in refusal of Western powers to account for London Conference
April	Organization of European Economic Co-operation set up in Paris
June	Social Democrats fused with Communists in Hungary
	Berlin blockade begins (June 24)
	Berlin airlift begins (June 25)
	Yugoslavia expelled from Cominform

1949

January	Comecon established
April	North Atlantic Treaty signed in Washington
May	Berlin blockade lifted (May 12)
July	Soviet atom bomb exploded
September	Trial and execution of Rajk and others in Hungary
October	Proclamation of People's Republic of China by Mao Zedong
	German Democratic Republic (East Germany) comes into being
November	Kostov repudiates his "confession" in Bulgaria show trial; convicted and executed

1950

February	Sino-Soviet Treaty of Friendship signed in Moscow
May	Idea of European Coal and Steel Community put forward by Robert Schuman, French Foreign Minister
June	Outbreak of Korean War
October	UN forces cross 38th parallel in Korea; China intervenes
December	Eisenhower appointed Supreme Allied Commander, Europe

1951

July	Three Western powers issue declaration formally terminating state of war with Germany
September	Japan Peace Treaty signed in San Francisco; China and the Soviet Union denounce its terms
	Western powers announce readiness to replace Occupation Statute by new relationship to enable West Germany to join European Defence Community (EDC)

1952

March	First of Soviet notes proposing German Peace Treaty upon basis of a withdrawal of foreign troops and a ban on entering military alliances
May	Bonn Agreement revoking Occupation Statute
	EDC Treaty signed in Paris

July	European Coal and Steel Community established
October	XIX Congress of the Soviet Communist Party (CPSU)
November	United States detonates H-bomb
	Eisenhower elected president
November – December	Trial and execution of Slansky and others in Czechoslovakia

1953

March	Death of Stalin
June	East Berlin uprising
July	Korean Armistice signed
	Imre Nagy replaces Rákosi as Hungarian prime minister, launches "New Course"
August	Soviet Union detonates H-bomb
September	Khrushchev becomes First Secretary of CPSU

1954

May	Fall of Dien Bien Phu
August	French Assembly refuses to ratify EDC Treaty
September	SEATO Treaty signed in Manila
	Khrushchev and Bulganin visit Beijing
October	Occupation of West Germany ended; West Germany and Italy accede to Brussels Treaty in West European Union

1955

February	Malenkov removed from Soviet leadership
March – April	Hungarian "New Course" reserved; Nagy removed from state and party position
May	West Germany joins NATO
	Warsaw Pact signed and joint command established
	Austrian State Treaty establishes Austria as a neutral state
	Khrushchev and Bulganin visit Yugoslavia
July	Summit Conference at Geneva
September	Adenauer visits Moscow; West Germany and the Soviet Union establish diplomatic relations
	Czech arms deal with Egypt
December	Khrushchev and Bulganin visit India, Burma and Afghanistan

1956

February	Khrushchev attacks Stalin and unveils peaceful coexistence at XX Congress of CPSU
April	Cominform dissolved
June	Riots in Poland; Gomułka returns to public life
July	Nationalization of the Suez Canal
October	Demonstrations in Budapest; Imre Nagy reappointed prime minister of Hungary
	Khrushchev leads Soviet delegation to Warsaw
November	Nagy renounces Warsaw pact, declares neutrality (Nov. 1)
	Soviet troops enter Budapest (Nov. 4)

1957

March	Rome Treaty on European Economic Community signed
June	Soviet "Anti-Party Group" ousted
August	First Soviet ICBM launched
October	Sputnik launched; Sino-Soviet secret atomic agreement
November	Conference of Communist Parties in Moscow; debates on revisionism and dogmatism; Mao Zedong speaks on prevailing wind and nuclear war

1958

March	Khrushchev replaces Bulganin as prime minister
May	Great Leap Forward begins in China
June	Imre Nagy executed
July	Khrushchev visits Beijing
November	Soviet Note on future status of Berlin
December	De Gaulle elected president of France

1959

January	Victory of Fidel Castro in Cuba
	XXI Congress of CPSU
February – March	Macmillan visits Moscow
June	Khrushchev renounces atomic agreement with China
September	Camp David meeting between Eisenhower and Khrushchev
	Khrushchev visits Beijing

1960

April	China attacks Khrushchev and Soviet Union in article entitled "Long Live Leninism"
May	U-2 shot down
	Paris summit breaks up
	Khrushchev issues new ultimatum over Berlin
June	Heated exchanges between Soviet and Chinese delegates at Congress of Romanian Communist Party in Bucharest
August	Soviet and East European technicians withdrawn from China
November	John F. Kennedy elected president of USA
	Summit meeting in Moscow of 81 Communist Parties; peaceful coexistence approved in face of strong Chinese opposition

1961

April	Bay of Pigs landing
June	Kennedy meets Khrushchev at Vienna summit
August	Berlin Wall put up
October	XXII CPSU Congress; Khrushchev attacks Albanian leadership
December	Albania severs relations with Soviet Union

1962

October – November	Cuban Missile Crisis

1963

June	China publishes 25-point indictment of Soviet Communist Party
	Hot Line agreement signed between USA and Soviet Union
August	Nuclear Test Ban Treaty signed by USA, Soviet Union and UK
September	West Germany opens trade mission in Poland
October	Romania and West Germany sign protocol establishing trade mission in Bucharest
November	Kennedy assassinated; Johnson becomes US president

1964

April	Central Committee of Romanian Communist party issues Declaration asserting equality of Communist parties
July	West Germany opens trade mission in Hungary
October	Khrushchev relieved of all posts; replaced by Brezhnev and Kosygin
	West Germany opens trade mission in Bulgaria

1956

February	Kosygin visits Beijing and Hanoi
	American bombing of North Vietnam begins

1966

March	XXIII CPSU Congress
April	Cultural Revolution begins in China
June	De Gaulle visits Moscow

1967

January	West Germany establishes diplomatic relations with Romania
April	Conference of European Communist Parties at Karlovy Vary in Czechoslovakia; agreement that no Eastern bloc country should open diplomatic relations with West Germany without prior agreement of East Germany
June	Six-Day War in Middle East
	Johnson meets Kosygin at Glassboro, New Jersey

1968

January	Dubček elected First Secretary of Czechoslovak Communist Party
March	Student demonstration in Poland suppressed
May	Vietnamese peace talks open in Paris; Johnson announces he will not stand in US presidential election
July	USA, Soviet Union and UK sign Non-Proliferation Treaty
August	Warsaw Pact invasion of Czechoslovakia
November	Nixon elected US president
	Brezhnev Doctrine of Limited Sovereignty

1969

March	Clashes on Sino-Soviet border at Damanski Island on Ussuri River
April	Dubček resigns as First Secretary of Czech Party; replaced by Gustáv Husák

September	West German elections; Brandt becomes Chancellor of SPD-FDP Coalition
October	Brandt announces readiness to negotiate with Soviet Union and Poland and declares need to establish dialogue with East Germany
November	West Germany signs Non-Proliferation Treaty

1970

March	Brandt meets Stoph, East German prime minister, at Erfurt in East Germany
April	SALT talks begin in Vienna
May	Second meeting between Brandt and Stoph at Kassel in West Germany
August	Soviet–West German Treaty of Non-Aggression signed in Moscow
November	Brandt visits Warsaw for signing of Polish–West German Treaty on renunciation of force and inviolability of frontiers
December	Riots at Gdańsk in Poland against food price increases; Edward Gierek replaces Gomułka as First Secretary of Polish Party

1971

March	XXIV Congress of CPSU
May	Erich Honecker replaces Ulbricht as First Secretary of East German Party
	Soviet Union signs Treaty of Friendship and Co-operation with Egypt
September	Quadripartite Agreement on Berlin (in force June 1972)
	Brandt visits Brezhnev in Soviet Union; agreement to work for Security Conference
October	People's Republic of China admitted to UN
December	Transit and Visitors' Traffic Agreements between East and West Germany (in force June 1972)

1972

May	West German *Bundestag* ratifies treaties with Soviet Union and Poland
	Nixon visits Moscow; SALT 1 Agreement and Declaration on Basic Principles of Soviet–American Relations
July	First round of European Security and Co-operation Talks in Helsinki
December	Basic Treaty signed between East and West Germany

1973

January	US–Vietnamese Armistice Agreement signed in Paris
June	Brezhnev visits Washington; agreement calling for prevention of nuclear war signed
July	President Sadat of Egypt expels Soviet advisers
September	East and West Germany admitted to UN
	US-backed coup overthrows Allende government in Chile
October	Arab-Israeli (Yom Kippur) War; American forces on nuclear alert
	Mutual Balanced Force Reduction (MNFR) Talks open in Vienna
December	Treaty between West Germany and Czechoslovakia annuls 1938 Munich agreement
	West Germany establishes diplomatic relations with Hungary and Bulgaria

1974

February	Alexander Solzhenitsyn expelled from Soviet Union

May	Brandt forced to resign over East German spy scandal; Helmut Schmidt becomes West German Chancellor
June	Nixon visits Moscow
July	Soviet Union signs Treaty of Friendship and Co-operation with Somalia
August	Culmination of Watergate scandal; Nixon resigns, replaced by Vice-President Gerald Ford
November	SALT 2 outline agreed by Brezhnev and Ford at Vladivostok
December	Trade Reform Bill approved in USA with Jackson-Vanik amendment (originally tabled December 1973) on Jewish emigration

1975

January	Soviet Union cancels 1972 Soviet-American trade agreement because of publicity given to emigration issue
April	Saigon capitulates and South Vietnam is taken over by North Vietnam
	Lon Nol's regime capitulates to *Khmer Rouge* in Cambodia
August	Final Act signed at Helsinki Conference on Security and Co-operation in Europe
	South African forces intervene in Angola
November	Angola achieves independence from Portugal; Cuban troops arrive in Angola in support of Agostino Neto's MPLA
December	Ford visits China
	Communist Pathet Lao takes over in Laos

1976

February	XXV Congress of CPSU
April	Deng Xiaoping removed from posts in China as a result of opposition conducted by Gang of Four
June	Strikes in Poland force government to withdraw food price rises
September	Death of Mao Zedong
October	Gang of Four arrested in China; Hua Guofeng becomes Party Chairman
	Soviet Union signs Treaty of Friendship and Co-operation with Angola
November	Carter elected US president

1977

February	Carter pledges support for promotion of human rights in Soviet Union in open letter to Andrei Sakharov; Brezhnev writes to Carter describing Sakharov as a "renegade who proclaimed himself an enemy of the Soviet State"
	Marxist coup in Ethiopia led by Lt. Col. Mengistu
March	Vance visits Moscow and proposes deep cuts in strategic weapons beyond levels agreed at Vladivostok in 1974; Russians reject
	Soviet Union signs Treaty of Friendship and Co-operation with Mozambique
March – June	Cuban troops support Katangan incursions into Shaba province of Zaïre
May	Cuban advisers arrive in Ethiopia
July	Rehabilitation of Deng Xiaoping in China
	Ogaden War between Ethiopia and Somalia; Cuban troops under Soviet command and Soviet arms tilt balance in favour of Ethiopia and are used to help Ethiopia suppress Eritrean separatist movement; Carter administration divided over appropriate response

October	Belgrade Security Conference to Review Helsinki agreements opens; ends six months later with little practical result
November	President Barre of Somalia tears up 1974 Treaty with Soviet Union and expels Soviet advisers

1978

April	People's Democratic Party of Afghanistan seizes power in military coup
June	Vietnam becomes member of Comecon
July	China breaks its alliance with Albania
August	Sino-Japanese Peace Treaty signed with "anti-hegemony clause"; Moscow denounces Treaty as a "threat to stability in Asia"
November	Soviet Union signs Treaties of Friendship and Co-operation with Ethiopia and Vietnam
December	Sino-American communiqué on normalization of relations Soviet Union signs Treaty of Friendship, Good Neighbourliness and Co-operation with Afghanistan Vietnam launches offensive into Cambodia

1979

January	Sino-American diplomatic relations established Deng Xiaoping visits United States and informs Carter of China's plans to teach Vietnam a lesson Shah of Iran forced into exile Guadeloupe Summit (Carter, Giscard, Schmidt, Callaghan) on modernization of NATO's IMF nuclear weapons
February	Culmination of Iranian Revolution; Ayatollah Khomeini returns to Tehran China launches attack on Vietnam
March	Revolution (New Jewel Movement) in Grenada Egyptian-Israeli Peace Treaty signed by Sadat and Begin in Washington China withdraws troops from Vietnam
April	Sino-Soviet Treaty of 1950 abrogated
May	Arrest of members of Charter 77 in Czechoslovakia
June	Summit between Brezhnev and Carter in Vienna; SALT 2 signed
July	Sandinistas overthrow Somoza in Nicaragua
November	Seizure of American embassy in Tehran; hostage crisis begins
December	NATO dual-track decision on deployment of cruise and Pershing by 1983 and negotiations as an alternative to deployment Soviet Union invades Afghanistan; Hafizullah Amin murdered in coup and replaced by Babrak Kamal

1980

January	Carter announces sanctions against Soviet Union and Carter Doctrine on Persian Gulf
February	Franco-German Summit in Paris of Afghan situation
April	Failure of mission to rescue hostages in Tehran; Vance resigns
May	Giscard d'Estaing meets Brezhnev in Warsaw
June	President Tito of Yugoslavia dies
July	American boycott of Moscow Olympics
August	Gdańsk Agreements on free trade unions in Poland; birth of Solidarity under Lech Wałęsa

September	Stanisław Kania replaces Edward Gierek as leader of Polish party
	Outbreak of Gulf War between Iran and Iraq
October	East Germany increases amount of currency to be exchanged by West German visitors and imposes four conditions for improvement of relations with Bonn
	Hua Guofeng resigns as premier in China; victory for Deng Xiaoping and further move away from Mao's legacy
November	Reagan elected US president
	Security Conference opens in Madrid
December	Brezhnev proposes Zone of Peace in Persian Gulf and Indian Ocean during visit to New Delhi

1981

January	Release of American hostages in Tehran
	Reagan, at his first press conference, claims detente has been a "one-way street" and accuses Russians of being cheats and liars
February	Wojciech Jaruzelski becomes prime minister of Poland
	Reagan administration claims to have evidence of "international communist conspiracy" in El Salvador
	XXVI Congress of CPSU
May	François Mitterrand becomes first post-war socialist president of France
July	Attack on party leadership at 9th Congress of Polish Party in Warsaw
October	Jaruzelski replaces Kania as party leader in Poland
November	INF talks begin in Geneva
	Reagan proposes "zero option" on INF weapons
	Soviet Union and West Germany sign gas pipeline contract
December	Martial Law declared in Poland; Wałęsa and other Solidarity leaders arrested
	Schmidt and Honecker say Poles have right to solve problems in their own way
	Reagan announces sanctions against Poland and Soviet Union; sanctions against Moscow include gas pipeline equipment but not grain

1982

June	START talks begin Geneva
	Reagan extends existing embargo on export of oil and gas equipment to Soviet Union to subsidiaries and licensees of American companies abroad
October	In West Germany, Schmidt forced from office as FDP defects and forms new coalition with CDU under Helmut Kohl
November	Death of Brezhnev; succeeded by Yuri Andropov
	Reagan lifts gas pipeline embargo
December	Martial law ended in Poland

1983

March	Elections in West Germany; CDU-FDP coalition continues (fierce-fought campaign over new NATO missiles)
	Reagan announces SDI
September	Soviet Union shoots down South Korean airliner

	Madrid Security Conference ends
October	American invasion of Granada
November	NATO begins deploying new missiles; Soviet delegations walk out of IMF and START talks; Honecker emphasizes need to limit damage

1984

January	Conference on Confidence and Security Building Measures and Disarmament in Europe opens in Stockholm
	Reagan visits China
February	Death of Andropov; succeeded by Konstantin Chernenko
July	Soviet and Eastern bloc boycott of Los Angeles Olympics (Romania takes part)
	West Germany loans DM 950 million to East Germany in return for further lifting of travel restrictions
August	Culmination of open split between East Berlin and Moscow on detente and East Germany's relations with West Germany; Honecker forced to cancel visit to birthplace in Federal Republic
October	Soviet Foreign Minister Gromyko meets Reagan in White House
November	Reagan elected for second term

1985

January	Meeting on arms control between Gromyko and Shultz in Geneva
March	Geneva arms talks resumed; umbrella approach on strategic weapons, INF weapons and space weapons
	Death of Chernenko; replaced by Mikhail Gorbachev
August	Gorbachev announces moratorium on Soviet nuclear testing; extended on three occasions to end of 1986
November	Reagan–Gorbachev summit at Geneva

1986

February	Corazon Aquino defeats Ferdinand Marcos in Philippines elections
	XXVII Congress of CPSU
April	American bombing raids in Libya
	Nuclear reactor explodes at Chernobyl in Soviet Union
June	Gorbachev proposes 30 per cent reductions in strategic weapons
	Reagan announces that by the end of the year the United States will not be bound by terms of SALT 2
July	Gorbachev's Vladivostok speech aimed at improving Sino-Soviet relations
August	American Senate approves Reagan's $100 million Contra aid request
September	Stockholm Security Conference ends with agreement on advance notice of military movements, presence of observers and verification
	Reagan offers not to deploy SDI weapons in space for seven years
October	Reagan–Gorbachev summit at Reykjavik collapses over SDI
December	Andrei Sakharov released from internal exile at Gorky
	Riots in Alma-Ata, USSR

1987

| *February* | At Moscow Peace Forum Gorbachev declares that no political objectives are worth the risk of nuclear war |

March	Gorbachev makes new proposals for INF agreement
September	Honecker visits West Germany
	Shevardnadze in Washington: agreement to dismantle INF weapons
October	13th Congress of Chinese Communist Party at Beijing: Deng Xiaoping and old guard stand down
November	Gorbachev's speech marking the 70th anniversary of the Bolshevik Revolution
	General Jaruzelski fails to win majority support for his economic and political reforms in Polish referendum
December	Jakeš replaces Husák as Czechoslovak party leader
	INF Treaty signed at Reagan–Gorbachev summit in Washington

1988

February	Ethnic conflict develops between Armenia and Azerbaidzhan over disputed enclave of Nagorno-Karabakh
	USSR Surpreme Court annuls sentence on Nikolai Bukharin
February – March	Demonstrations in Estonia, Latvia and Lithuania against 1939 Nazi-Soviet pact
April	International agreements in Geneva provide for USSR withdrawal from Afghanistan by February 1989
April – May	Polish strikes demand pay rises and legalization of Solidarity
May	Károly Grósz elected to replace Kádár as Hungarian party leader
	US–Soviet summit in Moscow
June	USSR Supreme Court annuls sentence on Zinoviev, Kamenev and Radek
June – July	XIX CPSU Party Conference in Moscow endorses proposals for political reform
September	Resignation of Polish prime minister Zbigniew Messmer; succeeded by Mieczysław Rakowski
	State of emergency declared in Nagorno-Karabakh
October	Mikhail Gorbachev elected chairman of the Presidium of the USSR Supreme Soviet
	Ladislav Adamec succeeds Lubomir Strougal as prime minister of Czechoslovakia
November	Miklós Németh appointed Hungarian prime minister
	CPSU Central Committee approves constitutional changes; passed into law by USSR Supreme Soviet on Dec. 1
December	Gorbachev address to United Nations
	Armenian earthquake centred on Spitak
	Resignation of Yugoslav prime minister Branko Mikulić after failing to carry budget

1989

January	Ante Marković appointed prime minister of Yugoslavia
	George Bush sworn in as new US President
	A leading member of the ruling party in Hungary repudiates the "counter-revolution" label previously applied to the 1956 uprising
February	Polish government opens talks with Solidarity
	USSR completes withdrawal from Afghanistan
	Václav Havel jailed for nine months in Czechoslovakia

March	National and largely competitive elections to the USSR Congress of People's Deputies; many officials defeated
April	Round table talks in Poland reach agreement on Solidarity's relegalization and political reforms including partially competitive elections
	Demonstrations in Georgia lead to 19 deaths
May	Hungary begins dismantling the fences along its Austrian border
June	Suppression of student demonstrations in Peking
	Polish elections produce victory for Solidarity in all but one of the freely contested seats
	Reburial of Imre Nagy in Budapest
July	Miners' strikes in the USSR
	Wojciech Jaruzelski elected President of Poland by a single vote
August	Tadeusz Mazowiecki of Solidarity becomes prime minister of Poland
	Czechoslovakian demonstrations to mark 21 years since crushing of Prague Spring
	Two million form human chain across Estonia, Latvia and Lithuania to protest at fiftieth anniversary of Nazi-Soviet Pact
September	Hungary lifts border restrictions for visitors from the GDR, swelling the flow of East Germans escaping to West Germany through the open border with Austria
	Solidarity dominates new coalition government formed in Poland
October	More escapees from the GDR are allowed passage to the West after taking refuge in West German embassies in Prague and Warsaw
	Reformists in Hungary's ruling Socialist Workers' Party secure its reconstitution as a Socialist Party
	The exodus of citizens and a wave of pro-democracy demonstrations throughout the GDR prompt the resignation of Erich Honecker as President and head of the ruling Socialist Unity Party; replaced by Egon Krenz
	Following approval by parliament of a multiparty system and free elections for 1990, Hungary is declared a republic on the anniversary of the 1956 uprising
	Warsaw Treaty Organization confirms abandonment of "Brezhnev doctrine"
	Eco-Glasnost demonstration crushed in Bulgaria
November	Amid a continuing wave of street protests, the authorities in the GDR unexpectedly abolish travel restrictions. Jubilation greets the breach of the Berlin Wall and in the next two days over four million East Germans visit the West
	Reformists oust Todor Zhivkov as President and party leader in Bulgaria
	New administration formed in the GDR under premiership of Hans Modrow; nearly half its members are non-Communists
	Massive street demonstrations in Czechoslovakia lead to the resignation of party leader Miloš Jakeš, to dialogue between the authorities and the opposition group Civic Forum, and to the abolition of the Communist Party's constitutionally guaranteed leading role
	Chancellor Kohl of West Germany visits the GDR and speaks of unification
December	Gorbachev meets the Pope in the Vatican, followed by a first "informal" summit meeting off the coast of Malta with George Bush
	1968 WTO intervention in that country condemned by Czechoslovakian Communist Party leadership
	Abolition of the SED's constitutional guaranteed leading role in the GDR

A new coalition government is formed in Czechoslovakia with a majority of non-Communist ministers

Communist Party in Bulgaria renounces constitutionally guaranteed leading role and calls free elections for June 1990

Resignation of Egon Krenz as East German party leader; replaced by Gregor Gysi and party renamed "Socialist Unity Party — Party of Democratic Socialism"

In the wake of the violent suppression of demonstrations in Timişoara, western Romania, protesters in Bucharest storm the Communist Party headquarters and overthrow Nicolae Ceauşescu; a broadly-based National Salvation Front takes power; Ceauşescu and his wife are executed

In Czechoslovakia the former reformist leader Alexander Dubček is named parliamentary Speaker, and the playwright and former dissident Václav Havel is sworn in as president

Lithuanian Communist Party declares itself independent of the CPSU

1990

January	Intercommunal riots in Azerbaidzhan ended by Soviet military
	14th Congress of League of Communists of Yugoslavia agrees to abolish constitutionally guaranteed leading role; Congress indefinitely adjourned after Slovene walkout
	Bulgarian National Assembly repeals constitutional guaranteed leading role of Bulgarian Communist Party
	11th Congress of Polish United Workers' Party; party reconstituted as Social Democracy of the Republic of Poland
	14th Congress of Bulgarian Communists Party; new programme and statute adopted
February	Central Committee of CPSU resolve to abandon constitutionally guaranteed leading role
	Council of National Unity formed in Romania following round table talks; to govern the country until multiparty elections later in the year
	Slovene League of Communists renounced links with the League of Communists of Yugoslavia; renamed the LCS—Party of Democratic Renewal
March	Elections in the GDR lead to formation of a predominantly Christian Democratic administration; Party of Democratic Socialism (formerly Communist party) in third place
	Following successes for the nationalist *Sajudis* movement in republican elections, Lithuania declares itself independent of the USSR
	USSR Congress of People's Deputies removes constitutionally guaranteed leading role of CPSU from Article 6 of the Constitution, and establishes powerful executive presidency
	Republican and local elections in RSFSR, Ukraine and Belorussia
March – April	Multiparty elections in Hungary, held in two rounds, lead to the formation of a coalition government dominated by the Hungarian Democratic Forum; Socialist (formerly Communist) Party in fourth place

A

ADAMEC, LADISLAV. Elected Chairman of the **Communist Party of Czechoslovakia** at an extraordinary congress held on Dec. 20, 1989, Adamec, who was born in 1926, spent a long time close to the centre of power before his elevation to the Party Presidium in March 1987. He was head of the Industry Department of the Party Central Committee from 1963 until his appointment as a Deputy Prime Minister in the Government of the Czech Socialist Republic in 1969. His inclusion in the Presidium followed his promotion to the post of Czech Prime Minister, which also brought him a Deputy Premiership in the Federal Government. He was thus well placed to take over as Federal Prime Minister when Lubomír Štrougal was forced to resign from that post in October 1988. During what proved to be a short period as head of government, Adamec made clear his commitment to economic reform and a modernization of Czechoslovak industry and later claimed to have unsuccessfully pressed his colleagues to adopt more wide-ranging reforms. Following the pro-democracy demonstrations in November 1989 he resigned from the Party Presidium, but stayed on as Prime Minister unitl Dec. 7 in what proved to be an abortive attempt to reach agreement on the composition of a coalition government with the opposition **Civic Forum**. His election as chairman revived a post which was abolished in the mid-1920s and resuscitated only for a short period between 1945 and 1953 when it was held by Klement **Gottwald**.

GW

ALBANIA. *Population*: 3,182,417 (1989). *Area*: 29,748 sq m. *Five main trading partners*: Italy, Federal Republic of Germany, Austria, France, Greece. *Urban population as percentage of total*: 35.5 (1989). *Birth rate*: 26 per thousand (1983). *Life expectancy*: males 67.9; females 72.9 (1982-83)

The Albanian population is on average very young, the average age being 26 years, and half the population is under 15. Families are typically large, those having five to seven members comprising, in 1979, 42.3 per cent of the total number of families. This is due to tradition and to the non-availability in ordinary circumstances of contraceptives. Some tendency has recently appeared for urban dwellers to have smaller families. The urban proportion rises only very slowly, state policy being to discourage migration.

Around 77 per cent of Albania is hilly or mountainous, the average elevation being over 670 m, which is about twice the European average. The country is well watered, 13 rivers having a length within Albania exceeding 100 km; precipitation is adequate, though mainly in winter and much greater in the northern alps than in the plains. Albania had land frontiers with Yugoslavia and Greece and a coastline (470 km in length) along the Adriatic Sea. The country is divided into 26 districts, the largest in area being Shkodër and Korçë. The capital is **Tirana**.

Albania is a one-party state, governed by the Party of Labour of Albania, (PLA), which is the successor to the Albanian Communist Party (founded Nov. 8, 1941). The PLA is a Communist Party in everything except name (which was adopted in 1948), and more wholeheartedly than most. In 1976 the country adopted the name of the People's Socialist Republic of Albania. The party first secretary and chairman of the Praesidium of the People's Assembly, i.e. the state president) is Ramiz **Alia**, who succeeded Enver **Hoxha** when the latter died on April 11, 1985. Party membership in 1981 was 123,000. The Politburo has 13 members including (apart from Ramiz Alia) the prime minister (Adil Çarçani), three deputy prime ministers, the ministers of internal affairs, industry and mining, and defence, and six other persons. Hoxha's widow Nexhmije heads the Democratic Front, which is the country's mass political organization. Other public bodies, all being under the control of the PLA, also exist.

History. Albanians are one of the most ancient races in Europe if (as is almost certain) they are descendants of the ancient Illyrians. Subsequent admixtures do not prevent the Albanian physical type from being obviously slimmer and narrower than the Serb one. During the seventh and eighth centuries the Illyrians were gradually compressed into the mainly mountainous strip, comprising the hinterland of the Strait of Otranto, which is modern Albania. Southern Albania (northern Epirus) was colonized by Greeks who have left archaeological remains. A Greek legacy of cultural oppression also stayed but since 1400 Albanian history has been dominated by Ottoman occupation which ended only in 1912, making Albania the last of the Balkan countries to be liberated. Scanderbeg, the Albanian national hero, led a revolt against the Turks in the third quarter of the fifteenth century. Following its eventual failure in the face of overwhelming odds some thousands of Albanians fled to southern Italy, where their descendants still live. Though Ottoman occupation was a misfortune for the Albanians, it would be more correct to describe this as a love-hate relationship. Ultimately, due mainly but not entirely to economic pressures, a majority of Albanians converted to Islam and some among them became the Sultan's most loyal troops. The northern clans, secure in their remote fastnesses, paid only nominal allegiance to the Porte and regulated their affairs primarily by the canons of *Lek Dukagjin*, a system of traditional laws of medieval origin. Many Turkish words passed into Albanian. At least 21 grand viziers of the Ottoman Empire were of Albanian origin, as was the royal house of Mahomet Ali in Egypt. Governors of the Albanian provinces often asserted virtual independence, though Ali Pasha paid ultimately with his head for doing so (1821). Islam as professed in Albania was especially the liberal Bektashi sect, and conflicts based on religion alone did not take place (there were sufficient other bases, however). Modern Albanians admit that the conversion to Islam delayed the nation's independence, but on the other hand contend that without it, their own identity would have been submerged.

Albanian independence began to be mooted in the nineteenth century. Individual citizens such as Lord Byron played some role in bringing the country to international notice, at a time when statesmen (notably Bismarck) were inclined to deny any existence of Albanian nationality. The Treaty of Berlin (1878) assigned a strip of northern Albania to Serbia but the local clans frustrated this intention. This Treaty instigated too the emergence of the League of Prizren—the chief event in the mobilization of Albanian nationalism. The League in 1880 declared itself a provisional government of Albania, but without lasting result. Independent Albania was proclaimed in 1912, mainly through the support of Austria-Hungary which wished to prevent Serbia from gaining access to the Adriatic, and a German, Prince William of Wied, was chosen by the Powers as its head of state. However, little could be achieved before the Great War during which various parts of Albania were occupied by foreign armies while by the secret Treaty of London (1915) the country was to be partitioned among Italy and Greece. However, the Treaty of Versailles upheld Albanian independence and Italian troops at Vlorë were ejected by the Albanians themselves.

Post-war Albania experienced a time of troubles but then a democratic government under the American-educated Fan Noli took over and enacted some liberal and overdue reforms. This government was overthrown by Zog who as King (1928 onwards) reigned until 1939 when Albania was invaded and occupied by Italy. Resistance was minimal, and King Zog fled. A puppet Albania, but enlarged through the addition of Albanian-settled parts of Yugoslavia following that country's defeat, was brought into the war on the Axis side. Italian rule was replaced by German (1943) but the following year, as the culmination of successful resistance operations led by Mehmet Shehu and Enver Hoxha, Albania was reborn as a Communist state (Nov. 29, 1944).

The subsequent political history of Albania cannot be written with assurance owing to gaps in the available information. Until his death the ruling party was dominated by Enver Hoxha. During most of the period until 1981 his long-term associate as prime minister was the former military chief, Mehmet Shehu. In December 1981 Shehu was liquidated. This was first stated to be suicide but later Shehu was accused of having been an agent of the Soviet, US and Yugoslav secret services, an unbelievable allegation. On the contrary after Shehu's death, and even before Hoxha's, Albania was starting to take tentative steps to emerge from her self-imposed isolation. That isolation remains intense yet it is now visibly relaxing. The attitude to foreign tourists has become more liberal, though mass tourism remains banned. Though internal reforms have in general not been enacted, foreign policy is opening up (see below). Ramiz Alia, who had clearly been envisaged as Hoxha's successor following Shehu's liquidation, took over the reins of power smoothly from Hoxha although he could not imitate his charisma. Statues of Hoxha have been erected in many cities and—as one concession to improved living—Tirana's central square is now adorned with illuminated fountains. However, the political system, which consistently, and of course fallaciously, records over 99.99 per cent in favour of the regime at general elections remains unchanged.

Recent political developments. The death in 1985 of Enver Hoxha, the dominant figure in post-war Albanian politics, prompted questions about the changes which his successor, Ramiz Alia, might introduce. Although Alia is not proposing an Albanian *glasnost'*, he has nonetheless relaxed some of the more austere features of his authoritarian regime. On taking office, he declared a partial amnesty for political prisoners, and foreign visitors to Albania are no longer made to conform to prescribed dress styles. He has also committed more resources to the consumer goods sector and introduced material incentives in industry and farming in an attempt to boost productivity.

Alia also realizes that he has to satisfy the aspirations of a young population increasingly exposed to a more sophisticated outside world via Italian and Yugoslav radio and television. He is clearly concerned that the gap between the population's expectations and reality and the current of democratization in Eastern Europe might increase the gulf between the PLA and society. In his speech at the eighth plenum of the Central Committee of the PLA, Alia blamed the "spread of modern revisionism" in the Soviet Union and Eastern Europe on numerous defects in those societies, but in particular on the ossified role of the masses in the management of those countries. This in turn illustrated the growth of social pressure from within Albanian society towards a more responsive style of government.

Although Alia declared that Albania would continue to oppose a return to private property and capitalism and resist the temptation of foreign credits (forbidden in the constitution), or permit the weakening of the leading role of the party, it is likely that his hawkish stance was aimed at placating the conservative survivors of the Hoxha leadership, in particular Hoxha's widow, Nexhmije, who was elected in 1986 Chairman of the Democratic Front of Albania. One of Alia's priorities in the 1990s will be to learn from mistakes in the Soviet Union and Eastern Europe where the growth of the bureaucracy and careerism and corruption within party ranks alienated the population at large.

Whether Alia succeeds in implementing modest reforms in the electoral system, including the possibility of more than one candidate running for party posts, and limiting the tenure of office for officials to five years, will depend on a number of variables: and first of all, his depth of perception of Albania's changing environment. Here his dilemma is that, on the one hand, throwing off four decades of Stalinist tradition under Hoxha at a stroke might jeopardize his position *vis à vis* the conservative bureaucracy and the army. On the other hand, Alia does not have the charismatic influence of his predecessor to justify to Europe's youngest population that continued Stalinist isolation and further economic sacrifices (Albania already has the lowest living standards in Europe) are essential to the country's future. Alia's room for manoeuvre will also depend on his ability to consolidate further his power base within the party. Soon after taking office as party leader he succeeded at the Ninth Congress of the PLA in promoting three candidate members (Çami, Murra and Bekteshi) to full membership of the Politburo (thus increasing the number of full members from 10 to 13), and in appointing three new candidate members. This indicates that he has surrounded himself with trusted colleagues who were carefully groomed under Hoxha's rule and do not pose a serious challenge to his leadership.

Following the election of a new People's Assembly in 1987, Ramiz Alia was also re-elected Chairman of its Presidium. Adil Çarçani was reappointed Chairman of the Council of Ministers, and the number of Deputy Chairmen was increased from three to four. The Ministry of Light and Foodstuff Industry was divided into two separate Ministries, and a State Control Commission was established at ministerial level. Finally, the pace of political reform in Albania may be determined by forces outside the party's control: mounting pressures both from within and outside may bring Albania in line with the democratization processes elsewhere in Eastern Europe.

Religion and atheism. All religious practices were outlawed in Albania in 1967. Mosques, churches and other religious buildings were closed and many mosques, in particular, have been demolished; others are turned over to different purposes, for instance as museums. Religion thus appears to be extinct, but probably continues to influence such matters as the small amount of pigkeeping. The Albanian rulers saw religion as divisive, since although a plurality of the population eventually converted to **Islam** there remained large minorities of Orthodox and Roman Catholic (respectively mainly in the south and the north); Islam also held back female emancipation. The first steps to limit religious practices were taken under King **Zog**. However, religious differences were not held as fanatically as in some other countries (for example, Yugoslavia); among the northern clans, customs based on religion tended to take second place to the code of *Lek Dukagjin*. The Albanian party still takes very seriously the propagation of atheism, but religious art is included among foreign tourist attractions.

Economy. This is of the Stalinist type, being centrally planned with virtually all means of production state- or co-operative-owned. However, the setting differs from the Soviet one: the country is far smaller, the economy had a more backward starting point, its production assortment is much simpler, there is less opportunity to become self-sufficient. As compared with the Soviet classical model, this has resulted in important policy differences. Incomes are much more egalitarian in Albania, which helps to mitigate the very low living standards. Nevertheless these, together with Romania's, are probably Europe's lowest. Growth policy has emphasized agriculture almost as much as (recently more than) industry, which is needed given the high population growth. Electrification has been emphasized. Albania, like the USSR, has emphasized heavy industry, in particular by building a steel works and engineering plants, but unlike the USSR there is special emphasis in Albania on producing spare parts. Prices are centrally fixed and remain unchanged over long periods, though cuts in retail prices are announced occasionally.

The same distortions tend to occur in the Albanian system as in the classic Soviet one: shortages of consumer goods, particularly simple types; unbalanced growth; repressed inflation; poor quality. The typical vices of a centralized system are less marked in Albania because the system is so much smaller and simpler, and at a more primitive stage. Albania still makes much use of all-out drives (in cleaning drainage ditches, clearing up, construction for a particular purpose) by all adults or by young people especially. In the short run these campaigns improve performance though at the cost of reducing leisure hours.

The economy is mainly regulated by ministries headquartered in Tirana, but also to a substantial extent on a district basis. For example, this is true of motor transport. The rail network, which enters or traverses 12 of the districts, transports about 50 per cent of freight measured by tonnes/km, but probably not more than 10 per cent reckoned by weight alone. Its construction has not reinforced centralizing tendencies as the network focuses on Durrës (the chief port) rather than the capital. The high percentage of the rural population also militates against extreme administrative centralization. On the other hand, Tirana's predominance is assisted by the fact that it is the educational and cultural capital as well as the economic and political one.

The economy is characterized by a very backward starting point and by mainly quite rapid but unbalanced growth. In the long run the tempo has fallen but there have been marked fluctuations. According to official statistics, average annual rates of growth of industry in successive five-year periods have been: 1955–60, 16.9 per cent; 1961–65, 6.8 per cent; 1966–70, 12.9 per cent; the drop in the middle period resulted from an abrupt cessation of Soviet bloc aid after 1960. In 1971–75 the tempo again fell, much more markedly in producer goods than in consumer goods. In 1976–80 the growth rate of producers goods remained much the same but that of consumer goods declined sharply. The latest complete five-year period, 1980–85, is not adequately

illuminated but growth appears to have fallen short of plan. During the current Five-Year Plan (1986–90) information is even more fragmentary: growth rates of producer goods may have continued to be about the same but are very low, of consumer goods also low: according to the 1989 plan, growth rates of industrial output were to be 6.8 per cent and of agricultural output 16.9 per cent, but it is often the case that Albanian economic plans are nowhere near fulfilled. Statistics are very sparse; the economy does however appear to suffer from serious problems, which in particular centre round agricultural performance and food supply (see below). In February 1989 the President warned of "serious repercussions" if agricultural supply did not improve and he proposed an enlargement of investment in agriculture, importation of wheeled tractors and other farm vehicles, and measures of reorganization. The fundamental problem is Albania's high rate of population growth (at least 2.0 per cent per annum, the highest in Europe), which cannot be matched by the growth of food output.

Mining. For its size Albania is rich in minerals, both metallic and non-metallic. Oil, natural gas, bitumen, lignite, ferronickel, chrome ore and copper are the chief ones. There is also phosphorite, dolomite etc. Albania is the world's third largest producer of chrome ore and consequently a significant exporter though the ore is of poor quality. Ferronickel is processed by the Elbasan Steel Combine, Albania's largest industrial undertaking, while copper wire is another important export. Oil is extracted for Albania's own needs and for export, the main oilfields being in Fier district (Patos, Ballsh) and Berat district (Qyteti Stalin); also in Vlorë district. The oil is viscous and its output seems to be static or declining, although recent statistics have not been released. Ferronickel comes from Librazhd and Pogradec districts, lignite from Tirana, Korçë, Tepelenë and Kolonjë districts. Other valuable minerals are found chiefly in the mountainous north-east of the country. The Myzeqe plain and the southernmost region (Gjirokastër and Sarandë districts) are not rich in minerals though prospecting continues.

Agriculture. This is almost completely socialized. Private plots, attached to individual homes, amount to only 200 sq m apiece but are thoroughly cultivated, growing mainly food crops. There being no counterpart to the Soviet-type collective farm market (where individual peasants can sell their surpluses), any sales of private produce are disorganized, and in part clandestine. The individual plots are invisible in official statistics, which claim 100 per cent socialization. This result is claimed to have been reached in 1967. The socialized sector of agriculture consists partly of state farms, or as they are termed "agricultural undertakings" (*ndërmarrje bujgësore*, or NB). Thus what proportion of the total cultivated area is socialized is not quoted, but may be about 99 per cent of the territory of co-operatives and about the same of the territory of co-operatives and agricultural enterprises together. Curiously, the number of agricultural enterprises is also not given, but appears to be about 25; the average area of such an enterprise being about 3.5 times that of an agricultural co-operative. The number of co-operatives is 421 (1983) but these are of two types: ordinary ones, then numbering 374, and "higher type" co-operatives, which then numbered 47. The distinction between these two is that "higher type" co-operatives receive state financed investments, which ordinary co-operatives do not.

The share of the co-operative sector, in this case *including* the contribution of individual plots, in total agricultural production was 73.6 per cent in 1983, having declined from 78.1 per cent in 1970. The number of co-operative families was 269,708 in 1983 and the total area cultivated by co-operatives 556,400 ha, out of a total of 709,800 ha. While agricultural enterprises manage their own machinery, co-operatives are served by machine tractor stations (the classic Soviet formula).

Cultivated land comprises fields, orchards, olive-groves and vineyards. The proportion consisting of fields, 82.9 per cent in 1983, has tended to decline as collectivization proceeded and with the progress of terracing of land. In 1983, 50.4 per cent of the cultivated land was producing bread grains; 10.2 per cent vegetables and potatoes; 17.5 per cent, industrial crops; 22.0 per cent, fodder and other. By comparison with 1938, the most striking difference is the reduction in the share of bread grains (83.5 per cent in 1938); within this total, wheat has displaced maize. The area under cultivation has increased by 2.4 times since 1938, thanks to the ploughing up of new lands, drainage of marches, desalination, irrigation and terracing. Investments have also been made in glasshouses, imported from Holland. Since 1985 congenital problems have been aggravated by frequent droughts. Total agricultural output is rising only very slowly: in all by 10.1 per cent between 1979–81 and 1987, according to authoritative Western estimates.

Recent economic trends. The needs for reforms leading to greater efficiency is as great in Albania as anywhere else in Eastern Europe, because of the necessity of switching from extensive to intensive economic growth. More ambitious plans may raise output in the short run but soon result in lowered efficiency and bigger environmental damage. Moreover, investment is not yielding the required results, as in oil prospecting. Even the virtues of competition have been admitted, by one commentator, but without action following. Alia clearly recognizes the need for reform, but he is not a determined reformer, and moreover reform is especially difficult owing to ideological objections, the PLA seeing all change as a betrayal of socialism. What has been done is therefore concerned mainly with cadres. Following an allusion by Alia in 1986, the need to reinforce cadres in the northern districts was stressed, so as to improve there the quality of local leadership and movements in that direction took place for periods of one to three years. A more bizarre approach was announced two years later: that administrative jobs must not be held longer than five years. Evidently favouritism in bureaucratic arrangements (and also in retail trade) has become a serious problem, yet more fundamental changes are not tolerated. Instead, reliance is placed increasingly on an admixture of foreign expertise.

Foreign relations and foreign policy. Albania maintains diplomatic relations with many countries but not with two superpowers, although she is a member of the United Nations. In most respects other countries are held at arm's length. Communist Albania was not always so isolationist. She collaborated economically with Yugoslavia until that country's break with the USSR (1948), then with the USSR (until 1960) and then with China (until 1978). Diplomatic relations were maintained with Yugoslavia and China but not with the USSR (see below). The US has not had diplomatic relations with Albania since 1944. Relations with the UK were broken as the result of a naval incident in the Corfu Channel in 1946 and it has not yet been possible to find a formula enabling them to be renewed; meanwhile, a sum of Albanian gold remains in Britain. During the 1980s Albania has initiated relations with other states including most notably the Federal Republic of Germany (September 1987). The FRG is now building the largest embassy in Tirana and trade between the two countries is on the increase. This is also true of Greece, with which a nominal state of war, which had existed since World War II, was terminated on Aug. 28, 1987.

Strategic situation and armed forces. Albania joined the **Warsaw Treaty Organization**

(Warsaw Pact) at the time of its signature, but withdrew from it in 1968. An alliance with China followed but since 1978 Albania has had no allies, and exhibits much concern for her security. According to the International Institute for Strategic Studies her armed forces number 42,000, including 22,400 conscripts. The conscription period is two years for the army, three years for the air force and navy. Due to the demographic features already mentioned there are unusually many males within military age groups. Women soldiers exist too (a small proportion of the total), while schoolchildren do military training every two weeks: they are frequently seen marching to target practice. Artillery and tanks are not infrequently seen. The country is peppered with innumerable unmanned pill-boxes of beehive shape. Uniforms are Chinese-style while equipment seems to be largely Russian (though obsolescent). Border guards and internal security forces exist as well and can be assumed to be especially well trained and armed. Emigration and visits abroad are banned and searchlights sweep the shore near to Greece Corfu; and though physical obstacles to defection are not obtrusive, intruders across the frontier are shot on sight. Albania is at the same time one of the most secretive of the world's countries. These precautions find some justification in Albania's turbulent history, including a threat from Yugoslavia and unsuccessful US and British attempts at subversion in the late 1940s. In recent years there has been no real danger to Albania but the overthrow of Communist regimes in Eastern Europe in 1989 is bound to intensify Albanian fears.

Rift with USSR. From 1948 to 1960 Soviet influence in Albania was strong and included substantial economic aid. This was reflected in Albanian allusions and attitudes. Since 1960 the situation has been quite different. On Nov. 16, 1960 Enver Hoxha at a conference in Moscow of 81 Communist parties denounced the **Khrushchev** line and moved instead very close to the Chinese one. In October 1961 the Soviet Union broke diplomatic relations with Albania. Since then the two countries have had neither diplomatic nor trade relations and Soviet citizens are barred from Albania. Although the Soviet Union has since then several times made overtures to Albania these have always been rejected. The reasons for the dispute were several. First of all, Albania was (and is) at a much earlier stage than the USSR in all respects. Hoxha's policies were essentially Stalinist; thus Khrushchev's criticism and denunciation of **Stalin** touched Hoxha directly. Khrushchev's call to other Communist

parties to denounce China seemed to threaten also Albania. Secondly, problems of excessive centralization which in the USSR loomed large, affected Albania much less, Albania being so much smaller.

Thirdly, the Albanian Communist leadership was alarmed by events in Poland and Hungary which it saw as resulting from Soviet revisionism. Albania particulary objected to Khrushchev's conciliatory policy towards Yugoslavia and to his repudiation of Stalin's attacks upon Marshal **Tito**. It objected also to what was seen as Soviet hints supporting Greek territorial claims (Greece and Albania remaining formally at war until August 1987). The Albanians also viewed the Soviet use of Sazan, where Soviet submarines were stationed, as overly aggressive. Economically, Enver Hoxha took exception to Khrushchev's advice that Albania should give up the effort to become self-sufficient in grain and should concentrate instead on producing Mediterranean delicacies; this affected in particular wheat-growing. As regards industry, the Russians saw as economically senseless the financing of the Elbasan steel combine which the Albanians considered as essential to their development. Since 1961 Albania has classified the Soviet Union together with the United States as aggressive and warmongering superpowers. The economic consequences of the break were initially most serious for Albania. The consequences in education have also been considerable. Albania drew closer to China which after an interval began to supply economic aid and advice. The eventual result has been to impel Albania to become more independent and self-reliant in both economic and foreign policy.

RH/PA

ALEKSANDROV, CHUDOMIR ASENOV. Bulgarian communist politician: First Secretary of Sofia city party organization 1979–84; Central Committee Secretary 1981–84 and again 1986–88; Politburo member 1984–88; First Deputy Chairman of Council of Ministers 1984–86; removed from leadership July 1988; Deputy Chairman of Ministers from February 1990.

A metallurgical engineer by training and early career, Aleksandrov (born in 1936) entered party work in his mid-thirties. Following various lower-level posts and service as Sofia party boss and junior Central Committee Secretary, Aleksandrov entered the Politburo in 1984. On his return to the Secretariat two years later he assumed the key responsibility for personnel matters and acquired the reputation of a radical reformist ("the Bulgarian Gorbachev") and the appearance of a possible successor to party leader Todor **Zhivkov**. In mid-1988, Aleksandrov was abruptly and unexpectedly purged from the Politburo and Secretariat, thereafter suffering the further humiliation of expulsion from the Central Committee and of "leaks" that his family had collaborated with the Nazis. The precise circumstances are still unclear, but presumably Zhivkov was either countering or pre-empting a move by Aleksandrov to supplant him: at any rate, since the previous year Aleksandrov had been calling publicly for the removal of ineffective and conservative party leaders and denouncing the remnants of a "personality cult". Aleksandrov's fall was also associated with an anti-reformist and hardline shift in Zhivkov's policies. With Zhivkov out of the way and reformism again in vogue, Aleksandrov's fortunes improved: his membership of the Central Committee was restored in December 1989, and in February 1990 he was appointed Deputy Premier. This is a post rather short of his former eminence, and it is possible that he will rise still further: his views are in tune with the times, and his years as party personnel manager will have given him ample opportunity to install friends in influential posts. But there will no doubt be some resistance among the successor leadership to the full reinstatement of such a powerful and popular rival.

RW

ALIA, RAMIZ. Alia was born in the northern town of Shkodër, Albania. As a student at the Tirana Gymnasium, he became active in the National Liberation Movement by becoming a member of the Communist Youth. In 1943 he joined the Communist Party at the age of 18. In 1944 he fought in Yugoslavia against the retreating German army for which he received a Yugoslav decoration. He was elected member of the Central Committee in 1948. Subsequent appointments included Minister of Education and Culture in 1955, candidate member of the Politburo in 1956, member of Party Secretariat in 1961, member of the Commission that drafted the new constitution in 1975, and Chairman of the State Presidium in 1982.

Since taking over the party leadership in 1985, Alia was made General Commander of the Armed Forces and Chairman of the Defence Council. He had the "correct" background as party ideologist, and gained Hoxha's respect in the 1960s in the Office of Propaganda and the Ministry of Culture when he devoted himself to the cultural revolution.

Alia combines the posts of First Secretary of the CC of the Party of Labour of Albania (PLA) and Chairman of the State Presidium of the People's Assembly.

PA

ALLIANCE OF FREE DEMOCRATS (HUNGARY — AFD, Szabad Demokraták Szsövetsége).

The origins of this important Hungarian opposition party are to be found in the dissident movement, the "Democratic Opposition", of the late 1970s. This was a rather loose-knit (and by no means numerous) circle of Budapest intellectuals, many of whom had been radical Marxists in the late 1960s and early 1970s, and some of whom had been associated with, or strongly influenced by, the "Budapest School" of philosophers around György Lukács. By the late 1970s, and especially after the Polish events of 1980–81, many of these intellectuals began a more or less thorough reappraisal of their political views, and came to emphasize principles much closer to classical liberalism, including human rights, individual freedom, and the importance of a legal framework as the underpinning of pluralist democratic political institutions. They also now fully accepted the necessity of the market economy. The main Hungarian *samizdat* publication of this period, *Beszélö*, was produced by members of this group.

In early 1988, as Hungarian politics began rapidly to open up, this group set up a "Network of Free Initiatives", as a sort of umbrella organization to co-ordinate the activities of various new groups which had sprung up. In November 1988, the Alliance of Free Democrats was set up as an offshoot of the Network. The first national congress of the AFD was held on March 19, 1989, at which a draft programme, which had been drafted by 21 social scientists, was discussed. This was formally approved after a month's adjournment on April 16. The programme was quickly recognized as a masterly piece of work, with lucid, straightforward and comprehensive proposals for thoroughgoing constitutional reform and economic reform, as well as social policy measures aimed to alleviate the problem of poverty. Indeed, it was the product of some of Hungary's finest economists, sopiologists, philosophers and legal specialists, many of whom had been leading government advisers but who had by now given up hope of seeing their ideas realized by the **Hungarian Socialist Workers' Party (HSWF)**-dominated government and had decided to throw their weight behind the AFD.

Two broad currents of opinion are in evidence within the AFD, a social-democratic current and a rather more libertarian current. The AFD is

21

uncompromisingly Western in orientation, and has come into bitter conflict with the **Hungarian Democratic Forum (HDF)**, particularly the latter's populist tendency. This conflict in certain respects has echoes of the inter-war populist/urbanist division in the Hungarian intelligentsia, and there are occasional anti-semitic undertones in the HDF's attacks. Although the two parties co-operated in the "Triangular Discussions" with the government at which basic constitutional reforms were negotiated in summer 1989, the AFD finally did not sign the agreement in September because it objected to the omission of three points which, it argued, vitiated the government: the HSWP's continued role in workplaces, the need for public disclosure of the HSWP's assets, and the role of the HSWP's armed militia, the Workers' Guard. The AFD also deeply disagreed with the institution of a directly elected presidency, which it saw as a dangerous loophole through which authoritarian rule might be sustained.

The AFD then set up a petition to Parliament requesting a referendum on these issues, which gathered 200,000 signatures and thus fulfilled the constitutional requirement. A referendum was therefore held on Nov. 27, which resulted in a narrow victory for the AFD position on the presidency. While in the summer, opinion polls were showing public support for the AFD of around 5 per cent, the party won much greater visibility after September, and an opinion poll in November showed that 10.1 per cent of the respondents would vote for the AFD in a general election. Good relations are enjoyed with **FIDESZ**, the **Hungarian Social Democratic Party** and the **Independent Smallholders' Party**. In the March– April 1990 general election the party secured second place with 23.8 per cent of the vote, and it subsequently constituted the principal opposition to the HDF-dominated government.

JB

ALLIANCE FOR GERMANY: (**Allianz für Deutschland**). This was an electoral pact formed by three right-of-centre parties in February 1990 to fight the March 18 elections. It included the **Christian Democratic Union of Germany (CDU)**, The **German Social Union (DSU)** and **Democratic Departure (DA)**. The parties did each stand in the elections, but there was a degree of co-operation and common policy. The Alliance emerged the clear victor, with 48 per cent of the vote, but this was largely because of the strong CDU showing, assisted by the West Germans. The DSU performed moderately, DA very badly.

Without an overall or two-thirds majority, the Alliance parties are to form part of the coalition government emerging from the elections.

JO

ANDROPOV, YURI VLADIMIROVICH. Soviet politician and General Secretary of the **Communist Party of the Soviet Union (CPSU)** from 1982 to 1984. Born in 1914 in the Stavropol region in southern Russia in the family of a railway official, Andropov went on to a water transport college, Petrozavodsk University and the Higher Party School of the CPSU Central Committee. After a short period Andropov became a Komsomol official and then from 1944 an official in the CPSU itself, first of all in Karelia and then from 1951 in the Central Committee apparatus in Moscow. From 1953 onwards Andropov was engaged in diplomatic work, serving from 1954 to 1957 as Soviet ambassador in Hungary. In 1957 he became a departmental head in the CPSU apparatus; in 1961 he became a member of the CPSU Central Committee, and in 1962 a member of the Secretariat. In May 1967, in a major shift of direction, Andropov became head of the KGB (Committee of State Security) and later the same year a candidate member of the ruling Politburo, becoming a full member in 1973. In May 1982 Andropov returned to the Secretariat, and in November of that year he was one of the leading candidates for the general secretaryship after **Brezhnev**'s death.

It had widely been expected that a decent interval would elapse before a successor was named as General Secretary, and indeed that a prolonged succession struggle might ensue. On Nov. 11, however, the day after Brezhnev's death, it was announced that Andropov was to be the chairman of the committee making arrangements for his funeral, and the following day it was announced that an emergency meeting of the Central-Committee had elected him to the vacant general secretaryship. Andropov's main rival for the succession, Konstantin **Chernenko**, had the task of proposing his candidacy to the Central Committee, where it was accepted unanimously. Brezhnev was buried on Nov. 15, Andropov making the funeral oration, and a week later the new general secretary made his first speech as party leader to the Central Committee, a brief but effective review of Soviet foreign and domestic policy. In May 1983 it became known that Andropov had succeeded Brezhnev as chairman of the Defence Council of the USSR, the body attached to the Politburo which oversees military and security matters, and in June he was elected to the vacant state presidency (chairmanship of the Presidium of the USSR Supreme Soviet), thus concentrating in his hands after only seven months the same combination of posts that Brezhnev had taken almost 13 years to accumulate.

Andropov's own health, however, was far from certain. An elderly man (already 68 when he assumed the party leadership) with a history of heart trouble, there were persistent rumours of incapacity from almost the outset of his period of office. Although a number of members of the "Brezhnev mafia" swiftly lost their positions, Chernenko remained prominent, making the opening speech at the June 1983 Central Committee plenum and reportedly chairing the Politburo in Andropov's absence. Andropov's effective authority in fact lasted for only a few months: he was last seen in public in August 1983 and unprecedentedly failed to attend the anniversary parade in Red Square on Nov. 7 and then the Central Committee plenum and the Supreme Soviet session the following month. It became known that Andropov was receiving kidney dialysis treatment at the Central Committee hospital near Moscow and that Mikhail **Gorbachev**, the youngest member of the Politburo and apparently the one most closely attuned to the general secretary's own thinking, was maintaining links between him and other members of the leadership. A series of "interviews" and statements, and an address that was circulated to the Central Committee plenum he was unable to attend, suggested that Andropov's intellectual powers were largely unimpaired. Nonetheless, explanations in terms of "colds" and "temporary causes" began to wear thin, and it was not entirely unexpected when on Feb. 11, 1984 the central press reported that Andropov had died two days earlier after a "long illness".

Although Gorbachev was later to emphasize the decisive break in Soviet policy that had taken place at the April 1985 plenum (the first he addressed as party leader), the change of political direction approved by the plenum was essentially a development of the reorientation that already began to take place under Andropov. Andropov's security background tended to obscure his earlier exposure to the Eastern European reform experience while Soviet ambassador to Hungary and a penetrating, somewhat puritanical intellect which was completely at odds with the complacency and corruption of the later Brezhnev era (he refrained, for instance, from promoting the careers of his own family, although his son Igor nonetheless emerged as a prominent Soviet diplomat). In some ways the most significant of Andropov's contributions was to the reformulation of Soviet **ideology**, particularly through an article on "The teaching of Karl Marx and some

questions of socialist construction in the USSR" which appeared in the party theoretical journal *Kommunist* in early 1983; its sober and realistic tone marked off the post-Brezhnev period from the optimism of **Khrushchev**, and even from Brezhnev's own somewhat complacent notion of "developed socialism".

There was a need, Andropov emphasized, for a proper understanding of the stage of development the USSR had reached. Any attempt to run ahead of that level of development would simply suggest tasks that were unrealizable. The Soviet Union, he insisted, was only at the beginning of the long historical stage of developed socialism; there should be no exaggeration of their closeness to the ultimate goal of full Communism, and there should be a proper acknowledgement of the difficulties that still remained. There could be no "ready-made solutions" to the Soviet Union's problems, Andropov told the Central Committee in June 1983; two years later, this was one of the terms that Gorbachev employed in explaining and justifying his programme of *perestroika*.

SLW

ANTALL, JOZEF. Leader of the **Hungarian Democratic Forum (HDF)** since October 1989, Antall became the first democratically-elected Prime Minister of Hungary after the elections of spring 1990. Antall, born in 1932, comes from a distinguished anti-Communist political family. His father was a founder-member of the **Independent Smallholders' Party**, and during World War II held the post of Commissar in charge of the 70,000 Polish refugees in Hungary who had fled their country after the Nazi-Soviet Pact. He also played a part in humanitarian activities to alleviate the plight of Jews in Hungary in the later years of the war. He held ministerial posts in the post-war coalition governments, until the Communist takeover.

Antall jnr was educated in the elite Budapest school, the Piarist Gymnasium, then studied history at Budapest University. He became a school teacher. During 1956, when his father returned to political life to establish the Smallholders' Party, Antall had his first opportunity to fulfil his own political ambitions: he became chairman of the Revolutionary Committee of Budapest Schools, and set up the Christian-Democratic Youth Alliance. After the suppression of the Uprising, Antall was imprisoned and was deprived thereafter of the right to teach. He began work as a librarian in 1960, and in 1964 he joined the Semmelweis Museum working as an archivist in the field of the history of medicine. In 1974, he became Director of this prestigious cultural institution. Antall was present at the founding of the Hungarian Democratic Forum at Lakitelek in September 1987, and played an important part in the Tripartite discussions between the various opposition groups and the **Hungarian Socialist Workers' Party** in the summer of 1989. He was elected president of the HDF in October 1989, but has retained close personal contacts with leading members (mainly of the older generation) of the Smallholders' Party. He has effectively steered the HDF away from the radical populist nationalism characteristic of some of its earliest supporters. Describing himself as a "patriotic liberal Christian Democrat", he has proved adept at building alliances across the right-of-centre of the political spectrum, and his personal emphasis on a conciliatory and moderate political style made possible early agreement with the main opposition party after the elections, the **Alliance of Free Democrats**, on the conduct of parliamentary business in an efficient manner. Lacking personal charisma, he had cultivated a distinguished *gravitas* which inspires confidence and lends dignity to the office of Prime Minister.

JB

ARMENIA. Armenia was proclaimed a Soviet Socialist Republic in November 1920. In 1922, together with **Georgia** and **Azerbaidzhan**, it became part of the Transcaucasian Soviet Federal Socialist Republic, and in 1936 it became a constituent republic of the USSR in its own right. It covers an area of 29,800 sq km, and its 1989 census population was 3,283,000 (or just over 1 per cent of the USSR total). The capital is Yerevan; several other towns in the republic suffered extensive damage during an earthquake in December 1988 in which an estimated 25,000 lives were lost. According to the 1979 census 90 per cent of the population were ethnic Armenians; there were also Azerbaidzhani and Russian minorities. Armenia is important for its cotton and subtropical crops, and it is rich in mineral resources. In 1990 the republic was subdivided into 37 districts. From 1988 onwards the republic has been profoundly affected by the dispute with Azerbaidzhan concerning the Nagorno-Karabakh autonomous region in that republic. (*See also* **Nationality Question in the USSR**)

SLW

ARMENIAN CHURCH. Armenia received Christianity in the third and fourth centuries, and broke from the Byzantine Church over a theological dispute in 451. The unique doctrinal position of the Armenian Monophysite Church and its use

of the Armenian language played an important part in the consolidation of Armenian national identity. Today religion is probably more closely linked with national feeling among Armenians than among any other Soviet nationality.

The Armenian Church suffered intense persecution in the 1930s, like other religions in the Soviet Union (*see* **Religion and Communism**). From World War II, however, it served as a useful instrument of Soviet foreign policy, particularly in relation to Armenians abroad. Armenians have traditionally seen the Russians as protectors against the Muslim Turks, a perception reinforced by the genocide of Armenians in 1915–16. The pro-Russian orientation of the Armenian Church eased its acceptance by the **Communist Party of the Soviet Union**. Since 1955 the Armenian Catholicos has been Vazgen I. An officially tolerated personality cult has arisen around him, to a greater extent than around any other religious leader in the USSR. Atheist propaganda has been downplayed in the Armenian Republic. In 1975 Vazgen claimed that 80 per cent of Armenians were believers and 60 per cent attended church. Its central position in Armenian culture makes the Church the principal focus on loyalty in the republic.

The Church has always supported Armenian nationalist demands: the annexation of Nagorny Karabakh (which has an Armenian majority) and Nakhichevan (which has an Azeri majority), both of which are in the Azerbaidzhani Republic; and the restoration of the territory around Mount Ararat, the symbol of Armenian national identity which is nevertheless located in Turkey. In 1988 the dispute between Armenia and Azerbaidzhan over Nagorno-Karabakh erupted (*see* **Nationality Question in the USSR; Islam**). The Armenian Party leadership proved incapable of persuading Moscow to accept the wishes of the population of the region to be transferred to Armenia. Vazgen I attempted to cool the nationalist passions which erupted, thereby risking a loss of influence with the people. As the party in the course of 1989 lost much of its authority, opposition informal nationalist groups increasingly came to the fore, with anti-Russian and secessionist slogans gaining ground. It seemed that the Church would have a further role to play in preventing bloodshed.

PJSD

ARMS CONTROL. As distinct from plans for general and complete disarmament, arms control negotiations emerged as a highly visible feature of global politics and East–West relations in the early 1960s. Arms control agreements fall into several categories. Preventive agreements are designed to avoid the intrusion of particular weapons into new areas and include the 1959 Antarctic Treaty, the 1967 Outer Space Treaty and the 1971 Seabed Treaty. The 1963 superpower "Hotline" accord and the 1972 US–Soviet Incidents At Sea agreement are examples of arrangements for managing possible crises. The confidence- and security-building measures provided for in the 1986 Stockholm Agreement exemplify measures crafted to make the occurrence of crises less likely as a result of miscalculation. The most well-known and, indeed, contentious agreements have been designed to prevent or limit the vertical or horizontal proliferation of nuclear or other types of weapons or their qualitative improvement. Examples of this kind of arms control endeavour include the 1963 Partial Test Ban Treaty, the 1968 Nuclear Nonproliferation Treaty, the dialogue on a Comprehensive Test Ban Treaty, the superpower Strategic Arms Limitation Talks and the multilateral negotiation of a Chemical Weapons Convention.

Restraints on nuclear weapons test explosions. In the 1950s progress towards a comprehensive test ban treaty (CTBT) was hindered by disagreement over a CTBT's link to other disarmament measures and many problems related to how such a treaty would be verified. These included the number and types of on-site inspections, the location and number of seismic monitoring stations to be set up and the organization of a control commission. In July 1963 the USA, USSR and UK agreed to focus on a limited test ban which could be verified without resort to seismic monitoring stations on Soviet territory or on-site inspections. The impetus to seek such modest, achievable arms control accords was provided by the experience of the Cuban Missile Crisis of 1962.

In October 1963 the USA, USSR and UK successfully completed their negotiation of the Partial Test Ban Treaty (PTBT). This banned nuclear weapons testing in the atmosphere, outer space and under water. Testing could therefore continue underground, allowing the three nuclear weapons powers to continue developing nuclear warheads. Most nations eventually signed the PTBT, with the exception of today's other two self-confessed nuclear weapons powers—France and the People's Republic of China (PRC). The PTBT was dismissed gratefully by some as a partial "clean air act". Despite declaratory claims to the contrary, which are usually made with an eye to public opinion, nuclear weapons powers have been wary of the constraints that a Comprehensive Test Ban (CTB) would place on their ability to proof-test and maintain the reliability

of their existing nuclear weapons stockpiles and to perfect new nuclear weapons. In the years of the Reagan administration the USA openly admitted its opposition to a CTB, based on the military need to continue testing and a profound scepticism that such a treaty could be reliably verified.

In July 1974 the USA and USSR signed a bilateral Threshold Test Ban Treaty (TTBT) limiting their underground nuclear weapons tests to 150 kilotons. In May 1976 they signed a companion Peaceful Nuclear Explosions Treaty (PNET) governing underground nuclear tests conducted for peaceful purposes. The PNET provided for on-site monitoring of peaceful nuclear explosions in certain circumstances relating primarily to the total expected yield of such explosions and both accords included several other co-operative measures designed to enhance their verification. The USA failed to ratify these treaties but both governments declared that they would abide by their terms.

Between 1977 and 1980 the USA, USSR and UK conducted tripartite negotiations to design a multilateral CTBT as President Carter announced his commitment to ending nuclear testing. Considerable progress was made. The USSR dropped its insistence on the right to continue with peaceful nuclear tests and on French and Chinese participation in a test ban from its inception. It also accepted in principle on-site inspections by challenge and the setting up on its territory of tamper-proof automatic seismic monitoring stations in response to US–UK verification concerns. The USA was worried about the possibility of undetectable "laboratory" explosions and it came to favour only a temporary test ban lasting for just three years. In 1980 the talks ground to a halt as the USA decided against further participation. The 40-nation Geneva Conference on Disarmament set up a committee to discuss a CTBT in 1983 but actual negotiations were not forthcoming due to the failure to agree on a negotiating mandate for the committee's work. This was largely at the insistence of the USA and UK who considered that further refinement of monitoring techniques was necessary before fruitful negotiations on a CTBT could begin.

In 1986 the USA and USSR began talks on improving the verification provisions attached to the 1974 TTBT and 1976 PNET so as to allow their submission for ratification by the US Senate. The USA continued to resist Soviet demands for a US commitment to seek a complete cessation of nuclear weapons testing. In 1986 and 1987 the USSR observed an 18-month unilateral moratorium but subsequently resumed nuclear testing, its public calls for US reciprocation having been rebuffed. In the new bilateral talks considerable progress was achieved in creating greater confidence in each side's ability accurately to gauge the size of the other's nuclear tests. Under the Joint Verification Experiment, each side sent a team of observers with equipment to monitor a nuclear test at the other's testing site and thereby improve calibration techniques. By 1989 there were still differences over the type of monitoring equipment to be allowed at on-site inspections but it seemed only a matter of time before agreement was reached on the additional verification measures to be attached to the TTBT and PNET as a protocol. This would allow the Bush administration to seek Senate ratification of the treaties.

Nuclear weapons nonproliferation. Underground testing of nuclear explosive devices was not banned by the 1963 Partial Test Ban Treaty and the three states that inspired the PTBT perfected the practice. The other two nuclear weapons powers — France and the PRC — continued with nuclear testing in the atmosphere while they developed the ability to test underground and did not sign the PTBT. In the mid-1960s the USA, USSR and UK led the effort to constrain the further spread of nuclear weapons and the ability to create them to other states. In 1968 the Nonproliferation Treaty (NPT) was signed. Its declared aims were to prevent the spread of nuclear weapons, promote the peaceful uses of nuclear energy and assist the process of nuclear disarmament. By 1989, 138 states had become parties to the NPT but important non-participants in the regime established by the Treaty included two nuclear weapons powers (France and the PRC) and a number of "threshold" or near-nuclear powers — Argentina, Brazil, India (which conducted a "peaceful" nuclear explosion in 1974), Israel, Pakistan and South Africa. While refusing formally to participate in the NPT, France indicated that it would do nothing to undermine the regime of nonproliferation, in which it shared a common interest with the other nuclear weapons states.

Article 6 of the NPT obliged the existing nuclear weapons powers to bring an end to their own vertical proliferation of nuclear weapons in return for the self-denying ordinance accepted by the non-nuclear parties to the Treaty. The NPT also provided for the transfer of peaceful nuclear technology from the leading powers in the spirit of Eisenhower's 1953 Atoms For Peace programme which had offered assistance to countries in developing nuclear energy programmes in return for guarantees that such help would only be used for peaceful purposes. The Programme

had led to the creation in 1957 of the International Atomic Energy Agency (IAEA) and its establishment of a safeguards system in the 1960s. Under the safeguards arrangements, which were incorporated into the NPT regime, non-nuclear states agreed regularly to submit to the IAEA reports on their civilian nuclear activity. They also agreed to permit IAEA inspectors to visit their nuclear facilities in order to check on these reports and confirm that no diversion of nuclear materials from peaceful to military purposes had taken place. States providing peaceful nuclear assistance to non-nuclear weapons countries directly were also obliged to insist on the application of IAEA safeguards to the recipients. The nuclear weapons powers themselves were not subject to the same intrusive verification of their nuclear activities although the USA and UK — and, since the mid-1980s, the USSR — have allowed the IAEA to visit designated nuclear facilities on their territory.

The fourth review conference of the NPT was scheduled for August 1990 and in 1995 the NPT parties are to meet to discuss the continuation of the NPT regime through the Treaty's extension. By 1989 there was growing pressure from non-nuclear-weapons parties to the Partial Test Ban Treaty for an amendment conference designed to convert the PTBT into a fully-fledged comprehensive test ban treaty, a move opposed by the USA and UK. This was one more recent manifestation of the dissatisfaction of the non-nuclear powers with the limited efforts of the nuclear weapons states to curtail their own vertical proliferation of nuclear weapons.

Strategic nuclear arms limitation.
    SALT I. In January 1967 the USA and USSR agreed in principle to talks on the limitation of strategic nuclear offensive weapons and anti-ballistic missile defences (ABM). The commencement of the Strategic Arms Limitation Talks (SALT) was delayed as a result of the Soviet invasion of Czechoslovakia in August 1968. The formal SALT negotiations began in November 1969. By the end of the 1960s the USSR was approaching a position of numerical parity with the USA in the overall number of land-based intercontinental ballistic missiles (ICBM) and submarine-launched ballistic missiles (SLBM). This created the basis for negotiations to constrain the further growth of, or even to reduce, the strategic nuclear arsenals of the two superpowers. Soviet deployment of an ABM system around Moscow in the mid-1960s and US development of ABMs threatened to unleash an offsetting offensive-defensive strategic arms race to add to the existing offensive strategic arms competition

between the two states. The ensuing SALT negotiations pursued many aims but it was hoped that the process would help to reduce the risk of nuclear war and to manage the strategic arms competition, perhaps even closing off some actual or potential areas of weapons rivalry.

At the outset of the SALT I talks the USA made clear its desire that an accord on offensive systems should only limit "central" strategic forces, i.e. ICBMs, SLBMs and heavy bomber aircraft. The USSR wanted to include US forward-based systems (FBS) — tactical aircraft based in Europe or on aircraft carriers and able to strike Soviet territory—in the total weapons ceiling to be agreed for the USA; alternatively, FBS should be removed. Although it was agreed to postpone the FBS question until the next stage in the SALT process, the issue highlighted the differences between US and Soviet definitions of what is or is not a strategic weapon. The Soviets initially gave priority to reaching agreement on restricting ABMs, while the USA placed equal emphasis on negotiating constraints in both offensive and defensive weapons.

The USA was eager to secure an overall cap on the continuing Soviet build-up of ICBMs and SLBMs roughly at the point of numerical parity with the USA, whose strategic weapons programmes were now focused more on qualitative improvements to its existing arsenal. The USA sought to maintain its lead in development of the technology of multiple independently targetable re-entry vehicles (MIRV) for use on its ICBMs and SLBMs through a ban on further testing, which the USSR rejected. The USA also wanted reductions in the number of "heavy" Soviet ICBMs which, if subsequently MIRVed, would pose a hypothetically destabilizing "hard-target" threat to the survivability of US ICBM silos. The USSR resisted limits on its growing SLBM force and serious constraints on missile modernization.

The Interim Offensive Arms Agreement and the Treaty on the Limitation of Anti-Ballistic Missile Systems (ABM) were signed in Moscow in May 1972. The Interim Offensive Agreement (SALT I Agreement) imposed a five-year limit on the numbers of ICBM and SLBM launchers each side could deploy. Bomber aircraft, in which the USA enjoyed a significant superiority, were excluded. ICBM launchers (silos) were frozen at the number already existing or being built — 1,054 for the USA and 1,618 for the USSR. The dimensions of ICBM silos were not be increased by more than 10–15 per cent and silos for light or older ICBMs were not to be converted into launchers for modern heavy ICBMs. The USA was limited to 710 SLBM launchers on 44 strategic missile-carrying submarines (SSBN) while

the USSR was allowed to increase its SLBM launcher force to 950 on 62 submarines.

The SALT I Agreement did not foreclose modernization of the superpowers' strategic arsenals: it did not limit the number of silo- and submarine-based missiles *per se* but their launchers, nor did it constrain either power from developing and deploying MIRVed warheads on their missiles. It did, however, provide greater predictability for each side in estimating in the crudest of terms the future threat it would face from the other. Verification of compliance with the Salt I Agreement and the ABM Treaty was to be by unilateral use of "national technical means" (a euphemism for intelligence satellites and listening posts). Interference with NTMs and deliberate concealment of activities directly relevant to the Agreement were banned. A Standing Consultative Commission (SCC) was to handle matters relating to the implementation of the two accords and be the forum through which questions of either sides' compliance would be handled in confidence.

The ABM Treaty was of unlimited duration and prohibited the deployment of ABM systems for a nationwide defence of the territory of either state or the creation of the basis for such a capability. The Treaty also prohibited the development, testing or deployment of land-mobile, sea-based, air-based and space-based components of an ABM system. Upgrading of non-ABM systems to give them ABM capability was banned. Restrictions were placed on the deployment of large phased-array radars in order to prevent the building of the base for a territorial defence against ballistic missiles. Exotic systems which could substitute for ABM radars, missiles or launchers were also banned. Each side was permitted to deploy two ABM systems: one for defence of the national capital and the other for protection of one ICBM field. The missiles (100), launchers (100) and radars allowed at these sites were specified in the Treaty. A 1974 Protocol to the Treaty reduced the permitted ABM deployment to one site and the USSR maintained its ABM system around Moscow while the USA decided not to proceed with any ABM deployment. The ABM Treaty restricted the competition in strategic defensive systems and thereby at least reduced one of the stimuli to the superpower competition in offensive weapons. It also seemed to symbolize both sides' acceptance of a mutual nuclear deterrence relationship founded upon the reality of "mutual assured destruction".

Many questions of possible Soviet noncompliance with the 1972 accords were dealt with to the satisfaction of the US government by quiet diplomacy in the SCC. By the mid-1970s, however, the good faith of the USSR became a subject of public debate in the USA and helped to weaken support for the SALT process in general. Soviet construction of a large phased-array radar near Krasnoyarsk became the central issue in a series of accusations of Soviet cheating made by the Reagan Administration in the 1980s.

The legacy of the SALT I period also included the 1971 Hotline Modernization Agreement updating the original 1963 US–USSR Hot Line Agreement by adding a satellite link to the existing direct radio and telegraph link between the two governments. The 1971 accord was itself amended in 1984 to provide for facsimile transmission over the direct communication link. In 1987 the two superpowers further strengthened their ability to communicate directly in normal and crisis times through agreeing to establish Nuclear Risk Reduction Centres in each other's capital. At the height of the early 1970s detente, the USA and USSR also signed an Accident Measures Agreement (1971), the Agreement on the Prevention of Nuclear War (1973) and an Agreement on the Prevention of Incidents at Sea (1972).

SALT II. The SALT talks resumed at the end of 1972 and eventually resulted in a treaty much more complex than its SALT I predecessor, the terms of which were observed after the end of the five-year period. The USSR initially demanded the withdrawal of US FBS and a ban on new US weapons such as the Trident SLBM and B-1 bomber under development. In late 1974 Ford and **Brezhnev** agreed on the goal of establishing an equal aggregate limit of 2,400 for both sides on the overall numbers of strategic nuclear delivery vehicles to be allowed under a SALT II treaty. Bombers were thus to be included in the count and the negotiations dealt additionally with modest constraints on qualitative improvements in the two arsenals. The two leaders also agreed to a limit of 1,320 on SLBM and ICBM launchers equipped with MIRVs. The USSR agreed to exclude US FBS from the talks and eventually dropped its demand for a ban on strategic air-launched cruise missiles (ALCM) in which the USA had a lead, agreeing to count ALCM-carrying bombers against the 1,320 subceiling on MIRVed launchers and to offer some constraints on the production of its own Backfire bomber. The SALT II Treaty signed in June 1979 did not greatly constrain the existing weapons programmes of the two sides. Yet it did contain some qualitative limitations and was much more detailed than the SALT I accord.

The Treaty itself was to expire at the end of 1985, the date originally agreed in 1974. A Protocol to last until the end of 1981 dealt with sys-

tems on which the sides had been unable to agree. A Joint Statement of Principles gave guidelines for subsequent strategic arms negotiations.

The Treaty's quantitative limits included the following: (i) equal overall numerical limits of 2,400 on ICBM and SLBM launchers and heavy bombers, to be reduced to 2,250 by the end of 1981; (ii) an aggregate ceiling of 1,320 on MIRVed ballistic missile launchers and heavy bombers equipped for launching ALCMs with ranges over 600 km; (iii) a subceiling of 1,200 on MIRVed ballistic missile launchers and a subceiling within this of 820 on MIRVed ICBM launchers; (iv) a freeze on the number of re-entry vehicles on current ICBM types, a limit of 10 such vehicles on the one new type of ICBM allowed under the Treaty, and a limit of 14 re-entry vehicles on new SLBMs; and (v) a limit on the number of ALCMs of over 600 km range that could be deployed on bombers.

The Treaty imposed some qualitative constraints on the two sides' weapons programmes, the most important of which was that each side could test and deploy only one new type of ICBM during the life of the Treaty. There were counting rules for associating MIRVs and their ceilings with corresponding launchers. Some kinds of ICBM test launches had to be notified in advance. The Treaty verification provisions were similar to those of SALT I but also included: a specific ban on the encryption of telemetry data from missiles being tested when verification would be impeded; co-operative measures to allow the other side remotely to distinguish aircraft with treaty-relevant missions (functionally-related observable differences).

The Protocol imposed a short-term ban on the deployment of ground-launched and sea-launched cruise missiles (GLCM and SLCM) of over 600 km range and deployment of mobile ICBM launchers. The Joint Statement committed the sides to seek substantial further limitations and reductions in their strategic nuclear arsenals and to resolve the problems covered temporarily in the Protocol.

The SALT II Treaty met much resistance in the US and Senate ratification was postponed after the Soviet invasion of Afghanistan. The Reagan administration was unhappy with the content of the treaty and decided not to seek its ratification but declared that it would not undercut it. The USSR stated that it would comply equally with SALT II. The USA began openly to accuse the USSR of violations of the SALT II and ABM Treaties and in 1985 threatened to retaliate through proportionate counter-violations of its own. In May 1986 President Reagan stated that the USA would no longer consider itself bound by the weapons ceiling incorporated in the SALT agreements.

START. The Strategic Arms Reduction Talks commenced in July 1982. The USA aimed for significant cuts in warheads on ballistic missiles. Its proposals gave priority to large reductions in the numbers of MIRVed ICBMs and would have had little effect on SLBMs and ALCMs, thus bringing about a major change in the structure of Soviet strategic forces while leaving US weapons programmes largely unconstrained. This US approach and its 1983 warhead "build-down" variant were rejected by the USSR as one-sided. Soviet proposals respected the differences in each side's strategic posture and called for slightly less radical reductions in the overall total of strategic missile launchers and heavy bombers on each side. They also called for a total ban on long-range cruise missiles. In December 1983 the USSR broke off the negotiations in retaliation for the beginning of the US deployment of intermediate-range GLCMs and Pershing II missiles in Western Europe. It also abandoned the US–Soviet talks on intermediate nuclear forces (INF) that had begun in November 1981 and covered "Eurostrategic" nuclear delivery systems.

Intermediate-range nuclear forces talks. The INF talks covered nuclear weapons with a range of 1,000–5,500 km. In December 1979 NATO adopted its "twin-track" decision to deploy from the end of 1983 464 US GLCMs and 108 US Pershing-2 ballistic missiles in Western Europe and to negotiate with the USSR on the limitation of US and Soviet intermediate-range forces deployed in or targeted against Europe. NATO equated the planned 572 US missiles with Soviet deployment since the mid-1970s of increasing numbers of SS-20 intermediate-range ballistic missiles (IRBM). SS-20 deployments had reinforced West European doubts about the reliability of the US nuclear guarantee. The USA initially proposed a "zero option": NATO would drop Pershing-2 and GLCM deployment if the USSR dismantled all its SS-20s (including those in the Far East). Shorter-range INF (SRINF) would be frozen and non-ground-based INF would be excluded from the talks. The USSR tried to include NATO's nuclear-capable aircraft and the British and French independent strategic nuclear deterrents in the count. All Soviet offers would have resulted in the maintenance of a Soviet monopoly in land-based IRBMs, as was the case, for example, with proposals in 1982 and 1983 to match Soviet missiles or warheads with British and French missiles or warheads (the latter were planned to expand considerably in the 1990s).

The beginning of US deployments in December 1983 in the face of an intense Soviet propaganda campaign led to Soviet abandonment of the INF and START negotiations until March 1985. Soviet SS-23 missiles were then deployed in East Germany and Czechoslovakia as a symbolic countermeasure by the USSR.

The **Gorbachev** leadership brought a gradually more flexible Soviet negotiating approach to the INF talks. This stemmed from an acceptance that the original SS-20 deployment decision had been made on narrow military grounds, without considering its possible political repercussions in Europe. It also reflected the Soviet leaders' increased reliance on arms control as a way of improving political relations with the West and recognition that progress in limiting strategic nuclear weapons in START could not be held hostage to the fruitless debate over what constituted a fair "Eurostrategic balance". In December 1987 the INF Treaty was signed, marking Soviet acceptance of a global double-zero solution to the problem of longer-range (LRINF) and shorter-range (SRINF) INF missiles and abandonment of the inclusion of UK and French nuclear forces in the treaty constraints. After the INF Treaty's entry into force, both sides would have three years to destroy LRINF and 18 months to destroy SRINF missiles on a global basis.

The INF Treaty involved the destruction of many more Soviet than US missiles. The only way in which pre-1983 US/NATO deployed forces were affected was through the West German government's agreement to remove from its territory 72 old Pershing IA short-range missiles operated by the FRG under a dual-key arrangement. According to the data provided in the Memorandum of Understanding attached to the INF Treaty, the USA would eliminate a total of 283 deployed and non-deployed launchers and 867 deployed/non-deployed missiles. The corresponding figures for the USSR were: 851 launchers and 1,836 missiles (SS-20, SS-4, SS-5, SSC-X-4, SS-12 and SS-23).

The Treaty was also notable for its unprecedented provisions for on-site inspections to verify compliance with its terms. Inspectors would be allowed to count the existing missiles at agreed places shortly after the Treaty entered into force. They could carry out inspections to ensure that bases and missile support facilities have been eliminated and could observe the destruction of missiles and launchers at elimination sites. For each of the subsequent 13 years the sides could undertake a specified number of short-notice inspections at agreed locations. Also for 13 years, American personnel would continuously monitor what leaves the machine-building plant at

Votkinsk in the USSR in order to check that the missiles and their components banned under the Treaty were not being built. Soviet inspectors would have the same rights outside a specified US plant. The Treaty's elimination of a whole class of nuclear weapons systems on a global basis and its intrusive verification procedures — and the successful implementation of the Treaty — breathed new life and optimism into the East – West arms control process.

In March 1985 the dialogue on strategic nuclear reductions had resumed in Geneva at the new Nuclear and Space Talks (NST). In the NST framework the START negotiations were resumed alongside those on INF and a third set of talks on space and defensive weapons. Reagan's March 1983 "Star Wars" initiative aiming to develop a space-based defence against ballistic missiles cast doubt on the survival of the 1972 ABM Treaty and thereby threatened to undermine the basis for superpower strategic offensive arms control. There followed an acrimonious debate between the superpowers, reflected in US – West European exchanges and domestic discord in the USA itself, over the SDI programme's compliance with the ABM Treaty. This injected a new and complicating element into the Reagan administration's broader public campaign alleging Soviet noncompliance with a range of arms control accords signed by the USSR. The USSR insisted that a future START agreement on reductions in offensive strategic weapons could only be achieved on the basis of continued US compliance with the ABM Treaty banning the creation of a nationwide defence against offensive missiles.

Both sides in the START talks supported the goal of significant reductions in the size of their strategic offensive arsenals. In 1986 the USSR proposed across-the-board 50 per cent cuts in launchers to 1,600 and a common ceiling of 6,000 on warheads. The USA wanted a specific sublimit on ballistic missile warheads of 4,800 within the 6,000 warhead ceiling, and a 3,600 sub-subceiling on ICBM warheads within the 4,800 figure. This reflected US concern with the large proportion of Soviet warheads placed on accurate ICBMs. But by 1987 both sides agreed on the overall goal of reductions in US and Soviet arsenals to a ceiling of 6,000 strategic warheads and 1,600 launchers. The new Bush administration obtained a pause in the talks between November 1988 and June 1989 while it reviewed the US position. At the time there remained a small number of issues that were difficult to resolve in the 300-page draft treaty.

The USSR wanted limits on nuclear-armed sea-launched cruise missiles which would,

unconstrained, undermine the effect of reductions in ballistic missiles, bombers and their warheads and in which the US Navy had a considerable and growing superiority. Moscow proposed that each side be limited to 1,000 SLCMs overall, with a sublimit of 400 nuclear-armed SLCMs. The USA was strongly opposed to constraints on its SLCM deployment plans and argued that insuperable difficulties in distinguishing between non-nuclear and nuclear SLCMs made any limits on them inadequately verifiable. The USSR came up with imaginative if not fully practical ideas on the thorny problem of SLCM verification techniques, an illustration of the much more positive Soviet attitude to co-operative verification of arms control agreements in the Gorbachev era.

The two sides also disagreed on the counting rules for air-launched cruise missiles (to be included under the 6,000 ceiling on warheads). The USA wished to count each ALCM-carrying heavy bomber as having 10 ALCMs, regardless of how many it could feasibly carry. The USSR wished to treat each bomber as carrying the maximum number of ALCMs it could hold. Soviet counting rules would force the USA to cut over 1,000 more ALCMs than would acceptance of US counting rules. The USA was opposed to deployment of mobile ICBMs; only the USSR had deployed these by 1989 — about 465 warheads were carried on mobile SS-24 and SS-25s. The Bush administration decided in April 1989 to seek Congressional support for the MX rail-mobile and Midgetman mobile ICBMs, which suggested that the two sides would agree on mobile ICBM deployment.

The USSR was only willing to accept the US-proposed sublimits on the number of ICBM warheads if the USA would also agree to a sublimit on the number of SLBM warheads. The USA resisted this, claiming that SLBMs on submarines promoted strategic stability by their invulnerability to attack while MIRVed ICBMs were destabilizing through their accuracy and consequent vulnerability as high-value targets for a first strike. The USA was also concerned to prevent the continued flight-testing and deployment of modernized versions of the Soviet "silo-busting" heavy SS-18 MIRVed ICBM while the USSR would agree only to a freeze on their deployed number.

The counting rules so far agreed in the START talks differed from those that applied in the SALT agreements of the 1970s, partly due to the new emphasis on limiting numbers of warheads as well as launchers. The estimated total inventories of START-accountable strategic weapons in 1989 are given in the table.

In considerable contrast to the SALT talks, the

START-accountable strategic weapons in 1989		
	USA	*USSR*
Deployed launchers	1,968	2,588
Total warheads		
SALT counting rules:	14,530	12,403
START counting rules:	9,868	10,953

discussion of verification provisions in START has — since 1986 — been both intensive and surprisingly fruitful. The USSR proved to be much more receptive to US verification concerns and, indeed, indicated that Moscow now accepted the central importance of adequate verification of future arms agreements to its own, as well as Western, security. In 1989 the USSR agreed in principle to President Bush's proposal that the verification measures negotiated for START should be tried out even before a START treaty is finally agreed as this would help strengthen support in the US Senate for such an accord's ratification. The on-site inspection rights under a START Treaty will be even more extensive than those agreed for the December 1987 INF Treaty.

It has been agreed that the resumption of the superpower strategic arms control process in 1985 would involve three sets of talks on strategic offensive forces, space weapons and intermediate-range nuclear forces. Strategic offensive and space weapons issues were to be "considered and resolved in their inter-relationships". In the Space Weapons talks the USSR sought to impose effective constraints on US efforts to develop a space-based ballistic missile defence system, which Moscow and many Western critics of the SDI programme believed to be in violation or potential nonconformity with the 1972 ABM Treaty. At the December 1987 Summit the two sides fudged their differences on the SDI-ABMT relationship and interpretation of the ABM Treaty, agreeing that they would both observe the Treaty as signed in 1972 while conducting their research, development and testing as required. The Soviet opposition to "Star Wars" and direct linkage of the issue with the prospects for a START accord gradually softened. The USSR still sought a ban on space-based testing of ABM components for a 10-year period. The USA would only accept non-withdrawal from the ABM Treaty for a number of years provided that it was allowed to conduct testing in space, that SDI systems could subsequently be deployed without further reference to the Treaty and that either side could abrogate the ABM Treaty if its supreme national interests were threatened.

In 1989 technological problems and pressures for substantial reductions in US defence spending promised ultimately to reduce the destabilizing implications of the US SDI programme for the superpower military balance and its ability to frustrate agreement in the START negotiations. Indeed, in February 1990 the USSR seemed to abandon its insistence that the USA recognize a Soviet right unilaterally to renounce the restraints which a START Treaty had imposed on strategic offensive weapons in the event that Moscow deemed US activities under the SDI programme to have violated the ABM Treaty. The two sides also appeared to have found a compromise-formula for restraints on sea-launched cruise missiles. Each party would accept the other side's declaration of the numbers and types of SLCMs in its inventory without the requirement to verify it.

Chemical and biological weapons disarmament. The use of chemical and bacteriological (biological) weapons was banned by the 1925 Geneva Protocol. The Protocol did not, however, prohibit the development, production or stockpiling of chemical and biological weapons. Multilateral negotiations for a comprehensive ban on these weapons began in the 1960s under the auspices of the United Nations and at the end of the decade it was agreed to address first bacteriological (biological) weapons. In 1972 agreement was reached on the Convention on the Prohibition of the Development, Production and Stockpiling of Bacteriological (Biological) and Toxin Weapons and on their Destruction. The Biological Weapons Convention (BWC) came into force in 1975 on the basis of ratification by the USA, UK and USSR. By 1989 there were 111 parties to the BWC. France and the PRC were not among them. The first Review Conference in 1980 occurred after reports of an outbreak of anthrax in Sverdlovsk in the USSR, behind which some parties claimed was a Soviet infringement of the BWC. The BWC contained no specific provisions for verification of compliance with its terms. In 1986 the second Review Conference agreed on certain voluntary measures designed to increase confidence in the Convention's effectiveness, including exchanges of information on the parties' research laboratories to reduce suspicion and bolster international co-operation in non-military bacteriological work.

Multilateral talks on a Chemical Weapons Convention (CWC) were downgraded during US – Soviet bilateral consultations between 1976 and 1980. These brought little progress largely due to differences over the requirements of a verification regime and Soviet resistance to intrusive on-site inspection measures. The Ad Hoc Committee on Chemical Weapons of the UN Geneva Conference on Disarmament began to meet again in 1980 with the aim to drafting a global ban on the development, production, acquisition, stockpiling or retention, and transfer of chemical weapons. It was also agreed that the CWC should include a ban on use of chemical weapons, reinforcing the prohibition contained in the 1925 Geneva Protocol. Membership of the 40-strong committee was balanced between NATO, the WTO and neutral and nonaligned countries known as the Group of 21.

The negotiations brought slow but steady progress towards a convention. Though the two superpowers were the major players in the talks, other states (notably the UK) made useful contributions to strengthening the elements of agreement between the USA and USSR and offering alternative formulae for resolving differences — primarily over verification of a CWC — in their approach. The superpowers possessed the largest chemical weapons inventories. Yet evidence of the accelerating spread of chemical weapons in the 1980s gave new urgency to the common interest both states shared in arresting their horizontal proliferation.

The US stockpile consisted of ageing chemical agents and weapons as the USA had announced a unilateral cessation of chemical weapons production in 1969. The USA produced no more chemical weapons until December 1987 when it began to produce advanced binary weapons. In March 1989 the USA announced the accelerated withdrawal of its unitary chemical weapons stocks from West Germany. The UK had unilaterally abandoned its chemical weapons in the late 1950s. Western governments estimated that the USSR possessed several hundred thousand tonnes of toxic agents in the face of the USSR's continued denials of the existence of any Soviet stockpiles, despite having the world's most extensive chemical warfare capability (both in terms of delivery systems for use of these weapons and equipment for defence of military personnel against them). It was only in 1987 that the USSR finally admitted to possession of chemical weapons and declared a stockpile of only 50,000 tonnes of toxic agent. In January 1989 the USSR declared that it would soon begin to dismantle its stocks of chemical weapons and reported the construction of a purpose-built plant for their destruction, calling on the USA to reciprocate.

By the late 1980s more than 20 countries were believed either to possess a chemical weapons capability or to be on the verge of developing one. The probability of the use of such weapons as a form of "poor man's atomic bomb" in Third

World conflicts was illustrated horrifically during the Iran–Iraq Gulf War. Iraq employed these weapons against Iranian soldiers and subsequently against some of its own Kurdish citizens. Western concern rose also about evidence of Libyan efforts to acquire a chemical weapons production capacity and there were reports of Syrian production of chemical weapons agents. Commitment to the 1925 Geneva Protocol, support for the Geneva negotiations on a CWC and for the role of the UN Secretary General in investigating allegations of chemical weapons use were expressed in the Final Declaration of the Paris Conference on Chemical Weapons held in January 1989.

In the Geneva Ad Hoc Committee agreement was reached on the elements of a CWC. These would include the following: (i) a declaration by all parties of their current chemical weapon stockpiles and production facilities; (ii) destruction of all chemical weapons stocks and production facilities over a 10-year period (though states would be allowed to keep one small facility to produce certain lethal chemical agents for protective, defensive purposes); (iii) toxic chemicals and chemicals important for production of chemical warfare agents (key precursors) would only be used by civil chemical industries for industrial and not military purposes; and (iv) an international commission would be set up to supervise compliance with the Convention.

By the end of the 1980s, provisions for the effective verification of compliance still remained a major obstacle to the final agreement of the CWC's text. The stance of the USSR on verification problems gradually shifted in the early 1980s and underwent considerable transformation after 1985 and the application of "New Political Thinking" to Soviet security policy. The USSR thus went some way to answering Western verification concerns. These were expressed in a rather extreme manner in the Reagan administration's demand for "anywhere anytime" challenge inspections of industrial facilities producing chemicals that could be used in the making of chemical weapons agents. The Soviet Union came to accept many Western demands concerning routine and challenge inspection of Soviet territory to verify Soviet compliance with destruction of weapons stocks and nonproduction of chemical weapons.

The more constructive Soviet attitude probably derived from an increased priority for restraining and US–Soviet competition on chemical weapons, related to the prospect of US deployment of binary chemical munitions. It may also have been driven by the recognition that the prevention of the proliferation of chemical weapons capability to many more states would also require their acceptance of intrusive verification. The verification problems associated with a ban on chemical weapons seemed so complex and their solution would require such a degree of military and industrial "openness" on the part of so many developed and developing states that only a convincing lead on the part of the major chemical weapons powers could bring an effective Chemical Weapons Convention to fruition.

It was agreed in the Ad Hoc Committee that a sophisticated verification regime would be set up at the levels of routine and "challenge" inspection. Routine on-site inspections would be allowed at various locations that states identified to the Convention and would be designed to verify: initial declarations of chemical weapons stockpiles and production facilities; the destruction of all chemical weapons stockpiles and production facilities; non-diversion of substances made by civil chemical industries to production of chemical weapons; the legitimate operation of the single small facility allowed for protective production of certain lethal chemicals.

Challenge inspections would also play a crucial part in providing a deterrent to any state that might be tempted to attempt to keep or acquire chemical weapons clandestinely in defiance of the Convention. The possibility as well as the actual exercise of challenge inspection rights in cases of suspected noncompliance would serve to enhance confidence in the arms control regime and therefore to prevent the breakdown of the Convention. Consensus on the specific details of challenge inspection in a global chemical weapons ban depended upon the USA and USSR themselves first reaching agreement over non-routine verification.

The superpowers began bilateral talks in 1985 on these issues. By mid-1989 they were close to agreement on the type of data they would exchange bilaterally about their stockpiles of chemical weapons and production facilities. They had agreed on the order in which their existing weapons stockpiles would be destroyed and on how to reach parity in their chemical weapons stocks within eight years of the Convention's entry into force. They also settled on a procedural framework to govern conduct of challenge inspections of stockpiles and industrial facilities suspected of producing chemical weapons.

In 1989 the Ad Hoc Committee evaluated the experience of some 15 countries which had conducted trial inspections of one of their own commercial facilities and sought to design a formula for international inspections of commercial enterprises that would meet the verification requirements of a CWC in confirming nonproduction of chemical weapons while not interfering with industrial operations or compromising commercial secrets. This, together with the rules governing challenge inspections and the pace of destruction of weapons stocks, was at the centre of the questions still to be resolved before a Convention could be agreed.

Conventional armed forces in Europe: confidence-building measures and arms limitation.

Confidence- and security-building measures. The 1975 Helsinki Final Act of the Conference on Security and Co-operation in Europe (CSCE), which involved all European states except Albania and also the USA and Canada, provided for voluntary confidence-building measures (CBMs) of limited application in Europe. The 1980–83 Madrid CSCE follow-up meeting agreed a mandate for the Conference on Confidence- and Security-Building Measures and Disarmament in Europe (CDE) which took place in Stockholm between 1984 and 1986. The Madrid mandate provided for the pan-European negotiation of confidence- and security-building measures (CSBMs) designed to reduce the risk of military confrontation in Europe as the first stage of a process of strengthening confidence and security and in achieving force reductions on the continent. The CSBMs were to cover the whole of Europe as well as the adjoining sea area and air space and were to be militarily significant, politically binding and accompanied by adequate and appropriate forms of verification. The mandate thereby promised a considerable improvement in the confidence-building regime that had applied in Europe as a result of the Helsinki Final Act.

It was only in the last round of the Stockholm Conference that the positions of the NATO and WTO states converged on key questions related to the nature of a notifiable activity, observation, verification and constraints. The Helsinki Final Act had provided for voluntary notification of manoeuvres and troop movements and in effect left it up to the notifying state to decide whether a particular activity was one that it should notify to the other states. Thus, the USSR had notified only 22 manoeuvres under the Final Act from 1976–83. In Stockholm NATO sought to get all "out-of-garrison" land activities above agreed thresholds notified. NATO and the neutral and non-aligned stated (NNA) wanted notification thresholds to focus on the major combat units rather than an abstract number of personnel on the move. The East, however, wished merely to lower the 1975 threshold of 25,000 men to 20,000. The West demanded the right of observers to monitor all notifiable activities in view of the post-1975 Eastern practice of inviting observers only to infrequent, "demonstration" manoeuvres and that the observers should be allowed reasonable on-site access. NATO proposed that each state should be entitled to execute a quota of on-site ground and air inspections which the host state could not refuse. Only at the very end of the last round did the USSR accept mandatory on-site inspection. The East wanted notification of independent air and naval activities, which NATO successfully resisted.

On Sept. 19, 1986 the Stockholm Conference adopted a CSBM regime that was much more detailed and precise than the CBMs agreed in 1975, applying to military activities at a much lower level of armed forces. The observance of the CSBMs was to be subject to verification, including the right to mandatory on-site inspection of suspect activities. The CSBMs, furthermore, were to enjoy a much larger zone of application, covering military activities occurring throughout the territory of the USSR West of the Ural Mountains.

The CSBM regime was accompanied by verification provisions making it difficult to undermine the purpose of constraining the ability of the WTO and NATO to prepare for surprise offensive military operations in Europe under the guise of exercises or manoeuvres without fear of detection. The CSBMs would thereby reduce the probability of unjustified fears of surprise attack arising. They would also have the desirable effect of constraining the ability of states to employ military exercises as a means of intimidating other governments or peoples either outside or within the same alliance system. The verification provisions included notably the right to on-site inspection from the air, ground or both, of activities which a party or parties to the Stockholm Agreement believed to be possible violations of the CSBM regime. The state whose military activities caused concern would have no right to refuse such a challenge inspection. However, no state was obliged to accept more than three inspections on its territory in any one calendar year or more than one inspection per calendar year from any individual participating state.

Weaknesses of the Stockholm Agreement included the exclusion of "alerts" from obligatory advance notification and invitation of observers unless the alert exceeded 72 hours. The accord also made no provision for the exchange of information on the organization and location of major formations in Europe as NATO's proposal to this effect was rejected by the WTO as too intrusive. An agreed data base, though not absolutely vital to a CSBM regime *per se*, would be a basic necessity for genuine military-political stability and indispensable in future negotiations on the actual limitation and reduction of conventional forces in Europe.

The Stockholm Agreement was the first major reflection of greater Soviet openness in military affairs and signified the USSR's acceptance of the Western argument that a reasonable degree of transparency in the military activities and deployments of the two alliances would enhance mutual confidence and security. During the Vienna CSCE follow-up meeting from November 1986 to January 1989 the 35 participating states assessed the implementation of the Stockholm CSBMs and sought to agree on the next stage of the CSCE's work in security matters. Indeed, the implementation of the Stockholm regime worked quite well, providing for a much greater flow of information about military activities in Europe and significantly increasing their transparency and predictability. Both NATO and WTO states took advantage of their inspection rights in order to reinforce the practice and acceptability of mandatory challenge inspections as well as to clarify uncertainties about the other side's behaviour. The experience gained in operating the Stockholm regime also afforded insights into the kinds of new CSBMs which might need to be associated with future agreements on the actual limitation or reduction of armed forces and armaments in Europe. Security and stability in Europe were thereby enhanced.

In January 1989 the Vienna Review Conference completed the mandate for a second stage of negotiations on improved CSBMs in Europe. The Vienna CSBM negotiations began in March 1989, where the NATO states favoured the continuation of a functional approach, focusing on proposals for an annual exchange of information on military structures, forces and equipment within the Atlantic-to-the-Urals area and associated verification measures for the data provided. The USSR and its WTO allies again brought up their demand that the CSBM regime should be expanded to embrace naval and air activities at large and thus bring to an end the exclusion of military forces in which (in the case of maritime power) the NATO alliance had a clear superiority. The CSBM negotiations were to be concluded in time for the next CSCE Review Conference scheduled for March 1992 in Helsinki.

Mutual and balanced force reductions (MBFR). The MBFR talks in Vienna began in 1973 with the goal of reaching agreement on the reduction of troops and armaments in Central Europe. The participants were the NATO members (USA, UK, Canada, Belgium, West Germany, Luxembourg and the Netherlands) and WTO members (USSR, East Germany, Czechoslovakia and Poland). Both sides eventually agreed in principle on reductions to 900,000 ground and air troops in the MBFR "guidelines area" and on an initial reduction of 11,500 Soviet and 5,000–6,500 US troops. The negotiations had progressed with frustrating slowness and by the time that MBFR was finally superseded in 1989 no breakthrough had been achieved on the major outstanding issues. These were related to provisions for verification of the withdrawal and non-reintroduction of forces in the reductions area in Central Europe and the inclusion of armaments as well as personnel in the reductions. After 16 years and 46 rounds, the MBFR talks were wound up without result in February 1989. Some lessons had been learned, however, from the MBFR experience: an agreed initial data base setting out the existing forces of both sides was vital to agreement and would require mutual on-site inspection; imbalances and asymmetries must be taken into account; and, as the West had argued, associated verification measures would have to apply not only to the process of reductions itself but also to the troops and armaments remaining after reductions have been completed.

Conventional forces in Europe negotiations (CFE). In 1989 the Vienna CSCE Review Conference approved a mandate that had been worked out by the 16 NATO and seven WTO states for negotiations on Conventional Armed Forces in Europe (CFE). These were to be conducted between the 23 NATO and WTO members and accompanied by meetings among all the CSCE participants to exchange information and views on their progress. In the "Group of 23" "mandate talks" that began in February 1987 between the two alliances on the subject of the future CFE, the East had focused on the withdrawal of nuclear arms as well as offensive conventional weapons from Europe. The WTO also indicated its readiness for reductions that would remove imbalances in particular weapons in which it had a numerical advantage. The two alliances eventually agreed on the goals of stability at lower levels of conventional arms and equipment and elimination of the potential for surprise attack and large-scale offensive action. This was to be achieved through reductions, limitations, redeployment provisions, equal ceilings and other measures. The Group of 23 also agreed on the necessity of an effective and strict verification regime which would include mandatory on-site inspections and exchanges of disaggregated information on arms, equipment and personnel in the armed forces of the participating states.

The final substantial issue was resolved in Autumn 1988 when it was agreed that nuclear weapons would not—contrary to WTO proposals —be the subject of negotiation in the CFE talks but that dual-capable conventional arms would not be excluded. The WTO also abandoned its efforts to include maritime forces in the scope of the CFE negotiations in the face of stiff NATO resistance, while continuing to press for confidence-building measures at sea and constraints on naval operations in the parallel pan-European CSBM negotiations. The geographical scope of the CFE talks, unlike the MBFR forum but reflecting the zone of application of the Stockholm Agreement on CSBMs, would cover the land area from the Atlantic to the Urals.

The CFE negotiations began in March 1989 at the same time and in the same building as the talks on CSBMs. Strictly speaking, the CFE talks were not to be a bloc-to-bloc forum, as they were to take place within the framework of the CSCE process. Yet they were to be conducted autonomously and only the 23 members of NATO and the WTO would determine their results. The atmosphere from March 1989 onwards proved to be surprisingly businesslike and reflected the high priority accorded to rapid achievement of a CFE accord on the part of the new US President Bush and Soviet President Gorbachev. The superpowers appeared anxious to cement their new co-operative relationship as quickly as possible through new arms control accords.

In November 1988 and January 1989 NATO and the WTO released their respective comparisons of conventional forces in the area from the Atlantic to the Urals. WTO figures for personnel and combat aircraft included naval forces. Some of the data are included in the table.

Comparisons of NATO/WTO conventional forces

	NATO estimate	WTO estimate
Personnel, NATO	2,213,593	3,660,200
Personnel, WTO	3,090,000	3,573,100
Tanks, NATO	16,424	30,690
Tanks, WTO	51,000	59,470
Artillery, NATO	14,458	57,060
Artillery, WTO	43,400	71,560
Combat aircraft, NATO	8,200	7,130
Combat aircraft, WTO	4,507	7,876

The unilateral reductions in Soviet military personnel and equipment in the European USSR and Eastern Europe, announced by Gorbachev in December 1988, indicated the USSR's willingness to begin to scale down its conventional military superiority in the European theatre. Yet, according to NATO, the unilateral Soviet reductions would still leave the WTO forces with a superiority over NATO in tanks and artillery of 2.4:1 and of 1.8:1 in combat aircraft.

Western proposals at the CFE talks in March 1989 called for overall ceilings for each alliance in the Atlantic-to-Urals area of 20,000 tanks, 16,500 artillery pieces and 28,000 armoured personnel carriers (APCs). Such cuts would involve highly asymmetrical cuts in WTO forces and remove their numerical superiority in these weapons. NATO also sought to limit the proportion of the total weapons in these categories which any single state could hold and to limit stationing of forces outside their own borders. The WTO proposals of May 1989 accepted NATO's proposal on tank and APC ceilings but called for a higher ceiling on artillery pieces (24,000).

The two alliances were in agreement on the principle of reducing forces and weapons to a level below that of the numerically inferior party. They also concurred on the need for a phased approach to reductions, with asymmetries first being eliminated through reductions to levels below current ones. They agreed on the desirability of first removing the capability to launch surprise attack and conduct large-scale offensive operations although they had differing views on the offensive qualities of certain weapons and the need to include them in a stage-one CFE agreement. The WTO sought specific limits on manpower while the West preferred its indirect inclusion in an accord. There was acceptance of the need to exchange detailed military information on the basis of agreed definitions and counting rules and WTO recognition of the NATO view that a comprehensive verification system would be essential, involving exchange of disaggregated information and mandatory challenge inspections by land and air. NATO proposals on data exchange, verification and "stabilizing measures" were presented in September 1989. The latter included suggested rules for the monitored storage of certain equipment items to be limited by treaty, prior notification of large-scale mobilization of reservists and of any major movement of treaty-limited items, e.g. tanks. In February 1990 WTO and NATO Foreign Ministers met in Ottawa to open negotiations on the US "Open Skies" proposal for aerial surveillance of installations and movements on the territory of the member-states of the two alliances. An "Open Skies" accord was confidently predicted by early summer 1990.

The two sides had difficulty agreeing over the exact subdivision of the Atlantic-to-the-Urals area in zones with sublimits on weapons deployed, on the rules affecting the stationing of forces outside national territory and on the proportion of armaments in Europe that could be held by any one state. NATO treated all combat aircraft in the same manner, while the WTO sought to exclude land-based air defence aircraft or to have them dealt with more leniently than strike aircraft and there were differences over the definition of combat aircraft and helicopters.

In May 1989 NATO proposed reductions by both sides to 15 per cent below the current NATO levels in combat aircraft and helicopters to ceilings of 5,700 and 1,900. NATO also proposed reductions in US and Soviet manpower stationed abroad in Europe to an equal ceiling of 275,000 and the demobilization of these forces on withdrawal. It suggested that agreement on superpower reductions should be reached within six to twelve months and the accord implemented by 1992 or 1993. Overall, the proposals made by NATO would have involved roughly a 50 per cent cut in Soviet forces stationed in Eastern Europe and the destruction of over half the USSR's tanks in Europe. The USSR reacted favourably to the NATO proposal on US and Soviet partial troop withdrawals from Europe and the desire for speedy progress to a first-stage CFE agreement that the initiative seemed to reflect.

On Feb. 8, 1990 NATO tabled compromise positions designed to bring the two sides closer together on issues related to tanks, APCs and aircraft, delimitation of subzones within the area of reductions and storage of military material. The large number of basic training aircraft held by the WTO states could be excluded from the count and there would be a separate upper limit on air defence interceptor aircraft and a reduced ceiling of 4,700 combat aircraft. NATO also responded to WTO calls for a more discriminating approach to reductions in combat helicopters and for inclusion of smaller tanks in the count.

NATO's February proposals confirmed President Bush's offer of Jan. 31, 1990 to reduce US military personnel in the Central European zone by 80,000 to a total of 195,000 in a first-stage CFE Agreement. The USSR would also be allowed to station 195,000 troops in Europe outside its territory. The new ceiling on US and Soviet troops in Central Europe was considerably lower than the 275,000 figure then under discussion in the CFE talks. The USSR welcomed this NATO initiative but rejected the West's desire to allow another 30,000 US personnel to remain in Western Europe outside the central area (e.g. in the UK), insisting on equal Soviet rights relative to the USA. The episode also drew attention to existing WTO demands for commitments to specific reductions in non-US foreign forces stationed in West Germany, particularly those of the

UK and France, which NATO resisted. Nonetheless, at the Ottawa meeting of Foreign Ministers the USSR accepted the Bush initiative.

Soviet acceptance of unequal ceilings on US and Soviet forces stationed abroad in Europe reinforced the growing optimism that a first-stage CFE agreement would be ready for signing before a summit meeting of CSCE states planned for Autumn 1990. It also reflected the growing pressure in Hungary, Czechoslovakia and Poland for the earliest possible withdrawal of Soviet forces from the territory of those allies. By early March 1990 it appeared that Soviet troops would have left Hungary and Czechoslovakia completely by mid-1991. Moreover, the future security orientation of a unified Germany was far from clear, generating new considerations to be incorporated into the European arms control policies of both superpowers and their allies.

In late 1989 the dramatic upheavals in Eastern Europe had strengthened Western hopes that the CFE negotiations might bring a massive reduction in the Soviet military threat to Western (and Eastern) Europe. Yet the political changes in the non-Soviet members of the WTO also cast some doubt over the survival of that alliance and its ability coherently to negotiate on the complex technical aspects of conventional arms reductions and their associated confidence-building and verification measures. By the spring of 1990 it might have appeared to some observers that the unexpected pace of political change in Eastern Europe — and especially the two Germanys — was sweeping away the ground from under the feet of the CFE negotiators on both sides in Vienna. (*See also* **Soviet Relations with the West**)

DS

AZERBAIDZHAN. A Soviet Socialist Republic was proclaimed in Azerbaidzhan in April 1920. From 1922, with **Georgia** and **Armenia**, it constituted the Transcaucasian Soviet Federal Socialist Republic as part of the USSR, and in 1936 it became an independent union republic within the USSR. Azerbaidzhan covers an area of 86,600 sq km; its 1989 census population was 7,029,000, or 2.5 per cent of the population of the country as a whole. According to the 1979 census Azerbaidzhanis accounted for 78 per cent of the republic's population; the remainder include Russians, Armenians and Daghestanis, agricultural output includes grain, cotton, rice and citrus fruit; the most important industry is the oil industry, particularly in the Baku region. Azerbaidzhan includes the Nakhichevan autonomous republic and the Nagorno-Karabakh autonomous region as well as 65 districts. Nagorno-Karabakh, an area of 4,400 sq km, had a 1987 population of 180,000 of whom the great majority (in the 1979 census, 75.9 per cent) are ethnic Armenians. A vote in the Nagorno-Karabakh assembly in February 1988 in favour of unification with Armenia led to continuing disturbances throughout the following years. (*See also* **Nationality Question in the USSR**)

SLW

B

BALCEROWICZ, LESZEK. Balcerowicz was appointed deputy chairman of the Council of Ministers and Minister of Finance in the **Mazowiecki** government of Poland endorsed by the Polish *Sejm* in September 1989. Forty-two years old at the time of his nomination, he is a graduate of the Main School of Planning and Statistics (SGPiS) and was employed there from 1970 specializing in international economic relations and the operation of economic systems. He undertook further economic studies in the USA between 1972 and 1974. From 1978 to 1981 he directed a group working on a social project for economic reform and was vice chairman of the Council of the Polish Economics Association in 1981 and 1982. During 1981 he was also a consultant for the network linking major enterprises organized by **Solidarity** directed to the formulation of an independent programme of economic reform. Until December 1981 he was a member of the **Polish United Workers' Party**. In recent years his interests have been directed towards free market solutions and the role of privatization in socialist economies. On appointment as minister of finance he undertook as a matter of urgency the formulation of a programme of economic stabilization and recovery, the outlines of which were made public in early October 1989. On Dec. 17 he presented to the *Sejm* the full economic package of the government, and on Dec. 23, 1989 a formal agreement with the IMF was signed which released a standby loan and further significant measures of economic assistance.

PGL

BAPTISTS IN THE USSR. The Baptist, Evangelical Christian and Pentecostal communities in the USSR derive from the influence of German and British church people visiting the Russian Empire, mainly in the nineteenth century. The Mennonites emigrated to Russia from Prussia at the invitation of Catherine II. (The Lutherans of Estonia and Latvia — *see* **Lutherans in the USSR** — received their religion from the dominant Baltic Germans.) In 1944, after a period of persecution shared with other religions in the Soviet Union (*see* **Religion and Communism**), the government allowed the formation of the All-Union Council of Evangelical Christians and Baptists (AUCECB). Many Protestant congregations refused to join the Council, seeing it as an instrument of central state control.

In 1960, under severe pressure form **Khrushchev**'s anti-religious campaign, the AUCECB sent out instructions to exclude children from worship, discourage the baptism of people under 30 and restrict proselytization. Opposition to the action of the AUCECB led to a split within the Baptist movement. Dissidents withdrew from the AUCECB and in 1965 established the Council of Churches of Evangelical Christians and Baptists (otherwise known as the Reform Baptists or *Initsiativniki*). After the state refused to recognize them, they were forced underground in 1970, under the leadership of Gennady Kryuchkov and Georgy Vins.

The Reform Baptists suffered severe persecution throughout the 1970s and early 1980s, with many pastors and laity being sent to labour camps and a number of unexplained deaths. Their efforts to worship were treated as hostile illegal political activities. They established underground printing presses, including the Khristianin Publishing House which printed Bibles. They produced a considerable literature on religious rights and repression, and created a network of committees to publicize in the West their persecution, and to support prisoners and their families. Many of them tried to emigrate, as did most of the Pentecostalist communities.

Meanwhile in the 1970s the government improved the conditions of the official AUCECB, hoping to win back the Baptist congregations to the recognized body. Both the official and unofficial wings experienced a considerable growth in support in the 1970s and 1980s. They tended to attract Russians and Ukrainians from less educated backgrounds (intellectuals were more likely to be attracted to the **Russian Orthodox Church** or **the Ukrainian Catholic (Uniate) Church**). Estimates of the total numbers of Baptists vary from one to three million. In April 1989, under *perestroika*, the oppressive instructions of 1960 were withdrawn. The persecution of unregistered Baptists was much diminished and most prisoners in camps for religious reasons were released.

PJSD

BELGRADE (Beograd). The Yugoslav and Serbian capital, Belgrade (1981 census population, 1,470,073) is located at the confluence of the Danube and Sava rivers. It is the commercial, industrial, political and cultural centre of the country as well as a transportation and communications hub. The city's industries include metal-work, textiles, chemicals, machine tools and food products. Repeatedly captured and recaptured over the centuries by Romans, Austrians, Turks and others, Belgrade became the Serbian capital in 1882 and the capital of the Kingdom of the Serbs, Croats and Slovenes (Yugoslavia after 1929) after World War I. Extensively damaged during World War II while under German occupa-tion, the city was liberated by Yugoslav partisans with Soviet support in 1944. As well as party and government headquarters, Belgrade houses the Serbian Academy of Sciences, a university, a Roman Catholic archbishopric, and an Orthodox Eastern patriarchate.

SLW

BELORUSSIA. Established in January 1919, the Belorussian Soviet Socialist Republic became one of the original members of the USSR in 1922. Together with the **Ukraine**, it enjoys represen-tation (together with the USSR) in the United Nations. Its area is 207,600 sq km; its 1989 census population was 10,200,000, or 3.6 per cent of the total for the country as a whole. Nearly 80 per cent of the population are Belorussian by nationality; Russians, Poles, Ukrainians and Jews are also numerous. Belorussia is important for its agricultural produce, including flax, potatoes, and meat and dairy produce; light and engineering industries have also been developed. In 1990 it was subdivided into six regions and 117 districts.

SLW

BENEŠ, EDVARD. Born in 1884, Beneš suc-ceeded T.G. **Masaryk** as President of Czechoslo-vakia in 1935. During World War I, from exile in France, he had been Masaryk's closest collabora-tor in the campaign for Czechoslovak indepen-dence and then served as his country's Foreign Minister from 1918 until his accession to the presidency. He resigned from the latter post in October 1938 after the Munich Agreement but in July 1940, in exile in London, resumed his posi-tion as president and head of the Czechoslovak government-in-exile. His conclusion of a Treaty of Friendship, Mutual Aid and Post-war Co-oper-ation with the Soviet Union in December 1943 was an early indication of a shift in Czechoslo-vakia's foreign policy from the primarily pro-Western orientation Beneš had pursued in the inter-war period to one which would involve a closer relationship with Moscow after World War II. That move reflected his disillusionment with Britain and France which had failed to defend

Czechoslovakia against Nazi Germany and his realization that the USSR would be the dominant force in East-Central Europe after the War. His hopes that, despite its closer links with Moscow, Czechoslovakia would remain a parliamentary democracy and a bridge between East and West were disappointed when the Communists seized power in February 1948. Beneš resigned the pres-idency once more in June that year and died the following September.

GW

BERECZ, JANOS. Leading ideologist of the **Hungarian Socialist Workers' Party (HSWP).** Berecz, born in 1930, began his political career in the Communist youth movement in Hungary, then went to Moscow for a period of study at the CPSU Academy of Social Sciences in 1963–66. On his return to Budapest, he worked as Secretary to the Party Committee in the Ministry of Foreign Affairs, then in 1972 was transferred to work in the HSWP Central Committee's Department of Foreign Affairs as its Deputy Head and, from 1974, Head. In 1982 he took the important post of Editor-in- Chief of the Party's daily newspaper, *Népszabadság*, and in 1985 he was promoted to Secretary of the HSWP Central Committee. The high point of his career came with his election to full membership of the HSWP Politburo in June 1987, and he thus became a leading contender to succeed **Kádár** as General Secretary of the party. Berecz was well-known for his relatively hardline position on ideological questions, and his best-known publication *Ellenforradalom tollál es feqyverrel* ("Counter-revolution with pen and arms", 1969), was the standard work of historical propaganda on the events of 1956. His efforts to win credibility in the increasingly influential reformist factions in the party were not success-ful, however, and also lost him support among the traditional hardliners. He lost the leadership battle to Károly **Grósz** in May 1988, and failed to win re-election to the Politburo in April 1989.

JB

BERLIN. Berlin, founded in the thirteenth centu-ry, is the former capital city of Prussia and of the German *Reich*. The city suffered devastating bomb damage in the latter stages of World War II. Since 1945 it has been under the control of Soviet, American, British and French forces, which each have their respective sectors of the city. "Berlin—Capital of the GDR" is the desig-nation used in the GDR for East Berlin, the Soviet sector of Greater Berlin. It is not recognized as the capital city by the Western powers, nor in principle by the West German government. In practice, as the seat of government and administration, it adopts such a role. In return, the GDR and the USSR do not recognize West Berlin as part of the Federal Republic of Germany. The population of East Berlin is approximately 1.3 million, that of West Berlin approximately 1.9 million.

Berlin has been a bone of contention between the three Western powers and the USSR since it was occupied. The first Berlin crisis occurred in 1948, when the Soviet forces responded to currency reform in the Western zones of Germany by sealing off water and road routes to West Berlin, in an attempt to prevent the foundation of a separate West German state. The Western allies replied with a massive transport of food and fuel through the air corridors to West Berlin, which lasted until May 1949.

As a result of Walter **Ulbricht**'s attempt to stem the flow of emigrants from the GDR, from Aug. 13, 1961 until Nov. 9, 1989 the Berlin Wall divided East from West Berlin. Passage in either direction was only via recognized border points. For GDR citizens permission to cross was hard to obtain; those who attempted to do so without permission risked being shot on sight. On the night of Nov. 9, 1989 the Wall (indeed the entire inter-German border) was opened for GDR citizens to cross freely. There are still formalities and specified border crossings, albeit a much greater number, but numerous agreements are beginning to join the two halves of Berlin together again. The city remains, however, under the terms of the 1971 Four Power Agreement, and any change in the status of Berlin as a result of union between the two German states would require a negotiated settlement.

JO

BESSARABIA. Now in the Soviet Union, this region has close associations also with Romania owing to its Romanian-ness and its history. The province is named after Basarab, a notable name in Moldavian history; under Stephen the Great (reigned 1457–1504) this was part of his kingdom. The Moldavian language is indistinguishable from Romanian except for being written in the Cyrillic script; even this (in 1989) was being altered. It is divided from Romania proper by the Pruth river. The southern part of Bessarabia contains various non-Romanian nationalities.

As long as hardliners prevailed within the Soviet Communist Party any question of Bessarabia's reuniting with Romania remained no more than academic, especially given that Romania itself was experiencing greater material hardships

than Bessarabia. The change of administrations in both countries—**Gorbachev** coming to power in the USSR and **Ceauşescu** being overthrown in Romania—has radically altered the situation. Soviet Moldavia (comprising the larger part of Bessarabia) belongs ethnically and linguistically to Romania, and although at the time of writing it still appears rather unlikely that the province will be allowed to secede, this can no longer be regarded as out of the question.

RH

BOBU, EMIL. Bobu was the Central Committee member of the **Romanian Communist Party** in charge of cadres and also chairman of the National Council of Problems of Economic and Social Organization under the Ceauşescu regime. He was also a Permanent Bureau member of the Political Executive Committee. Bobu fled with the Ceauşescus by helicopter at the time of the overthrow of the Ceauşescu regime but later separated from them. Captured, he was put on trial with other former Politburo members and was sentenced to life imprisonment.

RH

BRAŞOV. Second largest city of Romania but far smaller than **Bucharest** with a population under 350,000. Braşov is the country's second industrial city and witnessed a major demonstration on Nov. 15, 1987 which stemmed from grievances over pay and redundancies at the "Red Flag" tractor plant and was fuelled by anger at the local elite's relatively lavish life- style; it was brutally suppressed, though all details are not known.

Braşov was not named in early reports of the demonstrations leading to the overthrow of the **Ceauşescu** regime, but according to later reports large crowds assembled in the city centre on Dec. 21; no shooting took place then, but some, perhaps as many as 64, people were killed later. The local commander, Major-Gen. Ion Flora (or Florea) obeyed a telex received from the chief of staff, ordering him not to fire on the people. As reported in mid-January 1990, Flora was at that time heading the **National Salvation Front** in Braşov.

RH

"BREZHNEV DOCTRINE". A real if undeclared principle of Soviet foreign policy in the 1960s and 1970s, in terms of which the interests of the socialist community as a whole took precedence over the interests and wishes of any of its individual members. The doctrine emerged publicly in the aftermath of the intervention in Czechoslovakia by the USSR and five other **Warsaw Treaty Organization (WTO)** powers in August 1968 to end that country's experiment with "socialism with a human face". An authoritative editorial in *Pravda* entitled "The defence of socialism is the highest internationalist duty" explained the intervention in terms of the interests of the socialist countries as a whole, which took precedence over the wishes of any of the individual members of that community. **Brezhnev**, speaking to the 5th Congress of the **Polish United Workers' Party** in November 1968, explained that the **Communist Party of the Soviet Union** had always believed that each socialist country should choose the path of its socialist development in terms of its own specific conditions. But there were "general tendencies of socialist development, deviation from which could lead to a deviation from socialism as such". And whenever foreign and domestic forces hostile to socialism attempted to reverse the course of development of any socialist country towards the restoration of capitalism, and when a threat to the socialist cause developed in that country which was a threat to the security of the socialist community as a whole, this was "not only a problem of the people of the country in question, but a general problem and concern of all the socialist countries". This doctrine of limited sovereignty was written into the 1977 Soviet Constitution in the form of "socialist internationalism"; under **Gorbachev**, however, it was first informally and then officially repudiated, with the Soviet leadership joining with the other countries concerned to condemn the 1968 intervention as a mistaken and harmful act. By the early 1990s the "limits of the possible" in Eastern Europe were still being explored; a non-Communist government, a privatized economy and perhaps a decision to leave the WTO all appeared to be acceptable in principle provided Soviet security interests were not directly threatened.

SLW

BREZHNEV, LEONID IL'ICH. Soviet politician and General Secretary of the **Communist Party of the Soviet Union (CPSU)** from 1964 to 1982. **Khrushchev**'s successor as party leader, Brezhnev eventually became the longest-ruling General Secretary apart from Joseph **Stalin**, but his record of substantial economic and diplomatic achievement came to be obscured by the complacency and corruption of his later years of power and the Brezhnev period as a whole became known under **Gorbachev** as one of "stagnation". Brezhnev was born, according to his official biog-

raphy, in a metal-worker's family in what is now Dneprodzerzhinsk in the Ukraine in 1906. Brezhnev worked from the age of 15 but furthered his education on a part-time basis, latterly in a metallurgical institute in his home town. He rapidly gravitated towards party work, however, becoming a full-time official in 1938 and in February 1939 first secretary of the Dnepropetrovsk regional party committee. He continued his political work in the Soviet armed forces during the war, rising to the rank of major-general in 1944. After further local party postings Brezhnev became a republican party leader in Moldavia in 1950, and then in Kazakhstan in 1955. He had joined the party itself in 1931, and became a member of the Central Committee in 1952 (when he also became a junior member of the ruling Politburo).

Brezhnev moved into national office in 1960 when he took on the largely ceremonial duties of chairman of the Presidium of the USSR Supreme Soviet, or head of state. In October 1964, on Khrushchev's dismissal, he became party leader. Originally, after 1964, a "collective leadership", it had become a leadership "headed by Leonid Brezhnev" by the early 1970s. The Politburo had been listed in alphabetical order after 1964 to emphasize its collective character, but in 1973, after KGB chairman Yuri **Andropov** had joined it, Brezhnev's name contined to be listed first although this was a violation of strictly alphabetical principles. In 1976, at the XXV Party Congress, Brezhnev became the party's "universally acclaimed leader" and *vozhd'* (chief), a term previously used to describe Stalin. He became a marshal of the Soviet Union, and a bronze bust was unveiled in his birthplace. In 1977 he became head of state (or chairman of the Presidium) once again, and he was awarded the Gold Medal of Karl Marx, the highest award of the Academy of Sciences, for his "outstanding contribution to the development of Marxist-Leninist theory". In 1978 he received the Order of Victory for his wartime service, and in 1979 the Lenin Prize for Literature for his memoirs, which had been written for him by a literary aide who himself received the Order of Lenin a few days later. At the XXVI Party Congress in 1981 Brezhnev was hailed as an "outstanding political leader and statesman", a "true continuer" of **Lenin**'s great cause", and an "ardent fighter for peace and Communism". Unprecedentedly, the whole Politburo and Secretariat, Brezhnev included, were re-elected without change; Brezhnev's son, Yuri, a first deputy minister of foreign trade, became a candidate member of the Central Committee, and so too did his son-in-law Yuri Churbanov, a first deputy minister of internal affairs.

Brezhnev's 75th birthday in December 1981 brought these tributes to a new pitch of intensity. Seven of *Pravda*'s eight pages on Dec. 19 were wholly or partly devoted to the event, and tributes continued to appear in the central press throughout the following week. Brezhnev himself attended a ceremony in the Kremlin where he was invested with a series of distinctions by the leaders of the East European Communist states, who had come to Moscow for the occasion. The Soviet awards, which he had himself to authorize as head of state, included a seventh Order of Lenin and a fourth Hero of the Soviet Union citation. Mikhail Suslov, a few years his senior, remarked at the conferment of these awards that 75 was just the "beginning of middle age". Brezhnev's life was turned into a film, "Story of a Communist"; his wartime exploits in the Caucasus, little noted at the time, were presented as all but decisive turning-point of the struggle against the Nazis; and his memoirs were turned into a film, plays, mime, a popular song and a full-scale oratorio. He had more orders and medals than Khrushchev and Stalin combined, and more military distinctions than Marshal Zhukov, who had saved Leningrad and then liberated Berlin during World War II. Even a modest poem, "To the German Komsomol", written when he was 17, received front-page treatment when it appeared in *Pravda* in May 1982.

Brezhnev's personal and political powers, nonetheless, were clearly failing. According to the testimony of historian and commentator Roy Medvedev, Brezhnev began to suffer serious ill-health at the end of the 1960s and in January 1976 was briefly clinically dead following a stroke. For three months he was unable to work, as his speech and writing had been impaired, and thereafter he was constantly surrounded by doctors, with a fully- equipped ambulance following his car on trips abroad. His speech became increasing slurred, his breathing laboured, his concentration limited. Unkind anecdotes began to circulate: in one of these his eyebrows were "Stalin's moustache at a higher level", in another he was to have an operation to enlarge the chest so that he could accommodate his array of medals. Perhaps most seriously of all, his grip on affairs of state became increasingly infirm. The death of Mikhail Suslov, in January 1982, seems in retrospect to have been decisive. One of the Politburo's oldest and longest-serving members with acknowledged authority in both ideology and foreign affairs, Suslov had apparently served as king-maker in 1964, declining the general secretaryship for himself and then backing Brezhnev for the position. With Suslov gone the Brezhnev leadership began to disintegrate rapidly. At the end of the month

the death was reported of Semen Tsvigun, a first deputy chairman of the KGB and a close Brezhnev associate, rumour suggested it was a case of suicide precipitated by his impending arrest on corruption charges. At the beginning of March 1982 came the arrest of "Boris the gypsy" and other figures from the worlds of circus and entertainment on charges of smuggling diamonds abroad, bribery and currency speculation. All were close friends of Brezhnev's daughter Galina and their arrest showed that the general secretary's authority was no longer sufficient to protect them.

Still more significantly, in May 1982 a plenary session of the CPSU Central Committee took place at which Brezhnev (according to Western press reports) was unable to secure the election of his own protégé, Konstantin **Chernenko**, to the powerful position of Central Committee Secretary with responsibility for ideology which had become vacant with the death of Suslov. In a development widely seen as significant at home and abroad it was the head of the KGB, Yuri Andropov, who was elected to the position, apparently with the support of the armed forces lobby. All of this suggested that Brezhnev's political authority as well as his physical health were in decline, and reports circulating in the West in the early 1980s suggested that it had already been decided that Brezhnev would retire from the general secretaryship, retaining the much more ceremonial position of head of state. Brezhnev, in the event, anticipated any changes of this kind by dying suddenly on the morning of Nov. 10 1982, his health apparently undermined by a two-hour stint in the reviewing box at the anniversary parade in Red Square three days earlier. *Pravda*'s obituary mourned the passing of a "continuer of the cause of Lenin, a fervent patriot, and an outstanding revolutionary and struggler for peace and Communism, [and] an outstanding political and government leader of the contemporary era".

The Brezhnev era began to come under indirect attack during Andropov's brief general secretaryship, but the attacks became muted again under his successor Chernenko. It was not, in fact, until Mikhail **Gorbachev**'s assumption of the party leadership that Brezhnev and his period of rule began to be exposed to open and uncompromising criticism. For Gorbachev, addressing the XXVI Party Congress in 1986, the Brezhnev era was one of postponed decisions and missed opportunities, when a "curious psychology — how to change things without really changing anything" — had been dominant. By the end of the year, on the 80th anniversary of Brezhnev's birthday, the charges became much graver and more personalized. Brezhnev's wartime career, particularly the "brilliant episode" at the Malaya Zemlya beachhead in 1943, was warmly praised, and the early years of his general secretaryship were seen as a time of economic, social and cultural advance, including the attainment of strategic parity with the USA. In the later years of his life, however, there had been too much reliance on "habitual patterns and formulae", and a lack of openness had made it impossible to identify difficulties in time to deal with them effectively.

Criticism of the Brezhnev era became still more uncompromising over the years that followed. Brezhnev, Gorbachev explained in his address on the 70th anniversary of the revolution in 1987, had helped to bring about a change in methods of economic management soon after his accession. A programme of economic reform had been devised, and major schemes for the development of new parts of the country and new branches of industry had been elaborated. The country's scientific potential had increased, its defence capacity had been strengthened, and living standards had risen. Many developments in foreign policy had enhanced the Soviet Union's international prestige. The promise of these achievements, however, had been dissipated by a failure to carry the reforms through to their logical conclusion, and still more so by a failure to make the changes that had become necessary in social policy and political leadership. The gap between words and deeds had steadily widened, and a pre-crisis situation had developed in the economy. In the society at large, an unequal distribution of benefits had undermined public support for socialist principles and encouraged the growth of social alienation and immorality.

Brezhnev's faults of character were spelt out more fully in press commentaries. He had awarded himself four gold stars as a Hero of the Soviet Union for bravery in World War II when he did not deserve them, *Pravda* charged; and he had added the Order of Victory, which was formally speaking reserved for army commanders who gained important wartime victories. Such was his love of decorations, it was reported, that when he died more than 200 awards and other distinctions had to be carried behind his coffin. He was also greedy for applause, and had arranged for "organizational measures" to be taken to ensure that his speeches were greeted with prolonged ovations. The corruption of Brezhnev's immediate circle was exposed in other stories: Brezhnev's daughter Galina, for instance, was customarily addressed as "Madam" and speculated in diamonds, the price of which more than doubled during her father's administration. Her former husband became a Hero of Socialist Labour, and

she herself acquired a wholly spurious doctorate in philosophy. Readers of a weekly paper were regaled in early 1988 to accounts of the private life of Nikolai Shchelokov, Brezhnev's close associate who had also been Minister of the Interior. Shchelokov, it emerged, had a fleet of foreign cars for himself and his immediate family, a set of private flats, a private photographer, an architect, a "masseur", a cook and a biographer. He "acquired" old books from a library; he even had a film made about himself for his own private viewing at a cost to the state of about half a million rubles. His flat, an entire floor of the apartment block in which Brezhnev also lived, was crammed with antiques which had been confiscated from black marketeers.

There were few in the Brezhnev entourage, in fact, whose records could withstand scrutiny. His son-in-law Yuri Churbanov, already dismissed from his post at the interior ministry, was arrested in 1987 and brought to trial on charges of bribe-taking on a massive scale. He was sentenced to 12 years imprisonment in a harsh-regime labour camp at the end of December 1988 and stripped of his state honours. Galina herself, together with other family members, lost her special pension and other privileges earlier the same year, and Brezhnev's widow had to return his decorations to public custody. The city of Brezhnev, formerly Naberezhnye chelny, reverted to its original name in January 1988; so too did Brezhnev Square in Moscow and Leningrad, and the Brezhnev (formerly Cherry Tree) district in the capital (unkind humourists suggested that the Brezhnevs would soon become "Cherry Tree family"). Matters were taken further at the end of the year when it was decided that Brezhnev's name should be removed from every town, street, factory and institute that had been named after him following his death. Brezhnev's secretary, G. D. Brovin, was separately identified as connected with a major crime ring and was sentenced to nine years' imprisonment for bribetaking. Brezhnev, according to opinion polls, was already more unpopular than Stalin. The very name had become a curse, Brezhnev's grandson Andrei told *Moscow News*; people connected with the family had been forced out of their jobs, and their families and friends had deserted them.

SLW

BRUCAN, SILVIU. A former anbassador of Romania to the USA and the UN and a signatory of a letter criticising **Ceauşescu**, Brucan was put under house arrest towards the end of the Ceauşescu regime. An executive member of the **National Salvation Front**, Brucan quickly emerged as its leading ideologist although stating that he himself had no political ambitions.

RH

BUCHAREST (Bucureşti). Capital of Romania, population around 1.8 million, and the country's leading industrial and commercial centre. Bucharest's former reputed resemblance to Paris was severely damaged during the **Ceauşescu** era by a programme of construction of monumental public and party buildings and the destruction of historic monuments which drew wide international criticism. The city centre suffered severely during the overthrow of the Ceauşescu regime at the end of 1989, including fire damage to the presidential palace and the destruction of the national library. The television station and Otopeni airport also suffered. Other areas of the city are reported not to have been damaged.

RH

BUDAPEST. The Hungarian capital and its principal industrial, cultural and transportation centre. The city occupies an area of 525 sq km and had a population, in 1988, of 2,104,000 (about a fifth of the population of the country as a whole). One of Europe's oldest and most historic cities, Budapest became one of the two capitals of the Austro-Hungarian empire before World War I but was badly damaged when it was recaptured by Soviet troops in 1945 from German occupying forces. The city accounts for about half of Hungary's industrial production, with a wide range of output including machinery, iron and steel, chemicals, pharmaceuticals and textiles. Apart from party and governmental headquarters, Budapest accommodates a university (founded in 1635) and the Hungarian Academy of Sciences.

SLW

BULGARIA, PEOPLE'S REPUBLIC OF. *Population*: 8,989,000 (end-1988). *Area*: 110,912 sq km. *Top five trading partners* (1988): USSR (58.1 per cent); German Democratic Republic (5.5 per cent); Czechoslovakia (5 per cent); Poland (4.5 per cent); Federal Republic of Germany (2.9 per cent). *Urban population as percentage of total*: 66.2 per cent (1987); *Birth rate*: 13 per thousand (1989). *Life expectancy*: males 68; females 74 (1989).

Political background. The seat of a powerful empire and a relatively advanced culture in early medieval times, Bulgaria thereafter fell first under the influence of the neighbouring Byzantine state and then, at the end of the fourteenth century,

under Turkish rule. The latter ended in 1878, with the Russo-Turkish war and the Treaty of San Stefano, which created an independent Bulgarian state of considerably greater size than today's and with access to the Aegean. The Treaty of Berlin, occasioned by the Western powers' fear of Russian expansionism, promptly reduced this area by two-thirds. Bulgarian foreign policy in the succeeding 65 years was dominated by the aim of restoring the "San Stefano frontiers" (these territorial claims being bolstered by historical arguments on the extent of medieval Bulgaria): its pursuit brought Bulgaria on to the losing German side in both world wars. Domestically, a highly progressive and democratic ("Tirnovo") constitution was grafted at independence on to a peasant society unready for modern political forms. The results were predictable: politics were often violent, and for much of the time government took the form of royal or military authoritarianism.

The Red Army's entry into Bulgaria in September 1944 was swiftly followed by a coup in which the **Fatherland Front** anti-fascist coalition of parties, founded in the previous year, seized power. The **Bulgarian Communist Party (BCP)** was originally in a minority within this government, but by a combination of control of key ministries, Soviet support, and skilful use of "salami tactics", it emerged as the dominant force, excluding or subduing its original allies. In 1947–48, a one-party system was effectively established: all parties were outlawed except the BCP and its most important rival, the **Bulgarian Agrarian National Union (BANU)**, which was incorporated as a junior and entirely compliant partner in the Fatherland Front. This process of consolidating power involved a good deal of force and repression—for instance, BANU leader Nikola Petkov was tried and executed for treason—and the implementation of Communist policies of collectivization in the late 1940s was not notably gentler. As in other East European states, the Communist party eventually turned this repression against its own members: "Titoists"—largely "home Communists" who had spent the 1930s and the war years in Bulgaria rather than in Soviet exile—were exposed and purged in large numbers in 1949–50.

Leadership of the BCP and state passed from the veteran Comintern leader Georgi Dimitrov, who died in July 1949, to the ailing and aged Vasil Kolarov, who survived just six months in office. On Kolarov's death, power passed to Vulko Chervenkov, who consolidated his position by traditional Stalinist means. The death of Stalin in Moscow had its repercussions in Bulgaria: the BCP adopted its own version of the conciliatory "New Course", and Chervenkov was obliged in

1954 to give up the post of General Secretary, copying the separation of that office from the premiership that was then fashionable in Moscow. The successor chosen by him—Todor **Zhivkov** —turned out to be anything but the compliant supporter he had hoped for, and the political history of the next three decades is that of Zhivkov's gradual consolidation and resourceful maintenance of power, a process in which Chervenkov was rather early marginalized.

Recent political developments. Zhivkov's position was weakened in the second half of the 1980s by a variety of developments and difficulties. This weakening culminated in Zhivkov's overthrow in November 1989, when a leadership grouping headed by Foreign Minister Petur **Mladenov** succeeded in mustering a Central Committee majority against the veteran leader. Since then, the pace of politics has been hectic. Popular pressure has been mobilized and channelled by a highly effective opposition consisting of the **Union of Democratic Forces** and its constituent groups. This pressure has extorted various concessions from the BCP—or else, so strengthened the hand of the party's radicals as to allow them to force through these concessions. Zhivkov's associates have been removed from the leadership leaving only three members or candidates of the October 1989 Politburo in high office as of mid-February 1990; a good many even of those installed after Zhivkov's ousting have been judged insufficiently radical and therefore reassigned to obscurity. Mladenov himself was eased out as party leader after only three months and confined to the less influential post of President, being replaced at the head of the party by Aleksandur **Lilov**, a more convincing radical. Important political freedoms have been conceded, and relatively free elections scheduled for May 1990. To date the BCP shows no signs of suffering the fate of several other East European Communist parties: it has remained in power, it has avoided a disabling split, and it stands a good chance of emerging from the elections as at least the dominant partner in a coalition government— partly because it has been able to insist on an early date for these, giving the opposition little time to organize. But it is constrained to negotiate with the opposition at every turn, and its survival will now depend on its ability to operate effectively in the new competitive conditions. And Bulgaria's severe economic problems (see below) mean that this ability will be tested to the full.

Economic background.
(i) *Natural resources.* Bulgaria's natural endowments are mixed. On the one hand, the country has fertile soil and a warm climate: its agriculture is therefore capable of producing not only grain but also such eminently exportable items as tomatoes, grapes and tobacco. Bulgaria's sun and Black Sea beaches have also allowed the development of a lucrative tourist industry. On the other hand, Bulgaria's water resources are poor—a poverty aggravated by more or less constant drought during the 1980s. Expensive irrigation schemes have become an urgent necessity as a result, and the output and reliability of hydroelectric power have been adversely affected: it was the source of 10.7 per cent of Bulgaria's electricity output in 1980, but only 5.7 per cent in 1988 (the absolute output of hydroelectricity having dropped by 30 per cent over this period). Moreover, Bulgaria's mineral deposits are not over-abundant, nor of very high grade: the most important of these are lignite and brown coal, iron, lead, zinc, copper, and manganese, though pyrites, barite, fluorite, sulphur and asbestos are also mined, and recent finds suggest that the extraction of tungsten and molybdenum can be developed well beyond the level necessary for Bulgarian self-sufficiency. Oil is extracted, but in relatively small quantities — around 150,000 tonnes per year, enough to satisfy about 10 per cent of Bulgarian needs. Bulgaria's energy shortage has prompted a heavy dependence on imports of Soviet oil and on nuclear power, which accounted for 35.5 per cent of its output of electricity in 1988: the country has the third highest per capita nuclear generation of electricity in the world.

(ii) *Post-war economic development.* When the Communists came to power, the Bulgarian economy was dominated by peasant agriculture. The Soviet model of forced collectivization and rapid industrialization and urbanization, together with central planning, was applied, transforming Bulgarian economy and society. Thus: in 1945, 78 per cent of the population lived in the countryside, while in 1987 this figure was only 34 per cent; in 1939, 15 per cent of net material product originated in industry and 65 per cent in agriculture, while in 1987 the respective figures were 61 and 13 per cent. The structure of Bulgarian industry changed also: before 1945, it consisted of little more than light and food-processing branches, together with some coal-mining: since the war, engineering, metallurgical, electricity, and electrical appliance industries have been newly created —indeed, their development has tended to take precedence over that of both consumer-related branches and general infrastructure, creating serious disproportions. While Bulgaria's economy has in large measure been shaped by the "all-round" approach to national heavy industrial development prevalent in the early stages of Communist rule, the structure of its industry has also been affected by the planned division of labour within the **Council for Mutual Economic Assistance (CMEA)** — for instance, Bulgaria is the designated specialist in the production of fork-lift trucks and is (improbably) the world's largest producer of these. More recently, there have been serious efforts to develop the high-tech electronics and biotechnology industries, which have been designated as priority branches. Bulgaria is strong also in the production of certain chemicals.

(iii) *Foreign trade.* Bulgaria's foreign economic relations are dominated by trade with fellow CMEA countries, and its CMEA trade by trade with the USSR. Thus, in 1988, trade with CMEA countries accounted for 76.7 per cent of imports and 84.2 per cent of exports — the corresponding figures for trade with the USSR being 53.5 and 62.5 per cent. Raw material imports supplied by the USSR have been crucial in building up and supplying Bulgarian industry: especially important have been those of oil — though the terms of trade have shifted to Bulgaria's disadvantage in recent years. Outside the CMEA, the pattern of trade has traditionally involved a considerable deficit with the advanced capitalist countries, balanced by a considerable surplus with developing countries — notably those of the Arab World (especially Libya and Iraq). In real hard currency terms, however, this balancing has increasingly been more nominal than real, in that trade with the developing countries has often been conducted on the basis of very long term Bulgarian loans rather than of immediate payment. Bulgaria exports certain metals (steel, aluminium); farm products — notably tobacco, tomatoes and other vegetables; oil products and soda ash; and some engineering products — fork-lift trucks and electronic components — though for reasons of quality these find ready markets only in other CMEA countries, and not in the West.

Recent economic developments. Two trends have combined to make recent years problematic ones for the Bulgarian economy. The first has been a slowdown in economic growth. US government estimates of Bulgarian real GNP show an annual average of 6.4 per cent growth in 1961–65, 5.1 per cent in 1966–70, and 4.7 per cent in 1971–75 — healthy figures, higher than any other East European state in the first two periods, and higher than all but Romania and Poland for the third. But thereafter, rates declined sharply: from 1976 to 1980, growth was 1.0 per cent per annum, while cumulative growth between 1980 and 1988 was

no more than 12 per cent (indeed, Bulgarian sources have recently claimed that a growth figure of 6 per cent might be nearer the mark). This is no doubt an instance of the general tendency for economic growth to slow down after a certain point, once the possibilities of "extensive growth" have been exhausted (to take one crucial factor of production, Bulgaria's working age population actually declined by over 80,000 in the seven years following 1980). That Bulgaria's initial achievements were so impressive, and that her slowdown came later that most, simply reflects the fact that she was starting from a rather lower base. The second factor has been a shift in the country's external trade and payments position, itself an outcome of several different influences. The fall in oil prices in 1986 and again in 1988 affected Bulgaria's export earnings both directly (in that Bulgaria had been exporting refined petroleum products produced on the basis of Soviet deliveries) and indirectly (in that the hard currency available to some of Bulgaria's traditional Arab customers was reduced drastically). Simultaneously, the leadership had just embarked on an ambitious investment programme heavily dependent on inputs of Western capital goods, and was unwilling to let this programme be derailed by shortages of hard currency — believing, apparently (and wrongly), that the investments would soon generate hard currency exports. The result of all this was a mounting hard currency debt — the gross figure rose from $2.3 billion at the end of 1984 to an estimated $8.5 billion at end-1989 — and an increasing burden involved in servicing it. In the aftermath of Zhivkov's fall, officials began to talk of the possible need for rescheduling, though as of early 1990 no public moves in that direction had been made. Whether or not there is rescheduling, this debt will be a strain on Bulgaria's economy and a limitation on Bulgaria's potential as an export market for some time to come.

The country's economic troubles are not confined to the area of hard currency trade and payments. In the latter years of the 1980s, the Soviet Union — mindful of its own needs and shortages — has put pressure on Bulgaria to liquidate a large cumulative trade deficit by dramatically increased exports: thus, a Bulgarian deficit of 122 million foreign trade *leva* in 1985 gave way to a slight (56 million) surplus in 1986, a larger (381 million) one in 1987, and to 1988 and 1989 surpluses of 1,553 and 2,151 million *leva* respectively — large sums for an economy of Bulgaria's size, for the official exchange rate at the end of 1989 was 0.827 *leva* to the US dollar. Since a trade surplus between two soft-currency economies represents, in effect, an interest-free loan by the country in surplus to the country in deficit, these surpluses have been a source of considerable strain to the Bulgarian economy, pre-empting resources that might have been devoted to domestic needs or to hard-currency exports.

This—together with the economic slowdown, the debt problem and the labour shortages caused by the exodus of ethnic **Turks in Bulgaria** in 1989—has made Bulgaria's economic position at the end of the 1980s a problematic one. Shortages of consumer goods appear to have become acute in 1989, and the successors of Todor Zhivkov are faced with a situation in which they must simultaneously court popularity in newly competitive political conditions and administer harsh and unpopular remedies for the country's economic ills, about which they have been increasingly frank.

In the field of economic reform, the last decade or so of Zhivkov's incumbency was not an inactive period—indeed, its salient feature was in a superficial sense hyperactivity. In January 1982, a so-called "New Economic Mechanism" was instituted, under which planners were to hand down the minimum of targets to enterprises, which were to become financially self-supporting and to be guided in their activity by financial criteria and hence by pressures of the market. The measures passed in the rest of the decade—especially frequent in its latter half—were basically variations on this theme. Thus, 1986 saw the abolition of industrial branch ministries, their replacement with "voluntary" associations with a "guiding" rather than imperative function, and the devolution of many decision-making powers to lower levels. 1987 brought more decentralization—so much, indeed, that a partial recentralization was found necessary in December to counteract the resultant confusion—and a new two-tier system of banking which confined the State Bank to the role of a bank of issue with broad supervisory powers while setting up a more commercially-oriented "second tier" and break the monopoly (though not the primacy) of the Foreign Trade Bank in external financial transactions. Finally, in January 1989, the government issued the rather comprehensive "**Decree Fifty-six**"—despite the fact that the December 1987 regulations were said at the time of issue to be definitive to the end of 1990!

On paper, these reforms were by no means insignificant — Decree Fifty-six, in particular, was very far-reaching indeed. Their progressive impact, however, was severely limited by two factors. First, at least in Zhivkov's last three or four years, the reorganizations were so frequent that their net result was not so much change as uncertainty and confusion. Second, the centre—branch ministries to 1986, a newly created Ministry of Economic and Planning from 1987—was always left with the practical option of interference, and, for reasons of both self-interest and legitimate economic concern, generally exercised this option enough to impair seriously the working of the reforms.

Zhivkov's successors have to date introduced only one major economic reorganization measure: some branch ministries have been recreated, thus partially centralizing economic management. This is to be seen, however, as a temporary antidote to the confusion of the late Zhivkov period. The public pronouncements of the new regime suggest radical reformist intentions — Prime Minister Andrei **Lukanov**, for instance, has talked of the introduction of a full market system—and the newly influential opposition groupings, including the free trade union **Podkrepa**, seem well-disposed to free market ideas.

Foreign policy. Post-war, the salient feature of Bulgaria's foreign policy has been extreme loyalty to the USSR. No major instance of disagreement or disobedience can be cited, and long-serving party leader Todor Zhivkov was always effusive in his expressions of Bulgarian's devotion to the USSR—and is even rumoured to have pressed for his country's incorporation as the 16th Soviet Republic in the early 1970s. Bulgaria is a full member of both the CMEA and the **Warsaw Treaty Organization (WTO)**. In the latter capacity, Bulgaria is unusual in its exemption from the stationing of Soviet troops on its soil (contrast Poland, Czechoslovakia, Hungary and the GDR): given Bulgaria's strategic position on the WTO's southern flank, this can be assumed to reflect its reliability rather its unimportance. In 1989, Bulgaria's active forces totalled 117,500 — 91,000 of them conscripts — with the army accounting for almost 82,000 of these, the navy for nearly 9,000, and the air force for rather under 27,000. In addition, Bulgaria has around 470,000 reservists, and full-time paramilitary forces totalling 22,500.

As a Balkan country, Bulgaria naturally has its local interests and rivalries. Relations with Romania and Greece have generally been good, but those with Turkey and Yugoslavia have been complicated by question of nationality. Bulgarian–Turkish relations have been strained recently as a result of Zhivkov's policies towards Bulgaria's ethnic Turks, while there have been periodic polemics with Yugoslavia over the question of Macedonia: Bulgaria has maintained that Macedonians are linguistically and ethnically no more than a particular sort of Bulgarian, while

Yugoslavia has argued fiercely for their distinctness, accusing Bulgaria of depriving the Macedonian population of the Pirin region of its rights. While neither side in this dispute openly questions the territorial status quo, each is probably afraid of the other's possible claims—Bulgaria of Yugoslav desire to incorporate Pirin in its Macedonian Republic (in which 90 per cent of Macedonians live), Yugoslavia of Bulgaria's historic claims to the whole of Macedonia, which was granted to Bulgaria by the Treaty of San Stefano. Despite these problems, Bulgaria—especially its erstwhile foreign minister Petur Mladenov—has generally been enthusiastic about the development of multilateral relations in the Balkan area, and the first of a series of six-country meetings on a wide range of topics was held in Sofia in June 1989.

While Bulgaria's reputation in the international area has generally been good, there has been a tendency in the last decade or so for the country's image to be damaged by certain incidents and policies. Todor Zhivkov's actions toward Bulgaria's ethnic Turks is a case in point: this brought general disapproval, and condemnation from the Organization of Islamic States and various West European governments as well as from Turkey itself. Another example is the attempted assassination of the Pope in 1981: Bulgarian secret service involvement has never been proved, but was widely alleged—and taken as an example of Bulgarian willingness to do the USSR's "dirty work" for it. The signs are that Zhivkov's successors will be rather more careful of Bulgaria's international image.

RW

for three decades, most of this being in the villages. Completely subservient in matters of policy, it has nevertheless (or therefore!) enjoyed its share of appointments: its leader (Georgi Traikov 1947–74, Petur Tanchev 1974–89) has held the office of First Deputy President, while BANU members have occupied about a quarter of the seats in the National Assembly, around a fifth of those in the local councils, and four ministerial posts.

In the new political conditions after the ousting in 1989 of BCP leader Todor **Zhivkov**, radical changes in BANU's role and character can be anticipated. In December 1989, some members formed a breakaway "Nikola Petkov" BANU, declaring that the BCP could no longer automatically count on their support and that they were willing to form coalitions with any sympathetic party. BANU proper acquired a new leader (Angel Dimitrov) in that same month and has been indulging at least in the rhetoric of independence and assertiveness—most conspicuously, refusing to join the new government formed in February 1990 and vocally demanding the wholesale abolition of Article 1 of the constitution, which defines Bulgaria as a "socialist state". While it may be doubted whether BANU will break completely its links with the BCP, its survival as anything more than a "rump" in competitive conditions presumably depends on its ability to present itself as a genuine coalition partner genuinely championing rural interests—or at least, those of at least some significant part of the rural population.

RW

BULGARIAN AGRARIAN NATIONAL UNION (BANU).

Successor of the largest party in pre-Communist Bulgaria—a peasant party, hence understandably the most popular party in a predominantly peasant country. The left wing of this party under Nikola Petkov was originally a member of the **Fatherland Front**, founded in 1943, though it dropped out to become the main opposition as the intentions of the Communist Party (BCP) became increasingly clear in the immediate post-war years. In 1947, on the establishment of an effectively one-party system, the Communists chose to co-opt and incorporate rather than destroy this party, in view of its popularity in the villages. Since then it has served as a "transmission belt" for BCP policies, and has been been the BCP's junior partner ("little brother") in the Fatherland Front, and the only party apart from the BCP itself officially tolerated. Its membership has been stable at around 120,000

BULGARIAN COMMUNIST PARTY (BCP — Bulgarska komunisticheska partiya).

The foundation of the Bulgarian Communist Party (BCP) can fairly be dated to 1903, when, after a long history of internal feuding, the Bulgarian Social Democratic Workers' Party split into Broad Socialist and Narrow Socialist Parties—the latter, led by Dimitur Blagoyev, emphasizing doctrinal purity and denouncing "opportunism" in a manner roughly analogous to that of the Bosheviks in Russia.

In 1919, the party changed its name to "Bulgarian Communist Party" and affiliated to the new Comintern. The BCP enjoyed considerable electoral strength in the immediate post-war years —winning almost 20 per cent of the vote in the April 1923 elections to the National Assembly—but was limited in its influence by its unwillingness to co-operate with the largest party, the peasant Agrarians. When the Agrarian government of Aleksandur Stamboliski was overthrown by a military coup in June 1923, the BCP refused to help him and reserved its line only with a belated and futile attempt at an uprising in September of that year.

Thereafter, the BCP led a clandestine existence within Bulgaria, with much of its leadership in Soviet exile. Some of the exiles gained considerable prominence in the international Communist movement — notably Georgi Dimitrov, who became General Secretary of the Communist International in 1934. Dimitrov's prestige and the backing of **Stalin** allowed him to assert control over the BCP, defeating his main enemies, the "left sectarians", many of whom were purged as Trotskyites. The BCP in Bulgaria itself was limited in its effectiveness by political repression, but began to reassert itself as the tide turned against the Germans in the war.

The BCP gradually emerged as the dominant party in Bulgaria and established an effectively one-party system in the late 1940s. On Georgi Dimitrov's death in 1949 party leadership passed first, briefly, to Vasil Kolarov (a veteran communist who died within six months) and then to Vulko Chervenkov, the "Bulgarian Stalin", who consolidated his power with a purge of alleged "Titoists" in a process similar to that undergone in most other East European states at the time. In 1954, Todor **Zhivkov** was appointed First Secretary of the BCP, and gradually emerged as the dominant leader, a position which he occupied until his overthrow in November 1989. After Zhivkov, Petur **Mladenov** was General Secretary briefly, before he was replaced as party leader in February 1990 by Aleksandur **Lilov** (for the politics of these years *see* the entries for **Zhivkov** and for **Bulgaria**—Recent Political Developments).

Since the late 1940s the BCP has had most of the structures and attributes of a ruling Communist party: a monopoly of power, shared only nominally with a perpetually junior and in practice subservient partner (the **Bulgarian Agrarian National Union**); a strong First General Secretary; a Secretariat with a supervisory role in all areas of national life; a Central Committee nominally elected by periodic Congresses but in fact filled mostly by *ex officio* membership of the most important party and state officials; nomination from above, rather than election from below, as the real method of appointment of officials; a Politburo, meeting frequently, as the real locus of top-level decision making—government institutions being secondary; a regional party network making the party First Secretary the Number One official in his region, with considerable powers in practice; a BCP presence in all workplaces in the form of a party primary organization, with both mobilizing and supervisory functions; and a con-

cept of party discipline stressing the importance of unanimity and excluding at least the open existence of factions.

In the aftermath of Zhivkov's overthrow and the general atmosphere of change in Eastern Europe, the role and structures of the BCP have undergone considerable modifications.

The party has—under pressure—abdicated its monopoly of power both theoretically (by repealing the constitutional provision enshrining its leading role in Bulgarian society) and practically (by scheduling free and competitive elections for 1990). The new party statutes adopted at the special party congress held at the end of January 1990 affirm the right to form factions and to express dissenting opinions within the party—a provision that has acknowledged rather than occasioned the *de facto* emergence of various groupings, some (like the Alternative Socialist Association, the Bulgarian Road to Europe, and the BCP Democratic Front) apparently more reformist than the BCP leadership, others (like the Public Forum for the Restructuring and Protection of Socialism) decidedly less so. Further, since the Congress, the BCP has reluctantly conceded the opposition's demand that all workplace party cells be abolished.

The party's leadership structures have been overhauled too. The traditional Central Committee (CC) has been replaced by a Supreme Party Council (SPC), whose membership appears to have in practice a less *ex officio* character than that of its predecessor. Originally comprising 131 members (about half the size of the 1986 CC), the SPC was almost immediately enlarged to 153 when the new party leader insisted on the addition of 22 radical intellectuals to avoid the radicals' under-representation and the split that might result therefrom. The Politburo has been replaced by a 17-person Presidium of the SPC. The Secretariat and the office of General secretary have been abolished; henceforth the party leader will be the incumbent of the new post of SPC Chairman. Quite how significant these changes will be in practice remains to be seen. The abolition of the Secretariat seems likely to reduce—or at any rate to acknowledge a reduction of—the importance of the party as an administrative hierarchy. As to the other bodies, the SPC may be somewhat less unwieldy than the old CC, hence more able to exercise effective control over the top leadership, but otherwise changes in the methods by which (and the pressures under which) their members are chosen seem more significant than any novelty corresponding to the changes of name. The new statutes prescribe secret ballot as the method of election to party office, and this in combination with the plurality of candidates that is inevitable under new conditions should ensure a reasonable degree of democracy. Finally, these statues limit tenure in party posts to two-year terms: the contrast with the Zhivkov period will, however, be in the observance of this rule, rather than in the rule itself, which had previously existed but which was ignored as far as the top leadership was concerned.

The Manifesto adopted by the BCP for its Congress also marked various changes in the policies and image of the party: it expressed commitment to a market economy and to a multiparty political system; it omitted any reference to "democratic centralism" or "Marxism-Leninism"; it talked of a "civil society based on law"; it referred to the BCP as a party of "labour and intellect" (not of the working class). In the same spirit, the party daily *Rabotnichesko Delo* ("The Workers' Cause") has ceased to carry the slogan "Workers of the World Unite!" on its front page. And it appeared possible that the BCP would soon have a new name to match its new image—a decision deferred at the January congress. Favoured alternatives include "Bulgarian Socialist Party" and "Party for Democratic Socialism in Bulgaria (Communists)".

Politically, at the time of writing, the BCP seems in better shape than any East European Communist Party outside the USSR. It has avoided any major split—the radicals were skilfully conciliated at the January–February 1990 Congress (only a small minority of them left to form the Alternative Socialist Party), while the conservatives have nowhere else to go, and seem powerless to block the reformist direction of policy needed if the BCP is to survive in new political conditions (though they may still have some ability to impede its implementation, and there are signs that they have been exploiting anti-Turkish feelings in the provinces).

The BCP has almost completely renewed its top leadership, thus distancing itself from its discredited past and removing many top-level obstacles to reform. Only three of the 17 members of the Presidium elected after the Congress had been full or candidate members of the Politburo at the time of Zhivkov's ousting, and many even of those promoted to the leadership in his immediate aftermath of the coup have been discarded—presumably as insufficiently reformist. At the next level down, only about 10 per cent of the SPC had served on the old CC. Further the party would seem not to have suffered a mass exodus of disillusioned members (see below).

Opinion polls in mid-March 1990 showed 39 per cent support for the BCP—far more than for any other party or grouping, and enough to make it plausible that the BCP would emerge as the dominant partner in a coalition after the forthcoming elections (most likely with its old ally the Bulgarian Agrarian National Union). Similarly, the poll gave the Communist incumbent Petur Mladenov a 34 per cent presidential popularity rating, his nearest rival at 14 per cent being another Communist, the Prime Minister Andrei **Lukanov**. The most popular non-Communist was Zhelyu Zhelev of the **Union of Democratic Forces**, who scored only 9 per cent; support was otherwise very fragmented, with 37 possible candidates sharing the other 43 per cent.

At the beginning of 1990, an official claimed that the BCP had a membership of just over 984,000—an advance of somewhat more than 50,000 on its membership four years earlier. This is healthy figure, representing around 15 per cent of Bulgaria's adult population, and it suggests that the party suffered no serious loss of members in the aftermath of Zhivkov's fall. But the membership's age structure must be some cause for concern to the leadership, since over one third of members are pensioners, and a similar tendency is apparent in the fact that the party's youth wing, the Komsomol, declined in membership by one third (from 1.5 million to under 1 million) between June 1987 and January 1990. In the new political conditions, the future of the BCP will depend increasingly on its ability to appeal both to the electorate at large and to the young and the radical among its actual and potential supporters.

RW

BULGARIAN ORTHODOX CHURCH. Before the Communists came to power in Bulgaria, the Orthodox Church comprised 85 per cent of the population. It now has approximately 1,700 priests and 1,500 churches. Like other Orthodox churches (*see* **Relgion and Communism**), it had a tradition of subordination to the state and was able to accommodate itself to the Communist regime. The traditional friendship between Bulgaria and Russia was reinforced by ties between the **Russian Orthodox Church** and the Bulgarian Church.

That the Church was not seen as a threat to the ruling party is illustrated by the fact that, unusually in Communist systems, it received a subsidy from the state. More nationalist than the party, the Holy Synod claims Yugoslav Macedonia to be within its jurisdiction. The Church gave full support to the policies of the Zhivkov regime, which collapsed in November 1989, leaving the Church leadership discredited. The patriach of Bulgaria since 1971 has been Maksim (Minkov).

PJSD

BULGARISATION. The policy of more or less forcible assimiliation of Bulgaria's ethnic and religious minorities pursued from time to time by the country's post-war Communist regime. The most recent and conspicious instance is **Zhivkov**'s policy towards the ethnic **Turks in Bulgaria** in the mid-1980s, but a similar campaign was conducted against the Pomaks (ethnic Bulgarians of the Islamic faith) in the 1970s. The Bulgarian authorities have also, since the late 1960s, consistently denied the existence of an ethnically or linguistically distinct Macedonian minority in the Pirin area—a claim hotly disputed by the Yugoslavs, who are afraid of latent Bulgarian claims to the rest of Macedonia. The demonstrations by ethnic Bulgarians after the repeal of the anti-Turkish policy at the end of 1989 suggests that "Bulgarisation" may have some popular appeal with the Bulgarian majority, at least those in the areas with significant minority presence.

RW

C

ČALFA, MARIÁN. A graduate of Charles University's Law Faculty in Prague, Čalfa sprang to prominence when he replaced Ladislav **Adamec** as Czechoslovak Prime Minister in December 1987 and reached agreement with this opposition **Civic Forum** on the composition of a coalition government in which the Communist Party was given a minority of seats for the first time since February 1948. A Slovak, born in 1946, Čalfa worked for a number of legal and legislative agencies attached to the Federal Government from 1972 until his appointment in 1987 as Deputy Head of its equivalent of the Cabinet Office (*Úřad předsednictva vlády ČSSR*). In April 1988, he was made a Minister without portfolio in the Federal Government, where he had responsibility for legislation connected with the economic reform and other changes that were then being introduced.

GW

CEAUŞESCU, ELENA. The wife of Nicolae **Ceauşescu** of Romania, Elena held the positions of first deputy prime minister, chairman of the National Council of Science and Technology and vice chairman of the Supreme Council of Socio-Economic Development; she was also a full member of the Central Committee of the **Romanian Communist Party** and a member of the Political Executive Committee and its Permanent Bureau. In 1988 she for the first time delivered the main speech on Romania's national day. She had a propensity for receiving foreign honorary scientific degrees for which her qualifications seemed slender. Elena normally accompanied her husband on trips abroad and her profile in the media was second only to his. Nevertheless, she was far from popular in the country. Elena fled with her husband by helicopter at the time of the overthrow of the Ceauşescu regime, was captured, tried, sentenced to death, and executed with him on Dec. 25, 1989 (*see also* **Romania**—Overthrow of the Ceauşescu regime).

RH

CEAUŞESCU, NICOLAE. Secretary-general of the **Romanian Communist Party (PCR)** between 1965 and December 1989 and state President from 1974 to 1989 (in 1989 this was renewed for further five-year term, cut short by his execution on Dec. 25, 1989). Ceauşescu was also Chairman of the Council of State and of the Supreme Council of Socio-Economic Development. Born in January 1918 of peasant stock, he joined the Communist Party at the age of 14 and was first arrested a year later; he was in prison or a concentration camp between 1936–38 and 1939 –44. He then worked in Constanta and Oltenia. In 1948 Ceauşescu was appointed Deputy Minister of Agriculture, and helped to organize collectivization. In 1950 he was made Deputy Minister of the Armed Forces and put in charge of the army's political section. Having been in Romania throughout the war years Ceauşescu adhered to the "national" faction of the PCR and established himself as the natural successor to **Gheorghiu-Dej**, whom he succeeded in March 1965 when Gheorghiu-Dej died of cancer. Ceauşescu became First Secretary of the Romanian Communist Party at that time and its General Secretary in July 1965. He became Head of State in 1967.

Romania had already taken steps towards a more individual foreign policy and to reject Soviet proposals that Romania should remain predominantly agrarian: Ceauşescu carried these trends further. His decisive moment came in August 1968, when Romania, which had not taken part in the invasion of Czechoslovakia led by Soviet forces seemed itself threatened. His response was to declare all-out national resistance, which brought him instant popularity. Western governments too were attracted by his independence and on foreign visits both Ceauşescu and his wife were awarded honours. During a 20-year period Romania was on the whole favourably reported in the Western media; this then sharply changed, and in the final months of 1989 reporting became wholly negative. Within Romania, too, Ceauşescu's popularity steeply declined although his insistent nationalism probably continued to be approved by many.

The President filled numerous posts with members of his own family: these included his wife Elena **Ceauşescu**, who also held many posts, their son Nicu (made party boss at Sibiu), his son's wife, his brother Ilie (as Deputy-Minister of Defence) and many others. These appointments, at least in appearance nepotistic, were fixed points in an otherwise rather frequently changing complement of government posts. The President often made "working visits" to farms and other places, and his profile in these and other contexts was extremely high. His photograph appeared in

52

the press constantly, and his portrait was to be found in every public building, although it was not hung outdoors where, however, slogans such as "Ceauşescu — Heroism, Romania — Communism" were exhibited. The positive impact of all this on popular opinion was much less than Western visitors were inclined to think, but was reinforced by leaving out of the press all news that might disturb it and by the fabrication of congratulatory messages from foreign governments. The gigantic building operations in central **Bucharest** had also be seen as in part an emanation of the President's personality cult. While his image was larger than life it is clear nevertheless that Ceauşescu was an active and skilful politician.

Ceauşescu rejected all concepts of reform or *glasnost'* and was evidently determined to promote the current Romanian brand of socialism at all costs. His report delivered to the Party Congress on Nov. 20, 1989 was triumphalist in tone. However, even at that moment the likelihood of his completing another five-year term without a revolt against his rule appeared small to most outside observers. Speculation centred on whether, in the event of his death or retirement, his family would try to hold on to power; Elena Ceauşescu seemed to be well placed to make the attempt. But this was not to be (*see* **Romania** — Overthrow of the Ceauşescu regime).

The excesses of demolition and rebuilding, of other distortions in economic priorities, of nepotism in political life and of stifling of news reporting will remain Ceauşescu's lasting legacy, although the repayment of foreign debts and some other aspects can be assessed as positive achievements. In the aftermath of his overthrow no good word about the former President was to be heard anywhere, but this is an extreme assessment. Nicolae and Elena Ceauşescu performed a final service to their survivors and collaborators: the only important personages to suffer the death penalty, they became perfect scapegoats for all the ills of the regime they had personified.

RH

CENTRAL EUROPE. Central Europe, while a term of some historical significance and established political resonance, came into increasing prominence in the 1980s as, firstly, a way of establishing the cultural and political identity of certain nations on the margins of an increasingly decrepit Soviet empire and, secondly, a focus of identity for groups who felt themselves able to establish a more autonomous existence as the influence of the superpower blocs over Europe receded and more distinctive regional traditions

were able to assert themselves. For decades after the end of World War II Europe was either East and West and there was room for neither middle nor centre following the establishment of a dominant bipolar division. The situation began to change with the mounting evidence of the ideological and cultural sterility of late Brezhnevism in the Soviet Union and the growing possibilities in some parts of the region for resuming alternative identities, if only in an informal sense, in the social space that was left.

An important contribution to the process was made by the Czech writer Milan Kundera in an article published in 1983 on "The Tragedy of Central Europe" while, around the same time, certain Czechs, Hungarians and Slovaks began to hark back to the traditions and conventions of the Austro-Hungarian Empire which, further back in time, seemed to offer a more tolerable form of imperial rule than that provided by **Stalin**'s and even the post-Stalinist Soviet Union. At this stage views were expressed on a dominantly cultural plane and reflected the sentiments of *soi-disant* Central Europeans in distinction to Russians, rather than responses in a political vein to the nature and consequence of Communist rule. The Czech playwright Václav **Havel** emphasized a particular attitude, a "Central European mind, sceptical, sober, anti-utopian, understated". The Hungarian writer György Konrád referred to a "new Central European identity" and a Central European strategy. For Kundera in particular, Russia itself was excluded from Europe, a judgement that gave rise to considerable controversy and much discussion of the relation of Russia to mainstream European cultural development. Many thought it quite unreasonable to exclude Russia's cultural contribution from the European mainstream and mistaken to ignore the indigenous roots of some of the more violent and tragic episodes in Europe's history. Recent views of the Central European outlook have emphasized a different set of attitudes, including a profound suspicion of formal politics and the exercise of state power, a rejection of established ideological orientations, the projection of ethnical values into the political sphere and a strong endorsement of the idea of a civil society.

The relationship of a modern conception of Central Europe to other continental power also began to emerge as a major focus of attention. The idea of *Mitteleuropa* (Central Europe as the middle of Europe) had been a German conception which, not surprisingly, placed German peoples at the centre of the picture and promised — or threatened — an alternative form of hegemony exercised from Berlin or, possibly, Vienna over the people residing in the territories between the

German and Russian heartlands. This had been the implication of ideas prevalent earlier in the century which had been put by Friedrich Naumann in his book *Mitteleuropa*, published in 1915, against the implications of which the new Foreign Minister of Poland's new non-Communist government, Skubiszewski, explicitly warned in late 1989.

An alternative conception, closer to the ideas of those who brought the term back into currency in the 1980s, had been formulated by the Czech statesman Tomáš Masaryk. His view had encompassed the peoples between the Germans and Russians, ranging from the Lapps and Finns to Albanians, Turks and Greeks. It is this kind of idea, relating to the peoples situated between dominant (or potentially dominant or post-dominant powers) that has appealed more to the intellectual dissidents amongst Czechs, Slovaks, Hungarians, Slovenians and Poles. It is an idea that has had strong connections with aspirations for autonomy and the strengthening of links with the main currents of European culture. Not surprisingly, then, it has had a strong cultural dimension and has been articulated predominantly by writers and intellectuals, although barriers between dissidents and establishment, intellectuals and politicans began rapidly to dissolve in the late 1980s.

Whether Central Europe means more than the significance it has developed as a focus of traditional cultural identity distinct from and resilient to the tide of Marxist-Leninist ideology that has flowed from the East since 1945 remains to be seen. The relation of a German-based *Mitteleuropa* to the recently revived concept of Central Europe has become the subject of some speculation with the collapse of the **Honecker** regime in the German Democratic Republic and the growing salience of the question of German reunification. The notion of Central Europe, however, also received a great boost with the collapse of Communist regimes throughout the area in 1989 and the rise of an influential intellectual like Havel to assume the presidency of the Czechoslovak Republic. Whereas, too, Hungary and Poland had been somewhat isolated from their harderline Communist neighbours, that situation also changed with the shared experience of post-Communist rule. While the rejection of Stalinist rule had been as pronounced, if not more so, in Poland as in other countries and opposition movements had shared a number of characteristics with those in other countries, the idea of belonging to Central Europe had not been so strong as in the former dominantly Austro-Hungarian territories. Opportunities now grew both for independent association and co-operation and the reassertion of national traditions, which could well serve to drive a wedge between the different nations of the region as well as enhance their common orientations.

PGL

CHARTER 77 (CZECHOSLOVAKIA). Named after a manifesto published in Czechoslovakia on Jan.1, 1977 in which the 241 initial signatories committed themselves to campaign for human and civil rights, the Charter 77 movement sought to avoid organizational structures and to remain "a loose, informal community of people". Although it had little success in improving the human rights record of the Czechoslovak regime and many of the signatories suffered severely at the hands of the authorities as a result of their involvement, its activities had a number of positive consequences. The Charter succeeded in uniting the diverse opposition groups which had emerged after the suppression of the **Prague Spring** and helped keep the outside world informed of the regime's human and civil rights record. Associated with the Charter were smaller groups such as the *Committee for the Defence of the Unjustly Persecuted (VONS)*, founded in 1978, which concentrated on cases of political persecution. No less important however has its encouragement of a number of *samizdat* studies on topics largely ignored by the official media, ranging from the problems of pensioners and consumers to the state of the economy and the environment. Although the number of the Charter's signatories was never high (by 1985 it was reported to have reached 1,200), its moral authority among the people of Czechoslovakia was indisputable and contributed to the successful formation in November 1989 of the opposition **Civic Forum** and the emergence of Václav **Havel**, one of the Charter's original signatories, as the leading figure in that movement.

GW

CHERNENKO, KONSTANTIN USTINOVICH. Soviet politician and General Secretary of the **Communist Party of the Soviet Union** (CPSU) from 1984 to 1985. Widely regarded as a transitional leader after the death of **Andropov**, Chernenko was born in September 1911 in a village in the Krasnoyarsk territory. A member of the CPSU from 1931, he was educated at a teacher training college and at the Higher School of Party Organizers attached to the CPSU Central Committee. After a period of manual work in agriculture Chernenko became involved in Komsomol and then in party work, specializing in agitation and propaganda. In 1945 he became party first secretary in the Penza region, but then in 1948 he was sent to Moldavia to head the republican party organization's propaganda department. Leonid **Brezhnev** became the republican party first secretary in 1950, and their association at this time was decisive for Chernenko's subsequent advance. In 1956 Chernenko moved to Moscow to work in the central party and also in the government apparatus; in 1965 he became head of the general department of the Central Committee apparatus, and in 1976 he became a member of the Secretariat. In 1977, with Brezhnev's support, Chernenko became a candidate member of the ruling Politburo, and then the following year he moved up to full membership, becoming a prime and evidently favoured candidated for the succession when it became vacant after Brezhnev's death.

Chernenko was not, in fact, the successful candidate in November 1982, but his seniority was apparent in being chosen as the one who proposed Andropov's candidacy to the Central Committee and he remained prominent throughout the Andropov administration, chairing sessions of the Politburo in the General Secretary's absence. After Andropov's death there were again two principal contenders for the leadership: Chernenko, whose fortunes had revived with Andropov's illness, and **Gorbachev**, who was evidently Andropov's own favoured candidate for the succession. Chernenko was named to head the funeral arrangements committee, which suggested he would shortly be named the new General Secretary; but the formal choice took some time to arrange and appears to have divided the remaining Politburo members into two camps, a "Brezhnevite" faction supporting Chernenko and composed for the most part of long-serving members of the leadership like prime minister Nikolai Tikhonov, Kazakh party leader Dinmukhamed Kunaev and Moscow party secretary Viktor Grishin, and an "Andropovite" faction consisting of the younger, more reform-minded members who had joined or advanced within the leadership under the late general secretary. The choice fell finally on Chernenko, partly, it appears, because of his seniority and experience, and partly because a Gorbachev leadership would have been likely to last for an unduly lengthy period: Gorbachev at this time was just 52 and had been a full member of the Politburo for less than four years.

At all events, on Feb. 13, 1984, four days after Andropov had died, another extraordinary meeting of the Central Committee took place at which Chernenko, proposed by Tikhonov, was elected unanimously to the vacant general secretaryship.

It emerged subsequently that Gorbachev had also addressed the plenum, and unofficial reports suggested that he had been installed as a *de facto* second secretary with a power of veto, on behalf of the younger "Andropovite" faction, over leadership decisions. Gorbachev's greater prominence was apparent in, for example, his more advanced placing in the line-up of leaders beside Andropov's coffin, in the ranking he received in pre-election speeches and on other formal party and state occasions. In turn it indicated that the Chernenko leadership was a relatively evenly balanced coalition, containing both supporters of the late president Andropov's reforming policies and those who believed they had been pressed too far. These sharp internal divisions were sufficient in themselves to slow down the momentum of reform, quite apart from what the new General Secretary might have wished, and they persisted throughout his period of office as neither side could allow the other to gain a decisive advantage by adding to their supporters in the Politburo or Secretariat.

The state presidency and chairmanship of the Defence Council, as well as the party leadership, had become vacant on Andropov's death. It became known later in February 1984 that Chernenko had also assumed the chairmanship of the Defence Council, and in April 1984, on Gorbachev's nomination, the first session of the newly elected Supreme Soviet elected him to the vacant presidency. Chernenko was nevertheless, at 72, the oldest general secretary ever to have assumed this office, and he had a history of lung disease (emphysema) which caused difficulty in breathing. Perhaps inevitably, it was regarded as an interregnum from the outset. Two regular Central Committee plenums were held during Chernenko's period of office: the first, in April 1984, was devoted to the work of the soviets and educational reform, and the second dealt with land improvement. Neither plenum made any change in the membership of the Politburo or Secretariat or even in the membership of the Central Committee itself, and neither could be said to have initiated any major new departure in Soviet public policy (the educational reforms, which were of some importance, had been launched the previous year). Attempts to develop a modest personality cult around Chernenko's service in the border guards in the early 1930s had little success; nor could much be made of his undistinguished wartime service. A series of missed engagements suggested that Chernenko's health was already deteriorating, and official spokesmen had to admit that the recently-elected general secretary was suffering from a serious cold, or perhaps worse.

Chernenko was last seen in public at the end of December 1984. He failed to meet the Greek prime minister Papandreou on his visit to Moscow in February 1985, and failed to deliver the customary eve of poll address to the Soviet people in the republican and local elections later the same month. Although he was shown voting on television on Feb. 24 and was pictured in the central press receiving his deputy's credentials on March 1, rumours of the General Secretary's physical incapacity were strengthened rather than dispelled by his evident ill-health. Finally, on the evening of March 10, 1985, he died, the medical bulletin recording that he had expired as a result of heart failure following a deterioration in the working of his lungs and liver. The next day, with unprecedented speed, an extraordinary session of the Central Committee elected Mikhail Gorbachev as its third general secretary in three-and-a-half years; Chernenko, not without justification, has since been regarded as a relic of the Brezhnev era and at best an interruption to the reorientation of public policy that began to take place after the long years of Brezhnevite "stagnation".

SLW

CHERNOBYL. Energy and environmental policies throughout the world, not just in the Soviet Union, were powerfully affected by the nuclear explosion at Chernobyl in the Ukraine, USSR, in late April 1986. The accident appears to have arisen from an unauthorized experiment at the nuclear power station's No. 4 reactor, the aim of which was to discover how long the turbine could continue to provide electricity in the event of a loss of power. Under normal conditions, if there is a power failure, diesel engines at the site can provide emergency support within about 30 seconds. Soviet nuclear energy officials apparently believed that this time period had to be reduced, and tried to use the electricity generated by the turbine as it slowed down for this purpose. In the nuclear power industry this is known as a "turbine tripping experiment".

According to the closest studies of the disaster in the West, the experiment failed for two main reasons. First of all, the operators made a series of blunders, revealing their inexperience and inability to cope with the complexities of nuclear power. The second and ultimately much more important cause of the disaster was the design flaws in the RBMK type of reactor which was in operation at Chernobyl, and which generates 60 per cent of Soviet nuclear energy as a whole. Since the accident the chief designer of the RBMK has been dismissed from his post, and half of the 18 reactors of this type in the USSR have been shut down for alterations.

The experiment began in the early hours of Friday April 25, 1986. By 1 p.m. the reactor was at 50 per cent of its power and all the steam had been transferred to one turbine. An unexpected demand for electricity, however (the reactor was feeding the Hungarian grid), meant that the reactor remained at 50 per cent of full power. Nonetheless, the operator dismantled the automatic shutdown systems which, he felt, might prevent the test from taking place. Of particular importance was the fact that the emergency cooling system had been switched off.

Shortly after midnight on Saturday April 26 the operator made a mistake, causing power to drop to 30 megawatts (thermal), filling the reactor core with water and simultaneously causing a concentration of the gas xenon. By 1 a.m. the power was back up to 200 megawatts, mainly because the operator had pulled out almost all of the RBMK's control rods, some of which are used for emergency shutdowns. When the test began at about 1.25 a.m. the water in the reactor core began to boil rapidly. This led to a very rapid rise in power, so rapid that the reactor was destroyed before it could be shut down.

Soviet officials could therefore claim that the accident arose from an opertor's failure to observe established procedures. According to Western investigators, however, the basic cause of the disaster was the design of the reactor itself. The Soviet RMBK was designed in the 1950s as a military reactor and was subsequently brought into civilian use. Its design has been criticized for inadequate containment above the reactor (it is well protected from below); a more serious fault, however, is the instability of its operation at less than full power. This design fault had been pointed out by foreign nuclear engineers some years previously; Soviet nuclear officials had tried to guard against this fundamental fault by instructing their operators to avoid unsafe situations of this kind. But many operators and engineers are insufficiently trained and inexperienced for their jobs, and certainly in this case matters went appallingly wrong. The explosion (or explosions) at the reactor released between six and seven tons of material (or about 3.5 per cent of the fission materials in the reactor core) into the atmosphere. The material was released in two waves, the first on 26–27 April, and the second between 2 and 6 May, when the reactor core overheated a second time. The immediate casualties were firemen from the plant's fire brigade, who fought the blaze by themselves for about two hours, making heroic efforts not just to control the fire but to avoid it spreading to the No. 3 reactor. The main fire brigades arrived from Kiev at about 3.30 a.m. By 5 a.m. the main blaze had been extinguished, although virtually all the firemen had been seriously contaminated and some had already collapsed.

It took rather longer for party and state officials to decide upon an appropriate response. On the day of the accident children went to school near the plant in the usual way, and they were playing football in the streets that evening. Only on the afternoon of the following day (27 April) was an order given to evacuate Pripyat, in the immediate vicinity of the plant. Chernobyl, about 12 miles away, was evacuated between 2 and 6 May, and then in the face of the protests of local farmers. It was more than a week before adequate public warnings were issued (see also **Glasnost'**); up to this point, contaminated food was being eaten and life was proceeding more or less as normal. In Kiev, 80 miles to the south of the plant, the May Day parade went ahead as usual. There was widespread panic when the Ukrainian health minister issued the first public health warning over the radio on 5 May.

Over the following month about 135,000 people were evacuated from the northern part of Kiev region and from affected parts of the RSFSR and Belorussia. All had been subjected to high doses of radiation exposure. In addition, schoolchildren from Kiev and the Belorussian town of Gomel were moved elsewhere until September, and many others fled of their own accord. Initially a zone 30 km in radius was placed out of bounds, and early in May, once the graphite fire had been brought under control, efforts were initiated to decontaminate it by removing the topsoil that had been affected. This was undertaken by civilians, and later by soldiers, many of whom worked without proper protective clothing or living facilities. The most seriously affected victims of Chernobyl—about 209 people—were treated in Moscow's No. 6 Hospital, where Soviet doctors were aided by specialists from the USA and Israel. To date 33 people (mainly firemen and first-aid officials at the No. 4 reactor) are reported to have died from radiation exposure, and a further two are reported to have died as a result of physical injuries arising from the accident.

Estimates of the ultimate casualty figures have varied from a few thousand to half a million. A reasonably representative estimate is that at least 5,000 additional deaths will occur as a result of the explosion, most of them in the USSR but 45 of them in Britain. Professor Robert Gale, an American doctor who helped to administer bone marrow treatment after the explosion, has suggested an "upper" limit of 75,000 deaths. The total, whatever it is, will be higher than it would otherwise have been because of the lack of information and belated response on the part of the local authorities immediately after the accident. In addition, the environment in the areas affected will be seriously damaged for many years. Caesium-137, for instance, has a half-life of over 30 years, and strontium-90 a half-life of 29 years; it will take about eight times as long for each of these elements to disappear completely. The explosion is estimated to have released as much radiation into the atmosphere as the atomic bombs at Hiroshima and Nagasaki put together.

Apart from the immediate consequences of radiation, there have been political and legal consequences both within the USSR and outside it. The former director and chief engineer of the power station, for instance, were removed from their posts, expelled from the party, and put on trial in Kiev in 1987 (both received the maximum possible sentence, 10 years in a labour camp). Numerous local officials have been dismissed, although the Ukrainian party first secretary, Vladimir Shcherbitsky, managed to avoid direct responsibility (he finally left office in late 1989). A new Ministry of Atomic Power Engineering was established under the direction of the former head of a nuclear power station in Lithuania. There were consequences of many kinds abroad as well: in Italy, for instance, plans to add a further 10 to that country's existing four nuclear power stations were immediately suspended. Some Western governments, particularly the British, came under attack for their belated and unduly complacent public response. The nuclear power industry, already undermined by strictly economic comparisons, suffered a further and very serious setback. "Sellafield, twinned with Chernobyl" was the subject of a poster issued by British anti-nuclear activists soon afterwards.

In the USSR itself it appeared that the major consequences were likely to be economic rather than political, despite the fact that the party and government response was also slow and initially complacent. The economic cost will certainly be substantial: at least two billion rubles (about £2 billion) in direct losses, according to the then USSR finance minister Boris Gostev, speaking in September 1986; later, more inclusive estimates put the total cost at eight billion rubles, half from direct losses and half from the reduced output of the affected area. **Gorbachev** himself, in a television broadcast about two weeks after the explosion, used the opportunity to press for more effective international measures to improve nuclear safety, and went on to point out the obvious lesson in terms of the need to reduce the level of nuclear armaments. The explosion quite soon came to be regarded as a natural calamity, similar in many ways to World War II. There was the same kind of talk of "sacrifices" and "heroes"; public donations were invited to a fund for the relief of the victims; and all parts of the USSR played a part of some kind in resettling those who had been made homeless by the disaster. The science editor of *Pravda*, Vladimir Gubarev, wrote a gloomy play called *Sarcophagus* about the tragedy, which has been widely read and performed both in the USSR and abroad. Several Soviet spokesmen also pointed out that the USSR had not been the only country in which nuclear accidents had occurred; Windscale in Britain and Three Mile Island in the USA were also mentioned in this connection.

There has since been no suggestion, following Chernobyl, that the USSR should scale down its plans to increase the output of electricity from sources of this kind. It does, however, at least appear that future policy will place more emphasis upon the safer water-pressurised (VVER 1000) type of reactor, and that plants will be located rather further from major centres of population. The No. 4 reactor at Chernobyl itself has been encased in a concrete tomb from which no radiation now emerges, although the No. 3 reactor returned to service in 1987. A new radiology centre has been opened in Kiev under the auspices of the USSR Academy of Medical Sciences to monitor the 100,000 or more people who have been subjected to high levels of radiation, and greater powers have been given to the International Atomic Energy Agency (based in Vienna) to check the safety of Soviet nuclear installations. The IAEA itself staged the first-ever international post-accident review at its Vienna headquarters in September 1986, at which the Soviet delegation gave an exceptionally full and detailed presentation; it was followed by the adoption of an expanded nuclear safety programme, at the cost of an additional $2 million in 1987. The effectiveness of these and other measures must naturally be of concern not just to the population of the USSR but to all other countries, particularly those with their own nuclear industries.

SLW

CHRISTIAN DEMOCRATIC UNION OF GERMANY (CDU — Christlich-Demokratische Union Deutschlands). The CDU has for most of its history been one of the National Front parties in the GDR in alliance with the ruling **Socialist Unity Party of Germany (SED)**. It was founded in July 1945 as a party to represent the

Christian middle class, and was broadly equivalent to its West German counterpart. However, by 1946, under the leadership of Otto Nuschke, the CDU had entered into political alliance with the newly-founded SED. Since then it has scarcely had a voice of its own, and has served merely to organize and discipline those career-minded Christians who have not chosen or not been chosen to join the SED itself. In the GDR parliament the CDU has, like the other National Front parties (the **Liberal Democratic Party of Germany — LDPD**, the **Democratic Peasants' Party of Germany — DBD**, and the **National Democratic Party of Germany—NDPD**), a number of seats (52) decided in advance by an allocation on the unified election list. Its chairman from 1966 until the upheavals of 1989 was Gerald Götting.

The membership of the DCU in the GDR was at its height at the end of 1947 with 218,000. By the early 1960s only one third was left (70,000), but since then the party grew steadily to 140,000 in 1987. This should not be interpreted as a swelling of opposition to the SED, since the SED strictly controlled the membership of its allied parties and must therefore have favoured the greater organization and incorporation of non-Communist participants in the system.

The relationship of the CDU with the churches in the GDR has not always been a happy one. Although claiming to represent "socialist state citizens of Christian belief", the CDU came to symbolize compromise with the state rather more than defence of the Christian churches. When in the 1980s dissident groups protesting about militarism, nuclear weapons and pollution centred themselves on the churches, the CDU became even more remote.

The revolution of 1989 caused a major crisis for the CDU. Like most of the other parties it changed its leader—to Lothar **de Maizière**—and professed itself in favour of democratization and Germany unity. It did not, however, initially withdraw from the coalition government, as many of its members and the West German CDU were demanding. This compounded its already great implication in the old system and led to fears on the right and centre-right in the GDR and the Federal Republic that ground was being lost unnecessarily to the SPD and even the SED. In the run-up to the elections in March 1990, other parties emerged in the GDR threatening to take over the position of the CDU. One of these, the **German Social Union (DSU)**, was recognized as a sister party by the Bavarian CSU and was encouraged by some members of the CDU in the Federal Republic. However, pressure for unity within the GDR and from the Federal Republic led to the formation of the **Alliance for Ger-**

many, comprising the CDU, the DSU and **Democratic Departure (DA)**. With a massive input of West German CDU electoral campaigning and generous promises on the part of Chancellor Kohl, the Alliance scored a remarkable victory in the elections. The CDU was the principal victor, with 40.8 per cent of the vote and 163 of the 400 seats in the **Volkskammer** (parliament). Lothar de Maizière was charged with forming a coalition government in early April 1990.

JO

CIVIC FORUM (CZECHOSLOVAKIA — Občanské forum). Formed following the student-led demonstrations of Nov. 17, 1989 in Czechoslovakia, Civic Forum was set up by representatives of opposition groups to co-ordinate the campaign for the resignation of the country's Communist leadership and political reform. A brief statement of its programme, issued on Nov. 26, 1989, described it as an open association of citizens whose goals included the establishment of a democratic state based on the rule of law, free elections, an end to the Communist Party's power monopoly, a market-based mixed economy, welfare provision for the elderly, sick and needy by the state and voluntary agencies, a foreign policy based on friendly relations with neighbouring states and adherence to existing international commitments, action on the environment and promotion of culture and education free from state control. Civic Forum, whose main spokesman was the playwright Václav **Havel**, gained widespread support throughout the Czech Republic even among workers who backed its call for a two-hour strike on Nov. 27. By mid-December it had forced the Communist Party to accept a government in which Communists would hold only a minority of seats and which would include a number of Civic Forum's own nominees, among them two members of its Co-ordinating Committee, Václav Klaus, who became Finance Minister, and the Forum's press spokesman, Jiří Dienstbier, who was appointed Foreign Minister. A separate organization, "The Public Against Violence" (*Verejnosť proti násiliu*) was formed in Slovakia.

GW

CLUB FOR THE SUPPORT OF GLASNOST' AND DEMOCRACY (BULGARIA). Bulgarian dissident organization, comprising in late 1989 250 intellectual figures, around half of them **Bulgarian Communist Party (BCP)** members. Founded in the mood of disappointment arising after Todor **Zhivkov's** sharp turn against Chudomir **Aleksandrov** and the "left" of the BCP in mid-1988, the organization was subjected to official harassment in the first few months of its existence. This seems to have had remarkably little effect on the Club's resilience, and the organization came into its own with the fall of Zhivkov in November 1989. Since then it has become a leading element in the **Union of Democratic Forces**—an umbrella organization for Bulgarian dissident groups—to which it has contributed a chairman, Zhelyu Zhelev. Also prominent among its leaders is its own Chairman, Ivan Dzhadzhev. In late 1989 it became apparent that the Club, unlike certain other dissident groups, was intent on forming itself into a political party in opposition to the BCP. Its appeal, however, may prove to be limited by its liberal-intellectual character.

RW

COMINFORM. Acronym for the Communist Information Bureau, an information agency established in 1947 and dissolved in 1956. Its members were the Communist parties of Bulgaria, Czechoslovakia, France, Hungary, Italy, Poland, Romania, the Soviet Union and Yugoslavia. In 1948 the Cominform expelled the Yugoslav party because of the defiance of Marshal **Tito**; in 1956, as part of the reconcilation that took place between the USSR and Yugoslavia, it was dissolved.

SLW

COMMITTEE FOR WORKERS' DEFENCE (POLAND — KOR, Komitet Obrony Robotników). The Committee was set up in Poland in direct response to the repression of worker demonstrations which broke out in June 1976 following the announcement by the **Gierek** administration of immediate price rises for food products. The intensity of police repression was such that two people died shortly after, while heavy sentences were handed down on very dubious evidence. The formation of the Committee grew from the concern of a small number of concerned activists and intellectuals who attended the trials of accused workers and made contact with their families, and, arising from such an informal association of concerned individuals, the Committee formally constituted itself in September 1976 and composed an appeal to society and the authorities of the Polish People's Republic. The numbers of actual signatories were quite small and 14 people put their names to the original appeal, although others joined later. Once the Committee had dealt with activities arising from the 1976 events it broadened its remit and renamed itself the Committee for Social Self-Defence (*Komitet Samoobrony Społecznej*). It retained its association with the original conception and became known as KSS—"KOR".

The significance of the Committee was far greater than its small number of members might have suggested. It represented, firstly, a bridge between the different groups and contrasting strands of opposition that on previous occasions (most recently in 1968 and 1970) had remained separate and been dealt with individually by the authorities. Secondly, the organized basis of group activities, although loose and informal, provided a new element of continuity in the organization and programme of opposition activities. Thirdly, the ethical framework within which Committee activities were conducted, their appeal to constitutional provisions and alignment with the affirmation of **human rights** made in the Helsinki agreement encouraged the development of a particular attitude and framework which lent dignity and intellectual coherence to opposition activities. All these factors gained in significance as the crisis of the **Gierek** regime entered its terminal phase and opposition activities gained in intensity, culminating in widespread strikes during the summer of 1980. Many of those involved in KOR participated in different ways in the activities of **Solidarity** and other organizations which began operating in 1980 and 1981. Partly because of this and the progress that had occurred in the development of autonomous organization, KOR dissolved itself in September 1981.

PGL

COMMUNISM. In terms of the official theory of the USSR and other Soviet-type countries, this is the form of society that is both a necessary and desirable endproduct of social development. It is understood to have two phases: a lower phase, called socialism, and a higher phase, which is Communism proper. In a society of this kind there will be no state, all citizens will have the same relationship to the means of production, and the principle "from each according to his ability, to each according to his needs" will prevail. (*See also* **Ideology**)

SLW

COMMUNIST INTERNATIONAL (COMINTERN). An international organization of Communist and workers' parties, established in Moscow in 1919 and dissolved in 1943.

SLW

COMMUNIST PARTY OF CZECHOSLOVAKIA (KSČ — Komunistická strana Československa). Founded in May 1921, the Communist Party of Czechoslovakia enjoyed a high level of support in the inter-war period. In the 1925 parliamentary elections it was the second most popular party, with 13.2 per cent of the vote, and, although it fell to fourth place in those of 1929 and 1935, it retained the support of 10 per cent of the electorate, only 4 per cent less than the most popular Czech party at that time. After World War II, its appeal increased dramatically. In the May 1946 elections it won 38 per cent of the vote and 114 of the 300 seats in the Constituent National Assembly, and with the support of left-wing deputies from other parties it was able to win parliamentary approval and a semblance of constitutionality for its seizure of power in February 1948. The party's greatest popularity was achieved at times when it eschewed dogmatism and adapted its policies to Czechoslovak democratic traditions, notably between 1945 and 1948 when it was identified with a "specific Czechoslovak road to socialism" and during the 1968 **Prague Spring**. For most of its period in power, however, more hardline attitudes prevailed. Given the severity of the repression that followed 1968 and its failure quickly to respond to the spirit of reform spreading throughout Eastern Europe in the late 1980s, it seemed unlikely to retain the loyalty of more than a small proportion of the population once free elections were in prospect.

GW

COMMUNIST PARTY OF SLOVAKIA (Komunistiká strana Slovenska). Recognized as a separate party by the **Communist International (Comintern)** in February 1939 following the attainment of autonomy by Slovakia the preceding autumn, the Communist Party of Slovakia retained its organizational independence until September 1948 when it was subsumed within the unitary **Communist Party of Czechoslovakia**. The policy of destalinization begun in 1963 provided the Slovak Party, which retained its own Congress, Central Committee and Presidium, with the opportunity to pursue a slightly more independent course and to press in particular for satisfaction of Slovak grievances. Its representatives on the central Committee in Prague played a key role in bringing about the resignation of Antonín **Novotný** as Communist Party First Secretary in January 1968. Its support during the **Prague Spring** for the introduction of a federal system, which was seen by Slovaks as a guarantee of more equitable treatment, ensured the implementation of the one political reform not to be reversed after the **Warsaw Treaty Organization (Warsaw Pact)** invasion. After 1969 the Slovak Party was a less powerful influence within Czechoslovak politics partly because of the more authoritarian rule that prevailed in Czechoslovakia throughout the 1970s and 1980s and partly because government policies went a long way to placate Slovak interests.

GW

COMMUNIST PARTY OF THE SOVIET UNION (CPSU). (*Kommunisticheskaya partiya Sovetskogo Soyuza* — KPSS.) The CPSU is the longest-ruling party anywhere in the world, and although its role began to be placed in increasing doubt by the changes associated with "democratization", it still claimed to retain a dominant position in Soviet political life in the early 1990s just as it had done since the 1917 revolution. The party's dominant position in the society has traditionally been known as its "leading role", and until the late 1980s it was taken to be virtually the defining characteristic of a Communist political system. It was, for instance, to recover the "leading role" for local Communists that the Soviet Union and its allies intervened in Czechoslovakia in 1968 and appeared likely to do so in Poland during 1980–81 until pre-empted by the declaration of martial law. Although in the early 1990s the CPSU abandoned its constitutionally guaranteed leading role, as most of the East European parties had done, it nonetheless continued to lay claim to a "consolidating and unifying" position in the society; it sought to act as the society's "political leader", and regarded itself as the only political force capable of leading *perestroika* to a successful conclusion.

The "leading role of the party", or more modestly the party's "vanguard" role, derived from a number of circumstances, including the experience of tsarist rule (which forced parties to work conspiratorially) and the establishment of a centralized system of economic management. It derived also from a number of ideological sources, in particular the doctrine of the "vanguard party" which was formulated most fully by **Lenin** in works such as *What is to be Done?* (1902). In this book, Lenin argued that socialism would not necessarily come about through the automatic extension of trade union and other forms of economic activity by the working class. Strikes, Lenin argued, represented the class struggle in embryo, but "only in embryo", because the workers did not as yet have an awareness of the irreconcilable nature of the conflict between their interests and those of the capitalist class. This,

Lenin went on, could "only be brought to them from the outside", by the "educated representatives of the propertied classes — the intelligentsia". "There can be no revolutionary movement without a revolutionary theory", Lenin insisted, and the role of the vanguard could be fulfilled only by a party that was guided by this advanced theory. The struggle for socialism, in Lenin's view, must therefore place at least as much emphasis upon raising workers' consciousness as upon bread-and-butter economic issues, and within this struggle a role of particular importance devolved upon the intellectuals who possessed a knowledge of and commitment to the revolutionary theory by which the wider movement must be guided.

No less important was the question of party structure and organization, and it was upon this issue that Lenin and the Bolsheviks (majority group) split from the remaining Russian Social Democrats, thereafter known as the Mensheviks (minority group), at the Second Congress of the Russian Social Democratic Labour Party in 1903. Lenin argued in *What is to be Done?* that the first and most urgent practical task was to "create an organization of revolutionaries able to guarantee the energy, stability and continuity of the political struggle". Such an organization, Lenin insisted, must embrace "primarily and chiefly people whose profession consists of revolutionary activity"; and it must "inevitably be not very wide and as secret as possible", since it was essential to avoid police penetration. Lenin added that the professional revolutionary must "serve" the mass movement, not dominate it or "think for everyone"; he held that professional revolutionaries would be thrown up by the mass movement in "ever-increasing numbers"; and he insisted that his proposals were intended to be valid for Russian autocratic conditions only, in which an open organization would simply create a "paradise for the police". Lenin's principles have, none the less, been taken as the organizational basis of the ruling Communist parties of more recent years, and it is to his concept of the "vanguard party" — a relatively small group, centrally organized, of professional revolutionaries — that the Soviet Communist Party is officially dedicated.

The CPSU, in words at least, conforms closely to Lenin's dictates. The party is described, in its revised Rules adopted in 1986, as the "tried and tested militant vanguard of the Soviet people, which unites, on a voluntary basis, the more advanced, politically more conscious section of the working class, collective farm peasantry and intelligentsia of the USSR". It is not, in other words, a mass organization, admitting all who might wish to join it, but an elite group which, in theory at least, consists of those who have the highest levels of political knowledge and commitment in the society and who have been admitted into the party on that basis by the existing membership. The party is described in the Rules as the "highest form of socio-political organization" and as the "leading and guiding force of Soviet society"; it is based, officially speaking, upon what are called "Leninist norms of party life", in other words democratic centralism, collective leadership, inner-party democracy, the creative activity of party members, criticism and self-criticism, and broad publicity. The Rules, however, also make clear that the party is committed to "ideological and organizational unity, monolithic cohesion of its ranks, and a high degree of conscious discipline", and any form of group or factional activity is specifically prohibited (although it nonetheless became increasingly common in the late 1980s). Party activity, finally, is supposed to be based upon Marxist-Leninist theory and upon the party Programme, which defines the party's tasks as the "planned and all-round perfection of socialism" and the "further progress of Soviet society towards Communism". The party also regards itself as an "integral part of the international Communist movement".

The Rules lay down the organizational structure of the party. At the bottom are the primary party organizations (PPOs), formerly called cells, which are formed at workplaces and at residential locations throughout the USSR, wherever three or more party members are present. There were over 441,000 PPOs in 1990. The PPO is the organizational basis of the party; it admits new members, carries out agitation and propaganda work and seeks generally to improve the economic performance of the institution within which it is located. Meetings of members are held at least once a month, and a party secretary and (in all but the smallest PPOs) a party bureau are elected, who hold office for a year. Each PPO elects representatives to the level of the party immediately above it, the district level, which in turn elects to the regional level and then to the republican level of the party organization. At each of these levels conferences or congresses are held every five years at which party committees, bureaux and secretaries are elected, the latter consisting of full-time officials responsible for various areas of party work. At the apex of this system is the all-union Party Congress, which meets every five years; the XXVII Party Congress took place in February–March 1986 and the XXVIII was called, ahead of time, in July 1990.

Membership of the CPSU, according to its Rules, is open to any citizen of the USSR who accepts the party's Programme and Rules, takes an active part in Communist construction, works in one of the party organizations, carries out all party decisions and pays his or her membership dues (up to 3 per cent of monthly earnings). Admissions may be made from the age of 18, although those aged up to 25 inclusive may join only through the party's youth wing, the Komsomol. Applicants must submit recommendations from three existing members who have been members of the party for at least five years each and who have known the prospective member, professionally and socially, for at least a year. Membership is initially for a year-long probationary or "candidate" stage, after which a decision on full membership is taken by the members of the PPO to which application has been made. Once admitted, a member gains the right to elect and be elected to party bodies, to discuss party policies at party meetings and conferences and to uphold his opinions until a decision is made, to "criticize any party body and any Communist, irrespective of the position he holds", to address any question, statement or proposal to any party body up to Central Committee level and to demand an answer, and to attend any party meeting at which his conduct is discussed. Their duties, also set out in the Party Rules, are considerably more onerous, including the implementation and explanation of party policy, mastering Marxist-Leninist theory, and observing the "norms of Communist morality".

The party's total membership has increased steadily since the 1950s, both absolutely and as a proportion of the adult population, although the party authorities began to hold down the rate of growth in the mid-1960s and in the late 1980s non-recruitment and even resignations became a serious problem. The total membership in 1990 was just over 19.4 million, or about 10 per cent of the adult population. Some 45.4 per cent of members in the same year were workers by social origin, a proportion which rose steadily from the 1960s until less emphasis began to be placed on social origin as such in the late 1980s. Collective farmers accounted for about 11.4 per cent of party members in 1990, a proportion that has been falling slowly over the years, and white-collar staff accounted for the remaining 43.2 per cent. Women are rather under-represented in the party (see **Women's Issues**), at 29.9 per cent in 1990 as compared with just over half of the population, but their share of membership has been slowly rising and it accounts for about a third of all recruits (female membership, in fact, is relatively high as compared with the position in most Western countries). Of the nationalities, Russians account for rather more than their share of total party membership, at 58.6 per cent as compared with 50.8 per cent of the total population, but Georgians (and Jews) are more heavily over-represented than Russians, a result of their high educational and occupation standing and their predominantly urban residence. The level of party membership is lowest in the Central Asian republics and in Moldavia.

The "supreme organ" of the CPSU, according to the Rules, is the Party Congress, which is held every five years. (It is also possible to convene extraordinary Congresses if the circumstances require it.) The Congress hears and approves the report of the leading party bodies, it reviews and amends the party's Rules and Programme, and it elects the Central Committee and the Central Auditing Commission (which oversees accounts). It also "determines the line of the party in matters of domestic and foreign policy, and examines and decides the most important questions of party and state life and of Communist construction". The Party Congress is however too large and meets for too short a time to serve as a policy-making body in this sense, and in practice it serves mainly as a means of ratifying policies decided in advance as well as a periodic rally and morale-booster, particularly for the "best of the best" that are chosen as delegates by their local branches. The Central Committee's report, normally presented by the General Secretary, is the most important item of business considered by the Congress; it also receives a report delivered by a government spokesman on the new Five Year Plan. These are approved — in the past, unanimously — after a rather perfunctory debate, although individual speakers have increasingly taken this opportunity to press their regional or sectional demands.

Of rather more significance in a policy-making sense is the Central Committee, which is elected by the Party Congress to discharge its responsibilities in the intervals between Congresses. The Central Committee elected by the XXVII Party Congress in March 1986 had 477 members, of whom 307 had full membership and 170 had candidate or non-voting status. By January 1990, following a series of resignations, deaths and promotions, there were 249 full and 108 candidate members. The Central Committee is required to meet not less than once every six months; its responsibilities include the direction of the activity of the party and of its local bodies, the selection and appointment of leading functionaries, and the management of party institutions, the party press and the party budget. Its members constitute the closest approximation to the Soviet political elite, including — often, it appears, as of right — the leading party officials from the re-publican and regional levels as well as leading government ministers, trade union officials, diplomats, generals, heads or academic and scientific institutions, and a small but increasing number of "genuine" workers and peasants. The proceedings of the Central Committee are not normally published, but it seems clear that its periodic meetings serve as sounding-boards for the consideration of policy alternatives as well as occasions for the party leadership to announce new policies or to administer authoritative warnings about shortcomings in various areas of policy. Press reports of its meetings in the **Gorbachev** period suggested that they could also serve as an opportunity for the regional party leadership to express its misgivings about the course of *perestroika*.

The Central Committee met more frequently under Gorbachev than under his predecessors, and it was the occasion for more vigorous exchanges than at any time since the 1920s. Attempts were also made, as part of the effort to "democratize" party life, to involve the Central Committee membership more continuously in the process of policy formation. The most important development of this kind was the establishment of six Central Committee commissions in 1988, each of which was chaired by a senior member of the leadership. The commissions dealt with party matters, ideology, social and economic issues, agriculture, international affairs and law reform; each of them had a membership of about 20, and they met two or three times a year. The ideological commission, for instance, dealt in 1989 with the national question and the draft law on the press; the international affairs commission considered the Nazi-Soviet pact and the restructuring of Soviet foreign economic relations. The commissions, it became clear, were the occasion for sometimes vigorous debate, but it was less clear that they could take part in the shaping of party policy rather than its discussion and approval. They nonetheless represented a significant move towards a more open, participatory party of the kind that Gorbachev — and a wide section of party opinion — believed to be necessary.

Gorbachev and the CPSU. The process of "democratization", launched by the Central Committee plenum of January 1987, concerned the CPSU at least as much as other political institutions. The central idea, as the party theoretical journal *Kommunist* put it in early 1988, was that there should be a more restricted understanding of the party's role, involving a kind of "division of labour" in which the party stood aside from the direct management of public affairs, confining itself to a much more distant co-ordinating role.

The discussion that preceded the 19th Party Conference in 1988 saw very widespread demands for changes of this kind. There were calls, for instance, for party officials to spend more time working "with the masses" and less time in their offices, and for all party bodies from the Politburo downwards to present annual reports on their work. It was suggested that there should be party congresses every two years and party conferences during the intervals between them, as in Lenin's time, and that the existing membership, recruited to a large extent during the **Brezhnev** years of stagnation, should be reaccredited and if possible reduced. There was also some concern about the party's own finances, with calls for detailed income and expenditure statements. They knew more about the finances of the British Royal Family and President Reagan, one speaker at the party conference complained, than they knew about the income and expenditure of their own party.

Perhaps the most widely supported proposals, however, were that there should be a choice of candidate at all elections to party office, and that positions of this kind should be held for a limited period. Under the existing system of recommendation from above, wrote one contributor to the discussion, party posts were filled not by election but by appointment, and often for life. Instead of this there should be a "periodic renewal of elected and non-elected cadres", with maximum periods of tenure. Other contributors to the discussion that took place before the Party Conference called for a normal limit of two five-year terms in the same party position, and some called for the reintroduction of the compulsory turnover rules that had been brought in by **Khrushchev** but dropped by his successors. Party posts, it was agreed, should also be filled by secret and competitive ballot, and changes were suggested in the manner in which the General Secretary was elected, with some commentators calling for a party-wide ballot on the matter. There might, some thought, be age limits for party positions, such as 65 for Politburo and Secretariat members. And there should be changes in the party's own bureaucracy: it should be smaller, and should less obviously parallel the ministerial hierarchy.

Most of these themes found a place in Gorbachev's address to the Party Conference in June 1988. There had been "definite deformations in the party itself", Gorbachev told the delegates. Democratic centralism had degenerated into bureaucratic centralism. The rank and file had lost control over the leaderships that spoke in their name; officials had come to believe they were infallible and irreplaceable, and an atmosphere of comradeship and collectivism had been replaced by one of superiors and subordinates. Party and government had lost their distinctive functions, and the party apparatus had become too closely involved in economic and administrative rather than properly political affairs. The Conference, in its concluding resolution, agreed with Gorbachev that a "profound democratization" of party life was necessary. Towards this end, party primary organizations should be freed from "petty regimentation" by bodies superior to them. Membership should be determined by the moral and political qualities of applicants, not by their social background or centrally-imposed norms. Party meetings should be more open and constructive; and members must be given a greater role to play than simply attending and "rubber-stamping lists of candidates and draft resolutions". More records of party meetings should be published; and—a matter of "prime importance"—all posts up to Central Committee level should be filled by secret and competitive ballot for a maximum of two five-year terms.

Changes of this kind had already begun to occur: the first contested elections for party office, for instance, had taken place early in 1987, and similar changes had begun in the party's youth movement, the Komsomol, the previous year. The period that followed saw these principles applied still more widely. The party apparatus was restructured at all levels, and generally reduced in size by about 30 per cent. Central Committee commissions were introduced at republican as well as national level. A new journal, "*Central Committee News*", began to appear in January 1989: it contained a wealth of biographical, statistical and other material, and came out monthly in a large edition. The party's finances were discussed in its first issue, and also in *Pravda*. Members' dues, it emerged, provided the largest part of the party's income, but 19 per cent of expenditure had to be covered by contributions from party publishing houses and other sources. Most of the party's expenditure was incurred on maintaining the party apparatus at lower levels; the central party bureaucracy alone cost just over 50 million rubles a year to support, which was no more than 3 per cent of the party's total expenditure. Membership statistics were also reported more fully than ever before: among the 19.5 million members on Jan. 1, 1989 were 125 Eskimos, 7 Englishmen, three Americans, two "Negroes" and a single Canadian.

There remained some concern, at the start of the 1990s, that the CPSU had restructured itself less fully and swiftly than other institutions in Soviet life. Indeed there was nothing less than a "democratization gap" in the USSR, wrote a leading party official in 1989, between the CPSU and the society at large — and it was widening. Relatively few party secretaries, it emerged, were in fact being chosen by a secret competitive ballot; just 1 per cent of the party's regional first secretaries, for example, as compared with 74 per cent of the Congress of People's Deputies that had been elected in March 1989. This was a difference "hardly in favour of the party". District party committees, it appeared, still kept their records secret, the rank and file were "walled off" from their activities, and even members of elected party committees had no access to the meetings of the party bureaux that were nominally accountable to them. The "vanguard", in short, was "lagging".

There was also some evidence, in the late 1980s, that the party was beginning to lose members and more generally experiencing what party officials themselves described as a "crisis of confidence". Gorbachev, at the Congress in 1986, had called upon the party to lose its "infallibility complex". But it was far from clear what was to take its place. In the absence of a clear and binding conception of their role, some party members, particularly in the Baltic, joined the popular fronts, while others joined the movements that had been set up to oppose them. Some party members went on strike, and even headed the strike committees that emerged in the summer of 1989 in mining areas, while others called for public order to be maintained. Some felt that *glasnost*' had gone too far, and that the party was taking too much of the blame for the Stalin years; and they were concerned that the 1930s were being remembered almost exclusively in terms of repression, and not sufficiently in terms of social and economic achievement. For others, only an honest assessment of the past could prevent the recurrence of similar abuses in the future and establish the party's moral authority. Still others were disheartened by the party's failure to revive the Soviet economy and to overcome social and national tensions. Opinion polls made clear that the party's authority was falling; but without a coherent vision of the kind of society it was attempting to construct it was unlikely that the party's gradual demoralization, even disintegration, could be avoided.

The leadership of the CPSU. The Soviet party leadership, like that of most traditional Communist systems, was based in the late 1980s upon two key decision-making bodies: the Politburo and the Secretariat. Both were formally elected (more accurately, approved) by the Central Committee, which also, separately, elected the General Secretary. According to the Party Rules, the Politburo is supposed to "direct the work of the party" between meetings of the Central Committee. It is, in fact, the functional equivalent of a cabinet in a British-type political system, meeting weekly (usually on a Thursday) and taking key decisions in all areas of policy. The Politburo in January 1990 consisted of 18 members; the average age was about 60, rather younger than the Brezhnev Politburo of the late 1970s, and it included the first woman member for more than 20 years, Alexandra Biryukova, who had formerly worked in the central trade union bureaucracy. It was a better educated Politburo than all of its predecessors: three of its members (Medvedev, Yakovlev and Lukyanov) held higher doctorates in economics, history and law respectively, and Yevgenii Primakov, who joined as a candidate in September 1989, was a member of the Academy of Sciences and the former director of its important think-tank, the Institute of the World Economy and International Relations. It was, however, less representative of the party as a whole than the Politburos of earlier years, with only Vladimir Ivashko, the Ukrainian first secretary, heading a major non-Russian party organization.

Brief reports of Politburo meetings began to appear in the press from November 1982, and still fuller summaries of the discussions from late 1989. There was no typical agenda, but it seemed clear that meetings would normally start with Soviet domestic affairs—plan results, the energy industry, education or whatever—and then move to foreign affairs, more often by way of report than for the purposes of substantive discussion. Meetings normally concluded with "other matters", almost certainly a reference to appointments to leading positions. The Politburo meeting of Jan. 22, 1990, although on a Monday, was not otherwise untypical. The first and clearly most important item was the draft platform that was to be presented to the Central Committee in early February, covering (it later emerged) the further extension of political reform and the modification if not elimination of the Communist party's guaranteed leading role. The Politburo had a "thorough" discussion after which it "on the whole" approved the draft, instructing Gorbachev to prepare a further version taking into account the views that had been expressed. The Politburo also heard about Gorbachev's visit to Lithuania in December 1989 for discussions with its secessionist party organization, and approved recommendations on this issue for the forthcoming plenum. The other items were concerned with foreign affairs: contacts with the Japanese Liberal Democratic Party, and the discussions that had taken place between Gorbachev, **Shevardnadze** and the United Nations Secretary General on his recent visit to Moscow.

The Politburo, under Brezhnev, held relatively brief meetings, usually of an hour's duration. Politburo meetings, under Gorbachev, are known to last well into the evening, and an elaborate but changing network of committees attached to the Politburo carries out further work. One of these, for instance, was the commission set up in 1987 to review the sentences that were passed in the 1930s, 1940s and early 1950s and to rehabilitate those who were innocent; it took decisions of considerable political sensitivity and was latterly chaired by a close Gorbachev associate, Alexander Yakovlev. Not all meetings are chaired by Gorbachev in person; nor is the attendance necessarily limited to the formal membership. The editor of *Pravda*, for instance, is normally in attendance; the secretary of the national trade union council has also been present; and ministers and others will normally appear when their attendance is considered appropriate for a particular item on the agenda. Equally, a number of members based outside Moscow may attend less frequently than others. Not all the items on the agenda, it appears, are dealt with at the weekly meetings; in these circumstances the papers are circulated for the equivalent of a postal ballot. Again, Moscow-based members and particularly the full-time members of the Secretariat have a disproportionate influence on these decisions.

The Politburo works closely with the Secretariat, which is also elected by the Central Committee. In January 1990 there were 13 Central Committee Secretaries, including the General Secretary, and they normally met weekly on a Tuesday. The most important members, sometimes called "super-secretaries", were also members of the Politburo. The Party Rules say no more than that the Secretariat "directs current work, chiefly the selection of cadres [leading officials] and the verification of the fulfilment of decisions". This group of top-level officials, together with its counterparts at lower levels of the system, is in fact an institution of the utmost importance; it is the instrument through which the party's decisions are put into effect, it offers advice and information to the Politburo, and (given the party's broad conception of its leading role) it functions in effect as the administrative focus of the whole Soviet system. Some of the functions of the Secretariat, in the late 1980s, appeared to have been taken over by the newly-established Central Committee commissions (see above); the commissions, nonetheless, were headed by individual Central Committee Secretaries, and they were perhaps better conceptualised as adjuncts to the Secretariat rather than as a replacement for it.

The Secretariat's main responsibility is to guide the work of the Departments of the Central Committee, which are the party's full-time central bureaucracy. Under Gorbachev's predecessors there had been 20 or more departments, each of them responsible for a particular area of Soviet life and many of them responsible for supervising the work of a particular industrial ministry. In 1988, on Gorbachev's recommendation, the 20 departments that then existed were reduced to just nine. There was a Department of Party Development and Cadres, responsible for overseeing the inner life of the party itself and more general questions of appointments. The Ideological Department was responsible for questions of theory, and also for science and culture. There was a Socio-Economic Department, responsible for the general (but not day-to-day) management of social and economic matters, and an Agricultural Department, with corresponding responsibilities. A Defence Department was to supervise military industry (again without undermining the position of the relevant ministries). There was an International Department, to deal with the party's foreign relations and questions of foreign policy, and a Department of State and Law, responsible for political and legal reform. A General Department and Administration of Affairs were also required for day-to-day matters. The total staffing of the central party apparatus was 1,940, with 1,275 secretaries and others in addition. Reduced, as intended, by about 30 per cent, this was still a formidable party headquarters.

All of the party's leading bodies are in principle elective and accountable to those that elect them, but in practice, at least until the late 1980s, they largely dominated the congresses and conferences to which they were nominally responsible as well as lower levels of the hierarchy. There were several reasons for this. Perhaps the most important was Article 19 of the Party Rules, which required (in its 1986 formulation) that all party bodies be elective and accountable but also that there be "strict party discipline and subordination of the minority to the majority", and that the decisions of higher bodies were "obligatory for lower bodies". The decisions of leading party bodies could not therefore be openly challenged, at least without the risk of expulsion and other sanctions, and any attempts to form organized groupings or to establish direct links between party bodies at the same level in the hierarchy was explicitly prohibited. The Party Rules also specified various ways in which each level of the party structure supervised the level immediately below it. Of particular importance was the influence that was exerted over the election of leading officials at each level of the party by the level immediately above it. Although there was a secret ballot and although members had the "unlimited right to challenge candidates and to criticize them", it was normal, until the late 1980s, for a single list of candidates to be "recommended" by the party level immediately above and for it to be elected without opposition. Each level of the party hierarchy was also supposed to "direct" and "inspect the work" of the party bodies immediately subordinate to it, and to hear regular reports on their performance.

Leading officials at each level of the party organization, accordingly, could usually count upon the support of the party officials immediately superior to them and by whom they had been nominated, and had less need to pay attention to the wishes and opinions of those that nominally elected them. The Party Rules do in fact provide for the "free and business-like discussion of questions of party policy in individual party organizations or in the party as a whole"; every member has the right to criticize the conduct of any other member or (from 1986) any party body, and special party-wide discussions may be held when the circumstances require them. These are held to be basic principles of inner-party democracy, and severe penalties, even expulsion, are attached to any attempt to suppress criticism or to victimize those who have expressed it. The party press, however, is full of cases of this kind, with critics being forced to undertake less pleasant work or even to leave their employment for having spoken out of turn at party meetings, and it often requires the intervention of higher-level officials before the injustice can be corrected. Even in Gorbachev's CPSU it was still clear to most members that only "constructive", that was to say, mild and unspecific, criticism would be encouraged, and any more far-reaching criticism could well have adverse consequences for those that had expressed it, including their employment, their families' career prospects and perhaps even their liberty. It was not perhaps surprising, in these circumstances, that the CPSU continued to function in a centralized and hierarchical manner, rather than in the internally democratic manner for which the Party Rules ostensibly provided.

SLW

CORNEA, DOINA. A former teacher of French at Cluj university in Romania, Doina Cornea conducted a one-woman campaign against the **Ceauşescu** regime. Her health suffered as a result of consequent ill-treatment and she was kept under surveillance although not under house arrest.

RH

COUNCIL FOR MUTUAL ECONOMIC ASSISTANCE (CMEA). The CMEA, also known as Comecon, was created in January 1949 as a response to the announcement of the Marshall Plan, and possibly also as an element in **Stalin**'s campaign to rally the Communist faithful against renegade Yugoslavia. In the event, it remained largely a paper organization, concerned only with collecting statistics, during Stalin's lifetime, and did not develop into any kind of a policy vehicle until the mid-1950s. Its full members in 1990 were the USSR, Bulgaria, Czechoslovakia, the GDR, Hungary, Poland, Romania, Cuba, Mongolia and, since 1978, Vietnam. Albania was a founder-member, but stopped participating in 1961. Following its partial reconciliation with the USSR, Yugoslavia acquired observer status with the Council.

The reasons for the shadowy early life of the CMEA remain clouded in obscurity. One theory is that Vosnesensky, chairman of the Soviet State Planning Commission at the time of the birth of the Council, hoped to use the new organization as a framework for developing East European trade on a market basis, and as a complement to his plans for market-oriented reform within the Soviet Union itself. In March 1949 Vosnesensky was shot, and his policies abandoned. An alternative explanation is that the rationale of economic integration was lost under the pressures for short-term output maximization, always conducive to autarky, created by the Korean War.

In principle the supreme decision-making body of the CMEA is the annual meeting of Prime Ministers and Planning Commission chairmen, which normally meets sometime in early summer. But the decisions of the meeting are not binding, and the Council has, indeed, few "teeth" with which it can implement agreed policies. Two banks, the International Investment Bank, created in 1970, and the Bank for Economic Co-operation, which was set up in 1973, provide a partial exception to this rule. They have been of great importance in financing CMEA joint projects to bring Soviet energy to the smaller East European countries (hereafter EE-6). The International Investment Bank has, among other things, raised convertible currency loans to facilitate these projects.

Sometimes referred to as the East European Common Market, the CMEA has in practice been a signal failure of economic integration. We can distinguish a number of inter-related reasons for this. Firstly, the traditional model of central planning is inherently autarkic. Planners operate with physical quantities rather than prices. This is feasible, if at a cost, at the level of the domestic economy. Internationally it is impossible, because even trade between fraternal socialist countries must ultimately be couched in price terms, if only so that Balances of Trade can be compiled. In the absence of a special set of CMEA prices, the Council had adopted the practice of following world prices, with certain systematic modifications. Oil prices, for instance, are calculated on the basis of a five-year moving average of world prices. This is convenient, but has no general theoretical justification. It does in any case leave unsolved the problem of how to relate these prices to domestic prices, which are themselves of doubtful value as scarcity prices. Secondly, the technological deficiencies of the planned economies have meant that many of the investment goods required by all the member economies for their modernization plans have simply not been available within the CMEA region. Thirdly, specific sectoral problems, e.g. the huge Soviet grain deficit, have not been soluble on an intra-CMEA basis for a combination of organizational and climatic reasons. Neither of these latter two factors are, of course, independent of the planning system variable.

In the absence of a currency numéraire, CMEA trade is essentially carried on in a kind of vacuum. The "convertible" ruble is in practice not convertible. As a result, trade is generally balanced on a bilateral basis through clearing agreements. (There is a system of multilateral settlement for the joint energy projects, and a proportion of trade, around 10 per cent for Hungary for instance, is settled in hard currency. Above-quota deliveries of Soviet fuel to Eastern Europe has to be paid for in hard currency and at world prices.) In principle the clearing agreement system should keep bilateral trade flows more or less in balance from one year to the next. In practice, substantial surpluses do sometimes accrue. But while in the Western international economy trading surpluses are usually seen as a cause for satisfaction, bilateral CMEA surpluses dominated in inconvertible currency units are bad news. Thus we find that the CMEA is dominated by a kind of inverse mercantilism, with every partner trying to maximize its deficits. The period after the first oil shock of 1974 was dominated by big Soviet surpluses, as the CMEA oil price rose on the basis of a lagged adjustment to the world prices. In recent years, however, we have seen a tendency for the USSR to move into deficit with a number of CMEA partners. This partly reflects the collapse of world oil prices in 1985, but seems to reflect also a policy move on the part of Moscow to cut accumulated clearing account surpluses. The strength of CMEA reverse mercantilism was demonstrated at the end of 1988 and the beginning of 1989, after a decision to allow limited convertibility of domestic currencies for purposes of cross-border trade in consumer goods. Poles armed with worthless zlotys immediately invaded Czechoslovakia and the GDR, while new Soviet consignments of refrigerators, in dire shortage at home, were quickly bought up by fraternal consumers. By early 1989 the Soviet Union had banned the export of certain consumer goods to other CMEA countries.

This story provides yet another illustration of a general point that emerges from all the analysis of economic planning trends in Eastern Europe in recent decades. A little bit of reform is a bad thing —and so is a little bit of convertibility. Yet it is not difficult to see why the East European countries want to move towards convertibility; why, indeed, **Gorbachev** set the goal of a fully convertible CMEA ruble in his speech to the 1988 CPSU conference. Convertibility is the only way to multilateralize CMEA trade, the only way to build a bridge between domestic scarcities and international prices. It is also the only way to resolve the conflict over "hard" and "soft" goods. For while the smaller East European countries, particularly those with more sophisticated manufacturing sectors, have objected to the prices offered them by the Soviet Union for their industrial goods, Moscow has countered by pointing out that the bulk of East European deliveries to the Soviet Union are of goods which it might be difficult to sell at *any price* on Western markets. Soviet oil and gas, by contrast, can always find a ready market, at the going price, in the West. This argument, if taken to its logical conclusion, largely disposes of the argument about prices — the Soviet Union is exchanging something of value for something of no value. Of course Soviet industry and Soviet consumers are often happy enough to receive consignments from East European countries which have reached higher technological levels (e.g. the GDR), or enjoy special agricultural/climatic advantages (e.g. Bulgaria). But convertibility is an enormously enticing prospect, in terms of deepening the socialist division of labour, and simply in terms of settling arguments.

The actual structure of intra-CMEA trade reflects these problems and paradoxes. As a percentage of the total trade of individual countries, aggregate CMEA trade bulks large enough. Thus in 1988 the CMEA market took 58 per cent of total Soviet exports, according to official data. The price formula whereby CMEA trade and hard-currency trade is aggregated in official Soviet statistics tends to exaggerate the CMEA component, but even so CMEA trade must account for more than 50 per cent of total Soviet trade. For some member countries the figure is higher — over 70 per cent for Bulgaria, for instance—and for some lower, viz. Romania with under 50 per cent. But these shares have shown no upward trend over the past decade or so. There have been some successes of intra-CMEA specialization—most obviously the joint energy projects, but also transport equipment (Bulgaria—forklift trucks, Czechoslovakia—trams, Hungary—buses). In qualitative terms, however, intra-CMEA trade is marked by a striking absence of high-tech commodity exchange. Whether we look at the figures or at the policy history, then, the overall picture is one of stagnation.

Khrushchev was the first Soviet leader to try to bring some real division of labour into the CMEA, not just as a way of imposing Soviet priorities, but also in an attempt to settle disagreements between the more industrialized countries of the EE-6 and the predominantly agrarian countries of the Balkans. He failed, most obviously because of the Romanians' inflexibility over their plans to build up heavy industry, particularly the steel industry, but also because the more developed countries were reluctant to "pass on" the simpler forms of engineering production to their less industrialized allies. The most striking development in the period after Khrushchev's fall was the signature of an agreement between Czechoslovakia and Hungary, to run from Jan. 1, 1968, permitting limited commodity convertibility (i.e. Czech enterprises would be able to buy supplies in Hungary for Czech currency and vice versa). With Poland also interested, there seemed a genuine possibility of a real common market in north-east central Europe. But the Soviet invasion of Czechoslovakia in 1968 put a political end to this line of development. Perhaps for that reason, **Brezhnev** and **Kosygin** seemed largely content to leave the CMEA alone, and though the first CMEA "Complex Programme" was signed in 1971, it remained a dead letter, and no further Council summits were called until after the death of Brezhnev. The Concerted Plan of Multilateral Measures for the Period 1976–80 did provide an institutional framework for the joint energy projects. Further Concerted Plans were due to be signed for the periods 1981–85 and 1986–90, on the basis of long-term programmes for the main production sectors. But with the Romanians again worried about sovereignty, and the Hungarians, too, lukewarm, very little was in practice agreed. No doubt one of the underlying factors was the general downward trend in investment expenditure through the CMEA area. Be that as it may, the Council seemed, by the death of Brezhnev, to be in some danger of returning to the moribund status of the **Stalin** period.

Concern to bring a new impetus to CMEA integration grew steadily in urgency through the 1980s, at least in the Soviet Union, and in 1984 the first Council summit for 13 years was held in Moscow. Progress was initially hampered by a fundamental disagreement between the Soviet Union, on the one hand, and the EE-6 on the other. Moscow tended to see the future of the socialist division of labour in terms of joint enterprises. The others, fearing a loss of economic sovereignty and suspicious of Soviet pricing formulae (Moscow insists, for example, on using the standard moving-average world price formula for energy deliveries proceeding from joint projects), tended to favour increased marketization of intra-CMEA links. Strikingly, this was the case for countries like the GDR and Czechoslovakia, conservative on domestic economic reform, as much as for reform-minded Hungary. It was disagreements like this which condemned the Complex Programme for Scientific and Technical Co-operation, signed in 1985 and aimed at achieving meaningful integration in high-tech areas like electronics and robotization, to ineffectuality. But as Gorbachev's domestic *perestroika* programme grew in radicality, so the basis of the disagreement was rapidly eroded. By 1988 the Soviet position on poor quality East European deliveries was hardening, but at the same time Moscow was moving much closer to the East European position on the importance of market trading procedures, as Gorbachev's declaration on CMEA convertibility confirmed. The fruit of this new consensus was a "Collective Concept of the International Socialist Division of Labour in the Period 1991–2005". The new document was based on the earlier Complex programme, but sought to correct the latter's shortcomings by taking explicit account of reform trends and of the need for a degree of currency convertibility. But member states were not expected to work out a mechanism for multilateral co-operation and socialist integration until 1990, and no concrete measures were scheduled for introduction before 1991. For all the genuine strength of current reform trends in the domestic economies of the CMEA countries, it was still difficult to see the Council moving rapidly towards a genuinely integrated system. Meanwhile, the member countries had to respond to more immediate challenges.

One of the the most striking things about the new CMEA rhetoric of 1988 was the use of the term "single socialist market". Gorbachev himself quite consciously used the terminology of the Single European Act to underline how important it was for Eastern Europe to respond to the challenges currently emanating from Western Europe. Yet the predominant sentiment in the East in relation to the new phase of West European integration seemed to be one of dread rather than optimism, despite the signing of a General Accord between the EC and the CMEA in 1988, followed immediately by a Soviet request for full diplomatic links with the Communities. Did this reflect a fear that East-West barriers to trade might become stronger, that "voluntary" export restraints might increasingly be imposed by Brussels, rather than by national governments? Whatever the tenor of public statements, it was unlikely that this was the key element, except possibly for the GDR, whose special trading relationship with West Germany was threatened by the Single Market. Rather East European governments were simply afraid of the increased heat of competition and increasingly rigorous standardization which 1992 would, at least in principle, bring. Significantly, the Soviet government signed in 1989 an agreement with a West German organization which should help to bring Soviet industrial standards up to West European standards. But if the theory was that the single socialist market was a condition of effective integration into the wider European market, East European leaders could expect bitter disappointment. Countries like Poland and Hungary, already moving out of the Communist political orbit, would in any case almost certainly seek direct association with the European Communities. Other CMEA countries for which political and military alliance with the Soviet Union remained beyond question might find themselves pushed in the same direction, as indeed might the Soviet Union itself. The Single European Act was certainly a challenge to the CMEA, but it was a challenge which the Council was unlikely to survive in its existing form.

The true order of priorities is perhaps best discernible if we look at the trend in foreign trade legislation within CMEA countries. While progress on intra-CMEA matters has been painfully slow, most of the European member states have been taking decisive measures to ease the inward flow of Western capital, in particular by liberalizing the legislation on joint ventures. In the Soviet Union a new law of 1987 legalized joint ventures for the first time, and about 400 joint venture agreements had been signed by late 1989. Certainly most of these covered relatively small projects, and the experience of the other East European countries, which have permitted joint ventures for much longer, is that the interest of Western business in these agreements is still relatively slight. Until participation in joint ventures gives Western partners much freer access to domestic East European markets, and until transferability of profits can be absolutely guaranteed through fully convertible East European curren-

cies, attitudes are unlikely to change. That once again underlines the limited usefulness of limited forms of convertibility.

The three non-European members of the CMEA — Cuba, Mongolia and Vietnam — account together for less than 5 per cent of total intra-CMEA trade turnover. But this is nevertheless an important element within the aggregate trade of Council members, because it serves as a vehicle whereby aid—predominantly Soviet—is donated to the Third World members of the organization. There are two main ways in which aid is disbursed. One is through special purchase prices well above world prices, e.g. Cuban sugar. The other is through toleration of the build-up of very large negative balances on clearing account. In 1986, for instance, Vietnam was permitted to run a trade deficit of over Rb 1 billion with the Soviet Union. The corresponding figure for Mongolia was over Rb 0.7 billion. Gorbachev has made it very plain to his Asian and American CMEA allies that the era of blank cheques is over, and the Soviet Union would like to put its economic relations with the Third World as a whole on a much more business-like footing. The policy change has, however, still not made any significant impact on these deep-seated structural deficits.

DAD

CZECHOSLOVAK PEOPLE'S PARTY (Československá strana lidová). One of the four non-Communist parties included in the **National Front of the Czechoslovak Socialist Republic** since 1948, the People's Party has traditionally appealed to Christian sections of the Czech population. In national governments between 1948 and 1968, it was entrusted with the Ministry of Health. Two of its members were given posts in the "Government of national understanding" formed on Dec. 10, 1989, one as a Deputy Prime Minister and Chairman of the State Commission for Technology and Investment Policy and the other as a minister without portfolio. Since 1969 the People's Party has been allocated between 15 and 18 out of the 350 seats in the Federal Assembly and 14 or 15 of the 200 seats in the Czech National Council. Following changes in its leadership in November 1989, it reaffirmed its role as an ecumenical party appealing to Christian sections of the population.

GW

CZECHOSLOVAK PROTESTANT CHURCHES. While the **Roman Catholic Church** accounted for two-thirds of the total population of Czechoslovakia at the time of the

Communist rise to power, it was especially strong among the Slovaks, with the Czechs more evenly divided between Protestants and Catholics.

The Protestant groups include the Czechoslovak Hussite Church (formerly the Czechoslovak National Church), the Slovak Lutheran Church, the Evangelical Church of the Czech Brethren and the Reformed Church (mainly composed of Hungarians). These Churches were more susceptible to state control than the Roman Catholics, whose headquarters is outside the country. The Hussites and the Czech Brethren received relatively privileged treatment.

A senior theologian of the Czech Brethren was Josef Hromadká,who established the Christian Peace Conference and became a leading figure in the world ecumenicial movement. He advocated co-operation with the Communist Party and Christian-Marxist dialogue. The Christian Peace Conference worked with the Communist reformers of the 1968 **Prague Spring**, and Hromadká publicly opposed the Soviet invasion. After the invasion, the Protestant churches fell under the control of the **Husák** regime, and condemned those of their members who signed the human rights manifesto, **Charter 77**. Nevertheless, dissident movements developed in the 1980s among the Protestants, especially among the Czech Brethren.

PJSD

CZECHOSLOVAK SOCIALIST PARTY (Československá strana socialistická). One of the four non-communist parties in the **National Front of the Czechoslovak Socialist Republic** since 1948, the Czechoslovak Socialist Party emerged as the successor to the reformist National and Socialist Party (*Československá strana národně socialistická*) following a Communist-inspired purge of its membership in 1948. Between then and 1968 its leader was entrusted with the Ministry of Justice in the national government and in recent years a deputy chairmanship of the Federal Assembly. Since 1969 it has been allocated between 18 and 20 of the 350 seats in the Federal Assembly and between 12 and 14 of the 200 seats in the Czech National Council. Two of its members were given posts in the "government of national understanding" formed on Dec. 10, 1989—one as a Deputy Prime Minister entrusted with supervision of the Ministry of Agriculture and Food and the other as Minister in charge of the Federal Price Office.

GW

CZECHOSLOVAKIA. *Population*: 15.6 million

(est. 1988). *Area*: 127.900 sq km. *Top five trading partners*: USSR, German Democratic Republic, Poland, Hungary, Federal Republic of Germany. *Urban population as percentage of total*: 64 per cent. *Birth rate*: 13.8 per thousand (1987). *Life expectancy*: 71 years (1986).

General background. Czechoslovakia was created in October 1918 following the collapse of the Austro-Hungarian Empire. It brought together in one state the historical Czech Kingdom of Bohemia and Moravia which had been under Austrian rule since the early seventeenth century and Slovak provinces previously under Hungarian control. The Subcarpathian Ukraine (Ruthenia) also came under Czechoslovakia's jurisdiction between the two World Wars but was ceded to the USSR in 1945.

The two Western Slav peoples, the Czechs and Slovaks, have always formed a majority of the population but in the inter-war period almost a quarter of the country's then 13 –14 million inhabitants were of German nationality. A greater degree of homogeneity was achieved as a result of the expulsion of the Germans immediately after World War II, but sizeable minorities remain within the country's frontiers even today. As of the end of 1986, 9.8 million Czechs and 4.9 million Slovaks together made up 94.6 per cent of the total population of 15.5 million, and in addition there were 595,000 Hungarians, mostly in southern Slovakia, 72,000 Poles, 55,000 Germans and 48,000 Ukrainians. Although not recognized as an official nationality, the Gypsy population of the country is conservatively estimated at some 390,000.

In 1960 Czechoslovakia was renamed the Czechoslovak Socialist Republic (ČSSR) and since Jan. 1, 1969 has been a federal state comprising two republics of equal status, the Czech Socialist Republic, whose population on Dec. 31, 1988 was 10,360,000, and the Slovak Socialist Republic, which had 5,264,000 inhabitants. The supreme representative body is the Federal Assembly, a bicameral legislature, directly elected by the population, comprising the House of the People (*sněmovna lidu*) with 200 deputies (134 from the Czech Republic and 66 from Slovakia) and the House of the Nations (*sněmovna národů*) with 150 (75 deputies from each of the two republics). The Federal Assembly is elected for a five-year term and normally convenes for a few days twice a year. It is responsible for all legislative and administrative matters and elects a President who is the country's head of state. The President appoints the Prime Minister and government, subject to approval by the Assembly.

Each of the constituent republics has its own government and parliament or National Council (*národní rada*) but while the Czech National Council has 200 deputies, its Slovak counterpart has 150. Czechoslovakia is further subdivided into 10 regions (*kraj*), 112 districts (*okres*) and about 10,000 local units, each with its own national committee (*národní výbor*). Prague, the capital of the country and of the Czech Republic, and Bratislava, the capital of the Slovak Republic, also have regional status.

From February 1948 until December 1989 political power was effectively in the hands of the **Communist Party of Czechoslovakia (KSČ— Komunistická strana Ceskoslovenska)**, although four other political parties survived and are represented in the federal and republican parliaments and local government national committees. These are the **Czechoslovak Socialist Party**, the **Czechoslovak People's Party**, both active only in the Czech Republic, and in Slovakia the **Party of Slovak Renewal** and the **Freedom Party**. Although leading figures from these parties were allocated seats in the Czechoslovak government between 1948 and 1971, and participated in the governments of the Czech and Slovak Republics after 1969, the federal government was the exclusive preserve of the Communist Party between 1971 and late 1989. The formation of a "government of national understanding" on Dec. 10, 1989 left the Communist Party in a minority with nine out of 20 seats, while the Socialist and People's Parties were each awarded two posts and seven went to non-party members, among whom were two leading figures in the opposition **Civic Forum**. A further post remained vacant pending the election of a new Slovak Prime Minister, who like his Czech counterpart, is normally *ex officio* a Deputy Prime Minister in the federal government.

The Communist Party is a unitary organization which operates on the principle of democratic centralism. Although its primary organizations are predominantly in factories and other workplaces, above that level it is structured on a territorial basis to parallel the state administration. Party organizations in towns, districts and regions elect their own committees and presidia at conferences every two to three years. Slovakia has its own party organization which holds its congress every five years and elects a Central Committee, Presidium and Secretariat to enact party policy in that Republic within the framework set by the leadership in Prague, to which it is subordinate, but no equivalent organization has so far been created in the Czech Republic. A Committee for the direction of party work in the Czech Republic, however, was set up in October 1988 and draft party rules, published a year later, proposed the establishment of a Czech Communist Party with its own Committee and Presidium. Supreme authority is claimed to lie in the five-yearly Congress of the Communist Party of Czechoslovakia but in reality greater influence is wielded by the Central Committee which it elects and ultimate power is held by the Presidium and Secretariat nominally chosen by that Committee.

The inclusion of the Federal, Czech and Slovak Prime Ministers in the Communist Party Presidium reinforced its role as the real locus of policy-making. With the formation of the "government of national understanding", however, neither the new Federal Prime Minister, Marián **Čalfa**, nor his Czech and Slovak counterparts, retained places in the Party leadership. A shift of decision-making power to the government and parliament was clearly indicated by that move and it could be anticipated that it would be reinforced following competitive, multi-party elections in the spring of 1990.

Political history. Before the creation of Czechoslovakia on Oct. 28, 1918, Czechs and Slovaks had not lived in a common state since the Great Moravian Empire in the ninth century. Thereafter the Slovaks fell under Hungarian rule, but the Czechs established a kingdom of their own which played an important political and cultural role in Europe in the Middle Ages. With the emergence in the fifteenth century of the Hussite movement, named after John Huss (Jan Hus), the Rector of Charles University, Prague, who was burned at the stake for heresy in 1415, Protestantism became well established among the Czechs until their defeat by the Austrians at the Battle of the White Mountain in 1620 and the outbreak of the Thirty Years' War. The absorption of the Czech Kingdom in the Austrian Empire thereafter brought with it not only the destruction of the Czech nobility but also the eradication of Protestantism and an active Czech culture. The "Period of Darkness" which followed lasted until the nineteenth century when the works of philologists and historians sparked off a national reawakening that brought a revival of a Czech literary language, the beginnings of a modern literature, a national culture and a nationalist political movement that sought at first autonomy within the Austrian Empire and, when that proved futile, Czech independence.

A key role in the struggle for a Czechoslovak state was played by Professor Tomáš Garrigue **Masaryk**, Edvard **Beneš** and the Slovak Milan Rastislav Štefánik, who led the propaganda and diplomatic campaign among the Western Allies for recognition of their cause. Their activities were backed by Czech and Slovak prisoners-of-war in France, Italy and Russia, many of whom had deserted the Austrian army and volunteered for new Czech units fighting on the Allied side. The most important of these, the Czechoslovak Corps in Russia, which it was planned to transfer to the Western front, perhaps did most to capture Western sympathy for Czechoslovak indepedence when it became embroiled in conflict with the Bolsheviks in the summer of 1918.

Under the guidance of its two Presidents, Masaryk and Beneš, the Czechoslovak First Republic, from 1918 to 1938, was the only parliamentary democracy to survive intact in Central Europe for almost all of the inter-war period. Its stability was maintained despite the weaknesses created on the one hand by an electoral system which encouraged a multiplicity of political parties, reflecting ethnic as well as social cleavages, and which necessitated the frequent formation of coalition governments of relatively short duration, and on the other hand by the increasing disaffection felt by two of the three major national groups, the Slovaks and Germans, both of whom resented Czech dominance of the country's political life. While the former could well have been satisfied by some form of self-rule, the rise of Nazism in Germany in the 1930s and the extreme nationalism it evoked among the German minority intensified their hostility to the Czechoslovak state and stimulated demands for their incorporation within the Third Reich. That problem might well have been contained had not Britain and France acceded in the Munich Agreement of September 1938 to Hitler's plans for the annexation by Germany of Czechoslovakia's border regions (the Sudetenland), which were predominantly inhabited by members of that German minority.

Beneš' resignation from the presidency a month after Munich, in October 1938, signalled the imminent collapse of Czechoslovak democracy and restrictions on political life soon followed. In March 1939, Czechoslovakia disappeared altogether when Hitler occupied Prague, set up a German Protectorate of Bohemia and Moravia and granted the Slovaks their own state, albeit under German tutelage.

The outbreak of World War II permitted Beneš, by then in exile, to begin a campaign for the restoration of pre-Munich Czechoslovakia. Recognized by the Allies as the legitimate President and head of the London-based Czechoslovak government-in-exile by 1941, his realization that the Soviet Union would be a more powerful influence in East-Central Europe after the War led him to negotiate a Treaty of Friendship, Mutual Aid and Post-war Co-operation with Moscow in December 1943 and at the same time to reach a *modus vivendi* with the Communist Party leadership in exile in the Soviet capital.

Although Czechoslovakia remained a parliamentary democracy after its liberation in 1945, much had changed since 1938. Slovakia, where the strongest resistance to the Germans had been demonstrated in the Slovak National Uprising in August 1944, was given its own parliament and governing Board of Commissioners. Political life was however seriously curtailed by restrictions on the number of permitted political parties and the absence of a parliamentary oppostion to the all-party government. The most significant change however was the dramatically increased support for the Communist Party which won 38 per cent of the vote in the parliamentary elections in May 1946 (compared with 10 per cent in 1935). Since it was the largest party in the Assembly, its leader, Klement **Gottwald**, was appointed Prime Minister of a government in which all parties continued to be represented and in which Communists were awarded six other ministerial posts. However, that period of coalition government proved short-lived. The resignations of 12 non-Communist members of the Government on Feb. 20, 1948 provided the Communist Party with the opportunity to seize power by constitutional means. On Feb. 25 President Beneš reluctantly appointed a new government formed almost entirely of Communists and their sympathizers in other parties.

The ensuing months saw the steady adaptation of the political system to Soviet-type practices. On May 9, a new Constitution was approved declaring Czechoslovakia a people's democracy. On May 30 elections were held to the National Assembly on a single list of candidates which provided for some representation of the non-Communist parties, now purged of members unacceptable to the Communists and, after Beneš' resignation from the presidency on June 2, Gottwald was elected in his place.

In the years that followed, political repression struck not only the Communists' opponents but the Communist Party itself. The high point of the purges of that period came in November 1952 with the trial for conspiracy against the state of Rudolf Slánský, the Party's General Secretary, and 13 other leading Communist Party and government figures. Slánský and 10 of his co-defendants were subsequently executed.

Following the death of Gottwald on Mar. 14, 1953, a collective leadership was introduced with the election of Antonín **Zápotocký** as President and the appointment of Antonín **Novotný** as Communist Party First Secretary. In other respects the thaw in Moscow that followed

Stalin's death failed to reach Czechoslovakia. Demonstrations by workers in Pilsen and other Czech towns in June 1953 in protest at price increases and a currency reform that depleted the value of savings were brutally suppressed. Political trials continued, notably one in April 1954 in which leading Slovak Communists, including the late party leader and President, Gustáv **Husák**, were accused of bourgeois nationalism and sentenced to long terms of imprisonment.

Not even **Khrushchev**'s denunciation of Stalin at the XX Congress of the **Communist Party of the Soviet Union (CPSU)** in February 1956 brought about a radical change in policy. Destalinization was in fact delayed until early 1963 and followed Khrushchev's renewed onslaught on Stalin at the 1961 Congress of the CPSU. Nevertheless, that proved a decisive turning-point and Novotný, who had assumed the post of President alongside that of party First Secretary on Zápotocký's death in November 1957, somewhat hesitantly encouraged the introduction of economic and, even some political, reforms. His removal in January 1968 resulted from his failure to accommodate growing demands for change within the Party, discontent with the excessive personal power he retained and the animosity felt towards him and his style of leadership within the cultural intelligentsia, among proponents of reform and in the Slovak Party. His replacement as First Secretary, Alexander **Dubček**, then oversaw the introduction of a programme of radical changes that came to be known as the **Prague Spring**.

Soviet concern that Czechoslovakia's experiment in "socialism with a human face" during the Prague Spring might prove contagious elsewhere in Eastern Europe, including the Soviet Union itself, and that the USSR's strategic defences might be undermined if, as it feared, the Communist Party lost control in Czechoslovakia resulted in military intervention on the night of Aug. 20–21, 1968 by troops from the other Warsaw Pact states (except Romania). Initially Moscow's immediate goal of replacing the Dubček leadership failed when, confronted by the resistance of the population and the refusal of General Ludvík **Svoboda**, who had replaced Novotný as President in March that year, to accept the men chosen by Moscow, they backed down on that point. Nevertheless, the invasion brought a halt to the reforms and eight months later, on April 17, 1969, the Soviet leadership had its way when Dubček was forced to surrender the party leadership to Gustáv **Husák**.

Husák immediately set about reversing the 1968 reforms and ensuring Czechoslovakia conformed with a model of socialism acceptable in Moscow. Proponents of reform were expelled from the Communist Party and influential posts in other institutions and organizations. By 1971, a new Communist Party leadership had been formed consisting on the one hand of participants in the Prague Spring who, like Husák himself, were willing to come to terms with Soviet demands and on the other hand of men who had been party to the Soviet-led intervention and who could be relied on to prevent a resurgence of support for reform.

Any attempts to oppose the new orthodoxy were firmly suppressed and it was only with the publication of the **Charter 77** manifesto in January 1977 that opposition in Czechoslovakia found an effective mechanism for disseminating unofficial views that to some extent evaded the repressive measures of the regime and demonstrated the survival of democratic opinion within the country. Their efforts however had little effect on the Husák regime which appeared securely entrenched well into the 1980s.

Recent political developments. The election of Mikhail **Gorbachev** as General Secretary of the Soviet Communist Party in March 1985 and his commitment to a programme of radical reform confronted the Czechoslovak leadership with a serious dilemma. Throughout the 1970s and early 1980s they had proclaimed their close adherence to the Soviet model of socialism and lauded Soviet policy as the example Czechoslovakia should follow. As Moscow increasingly adopted changes resembling those of the Prague Spring reforms, they faced a choice between adhering to the hardline policies they had pursued since coming to power and abandoning their commitment to the Soviet example, or continuing to emulate Soviet practice and reversing the anti-reform policies they had followed for almost two decades. The latter option, especially insofar as it implied a rehabilitation of the 1968 reform programme they had spent much of their careers condemning, seemed an unlikely course which could only threaten their survival in office.

In practice, the leadership arrived at a compromise which involved the adoption of a Czechoslovak version of *perestroika* encompassing reforms in the economy and superficial gestures towards democratization and *glasnost'*. At the same time, they reiterated their condemnation of the Prague Spring and asserted that, whatever the similarities between Gorbachev's programme and the 1968 reforms in Czechoslovakia, they differed in their underlying purpose. The former, it was claimed, were designed to improve socialism while the Prague Spring reformers had planned to undermine it. Surprisingly, that line appeared to be accepted in Moscow and, when Gorbachev paid an official visit to Czechoslovakia in April 1987, he said nothing to contradict that view.

Nevertheless, a leadership which had remained almost unchanged since 1971 could hardly hope to survive unscathed for much longer. In December 1987, Husák, then aged 74, resigned as Communist Party General Secretary while retaining his seat on the Party Presidium and the post of President that he had assumed in 1975. He was replaced by Miloš **Jakeš**, the man who had been directly responsible, as Chairman of the Party's Central Control and Auditing Commission, for the purge of reformists from the Communist Party in 1970. It was a choice which promised little by way of radical change.

By the end of 1988 Jakeš had removed half the full members of the Presidium, including both the strongest proponent of a Czechoslovak *perestroika*, the then Prime Minister, Lubomír Štrougal, and its fiercest opponent, the Central Committee Secretary for international policy and guardian of ideological rectitude, Vasil Bil'ak. The new blood he brought in began the much-needed process of rejuvenation of a leadership which until then had contained no-one under 60, but it did little to strengthen commitment to reform at the top of the party.

At the same time, Jakeš began to introduce political changes similar, on the surface at least, to Soviet attempts at democratization. Secret ballots were recommended for the intra-party elections that were held in the first five months of 1988, and although very few primary organizations and only a minority of district conferences used that procedure to elect new committees, all but one of the regional conferences that year did so. In April 1988, two months before the Soviet party's conference introduced a limit on the tenure of key political offices, the Czechoslovak Central Committee anticipated that move by restricting the length of time such posts could be held to a maximum of 10 years.

The decision to convene the Party's XVIII Congress in May 1990, a year ahead of schedule, set a deadline by which it appeared the leadership hoped to have decided how far it could safely go in its concessions to political reform. The congress, it was announced, would be expected to approve not only new party statues but also a party programme and the draft of a new state constitution. When draft statutes were published on Oct. 31, 1989, they included the proposal that not only secret ballots but also competitive elections should be made compulsory within the Party. It seemed likely, too, that the new state constitution would give voters in parliamentary elections a

choice of candidates, as had indeed happened in a number of byelections for the Federal Assembly in April 1989.

Nevertheless, these changes were hardly far-reaching. There was no suggestion that the Communist Party might surrender its leading role and it seemed unlikely that any of the proposals would affect the position of the party leadership or the stability of the system. Nor did they make much impression on a population which, disappointed that Gorbachev had not insisted on more fundamental changes in Czechoslovakia, was beginning to show increasing signs of restiveness.

The twentieth anniversary of the **Warsaw Treaty Organization (Warsaw Pact)** invasion, on Aug. 21, 1988, provided the occasion for the first of a series of protests in which the readiness of an ever larger number of people to take part than had been the case in earlier years was clear. Demonstrations were repeated on Oct. 28, the seventieth anniversary of the foundation of Czechoslovakia, on Jan. 16, 1989, the twentieth anniversary of the suicide of the student Jan Palach, who had set himself on fire in protest at the retreat from reform after the invasion, and yet again in August 1989.

Despite the larger numbers, protest seemed still to be restricted to relatively few in relation to the overall population of the country and the sudden eruption of widespread demands for change in November 1989 came as a surprise to most observers as much as to a party leadership which had been boasting of the country's political stability only a month before. Fired by the success of East German demonstrators in forcing the departure of that country's leaders and the evidence that Moscow would respect the verdict of public opinion, Prague students took the opportunity of officially-sanctioned demonstrations on Nov. 17, organized to honour student victims of the Nazis in 1939, to demand radical changes. The brutality of the police response helped the protests spread, initially within the intellectual community in Prague, Bratislava and other major cities, but even before the new committee set up to co-ordinate opposition protests, the Civic Forum, led by the playwright and founder of Charter 77 Václav **Havel**, had demonstrated that their desire for reform was shared by the country's workforce, in a two-hour general strike on November 24, the entire Communist Party leadership had resigned.

Emergency sessions of the Central Committee between Nov. 24 and 26 elected a new General secretary, Karel **Urbánek**, and a 13-member Presidium in which all but three were new to the leadership. A draft Action Programme was produced which proposed that the Party should break with its recent policies and resume the democratic commitment it had adopted during the Prague Spring. By mid-December the Communist Party had agreed to give up its leading role in society and had accepted it would hold only a minority of seats in the coalition government which was being formed by Marián **Čalfa.**

Husák's resignation from the presidency on Dec. 10, 1989 removed the last remaining member of the leadership which had crushed the 1968 reform movement. On Dec. 29 he was replaced by Václav Havel who announced his intention of remaining President only until free elections could be held in 1990. The day before Alexander Dubček had returned to active political life with his election as Chairman of the Federal Assembly.

Yet by then it was clear that more than a revival of the Prague Spring was under way. Existing non-Communist parties were already attempting to establish independent identities, the Social Democratic Party, which has been swallowed by the Communists in 1948, was being reconstituted, and new parties were appearing (notably Farmers' and Green parties), all ready to compete with the Communists for public support. The Communist Party itself, at an extraordinary congress on December 20–21, changed its leadership once more and elected Ladislav Adamec, the former Federal Prime Minister who had resigned that post two weeks earlier, as Party Chairman (a post held by Gottwald between 1945 and 1953) and replaced Urbánek with the 36-year old Vasil Mohorita, who had been Chairman of the Socialist Youth Union until November.

Economic history. Czechoslovakia began with the distinct advantage that, although Slovakia remained primarily agricultural at the time of the country's foundation, Bohemia and Moravia were the most industrially developed regions of the Austro-Hungarian Empire. Major industries included coal-mining, metal-processing, textile and building and the country held a strong position in manufacture of glass, leather goods, cars and armaments. Agriculture in the inter-war period was among the most efficient in Europe, and Czechoslovakia was among the world's leading producers of hops, sugar-beet and potatoes.

Nevertheless, the country's prosperity depended on foreign trade and, although the establishment of a strong currency immediately after World War I and the successful replacement of traditional export markets within Austro-Hungarian Empire by new customers in Western Europe and the United States ensured a healthy development for much of the 1920s, the economy was hit severely by the international depression at the end of the decade. Recovery in the 1930s was slow and unemployment, which is estimated to have been over a million, or more than 15 per cent of the labour force, in 1933 remained high, at around 400,000, as late as 1937.

That experience in the 1930s fostered widespread sympathy for a shift to a socialist economy and, after World War II, the transfer of industry to state ownership began almost immediately. By early 1947, 80 per cent of workers and two-thirds of production capacity were in industries under state control. After the Communists' take-over in February 1948, nationalization was extended to all firms with more than 20 employees and in the following five years even small businesses and self-employed craftsmen were brought into the state sector. Collectivization of agriculture, begun in late 1949, was a more drawn-out process and as late as 1958, 30 per cent of agricultural land (including personal plots) remained in private hands. Two years later, however, the socialist sector accounted for over 90 per cent of arable land.

Socialization of the economy immediately after the war was accompanied by an attempt at state planning, though not yet on the Stalinist model. A Two-Year Plan covering 1947 and 1948, based on indicative rather than compulsory targets, restored living standards roughly to their pre-war level. After 1948 Soviet planning methods and Five-Year Plans were adopted which stimulated a period of rapid economic growth, distorted in favour of heavy industry and particularly armaments, at the expense of consumer goods, services and agriculture.

The shortcomings of the system began to make themselves felt in the late 1950s when declining rates of economic growth led to an abortive first attempt at reforming the centralized planning system in 1958. However, it was not until the early 1960s that a thorough-going economic reform was considered. A negative growth rate in 1963 and the abandonment of the 1961–65 Five-Year Plan created an economic crisis that convinced the leadership of the need for radical reform. In January 1965, the Communist Party Central Committee approved recommendations prepared by a team of experts under Ota **Šik**, Director of the Institute of Economics of the Academy of Sciences, which envisaged a shift to indicative planning, increased enterprise autonomy and some elements of the market.

Even after its approval, political obstacles remained in the way of implementing the reforms and it was only after the removal of Antonín Novotný as Party leader in January 1968 and Šik's appointment as a Deputy Prime Minister three months later that the prospects for a successful reform rose. The Warsaw Pact invasion in August, however, proved as fatal to economic reform as it was to political democratization, not so much because of the inherent character of the economic changes, as because of the political implications ascribed to them. In the eyes of many Czechoslovak reformers a decentralizing, market-oriented economic reform could not be achieved without parallel changes in the political sphere. As a result, the Husák leadership in the 1970s remained wary of economic reform and reversed even the initial steps towards its implementation that had been taken before Novotný's fall from power.

Nevertheless, there were some even within the party leadership who remained sympathetic to economic reform. Declining economic performance in the late 1970s after a reasonably successful period in the first half of the decade, combined with growing pressure to attain more efficient use of increasingly scarce energy, raw materials and manpower resources reopened the issue of reform of the economy. The measures introduced, however, were half-hearted despite the relative urgency of the problems the country faced, and it was only after the Soviet Union's commitment to *perestroika* that a more radical reform came into consideration.

Recent economic developments. By the mid-1980s Czechoslovakia had a reasonably prosperous economy by East European standards and developments under Communist rule had ironed out the stark contrasts between the industrialized Czech Republic and Slovakia. High levels of industrial investment in the latter, particularly in the 1970s, had brought Slovakia's share of the total "social product" from 45.8 per cent in 1948 to 71.9 per cent 40 years later and consumption levels, money incomes and retail turnover were reported to have reached 90 per cent of the levels in the Czech Republic. The country's foreign indebtedness, which had risen to 6.7 billion dollars in 1988 and the payments of which were reported to require 10 per cent of export earnings, was still low by comparison with other East European states. Prospects for the future however seemed gloomy. Much of the industrial infrastructure was antiquated and expensive in terms of energy, material and manpower and there was little likelihood that improvements in productivity could be achieved without radical systemic changes and new investment in modern technology. Although Czechoslovakia retained a strong position *vis-à-vis* the Soviet bloc, exports to the West suffered because of poor quality goods and lack of technical innovation.

The economic case for reform was therefore a strong one — although it required Soviet commitment to *perestroika* to gain its acceptance in Prague. The first indication that economic reform was again on the agenda in Czechoslovakia came at the Communist party's XVII Congress in March 1986 when Husák spoke of a need to change the "economic mechanism" in the light of the party's commitment to accelerated economic and social development by the end of the century, along the lines of proposals Gorbachev had made to the Soviet party congress only a month before. Ten months later, in January 1987, a document entitled *Principles governing the restructuring of the economic mechanism of the Czechoslovak Socialist Republic* was published which closely followed Soviet proposals for decentralization of economic decision making from the central planners to factory management, the introduction of full *khozraschet* (cost-accounting), and the requirements that factories become self-financing and operate in response to market demand rather than the arbitrary decisions of the planners.

Although those proposals received the Central Committee's approval in December that year, progress was slow until Ladislav **Adamec**'s appointment as Prime Minister in October 1988. Introduction of the New Economic Mechanism, as it came to be called, was to be advanced by a year, to Jan. 1, 1990, and Adamec announced the Government's commitment to radical changes in the structure of the economy in the 1990s which would see cutbacks in traditional industries such as mining and metallurgy, greater concentration on profitable sectors of heavy industry, a reduction in product range which was regarded as too broad, the development of a modern high technology sector appropriate to the 1990s, and expansion of the traditionally weak service sector.

With the creation of the coalition government at the end of the 1989 and the prospect of governments in future in which the Communist would at most be in a minority, economic policy was likely to be subject to radical revision. The broad goals set by Adamec of modernizing industry and introducing economic reform, of tying Czechoslovakia into the world economy and creating a convertible currency might remain the starting point but the scope for private enterprise could be expected to be greatly expanded and the opportunities for foreign investment were likely to increase especially in forms other than the joint enterprises favoured in the 1980s.

Foreign policy. During the First Republic Czechoslovak foreign policy was primarily oriented towards the West, although **Beneš**' awareness that the country's security against German expansionism depended on an effective system of alliances led him to sign treaties not only with France but also with the Soviet Union in the mid-1930s. France's failure to stand by Czechoslovakia in 1938 and its participation, with Britain, in the Munich Agreement convinced Beneš, however, that after World War II Czechoslovakia could no longer rely on the West. That, and his expectation that the Soviet Union would play a more powerful role in East-Central Europe after the defeat of Germany, led him to reach agreement with Moscow in December 1943 on a Treaty of Friendship, Mutual Aid and Post-war Co-operation which it was expected would establish a closer relationship between Czechoslovakia and the USSR in the post-war world.

Although Beneš hoped that Czechoslovakia would be able to act as a bridge between East and West after 1945, the Communist takeover in February 1948 put the country firmly in the Soviet camp. Since then it has been a loyal supporter of the Soviet Union and a reliable member both of the Warsaw Treaty Organization and the **Council for Mutual Economic Assistance (CMEA)** or Comecon.

The only period when it appears to have departed at all from its normal acceptance of Soviet leadership in foreign policy came during the Prague Spring when attempts were made to consider specific Czechoslovak interests within the boundaries set by its alliances and when suggestions were made, to no positive effect, that member-states should have a stronger voice in Warsaw Pact policy formulation. Hostility towards the Prague Spring on the part of the Soviet Union, East Germany and Poland led Czechoslovakia to look for moral support to others of its neighbours — Hungary, Romania and Yugoslavia — but there was never any question of abandoning its Warsaw Treaty commitments. The Warsaw Pact invasion in August 1968, which was followed in October by a Treaty on the stationing of Soviet troops on Czechoslovak territory, soured relationships, which were only too clearly based on *force majeure*, but the installation in power of a new leadership after 1969 led to a restoration of normal relations within the bloc.

In the period after Gorbachev's election Czechoslovakia had, it is true, more in common with its hardline allies, East Germany and Romania, than with those countries in which reforms were under way. Though hardly enthusiastic at the election of the non-Communist **Mazowiecki** government in Poland, it appeared to wish to make the best of the situation. Relations with Hungary, on the other hand, were placed under some strain in 1989 when Hungarian television broadcast interviews with Alexander Dubček and Václav Havel, despite Czechoslovak protests. An even more serious problem erupted in May that year when Hungary unilaterally decided to suspend work on the Hungarian section of the joint Gabčíkovo-Nagymaros project to construct a series of dams and hydroelectric stations on the Danube (*see* **Danube Dam**), on which work in Slovakia was already well-advanced. The issue remained unresolved with Czechoslovakia threatening to seek legal compensation when the Czechoslovak government changed in December 1989. Whether its successors will revise their views of the project remains to be seen.

The change of government in Prague seemed unlikely to bring a radical departure from Czechoslovakia's traditional foreign policy commitments in Europe. Even Civic Forum saw its Warsaw Pact and Comecon obligations as given until the disbandment of the two military blocs can be agreed between East and West, although any government in which it was involved could be expected to pursue more actively friendly policies towards the West.

GW

D

DANUBE–BLACK SEA CANAL. Envisaged 50 years ago, this project was partially completed during the 1980s at a cost of two billion dollars, half coming from a World Bank loan. The canal connects the Danube at Cernavoda with the Black Sea. The southern arm, which reaches the sea to the south of Constanţa, is finished while the northern one was still vigorously under construction in 1987. The largest investment project in Romanian history, this began to be undertaken by forced labour in 1949 but was abandoned in 1953, but recommenced in 1973 along a new route. During the earlier period the construction claimed many lives. The Canal shortens the route to the Danube by 340 km and has enabled traffic on the most navigable (Sulina) channel in the Danube delta to be reduced. Its economic viability appears nevertheless doubtful as it depends on whether through traffic along the Danube will increase sufficiently.

RH

DANUBE DAM. A joint Austrian-Czech-Hungarian enterprise, the Danube (Gabcikovo-Nagymaros) dam project was concluded in 1986 with approx. $400 million Austrian funding, to be repaid by 20 years' supply of two-thirds of the electricity generated. The dam was to be completed by 1993 and had long been delayed by environmentalists' protests, including a petition to the Austrian parliament by the "Danube Circle" group in Hungary. Work on the project occasioned further protests, involving up to 12,000 demonstrators. Although some members of the Hungarian Politburo commented suspiciously on the political motives that might lie behind this new-found interest in the environment, the demonstrations themselves were widely covered in the party and government press.

SLW

DĂSCĂLESCU, CONSTANTIN. The former Prime Minister of Romania and a member of the Permanent Bureau of the Political Executive Committee. This made him the second most influential person in the country unless (as is more likely) that ranking belonged to Elena **Ceauşescu**. Dăscălescu's profile in the media was not comparable with the President's and he appeared sometimes to be cast in the role of a high-level scapegoat: thus, in June 1988 he received an admonition in connection with dumping of toxic waste at Sulina.

RH

DECREE FIFTY-SIX (BULGARIA). Coming into effect in January 1989, Decree 56 of the State Council — supplemented by the Implementing Regulations issued in March of that year—set out a comprehensive economic reform programme. As such, it represented at least on paper the most radical variant of the "New Economic Mechanism" in operation in Bulgaria since 1982.

Decree 56's provisions included: a system that put all economic units on a profit-and-loss accounting system and reorganized them as share-issuing "firms", with provisions for employee shareholding and for the sale of stocks to Bulgarian citizens or foreign investors; detailed provisions for the bankruptcy of unprofitable state firms (hitherto more a theoretical than a real possibility); the abandonment of systematic production planning from above, firms being free to make their own plans on the basis of commercial considerations; a price-system based on free negotiation between firms, with the state fixing prices only for certain raw materials, transport services, and essential consumer goods; a more liberal attitude towards private and co-operative businesses (which were accorded a status equal to that of state-owned enterprises); regulations regarding foreign investment that were considerably more liberal than those contained in the 1980 law on the subject and that allowed, *inter alia*, 100 per cent-owned foreign subsidiaries on Bulgarian soil; and a radical decentralization of foreign trade, allowing firms to deal with foreign partners directly without the mediation of the Ministry of Foreign Economic Relations.

On paper, Decree 56's provisions were quite far-reaching: as such it can be seen as part of Bulgarian leader Todor **Zhivkov**'s attempt to save his position by demonstrating his reformism, and at the same time to use economic reform to avoid the necessity for political restructuring. In its practical impact, however, Decree 56 was not as radical as its seemed to be. In the political atmosphere of Zhivkov's last months, its implementation was sluggish or formalistic — often amounting to no more than a renaming and re-registration of existing units. And, insofar as substantial changes were actually involved, Decree 56—coming as it did only a year after a reorganization that was supposed to be the last till the end of 1990—proved more confusing than constructive. Above all, the decentralization involved was severely qualified by the fact that the state—in the form of the Ministry of Economy and Planning—retained the right to issue binding ordres to any economic unit, and a good deal of production was in practice covered by such "state orders", which became in effect ad hoc but quite extensive production plans.

As of early 1990 Decree 56 remained on the books, but it was likely to be superseded in the near future by more radical—and more genuinely radical—reforms, since the post-Zhivkov government is committed to the creation of a market economy and is unlikely to be replaced by any administration less favourable to that goal.

RW

DE MAIZIÈRE, LOTHAR. GDR politician, born 1940. In the space of five months, Lothar de Maizière emerged from relative obscurity as a lawyer, musician and lay church leader to be the prime minister designate of the GDR in early April 1990. His path to prominence depended on the autumn 1989 revolution and the election campaign, and victory by the **Christian Democratic Union of Germany (CDU)** in the spring of 1990.

Born the son of a lawyer in Nordhausen in the district of Erfurt, de Maizière joined the CDU as early as 1956. His French name stems from a Huguenot background. He studied first music (becoming a professional viola player), then law. From 1976 he was a member of the council of lawyers' associations, becoming a deputy chairman in 1987. He was involved in the defence of dissidents, and during this period came to know well Gregor **Gysi**, later chairman of the **Socialist Unity Party of Germany (SED)**. De Maizière was also active within the evangelical church, becoming a vice president of the synod in 1986.

The autumn of 1989 brought crisis to all the political parties of the GDR, and when the long-standing chairman of the CDU, Gerald Götting, was forced to resign, de Maizière was elected in his stead in November. He was considered to be relatively untainted by the CDU's collaboration with the SED. Also in November de Maizière was appointed to the new **Modrow** cabinet as a deputy prime minister with responsibility for church affairs.

During the run-up to the March 18, 1990 elections, de Maizière resisted demands from Chancellor Kohl that the CDU withdraw from co-operation with the **SED-PDS**. He did, howev-

er, take his party into the conservative **Alliance for Germany** with the **German Social Union (DSU)** and **Democratic Departure (DA)**. The election result, more of a triumph for Kohl than for de Maizière, nevertheless propelled the latter into the limelight. For several weeks he appeared undecided as to whether to aspire to the premiership himself. However, negotiations began with the **Social Democratic Party of Germany (SPD)** and the Liberals on a grand coalition, and when the **Volkskammer** (parliament) met on April 5, 1990, de Maizière was charged with forming a government. His relations with Chancellor Kohl have not been marked by cordiality, and in the lead-in to German unity he has pledged his party to defending vigorously the interests of the GDR population.

Before he became prime minister designate, de Maizière was touched by the **Stasi** scandal which brought down two party leaders, Wolfgang Schnur of the DA and Ibrahim Böhme of the SPD. De Maizière denied the accusations made against him.

JO

DEMOCRATIC DEPARTURE/DEMOCRATIC AWAKENING (GDR—DA, DEMOKRATISCHER AUFBRUCH). DA is one of the new political parties to emerge in the GDR in the train of the upheavals of 1989. It did not immediately establish a firm identity, but came to occupy a place on the centre-right. One local group at least, in Wittenberg, transferred to the **Social Democratic Party of Germany (SPD)** for this reason. Under the leadership of Wolfgang Schnur, DA participated in the **Round Table (Runder Tisch)** discussions and formed part of the **Alliance for Germany** with the **Christian Democratic Union of Germany (CDU)** and the **German Social Union (DSU)** for the election in March 1990. However, Schnur was forced to admit that he had collaborated with the **Stasi** and he resigned. His successor, Rainer Eppelmann, failed to undo the damage done to the party, and it achieved less than 1 per cent of the vote in the election and only four seats in the **Volkskammer** (Parliament).

JO

DEMOCRATIC PARTY (POLAND — Stronnictwo Demokratyczne). Until 1989 the Democratic Party of Poland was one of the two auxiliary parties in formal alliance with the **Polish United Workers' Party (PUWP)** which made up the official ruling coalition. In contrast to the **United Peasant Party**, whose main constituency was rural, the Democratic Party was intended to mobilize specific segments of the urban population—white collar workers, artisans and members of the intelligentsia. The post-war organization traced its roots back to a party founded in April 1939, which in turn drew on the traditions of clubs founded as part of a democratic and liberal movement to oppose pre-war authoritarianism and the succession of right-wing governments. It was one of the five parties that entered into the 1945 post-war government dominated by Communists and their representatives. The Democratic Party was part of the "democratic bloc" formed against the Peasant Party (PSL) in 1946 and it later continued to side with the Communist Party (PPR).

As the Stalinist dictatorship strengthened the party survived as a loyal partner of the Communist organizations and underwent further reorganization in September–October 1949. In 1950 it absorbed the Christian Democratic Party of Labour. The revised programme of the party committed it to the construction of socialism under PUWP leadership and to the extension of "craft co-operatives", which meant the elimination of private industry and small business. Its political role was henceforth negligible and the organization remained subject to Communist direction. At times of political relaxation and partial reform, like 1956–57, its leaders became more outspoken, established authorities were replaced and signs of heightened political activity appeared – although in this, too, the Democratic Party only followed the pattern of PUWP developments. Nevertheless, it was from the Democractic Party that proposals for some of the innovative changes in the late 1980s first originated, like those for the two-chamber parliament and a reformed presidency which were implemented in 1989.

In April 1989 it held its XIV Congress, at which Jóźwiak was elected the party's leader. A full commitment to further democratization in the spirit of the Polish Constitution of May 3, 1791 was expressed. There were clear signs at this stage that the party's view of its role in the ruling coalition was likely to diverge from the past pattern and that its programme at the round table (*see* **Round-table Agreement**) was in some ways closer to that of the opposition than that of the PUWP. It entered the election as a PUWP ally and, as agreed at the round table, gained 27 seats in the *Sejm* (6 per cent of the total number). It was awarded three places in the government of Tadeusz **Mazowiecki** and the head of the Democratic Party's parliamentary club, Jan Janowski, was made deputy premier. Responsibility was held by other members for the domestic market and the organization of a communications min-

istry. In 1989 the party had 140,000 members, an increase of 29,000 from 1985.

PGL

DEMOCRATIC PEASANTS' PARTY OF GERMANY (DBD — Demokratische Bauernpartei Deutschlands). The DBD is one of the two parties in the GDR (the other being the **National Democratic Party of Germany (NDPD)** which were founded at the instigation of the **Socialist Unity Party of Germany (SED)** to organize specific social groups. Founded in April 1948, the DBD was intended to draw the small peasantry and rural labourers into the communist sphere. It played a crucial role in the collectivization process of the late 1950s. It is one of the parties of the National Front (along with the **Christian Democratic Union of Germany — CDU**, the **Liberal Democratic Party of Germany — LDPD** and the **National Democratic Party of Germany—NDPD**) and, like the others, has 52 seats in the parliament. It has furnished government ministers, most recently Dr Hans Reichelt, who resigned in January 1990 as Minister for Environmental Protection and Water Management. In December 1989, as political upheaval shook the GDR, there was a surprise when the DBD chairman, Günter Maleuda (born 1931, DBD chairman since 1987) was elected president of the parliament (*Volkskammer*), defeating the expected victor, Manfred Gerlach of the LDPD. The latter, though, went on to become provisional Head of State.

The DBD's membership, like that of the other parties, was rising from the mid-1970s, with SED encouragement. In 1987 it stood at 115,000. At the same time, however, the SED revived its interest in another organization for rural workers, the *Vereinigung der gegenseitigen Bauernhilfe* (VdgB — Union of Mutual Peasant Aid). This was effectively a means of infiltrating the SED into the agricultural sector and, with about 425,000 members in 1984, the VdgB came to eclipse the DBD. In the wake of the revolution of 1989–90, however, the VdgB has suffered more loss of support because of its SED connections, and the DBD remains a political home for many co-operative farmers, for the time being at least. In the election of March 18, 1990 it held onto just over 250,000 votes (2.2 per cent) and took nine seats in the *Volkskammer*.

JO

"DEVELOPED SOCIALISM". Official Soviet theory employed in the **Brezhnev** period, indicating the stage of social development that the

USSR was supposed to have attained by the late 1960s. (*See also* **Ideology**)

SLW

DUBČEK, ALEXANDER. A Slovak, born in 1921, Dubček was First Secretary of the **Communist Party of Czechoslovakia** from Jan. 5, 1968 until April 17, 1969. Almost unknown to the public despite his having been party leader in Slovakia and a member of the Communist Party Presidium in Prague since April 1963, his identification with "socialism with a human face" during the 1968 **Prague Spring** quickly won him widespread popularity. The **Warsaw Treaty Organization (Warsaw Pact)** invasion of Czechoslovakia in August 1968 was a blow not only to the reform programme but also to Dubček's continuing faith in the understanding of the Soviet leadership for his aims. Abducted to Moscow on the night of the invasion, Dubček remained First Secretary despite Soviet plans to replace him, but was forced to make a halt to the reform programme and to agree to the stationing of Soviet troops in Czechoslovakia for the first time since 1946. At Soviet insistence, he resigned as First Secretary in April 1969 and after short periods as Chairman of the Federal Assembly and Czechoslovak Ambassador to Turkey, was expelled from the Communist Party. He returned to Slovakia where he found employment with the Slovak Ministry of Forestry. Dubček never abandoned his commitment to reform Communism and his continuing popularity was made apparent when he addressed the demonstrators in Bratislava and Prague in November 1989 under the auspices of **Civic Forum**. On Dec. 28 that year he returned to active politics as Chairman of the Federal Assembly.

GW

E

ECOGLASNOST (BULGARIA — Ikoglasnost). Bulgarian group, founded in early 1989 to exert pressure on ecological (*Eco-*) issues and to insist on openness of information (*-glasnost*) about them. Subject to harrassment and refused legal recognition for the first few months of its existence, this group took advantage of some relaxation during the CSCE conference on the environment in Sofia in October 1989 to stage a large demonstration that significantly contributed to Communist Party (BCP) leader Todor **Zhivkov**'s fall in November. Able to operate freely in post-Zhivkov conditions — the group received legal recognition in December 1989 — *Ecoglasnost* has gained strength and membership and has been one of the main elements in the opposition umbrella organization, the **Union of Democratic Forces**. Though the environment is central to the group's aims, the Bulgarian situation has made it inevitable that *Ecoglasnost* should have wider political concerns—if only to secure the political conditions in which those aims could be pursued. Thus, immediately after Zhivkov's fall, *Ecoglasnost* leaders were demanding an end to Communist dictatorship, freedom of speech, and dissolution of the secret police. *Ecoglasnost* has the makings of a Green Party: as of December 1989, while denying that it was, or wanted to be, a political party, it was considering the possibility of running "independent" green candidates in the following year's elections. There are signs that the post-Zhivkov leadership wants to co-operate with *Ecoglasnost*: at any rate, a circular sent from BCP headquarters to local organizations in December 1989 classified it as critical but constructive — in contrast to the free trade union **Podkrepa**.

Prominent among *Ecoglasnost*'s leaders are Petur Slabakov (chairman), Aleksandur Karakachanov (secretary), and Petur Beron (also secretary of the Union of Democratic Forces). A membership of 1,500 was reported at the beginning of December 1989: this is likely to grow fast.

RW

ELECTIONS AND ELECTORAL SYSTEM IN THE USSR. Soviet elections, like those of other Communist-ruled nations, were traditionally "acclamatory" exercises in which voters simply ratified a choice of candidates that had been made beforehand by the party authorities. Under Soviet election law, most recently the statute of 1978, there was in fact no limit to the number of candidates that could be nominated and placed on the ballot paper. **Stalin**, when the USSR Supreme Soviet was first established in the late 1930s, even assured a Western journalist that there would be a "very lively electoral struggle" for the seats that were available. Needless to say, no choice of candidate, still less of party or programme, was permitted throughout the period of his general secretaryship or that of his immediate successors, and it was not until the accession of Mikhail **Gorbachev** in March 1985 that electoral reform began to receive the attention of the leadership as part of a "democratization" of the political system as a whole.

Until Gorbachev's accession, Soviet voters were limited not just in the number of candidates from whom they could choose. In such "elections without choice", at least until 1987, the composition of each group of deputies was carefully determined by the party authorities leaving local officials the task of matching individual candidates to the gender, occupation and other parameters that were given to them. The right of nomination was reserved, under the constitution, for the **Communist Party of the Soviet Union (CPSU)** and other party-controlled organizations, and the few attempts that were made to challenge this monopoly were easily rebuffed. Voters could theoretically reject the single candidate, and at the local level they occasionally did. At the national level, however, no candidate was ever defeated, nor indeed returned by less than an overwhelming majority. At the last national elections, in 1984, the turnout had reached a giddy 99.99 per cent and the vote in favour of the single list of candidates — 99.94 and 99.95 per cent for the two chambers of the Supreme Soviet—was the highest ever recorded.

At the outset of his general secretaryship Gorbachev devoted relatively little attention to political reform, believing that the attainment of a more rapid rate of economic growth was (as he put it to the XXVII Party Congress in 1986) "the key to all our problems". A brief reference in the same speech, however, indicated that the General Secretary was aware of the need to make "correctives" in the electoral system, and this in turn became a central theme of his addresses to the January 1987 Central Committee plenum and to the 19th Party Conference in June 1988, the first such gathering for nearly 50 years. A limited experiment duly took place at the local elections of June 1987 in which a choice of candidates was provided in about 1 per cent of the constituencies, each of which returned several members. Gorbachev, in his speech to the Party Conference, suggested that competitiveness had made the elections "more lively, the voters more interested and the deputies more conscious of their responsibilities", and the resolution on political reform with which the Conference concluded committed the party to a "substantial renewal of the electoral system" in line with Gorbachev's report. The draft of a new electoral law embodying these very different principles was published on Oct. 23 and formally adopted on Dec. 1, 1988, after a brief but interesting public discussion.

The new electoral law made it clear that a choice of candidates was to become a normal rather than exceptional occurrence. Under Article 38 an unlimited number of candidates could be nominated for each of the seats available; the draft had specified that "as a rule" there should be a choice of candidate in each case, but the final text avoided this rather ambiguous formulation and made no definite requirement either way. The right to nominate, under the law, was extended to voters' meetings of 500 or more in addition to the Communist Party and other public organizations (Art. 37). Deputies were not allowed to hold governmental positions at the same time as they exercised their representative duties (Art. 11), in line with what Soviet lawyers called the "principle of incompatibility", and they must normally live or work in the area they represent (Art. 37). Candidates, under the new law, were required to present their, "programmes" to the electorate (Art. 45), and they had the right to appoint up to 10 campaign staff ("entrusted persons") to assist them (Art. 46). Voters, for their part, had to pass through a booth or room before casting their vote, even if (exceptionally) only a single candidate was standing (Art. 52). The new legislation was to apply to all future elections beginning with the national elections in March 1989; these, the Central Committee promised at its meeting on Nov. 28, 1988, would be "unlike all those that had preceded them".

The 1989 elections to the Congress of People's Deputies. Under the new election law the campaign was to proceed through two main stages. In the first, nominations were made and then approved by a selection conference in each constituency or in one of the social organizations (such as the CPSU) that had been given the right to nominate. In the second stage, the candidates that had been "registered" in this way were to compete among themselves for the support of

their electorate: in the ordinary constituencies up to election day, which was fixed for March 26, 1989, or in the social organizations up to a date that was to be fixed at some point during the previous fortnight. This was a new, elaborate and largely unfamiliar set of procedures; it was also one to which many citizens had strong objections. The representation that had been given to social organizations, in particular, appeared to violate the principle of "one person, one vote", and the holding of selection conferences to approve a final list of candidates was also unpopular. Who needed such "elections before elections", asked several correspondents during the discussion of the new legislation the previous autumn? It was pointed out, however, that some exercise of this kind was necessary so as to reduce a large number of nominations to more manageable proportions; and in any case this stage in the proceedings was bypassed in Estonia, most of Lithuania and some districts of Moscow precisely in order to leave such choices to the voters.

The selection of candidates in the social organizations took a variety of forms. At one extreme was the Council of Collective Farms, which approved 58 candidates for its 58 seats by an open vote in half an hour. The Communist Party itself caused some controversy by nominating no more than 100 names for the 100 seats it had been allocated under the constitution. As well as "authoritative representatives of the working class and peasantry" the list included most of the Politburo and Secretariat, together with a wide range of figures from science, education, culture and the arts (the Bolshoi soloist Yevgeny Nesterenko was perhaps the most unlikely inclusion). A somewhat more open process took place in the trade unions, which took seven hours and several rounds of voting to choose its 114 candidates for the 100 seats that were available. There was still greater controversy in the Academy of Sciences, where 23 candidates were chosen on Jan. 18, 1989 to contest the 20 seats available. The list did not include Andrei **Sakharov**, Roald Sagdeev and several other reform-minded and well-supported academics, and a continuing campaign of public and private lobbying took place in an attempt to secure their seats at a later stage.

The selection of candidates in the constituencies took a still wider variety of forms. A selection conference at Melitopol in the Ukraine, for instance, was packed out by officials to such an extent that it reminded one participant of a conference of party activists. Of the 33 who asked to speak only five were chosen, all of whom supported the local party first secretary; indeed only one of them raised the possibility that there might be another candidate. The party secretary was duly approved by an overwhelming majority. There were many cases of pressure by party secretaries on other candidates to withdraw; so successful were these efforts in Kazakhstan that all 17 of the republic's regional party secretaries were unopposed — a "strange monopoly" as *Pravda* remarked on 21 March. But there were also much more open exercises, for instance in Moscow's No. 1 territorial constituency, where 11 hours of discussion produced two academics as candidates after the poet Yevtushenko, the economist Gavriil Popov and the cosmonaut Igor Volk had all been rejected. Overall, according to a survey conducted under the auspices of the Academy of Sciences, about half of those polled described the selection conferences as "democratic" and about half described them as "controlled by their organizers"; this was probably close to the reality.

In the end, according to the Central Electoral Commission, 880 candidates were approved by the various public organizations to fight the 750 seats they had been allocated. Only 198 (22.5 per cent) were women, nearly half of whom represented women's councils; 15.9 per cent were workers and 10.3 per cent were collective farmers, all significantly below the proportions for which they had accounted within the outgoing Supreme Soviet. A much more substantial group of candidates (35.7 per cent) were employed in science, the health services and the arts, and no fewer than 778 (88.4 per cent) were members or candidate members of the CPSU. Some 2,895 candidates were selected to fight the 1500 constituency seats; in 384 constituencies, despite the intentions of the law, there was just a single candidate, but in the remainder there were two or more contenders, and in one of the Moscow seats no fewer than 12 candidates were approved. Again, just 16.6 per cent of the registered candidates were women, 25.2 per cent were workers, 12 per cent were collective farmers, and a massive 85.3 per cent were members or candidate members of the CPSU.

Voting in the social organizations began on 11 March, and concluded shortly before the national vote in the ordinary constituencies. Not all the seats, in the event, were filled: the Soviet Peace Fund, for instance, filled just five of its seven seats, and the Academy of Sciences only eight of its 20. This required a further round of balloting within the following two months in order to make up a full complement. More controversial candidates were often unsuccessful; the playwright Mikhail Shatrov, for instance, who was a candidate for the Union of Theatrical Workers, or the political commentator Alexander Bovin, who was seeking one of the Journalist Union's 10 places.

Many organizations simply nominated as many candidates as they had seats available; the Union of Friendship Societies, to take another example, put up five candidates for its five seats, all of whom were elected. The vote in favour of such candidates, however, was not necessarily unanimous, and even Gorbachev, standing for one of the Communist Party's 100 seats, had 12 votes cast against him (52 of the candidates were elected unanimously). The largest negative vote (78) was cast against the prominent conservative Yegor **Ligachev**, allowing Boris **Yel'tsin** a fairly well-rehearsed campaign joke: What would have happened if the CPSU had nominated not 100 but 101 candidates for the 100 seats it had been allocated?

Voting in the ordinary constituencies began in the Far East on the evening of 25 March (since it was already the following morning by local time) and lasted from 7 a.m. until 8 p.m. everywhere except **Armenia**, where it was arbitrarily extended by two hours. The first and in some ways most significant result was the turnout. Early forecasts indicated a level of 80–85 per cent; the final figure, according to the Central Electoral Commission, was 89.8 per cent — well down on the figure that had been reported in 1984 but a much more credible return. Turnout was highest in the Central Asian republics, where traditional forms of mobilization appear to have persisted: **Uzbekistan**, for instance, reported a turnout of 95.3 per cent, and in **Turkmenia** it was 96.1 per cent. Lower figures were reported by the Baltic republics (from 82.5 in **Lithuania** to 87.1 per cent in **Estonia**) and the lowest figure of all was returned by Armenia, where an active boycotting campaign was organized. Just 71.9 per cent of Armenian voters, according to the official return, took part in the election, and barely half (53 per cent) of voters in the capital, Yerevan, did so. In the end, according to the Central Electoral Commission, three of the 1,500 constituencies failed to yield a result because fewer than half of the voters had taken part. There were also substantial numbers of spoiled ballots, particularly because voters, unfamiliar with the new procedures, had left more than one name on the paper: in some areas this accounted for up to 10 per cent of all the votes.

The results, constituency by constituency, were still more remarkable. In 76 of the 1,500 seats in which three or more candidates had been standing none of them secured more than half of the vote and a run-off had to be declared between the two best-placed contenders. Still more surprisingly, even "sensationally" for *Izvestiya*, in 195 constituencies in which only one or two candidates were standing none of them secured more than half of the votes and the whole exercise had to be repeated within the following two months. A whole series of political leaders were successfully returned in the constituencies that did declare a result, including the party leaders, prime ministers and presidents of Estonia, **Belorussia**, Uzbekistan and Turkmenia, and the prime minister and president of the **Russian Republic**, by far the largest of the 15 union republics. There were also some outstanding votes for individual party secretaries, such as the Astrakhan and Tambov first secretaries who received 96 and 92 per cent respectively of the votes cast.

Much more striking, however, were the defeats that were suffered by party and state leaders at all levels. Altogether 38 district and regional party first secretaries were rejected, most of whom were members of the Central Committee. The losers included the Lithuanian prime minister and president, the Latvian prime minister, the party first secretary and mayor of Kiev, the mayor of Moscow, and the party first secretaries of Minsk, Kishinev, Samarkand, Alma-Ata and Frunze. The runaway success of former party secretary Boris Yel'tsin in the Moscow national-territorial seat (he took 89.4 per cent of the poll) was a particular snub to the central authorities, given the emphasis he had placed upon the abolition of privileges and the attempts that had been made to frustrate his campaign. The most spectacular defeats of all, however, were in Leningrad, where a whole series of officials failed to obtain a place including the regional first secretary (a Politburo member) and second secretary, the chairman of the city Soviet and his first deputy, the chairman of the regional Soviet and the city party secretary (who obtained a humiliating 15 per cent of the vote in a contest with a young shipyard worker). It was understandably some time before the full dimensions of this rebuff reached the columns of Soviet newspapers.

There is little doubt that these were the fairest, most "genuine" elections that have yet taken place in the USSR. There were, admittedly, some violations of the law. The very first voter at one of the polling stations in Alma-Ata was allowed to cast a ballot for his whole family. In the Leningrad constituency in which Solov'ev, the regional party first secretary, was standing unopposed, the voting booths were placed at the side of the polling station in clear violation of the law and of central directives. "Why not just put up a notice—straight ahead to the ballot box!" commented one indignant voter, who preferred to remain anonymous. And yet in other areas there was a close, almost obsessive concern with the letter of the law. There were several calls to the Central Electoral Commission, for instance, to

ask if pencils could be used in the voting booths instead of pens. And there were other questions: for instance, could a drunk be allowed to vote? And why were election posters still on display on the day of the election, when all agitation was supposedly prohibited? The experience of Western observers also suggested that close attention was paid to the law: polling stations, though sometimes in unsuitable premises, were properly furnished, and every effort was made to ensure that voters passed through a booth before casting their vote. Officials were on hand to answer questions, policemen preserved public order, and representations of the candidates kept a close eye on the whole proceedings.

The main objective of the exercise, from the point of view of the authorities, was less to select a group of deputies than to persuade the Soviet public to take a voluntary part in the political process. Some impression of their response is apparent in the results of a survey which was carried out by the All-Union Institute for the Study of Public Opinion in urban areas throughout the USSR. Over 80 per cent of respondents were familiar, at least in part, with the new procedure for the election of deputies. Some 48 per cent of respondents welcomed the new election arrangements, 13 per cent were against, and the remaining 40 per cent refrained from judgement. Asked to choose which methods of influencing state decisions were likely to be most effective, 14 per cent suggested election campaigns and voting; this came well behind appearances on the television or in the papers (49 per cent) and taking part in public opinion polls (38 per cent) but just ahead of participation in meetings and demonstrations (13 per cent) and well ahead of participation in newly-established informal organizations (7 per cent).

The level of turnout, in the absence of the usual pressures from agitators to take part and of falsification on the scale of previous years, was certainly consistent with the view that these were elections that engaged a widespread degree of public interest and support (even in the run-off and repeat elections that had to be held to make up a full complement turnout was still 74.8 and 78.4 per cent respectively). Newspapers reported that complete strangers struck up conversations about their voting intentions, and on polling day itself there were queues in some places to enter the polling station and then to enter the voting booth, where candidate choice was finally made. In one Moscow constituency extra voting booths had to be constructed as a matter of urgency, so great was the pressure to make use of them, and reports from other constituencies spoke of the sick and handicapped coming to the polling stations in person rather than waiting to be visited by officials. The new elections also received unprecedented coverage in the media, particularly on television where two regular programmes, "Power to the Soviets" and "Towards the Elections", gave candidates and voters an opportunity to air their views. In a few areas, such as Estonia and Moscow, there were actual "telestruggles" between the candidates themselves. Survey data indicated that television was the most important source of electoral information for 70.1 per cent of respondents, followed by the local and central press (54.3 and 53.4 per cent respectively).

If elections are about "sending messages to government", then several themes could be said to have been forwarded by voters to the authorities. To judge at least from the candidates' programmes, foreign affairs were of little interest, apart perhaps from a reduction in military spending. For the great mass of candidates, however, four other areas were of pressing concern. The first of these was the food supply; the second was the housing situation; the third was the environment; and the fourth was the political system itself, including freedom of information legislation, further reform of the electoral system, greater religious toleration and freedom of movement within and across Soviet borders. A survey in Leningrad of communications from voters to candidates found that these four were the top priorities. A poll by the weekly paper *Moscow News* found that the most important issues for its readers were the food supply and agriculture (41 per cent), human rights and democratization (39 per cent), inflation and prices (22 per cent), shortages (20 per cent), and housing and environmental pollution (both 19 per cent). In some of the republics, particularly in the Baltic, these concerns were intertwined with issues of a more directly nationalist character.

The impact of these very different electoral arrangements upon the political system more generally was less easy to define. In the short term a number of the defeated candidates were expected to resign their party and state posts; the Leningrad party leader and the Kiev party secretary were the first to do so, although there was no formal requirement to this effect. The election system itself came under close scrutiny, with considerable pressure for the abolition or at least reform of the representation of social organizations, and for the establishment of secret, equal and competitive voting directly to the Supreme Soviet, which under present arrangements is chosen from among its members by the Congress of People's Deputies. Further electoral reform is to be considered by the new Congress in conjunction with further reform of the Constitution itself and the adoption of new legislation on local and republican government, trade unions, and the legal system. A small but active group of reform-minded deputies formed an Inter-Regional Deputies' Group at the end of July 1989 to press for swift action on these and other matters.

The wider implications of these new-style Soviet elections, however, may also cast some doubt upon the way in which such exercises have traditionally been conceptualized. Among the functions of noncompetitive elections of this kind, it has been suggested, are political integration, legitimation, control through co-optation and co-responsibility. The 1989 Soviet elections appear in fact to have had some outcomes by no means so advantageous to the central authorities. The heavy defeats suffered by local party and state leaders, in particular, has placed the party's claim to rule in some doubt. The deputies that were returned to the Congress of People's Deputies drew their legitimacy from a popular mandate; the central authorities, in confronting them, had to rely upon their guaranteed quota of seats and unconvincing references to Leninism. The newly-elected deputies, moreover, were committed by their programmes to a series of improvements in popular living standards that the central authorities, with the best will in the world, would hardly be able to accommodate. The overwhelming success of nationalist candidates in the Baltic republics raised at least an implicit challenge to the existence of the state itself, when elections took place at lower levels of government in 1990 nationalist candidates were expected to secure a majority in republican assemblies, at least in the Baltic. Soviet elections, in the past, may indeed have contributed marginally to national integration and political legitimacy. Under the very different circumstances that prevailed in the late 1980s and early 1990s they appeared at least as likely to contribute to instability and territorial fragmentation.

SLW

ENERGY. The pattern of endowment with primary energy potential is extremely varied in Eastern Europe. At one extreme is the Soviet Union, richly provided with all the fossil fuels and with hydro-electric potential, and one of the world's principal exporters of oil and gas. (Oil alone accounts for some two-thirds of total Soviet exports.) At the other is Hungary, with very little fossil fuel and no mountains on which to build hydro stations. None of the other smaller East European countries is quite so poorly endowed as Hungary, but Bulgaria and Czechoslovakia have very limited domestic fuel resources. Yugoslavia has some coal and considerable hydro potential, but no oil. Romania has oil, though reserves are nearing exhaustion, and some gas. Poland is a major coal producer and exporter; East Germany can boast only of considerable stocks of low-grade brown coal, and the exploitation of these has caused very severe environmental problems. (See table showing the structure of energy production in the region.)

All the smaller East European countries import oil, gas or electricity from the Soviet Union, and this has, indeed, been the dominant commodity flow of trade within the **Council for Mutual Economic Assistance (CMEA)**. The dependence of these countries on the Soviet Union for energy supplies has in turn created a number of funda-mental tensions within the CMEA. At what prices should the Soviet Union deliver oil and gas to her allies? How should the Soviet Union view the exchange of "hard" (saleable on Western markets) energy materials for "soft" (not readily saleable on Western markets) East European manufactures? Up to 1989 intra-CMEA prices were calculated on the basis of a five-year moving average of world prices. This was disadvantageous for the Soviet Union, in relation to her energy exports to CMEA partners, in the period from the First Oil Shock in 1974 up to the collapse of world oil prices in 1985. It then turned to her advantage. With the world price of oil stable in 1990 at $15–20 a barrel, the formula is currently fairly neutral. None of this has prevented

The energy balance in Eastern Europe (in thousands of barrels per day or equivalent)			
	1988	*1989[1]*	*1990[1]*
Bulgaria			
Total energy production	231.71	233.91	246.85
Coal	118.52	118.36	122.08
Oil	6.38	6.70	7.10
Gas	0.24	0.25	0.26
Primary electricity (hydro, nuclear etc.)	101.57	103.60	112.41
Other	5.01	5.00	5.00
Czechoslovakia			
Total energy production	1,055.89	1,062.06	1,074.18
Coal	883.77	874.93	870.56
Oil	3.17	3.20	3.20
Gas	12.29	12.23	12.16
Primary electricity (hydro, nuclear etc.)	150.67	165.74	182.31
Other	5.99	5.96	5.95
GDR			
Total energy Production	1,476.3	1,489.4	1,517.4
Coal	1,345.9	1,356.0	1,381.2
Oil	1.0	1.0	1.0
Gas	48.8	48.5	48.3
Primary electricity (hydro, nuclear etc.)	78.1	81.4	84.6
Other	2.6	2.5	2.4
Hungary			
Total energy production	368.95	368.96	370.87
Coal	122.82	122.95	123.19
Oil	38.68	38.49	38.34
Gas	132.24	131.44	130.65
Primary electricity (hydro, nuclear etc.)	63.34	63.97	66.34
Other	11.87	12.11	12.35
Poland			
Total energy production	2,596.89	2,634.61	2,672.88
Coal	2,477.14	2,514.29	2,552.01
Oil	3.43	3.41	3.39
Gas	85.05	85.13	85.26
Primary electricity (hydro, nuclear etc.)	19.50	19.87	20.21
Other	11.77	11.89	12.01

Romania

Total energy production	1,094.31	1,089.86	1,090.55
Coal	244.43	256.65	266.91
Oil	181.56	177.02	172.59
Gas	579.83	568.23	562.55
Primary electricity (hydro, nuclear etc.)	53.41	52.34	52.34
Other	35.09	35.61	36.15

Soviet Union

Total energy production	33,601.65	33,807.92	34,539.42
Coal	6,280.24	6,248.84	6,280.08
Oil	12,289.25	12,043.46	11,923.03
Gas	12,625.70	13,130.73	13,918.57
Primary electricity (hydro, nuclear etc.)	1,908.95	1,889.86	1,927.66
Other	497.51	495.03	490.08

Yugoslavia

Total energy production	715.62	734.80	751.63
Coal	394.07	409.83	421.31
Oil	74.63	74.03	73.29
Gas	55.01	56.11	57.23
Primary electricity (hydro, nuclear etc.)	165.47	168.12	172.82
Other	26.44	26.70	26.97

[1]Estimates

Source: WEFA.

the Soviet government from continuing to complain bitterly about the quality of the deliveries of the East Europeans to the USSR. At the same time some of the smaller East European countries, notably Hungary, have been very unhappy about the terms on which they participate in joint ventures relating to the production and shipping of Soviet energy to the rest of Eastern Europe. In 1989 the CMEA started to move towards a new pricing formula which would be based more directly on world prices—but taking quality into account.

Eastern Europe finds itself moving into the 1990s faced with a number of fundamental energy dilemmas. The relative poor endowment of the East Europeans with primary fuels has induced a heavy dependence on nuclear power which looks environmentally hazardous in the post-**Chernobyl** world. In Bulgaria, for instance, the share of nuclear power in total electricity production reached 35.6 per cent in 1988. The comparable figure for Czechoslovakia is 26.6 per cent, and the trend for both countries is still upwards. From the point of view of East Germany, however, with its bleak profile of coal-induced environmental decay, nuclear energy still looks like an attractive alternative — even from the environmental point of view. Yugoslavia, having spent years and millions of dollars searching the Adriatic Sea fruitlessly for oil, faces a choice between trying to develop the domestic energy base — at whatever cost — or trying to export enough to be able to afford to import the bulk of fuel requirements. The problem there is that Yugoslavia's export performance has never been strong enough to guarantee that energy dependence on the outside world does not lead straight to external debt problems.

But the biggest energy dilemmas in the region are those facing the Soviet Union. Rapid growth in the Soviet economy under **Stalin** would have been inconceivable without abundant, cheap domestic energy resources. And it was precisely as fuel extraction costs started to escalate dramatically in the early 1970s that the secular slowdown in Soviet growth rates set in. By the early 1980s the aggregate level of oil production had actually started to fall, though gas output continued to grow rapidly. One of the early triumphs of the **Andropov/Gorbachev** leadership was to extract new growth from the oil industry. But by 1989 oil output was again falling, as also was coal output, with industrial unrest in the mines exacerbating an already difficult situation. Even more worrying, the growth rate of gas production was falling off sharply.

But these gross production trends are by no means the most disturbing tendencies in the Soviet sector. It has been argued by Soviet energy specialists that Soviet energy strategy is, in fact, completely misconceived in that it concentrates on great energy output, rather than on *net* output

ENERGY

—after subtracting the enormous energy requirements of the Siberian fuel industry itself. Existing plans envisage a peaking of gross gas output in the year 2005. But this would actually imply a peaking of net gas output as early as 1990. An alternative strategy, put forward by Professor D. Aksenov of the Subkin Oil and Gas Institute, would hold gross gas output at the 1990 level. That would release funds for investment in energy-saving technology, and would yield an overall economy of more than Rb 150 billion in terms of capital investment.

Aksenov's argument, of crucial importance in itself, points also to a more general argument. Whatever difficulties Eastern Europe may have on the energy production side are essentially relative — relative to the central problem of *energy consumption*. Coefficients of energy utilization to national income are two or three times as high in Eastern Europe as in the Western industrialized countries. And the 1980s showed few clear-cut trends for the situation to improve, as illustrated in the table showing changes in energy intensity.

Changes in energy intensity[1] in the European CMEA (annual percentage change)

	1981–85	1986	1987
Bulgaria	−1.9	−1.8	—
Czechoslovakia	−1.2	−0.5	−0.5
GDR	−3.1	−3.5	−1.3
Hungary	−2.3	−0.2	−1.8
Poland	1.6	−4.2	0.6
Romania	−3.1	−5.4	—
Soviet Union	−0..9	−2.4	1.3

Ratio of gross primary energy consumption to net material product in "constant" prices

Source: United Nations, Economic Commission for Europe, *Economic Survey of Europe in 1988–1989*, p.142.

If we take elements of concealed inflation in national income reporting into account, these figures present an overall picture of stagnation in energy utilization efficiency levels. Only in the case of Hungary can we be fairly sure that a real improvement has taken place. In Romania genuine reductions in energy consumption coefficients have been achieved, but only at the cost of draconian power supply cuts to the population.

In Yugoslavia, for which exactly comparable figures are not available, energy intensity seems to have grown steadily during the 1980s. Behind this trend lies a very special Yugoslav problem. The system whereby the great bulk of state and

para-state functions are devolved to republics and provinces has played havoc with industries like electricity, which demand a highly integrated, centralized form of organization. All strategic decisions touching on the construction of new capacity, the development of the transmission grid etc. have to be taken by a committee of the eight regional power organizations. The result is that no decisions are taken, which leads in turn to serious and escalating losses of economies of scale and much sheer wastage of primary energy materials.

What is the future of *nuclear power* in Eastern Europe? Bulgaria seems set to continue to expand this element in her energy balance, though the dramatic political changes of the late 1980s and early 1990s could change this. In Yugoslavia, nuclear generation has been sharply de-emphasized since Chernobyl. In the Soviet Union, the experience of Chernobyl has already produced a major rethink of the role of nuclear power, with popular environmentalist pressure against atomic power stations developing as a key component in the Soviet democratization process. The Soviet long-term energy plan for the period up to the year 2000 has been revised to accommodate a reduction in the role of nuclear energy, though atomic power stations will still, on this scenario, be producing around 6.5 per cent of the total Soviet energy balance in the year 2000, by comparison with a figure for the late 1980s of 2.2 per cent. We cannot exclude the possibility that faltering production trends in the primary energy sectors may pressure the Soviet government into renewed emphasis on nuclear generation. But here, as with every aspect of the Soviet energy balance, the key issue is efficiency of utilization. Thus Boris Paton, president of the Ukrainian Academy of Sciences, has argued that if the Ukraine could reach the energy utilization coefficients of the Western industrial countries, the savings thus generated would be the equivalent of the output of seven Chernobyls. (Chernobyl is, of course, in the Ukraine.)

DAD

ENVIRONMENTAL PROTECTION.

The conceptual basis of environmental management. Environmental management involves a complex of activities that are initiated and overseen by governmental units at various levels of society. The specific activities can only be accomplished with the co-operation of industry, agriculture, government, educational organizations, and private individuals. Improvement in environmental conditions is sought in the Soviet Union and the countries of Eastern Europe because the damage to their national economies is very great indeed and, in some regions of the USSR and Poland, pollution is an impediment to life expectancy and public health. The environmental laws in Eastern Europe and the Soviet Union are being developed around two main concepts — resource conservation and nature protection.

Resource conservation. This is understood to mean that industry, in particular, must undertake to avoid or to reduce the formation of production wastes. Since wastes are inevitably generated and resource conservation can only be achieved gradually, the economic programmes of the Soviet Union, the German Democratic Republic, and Czechoslovakia (among others) provide that enterprises must identify the useful components in their wastes so that they can be recycled and reused. As a result, nature should benefit from the slower expansion of extractive industries (such as mining and forestry, which are environmentally disruptive) and a reduction in the requirements to develop additional sites for solid waste disposal (which displaces land that could otherwise be put to more profitable uses).

The resource conservation provisions in the 12th Five-Year Plan for the Economic and Social Development of the USSR 1986–90 (hereinafter cited as 12th FYP) required industry and agriculture to lessen their impact on nature by reducing the consumption of fresh water, raw materials, fuel and energy per unit of production, and the metal content of metallurgical products. During the 12th FYP it was envisaged that such savings would offset as much as 65 per cent of the anticipated additional consumption in these areas across the national economy. For the period of the 13th economic plan (1991–95), the same general objectives will obtain although the specific targets had not been announced by early 1990.

Water conservation. Industry and agriculture can (and do) curtail the volume of fresh water they withdraw from rivers, lakes and subterranean reservoirs by recycling water that would otherwise be released as sewage. Current requirements in the USSR are for these two sectors to reduce consumption by 10 to 15 per cent. In the GDR (which relies heavily on groundwater resources), a 5 per cent reduction in water consumption is envisaged. In Bulgaria and Czechoslovakia, the state plans single out the need for water conservation. Extensive use of recycled water reduces the volume that treatment installations must handle, although one trade-off is that the remaining waste water contains higher concentrations of pollutants and may be more difficult and costly to clean relative to the volume of water flow. The factories may require water purification facilities to prevent the damage that contaminated water can cause to production equipment. However, most recycled water is not cleansed prior to reuse and otherwise it is not treated to the standards required for release into the waterways; for this reason recycling techniques (especially simple repeat-use systems) are regarded by Soviet planners as a lower-cost alternative to waste water treatment.

A decree issued in January 1988 requires a 15 per cent reduction in municipal and domestic water consumption throughout the USSR. The water conservation programme suffers from the poor repair of the water supply and sewerage infrastructures, which are the responsibilities of local councils, housing authorities, and industrial ministries. Water losses are extensive; in 1986, government statistics indicated that annual losses amounted to 40 cu km. Several studies have shown that, in towns and cities of the Russian Republic, fresh water consumption could be reduced by as much as 35 per cent by making repairs to the water infrastructure. In **Moscow**, water is supplied for all purposes at a rate of 600 litres per capita each day (elsewhere, the eventual goal for daily water supplies is 300 litres per capita, presumably much of this amount would be consumed by local industry and government). Moscow's water is not evenly distributed. In some suburbs, water supplies are rationed (for example, hot water supplies are provided only at certain hours of the day and night). The city, where losses reach an estimated 1.5 million cu m per day, is relying on the completion of the Rzhev Canal and waterworks to provide an additional water to the Moscow area.

Energy and fuel conservation. The savings of electric power and fuel are not as easy to achieve as water recycling. Energy savings depend primarily on the efficiency of the production technologies and the type and quality of fuel and to some extent on the idiosyncratic patterns of individual operators. In 1987, 1665 billion kilowatt hours (kWh) of electric energy were produced, of which 35 billion kWh were exported. Of the 1,630 billion kWh produced for domestic consumption, industry consumed 957 billion kWh (60 per cent) and agriculture 160 (including 25 billion kWh for rural households). After the electric power used to operate the electric stations is subtracted from the industrial share, 62 per cent of the electric power supplied to industry was used to power its motors and 28 per cent for other purposes. The target is to reduce the amount of electricity consumed per unit of output. This

91

requires reconstruction or replacement of basic production technologies and power plants, although the immediate efforts involve the less costly adjustments to operating schedules, turning off lights, and so forth. The resource conservation initiative yielded savings of 25 million tonnes of fuel and energy resources in 1988. In addition, 155 gigacalories of secondary fuel resources were claimed in 1988 by tapping waste heat. In comparison, 20 million tonnes of standard fuel were economized in 1986.

The nature and location of the fuel supplies in the Soviet Union and Eastern Europe also constrain the potential for resource conservation. An important consideration is the necessity to transport fuel and energy supplies over long distances. Usually, it is most economical to transport electric power rather than coal, oil, or gas to Soviet industry, even though as distances involved increase, a large amount of electric power is consumed in the transportation process. Since the 1970s, however, the export of oil and gas from the USSR to Eastern and Western Europe have occasioned the construction of pipelines over thousands of kilometers; coal is also transported over increasingly long distances because of the deteriorating quality of the deposits in Western regions. About three-quarters of coal consumption occurs in the Western RSFSR and the Ukraine, where there is heavy demand by the metallurgical and electric power industries. Transportation in any form requires energy to operate the system; and energy savings are constrained by the available technologies and are jeopardized by the lack of repair and maintenance services. These constraints and the insufficient diligence by operators led to the loss of many lives, energy supplies, and extensive environmental damage as a result of a gas pipeline explosion in Siberia during 1989. Losses of coal, oil and gas during shipment are as high as 20 per cent (some analysts estimate this to be much higher), which can be partially avoided by covering and repairing the wagons on the trains. Coal-slurry systems, which are more efficient in respect of low wastage, are not appropriate for long-distance transport. It is noteworthy that the 500,000 tonne capacity steel mills constructed during the 1980s have electric furnaces and process significant quantities of scrap.

Raw materials conservation. Bulgaria directs about 20 per cent of its nature protection budget to the introduction of non-waste and advanced technologies and recycling of water. In the GDR, it is planned that by 1990 secondary materials of all types in the volume of 35 million tonnes will satisfy 15 per cent of the national demand for raw materials. In Czechoslovakia, a long-term programme to the year 2010 has been established; the financial requirements for implementation of the programme are valued at 60–100 billion korunas, amounts that are likely to be inadequate and unavailable. During the 8th FYP (1986–90), investments of 10–15 billion korunas are being made for the introduction of low waste and non-waste technologies and scrap processing equipment.

The 12th FYP in the USSR called for reductions in the use of metals over the national economy by 13–15 per cent or six million tonnes. An estimated 30 per cent of rolled metal products (production is 135 million tonnes annually) goes immediately to scrap. However, three-quarters of the rolling mills are obsolete and require reconstruction or replacement. Since this is one of the most capital-intensive areas of metallurgical construction, progress will be slow. The resource conservation programme in the USSR is making headway in some industries—for example, 1988 statistics indicate that the machine-building industry saved four million tonnes of metals, including 2.5 million tonnes of rolled ferrous metal, 0.3 tonnes of steel pipe, and 60,000 tones of nonferrous metal. Similarly, the construction industry reported savings in 1988 of 500,000 tonnes of rolled ferrous metals and three million tonnes of cement. Soviet sources do not indicate the nature of the savings, although it is likely that some were achieved by manipulating inventories. In comparison, data for 1986 indicate that resource conservation initiatives for all sectors of the economy produced savings of 35,000 tonnes of ferrous metal products, and 80,000 tonnes of various types of pipe.

Resource conservation is looking for an additional method of savings—that is, not forming wastes in the first place. In the metallurgical industry, the obstacles to resource conservation are that many, but potential gains appear to make the investment attractive from a national economic perspective. For example, attention is being given to deeper refining of mineral ores; wastage in the USSR and East Germany is believed to be at 93 and 97 per cent, respectively.

Nature protection. In the present economic context, this means pollution abatement and amelioration of polluted land and water. Nature protection also involves construction of flood controls, dams, bridges, and erosion prevention along coastal areas amongst a host of other construction activities, and it refers to the creation of forestry preserves and the protection of endangered species of plants and wildlife. In the Soviet Union and in Eastern Europe most such activities are undertaken as economic rather than environmental protection activities, and the related investments are external to the nature protection budgets (for example, they may be designated in the agricultural budget as water management construction) where the ecological implications of construction work, in particular, are not emphasized.

State budgetary allocations for nature protection are currently directed almost entirely to the construction and operation of pollution abatement installations. Only in Bulgaria, where fully half (824 million levs) of the state nature protection budget (1.3 billion levs) was allocated in the 9th FYP, does it appear that attention is paid to improvement of land that has been contaminated or ecologically damaged due to industrial or agricultural activities. The nature protection budgets also include expenditures on forestry management, although in the USSR the nature of the work and the amount of the expenditures have not been specified. In the past, allocations for "geological exploration" also appeared in the nature protection budget, but such costs may now be borne elsewhere in the USSR state budget.

The state capital budget for nature protection represents only part of nature protection expenditures. Other funds are included in the operating budgets of individual ministries, and elsewhere in the state capital budget under the provisions for reconstruction, retooling, replacement and repair of existing plant and equipment. In 1988, for instance, the total amount expended was about 11 billion rubles for all purposes, including capital construction as above, but exclusive of the costs of regulatory agencies. Originally, it was thought that as much as 15 billion rubles would be allocated in the USSR for capital construction in the environmental area in the 12th plan period. However, the level that has been allocated in the annual economic plans is about 13.5 billion rubles. Over the period 1986–90, about 70 per cent (9.4 billion rubles) of the capital investment in nature protection was for water management (i.e. water recycling and waste water treatment). The total is somewhat larger than the construction budget during the 11th plan period (1981–85) when eight billion rubles were allocated to water management in the nature protection budget, although the share during the 11th plan period of total funds available was somewhat higher. However, due to the recent outbreak of inflation, which is between 10 and 15 per cent, the funds available for water management construction will purchase marginally less than in the previous plan period.

Soviet industry and municipalities usually filter effluents and rely heavily on diluting waste water (which is often still highly contaminated) prior to release as a means of reducing the harm to the recipient environment. About two-thirds of Soviet cities have primary waste water treatment installations, and of these about 30 per cent have secondary waste water treatment (using biological or chemical methods). So far, there are no data for the number of rural households that have sanitation systems, which may be uncommon except on the wealthier collective and state farms. Untreated municipal and industrial effluents are still released into rivers and streams, which relies on the volume and flow of the waterways to dilute the wastes. In Central Asia, water resources have been over-subscribed because of the dry climate, a large population, widespread irrigation and thirsty crops (such as cotton and rice), and an increasing presence of industries which are dependent on high-volume water consumption. The region has not achieved high levels of industrial water recycling and effluent treatment; for example, 78 per cent of industrial water in Turkmenia and 62 per cent of that in Azerbaidzhan is fresh water. (The problem is not limited to Central Asia—for example, Estonian and Moldavian industry have similar or worse performances in this area.) The ecological consequences are seen in the massive dust storms that spread dust, aerosols and salts over agricultural areas in Uzbekistan and Kazakhstan; the evaporation of the Aral Sea and loss of the fishing industry and displacement of the villages surrounding the seabed; and most importantly in the extraordinary levels of infant mortality and the spread of disease throughout the area. In the Ukraine, where the seasonal water tables vary precipitously, surface and ground water resources are so constrained that industrial expansion is strictly controlled. Officially, about 70 per cent of industrial and municipal effluents in the Soviet Union are subjected to environmental regulation. Of this, an estimated 28.6 billion cu m are not clean on release, and such effluents subject to mandatory cleansing in the West may be excluded from regulation in the Soviet Union. The lowest attainment of recycling and repeat use water is in Lithuania at 22 per cent of supply; the highest are supposedly in Turkmenia and Kirghizia at 95 per cent.

Water pollution is one of the main environmental concerns in a number of Eastern European countries, such as Bulgaria and Hungary which are singling out the issue in their current investment programmes. The data presented for each of the Eastern European countries and the Soviet Union are not comparable. In Czechoslovakia, the Odra and Ostravica rivers are particularly polluted and their water flows affect water quality in

Poland. The data concerning water pollution in Poland indicate the problems there are extensive. A report issued by the official publication *Wiadomosci statystyczne* in 1987 said that 38 per cent of the inland waters are polluted, while *Aura* said in 1988 that no rivers complied with pollution standards. The former source also said that 43 per cent (4.6 billion cu m) of waste water is discharged without purification and a further 34.1 per cent is partially treated. The two areas of **Gdańsk** and Szczecin are located in coastal areas where the ports and industrial activities have caused bacteriological and chemical pollution of coastal sea water, and the lower reaches of the Vistula and Oder rivers.

USSR state budget allocations for air pollution controls were about 10 per cent (1.4 billion rubles) of the capital budget for nature protection (13.4 billion rubles) during the 12th plan period. This represented a nominal increase over expenditures during the 11th plan period (1981–85) when 8 per cent (899 million rubles) of the state capital budget for nature protection (11.1 billion rubles) was directed to air pollution controls. Some of the allocations were probably absorbed by inflation-induced cost increases; and not all of the budgets are being spent each year, probably due to the lack of appropriate equipment. Of the funds allocated for the construction of air pollution controls in the USSR as a whole, the ferrous and non-ferrous metallurgical industries absorbed over 50 per cent during the 12th plan period in comparison to about 80 per cent during the 11th plan period.

There is, as yet, no co-ordinated programme of investment in air pollution control in the Soviet Union; most investments to date relate to dust trapping, less to contain sulphur dioxide and other toxics. The apparent targets for air pollution controls are the result of the 1986 European agreement by which the USSR agreed to cut its emissions of sulphur dioxide by 30 per cent by the early 1990s; although such reductions are unlikely within the time frame. Such emissions are a particular concern for the fossil-fuelled electric power industry; the electric power industry's programme for decommissioning old power plants has fallen far behind schedule. In the wake of the **Chernobyl** explosion, the construction of nuclear power installation has virtually halted in favour of coal and gas-fired electric power. Reliance on fossil fuels can be environmentally risky, as much of the coal contains high levels of ash and/or sulphur; the gas deposits being exploited in Astrakhan, for instance, bear an extraordinary level of hydrogen sulphide which is lethal in small doses. Northern petroleum deposits represent environmental problems in respect of the fragile ecological environments where exploration and extraction takes place, and native populations throughout Siberia have expressed grave reservation about the damage.

The responsibility for air quality monitoring and regulation is split at the national levels amongst the USSR Committee on Nature Protection, the State Committee on Hydrometeorology, and the State Committee for Atomic Power. Additionally, the republics (especially Estonia), regions (such as the Sumi *oblast*), and localities (such as Odessa and Erevan) are developing their ecological expertise. Initial steps have been made to establish the essential regulatory infrastructure. For example, state standards were promulgated in 1986 by the State Committee on Hydrometeorology and the USSR Ministry of Health concerning the arrangement, concentration, and responsibilities of air quality monitoring stations. These will be established according to a population-based formula: one station — up to 50,000 population; two to three stations — 100,000–200,000 population; three to five stations — 200,000–500,000 population; five to ten stations — over 50,000 population; 10–20 stationary and route stations — over one million population.

Emissions standards have been set by the USSR Ministry of Health and the USSR State Committee on Hydrometeorology for several hundred substances that have been judged to be a danger to public health. The number of substances that are subject to regulatory control is contentious; insufficient scientific data and technological expertise, unavailability of equipment and personnel, and budgetary constraints preclude compliance by many enterprises. The USSR Ministry of Health insists that regulatory standards must be issued where the scientific basis for environmental controls has been established. The contrary opinion is that large-volume pollutants, such as dust and sulphur dioxide, are the only ones that can be controlled at the present time, and that localities should proceed with pollution controls for small volume contaminants (from a national perspective) that are important within their jurisdictions.

Soviet data on air pollution are few and not fully explained when they are reported. They do suggest that there is an extremely high level of pollution; 100 cities in the Soviet Union have recorded air pollution levels (presumably this was ascertained by one-time testing of designated substances) at ten times or more than regulations permit. The total amount of pollutants released into the air from stationary sources are represented as 64.1 million tonnes, and half of the total are generated by the metallurgical and electric power industries. Of the total released, 15.6 million tonnes are comprised of solids (i.e. particulate matter such as ash and dust), and 48.5 million tonnes are gaseous or liquid (probably steam) in form. Of the latter, sulphur dioxide comprises 18.6 million tonnes (38.4 per cent); nitrogen oxides 4.5 million tonnes (9.3 per cent); and carbon monodizes 15.5 million tonnes (32.0 per cent). "Other" gases total 9.9 million tonnes (20.4 per cent); these are not characterized in Soviet data, which probably comprised volatile organic compounds and hydrocarbons.

In practice, factories rely on climatic conditions and the efficiency of tall smoke stacks to direct the plumes into the upper atmosphere and away from the immediate area. Most enterprises have dust traps (installations to contain dust and particulate matter) although about half such installations are more than 10 years old and are inefficient or inoperable. Some enterprises reduce the emissions of substances, such as sulphur dioxide, by using, in addition, a combination of more advanced technologies such as Venturi tubes, cyclones, and electrostatic precipitators. The construction programmes for most industries have been devised so that factories are surrounded by "sanitary zones" (a Soviet term for land surrounding industrial sites) and residential areas are located at prescribed distances from the enterprises. The problem, of course, is that cities have grown up around the industrial sites (which once may have been some distance from residential areas), and now require either the plants or the housing to be relocated. The habitual reliance on tall smoke stacks and the lack of adequate controls on pollutants such as sulphur dioxide means that the pollutants are transported significant distances down-stream. For example, emissions from metallurgical plants on the Kola Peninsula affect Scandinavia, and those from Kazakhstan affect the People's Republic of China.

In Eastern Europe, the deterioration of air quality is especially serious. In Poland, pollution has reached critical points in cities, and there is evidence of pollutants entering the food chain, which represents a further threat to public health. Officially, 8 per cent of forests are damaged by gaseous emissions, which included 1.8 million tonnes of dust and 6.1 million tonnes of sulphur dioxide emitted annually. In the GDR, as elsewhere in Eastern Europe, air pollution is significantly linked to the use of low quality coal.

The legal basis for nature protection. The history of environmental law in the Soviet period dates back to **Lenin**, and each of the subsequent Soviet constitutions has guaranteed the rights of citizens to ecologically safe environments. The adminis-

trative laws, decrees, and regulations of which there have been many hundreds over the years, are however rarely enforced. In the past, it appears that environmental laws and regulations represented goals of what should be done, without any real expectation of compliance. Until the 1970s, when hopes were briefly raised by a flurry of new policy-making, most Western observers until the mid-1980s tended to dismiss the environmental issue as unrelated to Soviet economic and investment priorities.

In the Soviet Union, the work to revise and co-ordinate existing environmental law is being conducted in the Institute of State and Law of the USSR Academy of Sciences; latterly it will be considered by the Supreme Soviet and the Central **Committee of the Communist Party of the Soviet Union**. An authoritative collection of Soviet laws and decrees on environmental protection and resource conservation was published in 1986. The current attention to environmental protection, according to Soviet sources, was occasioned by developments initiated in the 1970s in Siberia, Central Asia and the Soviet Far East, where fragile ecological environments were endangered by economic activities. Environmental pollution caused by economic development in Western areas of the Soviet Union are now linked in the Soviet press to extensive deterioration in morbidity and mortality indicators, and birth abnormalities, although relevant scientific data have been suppressed since the early 1970s. Similar situations obtain in Eastern Europe.

Administrative leadership. The USSR State Committee on Nature Protection (USSR *Goskompriroda*) was created by decree in January 1988 to lead the development and implementation of environmental programmes in the Soviet Union. The decree was sweeping in its mandate which included all functions from international co-operation, provision of ecological expertise and material supplies, public education and propaganda. However, the decree left unresolved fundamental issues of financing nature protection initiatives, the institutional means and routes for enforcing and appealing decisions, and the legal competence of existing regulatory agencies. In addition, the role of party organizations in arbitrating environmental decisions has in the past been considerable, and this area has also been left unresolved. According to the decree, local soviets will assume an increasing level of responsibility for nature protection. The first director of USSR *Goskompriroda*, F. T. Morgun, was appointed after several months' delay. Morgun was succeeded in the summer of 1989 by

N. N. Vorontsev, a non-party biologist and member of the Congress of People's Deputies.

Early in 1989, the director of USSR *Goskompriroda* was described by the publication *Priroda i chelovek* as a "General without an army", while many others have charged since that all that has happened is the creation of a new, amorphous, bureaucratic giant. Now, after two years, there is an organizational chart for the State Committee. It shows five levels in the national bureaucracy, and there are supposed to be corresponding bureaucracies in the republics, *oblasts*, *krais*, and localities. None of the nature protection agencies are fully established, but judging by reports in the Soviet press, some local protection officials are very active. Many of the largest production ministries have created "Nature Protection Committees", and a few have *Goskompriroda* representatives on them. (The committees develop plans for investment in nature protection installations that are needed by their enterprises.) USSR *Goskompriroda* also has the assistance of the USSR Academy of Sciences, which has placed ecology very high on its list of priorities, and has established several committees to investigate problems such as water shortages around the Aral Sea and pollution at Lake Baikal.

USSR *Goskompriroda* has not succeeded thus far in asserting its authority over other bureaucracies. Such struggles must be resolved by government and party leadership at the highest levels, and it was hoped that the omnibus environmental legislation expected in 1990 would clarify jurisdictional responsibilities. In particular, large production ministries and other State Committees have resisted the direction of USSR *Goskompriroda*, which does not control their budgets and whose bureaucratic status is not greater, and in economic terms is often less, than their own. Questions remain whether authority for the monitoring stations operated by the State Committee on Hydrometeorology and the USSR Ministry of Public Health, for instance, will be transferred. It is unknown if responsibilities for protection of coastal zones and inland waterways will be retained by the USSR Ministry of Fisheries. Similarly, it is not certain who (or if) there will be environmental reviews of the decisions taken by the USSR Ministry of Water Management (which is roundly criticized for construction activities that have caused many ecological disasters, including the massive shrinkage of the Aral Sea). The transfer of enterprises formerly under central ministrial jurisdiction to republican authorities will ease some of the obstacles to environmental regulation; for example in Estonia, 90 per cent of industry was formerly under Moscow's control. From 1990, a total of 75 per cent of industry will be subjected to Estonian environmental and economic authority.

Apart from monitoring of ecological conditions, the USSR State Committee on Nature Protection requires an intricate network of testing and laboratory facilities to support the full range of regulation-making and enforcement activities. In December 1988, F.T. Morgun announced that nine research and scientific laboratories would be established. The main one—called "Ecology"—is in Moscow. Others are to be located in **Leningrad**, Perm, Novosibirsk, Irkustak, Khabarovak, Vladivostok, Noril'sk, and Petropavlovsk-Kamchatka. The USSR *Goskompriroda* laboratories are to be supplemented by facilities developed under republican auspices. Some laboratories, called "Eko-centres", are to be designed according to the mix of industry and agriculture in specific *oblasts* or *krais*. In the interim, the ecological movements and administrators will rely on laboratories operated under the auspices of the USSR and republican academies of sciences, universities, and industrial research units for scientific data and research expertise. The existing facilities, such as the research institutes at Lake Baikal, are not well established and the quality of consequent recommendations will depend on their being adequately staffed, funded and equipped.

Integration of environmental protection into economic decision making. It is well known that the Soviet economy must undergo radical reforms in order to be an efficient provider of food, consumer durables, and industrial commodities (*see* **USSR**—Economic background). These reforms will also determine the success of the environmental programme, where economic obstacles are the root of many ecological disasters. In the past, industry has been starved of investment—some particularly serious sources of pollution desperately so. In other cases, the lack of investment was not because there was no financial backing, but because the choice was made for the industries to use money, resources, and manpower at their disposal to expand their presence in the national economy. This investment pattern meant that few resources were left over to streamline or modernize, or for the upkeep of plant and equipment. Now, the age structure of key industrial infrastructure, such as rail transportation and electric power, suggests that the declining efficiency in the Soviet economy could continue unless the problems are addressed effectively and rapidly. One result is that enterprises and ministries will continue to adopt cost avoidance attitudes and practices. Cost avoidance (in Soviet terminology to take a "residual approach") meant, in the past, that existing pollution control installations were not systematically maintained, repaired and replaced because they were not and are still not productive investments within the terms of Soviet economic planning.

To address these problems, the state capital budget for industry has been substantially revised so that enterprises will be retooled and reconstructed. The objective of the activities is to re-establish the industrial base, and to secure simultaneous improvement in production in qualitative and quantitative terms. At the same time, modernized industries, it is anticipated, will have a lesser impact on nature. By 1990, over half of the capital budget will have been given over to the reconstruction and retooling of existing plant. This is, therefore, to be the main vehicle to lessen the impact of industry on the environment, leaving the nature protection budget to cover areas not subject to remedial investment or to pick up the residual toxic emissions and effluents. The environmental gains from retooling and reconstruction have not been elaborated so far, and new issues of old technologies are often used rather than more efficient designs. In effect, therefore, the shift of the capital budget may stabilize production in some industries, but as presently implemented it is largely unresponsive to the environmental factor.

There are important successes linked to the reinvestment programme. For example, the metallurgical industry is replacing the open hearth furnaces, and with new technologies metallurgical pollution many be more easily managed. It is important to note that electric furnaces transfer the pollution to another sector of the national economy where, as it happens, there is no or little investment in pollution controls. In principle, though, gaseous wastes from electric power plants are somewhat different in composition and should be easier to manage, but pollution continues to be generated at the reconstructed metallurgical sites as well. So, both industries require pollution abatement installations, and if these are not provided to the electric power stations, the metallurgical industry's solution amounts to one step forward and a few more backward.

A fundamental question relates to the importance of reinvestment in existing plants, and whether adequate attention is being given to the restructuring of the entire Soviet economy into new types of industry. A good case is that of the Soviet chemical industry, where the future of the industry in economic and ecological terms probably requires a resolution of the policy split between extensive and intensive investment. At present, the arguments centre on the Tyumen petrochemical development, which with other

similar developments will offer to the Soviet economy materials, such as plastics, to replace the use of metals (for which the resource base is declining) and other less efficient substances as clay and cement. In the maximum estimate, the Tyumen petrochemical development will cost upwards of 100 billion rubles, and it is hardly coincidence that the requirements for reconstruction and development of existing plants industry-wide are valued on the same order of magnitude.

There are other many issues that must be addressed during the reforms of the Soviet economy. Amongst these, the need for educational and labour training that will supply environmental cadres may be the single greatest obstacle to an ecological *perestroika*. At present, the numbers of individuals engaged in ecological studies or studies adaptable to ecological management are few, and in fields such as chemistry the enrolments already fall short of industrial requirements. Most educational activities by the USSR State Committee on Nature Protection appear to take the form of propaganda for purposes of public education, which is an essential element in furthering nature protection. Propaganda is a motivational tool, but cannot meet the requirements for skilled researchers and practitioners.

MT

ESTONIA. A Soviet regime was briefly established in Estonia in 1917–19, but the incorporation of the republic into the USSR as one of its constituent members occurred in 1940 following the Nazi-Soviet Pact of 1939, in which the Baltic republics had been allocated to the USSR. Many Western governments refused to recognize the incorporation of Estonia into the USSR *de jure* and in 1989 and 1990 the Estonian Supreme Soviet declared the incorporation invalid in terms of international law and Soviet laws inoperative in the republic. Estonia occupies an area of 45,100 sq km, and its 1989 census population was 1,573,000; according to the 1979 census 65 per cent of the population were ethnic Estonians, with a large minority of Russians accounting for a further 28 per cent. The capital is Tallinn, and the republic is divided into 15 administrative districts. Agriculture and dairy farming are the chief occupations; there is an important timber industry and large deposits of high-quality shale, phosphorite and peat. Living standards are the highest in the USSR and this has encouraged substantial immigration from elsewhere, particularly of blue-collar workers from the Russian Republic. Together with the other two Baltic republics,

Estonia lent its support to a strongly assertive nationalist movement from the late 1980s onwards. (*See also* **Nationality Question in the USSR**)

SLW

EVANGELICAL CHURCH IN THE GDR. The Evangelical Church was the traditional church of the vast majority of the population of what became the German Democratic Republic (14 million out of 17 million at the end of the war). The remainder were linked with the **Roman Catholic Church**. The Evangelical Church had a relatively privileged position in the years of Walter **Ulbricht** and Erich **Honecker**. Despite atheist propaganda, and, more effectively, discrimination against believers, the Federation of Evangelical Churches (BEK) could still claim seven million members by the late 1980s.

Up to 1969 the East German Evangelical Churches remained part of a single Evangelical Church covering the FRG and the GDR, and therefore formed a living embodiment of continuing German unity. The 1969 split into Eastern and Western wings reflected a tendency to come to some partial accommodation with the GDR authorities; in 1971 the Synod elaborated the idea of the "Church in socialism", seeking to persuade the government that it should not be regarded as a hostile force. Nevertheless, the Church never came under state control; it defended believers' rights, although not as strongly as some within it would have liked, and it spoke out particularly against militarism in the GDR. It appears to have benefited from West German pressure on East Berlin to minimize persecution of the churches.

In March 1978 there was a historic meeting between Honecker and the Evangelical leadership. This helped to secure the position of the Church in society, with greater freedom to publish and to make religious broadcasts, and permission to build more new churches. From 1980 onwards, the Evangelical Church became an umbrella for the emerging peace movement. Local churches organized peace festivals involving services with thousands of people, and activists organized large demonstrations against Soviet porposals to deploy intermediate-range nuclear forces in the GDR. In 1982 the authorities banned people from wearing the "swords into ploughshares" emblem, which had become popular among young supporters of the peace move-

ment. The same year, Pastor Rainer Eppelmann and the Marxist Robert Havemann were among the launchers of the Berlin Appeal, which called for the withdrawal of all foreign soldiers from both German states and the establishment of a nuclear-free zone.

The Honecker leadership disapproved of the independent peace movement but refrained from a frontal assault. In 1983, the First Secretary himself headed the celebrations for the 500th anniversary of Martin Luther, seeking to prevent the Evangelicals and the peace activists from seizing the initiative. The party portrayed the Protestant leader as part of the tradition in German thought which culminated in the building of socialism in the GDR.

The rise of **Gorbachev** and the beginnings of *glasnost'* and *perestroika* in Eastern Europe gave a powerful boost to the peace movement and the independent thinkers inside the Evangelical Church. A mass civil rights movement developed, involving people who had little in common with the Church leadership or Evangelicalism generally, but the Church continued to give it protection. The Honecker regime became alarmed. In November 1987 the security police raided the Zion Church in East Berlin, a dissident centre. Thereafter it cracked down on Church-based groups, dispersing their demonstrations.

During Honecker's last days, and through the interregnum of Egon **Krenz**, the Nikolaikirche in Leipzig provided a focus for weekly meetings and demonstrations, demanding human rights and free elections. As emigration from the GDR became possible in late 1989, Church leaders joined the regime in calling on people to stay in the GDR and work to improve it. In December 1989 the Protestant and Catholic churches chaired the "**Round Table**" which brought together Communist and opposition forces in an attempt to find a way out of the crisis caused by the collapse of legitimacy of the institutions of the GDR.

As the question of German political unification was posed more urgently in late 1989 and early 1990, the churches became alarmed at the growth of German nationalism and its possible consequences for European security. Whereas in the past the Evangelical Church had sought to keep alive the idea of German unity, its leaders, paradoxically, became practically the last defenders of the continued existence of a separate socialist state in East Germany.

PJSD

F

FATHERLAND FRONT (BULGARIA — FF Otechestven Front). Originally a "popular front" type organization set up in Bulgaria in late 1943 and uniting various left-wing parties and factions opposed to the right-wing pro-German government, the Fatherland Front (FF) came gradually under the control of the Bulgarian Communist Party (BCP) during the latter's consolidation of power in the late 1940s. Since 1948, it has incorporated the only two legal parties in Bulgaria — the BCP and BANU (the **Bulgarian Agrarian National Union**) — but it has functioned as a mass organization, with a membership several times greater than that of the two political parties combined. Formally it has been the organization which has put forward the approved candidates, party and non-party, in Bulgaria's uncontested elections for seats in the National Assembly and more local councils – though in practice the BCP has been the real decision maker.

Undoubtedly, the FF's role is called into question by post-**Zhivkov** developments. Two possibilities suggest themselves. The first is that the FF will simply disintegrate, given the emergence and likely deepening of differences between the BCP and BANU, and the availability of yet other alternatives to the public hitherto monopolised by the FF. The second is that it may survive as a forum for vigorous debate and pre-electoral competition within a broad but stable coalition.

RW

FIDESZ (HUNGARY — Alliance of Young Democrats). FIDESZ (*Fiatal Demokraták Szövetsége*) was set up in Hungary on March 30, 1988 as an alternative, unofficial and independent youth movement. From the start it took an uncompromisingly radical and oppositional stance. At first it was banned, and individuals associated with it suffered a certain amount of harassment by the authorities, but it was able to hold its first national congress on Nov. 19–20, 1988. The movement appeals to the 16–35 year age group, and an important element within the membership comprises law students and young lawyers. In fact it is a sort of hybrid youth movement-cum-party, and intended to put up its own candidates in national elections. Its programme has much in common with that of the **Alliance of Free Democrats (AFD)** although FIDESZ is not the AFD's "youth wing" and in certain respects is much more radical than the latter.

According to recent information leaflets, "for FIDESZ, the source of all progress lies in humanism; European culture; respect for national and communal identity; the self-regulating market economy; social security; the self-organization of society; parliamentary democracy and the fullest possible freedom of the individual". FIDESZ has adopted a particularly outspoken and controversial position on the issues of 1956, neutrality and the stationing of Soviet troops in Hungary. At the funeral of Imre **Nagy** on June 16, 1989, a leading representative of FIDESZ, Victor Órbán, made a impassioned speech in which he drew the conclusion that "democracy and communism are incompatible", and called for the withdrawal of Soviet troops. The speech caused something of a storm, but the FIDESZ leadership backed Órbán. FIDESZ was represented at the "Triangular Discussions" with the **Hungarian Socialist Workers' Party (HSWP)** in summer 1989, and, like the AFD, refused to sign the final agreements. In the November referendum on the issue of the presidency, FIDESZ sided with the AFD and other parties opposing the direct election of the President. It secured 5.4 per cent of the vote in the March – April 1990 elections.

JB

FREE GERMAN TRADE UNION LEAGUE (FDGB — Freier Deutscher Gewerk Schaftsbund). The FDGB was until 1990 the monopolistic trade union organization of workers and other employees in the GDR. Originating in the early phase of reconstruction after World War II, the FDGB came to be inextricably linked with the ruling **Socialist Unity Party of Germany (SED)**. The former Social Democratic tradition of the trade union movement was thus destroyed, as were rival Catholic and liberal unions. Conflict in labour was not admitted in the GDR, so the FDGB's function came to be state- and party-supportive, with only limited scope for representing genuine grievances on behalf of the workforce. The FDGB consisted of 16 trade unions, in which were organized over nine million members, that is over 90 per cent of eligible employees.

The revolution of 1989 soon brought change in the FDGB. Its chairman and Politburo member since 1975, Harry Tisch (born 1927), was one of the first casualties of grassroots pressure. He resigned at the beginning of November 1989 because, he said, he had lost the confidence of the members. Demands were made for his arrest on corruption charges. As other trade union leaders went the same way, Tisch's position was taken by Annelis Kimmel, former leader of the Berlin trade union organization. She too was replaced at the beginning of February 1990 by Helga Mausch of the **National Democratic Party of Germany (NDPD)**. At the same extraordinary congress of the FDGB it was agreed that individual unions should have more autonomy and that the FDGB should remain only as a limited umbrella organization. As the economic crisis in the GDR developed in 1990, labour unrest had already begun to overtake the previous role of the FDGB.

JO

FREE GERMAN YOUTH (FDJ — Freie Deutsche Jugend). Originally presented not as a Communist youth organization but as a free movement, the FDJ of the GDR was in fact from the outset a junior partner of the KPD Communist Party of Germany and then the **Socialist Unity Party of Germany (SED)**. Its first chairman, from 1946 to 1955, was the future GDR leader, Erich **Honecker**. Again, from 1974 to 1983 the leadership of the FDJ provided the training ground for high office, this time for Egon **Krenz**. He was followed by Eberhard Aurich.

As the only officially permitted youth organization, the FDJ has played an infiltrating role in all educational institutions and its members engage in industrial and agricultural work. Its primary purposes have been to indoctrinate young people in official ideology, to promote military training and to groom future members of the SED. Its 2.3 million members (1981) ranged in age from 14 years to over 24 years.

As monopolistic organizations in the GDR lost ground to reform and pluralist democracy, the FDJ attempted to prove itself as responsive to change. In its existing form, however, it appeared to have little or no future.

JO

FREEDOM PARTY (CZECHOSLOVAKIA — Strana slobody). One of two small Slovak non-Communist parties included within the **National Front of the Czechoslovak Socialist Republic**, the Freedom Party was founded in April 1946 as the result of a split in the Democratic Party (*see* **Party of Slovak Renewal**). It has been allocated four of the 350 seats in the Federal Assembly and seven of the 150 in the Slovak National Council since the creation of those bodies in 1969.

GW

G

GDAŃSK. Located at the mouth of the Vistula river on the Baltic coast of Poland, population 461,500. Forming part of "tri-city" with the port of Gdynia and the resort of Sopot, the conurbation includes 759,500 inhabitants. Already a centre for overseas trade in the tenth century, Gdańsk became the seat of the dukes of Pomerania, who severed early Polish connections in the late twelfth century. In 1308 it was conquered by the Teutonic Knights and not returned to Polish authority until the middle of the fifteenth century. With the extensive growth of trade in the sixteenth and seventeenth century it developed as a major European port, acquiring a distinctive architectural identity and a reputation for furniture-making and metal-work. After the Second Partition of Poland in 1793 the city passed to the Prussians, and its subsequent development under German auspices as Danzig in combination with Polish historical associations and a commanding position over the outlet to the sea of Poland's major waterway produced a decidedly mixed historical legacy.

This mixture was reflected in the treaty agreed in 1919 at Versailles, whereby Danzig became a free city while Poland was given responsibilty for its foreign affairs and control over an internal customs area, retaining also use of the port, rail and waterways. At the same time the Polish government attempted to build up its own resources and economic network, including a new port at what was originally the neighbouring fishing village of Gdynia. After the conclusion of a non-aggression pact with Germany in January 1934, Polish foreign minister Beck, believing that the main threat to Polish security lay to the east, did little to oppose German claims over the city (which were strong on ethnic grounds — in distinction to the more Polish Pomeranian hinterland) or oppose the Nazification process. German demands with respect to Danzig and full rights for a passage through Polish territory became more pressing after the occupation of Austria and the Munich agreement. It was following a German attack on the Polish garrison at Westerplatte and the Polish post office that World War II broke out.

Most of the historical centre was destroyed during the war but has later been rebuilt. Its surviving German population, too, either fled to Germany or was transferred soon after the war. During the process of post-war reconstruction and development particular emphasis was placed on the Gdańsk shipyard, named in the late 1960s after the Soviet leader **Lenin**. It was in the towns along the northern coast, including Gdańsk, that worker response to the 1970 price rises was swiftest and most pronounced. In 1980 the strike at the Gdańsk shipyard also received the greatest prominence, in no small part due to the role played by Lech **Wałęsa**, and the agreement signed there was one of the major bases on which the **Solidarity** union was formed. The union's headquarters have remained in Gdańsk. Prime Minister **Rakowski** announced the closure of the shipyard on economic grounds in October 1988, although many interpreted this rather as an aggressive political gesture. A special *Sejm* commission set up in 1989 to investigate the conduct of the Rakowski government reported in December 1989 and concluded that the decision to close the shipyard was made with undue haste and insufficient consultation. In early January 1990 the government announced that it had dropped the closure plans.

PGL

GEORGIA. Georgia, briefly an independent state after 1918, became a Soviet Socialist Republic in 1921. Together with **Armenia** and **Azerbaidzhan** it constituted the Transcaucasian Soviet Federal Socialist Republic in 1922, which became a member of the USSR in the same year. In 1936 Georgia became one of the constituent republics of the USSR. Georgia occupies an area of 69,700 sq km and had a 1989 census population of 5,449,000, just under 2 per cent of the USSR total. In the 1979 census Georgians accounted for 69 per cent of the population; Armenians accounted for a further 9 per cent and Russians for 7 per cent. The capital is Tbilisi. Georgia enjoys a mild climate and has abundant natural resources; its agricultural output includes grain, tea and citrus fruit, and its industrial output included manganese and light engineering goods. Georgia contains two autonomous republics, one of them Abkhazia, and an autonomous region; there were 65 districts in 1990. Always strongly nationalist in a cultural sense, Georgia was one of the republics where a strong wave of political nationalism was apparent in the late 1980s. (*See also* **Nationality Question in the USSR**)

SLW

GEORGIAN ORTHODOX CHURCH. Georgia accepted Christianity from Byzantium in the fourth century, six centuries before the Russians. In 1811, following Russia's annexation of Georgia, the Georgian Orthodox Church was incorporated in the **Russian Orthodox Church**. This position was interrupted only during the period of Georgia's independence, between 1917 and 1921, since after the Bolshevik reconquest of Georgia the Georgian Church was again subordinated to the Russian body. In the 1930s, the Georgian Church suffered severe persecution (*see* **Religion and Communism**), but in 1943, when Stalin improved the situation of most religions in the USSR, the Russian Church granted the Georgians autocephaly.

The Georgian Orthodox Church has been headed since 1977 by the Catholicos-Patriarch of all Georgia Iliya II (Shiolashvili). Under his predecessor, David V, the Church was involved in corruption scandals involving the theft of Church property, which implicated the Georgian KGB and senior Georgian Party and government figures. Patriarch Iliya II brought the Church out of its crisis, filled all the vacancies among the diocesan bishops and re-opened a large number of churches. (Possibly Eduard **Shevardnadze**, as party leader in Georgia, created a more tolerant environment for the Church.) Whereas under **Khrushchev**, most services had been conducted in Russian, owing to the lack of native priests, Iliya II emphasized the importance of the Georgian language and the role of the Church in defending Georgian national culture.

While normally defending the policies for the Soviet government, in 1980 Iliya II signed a statement condemning the Soviet invasion of Afghanistan. The advent of *glasnost'* allowed further opportunities for the Georgian Church, but it also brought in its wake an upsurge of violence and intolerance between the Georgians and other peoples of the republic (*see* **Nationality Question in the USSR**). Some of the emerging nationalist informal groups and opposition parties which emerged from 1987, like the National Democratic Party of Georgia, the Society of St Iliya the Just and the Ilya Chavchavadze Society took an openly Georgian Orthodox orientation. Iliya II reacted cautiously to the new challenges. In 1988, a new Theological Academy was established in Tbilisi, and the Theological Seminary was transferred there from Mtskheta. On April 9, 1989, prior to the massacre of demonstrators in Tbilisi, the Patriarch appealed to the crowd to disperse, warning of a forthcoming disaster. Since the killings, there has been an upsurge of Georgian nationalism and separatism in which the Church has been an important focus.

PJSD

GEREMEK, BRONISŁAW. Chairman of the Solidarity-backed Citizens' Parliamentary Club (*Obywatelski Klub Parlamentarny*) in the Polish *Sejm*, he was born in Warsaw on March 6, 1932. He graduated from Warsaw University in 1954 and was a member of the Academy of Sciences from then until 1960. From 1960 to 1965 he lectured in Paris at the Sorbonne. He then returned to the Academy of Sciences to head the Research Unit on the History of Medieval Culture. He was a member of the **Polish United Workers' Party (PUWP)** from 1950 to 1968. From 1976 he became active in dissident circles and was an adviser to the Interfactory Founding Committee of **Solidarity** in 1980, later acting as chairman of the council of the centre for social and occupational affairs attached to the Co-ordinating Commission of the union. He was interned for a year from December 1981 and was again arrested in May 1983. In March 1985 his employment at the Academy of Sciences was terminated for political reasons. He was elected to the *Sejm* in Suwalki province on the first round in June 1989, and proposed by Lech **Wałęsa** on June 23 to chair the Citizens' Club.

PGL

GERMAN DEMOCRATIC REPUBLIC (GDR). *Population*: 16.4 million. *Area*: 108,333 sq km. *Top five trading partners*: USSR, Federal Republic of Germany, Czechoslovakia, Poland, Hungary. *Urban population as percentage of total*: 77. *Birth rate*: 13 per thousand. *Life expectancy*: males 70; females 76.

The German Democratic Republic (GDR) is the state founded in 1949 from the Soviet Occupation Zone of Germany after World War II. It comprises the central portion of the former German Empire, namely the territories and former *Länder* of Mecklenburg, Brandenburg, Saxony-Anhalt, Thuringia and Saxony. It claims as its capital the Soviet sector of **Berlin**, and does not include the enclave of West Berlin. The GDR has a northern coastline on the Baltic Sea, borders the Federal Republic of Germany in the west and south-west, Czechoslovakia in the south-east, and Poland in the east. About two-thirds of the country forms part of the low-lying North German plain; the remainder is more elevated, rising over 1,000 m in the southern Erzgebirge and in the western Harz. About 55 per cent of the territory is cultivated, and 27 per cent is forest. The principal rivers are the Elbe, the Spree, and the Oder and Neisse, which form most of the border with Poland. There is a network of lakes in the north and centre of the country. The climate is temperate, with cold winters not infrequent.

The road and rail systems are well developed, but they are in bad condition in many areas. Efficient transport is also hindered by the tight borders which were built between the two German states and between the GDR and West Berlin, which cut across previous lines of communication. There are nuclear power stations in the GDR, but the main domestic energy source is lignite, which is mined in the south of the country and which has caused major environmental damage.

Population density in 1987 was 154 people per sq km, which is average by European standards. The most densely populated areas are in the industrial centres south of the country. The population has fallen almost continually since the founding of the republic, through a low birth rate and periods of emigration.

The GDR has overwhelmingly a German culture, but there are about 100,000 Sorbs who speak a West Slavic language and live mostly in the south-eastern districts of Dresden and Cottbus. In 1989 there were also about 90,000 foreign workers in the country, from a variety of mainly African and Asian countries. The territory of the GDR is of a predominantly Protestant tradition, but Catholic allegiance is present too. Between four and five million people were members of a church in the late 1980s.

The population is predominantly urban, with 77 per cent of people living in communities of 2,000 and above and over one quarter of the population living in cities of over 100,000. Of these the largest by far is "Berlin—capital of the GDR" (East Berlin), with 1.3 million inhabitants, followed by the three Saxon cities of **Leipzig**, Dresden and Karl-Marx-Stadt (formerly Chemnitz).

Until 1952 the GDR consisted of five *Länder*, but these were replaced by the 14 districts (*Bezirke*) which form the administrative structure today: Rostock, Schwerin, Neubrandenburg, Magdeburg, Potsdam, Frankfurt a.d. Oder, Erfurt, Halle, Leipzig, Cottbus, Suhl, Gera, Karl-Marx-Stadt, and Dresden. Berlin (East Berlin) constitutes, as far as the GDR authorities are concerned, a fifteenth district. Each of these districts has political, administrative and economic structures and substructures, but the "democratic centralism" of the GDR has meant until recently that the district authorities received instructions from above.

The constitution of the GDR, as amended in 1974, enshrines a multitude of political and human rights which have until the recent changes been blatantly ignored. The party's leading role is entrenched in the Constitution, but this claim has now been abandoned. The constitution also binds the GDR irreversibly to its alliance with the USSR.

The GDR has been governed by a complex interaction between party and state. Most state functions at national and local level are also covered by party secretaries. Constitutionally, the parliament or People's Chamber (*Volkskammer*) is the highest organ of state, but since there have not been free elections, this body has been a rubber-stamp for the ruling party. Only in the course of the revolution of 1989 did the People's Chamber begin to exercise its rights. The presidency of the GDR was abolished in 1960, and the Head of State is the Chairman of the State Council (*Staatsrat*). This post has been occupied since 1976 by Erich **Honecker** (1976–89), briefly by Egon **Krenz** (1989), and provisionally by Manfred Gerlach of the **Liberal Democratic Party of Germany (LDPD)** (1989–90). The Council of Ministers (*Ministerrat*) is officially the government of the GDR, but until recent events it was overshadowed by the **Socialist Unity Party of Germany (SED)** party apparatus. The Prime Minister (Chairman of the Council of Ministers) was Willi **Stoph** from 1976 to 1989, when Hans **Modrow** took over. In view of the collapse of the party his cabinet took charge of governing the country, pending elections on March 18, 1990.

The history of the German left before 1945. The GDR was founded only in 1949, but it had earlier roots. During the last quarter of the nineteenth century the **Social Democratic Party of Germany (SPD)** became the largest socialist party in the world. In 1891 at Erfurt in Thuringia it adopted a Marxist programme, but in general the party pursued political and economic change through legal reformist activity. On the eve of World War I the party had about one million members and the trade unions associated with it about 2.5 million. The city of Berlin and the industrial cities of Saxony were heartlands of German Social Democracy. By 1912 the SPD was the largest party in the *Reichstag*, without being permitted any role in government. Despite an internationalist and anti-imperialist programme, the SPD parliamentary party approved funds for the German war effort in 1914. This helped to provoke a split in the party in 1917, when the left formed the USPD (Independent Social Democratic Party of Germany). It was from within the radical left of the USPD that the KPD (Communist Party of Germany) emerged at the end of 1918. Two of its early leaders were Rosa Luxemburg and Karl Liebknecht.

In November 1918 privations amongst the population, mutinies in the navy, and the collapse of the German war effort on the western front combined to produce a revolution in Berlin and other German cities. After the abdication of Kaiser Wilhelm II, the SPD and USPD took charge of a provisional government. The SPD quarrelled with its ally, however, and the USPD soon left the coalition. Force was used to quell communist uprisings in Berlin and Munich, which resulted in the murders of Luxemburg, Liebknecht and others.

The initial parliaments of the new republic met in the Thuringian town of Weimar, and a so-called Weimar governmental coalition was formed between the SPD, the Catholic Centre Party, and the DDP (German Democratic Party). This did not survive the political and economic crises of the early republic, however, and the SPD played at most a minor role in government until 1928–30. At municipal and state level, however —most notably in the largest state of Prussia and its capital of Berlin—the SPD initiated major programmes of social welfare.

In the hyper-inflation year of 1923 the states of Thuringia and Saxony were the scenes of attempts by the KPD, in local coalition with the SPD, to take Germany back onto a revolutionary path. The entry of Communists into the state governments moved the Reich government to adopt the reserve powers of SPD Reich President Ebert and remove the KPD influence. The Weimar Republic was beset by major economic crises, and these compounded the breach between the SPD and the KPD. The latter, under the leadership of Ernst-Thalmann and increasingly directed from Moscow, attacked the SPD for its reformism and collaboration with bourgeois parties and state institutions. By the final years of the republic the KPD line, derived from Stalin, was to denounce the SPD rather than Hitler's National Socialists as the main enemy, so-called "social fascists".

From 1930 parliamentary government was all but dead in Germany, as Chancellor Bruning used President Hindenburg's powers to rule by decree. The SPD tolerated much of his legislation, but was excluded from power. Meanwhile, the political extremes of right and left made strong advances, benefiting from the economic depression and mass unemployment. The Nazis gained strength from an apprehensive and impoverished middle class, and the KPD won support from the working-class unemployed. In the November 1932 elections the Nazis won 196 *Reichstag*

seats and the KPD 100, drawing closer to the SPD's 121.

Although the KPD and SPD had jointly more seats than the National Socialists, the gulf between them weakened their resistance to the Nazi threat. When Hitler was appointed Chancellor in January 1933, both parties were banned, trade union offices were destroyed, and Social Democrats and Communists were despatched to concentration camps, where many — including Thalmann—died, or were forced into exile. The USSR was the destination of many Communists, including future GDR leaders Wilhelm Pieck and Walter **Ulbricht**. They and others were schooled in the harsh world of Stalinism and many did not survive the purges. In 1943 in Moscow Ulbricht helped to found the National Committee for a Free Germany in preparation for the reconstruction of Germany after the defeat of the Third Reich, and the introduction of a Communist system.

The pre-1945 experience defined the emergent socialist state in a variety of ways. The GDR derived from a long tradition of German revolutionary socialism which had then been distorted by Stalinism. The inability of the left to stop Hitler was, though, seen by many Social Democrats as a reason to join forces with the Communists. The Communists were only too keen to assert their authority on the amalgamated political left. The sufferings of both Social Democrats and Communists at the hands of the Nazis and the barbarism of the Hitler regime also gave to the GDR a specific "anti-fascist" purpose and rhetoric which it has maintained to the present day.

The occupation of Germany 1945–49. As the Third Reich disintegrated, Soviet, American, British and later French troops occupied Germany. Four occupation zones were devised, and the USSR took control of the territories of Mecklenburg, Saxony, Saxony-Anhalt, Thuringia, Brandenburg, Danzig, Silesia and West and East Prussia. The last four regions were allocated to Polish or Soviet administration, and only central Germany became the Soviet Occupation Zone proper. Berlin, which was situated in the Soviet zone, was also divided into sectors and placed under four-power authority.

The Soviet Military Administration in Germany (SMAD) purged heavily implicated Nazis from positions of power and confiscated large industrial and agricultural property. Much industrial and transport equipment was dismantled and removed to the USSR. As the political exiles returned, SMAD permitted the KPD and the SPD to regroup, and approved the formation of two new non-socialist parties, the **Christian Democratic Union of Germany (CDU)** and the LDPD (Liberal Democratic Party of Germany). These were later joined in the so-called National Front of all parties by a peasants' party, **the Democratic Peasants' Party of Germany (DPD)**, a party for ex-officers, some ex-Nazis and the middle class, the **National Democratic Party of Germany (NDPD)**, by the trade union confederation **Free German Trade Union League (FDGB)**, and by the Communist youth organization **Free German Youth (FDJ)**.

Although the ruling party for most of the GDR's history is often loosely termed "the Communist Party", it was in fact an amalgamation of the two previously warring factions of the German left, the SPD and the KPD. In recognition of the alleged new harmony, the party which emerged in April 1946 was called the **Socialist Unity Party of Germany (SED)**. At its head stood the joint chairman, Wilhelm Pieck of the KPD and Otto Grotewohl of the SPD. At the foundation of the party, the SPD membership stood at around 679,000 and the KPD's at 619,000. This apparent pre-eminence of the SPD did not prevent the KPD element from acquiring a rapid dominance of the party. Communists were more likely than their Social Democratic allies to be appointed or promoted to party posts and in January 1949 the principle of parity between the two was abandoned. Furthermore, the party soon became a more centrally directed organization, with real power in the hands of the small Politburo. This had a Communist majority and here, as in the rest of the party, the Social Democrats found themselves pushed into a subordinate position. The other parties of the SED-dominated National Front were also forced into an orthodox line, but they maintained a function of providing a political home for those who for reasons of religion, class or ideology were thought unsuitable for membership of the SED.

In the autumn of 1946 local and regional elections were held in the Soviet zone, and the SED achieved a substantial plurality but no overall majority. However, in the one place — Berlin — where the SPD had been able to retain an existence separate from the KPD, it became clear how the Communists had hijacked the German left in the Soviet zone. The SED came third behind the SPD and the CDU in Berlin as a whole, and only second to the SPD in the Soviet sector.

The political paths of the Soviet zone on the one hand and the western zones on the other were now diverging in many ways, despite the professed intentions of both sides to maintain one German state. In early 1947 the American and British zones formed so-called Bizonia, with a united administration. In June 1948 the Western occupying powers introduced currency reform, providing an excuse for a similar reform in the Soviet zone and the blockade of the Western sectors of Berlin. The Western powers responded with a massive airlift of essential supplies, which helped to keep West Berlin free of Soviet control.

It was in fact the West Germans who first established a separate state by promulgating the Basic Law of the Federal Republic of Germany in May 1949, but the intentions of the SED and their Soviet mentors had already become clear. On Oct. 7, 1949 the German Democratic Republic was established and SMAD was dissolved. Wilhelm Pieck became president and Otto Grotewohl prime minister. By the end of the year diplomatic recognition had been accorded by the USSR and by the new socialist states of Eastern Europe and the Far East.

The Ulbricht era 1950–71. Pieck and Grotewohl were not to be the men who dominated the early history of the GDR. Walter **Ulbricht** was elected to the Politburo in January 1949 and as secretary general of the SED in July 1950. He then shaped it in his image, as disciplined, orthodox and Marxist-Leninist. Those who did not conform were purged from the party.

The first major crisis of the GDR came in the summer of 1953, after the death of **Stalin**. The raising of work norms by at least 10 per cent provoked an uprising of workers in East Berlin and other cities on June 17. It was explained officially as the work of paid criminal elements from West Berlin, and was violently suppressed by Soviet troops. The new norms were retracted, however. Ulbricht himself survived by pinning the blame on others and purging them from the leadership.

In the 1950s the GDR began to establish itself as a distinct independent state, although it relied heavily on Soviet policy. In 1950 the GDR joined the **Council for Mutual Economic Assistance** (CMEA, or RGW in German). In 1954 the USSR recognized the sovereignty of the GDR. In 1956, after the Federal Republic of Germany had joined NATO, the GDR formed its own **National People's Army (NVA)** and Ministry for National Defence, and joined the **Warsaw Treaty Organization (Warsaw Pact)**.

The GDR economy in the 1950s faced massive problems of reconstruction and the perceived need to compete with and overtake the economic performance of the Federal Republic. In mid-decade a so-called "new course" allowed some private enterprise to continue, but this was replaced by a concerted drive for full socialization. Centralized state planning was instituted on a seven- (later five-) year basis; most industry was nationalized; and a programme of agricultural collectivization was launched, culminating in the almost complete eradication of individual peasant farming by 1960.

Political repression and evidence that the economy of the Federal Republic was providing opportunities and a standard of living impossible in the GDR led to emigration westwards of over 100,000 GDR citizens each year. The city of Berlin was the favourite route, and in 1961 the Ulbricht regime decided in consultation with the USSR to seal it off. On Aug. 13, 1961 a wall was built between the Soviet sector and West Berlin and around the territory of West Berlin. At the same time the frontier between the GDR and the Federal Republic was tightly sealed.

The 1960s saw new twists and turns in an attempt to speed economic advance. Production incentives were introduced and aspects of the economy were decentralized. In 1965 nine new industrial ministries replaced the overall Economic Council. From 1968, however, partly in response to the events in Czechoslovakia which GDR troops had helped to halt, centralized planning returned to the forefront.

The GDR under Honecker 1971–89. The years 1970–71 saw significant changes for the GDR. Ulbricht responded only reluctantly to overtures being made by the new Chancellor of the Federal Republic, Willy Brandt, to reach an accord between the two German states. He was also not in favour of proposals for a four-power agreement on Berlin. Ulbricht's concern was that the separate identity of the GDR, enforced by the Berlin Wall and fostered in such aspects of GDR life as sport (the GDR fielded a separate Olympic team in 1968), would be eroded by closer contacts between the Germanies and a more relaxed situation in Berlin. His stance, combined with a worsened economic situation in 1970, led both domestic critics and the Kremlin to drop him. In May 1971 Ulbricht was replaced as First Secretary of the SED by Erich **Honecker**, his long-time protégé.

Brandt's *Ostpolitik* (eastern policy) led from meetings with Willi **Stoph** in Erfurt and Kassel in 1970 to detailed negotiations on the character of future inter-German relations. In December 1972 the two Germanies signed the so-called Basic Treaty, in 1973 both were admitted to the United Nations, from 1973 the GDR began to receive diplomatic recognition by foreign states (Britain in 1973, the USA in 1974), and in 1974 the GDR and the Federal Republic established permanent missions (below embassy status) in Bonn and (East) Berlin respectively. The agreements between the two German states did nothing to alter the Federal Republic's constitutional claim to rule on behalf of all Germans, nor the GDR's insistence on its status as a sovereign state, but they did open the way for increased trade, some relaxation of travel restrictions, and co-operation in numerous other fields.

Meanwhile the USSR, USA, Britain and France signed in September 1971 the Four Power Agreement on Berlin. This went a long way towards regularising the status of the city and avoiding the tensions of 1948 and 1961. The western powers conceded that West Berlin was not strictly part of the Federal Republic of Germany, while the USSR pledged to keep open the transit routes to that part of the city. West Berliners were also to be allowed greater access to the territory of the GDR.

The economic troubles of the early 1970s were eased somewhat by the new centralized policies, but with a time lag the oil crisis hit the GDR too, as the USSR increased its prices to its allies. Domestic industrial production in the GDR was inadequate and the ties to the CMEA partners made it difficult to develop strong exports to earn hard currency. Debt to the West was growing alarmingly.

The 1980s began in economic and political gloom. High debt levels and poor economic performance combined with international tension over Afghanistan, Poland and nuclear weapons in Europe. Within the GDR there arose a dissident church-based peace movement, which gathered considerable support before being weakened by police repression, the forced emigration of many of its activists and eventually by a diminution of superpower tension. This peace movement was, however, a precursor of what was to emerge later.

By the mid-1980s the economic and political situation of the GDR seemed to be much improved, but this must now be regarded with some scepticism. It is no coincidence that what was to be the highpoint, the year of 1984, with record economic performance and a proposed Honecker visit to the Federal Republic, was the 35th anniversary of the GDR. Early in the year large numbers of citizens were permitted to emigrate, in an attempt to rid the country of malcontents. The economy did seem to be on the upturn, with a reported record growth rate of 5.5 per cent in Net Material Product. A hard-currency trade surplus was achieved, and foreign debt stabilized so much that Western credit was once more forthcoming. The only disappointments for Honecker were that the GDR had to boycott the Los Angeles Olympics and that in its dying throes, the old Kremlin leadership instructed him not to accept the invitation to visit the Federal Republic.

With hindsight it can be seen that much of this achievement was contrived and based on weak premises. The GDR economy did pick itself up out of the recession of the early 1980s, even if allowance is made for the deliberate falsification of statistics which has since been admitted. However, the recovery, particularly on the hard currency side, was based largely on the import, processing and re-export to the West of oil products. The rest of GDR industry was less dynamic and was building up problems for the future. Lignite production, for instance, was boosted strongly — from around 278 million tonnes in 1983 to 312 million tonnes in 1985 — but stagnated thereafter as mining became more difficult, and meanwhile exacerbated the dreadful pollution associated with it. Other industries were starved of investment as money was pumped recklessly into microtechnology. The provision of the population with consumer goods, however, did not improve sufficiently, and staple prices for food, accommodation and transport could only be kept down by increasing the large state subsidies. These, it has since been conceded, were funded by hard-currency borrowing not revealed in the state budgets of the Ministry of Finance.

Erich Honecker meanwhile adopted the role of world statesman. His initial setback over the visit to the Federal Republic was overcome when he set forth for Bonn in September 1987. This was a personal triumph for him and for his perception of the GDR, but it was, of course, the same Mikhail **Gorbachev** who allowed him to travel who was later to be his undoing. The Bonn visit was one of many around the world, including several to NATO countries. As the 40th anniversary of the GDR approached, Honecker could look with some pride on the international acceptance of the GDR, on apparent economic advance and on a successfully imposed social and political peace.

The revolution of 1989. From the summer of 1989 the GDR was in the process of collapse as an independent state. Unlike the other countries of Eastern Europe which had similarly undergone upheaval, the GDR had primarily an ideological rather than a national identity and the population had an alternative national focus in the Federal Republic. Once the strictures on freedom were lifted, the extent of the internal crisis was revealed in full and the GDR lost its justification. All its citizens have an automatic qualification for citizenship in the Federal Republic, and many made use of this, deciding that the pace of change in the GDR was too slow and the prospects too

unreliable. This was the main problem confronting the governments in East Berlin and in Bonn. German unity was set as a goal by both, and Mikhail Gorbachev removed the Soviet objection, but the GDR was losing people and collapsing internally in a way beneficial to neither German state nor to other interested powers.

The long-term origins of this revolution were various. In respect of political dogmatism, police harassment, corruption, and economic ineptitude, the GDR shared the characteristics of the Eastern European states and the USSR. Some aspects were less, some more prominent than elsewhere. The economy, for instance, benefited from West German direct or indirect involvement and managed to provide for the population better than in Poland. Corruption was probably less rife than in Romania, although revelations since October 1989 showed that the apparent sea-green incorruptibles of the party leadership were anything but that. The party apparatus, the official dogma, and the police state were very highly developed, with little room for manoeuvre for the individual. Most importantly, though, the population was literally walled in, with only limited opportunities to travel to allied states.

These tensions within the system were kept under control by allowing or forcing emigration of persistent critics, by maintaining low staple prices at high cost, and by regimenting and spying on the population at all junctures. The attempt was made to generate a new national GDR identity through sporting triumphs and a manipulation of German history. It cannot be denied that the policy of the regime enjoyed some degree of success, and it has been clear since the *Wende* (turning point) that there were many in the GDR who wished to retain important aspects of socialized production and the welfare state. Many more took some pride in the achievements of the GDR and resented being regarded as the poor cousins of the West Germans. What rankled, however, was the feeling that, by not allowing free travel or free comment, the regime treated the population as children, not as adults. This impression was frequently articulated in church circles, the only forum with any degree of autonomy and the original focus of the peace movement earlier in the 1980s and the demonstrations of 1989.

The GDR was squeezed from two sides. The example of the Federal Republic was everpresent on the television screens in most of the GDR and also in family and friendships contacts. It also kept alive more than anything else the frustration of not having freedom of travel. From the mid-1980s a new ingredient was added: the spectacle of political openness and reform emanating from the USSR and taken up in Poland and Hungary.

In mid-1989 several events took place which hastened change. Communal elections were held in May, and the authorities made great play of new regulations which allowed foreigners the right to vote and to stand for election, and which permitted groups other than the established parties to put forward names for candidature. This latter concession meant nothing in practice, but it had excited some expectations, and opposition groups braved the police in an attempt to monitor for themselves the probity of the elections. The official results did show a significant increase in the registration of opposition to the unitary official list, but maintained the fiction of near unanimity. That it was a fiction was clear from the gross discrepancy between the observations of the unofficial monitors and the final counts. For the first time there was noticeable public indignation about the fraudulence of the "democracy" in the GDR. In June indignation was mixed with fear as the citizenry of the GDR saw West German coverage of the Tiananmen Square massacre and GDR reports approving the Chinese leadership's response. Egon **Krenz**, who had just been in charge of the electoral commission, was sent to Beijing to give congratulations in person. All pronouncements by leading party figures — Erich and Margot Honecker, Kurt Hager, Joachim Herrmann, Günter **Mittag** and others — were to the effect that nothing was going to change in the GDR, and by supporting the Chinese they implied that violence would be used if necessary. They had now displayed fully their contempt for the freedoms growing in allied states and for their own population. In one sense their stance was quite logical; they knew that reform in the GDR would mean the end of the GDR, and they were right.

The month of July 1989 shook the GDR in two ways. On July 8 illness forced Erich Honecker to return home early from the Warsaw Pact summit in Bucharest. In his absence from the forefront there followed a period of drift as dialogue between the two Germanies all but ceased. This was critical, since July also saw the beginnings of a mass exodus of GDR citizens via the Hungarian-Austrian border. Thousands became tens of thousands as the Hungarians lifted all restrictions on Sept. 10, and these were joined in the Federal Republic by others who had fled through Poland and Czechoslovakia. As significant, though, were the demonstrations in cities of the GDR, particularly in Leipzig, by those who declared that they wanted to stay but that they wanted reform. "We are the people", was the slogan chanted.

In the face of all this, the SED regime prepared the grandiose celebrations of the 40th anniversary of the GDR on Oct. 7. This exercise, far from bolstering the regime, helped to finish it. Erich Honecker, now remarkably recovered, jumped up and down with excitement, but received a clear enough indication from his main guest, Mikhail Gorbachev, that resisting change was fatal. East Berlin was practically sealed off from the outside world for fear of coverage of unwelcome events. Away from the official ceremonies, the first week of October saw swelling demonstrations and brutal police intervention, notably in Leipzig, Dresden, and East Berlin. Only on Oct. 9 was a march of 70,000 allowed to proceed unhindered in Leipzig. In Dresden and Leipzig SED officials began to talk with opposition representatives.

Within the SED leadership Egon Krenz, Gunter **Schabowski** and others had already begun to scheme the ouster of Honecker, Mittag and Herrmann, and on Oct. 18, Krenz took over as party secretary. Far from bringing the process of change to an end, however, the mass demonstrations grew remorselessly, until around one million marched on the streets of East Berlin on Nov. 4. The exodus from the country continued, but the main pressure was now from those who demanded thorough-going democratic reform. On Nov. 7 the Stoph government resigned, the next day a new Politburo was elected and included for the first time Hans **Modrow**, and on Nov. 9 Schabowski announced at a press conference that GDR citizens could henceforth travel without hindrance. In advance of the official introduction of this measure the following morning, East Germans rushed to border crossings in Berlin and elsewhere and effectively forced the frontier open themselves.

From that point millions of East Germans visited the Federal Republic. Most returned home, but the steady haemorrhage of population continued into the first months of 1990, when 2,000 a day were leaving. This caused a dramatic downturn in the GDR economy, whose previous performance was in any case now admitted to be a fabrication by Mittag and his associates. The social and health services in the GDR also began to collapse as trained personnel moved westward.

Egon Krenz attempted to belie his former hardline image and promised far-reaching changes in every aspect of life in the GDR. He refused, however, to countenance the demands for German unification which were starting to be heard in the continuing mass demonstrations and he clung to the basic socialist structures of the society and economy. Meanwhile the real authority in government moved to the new prime minister, Hans Modrow. On Dec. 6 Egon Krenz was deprived of his party and state functions, and three days later Gregor **Gysi** was elected chairman of the SED, which subsequently change its name to **SED-PDS** and abandoned its monopoly of power in the GDR.

Round table discussions between government and opposition groups commenced on Dec. 7, and agreed that elections would be held in May 1990. These were later brought forward to March 18, as the crisis in the GDR and the urgency of negotiation with the Federal Republic became pressing. When in February Hans Modrow himself admitted the inevitability and desirability of German unity, the path for the GDR became clear; it was soon to be subsumed in a larger Germany. What was far from clear was which mechanisms could be devised to halt the outflow of people from the territory of the GDR, to regulate currency exchange, to rebuild the East German economy and to place a new Germany within the context of international power relations.

The elections of March 18, 1990 brought a radical change to GDR politics. Contrary to early indications, the conservative parties reached agreement on an electoral "**Alliance for Germany**" and, with massive support from the West German CDU and CSU, romped to victory. The CDU gained 40.8 per cent of the vote and the DSU 6.3 per cent. The once hopeful SPD limped behind the CDU with 21.9 per cent, while the PDS (the former SED) performed creditably with 16.4 per cent. The result did not, however, give the CDU and its allies an absolute majority in the 400-seat *Volkskammer* (CDU: 163 seats; DSU: 25; **Democratic Departure (DA)**: four), let alone the two-thirds majority required for constitutional change. CDU leader Lothar **de Maizière** therefore began negotiations on a grand coalition drawing in the Liberals (21 seats) and the SPD (88 seats). The CDU triumph seems to have represented a large vote for German unity and decisive rejection of the Communist past. It was particularly strong in the southern regions of Saxony and Thuringia, which had had before 1933 a long Social Democratic tradition and which had spearheaded the revolution of 1989. Whether the CDU can hold onto this backing through the travails of forging German unity is open to question.

JO

GERMAN SOCIAL UNION (DSU—Deutsche Soziale Union). The DSU is a new party of the right in the GDR, founded in **Leipzig** in mid-January 1990, by Hans-Wilhelm Eberling, pastor at the Thomaskirche. It stands for German unity, Christian values, and a restoration of the old *Länder* in the territory of the GDR. The significance of the DSU is that it proposes to seize political ground from the old National Front parties, especially the **Christian Democratic Union of Germany (CDU)** and the **National Democratic Party of Germany (NDPD)**. The DSU quickly gained support from the CSU in Bavaria, one of Chancellor Kohl's coalition partners in Bonn, and then helped to form the **Alliance for Germany** electoral pact. In March 1990 the DSU was overshadowed by the success of the CDU, but scored a respectable 6.3 per cent of the votes and 25 *Volkskammer* (parliament) seats.

JO

GHEORGHIU-DEJ, GHEORGHE. Former Romanian party leader. He was born in 1901 and joined the Communist Party in 1930. Having spent the war in prison he led the **Romanian Communist Party** (then under another name) from 1944 to 1965, as head of its "nationalist" faction (though the real leader may have been Ana Pauker, who was purged in 1952). Gheorghiu-Dej pursued a "Romania first" policy in industrialization. He died in March 1965.

RH

GIEREK, EDWARD. Born January 1913 in Silesia (Katowice province) to a mining family. After his father's death in a mining accident he emigrated with his mother in 1923 to France where, from the age of 13, he also worked as a miner. He became active in the trade union movement and in 1931 joined the French Communist Party (PCF). Arrested in 1934 after a miners' strike, he was deported to Poland. In 1937 he again emigrated and took up employment in Belgium as a miner, once more joining the local Communist party and later taking part in the resistance movement under the German occupation. After World War II he organized Polish and Communist support activities and returned in 1948 to Poland, where he was employed in the organization of the Polish Workers' Party (PPR) Central Committee. In 1949 he returned to Katowice as a secretary of **Polish United Workers' Party (PUWP)** provincial committee and began studies at the Cracow Mining and Metallurgy Academy where he gained an engineering diploma.

In 1954 he was elected to the Central Committee and appointed to its apparatus as director of the Department of Heavy Industry. In 1956 he became a CC secretary and joined the Politburo, and in 1957 was directed back to Katowice to act as first secretary of the provincial committee.

From 1952 he was a deputy to the *Sejm*. It was in Katowice, during the period of Wladyslaw **Gomuɫka**'s rule, that his national reputation was made and he became known as an efficient manager of the leading modern industrialized region of Communist Poland. Wages were certainly higher in Katowice and the shops better stocked with consumer goods, as mining and heavy industry were favoured in the distribution process affecting consumption as they were in the sphere of investment and capital goods. It was only later realized that this pattern of development brought appalling costs in terms of pollution and its affect on public health, and that the privileged status of Katowice's inhabitants rested on an insecure base.

His ambitions were not restricted to the Katowice region, though, and it became clear during the political conflicts of 1968 that he was likely to play a major part in the looming succession struggle. In the immediate aftermath of the workers' demonstrations of December 1970 he was appointed PUWP first secretary. He was seen as being not only more efficient and attuned to the needs of a modern industrial Poland but also, with his lengthy experience as a miner, closer to the needs and demands of the working people than the aloof Gomuɫka. This proved to be ironic as Gierek introduced organizational changes in the party and goverment which increased the isolation of the top leadership and he adopted an economic policy which involved taking on extensive foreign debts which helped to take the Polish economy into a state of major crisis by the end of the decade. While making use of his foreign experience during the atmosphere of detente in the 1970s his efforts ultimately bore little fruit in either political or economic terms.

After the failure of his attempt to raise food prices in 1976 he took further measures to achieve this in July 1980, setting off in response a wave of strikes to which he initially took a cool attitude, allowing local leaders to make ad hoc agreements and grant pay rises to the workers. This strategy did not succeed and the strikes took on a major national dimension, the attitudes of their participants hardening in major industrial centres like **Gdańsk**. Gierek proved to be unable to master the crisis and, having dropped several of his former colleagues at the IV CC Plenum on Aug. 24, suffered a heart attack in early September and was replaced as first secretary at the VI Plenum on Sept. 5, 1980 by Stanisɫaw **Kania**. As a token of the even-handedness of General **Jaruzelski** in introducing the **State of War** he was "interned" in December 1981, although under conditions rather different from those experienced by most **Solidarity** activists.

PGL

GLASNOST' ("openness" or "publicity"). Secrecy is a very well-established Russian tradition. In Tsarist times not only only military but also quite harmless social information was withheld from the population at large, and especially from foreigners. The Bolsheviks briefly abolished secret diplomacy and other customs of the past when they came to power, and indeed there was consternation in Allied capitals when they published the annexationist secret treaties on which the conduct of the war had been based. Older practices, however, soon reasserted themselves, and for many Western students of Soviet affairs control over the flow of information came to represent a basic element in the Communist system of power (it was, for instance, one of the issues about which Soviet negotiators were most concerned during their dealings with the Czech reformists in 1968). Western journalists have generally been compelled to live within a separate foreigners' compound and operate under great restrictions; Soviet official statistics, until recently, left out whole areas of social and economic life from crime and mortality rates to balance of payments and road accident data; and the official media, at least until the early 1980s, typically presented an almost unvarying diet of champion milkmaids and heroic shockworkers marching forward to a fully Communist society in contrast to the unemployment, poverty and hopelessness of the capitalist West.

Although this picture was already beginning to change in the 1960s, it was not until **Gorbachev**'s accession that shortcomings in the official media —and indeed in the quality of Soviet public life in general—became the object of close attention at the very highest levels of the leadership. From the outset Gorbachev committed himself to a policy of openness or *glasnost'*, embracing not only the printed media but also radio, television and all areas of the creative arts. There were several reasons for this change. In the first place, Gorbachev appears to have believed that *glasnost'* would of itself help to bring about a more energetic and constructive atmosphere in the Soviet workplace and thus to reverse the economic stagnation of the later **Brezhnev** years. "Broad, up-to-date and honest information", he told a conference in December 1984, "is a sign of trust in people, respect for their intelligence and feelings, and their ability to make sense of developments". Equally, it raised the level of labour activism, reduced bureaucracy and helped to avoid errors in party and state work. "The better the people are informed", he told the Central Committee that elected him, "the more consciously they act, the more actively they support the party, its plans and programmatic objectives". People, he wrote in his *Perestroika*, "should know what is good, and what is bad, too, in order to multiply the good and combat the bad"; *glasnost'* would help them to gain a better understanding of the Soviet past and present, and "on the basis of this understanding, to participate in the restructuring effort consciously".

The monotony and other failings of the official media had in any case attracted a lot of public criticism. The daily paper *Sovetskaya Rossiya* reported the case of V.D. Polyakov of Kaluga, a well-read man who followed the central and local press and never missed the evening TV news. He knew in detail what was happening in various African countries, Polyakov complained, but he had "only a very rough idea of what was happening in his own city". After studying a file of the local paper, *Sovetskaya Rossiya*'s correspondent had to agree: he couldn't find an answer to a single one of the questions of public interest that Polyakov had raised. Nor was this an isolated case. In the Black Sea resort of Pitsunda, for instance, the peace of an August evening had suddenly been broken by a series of explosions. Frightened holidaymakers tried in vain to find out what had happened, and rumours spread rapidly. But not a word of explanation appeared in the local paper, though it did find the space to cover an unprecedented flood in South East Asia, a volcanic eruption in Latin America and a train collision in France. It eventually emerged, from a Moscow rather than a local publication, that Soviet sailors, at considerable risk to their lives, had been disarming some German bombs that had been left behind after World War II. In October 1985, another correspondent wrote in the same paper a few months later, there was a major earthquake in Tadzhikistan in Soviet Central Asia, but no details were made known other than that "lives had been lost". At about the same time there had been an earthquake in Mexico and a volcanic eruption in Colombia; both were covered fully with on-the-spot reports, including details of the casualties that had been suffered. Was Tadzhikistan further from Moscow than Latin America?

Readers and journalists also began to complain that when information was provided, particularly from abroad, it was too often partial and inaccurate. Soviet journalists, as the commentator Fedor Burlatsky pointed out in early 1987, had allowed a series of "gaps" to appear in their reporting of such matters. They had had little to say, for instance, about the "new technological revolution" that was taking place in Japan and the West based upon advanced electronics, or about the emergence of newly industrialized states in the developing world. There would, he believed, be no industrial revolution in the USSR itself so long as Soviet people compared their efforts, not with the best that had been achieved elsewhere, but with what earlier Soviet generations had accomplished as long ago as 1913. Soviet reporting on the Third World was particularly unhelpful, wrote D. Vol'sky, another contributor to the debate. The developing world had turned out to be far more complicated and heterogeneous than Soviet journalists had depicted it, although the truth of this fact tended to become apparent only after the event (after, for instance, the fall of the left-inclined Ne Win administration in Burma). Only then, complained Vol'sky, did it become known that the "national patriotic forces", on coming to power, had behaved like feudal or even pre-feudal princes, that "important industrial projects" had been undertaken to indulge their vanity, and that "progressive transformations" had often led to economic catastrophe and in turn to their own downfall.

The point was not simply that the official media were silent or one-sided on many issues of the day. The truth, as the daily paper *Sovetskaya Rossiya* pointed out, would eventually emerge. The problem was that if those who were responsible failed to explain the real state of affairs at the earliest opportunity, it would be replaced by gossip, conjecture and exaggeration. The shortcomings of the official media, in particular, encouraged a greater degree of interest in Western radio and TV broacasts than would otherwise have been the case. Perhaps 2 per cent of the Soviet population were able to listen to foreign radio broadcasts in 1940 and about 8 per cent could do so by 1950, it has been estimated, but about 50 per cent of the population were able to do so by the 1970s. The BBC alone was estimated to have at least 18 million regular listeners in the USSR in the late 1980s, when jamming was suspended; the foreign radio audience as a whole was estimated at about 67 million, a significant proportion of the adult (and still more of the urban and better-educated) population. Viewers in the Baltic and some other peripheral areas had direct access, in addition, to foreign television programmes, which they generally preferred to domestic ones. The danger of failing to report fully and promptly on the whole range of foreign and domestic developments was that, increasingly, the information deficit would be satisfied by "foreign voices with anti-Soviet overtones", as *Sovetskaya Rossiya* put it.

The poor quality of official information contributed towards a still more serious outcome: inadequate discussion of policy alternatives, ill-considered decisions and in some cases wasteful and damaging "projects of the century", such as the Baikal-Amur mainline railway across Siberia, completed in 1985, or the ambitious plan to divert the Siberian rivers southwards, finally abandoned in 1987 (the same ministry, *Izvestiya* reported, had even made plans to irrigate the Sahara desert). Some of these issues were taken up in an article on Soviet sociology by the head of its professional organization, Tat'yana Zaslavskaya, early in 1987. The problem, Zaslavskaya wrote, was not simply the poor state of Soviet sociology in comparison with the position in Eastern Europe, let alone the USA. Still more serious was the quality of public information: the census had become a steadily less useful source of data on social development since the late 1950s, and whole areas—crime, suicide, the distribution of income, drug abuse, alcohol consumption and environmental pollution in the major cities and republics—were omitted from official sources. The USSR, she charged, held one of the last places in the world among developed nations in the provision of social statistics, and things had become worse in the late 1970s when several categories of information (such as inter-regional and urban-rural migration) had disappeared entirely from published sources. If people, she argued, were denied information on the conditions under which they lived, they would hardly assume a more active role in public life; and if sociological "feedback" was ignored there would be more mistaken decisions by the authorities. It was considerations of this kind—to activate the "human factor" and to avoid costly errors—that appear to have contributed most directly to Gorbachev's commitment to *glasnost'* in all fields of public and cultural life.

Glasnost', under Gorbachev, led to a steady widening of the range of legitimate public debate and of the sources of information that were available for such purposes. One of the most notable of the changes related to the Soviet past occurred where a series of figures that had previously been ignored or denigrated – Bukharin and **Trotsky** were prominent examples—began to be restored to historical record. Many episodes of the Soviet past, from collectivization to the revolution itself, began to be discussed more openly and in many cases with the participation of foreign historians; and Russian pre-revolutionary writers, even open opponents of the early Soviet regime, became available again in libraries and in journals. No less important, the quality of public information steadily improved, particularly so far as official

statistics were concerned. As Zaslavskaya and others had remarked, the quality of public information had steadily deteriorated over the Brezhnev period as problem after problem was "resolved" by simply discontinuing the publication of any information about it. The census, for example, has always been a vital instrument for planners and government officials as well as for social scientists. Under Brezhnev, however, it became steadily less useful; the 1979 census was published five years after it had taken place. The annual statistical handbook, similarly, became slimmer and slimmer as the 1970s progressed, as social problems—such as a fall in life expectancy—were "resolved" by the simple expedient of ceasing to publish information about them.

A very different approach to the provision of information has been followed in the Gorbachev era under a central statistical administration which has itself been given a new name—the USSR State Statistics Committee—and a new head, appointed in 1987. In one of the most notable developments, the annual statistical handbook reversed the diminishing trend of the 1970s and became larger and more detailed. The first "Gorbachev" issue, published in 1986, was almost 30 pages larger than its predecessor; more important, it contained a wealth of information that had not been available for some time. Figures for infant mortality, for instance, were again reported: at 26 per thousand live births they compared poorly with those for the development capitalist nations, although there were enormous regional disparities. Life expectancy figures returned were 64 for men and 73 for women; though an improvement on the figures belatedly provided for the late 1970s, they were still up to 10 years less than those for other industrial nations. Later issues continued this improvement in the quality and quantity of date provided; particularly welcome was a more rigorous approach to definition and an attempt to secure greater international comparability. The annual handbooks were followed from late 1988 by a series of sectoral volumes dealing with population, labour, industry and so forth, some of them containing data last reported in the 1920s.

The handbook on population, for instance, published in 1988, contained the first-ever systematic data on abortions in the USSR (*see also* **Women's Issues**). The figures reported were, by international standards, remarkably high. There were 101.2 abortions for every thousand women aged between 15 and 49 in 1986, it emerged, and still more in the RSFSR and other European republics. As an article in the weekly paper *Nedelya* pointed out, the rate of abortions in the Russian Republic was about 25 times higher than it was, for instance, in West Germany, and several times higher than the rate in Britain and the USA. There was a similar degree of openness about other social problems, such as prostitution, drugs, crime and juvenile delinquency. The first useful figures for troop and weapon numbers appeared in early 1989; the same year saw the first meaningful figures for Soviet military expenditure (about four times as high as those that had been previously reported), and the first figures for the Soviet foreign debt and the cost of the war in Afghanistan. Many previously unpublishable writers returned to the pages of Soviet books and journals, including Pasternak and **Solzhenitsyn**, and there was a greater degree of interaction with the outside world, including live interviews of visiting politicians and "telebridges" between Soviet and foreign studio audiences.

Asked in a poll in 1989 what had been the most important outcome of **perestroika**, the largest single group of respondents cited "*glasnost*', truthfulness of information in the press, radio and television". Economic reform — the transfer of enterprises of self-financing and new forms of management — came second with 54 per cent, and changes in the government and electoral system came third with 46 per cent. It was, of course, much easier to allow the publication of (for example) *Doctor Zhivago* than to fill the shops with foodstuffs. And yet the scale of the change, in just three or four years, was remarkable. As Andrei **Sakharov** — whose release from administrative exile at the end of 1986 was in itself a notable development — put it, the authorities themselves were now publishing things for which people would a short time previously have been arrested. The new changes were clearly popular — Soviet newspapers and journals, for example, increased circulation, some at a spectacular rate, and there was an estimated fall of about half in the number of Soviet citizens who regularly listened to Western radio broadcasts.

These changes notwithstanding, there was much about the operation of *glasnost*' in the late 1980s that was precarious, ambiguous and incomplete. *Glasnost*', in the first place, did not and was not intended to mean an unqualified "freedom of the press". The word itself meant "publicity", or an explanation of the decisions that had been taken, at least as much as "openness", or the ability to challenge them; it was possible to be controversial in support of *perestroika*, but not (broadly speaking) against it. Indeed it was sometimes easy to forget the extent to which the press, radio and TV continued to conform to longstanding Soviet conventions. The front page of *Pravda* on a random date (Nov. 21, 1987) was reasonably typical of at least the earlier Gorbachev years.

The top right-hand corner carried a report of the previous day's Politburo meeting. The main feature, under the heading "Continuing the cause of October", pictured a veteran party member enrolling a new recruit, a statue of Lenin and a champion furnace-worker from Western Siberia. Another lead story, "They light the creative sparks", dealt with a family of metal workers in Kaluga, three of whose members — a father and his two sons — had received medals for their production achievements. "News from Orbit" dealt with the scientific spacecraft "Peace" on which Yuri Romanenko and Alexander Alexandrov were continuing their work and "feeling fine". At the bottom of the page, "Universal Interest" described the reception of Gorbachev's book *Perestroika* in London, Ottawa and Brasilia. For at least one Soviet citizen, writing in *Pravda* at the end of 1986, there was nothing in the papers apart from leaders' speeches that could not have appeared some 10 or 20 years earlier. And it was certainly difficult to find, even in academic quarterlies and the most controversial weeklies, any direct criticism of **Lenin**, the October Revolution, the party's leading role or of its leaders individually.

There were several other areas in which press discussion and criticism, though it existed, was muted and intermittent. The then editor of *Pravda*, Viktor Afanas'ev, speaking to the 6th Congress of Journalists in March 1987, singled out several of these continuing "'forbidden zones' for criticism" in his address. One of them was the Soviet space programme (in common, it may be remarked, with its counterparts in some Western countries). The spaceships were invariably "working normally", the cosmonauts were always "feeling fine". And yet work in space was well known to be dangerous and heroic. Another "forbidden zone" was the environment, where a great many meetings were necessary before articles could be cleared for publication. Only with great difficulty and with the personal intervention of a Central Committee Secretary, Afanas'ev revealed, had *Pravda* been able to "push through" its articles on the pollution of Lake Baikal and on the scheme to divert the Siberian rivers southwards. All kinds of methods were used to pre-empt criticism. The local party secretary, for example, might take the earliest possible opportunity to criticize the central press so that any subsequent publications could be presented as revenge. Articles in the press might also be ignored. The most common response, however, was a purely formal one, acknowledging the substance of the criticism but failing to take any practical steps to deal with the problem that had been identified. And "preventive measures" were also practised, including phone calls to the editor and threats of dismissal to the journalists in question.

Several other topics proved particularly controversial in the early Gorbachev years. One of them was the "special schools", in which a particular emphasis was placed upon the sciences or (more commonly) a foreign language. In many of these schools, as the Moscow local paper discovered, there was a very high concentration of the children of officials, and the schools themselves were concentrated in certain districts of the capital where the bulk of the population was made up of senior government employees and white-collar professionals. The children came to school in official cars, and the schools themselves were sometimes "palaces" with fountains and swimming pools. The paper came under very heavy pressure from "influential papas" to drop its investigation, and the subject largely disappeared from newspaper columns after this particular episode had been concluded. Another difficult subject was the related issue of privilege. One of the earliest sensations in the press in the period after Gorbachev's accession was an article entitled "Cleansing", which made it clear that there was widespread concern about the abuses of position that had become particularly marked during the later Brezhnev years. He had become convinced, wrote one of *Pravda*'s correspondents, that an "immobile, inert and viscous 'party-administrative stratum'" had formed between the party and the working class, which was by no means interested in radical change. Another reader pointed out that social inequalities had been deepened by party, state and other officials who had taken advantage of "all kinds of special canteens, special shops, special hospitals and so forth". By all means let managers earn more than ordinary workers, if they deserved it; but they should stand in line for goods like everyone else.

Glasnost' also registered some signal failures. The failure to report fully and promptly on the nuclear explosion at **Chernobyl** was an early example. The explosion, the world's worst nuclear disaster to date, took place early on the morning of Saturday April 26, 1986. On the Monday morning Swedish monitoring stations reported heightened levels of radiation and traced the source to the Ukraine. The first official Soviet response was the Monday evening TV news, which included a brief announcement that an "accident" had taken place at the Chernobyl plant, that one of the reactors had been "damaged" and that aid was being given to those who had been injured. A longer bulletin the following evening gave a fuller version of the events and reported for the first time that lives had been lost.

The first press reports referred similarly to "dangerous conditions" rather than radiation, and it took more than a fortnight for the story to reach the front page of *Pravda*. Gorbachev's first public response was a TV broadcast on May 14, nearly three weeks after the explosion had occurred. Four years later the full facts, including the detailed report that was presented to the International Atomic Energy Agency, had yet to be presented to the Soviet public. The media response to the Nagorno-Karabakh conflict in 1988 was also incomplete and belated: the first reasonably full picture was given in an extended TV documentary on April 26, 1988, itself incorporating some of the amateur footage that had been seen for at least two months on TV screens in the West.

Glasnost' was accordingly, at best, in its early stages by the end of Gorbachev's first five years of office. Some taboos remained, although many fewer than had been the case under his predecessors. The central press was much more enterprising than its local counterparts, where officials preferred a "pocket editor" to one inclined to challenge their decisions. *Glasnost'* was very popular among intellectuals, less so among ordinary workers, and not at all to the taste of party and state officials at all levels, nearly all of whom complained of "sensationalism" and "irresponsibility" and some of whom pressed for journalists to be made legally answerable for the accuracy of their stories. Gorbachev personally enjoyed a close relationship with the press, and frequently drew editors and others into his confidence; but he took open issue with the editor of the weekly paper "*Arguments and Facts*" in late 1989 when it appeared to suggest that other figures in Soviet public life enjoyed greater popularity than he did, and there were still no adequate guarantees against political interference in the work of the media. The law on the press, published in December 1989 after three years of discussion, nominally abolished censorship other than for state security and established a limited "right of information" for the ordinary citizen, but publications still had to be "registered" and attempts to change the existing political and social system were explicitly prohibited. *Glasnost'*, for all its achievements, was a long way from an unqualified "freedom of the press"; its meaning in any instance depended upon the changing and precarious balance between "conservative" and "reformist" sentiment at every level of the society.

SLW

GLEMP, CARDINAL JÓZEF. Born to a peasant family in December 1929 in Central Poland

(Bydgoszez province). During World War II he worked as a farmhand and finished secondary school in 1950. He studied Polish language and literature before entering a seminary in Gniezno, being ordained in 1956 and then serving for two years as a parish priest. Between 1958 and 1964 he studied in Rome and took a double doctorate in canon law and civil law, then becoming an advocate to the ecclesiastical court of the Roman Rota. When he returned to Poland in 1964 he began work in Gniezno in the Metropolitan Curia and in 1967 transferred to **Warsaw** to work in the office of the Polish primate. He later became Cardinal Wyszyński's secretary and chaplain. Glemp also lectured at the Warsaw Catholic Theological Academy, continued to publish, and acted as a member of the episcopal commission on the revision of canon law as legal adviser to the primate's secretariat. In March 1979 he became Bishop of Warmia, based in Olsztyn.

Following the death of Cardinal Wyszyński, Glemp was in July 1981 named Archbishop of Gniezno and Warsaw and thus primate of Poland in succession to Wyszyński. The installation of the **State of War** later in 1981 placed the new primate in a highly sensitive situation that exposed him to some criticism. In a sermon preached on the day that martial law was announced (and later broadcast on television) he urged holding back from opposition as indignation and protest "may not yield the expected results...the exceptional nature of martial law is dictated by higher necessity, it is the choice of a lesser rather than greater evil". Emphasis was placed on keeping the lines of communication open with the military authorities and seeking a way out of the current conflicts through negotiation rather than conflict. Other members of the Church, though, were more keen to maintain a closer identity with **Solidarity** activists and Glemp was criticized by some priests for seeming to organize a joint programme with the military authorities.

In February 1983 he was made a Cardinal and later that year, in June, the Pope made a further visit to his home country, a presence that was interpreted both as a gesture of support for the position of the Polish Church under martial law and as an expression of sympathy for those who stood out against accepting the obvious realism of accommodating to the logic of military force. Controversy about Glemp's performance and attitudes did not abate with the ending of the State of War. In 1989 his behaviour concerning the Carmelite convent at Auschwitz and more general views on Polish–Jewish relations gained considerable publicity even amidst the drama surrounding the installation of a Solidarity-led government. Despite an international agreement

reached in 1987 to transfer the existing convent no effective action to implement it had been taken, and Glemp's reference to Jewish anti-Polish sentiments did not help the situation. Towards the end of 1989 he attracted further criticism for becoming a patron of the National Christian Party and making what some considered to be ill-advised remarks on the identity of Polish nationality and Catholicism in connection with this political association.

PGL

GOMUŁKA, WŁADYSŁAW. Born in February 1905 in Krosńo, Poland, after his father had returned from an unsuccessful attempt at settling in the United States. His education did not go further than primary school, after which he began work as a locksmith and became active in the trade union movement. From 1923 he held various posts in the union of the chemical industry, joined the socialist party in 1926 and the illegal Communist Party soon afterwards. Following several terms of imprisonment the party sent Gomułka in 1934 to the Lenin School in Moscow. Returning to Poland in 1935 he was again arrested and spent the following four years in prison, where his life was in far less danger than if he had stayed in Moscow at the height of the purges. At the onset of hostilities he escaped from prison and became active in the underground movement, becoming secretary of the newly founded Polish Workers' Party in 1942. After the death of its first two leaders he became First Secretary in November 1943.

When Soviet-sponsored groups set up a provisional Polish government in Lublin in the first area of modern Poland liberated by the Red Army Gomułka was made vice-premier and minister for the recovered territories, the lands of pre-war Germany allocated to Poland in recompense for the eastern areas taken by the Soviet Union. This provided him (and the Communists) with a major power base in the post-war years as they consolidated their hold over the country and squeezed non-Communist forces out of public life. In August 1948 Gomułka fell victim to the intensification of **Stalinism** in Eastern Europe and was accused of right-wing tendencies and nationalist deviation. Although ousted from the leadership of the **Polish United Workers' Party (PUWP)** and gradually removed from his official appointments his life was again spared and he ended up under arrest in 1951. Quietly released in 1954 his name again came up as possible candidates for inclusion in the party leadership were considered as a situation of growing urgency developed in Eastern Europe after **Stalin's** death and

Khrushchev's revelations at the XX Congress of the **Communist Party of the Soviet Union (CPSU)**.

Re-elected to the PUWP leadership in October 1956, Gomułka faced up to the hostile Soviet delegation headed by Khrushchev and persuaded them of the advisability of accepting the reconstituted Politburo. Seen at the time as a considerable victory of the Poles and a major turn away from Stalinist practices, the atmosphere of reform and political liberalization proved to be short-lived. Gomułka soon restored control over party revisionists and tightened the grip of the leadership over the press and public life. After a period of satisfactory economic growth in the late 1950s the economy also settled down to some years of stagnation and poor performance. Student and intellectual opposition coalesced with conflict within the PUWP in 1968 and was followed by extensive worker unrest in 1970, which provided the conditions for his removal from office on Dec. 22. He died in retirement on Sep. 1, 1982.

PGL

GORBACHEV, MIKHAIL SERGEEVICH. General Secretary of the **Communist Party of the Soviet Union (CPSU)** Central Committee from March 1985; Chairman of the USSR Supreme Soviet Presidium from 1988 to 1989; Chairman of the USSR Supreme Soviet from May 1989; President of the USSR from March, 1990.

Gorbachev was born, according to his official biography, on March 2, 1931 to a peasant family in the village of Privol'noe in the Stavropol territory in southern Russia. His mother still lives in the village of his birth, where she is reported to be a regular attender at religious services. Gorbachev's father was wounded in the war and he was brought up mainly by his grandparents. He worked first as a mechanic at a machine-tractor station, and then in 1950, with the help of his local party organization, enrolled in the Law Faculty at Moscow State University. Gorbachev was a Komsomol activist while at university, and joined the CPSU itself in 1952. He graduated in 1955, the first Soviet leader since **Lenin** to have received a legal training and the first to graduate from the country's premier university. The Czech Communist and later dissident Zdeněk Mlynář, who was his classmate and close friend at this time, later recalled Gorbachev's openmindedness and his enthusiasm for Hegel's dictum that the truth was "always concrete". His years near the front during the war, Mlynář believed, gave him appreciation of the human suffering involved, and he was ready even in 1952 to take issue with the purges (Lenin, he pointed out, had allowed his Menshevik opponents to emigrate).

After graduation Gorbachev returned to Stavropol where he worked in the Komsomol and party apparatus, later completing a correspondence course at Stavropol Agricultural Institute. In 1966 he became first secretary of the city party committee, in 1970 he was appointed to head the territorial party organization, and the following year he joined the Central Committee as a full member. In November 1978 Gorbachev replaced his mentor Fedor Kulakov in the Central Committee Secretariat, taking responsibility for agriculture. In November 1979 he became a candidate, and then in October 1980 a full member of the ruling Politburo. He was already a deputy to the USSR Supreme Soviet, and to the Supreme Soviet of the Russian Republic.

It is not customary for a Soviet leader to discuss his personal affairs with the mass media, but Gorbachev did venture some information on this subject when he was interviewed by the Italian Communist paper *L'Unità* in May 1987. His main weakness, Gorbachev believed, was that he had too many interests. He had enrolled in the law faculty at university, for instance, but had originally intended to study physics. He liked mathematics, but also history and literature. In later years he had turned more and more to the study of economics, while remaining interested in philosophy (this was not, to put it mildly, the intellectual background of his immediate predecessor, Konstantin **Chernenko**). Interest in the General Secretary's personal affairs was hardly satisfied by such revelations and there were further queries in the spring of 1989. Did Mikhail Sergeevich, for instance, like fishing? And why did *glasnost'* not apply to the person who had introduced it? Gorbachev obliged with some further information in an interview in a Central Committee journal later the same year. He earned 1,200 rubles a month, he explained, the same as other members of the Politburo. He had a considerable additional income from royalties and other sources (his book *Perestroika* alone appeared in more that 100 countries), but he had donated any earnings of this kind to the party budget and various charitable causes. Literature, theatre, music and cinema remained his hobbies, although he had less and less time to devote to them.

Apart from his relatively modest years and evident openmindedness, there were also some clues in Gorbachev's speeches before his assumption of the General Secretaryship as to the direction of policy he was likely to pursue. Perhaps the clearest indication of this kind was a speech Gorbachev delivered to an all-union conference on ideology in December 1984. The speech contained positive references to self-management, which Lenin had "never counterposed to Soviet state power", and drew attention to the various interests of different social groups and to the need for a greater measure of social justice (which had become a coded form of attack upon the **Brezhnev** legacy). There was enormous scope, Gorbachev went on, for the further development of the Soviet political system, and of socialist democracy. This was partly a matter of developing all aspects of the work of the soviets, and of involving workers more fully in the affairs of their own workplace. It was also a matter of securing a greater degree of *glasnost'* or openness in party and state life.

Gorbachev's electoral address of February 1985, made at a time when Chernenko's serious illness was widely known, repeated many of these themes, combining almost populist references to Soviet power as a form of rule "of the toilers and for the toilers" and to the need for the party "again and again to check its political course against the rich experience of the people" with more abrasive remarks about the need for self-sufficiency in enterprise management and for greater labour discipline. These speeches, in effect an election manifesto to the Central Committee "selectorate", made it clear that Gorbachev would continue **Andropov**'s emphasis upon efficiency and discipline but also that they would be placed within a broader framework involving democratic reform and a reassertion of the moral values that were, for Gorbachev, implicit in socialism. (For Gorbachev's subsequent career *see* **USSR**—Recent political developments.)

SLW

GORBACHEV, RAISA MAKSIMOVNA.

Wife of Mikhail **Gorbachev** and a member of the board of the USSR Cultural Fund. Raisa Maksimovna Titorenko was born, according to her official biography, in the town of Rubtsovsk in Siberia in 1932, the daughter of a railway engineer. She did well at school and then enrolled in the philosophy faculty of Moscow University. It was at university that she encountered the future General Secretary; if subsequent accounts are to be believed, they met during a class in ballroom dancing. The Gorbachevs married in 1953 and then moved to Stavropol two years later after their graduation. Raisa Gorbachev took the opportunity to pursue some sociological research into daily life in local collective farms, receiving a candidate of science degree (roughly equivalent to a Western doctorate) in 1967. After their return to the capital in the late 1970s she lectured for

some years at Moscow University. The Gorbachevs have a daughter, Irina, who was born in 1959 and who is a doctor by profession, and two grandchildren. Previous party leaders' wives have played a very discreet role in Soviet public life: it was not even known that **Andropov**'s wife was still alive until she appeared at his funeral in 1984. Raisa Gorbachev, however, swiftly came to play a prominent part in Soviet public life and especially in international affairs, where she became a Soviet "First Lady" accompanying the general secretary on his travels (even when, at Reykjavik, Nancy Reagan stayed at home). Her views are believed to exercise a strong influence upon the general secretary himself; they certainly discussed "everything" at home in the evenings, Gorbachev told an NBC interviewer in late 1987 in remarks which were censored for Soviet domestic consumption. Important as a role model for Soviet woman at home and abroad, her stylish dressing and expensive tastes also came in for criticism and they were reported to have been among the issues that were raised in Boris **Yel'tsin**'s attack on the leadership and its policies in late 1987.

SLW

GOTTWALD, KLEMENT. Czechoslovakia's first Communist Prime Minister, from 1946 to 1948, and its first Communist President, from 1948 to 1953, Gottwald was elected the Communist Party's General Secretary in 1929 and in that capacity was responsible for the Bolshevization of the party in line with the policy of the **Communist International (Comintern)**. His commitment between 1945 and the Communist takeover in February 1948 to a "Czechoslovak road to socialism" based on the country's parliamentary traditions won him a degree of popularity at home. In the end his overriding loyalty to Moscow, his part in imposing the Stalinist system in Czechoslovakia after 1948 and his responsibility for the political repression that followed, which culminated in the trial of 14 of his senior colleagues, including the Communist Party's then General Secretary, Rudolf Slánský, tarnished his political record. Born in 1896, he died on March 14, 1953 shortly after returning from **Stalin**'s funeral in Moscow.

GW

GREAT FATHERLAND WAR. The term used in the USSR to describe that country's participation in World War II from the Nazi invasion of June 1941 to the end of hostilities in 1945 (also known as the Great Patriotic War). Soviet losses, including at least 20 million men, were the heavi-

est sustained by any country in any war and greatly influenced the country's negotiators in seeking a post-war settlement that would strengthen the security of the USSR. More generally it continues to influence the country's demographic structure and it represents a powerful support for any leadership that appears to promise peace and security, although often on terms that other countries have found difficult to accept.

SLW

GROMYKO, ANDREI ANDREEVICH. Soviet politician and veteran foreign minister. Born 1909 in a village in Belorussia but a Russian by nationality, Gromyko trained as an economist in the 1930s and eventually, in 1956, completed a higher doctorate in economic science. In 1939, however, he entered the Soviet diplomatic service, becoming Soviet ambassador to the USA in 1943. Present at the establishment of the United Nations (and at many other wartime conferences, including Yalta), he became the Soviet representative in the UN Security Council from 1946 to 1948, serving thereafter as deputy and then first deputy foreign minister, and then from 1952 to 1953 as Soviet ambassador to Great Britain. From 1953 to 1957 again a first deputy foreign minister, he was then promoted to the foreign ministry itself and held the same position for nearly 30 years (to 1985). A party member from 1931, Gromyko became a candidate member of the Central Committee in 1952, and a full member between 1956 and 1959 and then continuously from 1961 until his resignation in 1989. Gromyko became a member of the ruling Politburo in 1973, in which capacity he directed **Brezhnev**'s programme of detente with the West although (Brezhnev told Western newsmen) he was less than enthusiastic about it.

Although it was Gromyko who proposed **Gorbachev** to the Central Committee as the new General Secretary in March 1985, Gromyko's career soon went into eclipse. In July 1985 **Shevardnadze** became foreign minister, an appointment which tended to strengthen Gorbachev's personal command of Soviet foreign relations, and Gromyko became head of state or chairman of the Presidium of the USSR Supreme Soviet, a largely ceremonial post he held until Gorbachev succeeded him in 1988. Gromyko left the Politburo in the same year, and was one of the large number of veterans who retired from the Central Committee itself in early 1989. Gorbachev, on his retirement from the presidency, went out of his way to praise Gromyko's record of public service, but there had already been open criticism of the Brezhnev–Gromyko

legacy in foreign policy, not only for specific decisions such as the intervention in Afghanistan, but also for its "dogmatism", "subjectivism" and undue reliance on military rather than political forms of security. There was nonetheless a full official funeral when Gromyko died shortly afterward, in July 1989. Gromyko published his memoirs in two volumes in 1988; they were felt to have dealt much too discreetly with the **Stalin** years, which had a disproportionately heavy impact upon the diplomatic service.

SLW

GRÓSZ, KÁROLY. General Secretary of the **Hungarian Socialist Workers Party (HSWP)** from May 1988 to October 1989. Grósz, born in 1930, began his political career as a party activist in Borsód County, and rose to be editor of the local daily newspaper. In 1961 he was promoted to Secretary of the HSWP Committee at Hungarian Radio and Television, and he moved on from there to become Deputy Head of the HSWP Central Committee's Department of Agitation and Propaganda in 1968. He had a brief spell as HSWP First Secretary in Fejér County in 1973–74, then returned to the Department of Agitation and Propaganda as its Head until 1979. He was then transferred back to Party regional work as Borsód County First Secretary, and was promoted in 1984 to the key post of First Secretary of the Budapest Party Committee. He thus became an important contender for the Party leadership as **Kádár** weakened; he had acquired a very firm base of political support in the party apparatus both at the centre and in the regions, and had a reputation as a tough character of hard-line convictions.

No doubt sensing a challenge to his power, Kádár moved Grósz to the post of Prime Minister in July, 1987, probably expecting thus to weaken Grósz's political influence. But Grósz used this as an opportunity to widen his support. He launched an energetic campaign of consultation with a wide range of expert and elite groups, declared himself more flexible on the question of reform and prepared to conduct a dialogue even with the unofficial opposition. His economic programme, presented to Parliament in September 1987, made a very favourable impact both at home and abroad with its frank and jargon-free criticism of the state of affairs. As a result, the prestige of the position of the Prime Minister and government was greatly enhanced at the expense of the party under the rapidly aging Kádár.

When Grósz took over from Kádár as party leader in May 1988, expectations of more effective policies to deal with the economic crisis were raised, but Grósz's new-found reforming vigour quite soon ran out of steam. His basic authoritarian political instincts began to reassert themselves and he lost public confidence and also encountered growing conflict with the increasingly radical reformist faction within the HSWP. In June 1989, his authority was significantly weakened when the Central Committee set up a four-man Presidium of the HSWP in which he had to share power with the radical reformers Rezsó **Nyers**, Imre **Pozsgay** and Miklós **Németh**. He was unable to accept the transformation of the HSWP into the democratic Hungarian Socialist Party at the special congress in October 1989, and instead allowed himself to become the focus, and unofficial leader, of various traditionalist Communist groups which have subsequently been working to re-establish the HSWP.

JB

GYSI, GREGOR. GDR politician, born 1948. Gregor Gysi was born in Berlin to a partly Jewish family. His father, Klaus Gysi, had been a Communist before the Nazi period and after the war rose within the **Socialist Unity Party of Germany (SED)** to become party secretary for religious affairs. A souring of relations with the churches, however, forced his resignation in July, 1988.

Gregor Gysi trained as a lawyer in the 1960s and joined the SED in 1967. From 1971 he practised as a lawyer and in 1988 became head of the council of lawyers' associations. He used his legal skills to defend dissidents in conflict with the authorities and this gave him a reputation for fair-mindedness and willingness to countenance reform. Gysi was a member of the group of party activists which engineered the downfall of **Krenz**, and he was a member of the temporary commission which succeeded him.

On Dec. 9, 1989, Gysi was elected to the unenviable post of Chairman of SED, and at the party congress waved a broom in the air to show his intentions. He led a party committee of 100 members, practically all of whom were new to the party leadership. Almost all of the old guard, including those who had instigated the *Wende* (turning point), were expelled from the party. Gysi tried to save the party by stressing its democratic potential (it changed its name to the PDS— Party of Democratic Socialism) and its break with the past. He fought a good election campaign in the circumstances, and the PDS emerged with 16.4 per cent of the votes and 66 seats.

JO

H

HAVEL, VÁCLAV. Czechoslovakian president, born in 1936, Havel sprang to prominence in the early 1960s as the leading playwright at the Theatre on the Balustrade (*Divadlo na Zábradlí*) in Prague with the political satires "The Garden Party" (*Záhradní slavnost*) in 1963 and "The Memorandum" (*Vyrozumění*), two years later. In 1968, he played a prominent part in debates over political reform, notably with an article "On the Theme of Opposition" in the Writers' Union weekly, *Literární listy*, in which he argued for a multi-party system as the only certain mechanism to prevent an abuse of power by government. After 1969 Havel's work was banned in Czechoslovakia although his later plays were presented in the west. One of the initial signatories of, and spokesmen for, **Charter 77**, he was also closely invloved with VONS (the Committee for the Defence of the Unjustly Persecuted), founded in 1978, and contributed to the *samizdat* literature on political themes. A repeated target for the regime because of his activities, Havel was imprisoned on a number of occasions but never wavered in his commitment to civil rights, tolerance and democracy. He was at the forefront of the demonstrations in favour of political reform in 1988 and 1989 and was a natural spokesman for the opposition movement during the pro-democracy protests in November 1989. He led the **Civic Forum** negotiators who forced the Communist Party to agree to the formation of a government with minority Communist participation on Dec. 10, 1989 and on Dec. 29 he succeeded Gustáv **Husák** as President of Czechoslovakia.

GW

HONECKER, ERICH. Former GDR statesman, born 1912. Honecker was the second political leader of the GDR. He succeeded **Ulbricht** at first secretary of the **Socialist Unity Party of Germany (SED)** in May 1971, became head of state (Chairman of the State Council) in 1976, and was forced out of office only in October 1989, after he officiated at the 40th anniversary celebrations of the state. Honecker supervised the entry of the GDR into the international community, while sparing little in the suppression of domestic political dissent. His dismissal began the revolutionary process which is moving towards the absorption of the GDR into a unified German state.

Erich Honecker was born in the Saar in western Germany to a Socialist then Communist mining family. In his autobiography he claims to have been impressed by the Russian Revolution, although he was only five years old at the time. He was involved in political acivities during his youth, joining the KPD (Communist Party of Germany) in 1929. In 1930–31 he was sent to train in Moscow. The accession of Hitler to power did not immediately affect the Saar territory, but Honecker was active in the *Reich* too, using several pseudonyms. He was arrested in 1935, and served 10 years' gaol in Brandenburg–Görden. After the war his career in the SED was solidly upwards: he chaired the party youth section, **Free German Youth (FDJ)**, from 1946 to 1955; he became a Politburo member in 1958 and was responsible for security and defence; in 1961 he supervised the construction of the Berlin Wall; he was Ulbricht's chosen successor, but in 1971 he was also Moscow's choice to replace his awkward mentor.

Honecker's years in power were characterized by apparent economic success, a much enhanced international profile for the GDR, and fluctuating phases of domestic accommodation and repression.

By the mid-1980s the official picture of the GDR economy presented by Honecker and his associates was of a major industrial state enjoying buoyant growth and moving rapidly into modern technologies. Much of this was a deception.

Honecker clearly enjoyed the role of international statesman, but his string of prominent visitors and his own visits abroad were intended to impress upon the domestic population the independence and international respectability of the GDR. This did increase as the GDR signed the Basic Treaty with the Federal Republic of Germany in 1972 and entered the United Nations in 1973. Honecker's rapprochement with the Federal Republic culminated in his official visit in September 1987. He also visited Paris and Rome, but was not allowed time to fulfil his ambition of being received in London and Washington.

At home Honecker appeared as a tough, ascetic, but not entirely cold character. He was prepared to be conciliatory on occasions, as with the churches from 1978, but individual or collective opposition was stamped on smartly. Honecker took a personal interest in censoring the press and in spying upon suspected dissidents. He enjoyed hunting, and revelation in 1989–90 of his numerous hunting lodges and other excessive perks of office caused resentment.

There were many signs of crisis in the GDR in the late 1980s, as **Gorbachev** sought change and the GDR economy faltered. Honecker's fall from power began when he had to return suddenly from Bucharest in the summer of 1989 for a gall bladder operation. During his enforced absence from the scene, GDR policy drifted in the face of mass exodus of GDR citizens via Hungary and Austria. Growing street protests and police brutality then followed, marring Honecker's triumphant celebration of 40 years of the GDR. His adamant resistance to change was now seen as a liability by Politburo colleagues and on Oct. 18, 1989 he was dismissed "on health grounds" and replaced by Egon **Krenz**, the man groomed by him for the succession. At first Honecker's exit seemed fairly dignified, but then he was arrested and expelled from the party. He faced corruption charges, but became seriously ill with cancer. Forced to leave the luxury party compound at Wandlitz, Honecker and Margot Honecker lived first in a church home for the elderly, until they were forced out by popular protest.

JO

HOXHA, ENVER. First Secretary of the Party of Labour (PLA) of Albania; born 1908 in the southern town of Gjirokastër.

In 1930, after attending the French Lycée in Korçë, Hoxha was awarded an Albanian government scholarship to study at the University of Montpellier; from there he moved to Paris where he joined the French Communist Party and published various articles in the French daily *L'Humanité* attacking the **Zog** government in Albania. After a spell as Secretary to the Albanian Consul in Brussels, he enrolled as a law student at the University of Brussels, but left before graduating.

In 1936 he returned to Albania and taught French at the Lycée in Korçë, where he joined the Puna (Labour) group of Communists. In 1941, when most Albanian Marxist groups were amalgamated under Yugoslav guidance to form the Albanian Communist Party, Hoxha became its Secretary General. When the Albanian National Liberation Movement was set up in 1942 Hoxha became the dominant figure, and was appointed Chief Political Commissar of the National Liberation Army.

When the People's Republic was proclaimed in 1946, he held the posts of Prime Minister, Minister of Defence and Foreign Minister. In 1953 he relinquished his government posts, preferring to rule through the party.

In 1948, after several years of internecine struggle with his Communist rival for power, Xoxe, the Soviet-Yugoslav quarrel gave Hoxha the opportunity to purge Xoxe and have him executed in 1949. By 1956, after several more rounds of purges, Hoxha was the only active member of the original 1941 Central Committee. When the Sino-Soviet dispute came to a head in 1960, Hoxha declared his party's support for China. Albania's rift with the USSR, contributed to by various circumstances including Hoxha's personality and his aspiration that Albania should achieve the maximum political and economic independence, followed. Chinese economic aid in part replaced Soviet. However, from 1972 onwards Hoxha showed his displeasure at China's overtures to the USA; by 1978, his party's newspaper *Zëri i popullit* was referring to the Chinese as "imperialists", whereupon China's aid to Albania was cut off. In the wake of her break with China, Albania constructed myriads of pillboxes; Hoxha capitalized on this by claiming that internal and external enemies perpetually threatened Albania's security, and thus succeeded in maintaining a totalitarian system.

Hoxha ensured a smooth transfer of power to Ramiz **Alia** by eliminating the strongest candidates in the struggle for power. The 1981 purges included Mehmet Shehu, the long-serving Prime Minister, Kadri Hazbiu, the Defence Minister, and Feçor Shehu, the Interior Minister.

Enver Hoxha is buried in the Martyrs' Cemetery overlooking **Tirana**. Numerous statues of him have been erected, for instance in Tirana (Scanderbeg Square) and Gjirokastër. Hoxha was survived by his wife Nexhmije, who on March 2, 1986, became chairman of the Democratic Front, which is Albania's mass political organization.

PA

HUMAN RIGHTS. Communist rule in the USSR and Eastern Europe has been widely recognized for its social and economic achievements, such as the elimination of illiteracy, low levels of unemployment, and comprehensive arrangements for education and health care. But there are very few, in the West at least, who would be inclined to argue that Communist governments have made a comparable contribution to the enlargement of human liberty. Marx had supposed, broadly speaking, that once capitalism — which was the last of the class-divided and antagonistic societies — had been replaced by socialism, there would be no more need for a separate administrative structure and the state could simply "wither away". In the USSR and the other Communist states of Eastern Europe, however, there has been little sign of a process of this kind: the Communist states, on the contrary, have been large, powerful and authoritarian institutions in which the rights and liberties of the citizen (as least in Western terms) have been systematically restricted.

The USSR and the East European states (at least until the late 1980s), however, did not claim to have constructed a form of democracy which conformed to Western liberal theory. On the contrary, they had and still have a democratic theory of their own, which in line with Marxist and some other older theories of democracy places far more emphasis upon the content of democracy rather than its form, and upon the socio-economic rights of citizens rather than their formal independence of state power. In terms of this theory (which is still upheld in the USSR, although largely abandoned by the post-Communist governments in Eastern Europe) the USSR and its Communist allies have constructed a society far more democratic than any that exists in the capitalist West, and one that offers a far wider range of genuine human rights to the mass of its citizens. Even in Western terms, moreover, there have been considerable variations in the extent to which individual liberties have been respected in the USSR and Eastern Europe, and there has been a slow but steady development of what is called "socialist legality", or the observance of established legal procedures, in all of these countries. An adequate assessment of human rights and democracy in the USSR and Eastern Europe must take account of all of these circumstances.

The Soviet and orthodox Communist theory of democracy and human rights is based upon classical Marxist theory, in terms of which there can be no "democracy" in the abstract but only particular forms of class democracy depending upon which social group owns the means of production and thereby, it is thought, holds political power in the society in question. In the Soviet Union, as in the other Communist ruled states, the means of production — factories, farms and so forth — belong to the people as a whole, and it is the working people, not a narrow and exploiting group, who control the national resources and make sure that they are used for the benefit of all members of the society. As the current edition of the *Great Soviet Encyclopaedia* puts it, bourgeois democracy, of the kind that exists in Western countries, is a "form of dictatorship of capitalists over proletarians and other semi-proletarian and non-proletarian working classes and strata of the population. It is characterized by a blatant contradiction between the declared 'power of the people' and the actual domination of the exploiters". In the USSR and the other Commu-

nist countries, on the other hand, there is "complete accord between the form and content of democratic institutions, laws etc. and the power of the workers".

These principles of socialist democracy, it is argued, are fully applied in the contemporary USSR, as in the other Communist-ruled states of Eastern Europe. All power in the USSR belongs, according to the constitution, to the people, who exercise it through the soviets of working people's deputies which they elect and which alone have law-making powers. The people, it is pointed out, are themselves well represented in these bodies, in line with the Soviet principle that working people should administer the state directly rather than leave it to a professional class of politicians. The soviets at all levels of the system (*see* **USSR**—State structure) are indeed representative of all sections of the nation; there were more women in the USSR Supreme Soviet in the 1980s, for instance, than in the British, French, Italian and American parliaments put together. It is of course accepted that the **Communist Party of the Soviet Union (CPSU)**, whose members are a small proportion of the total population, plays a "leading" or "guiding" role in the work of such state bodies. But, it is argued, workers and peasants constitute a majority of the party's members, and for them it is an instrument of rule, a means of ensuring that their interests are reflected in the policies pursued by the Soviet government. What could be more "democratic" than that?

The Soviet Constitution, it is argued, extends there principles further. Unlike the constitutions of capitalist states, which do no more that proclaim the rights of citizens in purely abstract terms ("the right of everyone to dine at the Savoy", though few will be able to afford to do so), the Soviet Constitution purports actually to provide the means by which the rights it contains can be enjoyed. The right to education, for instance (Article 45), is "guaranteed" by the free provision of all forms of education, by the payment of scholarships and grants, and in other ways. Similar means are provided by which the other rights mentioned in the constitution, such as the right to work, to housing, or to health care, can also be enjoyed in practice by all citizens. The constitution also provides and again formally guarantees a wide range of civil liberties, including freedom or speech, of the press, of assembly, of mass meetings and of street processions and demonstrations, which is supposedly guaranteed by "putting public buildings, streets and squares at the disposal of working people and their organizations, by the broad dissemination of information, and by the opportunity to use the press, television and radio" (Article 50). Similar rights are specified in other Communist constitutions.

Most of these rights, however, are qualified in various ways. The right of freedom of speech, of the press and of assembly, for instance, is guaranteed only in so far as it is "in accordance with the interests of the people and in order to strengthen and develop the socialist system". Any meeting or publication which is held to be unlikely to strengthen the socialist system may therefore quite legally be prohibited. The right of freedom of scientific, technical and artistic work and the right to associate in public organizations (Articles 47 and 51), similarly, are granted only in so far as they are "in accordance with the aims of building Communism". Further more general restrictions are contained in Article 39, which states that citizens' enjoyment of their rights must "not be to the detriment of the interests of society or of the state", and in Article 59, which states that citizens' performance of their duties and freedoms is "inseparable from the performance of their duties and obligations", including the duty to perform socially useful labour, to protect state property and to bring up their children to be "worthy members of socialist society". Nor can an interpretation of any of these points be taken to a Soviet court with any prospect of success, given the control that the authorities have had (and still had in the early 1990s) over their personal and individual decisions.

It would, of course, be wrong to suggest that the Western liberal democracies, still less the non-Communist world as a whole, are entirely above reproach in matters of human rights. In many Western countries, for instance, Communists (as well as right-wing extremists) are debarred from a variety of forms of public employments, including not only the police and diplomatic service but also (in some countries) teaching posts in secondary and higher education. The considerable costs of taking legal action, moreover, may make it difficult for many citizens to take advantage of the extensive civil rights with which they have theoretically been endowed, while the class origins and upbringing of judges in many Western countries may give at least the impression that cases involving (for instance) trade unions or the rights of private property will receive less than an impartial hearing. Nonetheless, as even Soviet and other Communist sources acknowledge, public pressure over the years has led to a series of concessions to popular demands in many of the capitalist countries, such as extensive civil and trade union rights, a substantial public sector in the economy and comprehensive non-contributory health

schemes. It would be difficult to give a comparable list of major measures of public policy that have been pushed through by public pressure against the wishes of the authorities in the USSR or the Communist-ruled states of Eastern Europe.

Indeed the whole area of popular control over executive action, whether in the party or the state or in other areas, is one in which Communist governments have been notably deficient. How, for instance, could a legislature such as the USSR Supreme Soviet, which met for only a few days a year, be expected to monitor the stream of decisions that flowed every day from the Soviet government and its agencies? (The establishment of a working parliament in 1989 was in part a recognition of this deficiency.) How could a Party Congress or a Central Committee be expected to hold the Politburo and Secretariat to account, when they met so infrequently and had in any case been largely selected by those bodies? And how could the press and mass media generally, which were controlled by the party and state authorities, be expected to permit regular and serious criticism of their activities?

The peoples of the USSR and the other Communist-ruled states, even before the changes of the late 1980s, were not entirely without means of influencing the governments that ruled in their name; but they lacked the ultimate sanction, a general election at which they could be removed from office. Communist leaders, for their part, were not simply protected from the whims of the electorate, but also disposed, through their control of the economy and the courts, of the means of depriving critics of their jobs and if necessary also of their freedom. In these circumstances it was not perhaps surprising that the USSR and Eastern Europe, their democratic and humanistic credentials notwithstanding, tended in practice to operate in an authoritarian and sometimes in a repressive manner. Entering the 1990s, it was widely acknowledged even in those states in which Communists still retained power that an answer to these problems was more likely to be found in the theory and practice of liberal democracy than in **Marxism-Leninism**.

SLW

HUNGARIAN DEMOCRATIC FORUM (HDF—Magyar Demokrata Fórum). The origins of this important Hungarian opposition movement date back to a meeting which took place on Sept. 27, 1987 at the home of Sándor Lezsák, a populist writer, in the village of Lakitelek in south-east Hungary. About 150 leading reform economists, social scientists, historians and writers gathered for a critical discussion of the state of the nation, the economic crisis, and the manifest failures of the government and the political system. Many of the participants were well-known members of the ruling **Hungarian Socialist Workers' Party (HSWP)**, and the meeting was addressed by the party's leading reformist, Imre **Pozsgay**. The original aim was to form a free discussion forum for intellectuals of all shades of opinion who were concerned with finding a way out of the mounting crisis. The HSWP leadership under János **Kádár** greeted this new autonomous movement with considerable hostility, and several of its adherents within the party were subjected to disciplinary measures in th early months of 1988.

After Kádár's removal from power, the conditions for open political activity became much easier, and the HDF held a formal inaugural meeting on Sept. 3, 1988, again at Lakitelek, with 364 members in attendance. It was now decided to transform the HDF from a loose-knit intellectual discussion club into a "political movement". The aim was said to be "to build a bridge between the state and society", to promote broad public discussion on key issues facing the country and to further democratic reform of the political system. But it was not intended to be a political party, nor to stand in opposition to the HSWP. It would, however, nominate candidates in future local and national elections. A nine-man presidium was elected, dominated by literary figures and historians well known for their populist views. Official permission was given for the movement to publish its own fortnightly magazine *Hitel* ("Credit").

The movement retained close links with reformers within the HSWP, and received a fairly warm official welcome and substantial media coverage. It was particularly prominent in subsequent months in its outspoken stance on the Danube Dam project and the position of the Hungarian minority in Romania (*see* **Hungarian Minorities**). By the time of its first National Congress, held in Budapest on March 11, 1989, it had gathered 15,000 members. The Congress was attended by a representative of the HSWP, by the speaker of the National Assembly, and by the Ambassadors of the USA and the UK and other diplomats. The 700 delegates attending amended the original statute of the movement to exclude HSWP members from holding leadership positions in the HDF, but there was continued uncertainty among the delegates as to whether the HDF should aim to become a political party. The populist-dominated leading group in the HDF strongly preferred to develop the movement as a force for consensus and national unity, and, for the time being, this view prevailed. However, as the movement grew, a greater diversity of views

appeared within it, and the originally dominant populist current was joined with liberal and Christian-Democratic currents which were more strongly oriented towards Western European models, and the transformation of the movement into a party became accepted as inevitable.

During the summer of 1989, the HDF put up candidates (with the support of the other opposition parties) in four parliamentary by-elections, and won each one convincingly against the official HSWP candidates. By late summer, the HDF seemed to be by far the most powerful and effective party in Hungary, and looked set to win a future general election. However, in September, sharp conflict between the HDF and other opposition parties, especially the **Alliance of Free Democrats (AFD)**, broke out at the "Triangular Discussions" at which major constitutional reforms were being negotiated. The source of the conflict was the controversial issue of the new presidency. The HDF broke ranks with the other opposition parties to side with the HSWP in favour of a directly-elected presidency. The AFD suspected a secret deal had been concluded between the HSWP and the HDF, according to which the HDF would support Imre **Pozsgay**'s candidacy for the presidency, and thus guarantee his election, in exchange for an HDF appointment to the post of Prime Minister. When the issue was put to a referendum in November 1989, the HDF urged its supporters to boycott the ballot. But both the level of the turnout and the results of the ballot were a blow to the HDF, demonstrating a certain popular mistrust of the HDF's continuing close links with the by now discredited ruling party. The forum, in the event, secured 42.7 per cent of the vote in the March–April 1990 general election, and its president, Jozsef **Antall**, became prime minister in an HDF-dominated government.

JB

HUNGARIAN MINORITIES. There are substantial Hungarian minorities living in Romania and Czechoslovakia. Concern at the position of these minorities on the part of the Hungarian government and Hungarian public opinion has given rise at various times to political tensions between Hungary and its neighbours. The most serious problems have arisen in Romania, where an estimated two million Hungarians live in the region of Transylvania, which was part of the Hungarian Crown lands until the end of World War I, and was ceded to Romanian by the Treaty of Trianon (1920). From the early 1970s, the Romanian regime of Nicolae **Ceauşescu** began to withdraw facilities for separate educational and cultural provision in the Hungarian language and to intro-duce various measures in administration, employ-ment and travel which were discriminatory against ethnic minorities. This was a result of the increasing emphasis on Romanian nationalism in the ideological legitimation of the Ceauşescu regime as it strove for increasing independence from the Soviet Union and the **Warsaw Treaty Organization (Warsaw Pact)**.

In the 1980s, as the economic situation in Romania worsened, Hungarians in Hungary became more and more worried about the plight of their co-nationals in Romania. The Hungarian government, which up until the 1980s had been careful to avoid upsetting relations with the Romanian regime and was wary about fomenting Hungarian nationalism, now began to respond to popular pressure on this issue, possibly intending to use this as a safety valve, given the mounting economic problems in Hungary too. This became particularly noticeable once Károly **Grósz** emerged as the new Hungarian leader. As the Hungarian press and political arena opened up from 1987 onwards, the issue became ever more prominent in Hungarian politics. In the course of 1987, about 10,000 Hungarians from Romania fled to Hungary and sought political asylum. In June 1988, an unofficial demonstration, in which an estimated 50,000 took part, was staged outside the Romanian Embassy in Budapest in protest against Ceauşescu's policy of "systematization" of villages (i.e. destroying traditional peasant dwellings, and with it peasant culture, under the guise of modernization of rural life). Károly Grósz attempted to negotiate with Ceauşescu to ease the tension in the two countries' relations at a meeting in Arad in August 1988, but his efforts were widely regarded by the Hungarian public as wholly ineffective, and led to a sharp drop in his standing in Hungary.

In March, 1989, Hungary joined Sweden in calling for a United Nations enquiry into human rights abuses in Romania, and at the same time applied for UN aid in dealing with problem of Hungarian-Romanian refugees, of whom there were by now estimated to be at least 20,000 in Hungary. Tension between Hungary and Romania again began to mount in late 1989 over the case of a Hungarian Calvinist pastor, László Tökés, from **Timişoara**, Transylvania, whom the Romanian authorities wished to evict from his home. On the weekend of Dec. 16–17, about 200 Hungarian parishioners demonstrated in Timişoara against the arrest of their pastor. This demonstration esca-lated into a massive general popular revolt, in which Romanians joined Hungarians, indicating a remarkable ineffectiveness in the authorities' use of nationalism as a means of social control.

The bloody repression with which the Romanian authorities met this demonstration (early esti-mates suggested as many as 4,000 people lost their lives in Timisoara) proved unsuccessful in suppressing the popular upsurge, and the events at Timisoara precipitated the downfall of the Ceauşescu regime only days later.

About 600,000 Hungarians also live in Czechoslovakia, the vast majority of them in Slovakia, where they constitute some 11 per cent of the population. Complaints about discrimina-tion against Hungarians and restricted cultural rights surfaced in the 1970s and 1980s, and a Hungarian spokesman, Miklós Duray, joined the Charter 77 human rights opposition movement. Contacts between this minority and Hungarians resident in Hungary have been relatively easy, particularly in comparison with the gross restric-tions imposed on similar contacts by the Romanian authorities, and the issue has not been a major source of friction between the Hungarian and Czechoslovak government.

JB

HUNGARIAN SOCIAL-DEMOCRATIC PARTY (HSDP — Magyarországi Szo-ciáldemokrata Párt).

One of the so-called "his-torical" parties of Hungary which existed in the pre-Communist period and have now reappeared in the current democratic ferment. The party was founded in December 1890 from the previously existing Hungarian General Workers' Party. It had a brief period of alliance with the Communist Party of Hungary under Béla Kun in 1919, which was a disaster for it. It reconstituted itself on Aug. 24, 1919 after the collapse of the Hungarian Soviet Republic. It was able to operate legally in the inter-war period, and its leaders were resolute in resisting Communist infiltration. It was closely linked with the trade union movement, and enjoyed strong support among the Budapest working class. At the end of World War II, after the liberation of Hungary in April 1945, the HSDP claimed a membership of 50,000, which rose rapidly to 400,000 by the year's end. It fought the free elections to Budapest Council in October 1945 in alliance with the Hungarian Communist Party, but decided to fight the November 1945 General Election on its own. It won 17.41 per cent of the vote, coming second to the massively successful Smallholders' Party and beating the Communist Party. It was particularly strong in Budapest.

This success made it a prime target for Com-munist "salami tactics". Many of the HSDP's leaders were strongly sympathetic to the Com-munists, and they worked from within to effect the merger with the HCP which took place in June 1948. While some Social Democratic politicians went on to have successful careers in the Hungarian Workers' Party, others fell victim to the Stalinist purges of the early 1950s. Those who refused to accept the merger and join the HWP also suffered political repression (if they did not succeed in fleeing the country).

The HSDP briefly reappeared in 1956, when Anna Kéthly, an opponent of the 1948 merger who now became the party leader, joined the coalition government of Imre **Nagy**. The HSDP was suppressed again after the Soviet invasion put an end to the revolution. One Nov. 28, 1988, an Interim Executive Committee of the Hungarian Social-Democratic Movement was set up, chaired by András Révész, who had been Kéthly's deputy in 1956. About 40 other survivors were also involved. The HSDP was formally re-established on Jan. 9, 1989. Potentially, it posed a great challenge to the HSWP, and an opinion poll in March 1989 showed it to enjoy the greatest popular support of any of the new opposition parties (13 per cent expressed a preference for it). However, it has been seriously damaged by bitter internal conflicts over the direction it should take. The old guard are deeply suspicious of the large number of younger recruits who have come from the HSWP, and in February 1989 they rejected the proposed leadership of the well-known political scientist Mihály Bihari, who had been a prominent reform Communist associated with Imre **Pozsgay**.

The older generation's understanding of "social democracy" is rooted in the radical but non-Soviet Marxism of a previous era, while the younger members look to contemporary West European models. They advocate a Western-style capitalist mixed economy with developed welfare state, free trade unions, and representative democracy. This division produced a split at a national congress in November 1989, when a minority broke away to form an Independent Social Democratic Party, which attacks the current HSDP line as "bourgeois liberalism", and also refuses membership to former HSWP members. The leader of the HSDP is Anna Petrasovits. According to an opinion poll in November 1989, 9.1 per cent of the electorate would support the HSDP in a free election. This represents a drop since the earlier poll in March. It has lost support probably mainly to the **Alliance of Free Democrats (AFD)**. The HSDP joined with the AFD and others in opposing the direct election of the President in the November 1989 referendum, but it attracted a negligible level of support in the general election in March–April 1990.

JB

HUNGARIAN SOCIALIST PARTY (HSP) *see* **Hungarian Socialist Workers' Party**.

HUNGARIAN SOCIALIST WORKERS' PARTY (HSWP — Magyar Szocialista Munkáspárt). The Hungarian Socialist Workers' Party is the name by which the Communist Party in Hungary has been known since 1956. The origins of the Party date back to March 24, 1918, when Béla Kun founded a Hungarian Section of the Russian Communist Party (Bolsheviks) from leftist sympathizers among the half-million Hungarian prisoners of war in Russia. On Nov. 4, 1918, the establishment of a Communist Party of Hungary (CPH) was proclaimed, and later the same month it returned to Hungary and was re-established in Budapest on Nov. 24. A recruitment drive was launched and by January 1919 a membership of 10,000 was claimed. In March 1919, the CPH came to power in coalition with the **Hungarian Social-Democratic Party (HSDP)** after the collapse of the Károlyi government. In anticipation of an imminent world revolution and Soviet aid, a Hungarian Soviet Republic was set up which lasted a mere 133 days. Some much-needed radical social reforms were carried out, but were accompanied by highly unpopular coercion and terror which discredited Communism in the eyes of the population, in particular among the peasantry.

After the collapse of the Soviet Republic, Hungarian army officers spearheaded an anti-Communist "White Terror", and large numbers fled abroad. Because a significant proportion of leading Communists were of Jewish origin, the new regime was able with some success to mobilize popular anti-semitism as a further means of undermining support for the Communists. Under Horthy, the CPH was outlawed and the membership melted away to possibly only a few hundred in emigration or in the underground party. Béla Kun and his associates went to Moscow, where most of them perished in the course of Stalin's purges. (The Soviet Union officially admitted in 1989 for the first time that Kun himself was in fact executed by firing squad in August 1938 as an alleged Trotskyist.) The illegal "home" party ceased to exist after 1936, when the **Communist International (Comintern)** ordered its members to infiltrate the trade union movement and the HSDP. Thus, by the time of World War II, the CPH was in complete disarray.

The party's leadership regrouped and was built up in Moscow during the war under Mátyás **Rákosi**. The Red Army moved westwards to liberate Hungary in 1944, and on Dec. 21 a Hungarian National Independence Front was set up in Debrecen with Soviet backing, which included a number of parties but was effectively dominated from the start by the CPH and was used by the Soviet Union as a means of securing control of Hungary. Meanwhile, home Communists had re-emerged after the German occupation of Hungary in 1944 as one group in the resistance in Budapest. Tensions between the Moscow-trained leadership and the home Communists over questions of strategy and tactics soon became apparent after liberation in April 1945, and were to play a fateful role in the party's history. The home Communists tended to favour a more rapid and radical transformation of Hungary, and were not happy with the coalition strategy imposed by **Stalin** in the immediate post-war period. The "Muscovite" faction was, on the other hand, absolutely disciplined to follow Stalin's wishes at all times. The party set about a vigorous recruitment drive to build up support, after its rather weak performance in the elections of 1945, in which it won under 17 per cent of the vote as compared with the Smallholders' Party's 57 per cent. Membership rose from an estimated 30,000 in February 1945 to 608,728 in January 1946, largely through the indiscriminate admission of former fascist Arrow Cross activists and through the political manipulation of the peasantry, who were promised land in the Communist-administered land reforms.

By 1947, Stalin's strategy had changed from supporting coalition governments and gradualist policies based on local specific conditions to securing total domination of politics in Eastern Europe through the imposition of a Communist monopoly of power and the transformation of each country's social and economic system in line with the Soviet model. In Hungary, Rákosi applied his notorious "salami tactics" to the rival non-Communist parties, slicing away their support. An enforced merger in June 1948 allowed the Communist Party to swallow up the Social-Democrats, and brought the membership of the thus formed Hungarian Workers' Party (HWP) to 1,128,130. After the complete monopolization of power by the HWP, a purge was effected to weed out less reliable elements. The purge was also connected with Stalin's increasing paranoia about infiltration of the Communist movement by "enemies" of various types, including not only Western "imperialist" agents but also "Titoists" (insubordinate national Communists). Many home Communists in Hungary were vulnerable to the latter charge, most notably Lázsló **Rajk**, who was executed in 1949. Other leading Communists (as well as non-Communists) were imprisoned. Overall, the purges reduced the HWP's membership to 862,603 by January 1954.

Despite the purges, the party leader Mátyás Rákosi still faced considerable opposition on account of the disastrous impact of Stalinist policies on the economy. After Stalin's death in 1953 a faction grew within the HWP, especially among party intellectuals, in favour of a "New Course" similar to that being implemented in the Soviet Union at this time. Imre **Nagy** was brought back under direct Soviet orders as Prime Minister, but the hardline faction of Rakosi continued to dominate the HWP leadership, and proved able to remove Nagy in April 1955. The XX Congress of the **Communist Party of the Soviet Union (CPSU)** in February 1956 had an enormous impact on the HWP, rekindling open conflict, but the hardliners clung to power with extraordinary, and ultimately catastrophic, tenacity. Rákosi was replaced as Party leader finally in June 1956, but his successor, Ernö Gerö, was well known as an equally intransigent Stalinist. The despairing membership began to drift away, and when the revolution broke out in late October, the party simply collapsed. János **Kádár** was appointed as the new leader on Oct. 25, 1956, and on Nov. 1 he announced that the HWP had been abolished. It was to be succeeded by a new Hungarian Socialist Workers' Party (HSWP), with a reported membership in December 1956 of 37,818 (as compared with the 871,497 members of the HWP in August 1956).

Kádár slowly built up the HSWP's membership to 394,910 by December 1957, to reach 498,644 by December 1961. In this period, inevitably he had to rely heavily on old hardliners to make up the numbers, but he was also determined not to allow a repeat of the mistakes of the Rákosi leadership, and thus insisted on a "two-front" struggle against extremes, not only on the "revisionist" right but also on the "dogmatic" left. By the time of the VIII Congress of the HSWP in November 1962, Kádár (with **Khrushchev**'s support) had reached a secure position in the party from which he was able to announce "whoever is not against us is with us", signalling a more flexible and pragmatic approach in ideology and policy. This underpinned the strategy of reform which he launched in 1963. Party membership grew steadily thereafter, drawing in many able and ambitious people interested in promoting the cause of gradual reform from within. Membership reported at the X Congress in November 1970 stood at 662,000; by January 1975 it had reached 765,566. At the XIII Congress in March 1985 it was reported as 8,770,992.

In the 1980s, the HSWP once again found itself deeply divided and facing what proved to be a terminal crisis. Kádár was replaced as party leader by Károly **Grósz** at a special HSWP conference in May 1988, but this change was not adequate to solve the conflicts. The basic issue was the scope and pace of the reform programme, which the numerous reformists in the leadership and among the rank-and-file now wished to extend to political reforms. Many members, including the leading reformist Imre **Pozsgay**, no longer supported the HSWP's monopoly of power. Conflict with the more conservative HSWP leadership of Grósz weakened the party, and membership began to drift away in 1988 and especially in 1989. The conclusive sign of a general crisis of self-confidence in the party came with the Central Committee's decision in February 1989 to reintroduce a multi-party democracy. A new four-man leadership was set up in June 1989, bringing in the respected reform economist Rezsö **Nyers** as party President to stiffen Grósz's resolve to introduce more decisive changes. Imre Pozsgay and the Prime Minister Miklos **Nemeth** were also included.

The party set up negotiations with the emerging new opposition parties in order to effect a peaceful transition to democracy. It also made preparations to transform itself from a Leninist type of ruling party into a democratic, vote-winning party. A special Congress was convened in October 1989, at which a majority of the delegates (elected democratically by secret ballot) voted to rename the Party the Hungarian Socialist Party. All previous HSWP members (720,000 had been reported at this congress) were invited to register for the HSP. To prevent an outright split, Nyers, who was elected leader of the HSP, insisted on some compromises between reformist radicals and conservative groups, particularly on the question of maintaining party basic groups in the workplace. But this compromise was ineffective, in that it was inadequate to keep the conservatives in the party while it alienated many reformists, and served in general to feed popular cynicism about the real meaning of the changes.

As a result, only about 30,000 members had signed up by November 1989, and a public opinion poll conducted at this time showed only 10.5 per cent of the population would vote for it in a free election (as compared with the 36.5 per cent who expressed a preference for the HSWP in a similar poll conducted in March 1989). The HSP was badly damaged at the outset by the decision of the Hungarian National Assembly in October to outlaw party organizations in workplaces, which disorganized its recruitment drive. Moreover, the old group of conservatives decided to re-establish the HSWP, claiming a membership of 120,000. Their likely electoral support, however, appeared to be even more restricted than that of the HSP: an opinion poll in November showed

only 4.2 per cent support. The HSWP, in the March–April 1990 elections, attracted negligible support; the HSP itself, however, secured no more than 8.5 per cent of the vote.

JB

HUNGARY. *Population*: 10,588,600 (January 1989). *Area*: 93,030 sq km. *Top five trading partners*: USSR, Federal Republic of Germany, German Democratic Republic, Austria, Czechoslovakia. *Percentage of population that is urban*: 59.4. *Birth rate*: 11.9 per thousand (1987). *Life expectancy*: males 65.7; females 73.3 (1987).

Political background. An independent Hungarian state emerged from the collapse of the Austro-Hungarian Dual Monarchy at the end of World War I. The leading liberal opposition politician, Count Mihály Károlyi, tried to set up a modern liberal republic, but the attempt failed, due to lack of recognition by the Allied Powers and the threat to the territorial integrity of the former Hungarian Crown lands posed by the foundation of the new "successor states" of Yugoslavia, Czechoslovakia and Romania. Károlyi was forced from office in March 1919 by Béla Kun, who then established a brutal communist dictatorship. The "Hungarian Soviet Republic" lasted only four months, but it left a deep impact on the population in the form of ingrained hostility to Communist ideology. It was suppressed in August with the help of the Romanian army, which occupied Budapest. A counter-revolutionary government, formed in Szeged under Admiral Horthy, returned to Budapest in November. Horthy ruled Hungary as Regent from March 1920.

The Treaty of Trianon, signed in June, 1920 deprived Hungary of over 70 per cent of its former territory, and the population was reduced from 20.9 million to 7.8 million. Large numbers of ethnic Hungarians found themselves outside Hungary, mainly in Czechoslovakia and Transylvania, which now became part of Romania (*see* **Hungarian Minorities**). The peace terms were deeply resented in Hungary, and revision of Trianon was the dominant motif of inter-war politics, along with a deeply conservative approach to domestic affairs. In particular, much-needed land reform was fudged, and considerable problems of rural impoverishment resulted. Horthy established an authoritarian, "law and order" regime which enjoyed fairly widespread support in a population tired of war end revolution, and the country was ruled by a succession of right-wing governments. The Communist Party (HCP) was outlawed, and the non-Communist left had little room for manoeuvre. Parliament was dominated by the government, but the regime was committed to the rule of law and there was a relatively free press.

In its pursuit of revision of the Treaty of Trianon, Hungary was drawn into alliance with the Axis powers. Thus in 1938 and 1940, Hungary regained parts of Slovakia and Transylvania, and in April 1941, Hungarian troops occupied Vojvodina in support of the war declared by the Axis on Yugoslavia. In June 1941, Horthy took Hungary into war against the Soviet Union alongside Nazi Germany. However, Horthy was never a wholly pliant puppet of Hitler (for example, he did not implement the most brutal anti-semitic measures which Hitler wanted). He maintained covert links with the Western allies, and in 1944 tried to take Hungary out of the war. But in October the Germans occupied the country, arrested Horthy and installed a puppet regime of the fascist "Arrow Cross" movement. The following months saw some of the bitterest fighting of World War II as the Soviet Red Army struggled to repulse the Germans from Hungarian territory. The country was liberated on April 4, 1945.

The HCP was re-established at the end of the war in the Soviet Union under the leadership of Mátyás **Rákosi**, who returned to Hungary with the Red Army and set up a provisional government in Debrecen, drawing in representatives of other parties in addition to the Communists. During the period of coalition government, the HCP rapidly—and indiscriminately—built up its membership from an estimated 30,000 in February 1945 to 887,472 in June 1948. A significant proportion of recruits included not only opportunists but also rank-and-file former members of the Arrow Cross movement. But this recruitment did not translate into great success at the ballot box. In the November 1945 elections, the HCP won 16.95 per cent of the vote as compared with the centrist Smallholders' Party, which won 57.03 per cent, and the Social Democrats, who won 17.41 per cent and proved particularly strong among the working class in the capital. And, despite considerable political pressure (backed by the Soviet representatives in Budapest) and outright electoral fraud, the HCP still only managed to win the elections of August 1947 with 22.27 per cent of the vote. In the meanwhile, the HCP's main rivals, the Smallholders and the Social Democrats, were being undermined by Rákosi's notorious "salami tactics", which successfully whittled away both their political support base and the integrity of their leaders, who were either imprisoned or forced into exile, or alternatively chose to co-operate with the HCP. By the end of 1947, the Smallholders were forced

out of existence, and in June 1948, the HCP induced the Social Democrats to merge with them to form a new Hungarian Workers' Party (HWP). From this point, Hungary became, effectively, a one-party state, although the National Peasants' Party, closely allied with the HWP, continued to exist until 1956.

From 1949, Hungary lived through a Stalinist "proletarian dictatorship" of extreme ruthlessness and severity. The Soviet economic model of near-complete nationalization and centralized state control of the economy, collectivization of agriculture, priority development of basic heavy industry and a forced pace of growth at the expense of popular consumption was imposed without regard to its appropriateness for Hungarian conditions. Political life was dominated by political purges within the HWP, which were initiated by Stalin but which were pursued with some vigour by Rákosi as a means of despatching his rivals and potential opponents. The most prominent victim of the show trials which took place at this time was the former resistance leader and subsequently Minister of the Interior, László **Rajk**.

By the time of **Stalin**'s death in 1953, the tensions created by this pattern of economic and political misrule were coming to a head. Rákosi was summoned to Moscow by the new Soviet leaders and instructed to introduce a "New Course" to ease the economic situation and improve popular consumption. Imre **Nagy**, a leading Hungarian Communist who had been under house arrest, was to take over as Prime Minister, but Rákosi was allowed to retain the top party post. Nagy began to implement a series of more popular economic policies, but continually ran up against the opposition of the unreconstructed Stalinists in the Party, led by Rákosi who eventually proved able to oust Nagy from his post in April 1955. By this time, the party itself was deeply divided and the population was frustrated and despondent. Nagy, in retirement, became the focus of the hopes of "revisionist" marxists in student and intellectual circles.

Khrushchev's denunciation of Stalin's crimes in the secret speech to the XX Congress of the **Communist Party of the Soviet Union (CPSU)** in February 1956 had a devastating impact in Hungary. Rákosi's position immediately became untenable, and he was finally forced from office in July 1956, only to be replaced by his close associate, Ernö Gerö. The inability of the party leadership to make any credible changes only heightened conflict within its ranks, and led to its accelerating disintegration as the membership deserted en masse. The first signs of the impending revolt came in early October with the huge crowds which gathered in Budapest on the day of the ceremonial reburial of László Rajk, who had been posthumously rehabilitated. The simultaneous crisis in Poland fuelled the ferment. When news arrived in Budapest of **Gomułka**'s election to leader of the **Polish United Workers' Party**, a crowd of demonstrators gathered to demand the return of Nagy. But the Central Committee which gathered on Oct. 22–24 to reinstate him as Prime Minister, also called upon Soviet troops stationed near Budapest to restore order, which precipitated the armed national uprising. In his efforts to win back the people's confidence and restore order, Nagy negotiated, with the apparent agreement of Soviet representatives in Budapest, a new multi-party coalition government and the promise of free elections. When he discovered, on Nov. 1, that the Soviets were reneging on their agreement to withdraw their troops and in fact were re-invading the country Nagy felt compelled to announce Hungarian withdrawal from the **Warsaw Treaty Organization (Warsaw Pact)** and neutrality. In the course of the bitter fighting which followed, an estimated 25,000 people were killed, 150,000 injured and 200,000 left the country. Nagy was arrested when he tried to leave the country under Yugoslav protection, and was executed after a secret trial in 1958.

Communist rule was restored under János **Kádár**, who had been a supporter of Nagy, and had been elected party leader on October 25. But he disappeared on Nov. 1, resurfacing as leader of a Soviet-backed "Workers' and Peasants' Government". The HWP was dissolved, and a new **Hungarian Socialist Workers' Party (HSWP)** was set up. Several years of harshly repressive rule followed and large numbers of leading participants in the uprising were sentenced to long terms of imprisonment. But Kádár was not a brutal Stalinist after the manner of Rákosi. He saw himself as a realist, compelled to force his country to face the inevitability of their subordination to the Soviet Union. And once control was restored to Moscow's satisfaction, Kádár set about a gradual process of reconciliation with society through a more pragmatic approach to rule, which aimed to make people's lives more comfortable. In 1961 he pronounced his famous dictum, "whoever is not against us is with us", thus reversing the traditional Leninist slogan and signalling an end to the insistence on full ideological conformity and active commitment to the party line. An amnesty released most of the political prisoners.

Kádár was also receptive to the idea of economic reform, and during the 1960s teams of economic experts were set to work on the elaboration of a comprehensive proposal for a "New Econo-mic Mechanism". Which was approved by the Central Committee in 1966 and implemented on Jan. 1, 1968 (see below). But political reform was not allowed to come onto the agenda, especially after the events in Czechoslovakia of 1968. Kádár adopted a more flexible and tolerant style of rule with limited, bureaucratized, but not insignificant opportunities for the expression and incorporation of interests, and a sizeable proportion of the party membership came to include various shades of reform-minded people. But political change of this limited kind was not enough to guarantee the consistent implementation of the economic reform, and in the early 1970s there emerged a groundswell of reaction from vested bureaucratic interests in the sectoral ministries and large enterprises, the regional party apparatus, diehard ideologists and the official Trade Union leadership. There groups coalesced to form a majority on the HSWP Central Committee, and thus were able to force substantial modifications to the economic reform which undermined its effectiveness. Moreover, leading reformist politicians, including the architect of the New Economic Mechanism, Rezsö **Nyers**, were excluded from the party leadership, and greater political and ideological conformity was enforced in intellectual life. Nevertheless, by contrast with Czechoslovakia or East Germany, political life in Hungary in the 1970s remained relatively relaxed. The reform was never officially repudiated and, importantly, the reformists were by no means excluded from the party altogether.

By the end of the 1970s, it became clear from increasing economic difficulties that the reform reversal had been a mistake, and pressure began to mount from economic experts for a "reform of the reform", which met with support from reformists within the party, who by now were also convinced that the economic reform had to be more radical than before and that fundamental political reform was essential too. But Kádár proved unwilling to lead a reform of this type and played an increasingly obstructive, conservative role. The substantial popularity and personal authority which he had accumulated since the 1960s began to evaporate rapidly as economic difficulties degenerated into open crisis in the 1980s. Moreover, Kádár was now ageing, his health was failing, and his grip on the day-to-day running of the party was weakening. As the leading contender in the emerging succession struggle put it, the Kádár era was reaching its "biological limits".

Recent political developments. After a disastrous economic performance in 1985, the pace of political change began to accelerate. The government's fond hopes that the economic crisis had been successfully weathered were dashed, but the government reshuffle at the end of 1986 did nothing to restore confidence. Divisions at the top, among leading party personalities, became increasingly open, and three candidates for the succession to Kádár emerged: Károly **Grósz**, the reputedly hardline Budapest Party Secretary; János **Berecz**, the leading party ideologist; and the radical reformist Imre **Pozsgay**, the former Minister of Culture whom Kádár had shunted into the political side-alley of the Patriotic People's Front (PPF) in 1982. Grósz posed the most powerful challenge, and was moved by Kádár to the less advantageous post of Prime Minister in June 1987. But Grósz used this post to great effect, making convincing efforts to consult with a wide range of specialists outside the apparatus and showing himself open to dialogue. He thus greatly enhanced his chances in the leadership contest by broadening his political base beyond the party apparatus, where he already enjoyed strong support.

As a result, it was Grósz who took over the party leadership in May 1988. However, his performance rather rapidly began to falter, and no improvement in the economy came about. Meanwhile, Imre Pozsgay, who was reputed to be **Gorbachev**'s preferred candidate for future leader, was building up a sizeable personal following among the reformist intelligentsia, and using his position in the PPF to promote controversial reformist ideas. He even supported the formation of a new informal political group, the **Hungarian Democratic Forum** (HDF). Evidence of Pozsgay's growing influence was his promotion to the government as Minister of State charged with promoting dialogue with society and political reform. But the cause of reform was further strengthened by the formation of a new government in November 1988 under Miklós **Németh**, which brought in Reszö Nyers as Minister of State in charge of economic reform.

Meanwhile, signs of broader public unrest were appearing, with increasingly well-supported unofficial demonstrations in favour of political reform in general and also touching on sensitive issues such as the plight of the Hungarian minority in Romania (*see* **Hungarian Minorities**) and the environmental impact of the Danube dam project. By late 1988, a proliferation of political groups and embryonic parties had begun to emerge, and a new Law on Associations was promised. In January 1989 the National Assembly (*Orszáqqyülés*) passed this new Law, although the question of political parties remained ambiguous. The decision of the HSWP Central Committee in Feburary to accept the rein-

troduction of a multi-party system took the nation by storm. From this point onwards, political reform was generally understood as the transformation of Hungary into a fully democratic state in the Western sense. Pozsgay set up a negotiating forum (the "Triangular Discussions") including representatives of the main opposition political groupings (the "Opposition Round Table"), the HSWP, and the official social organizations such as the Trade Unions. This forum finally set to work in June 1989 to hamner out the basic constitutions amendments necessary for the peaceful transition to democracy.

In the course of 1989, numerous parties constituted themselves, including the HDF, the **Alliance of Free Democrats (AFD)**, the **Hungarian Social Democratic Party (HSDP)**, the **Independent Smallholders Party (ISP)**, the Alliance of Young Democrats (FIDESZ), and a plethora of other parties and new interest associations. In the summer, four parliamentary by-elections were held in which opposition candidates were able to stand for the first time. In each case they won convincingly. Moreover, public opinion polls conducted in the summer showed the likely electoral support of the HSWP in free elections to be no more than about 30 per cent, and the HDF appeared to be the strongest political force. Moreover, by this time open crisis was evident in the party as dissatisfaction with Grósz's leadership grew. "Reform Circles" sprang up among the rank-and-file membership to promote more decisive change. In June 1989, the Central Committee set up a new four-man Presidium, in which Grósz, as General Secretary, was joined by the well-known reformers, Pozsgay, Nyers (now promoted to President of the party), and Prime Minister Németh. Radical reform of the party itself now came onto the agenda, with Nyers and Pozsgay advocating its transformation into a Western-style democratic socialist party. A special Party Congress was called for October to effect such a transformation.

In mid-September, the "Triangular Discussions" produced agreement on the establishment of a new presidency (to be directly elected before the end of the year), a new Constitutional Court, the legal position of political parties, a new electoral system, and amendments to the Criminal Code. But deep divisions between the oppostion parties had occurred, in particular, between the HDF and the AFD over the question of the presidency. The latter opposed the establishment of a powerful presidency and preferred to vest ultimate authority in a democratically-elected Parliament, to whom the Head of State should be accountable. The AFD and two other parties refused to sign the agreement on these grounds, and also because they were dissatisfied with the failure to address the issues of the HSWP's role in workplaces, the HSWP's assets, equal access to the mass media for all political parties, and the continued existence of the party's private militia, the Workers' Guard. Although they did not veto the agreement, the AFD subsequently set about organizing a petition to Parliament for a public referendum on these issues.

On Oct. 12, the HSWP special congress met, and in a historic vote, the majority of delegates agreed to transform the party and rename it the Hungarian Socialist Party (HSP). Nyers was elected its President, and it was agreed to put forward Pozsgay as the HSP candidate for the forthcoming presidential election. Nyers invited all former HSWP members to sign up for the HSP by the end of October, but his hopes for successful recruitment were dashed by two developments. Firstly, the National Assembly swung into action in full accord with the spirit of the times and passed resolutions outlawing party activities in the workplace. This effectively undermined the organizational base of the former HSWP. But a further blow to the new HSP was the unexpected resuscitation of the HSWP itself, with the support of many old faces from the Kádár era including Grósz, who refused to join the new HSP and insisted that the October Congress had not legally abolished the HSWP. As a result of these embarrassing blows, Nyers managed to gather only 10,000 recruits by the end of October, out of the 720,000 members of the former HSWP.

The National Assembly approved the constitutional amendments emanating from the "Triangular Discussions", and on Oct. 23 — the thirty-third anniversary of the 1956 uprising, now declared a "day of national reconciliation" — the Speaker of the Assembly and acting President Matyás **Szürös** declared that Hungary was now a "Republic". The preamble to the new constitution describes this as "an independent, democratic, legal state in which the values of bourgeois democracy and democratic socialism prevail in equal measures".

The remarkably smooth course of events was upset somewhat in November 1989 when the Hungarian electorate voted in a referendum by a very narrow majority in favour of the AFD's arguments on the question of the presidency. A general election was thus to be held first, and the President would be elected by and accountable to the new, democratic National Assembly. The main effect of this was to weaken dramatically the chances of the hitherto front-running presidential candidate Imre Pozsgay. Moreover, the HDF, which opposed the referendum and urged a boycott, was seriously weakened as an electoral

force by the popular perception of it as too closely associated with the now discredited ruling elite. The standing of the AFD, on the other hand, improved greatly. In the event, in the election which took place in two rounds in March and April 1990, the HDF was a convincing victor with 165 of the 386 seats and 42.7 per cent of the vote. The AFD came second, with 92 seats and 23.8 per cent of the vote, followed by the Independent Smallholders' Party (11.1 per cent) and the Socialist Party (8.5 per cent). The new government was a coalition one, dominated by the Democratic Forum; the results taken as a whole, were highly reminiscent of the last such exercise in the pre-Communist era, in 1945.

Economic Development. Until 1968, the Hungarian economy was organized along traditional Soviet-type command planning lines (although agricultural co-operatives, which were re-established in the late 1950s after the 1956 crisis, were significantly more decentralized and allowed more room for individual farming than Soviet collective farms). Economic performance in the Stalinist period had been characterized by extreme disequilibrium, as excessive rates of growth of industrial production were enforced through very high levels of investment, particularly in heavy industry, at the expense of development in agriculture, light and consumer goods industry, and also at the expense of the population's standard of living. The pattern of investment was irrational in view of the country's natural resource endowment: for example, a massive steelworks was constructed which was entirely dependent on imports for inputs of iron ore and coking coal. The adverse impact of these ideologically-impelled economic policies on society became fully apparent in the popular revolt of 1956.

After 1956, the **Kádár** regime demonstrated an awareness of the untenability of the Soviet model of autarkic industrialization for a small country, poor in raw materials and inevitably heavily dependent on foreign trade. A commission of experts was set up in early 1957 to consider the question of economic reform, but its proposals, which owed much to the Yugoslav self-management model, were rejected as they were politically unacceptable at this time. Some partial reforms were introduced, but these proved insufficient to bring about a real turnaround in economic performance. But by the early 1960s, Kádár was more confident of the political stabilization of the country, while unmistakeable evidence of the need for more far-reaching reform was emerging from Hungarian economic performance, particularly in the foreign trade deficit and balance-of-payments difficulties. The basically pragmatic political perspective of the regime at this time made it receptive to reformist ideas in the economy, and in 1963, the HSWP Secretary for Economic Affairs, Rezsö Nyers, set up a team of experts to work on the outlines of a proposal for comprehensive reform, with the support of Kádár. The HSWP Central Committee finally accepted a fairly detailed blueprint for reform at the end of 1965, and with this essential political backing, the New Economic Mechanism (NEM) was carefully prepared for introduction from Jan. 1, 1968.

The NEM represented a "regulated market" model of economic reform. Enterprises were to be freed from detailed central directives, and were now required to determine their own production plans. Their basic goal thus changed from fulfilling commands set by their bureaucratic superiors to the pursuit of profit from sales, and so to the satisfaction of customers' requirements. Managerial incentives and workers' bonuses were tied to profit, and the enterprises were to finance their investments from retained profits and from interest-bearing bank credits, rather than from direct budgetary grants as before. Central planning was not to be abandoned altogether, but to focus on long-term, general economic strategy. The connection between the central planners' objectives and enterprise economic activity was to be assured by means of a set of instruments in the hands of the central authorities which would allow them to manipulate the market economic environment in which enterprises operated. These instruments included a set of price controls (which were, however, intended to be temporary and to be gradually released as the market developed); centralized sectoral quotas for the allocation of investment credits; central control of the average basic wage level; and a set of rules determining the use of enterprise funds.

In the first few years of its operation, the NEM worked quite successfully, accompanied by a satisfactory rate of growth and improvements in both internal and external equilibrium. The good performance of agriculture since the early 1960s provided a useful reserve to tide the economy over the inevitable uncertainties of the transition to a more market-oriented system, while at the same time, Hungary's terms of trade were favourable. However, as early as 1972, the regime began to backtrack in its commitment to the reform for a variety of mainly political reasons. There had always been highly-placed ideological opponents of the reform who were quite soon joined by certain powerful vested interests which found themselves threatened by its operation. A particularly influential "lobby" was that of the

managers of the large monopoly enterprises, supported by sectoral ministries, who resented the increasing pressure on them in the new, more stringent economic environment, and found themselves unable to retain their workforce in the face of competition from dynamic new firms set up by the agricultural co-operatives. The trade unions began to agitate, in alliance with these industrial monopolies and ministries, for across-the-board wage rises for workers in traditional industrial branches which were being squeezed by the new financial pressures. A campaign against high rural incomes was part of this bureaucratic backlash. Peasants were said to be profiting at the expense of the urban working class, and anxiety about inflation in consumer goods and food prices was whipped up.

The government, anxious above all to avoid open public unrest, introduced a set of "temporary" measures to soften the impact of the reform through "exceptional" concessions to key large firms. Moreover, after 1973 and the onset of the world economic recession, further measures were taken to protect the domestic economy from the drastic changes taking place in the world market. The objective of gradually bringing Hungarian domestic prices in line with the world market was abandoned, and with it, a basic precondition of the success of the economic reform was lost. Throughout the 1970s, although the rhetoric of reform was maintained and centralized directive planning was never restored, in practice, enterprises proved able to avoid the market and concentrated on negotiating concessions and subsidies on prices, wages, investments and so on with their bureaucratic superiors in the sectoral ministries. Economic growth was sustained at a high level of 5–7 per cent until 1978, real wages and consumption grew steadily, and high levels of investment were recorded, but virtually no structural change or adjustment to the changes in the external environment took place. The result of this was, by the end of the decade, a serious problem in the external economic balance with rising debt, trade and balance-of-payments deficits.

After the second world oil price shock in 1979, the Hungarian economy was clearly in serious difficulties, and measures to restore balance by slowing down the growth rate were introduced. A massive deterioration in the Hungarian terms of trade had taken place by the early 1980s with both the West and the Soviet Union, Hungary's main energy source. The government and party leadership was forced to concede that the stalling of the economic reform in the mid-1970s had been a mistake, and a renewed drive for economic reform began in the early 1980s. Competitive wholesale pricing was introduced in January

1980, and regular consumer price rises began to be allowed in order to reduce the level of subsidies on food, energy, rents and public transport. An increased role for the small-scale private sector in consumer services was allowed with the introduction of leasing arrangements for previously state-managed restaurants and shops. The sectoral ministries, which had been the key institutional base for anti-reform interests, were abolished with the creation of a merged Ministry of Industry in 1980, which had no direct links to enterprises. Some of the giant monopoly enterprises were broken up into more economically appropriate small and medium-sized units, and provisions for subcontracting work within large enterprises to groups of employees added further flexibility to the management system. Workers' councils were introduced in 1984 as a further means of assuring enterprise autonomy and self-management. Reform of the banking system was introduced in 1985 which separated the Hungarian National Bank from the commercial credit banks. All these measures were greeted as positive developments, but they were not fully or consistently implemented (subsidies to large enterprises, for example, continued at high levels) and thus did not prove adequate to halt the growing economic crisis, particularly the problem of mounting debt.

In 1982, Hungary suffered a serious hard currency liquidity crisis when foreign depositors withdrew $1.3 billion in short-term deposits in the first three months, cutting Hungary's hard currency reserves to less than $500 million. At this point, Hungary applied to join, and was accepted by, the IMF and World Bank and thus received financial help which enabled it to weather the crisis and restored Western confidence. Some progress in reducing hard currency debt had been made between 1980 and 1983, when gross debt fell from $9.1 billion to $8.3 billion. However, on the basis of rather slender evidence of an upturn in the economy, the government introduced an ill-advised policy of accelerating economic growth again. Without the necessary restructuring of the economy, such growth could only lead to renewed tensions in the trade balance with the West. As a result of this policy, and the relatively easy access to Western credit which Hungary enjoyed on account of its very favourable reputation in the West, hard currency debt jumped from $8.8 billion at the end of 1984 to $17.7 billion at the end of 1987. At the same time, economic performance weakened steeply and steadily from 1985.

The depth of the economic crisis by 1987 was contributing to growing political instability at the level of the top leadership, and to growing pressure from reformists within the elite for further radical reforms to bring about a fully marketized economy without the traditional qualifying adjective of "socialist". Major restructuring, it was accepted, required the consistent application of the new law on bankruptcy passed in 1985, and provision for unemployment, which could rise to at least 200,000. A thoroughgoing austerity policy, which has been insisted upon by the IMF as a condition for extensive financial aid, will have a very damaging effect on the population's standard of living, and open inflation has risen from 7–6 per cent per annum in the mid-1980s to over 15 per cent in 1988 and over 20 per cent in 1989. Priviatization of substantial areas of economic activity is underway, with the sale of state assets to foreign purchasers, alongside legal reforms to encourage joint ventures and other forms of foreign participation and investment in Hungary. The enormous social tensions generated by policies and reforms of this type have been the major contributory factor in the disintegration of the HSWP's monopoly of power, and it was widely hoped that the free elections in 1990 would establish a government with sufficient popular legitimacy to carry out the necessary measures. The formation of a coalition headed by the Hungarian Democratic Forum, following the elections, was widely expected to satisfy this requirement.

Foreign policy. For most of the period of Communist rule in Hungary the country could almost be said not to have had a foreign policy, unless it were complete subservience to the Soviet line at all times. In 1956, however, the demand for Hungarian withdrawal from the Warsaw Pact and the acquisition of neutral status was raised as one of the main demands of the insurgent population. Imre Nagy tried to negotiate the removal of Soviet troops from Hungarian soil with the Soviet Politburo representatives in Budapest at the height of the crisis. When he discovered that the Soviet Union had in fact reinvaded the country, he felt he had no other option but to accede to the demand of his people for neutrality. After 1956, the Kádár regime was extremely careful not to depart from the Soviet position in international affairs on any issue. This may have been seen by both sides as a condition for Soviet toleration of the less orthodox economic policies and more relaxed approach in domestic politics that emerged from the mid-1960s.

However, at the start of the 1980s, a marked change occurred in this pattern. Hungary found itself in an unexpected informal alliance with the GDR in resisting Soviet demands for greater unity within the Warsaw Pact against the West. Hungary, like the GDR, had built up an enormous degree of economic dependency on the West; the Kádár regime had become committed to detente and opening up to the West as part of its struggle to retain the confidence of its population and win some legitimacy as a genuine representative of Hungarian national interests. This difference with the ageing Soviet leadership under **Brezhnev** began to become apparent after the Soviet invasion of Afghanistan, which was seen by the Hungarian side as a great mistake. It became more acute in the wake of the Polish crisis, and culminated with the high point of East–West confrontation in 1982–84 at the time of the crisis over the stationing of intermediate-range missiles in Europe. The HSWP Secretary in charge of foreign affairs, Mátyás Szürös, made a series of public pronouncements in 1983 and 1984 on the role of national interests in the co-ordination of socialist foreign policies, clearly advocating their primacy as against the Soviet attempt to enforce uniformity and subordination to its own great power interests. Szürös also supported Erich **Honecker** at this time in arguing for the "special role" of small nations in Europe as a bridge between East and West, a role which, moreover, was argued to be particularly important at times of heightened international tension. Honecker and Szürös did not defeat the Soviet Union on this occasion, but the rapid changes which took place after the accession of Mikhail **Gorbachev** to the Soviet leadership eventually vindicated their position. By 1989, as it gradually became clear that the Soviet Union was genuinely renouncing the "**Brezhnev doctrine**", Hungarian foreign policy developed rapidly with an irresistible momentum: by the end of that extraordinary year, the aspiration to neutrality had not only re-emerged but had become the generally accepted position of all the major political parties. The main source of debate was not whether, but when and how.

The second major feature of Hungarian foreign policy in recent years has been the focus on the position of Hungarian minorities abroad, particularly in Romania, where an estimated two million live. Relations with the Romanian regime under **Ceauşescu** became extremely strained from the mid-1980s on. Hungary took the hitherto unprecedented step for a Soviet-bloc state of denouncing a fraternal ally for its human rights violations at various international gatherings under the CSCE. Eventually, Hungarian intelligence played some part in the overthrow of Ceauşescu in December 1989 by supplying the Romanian army with information on **Securitate** movements, derived from intercepted radio signals. Immediately after the defeat of Ceauşescu, the Hungarian Foreign Minister Gyula Horn went to Bucharest to offer support and to reassure the new government that Hungary had no interest in pursuing territorial revisions as the solution to the national minority issue: the solution was to be found in democratic reforms and freedom of movement across frontiers. Romania agreed to the provision of Hungarian aid to support the revival of Hungarian-language education and cultural facilities, and to the reopening of the Hungarian consulate in Cluj.

JB

HUSÁK, GUSTÁV. Born in 1913, Husák was a leading figure in the **Communist Party of Slovakia** during World War II and a key participant in the Slovak National Uprising against the Nazis in August 1944. In 1951 he was arrested and, despite his refusal to confess his guilt, was sentenced in 1954 to life imprisonment on charges of "bourgeois nationalism". Released in 1960, he returned to political life in March 1968, first as a Deputy Prime Minister and then from August as First Secretary of the Communist Party of Slovakia. Although not privy to the Soviet-led invasion in August 1968, Husák proved ready to fall in with Soviet wishes and dismantle the **Prague Spring** reforms following his appointment as First Secretary of the **Communist Party of Czechoslovakia** in April 1969. From 1975 he combined that post with the presidency of Czechoslovakia but his personal imprint on policy can be detected with certainty only in the more positive policies towards Slovakia during his leadership. His authoritarian attitudes blended with the hardline regime of the 1970s and early 1980s, but the worst features of that period may be attributed as much, if not more, to the consensus within the leadership as to Husák's personal preference. He showed little evidence of sympathy with the reformist policies under way in the Soviet Union after 1985 but his resignation as party leader in December 1987 seems likely to have been the result of personal rivalries and his declining health. He remained President until Dec. 10, 1989 when public pressure secured his resignation from that post five months before the completion of his third term as head of state.

GW

I

IDEOLOGY. At least until the changes of the late 1980s the USSR and the countries of Eastern Europe were ruled by Communist parties formally dedicated to **Marxism-Leninism**. The largest of these states, the Soviet Union, is still controlled by a party which claims to base itself upon a formal ideology of this kind, whose ultimate objective is the establishment of a fully Communist society. For this reason, it is sometimes referred to in the West as a "Communist society". This is not, however, a description that the Soviet authorities themselves accept. Communism, in their view, is a state of affairs that will be achieved only at some unspecified point in the future, when the development of productive forces makes the distribution of goods to all in accordance with their needs a real possibility, and when Communist, collectivist values have been embraced by the population at large. Until that point is reached, the USSR (and the East European societies that are modelled upon it) are held to be more properly described as "socialist" societies. In societies of this kind the means of production (factories, farms and so forth) have been taken into public ownership, and there is no longer a capitalist class who make a living from employing others. Equally, however, the state still exists (as it is not supposed to do under Communism) and the distribution of rewards is determined by the work that people do, rather than by their needs. Only when the higher stage of Communism has been reached will the state "wither away", separate classes disappear, and distribution be determined by people's needs rather than their work.

In the Soviet case, the single most authoritative statement of the official ideology is the Programme of the **Communist Party of the Soviet Union (CPSU)**, a new and revised version of which was adopted by the XXVII Party Congress in 1986. This defines Communism in the following terms:

Communism is a classless social system with one form of public ownership of the means of production and with full social equality of all members of society. Under Communism, the all-round development of people will be accompanied by the growth of the productive forces on the basis of continuous progress in science and technology, all the springs of social wealth will flow abundantly, and the great principle "from each according to his ability, to

each according to his needs" will be implemented. Communism is a highly organized society of free, socially conscious working people, a society in which public self-government will be established, a society in which labour for the good of society will become the prime vital requirement of everyone, a clearly recognized necessity, and the ability of each person will be employed to the greatest benefit of the people.

The achievement of a Communist society of this kind is described in the Programme as the CPSU's "ultimate goal"; the much more general transition from capitalism to Communism on a worldwide scale is described, despite its "unevenness, complexity and contradictoriness", as "inevitable".

The 1986 Party Programme replaced the version adopted under Nikita **Khrushchev** in 1961, which was best known for its promise that Communism in the USSR would be established "in the main" by 1980. The construction of Communism, the 1961 Programme promised, would be carried out by a series of stages. During the 1960s, the world's richest and most powerful capitalist country, the USA, would be overtaken in per capita production, hard physical labour would disappear, the Soviet people would all live in "easy circumstances", and the USSR would have the shortest working day in the world. By the end of the 1970s, the Programme went on to promise, an "abundance of material and cultural values for the whole population" would have been created, a single form of property—public ownership—would prevail, and the principle of distribution according to people's needs would be close to attainment. By the end of the 1970s, the Programme suggested, a Communist society would "in the main" have been constructed in the USSR, to be "fully completed" in the subsequent period. The Programme concluded with the pledge: "The Party solemnly proclaims: the present generation of Soviet people shall live in Communism!"

Not simply was this Programme (the party's third) not fulfilled; it soon became unmentionable, at least in print, and no more was heard of the dates by which its ambitious targets were to be achieved. Leonid **Brezhnev** (party leader from 1964 to 1982) introduced the concept of "developed socialism", which was a stage of socialism that would last for many years before a transition to Communism could be contemplated. His successors Yuri **Andropov** and Konstantin **Chernenko** (party leaders from 1982 to 1984 and from 1984 to 1985 respectively) made it clear that the Soviet Union was "only at the beginning" of the stage of developed socialism, and called for more attention to be given to immediate and practical tasks rather than to what **Lenin** had called the "distant, beautiful and rosy future". The Programme became increasingly out of line with these directives, and in 1981 it was decided to redraft it. The drafting commission, chaired by **Gorbachev** after his accession to the party leadership, published a preliminary version of the new Programme in October 1985 for national discussion; a final, slightly amended version was adopted by the XXVII Party Congress in March 1986. Gorbachev told the Congress that some had argued this should be called a fourth Party Programme, not a new version of the third, because the changes it contained were so considerable.

The 1961 Party Programme, for instance, described itself as a "programme for the building of a Communist society"; the 1986 version talks only about the "planned and all-round perfection of socialism" with a view to a "further advance to Communism through the country's accelerated socio-economic development". In 1961 it was argued that socialism alone could abolish exploitation, economic crisis and poverty; the 1986 version claims only that socialism offers "advantages" and is a superior form of society to capitalism. No dates or stages are presented through which the transition to full Communism is to proceed (forecasts of this kind are described as "harmful"); and there are no references, as in the 1961 Programme, to the increasing provision of free public services, a guaranteed one-month paid holiday for all, or the withering away of the state, a classical Marxist goal. (Some had always maintained that the only thing that would wither away was the *idea* that the state would wither away — they turned out to be right.) Indeed there are few references to "Communism" of any kind in the new Programme; much more emphasis is placed upon eliminating defects in contemporary Soviet society such as profiteering, parasitism and careerism. All this is in line with the tendency of recent years to retreat from long-term and sometimes utopian goals and to place much more emphasis upon short-term, practical and even disciplinarian objectives.

The new Programme (which is likely to remain in force for some time) presents an analysis of both domestic and international affairs. On the domestic front, the Programme puts forward what it describes as a programme for "social progress" leading ultimately to the construction of a fully Communist society. The Bolshevik revolution of 1917 is held to have been a "landmark in world history" which determined the main trends of development worldwide and launched the "irreversible process of the replacement of capitalism by the new, Communist socio-economic formation". The basic means of production passed into popular ownership, industrialization and collectivization transformed economic life, and a "cultural revolution" took place which brought about the "development of creative forces and the intellectual flowering of the working man". By the end of the 1980s, a socialist form of society is held to have been "essentially built" in the USSR, which was fully and finally established after the defeat of Nazi Germany in World War II.

In a fully developed socialist society such as the USSR is now supposed to have become, productive resources are owned by the people and there is rapid economic and technological advance. There are equal rights to work and pay and a wide range of social benefits is available. There is equality between the different social groups, between men and women, and between the nationalities, and "genuine democracy — power exercised for the people and by the people" is in operation based upon the "broad and equal participation" of ordinary citizens. More generally, a "socialist way of life" is supposed to have come into existence on the basis of the principles of "social justice, collectivism and comradely mutual assistance". Further advances towards Communism will take place (the Programme explains) as the economy becomes able increasingly to satisfy all reasonable needs and as the "truly humanistic Marxist-Leninist ideology" becomes dominant. Internationally, at the same time, more and more countries are believed to be associating themselves with socialist principles as the "general crisis of capitalism" continues to deepen.

The Party Programme is the single most important statement of the official ideology in the USSR, but the ideology as such — Marxism-Leninism — draws upon a variety of other sources including the writings of Marx, Engels and Lenin and other party documents. The official ideology — Soviet Marxism-Leninism — may be divided into four main parts. The first of these, *Dialectical Materialism*, teaches that it is concrete reality, rather then ideas or doctrines, which is the motive force of chance, and that change takes place "dialectically" or through a struggle between opposing forces. The second part is called *Historical Materialism*. According to this part of official doctrine, social development necessarily proceeds through a series of stages from primitive society to slave society to feudalism and capitalism and then finally to socialism or Communism. These stages follow the overthrow of one previously dominant class by another, which itself becomes dominant, until in the last of these revolutions the working class overthrows capitalism and establishes a Communist society.

The third part of the doctrine, the *Political Economy of Capitalism*, analyses the economic aspect of these changes. Capitalism, it teaches, contains deep and irreconcilable "contradictions" or antagonisms, which guarantee its ultimate downfall; the socialist system which succeeds it is held to be the only form of society that can bring about the full and increasing satisfaction of human needs. The fourth part, *Scientific Communism*, deals with what are considered to be the main features of the present situation, both in the capitalist world (which is experiencing ever-deepening economic crisis) and in the developing countries (which are considered to be carrying out an increasingly successful struggle against colonial and "neo-colonial" rule). Within the USSR itself it is claimed that a transition from socialism to full Communism is taking place, based upon three inter-connected processes: the development of a technologically-advanced society of material abundance, the elimination of differences between town and country and between mental and manual work, and the establishment of a firm commitment to Communist values among the population at large.

To many these may seem unrealistic, and perhaps also undesirable goals. Capitalism, whatever its economic difficulties, is arguably no nearer to being replaced than it was in 1917, at least in the major capitalist countries of Western Europe and North America. Nor does the experience of the USSR and the countries of Eastern Europe suggest that the overthrow of capitalism is in itself sufficient to guarantee the establishment of a free and equal, or even of a more prosperous society. Marxism-Leninism, however, has at least historically provided a means by which the party leaderships can justify their rule, and a vocabulary through which political discourse can be expressed; and although there was little evidence, even before the changes of the late 1980s, of a mass commitment to specifically Marxist values, there had always been strong support in many of these societies for broadly egalitarian social policies and an interventionist state—values that will certainly be compatible with Marxism-Leninism, if not a product of it. Entering the 1990s, nonetheless, official ideology in the USSR and Eastern Europe had reached a state of what was probably terminal decline. In some of these societies, such as Poland and the GDR, it had been directly repu-

diated at the polls; and even in the USSR itself there was an increasingly open acknowledgement that Marxism-Leninism as such provided few answers to the country's problems. For a small but growing number, indeed, the official ideology, through its denial of political and economic diversity, was better seen as a source of the country's problems than as a solution to them.

SLW

ILIESCU, ION. The first chairman of the **National Salvation Front** in Romania and in early 1990 its apparently secure leader.

RH

INDEPENDENT SMALLHOLDERS' PARTY (HUNGARY — ISP, Független Kisgazdapárt). One of the so-called "historical" parties of Hungary which existed in the pre-Communist era and has re-emerged in the very recent period of democratization. The origins of the party lie in the inter-war period, when it represented not only the more prosperous peasantry but also provincial lawyers and other members of the professional classes. After 1945, the importance of the party grew as it became the major non-left-wing political force once all other parties to the right of it had been abolished. Its electoral support in the urban areas now became substantial. In the Budapest Council elections of Oct. 7, 1945, it won over 50 per cent of the vote. In the Nov. 4 General Election, it won over 57 per cent of total votes cast; its list came first in every electoral district in the country; and it won an outright majority in all but three of the 16 electoral districts. But its support was inexorably whittled away by the notorious "salami tactics", applied by the Hungarian communists under **Rákosi**, and the party showed signs of disintegration by the summer of 1947 after the arrest of its leader, Béla Kovács, by the Soviet occupation authorities in Hungary. The party disappeared completely by 1948, but some of its old leaders reappeared on the political stage for a brief moment during the 1956 revolution, and were invited to join Imre **Nagy**'s coalition. Again it was suppressed after the Soviet invasion, but interestingly enough, no formal document or decree concerning its outlawing at this time could be produced by the Hungarian authorities in 1989, when the question of its relegalization arose.

The first moves to reconstitute it were made at a meeting in Budapest on Oct. 28, 1988, attended, among others, by 16 former parliamentary deputies of the party. At this stage, while the legal status of parties was still unclear, the supporters styled themselves the "Béla Kovács Association". Branches were set up in Szentendre on Nov. 12 and in Budapest on Nov. 18. The first national congress of the Independent Smallholders' Party was convened on March 23, 1989 and a second congress was held on June 3–4. Estimates of the membership in mid-1989 stood at about 6,000, and a public opinion poll conducted in the early summer showed that 5.4 per cent of the population would have voted for them in a free election. Electoral support seems likely to remain restricted to the older generation, but the party may draw new supporters among the still small but rapidly increasing stratum of Hungarian entrepreneurs. The ISP was represented at the "Triangular Discussions" on political reform, and was among those parties which signed the final agreement on constitutional changes with the **Hungarian Socialist Workers' Party (HSWP)**. But it has good relations with the **Alliance of Free Democrats** and decided to side with them in the November 1989 referendum. In the March–April 1990 general election it took third place with 11.1 per cent of the vote, and it subsequently entered the **Hungarian Democratic Forum (HDF)**-dominated government.

JB

INFLATION. The inter-war period in the Soviet Union was characterized by a recurrent tendency to price instability. In the course of the Civil War (1918–21) the old Russian currency was reduced to worthlessness by hyper-inflation, as the new Soviet government followed a conscious policy of using currency issue to raise revenue, and possibly to destroy capitalism at the same time. After the proclamation of the New Economic Policy (NEP) in 1921, a new Soviet currency, the *chervonets*, was introduced (1922–24). The *chervonets* was backed by gold, and the overall price level remained fairly stable throughout the NEP period. With the introduction of centralized planning for crash industrialization from 1929, however, price stability began to break down again. Highly ambitious production targets were fulfilled only on the basis of gross over-shooting of targets for costs, particularly labour costs, as enterprises took on new labour in excess of planned levels. In order to provide the finance for these over-shoots, the State Bank started to increase emissions of new currency sharply again. Meanwhile delays in the completion of new investment projects limited the flow of goods coming on to the market. The result was a new "scissors" movement, and the aggregate price level rose by over 150 per cent from 1928 to 1932, with average wages rising by a good deal

less. The price level rose by a further 100 per cent or so from 1932 to 1937.

In the smaller countries of Eastern Europe the inter-war trend was strongly deflationary, especially after 1929. Conservative policies in the wake of the Wall Street Crash and the subsequent collapse of world agricultural prices ensured the maintenance of stable prices, though the price paid in terms of unemployment and general welfare levels was high.

The immediate post-war period was marked by a high degree of price stability throughout Eastern Europe. Open inflation only began to develop in the Soviet Union in the late 1980s, as the authorities started to liberalize a price structure previously almost wholly under the control of Moscow bureaucrats. By 1989 the Soviet rate of inflation was at least 10 per cent. Elsewhere in Eastern Europe socialist inflation has a longer history, usually as a function of a swifter rate of progress towards some kind of market socialism. Thus in Yugoslavia inflation has been a major problem since the 1960s, and has escalated to hyper-inflation in the 1980s, with the annual rate of inflation reaching 2000 per cent at the end of 1989. The rate of inflation in Poland was of the same order at that time. In Hungary there has been significant inflation, a good deal of it "planned" since 1968, but it has not, up to now, spilled over into hyper-inflation. The average inflation rate from 1981 to 1985 in that country was around 7 per cent. It then fell a little in 1986, to accelerate to 17 per cent in 1988, and to over 30 per cent in 1989.

The pattern of underlying inflationary pressure is, however, fairly uniform throughout Eastern Europe. The bulk of it originates from government policies which have sought to by-pass the market in the economic and social development spheres. The financing of loss-making "political factories" and collective farms, of housing programmes coupled with very low rents, and in the Soviet case of a military budget representing some 13 per cent of national income, has placed intolerable strain on the budget and the money supply.

In the Soviet case those two dimensions have, indeed, been very closely linked. Because the Soviet economy remains essentially a centrally planned one, virtually all financial transactions relating to the economy go through the central budget, in addition to more conventional items like administration, social services and defence. (This may change if and when current proposals for republican financial autonomy are implemented.) So loss-making in industry and agriculture has a direct impact on the expenditure side of the budget. The Soviet budget deficit escalated dramatically in the late 1980s, growing from Rb 18 billion in 1985 to Rb 120 billion (some 20 per cent of national income) in 1989. This rapid growth is partly the result of the collapse in world oil prices in 1985, partly due to revenue losses incurred through the anti-alcohol drive. Beyond that, it reflects **Gorbachev**'s failure to stop the further growth of subsidization in the Soviet economy, particularly in relation to agriculture. Because there is no money market in the Soviet Union, and against a background of reluctance to borrow abroad to finance budget deficits, the Soviet government has only one means of covering these deficits — by printing some money. Thus the Soviet budget deficit has an immediate inflationary impact. In the past the inflationary pressure has been repressed, and has manifested itself through lengthening queues, rapid growth in savings deposits and a burgeoning second economy, rather than through price increases. As a result, the pent-up inflationary pressure is so great that a Polish/Yugoslav-type hyper-inflation cannot be excluded as a future possibility in the Soviet Union. Thus the future of Gorbachev's *perestroika* programme is crucially dependent on cutting the budget deficit and reducing inflationary pressure.

In Yugoslavia the pattern has been more complex. With decentralization to the level of the firm and the republic, the federal budget came to account for a fairly small proportion of total Yugoslav national income. But budget deficits at republican level have been equally potent sources of inflationary pressure. Beyond that, control over the supply of money in the Yugoslav case has been complicated by factors peculiar to that particular system of market socialism. As in the Soviet Union, budget deficits are inflationary because in the absence of a money market they can only be covered through the issue of primary money. In addition, however, the Yugoslav system features a monetary institution unique in world banking practice — that of "selective primary emissions". Quite apart from being the government's banker, the National Bank in Belgrade is obliged to issue primary money for specific earmarked purposes. Republican national banks have parallel obligations. In principle, selective primary emissions are largely geared towards the financing of exporting and the procurement of agricultural produce. In practice, they have been diverted to all sorts of essentially political priorities. It is through selective credits that regional **League of Communists** leaderships have ultimately found the money to keep loss-making enterprises going, and to fund "favoured" local projects. Finance for commercially dubious projects has often come initially through the emission, by the enterprises and commercial banks concerned, of bills of exchange of one sort or another. This tends to result in periodical build-ups of "near-money". As holders of near-money come to seek conversion of their "assets" into real money, extreme pressure is placed on the National Bank to increase the supply of money through selective primary emissions, in order to prevent widespread bankruptcies, with all that that would imply in social and political terms.

The inflationary pattern in Yugoslavia bears one more rather special characteristic. Yugoslavia's trade with the rest of Eastern Europe is organized on the basis of a CMEA-typical set of bilateral clearing agreements. Yugoslavia has tended to run very big surpluses on these clearing accounts, and the cumulative surplus in 1990 stood at over $2 billion. This is unsatisfactory from a purely trading point of view. In addition, however, it adds fuel to inflationary pressure because any Yugoslav exporter delivering to Eastern Europe can claim immediate payment from the National Bank in domestic currency. The corresponding deliveries from the **Council for Mutual Economic Assistance (CMEA)** may come through months or years later, or not at all. In a word, trade with the CMEA area tends to increase demand much more certainly than it increases supply. Attempts to bring this problem under control by introducing a waiting period between exports to the CMEA and payment in dinars have predictably run into regional complications. Exporting to the East is mainly concentrated in Serbia, located in the eastern part of Yugoslavia, and plans to change the financial procedures covering this trade tend to be seen as yet further proof of a Croatian/Slovenian conspiracy against the Serbs.

As the Soviet Union moves gingerly towards the idea of an independent and politically neutral central bank, planning money supply in the interests of price stability on the model of the West German Bundesbank, and towards the creation of some kind of money market, as Yugoslavia prepares to introduce a "new" convertible dinar pegged to the Deutschemark, as Poland makes plans to clear her budget deficit by 1990 and introduce strict monetary discipline, there are some prospects that the end of the period of repressed inflation in Eastern Europe will not simply be succeeded by a period of generalized open hyper-inflation. But the countries which remain under Communist-dominated one-party systems stand a less good chance of succeeding in the battle against inflation than countries in which the transition to institutionalized political pluralism has been made. The notion that being a Communist activist gives you a "licence to print money" is deeply rooted amongst the old political cadres of Eastern Europe. This in itself may, however, accelerate the trend towards political pluralism throughout the region.

A phenomenon highly specific to the CMEA region is that of concealed inflation in "constant price" national income data. In principle, production series in current prices should be deflated to some common price base in order to produce comparable output figures for different periods. In practice, in Eastern Europe, this process of deflation has often been done only to a partial extent. In the Soviet Union, for instance, the machinery index is a notorious vehicle for concealed inflation, as "new" machines are allocated putative constant-price-base prices which greatly exaggerate their actual productivity by comparison with "old" machines. This is partly due to the tendency for new machines to carry *current* prices many hundreds of per cent greater than those of the machines they replace, which in turn reflects the pressure of excess demand at given prices, i.e. the pressure of repressed inflation. "New" consumer goods often evince the same problem, and for the same reason. The element of concealed inflation may vary considerably in amplitude between different East European countries. It is generally reckoned to be comparatively high for the GDR, and comparatively low for Czechoslovakia. There is no evidence of any significant problem of this nature in Yugoslavia. The official line in the Soviet Union is that concealed inflation was a major problem under **Brezhnev**, but has now been eradicated from official Soviet statistics. Close analysis of current Soviet statistical reporting does, however, suggest that the problem may, if anything have actually worsened in the **Gorbachev** period.

DAD

INFORMATION TECHNOLOGY. Information and communications technology is one of the weakest areas of the economies of Eastern Europe. Even in the GDR, the most advanced of the countries of the **Council for Mutual Economic Assistance (CMEA)**, the absence of computerization and the poverty of the telephone system is one of the first things that strikes the traveller. Indeed the failure to keep abreast of the micro-electronics revolution of the 1970s and 1980s was one of the main "qualitative" factors behind the slowdown in East European growth rates over those decades. The need to fill the yawning gap this failure has left presents one of the most concrete illustrations of the vital necessity of *perestroika* in the countries concerned.

We can distinguish four main reasons for the CMEA information technology lag:

(i) Political conservatism: the stability of the **Brezhnev** period was to a considerable extent based on the principle that no-one was ever fired. This tended to produce a gerontocratic pattern ill-suited to the absorption of new technology. In the Soviet Union the quadrupling of oil prices in 1974, which greatly benefited the Soviet Union as a major oil exporter, tended to reinforce the mood of complacency. This contrasts starkly with the Japanese reaction. With no energy resources of their own, the Japanese reacted to the first oil shock by throwing enormous resources into the development of energy-efficient micro-electronic technology.

(ii) Internal security concerns: Brezhnevite stability, in the USSR and elsewhere in Eastern Europe, was also centrally based on the comprehensive suppression of freedom of expression. Against such a background, any machine capable of producing multiple copies took on the character of a strategic good. With photocopiers guarded as if they were nuclear missiles, it is hardly surprising the word-processing technology did not take off rapidly once it became available.

(iii) Traditional planning systems: with their emphasis on quantity rather than quality, and their hostility to radical technical change, these were unable to provide an environment conducive to a technological revolution. East European managers found it simpler to carry on earning their bonuses for producing more of what they had always produced. The quality-insensitivity of Soviet-type economic systems may also have contributed to problems with the supply of silicone of the purity required for the manufacture of silicone chips.

(iv) Western strategic embargo: the CoCom agreement, subscribed to by all the NATO countries except Iceland, and also by Japan, covers a list of "strategically sensitive" items which can only be exported to **Warsaw Treaty Organization (Warsaw Pact)** countries under special licence. Nearly two-thirds of the CoCom "Industrial List" (there are separate lists for armaments and atomic energy) relates to electronics, computer equipment and telecommunications products. In the realm of computers, for instance, machines with a capacity of 2–16 bits are subject to licensing at the level of national governments. Above that, agreement must be reached between all the CoCom signatories. Licences have in the past rarely been granted, and it has been virtually impossible legally to export a 32-bit computer from a CoCom country to Eastern Europe. There is a separate US Commodity Control List which is rather more comprehensive that the CoCom list.

CoCom has been a less crucial obstacle to the development of East European information technology industries than might appear *a priori*. Not all the advanced industrial countries are members (Sweden and Switzerland are the most important non-members), and it is very difficult to stop individual smuggling. Most importantly, the technological obtuseness of traditional central planning has ensured that, even when Western hardware is acquired by East European countries, it is poorly applied, and provides little boost to domestic electronics design and production capacities.

Against this background, the success rate in the assimilation of micro-electronic technology has varied somewhat between product groups and between countries. In the Soviet Union, following on a decision of the Council of Ministers taken in August 1988, production of video-recorders grew by some 70 per cent in 1989, to reach an annual production level of over 100,000. In contrast, Soviet attempts to develop robot technology have been a dismal failure, and the Soviet authorities stopped reporting production levels of robots in 1988. Efforts to solve the problem through co-operation with Czechoslovakia have provided one more illustration of the ineffectuality of the CMEA as a vehicle for technical co-operation. Soviet efforts to produce personal computers has been another disaster story. In 1987 the *Agat* school computer had to be withdrawn from production because it simply did not work. The replacement, *Korvet*, remains unproved. The critical shortage of reliable computers in educational establishments means that a new generation of Soviet students are growing up without basic computer literacy. A 1988 contract with the Chicago Trading Group to set up three assembly lines for PCs in the Soviet Union, and a deal the following year to buy $850 million of personal computers from the West German firm Siemens will ease but not solve the problem.

The one CMEA country to achieve some real development in micro-electronics is Bulgaria. Output of the electrical machinery and electronics sector grew at an average rate of 13.7 per cent from 1984 to 1988. There are probably substantial elements of concealed inflation in that figure, as "new" products have been introduced. Even so, there can be no denying Bulgaria's comparative success in this area. But the country's electronics industry is still not capable of competing on the world market, and this is presenting increasing problems in terms of international trade patterns. A large proportion of Bulgaria's electronics output is shipped to the Soviet Union. Recent years have, however, withnessed a growing Bulgarian surplus in trade with the Soviet Union, as Soviet deliveries of fuel have been cut. Because the trade is balanced bilaterally, these surpluses cannot be converted into hard currency or goods from other countries. Up to now, the accumulated surpluses have probably only been wiping out accumulated deficits from the era of high oil prices. In the future, however, Bulgaria will have to seek new markets for her electronics output.

The history of modern micro-electronics in Yugoslavia has been rather different from that in the other East European countries. Unhampered by CoCom restrictions or central planning, information technology could have been a major growth area in Yugoslavia, as in other "newly industrializing countries". In practice, micro-electronics development has been a disappointment, mainly because the politically conditioned fragmentation of the country makes any kind of integrated, national development strategy impossible. Domestic production of video-recorders has been set up, but can only survive on the basis of very heavy protection. There are some internationally rated electronics companies in Yugoslavia, like Iskra of Ljubljana, which operates a rather Japanese-style pattern of co-operation with small private companies. But the director of Iskra reckons that his firm is a generation behind leading companies in terms of actual production. Shortage of trained design engineers has been a major specific bottleneck for Iskra, and indeed for the Yugoslav industry as a whole. There can be no doubt, however, that were Yugoslavia able to solve its basic systemic problems, the information technology sector could provide one of the springboards for future development.

The future of the information industry among the six Eastern European CMEA members is clearly intimately tied in with the unfolding of political conditions in the aftermath of the momentous events of 1989. If the early 1990s see the emergence of a group of market economies in Eastern Europe owing at most purely symbolic allegiance to the Warsaw Pact, or if, indeed, the Warsaw Pact (and possibly also NATO) simply ceases to exist in its present form, then the principal obstacles, external and internal, to a rapid information technology revolution will disappear. In the case of East Germany, the removal of barriers to free movement between the two Germanys will in itself almost certainly be enough to work a miracle in the level of computer and telecommunications technology in the GDR. If Bulgaria chooses to open up to international capital the existing electronics base could certainly be transformed into a competitive force on the world market. For the Soviet Union itself, however, the situation will be more complex. Some degree of strategic embargo is bound to continue to apply to that country for the foreseeable future, though the indications as of 1990 were that CoCom restrictions would be significantly relaxed. Beyond that, there is no immediate prospect for the transformation of the Soviet economy into a fully-fledged market system. Where there are real prospects is in the area of specific joint ventures. The San Francisco–Moscow Teleport, opened in 1988, made it possible for the first time to transmit faxes between the USA and the USSR. Another joint venture involving the British firm GPT started installing modern business telephone systems in Moscow in 1989. Fargo Management and Consulting of Toronto are planning to set up photocopying and custom printing facilities in the USSR in co-operation with the Moscow publishing house Kniga. Significantly, two of the new Chinese-style special economic zones to be set up in the Soviet Union in the early 1990s—those at Vyborg and Novgorod—will specialize in electronics. Even with special economic zones, however, the Soviet trading regime is unlikely to be attractive enough to cause a stampede of Western electronic firms into joint ventures until **Gorbachev**'s *perestroika* policies have gone a great deal further.

DAD

INTER-GERMAN TRADE. The GDR has treated trade with the Federal Republic of Germany as foreign trade, while the latter has not. This has meant that special trading terms have been devised, very much to the advantage of the GDR. All transactions are conducted in so-called "accounting units", which assume a false parity between the Deutschemark and the East German foreign trade Mark, the Valuta Mark. Over and above reciprocal trade, the GDR can make use of DM 850 million interest-free "swing" credit. GDR trade with the Federal Republic accounts for at least 8 per cent of the GDR's total trade turnover and about 60 per cent of the GDR's trade with OECD countries. Because of the special trading conditions, the GDR has been described as a surrogate member of the EC. This was not the case, but the GDR appeared likely in the 1990s, through the Federal Republic, to become an actual member.

Inter-German trade covers a wide range of products, most notable of which are oil products, fuels, mining products, chemicals, machinery and metals. In 1984 the GDR had a trade surplus with the Federal Republic of DM 1.3 billion, but since then only deficits have been recorded: DM 0.4

billion in 1988. The GDR's accumulated debt to institutions in the Federal Republic at the end of 1988 was around DM 4.5 billion. The general level of trade has stagnated because of the GDR's failure to produce sufficient competitive quality goods and its obligations to the USSR. In the new political conditions of 1990, however, West German involvement in the GDR economy was likely to expand enormously.

JO

ISLAM. In the USSR, there are about 55 million people belonging to nationalities which traditionally adhered to Islam, nearly one fifth of the population. There are around four million in Yugoslavia, 1,500,000 in Albania, around 1,200,00 in Bulgaria and much smaller numbers in Romania and Poland.

The 1989 USSR census showed that the Muslim nationalities were continuing to grow rapidly in their numbers, although not quite as rapidly as before. Among the age cohort of normal entry into the armed forces, over one third come from Muslim nations. The Muslims do not, however, represent a united force, threatening Moscow's domination of the Soviet Union. They are divided by nationality, language, denomination, geography and clan.

The principal Muslim nations are the Uzbeks (who with 16,700,000 in 1989 constituted the third largest national group in the USSR), Kazakhs (8,100,000), Azeris (6,800,000), Tatars (n.a.), Tadzhiks (4,200,000), Turkmenians (2,700,000), Kirghiz (2,500,000) and Bashkirs (n.a.). The Uzbeks, Kazakhs, Azeris, Tadzhiks, Turkmenians and Kirghiz have their own Union Republics, while the Tatars and Bashkirs have Autonomous Republics within the RSFSR. Some of the smaller Islamic nationalities have their own Autonomous Republics or regions.

Nearly all of the Islamic nationalities speak Turkic languages, but the Tadzhiks speak Farsi. Most Soviet Muslims are Sunni and therefore perhaps less susceptible to Shi'ite influences from Iran. The Shi'ites are limited to about 70 per cent of the Azeris. For them, sympathy with the Azeri minority across the border in Iran, where the Azeri language lacks official recognition, may be stronger than Shi'ite solidarity. Moscow has a long-standing policy of seeking to isolate rank-and-file Soviet Muslim from their co-religionists abroad.

Islam is as much a culture and a way of life as a religion, and it is not considered obligatory to fulfil all the requirements of prayer and ritual to retain one's status as a Muslim. It is difficult to estimate the religious commitment of Soviet

Muslims. While Western analysts often draw a distinction between "official" and "unofficial" branches of Soviet Islam, depending on whether or not the mosques and mullahs are registered, in practice the two merge into one another. Statistics for the numbers of mosques and mullahs have been unreliable. On the other hand, traditional Muslim rites such as male circumcision and religious burial seem universal, and religious marriage ceremonies are very common.

During the **Great Fatherland War**, the Soviet authorities established an official structure for Muslims, placing their own appointees in charge. There are four Spiritual Directorates. The most important is in Tashkent, covering Central Asia and Kazakhstan; the others are in Ufa, covering the Muslims living in the European part of the USSR, the Volga region and Siberia; in Makhachkala, covering the Northern Caucasus; and in Baku, covering Transcaucasia and also all the Shi'ites in the Soviet Union. The directorates are responsible for the upkeep of mosques, the employment of priests, and the maintenance of the *madrassah* (seminaries) in Bukhara and Tashkent. They play an important role in Soviet foreign policy in relation to the Muslim countries, with the leaders frequently travelling abroad and receiving guests. Their duty is to present a rosy picture of the situation of Soviet Islam to foreigners. A periodical, *Muslims of the Soviet East*, facilitates this.

The Muftis who head the directorates have sought to adapt Islam to Soviet conditions, relaxing requirements such as the *hajj* (pilgrimage to Mecca) and the need to pray five times a day. They have argued that Communism and Islam are motivated by the same social ideals, but Communism lacks a spiritual dimension which can only be filled by Islam. Outside the religious structures, all the republics have Unions of Writers and societies for the preservation of historical and cultural monuments which have shown increasing boldness is defending the Islamic elements in the national cultures. Perhaps more dangerous to the political regime are the Sufi brotherhoods, originally in the Northern Caucasus but now also in Central Asia. These secret societies were formed in opposition to Tsarist colonialism. Their actual strength and political significance remains obscure.

Official Soviet policy has been to develop the cultures of the different nationalities, to prevent the emergence of pan-Islamic or pan-Turkic feeling. As a result, Soviet Muslims have overlapping identities, seeing themselves as Muslims, as members of a particular nationality, from a particular area and perhaps belonging to a particular clan. The different nationalities show uneven levels of attachment to Islam; for the Uzbeks, it is central to their culture, but it is of much less significance to the Kazakhs.

Soviet propagandists have long denounced the idea that Islam is essential to the national cultures of the Muslim nations. They attack Muslim religious practices and the cult of "holy places". Religious literature is in such short supply that Soviet soldiers of Muslim background in Afghanistan reportedly traded their weapons for copies of the Koran. The Soviet press, especially from 1983, has complained about the growth of Islamic fundamentalism. It has referred to subversive radio broadcasts from Iran and sabotage and terror by Afghan *mujahaddin*.

Yuri **Andropov**'s anti-corruption campaign, continued by **Gorbachev**, created alarm among religious Soviet Muslims. They feared that Moscow was sending Russians into powerful positions in Central Asia on the pretext of fighting corruption but with the real intention of weakening Islam. Gorbachev's speech in the Uzbek capital, Tashkent, in November 1986, which strongly attacked religion, strengthened these worries. His appointment of a Russian First Secretary in Kazakhstan in the following month led to the Alma-Ata riots (*see* **Nationality Question in the USSR**). Here nationalism and clan solidarity appear to have been more important than Islam.

Perestroika has been slow to arrive in Central Asia, apart from the anti-corruption campaign, but a demonstration in Tashkent in early 1989 led to the replacement of the old Grand Mufti, seen as too closely linked to the Brezhnevite political leaders of the region, by a new young leader, Mamayusupov Muhammadsaddyk.

The Islamic identity is not sufficient to prevent rivalry based on identities. Thus in 1989, for example, there were clashes between Uzbeks and Meskhetian Turks in Ferghana and between Kazakhs and immigrants from the Caucasus in Novy Uzen. Rivalry between Uzbeks and Tadzhiks over territory is long-standing.

On the other hand, the Muslim peoples have shared interests which do not necessarily coincide with those of Moscow. Their desire for religious freedom, for greater use of their native languages and for more economic autonomy, which were suppressed in the Brezhnev years, seem more compatible with those of *perestroika*. The Gorbachev leadership, however, has stopped the plan to reverse part of the flow of Siberian rivers into Central Asia, which the local leaders see as essential for economic development. Moscow is generally unwilling to continue subsidizing the development of the Muslim areas.

The change in investment policy, to the disadvantage of the Central Asians, comes at a time when they have lost any representation in the Politburo, although one Tatar was admitted to the Secretariat in November 1989 and Gorbachev has spoken of increasing non-Russian representation. If the locus of decision making shifts from the party to the soviets, however, the Muslims will benefit, because they are well represented in the new Supreme Soviet, especially in the Soviet of Nationalities, which is chaired by the Uzbek Rafik Nishanov.

At the beginning of 1990 Moscow's biggest problem by far in relation to Soviet Muslims was the need to restore order in Azerbaidzhan. The anti-Armenian pogroms of January 1990 were accompanied by a collapse of the republican party and government authority, with the Popular Front of Azerbaidzhan apparently enjoying mass support. Moscow had no alternative but to send its armed forces to recapture Baku. The Popular Front had within it a wide range of political tendencies, from social democratic to Muslim fundamentalist. The Nakhichevan Autonomous Republic, an Azerbaidzhani enclave between Armenia, Turkey and Iran, declared its secession from the USSR. The impact of the Azerbaidzhan revolt and its suppression on Soviet Muslims elsewhere was still to be felt.

All Muslims in the Balkans are Sunni, other than the Bektashi in Northern Albania, who are Shi'ite. In Yugoslavia, approximately two million of the Muslims are Slavs who were converted to Islam when the South Slav lands formed part of the Ottoman Empire. Most of these live in the republic of Boznia-Herzegovina, where they are the largest ethnic group. These Muslims were recognized as a separate nationality only in 1961, as "ethnic Muslims". This was apparently to avoid the polarization of Yugoslavia between the northern nationalities (Croats and Slovenes) and southern nationalities (Serbs, Macedonians, Montenegrins and Albanians). (See **Nationalism and Communism in Eastern Europe**.) A further 1,700,000 Muslims are ethnic Albanians, mainly in Kosovo. Yugoslavia was concerned to develop its relations with Arab countries, and the religious conditions for Muslims were made more favourable.

Not surprisingly, the revitalization of world Islam in the 1970s and 1980s led to a growth in the religious life of Yugoslav Muslims, who were allowed easier links with foreign Muslims than their Soviet counterparts. This also had a political dimension, which was unwelcome to the authorities, who tried to separate Muslim ethnicity from religious extremism. Encouraged by the Iranian revolution, there was an upsurge in both ethnic Muslim and Albanian nationalism. In September 1983, 13 Muslim activists received severe prison sentences for disrupting the "brotherhood" of the Yugoslav nationalities; in 1987 three more were sentenced for allegedly seeking to establish an Islamic state, and it was rumoured that the accused had links with Iran. The Albanian nationalism was more closely related to economic grievances, and the desire of the Albanians for Kosovo to obtain the status of a republic within Yugoslavia, but the expression of Albanian nationalism against the Serbs undoubtedly had a religious dimension (see also **Serbian Orthodox Church**).

In Albania itself, where 70 per cent of the population was Islamic, all religious practice has been banned since 1967. Worship is therefore mainly performed secretly, in believers' homes, but at present it is difficult to assess how widespread this is.

Muslims in Bulgaria comprise at least one million ethnic Turks and around 200,000 "Pomaks", Bulgarians who were forcibly converted to Islam under the Ottomans. In 1984 the **Zhivkov** regime began a campaign against Islamic religious practices and also tried forcibly to persuade the Turks to adopt Bulgarian names. In summer 1989 the authorities moved again against the Turks, reportedly killing some of those demonstrating for religious freedom. The regime then encouraged or forced around 300,000 Turks to move to Turkey, without most of their possessions (see also **Turks in Bulgaria**).

Following the fall of Zhivkov in December 1989, the **Mladenov** leadership announced that Turks would be allowed to revert to their old names, and that all Muslims would be able to practise their religion. In January 1990 Bulgarian chauvinists, probably linked with the party apparatus, demonstrated in Kurjali and Sofia against these reforms, and a general strike spread through the country. While the government stood its ground, the events showed that old enmities could still be manipulated for political gain.

PJSD

J

JAKEŠ, MILOŠ. General Secretary of the **Communist Party of Czechoslovakia** from December 1987 until November 1989, Jakeš's early career was devoted to the economic activities of local government (including the period between 1966 and 1968 when he was a Deputy Minister of the Interior). He owed his promotion to the post of Chairman of the Communist Party's disciplinary body, the Central Control and Auditing Commission, in March 1968, to his friendship with Alexander **Dubček**, with whom he had studied between 1955 and 1958 at the Higher Party School in Moscow. In that post he was responsible for the expulsion of proponents of reform from the Communist Party in 1970 in a purge which affected one-fifth of the membership. In 1977, he was made a candidate member of the Communist Party Presidium and the Central Committee Secretary in charge of agriculture. Four years later he was promoted to full membership of the Presidium and the Secretary responsible for economic policy. His readiness in that last capacity to sanction some experiments in the economy, combined with his hardline record in ideological and political matters, made him acceptable, in the eyes of his Presidium colleagues, as a successor to Gustáv **Husák** as party General Secretary in December 1987. In that post he supported moves towards reform of the economic system but avoided other than superficial changes in the political sphere, refusing to countenance rehabilitation of the 1968 **Prague Spring**. He resigned from the party leadership on Nov. 24, 1989 after a week of public demonstrations demanding his dismissal and political reform.

GW

JARUZELSKI, GEN. WOJCIECH. Born in July 1923 near Puławy, Poland (Lublin province) into a family of landed gentry and attended a Jesuit boarding school. He was in the Soviet Union after the outbreak of war (the precise circumstances of the move remain unclear) and worked there as a labourer until 1943, his father dying in the country at some stage during the war. He then entered the renowned Ryazan military training academy and joined the Polish army raised in the Soviet Union by Gen. Berling. Jaruzelski fought with the army for the whole of its westward campaign, finishing as head of a regimental reconnaissance unit. Until 1947, the year he joined the Communist Party, he was occupied fighting anti-Communist Polish partisans. After that he underwent further training at the Higher Infantry School and then the General Staff Academy, subsequently becoming a lecturer himself, head of the administration of military academies and officer schools and deputy head of the Main Combat Training Commission.

In the critical year of 1956 he became the youngest general in the Polish Army at the level of brigadier and, from 1957, led the 12th Mechanized Division. Promotion in critical political areas followed with his appointment in 1960 to head the Main Political Administration of the Armed Forces and, two years later, as vice-minister of defence. He was then made Chief of General Staff in 1965 and, in 1968, Minister of National Defence in time to oversee Polish preparations for its part in the invasion of Czechoslovakia by the **Warsaw Treaty Organization (Warsaw Pact)**. From 1964 he was a member of the Central Committee of the **Polish United Workers' Party (PUWP)**. He had also risen to become division general in 1960 and general of arms in 1968. The fall of **Gomułka** saw a further consolidation of his political status and he was made candidate member of the PUWP Politburo in December 1970 and a full member one year later. Towards the end of the **Gierek** period he developed a reputation for an insistence on dealing cautiously with the increasingly restive population, and is supposed to have said he would not give the order to fire on Polish workers.

Under the crisis conditions of 1981 the sphere of political responsibility widened with his election in February as Prime Minister and replacement of **Kania** as leader of the PUWP in October, this being followed eight weeks later by his announcement of a **State of War** and the suspension of many civic freedoms in the name of martial law. These developments tarnished Jaruzelski's image as a patriotic soldier largely above politics. Further, it took time for him to pass some of these posts to others — to Gen. Siwicki as Minister of Defence in November 1983 (although at the same time he took on the presidency and chair of the National Defence Council), to Zbigniew Messner as Prime Minister in November 1985 and to Mieczysław **Rakowski** as party leader on July 29, 1989. His role nevertheless remained a dominant one through the 1980s and he was elected to the newly strengthened office of president on July 19, 1989.

PGL

K

KÁDÁR, JÁNOS. The dominant political figure of post-World War II Hungary, leader of the **Hungarian Socialist Workers' Party (HSWP)** from its foundation in 1956 until May 1988. Born János Czermaník in 1912, a mechanic by original profession, Kadar joined the illegal Hungarian Communist Party (HCP) and Young Communist League in 1931, joining the secretariat of the latter organization the following year. He remained in Hungary throughout the Horthy era, serving two years in prison from 1935–37 for illegal political activity, after which he joined the (legal) **Hungarian Social-Democratic Party**. During World War II, he helped to set up the underground HCP and was active in the resistance movement, working closely with László **Rajk**. After liberation, he was elected to the Central Committee and Politburo of the re-established HCP, and from 1945 to 1948, he held the key posts of Secretary Party Committee of Greater Budapest and Deputy Chief of Police. In addition, he took on the post of Deputy General Secretary of the Party from 1946. In 1948, he took over from Rajk as Minister of the Interior, in which capacity he was implicated in the unlawful arrest, trial and execution of Rajk (one of his closest friends) in 1949. But by 1950, his turn came too: he was dismissed from all his posts, and expelled from the party by the **Rákosi** faction. In 1951, he was arrested on trumped-up charges and imprisoned without trial until 1954, when he was released, rehabilitated and restored to his former post of Budapest Party Secretary.

Kádár played a crucial role in the events of 1956. His sympathies were clearly with the cause of Khrushchevite reformism and against Rakosi and his faction. In July 1956, he was brought back into the Central Committee and Politburo of the party, and on Oct. 25 he was elected to replace the discredited Erno Gero as its First Secretary. He joined the multi-party coalition government under Prime Minister Imre **Nagy**, and was believed to be fully committed to that government and its new policies. On Nov. 1 he announced the disbandment of the HWP and the formation of a new Hungarian Socialist Workers' Party, but when news came that same day that Soviet troops were re-entering Hungary, Kádár disappeared. He resurfaced on Nov. 4 at the head of a "Revolutionary Workers' and Peasants' Government" set up to restore Soviet control of Hungary, and brought back to Budapest by the Soviet Army. From that time until 1958 he combined the post of Prime Minister with that of party leader, and thus must be held directly responsible for the harsh repression which took place in those years in which Communist rule was restored, including the execution of Imre Nagy in 1958. Clearly, the Soviet Union had the dominant role in defining the terms of "normalization" in Hungary, but Kádár's preparedness to oversee the process must be taken as an important indication of the priority he attached to loyalty to Moscow over the values of national independence, democratic freedom, and personal moral integrity.

Kádár was a pragmatic realist rather than a fanatical Communist, and, having forced his fellow-countrymen to submit their inescapable subordination to the Soviet Union, he set about making their lot more comfortable in material terms. In fact, in the first six months of his rule he had set up a committee of economic experts to work on a proposal for economic reform. But this was rejected as impracticable in the fraught political circumstances of 1957. It was not until 1961 that Kádár felt fully assured of his own personal control of the party, and that Moscow felt fully assured of the political stabilization of the country, both of which were essential preconditions for reform. The "Kádár era" proper dawned at the end of 1961, when Kádár pronounced the famous dictum, "whoever is not against us is with us", which signified an important departure from the previous mistrustful and coercive relationship with the population. It implied that those who were hard-working, conscientious and law-abiding could expect to do well, to be rewarded and promoted without having to conform overtly to strict ideological discipline and without having necessarily to be party members.

This approach was particularly successful in regaining the confidence of the intelligentsia, who were then set to work on the task of devising a "New Economic Mechanism" (NEM) (*see* **Hungary** — Economic development) which would ensure the improved economic performance essential to winning over the rest of the population. Kádár's own contribution to the economic reform was that of political patron, without whose support it would never have been implemented. He defended this departure from Stalinist orthodoxy in the economy against quite strong ideological opposition from the party's "left", but, true to his centrist leadership style, he also curbed any aspiration on the reformist "right" to carry the reform into the political sphere. This propensity to initiate reform, but then to compromise, which was so characteristic of his entire period of rule, was eventually to lead not only to the failure of the NEM in the 1970s, but to the political crisis of the 1980s which eventually swept him from power.

Kádár's position as party leader first began to weaken at the beginning of the 1980s, when it became clear that the modifications of the economic reform in the mid-1970s had been an enormously costly mistake. Certain leading reform economists broke ranks and began urging a "reform of the reform", which Kádár found intolerable. Thus he put himself firmly in the "conservative" camp in the party, and thereafter found himself on the defensive. Morever, he was ageing, his health was less robust, and he was clearly losing his grip on day-to-day affairs in the apparatus and also his previous sensitivity to the popular mood. The considerable respect and genuine public support he had built up since the 1960s began to evaporate. He was finally removed from power at the special HSWP conference in May 1988; he was shifted to the newly created, ceremonial post of party President, but was excluded from the Politburo. One year later, he was relieved of this post and his Central Committee membership, officially for health reasons (in April, serious respiratory illness had been diagnosed). But the new leader Károly **Grósz** also let it be known that he had been "unable to come to terms with political changes". He was admitted to hospital seriously ill and died on July 6, 1989, by coincidence on the same day that the Hungarian Supreme Court annulled the verdict of treason passed on Imre Nagy in 1958. Kádár's funeral on July 14 was attended by over 100,000 people, and obituaries, while openly recognizing his mistakes, also paid respectful tribute to his search to build "national consensus" after the trauma of 1956.

JB

KANIA, STANISŁAW. Leader of the **Polish United Workers' Party (PUWP)** from September 1980 to October 1981. Born to a smallholding family in Krosno province in March 1927. At the age of 15 he began work for a blacksmith and two years later in 1944 became active in the resistance and joined the Peasant Battalions. At the end of the war he organized a local branch of the youth movement in his village and joined the Polish Workers' Party (PPR) in April 1945. He rose up the hierarchy of the youth organization and became vice-chairman of its provincial committee in Rzeszów. He also held several party posts

and was a member of the party committee executive in Rzeszów, too. Having passed through the central school of the PUWP in 1952 he became head of rural youth department of the national youth organization and a member of its national Presidium. In 1958 he assumed responsibility for the agricultural department of the Warsaw party committee and later became a secretary of the committee.

In 1968 he became head of the Central Committee administration department and in April 1971 a Central Committee secretary. He was a candidate member of the Central Committee from 1964 and a full member from 1968 (a position he held until 1986). In 1971 he became a candidate member of Politburo and was made full member in 1975. Kania was closely involved in the activities surrounding the consolidation by Edward **Gierek** of his leadership and he took over Moczar's responsibilities within the CC secretariat for the military and internal security before the latter's removal as CC secretary in June 1971. He was first elected to the *Sejm* in 1972, remaining a deputy until 1989 when he was one of the candidates on the national list who failed to get elected. Around the mid-1970s he also assumed responsibility within the Central Committee for church-state relations.

He played a central role in the party leadership at the time of the 1980 strikes and was instrumental in the rejection by the party of the proposal that they be forcibly crushed. When Gierek fell ill at the beginning of September a CC Plenum was assembled at which Kania was elected first secretary. His rather ill-defined ideas of political reform and the creation of a new role for the party through which it could restore its credibility now became official policy, though many within the party-state establishment continued to fight a rearguard action against **Solidarity** and political reform. Kania fought off hard-line attacks on his position and steadily prepared the party for its Extraordinary Congress, finally held in July 1981, managing to link the forces in the party seeking more radical reform with the political preparations for the Congress. When it opened he was re-elected first secretary, though was not given the free political hand he apparently sought. As the party moved on to the offensive and relations with Solidarity worsened Kania's position weakened, and his proposal to resign the leadership was accepted by the CC in October, the leadership of the PUWP passing to Gen. **Jaruzelski**. He retained a higher status than most former party leaders, however, and was chairman of the *Sejm* committee for self-government affairs until the elections of 1989.

PGL

KARDELJ, EDVARD. Born in Ljubljana (Slovenia) in 1910; joined the Yugoslav Communist Youth Organization in 1926 and the Communist Party of Yugoslavia (CPY) in 1928. During the 1930s he was imprisoned for illegal political activities. He studied at the Lenin School in Moscow; he joined the Central Committee of the CPY in 1937 when **Tito** became its Secretary-General, and remained a member of the Committee until his death in 1979. He served as Vice President of the Federal Government from 1946 to 1953, and as Foreign Minister from 1948 to 1953. Kardelj was Tito's closest colleague and was credited with the development of the ideological basis of self-management.

PA

KATYN. The name of a village in Soviet Russia which has occupied a critical place in Polish-Soviet relations and come to symbolize much of the post-war antagonism in East European political relations. It was in a forest outside the village that the bodies of over 4,000 Polish officers, deported from Poland by Soviet forces in 1939, were found in April 1943. These facts were beyond dispute, but little else has been. The graves were discovered by German forces when they occupied the area, and they were happy to sow discord amongst the Allies by assigning responsibility to the Soviet occupying forces of Eastern Poland between 1939 and 1941. The Soviet Union blamed Germany, while both Poles and Germans called on the International Red Cross to investigate the site. This was regarded by the Soviet leadership as a hostile act on the part of the Poles and provided the basis for the Soviets to break off diplomatic relations with the Polish government-in-exile two weeks after the discovery.

This clearly reflected long-lasting tensions between the two countries and was used by the Soviet leadership to distance itself from the official Polish government in the pursuit of longer-term strategic aims. Polish determination, though, also served to isolate its government from the one ally whose attitude was bound to be crucial to its future fate and its stand did nothing to strengthen its position within the alliance. Nevertheless, the original investigation and subsequent research only strengthened the case against Soviet representatives for having murdered the Polish officers whose remains were discovered at Katyn — and, by implication the remaining 10,000 of the Polish officer corps of whom nothing was heard after 1940. For obvious reasons, the Western allies were not anxious to make an issue of the affair and remained agnostic during the war years—and the subsequent period. The Soviet authorities resolutely held to the theory of German guilt for the massacre and during the years of Communist rule in Poland the issue remained one surrounded by an eloquent silence. As such, "Katyn" became a symbol of the unacknowledged truth about Stalinist designs on Poland and the nature of the post-war dictatorship.

The subject was, of course, well aired in informal discourse and in underground Polish publications. As late as 1985, though, the Soviet authorities erected a monument at Katyn with an inscription referring to the victims of Nazi aggression. But the changes introduced under **Gorbachev** towards the Soviet historical heritage and relations with neighbouring countries also involved an agreement to fill in the "blank areas" on the map of Soviet-Polish relations and, beginning in 1987, the question of Katyn slowly began to come to the surface. It increasingly became the subject of public discussion in Poland, although Soviet authorities continued to be evasive. In October 1989 the Polish Prosecutor-General requested further investigations from the Soviet side.

PGL

KAZAKHSTAN. The Kirghiz (in 1925 renamed Kazakh) Autonomous Soviet Socialist Republic was formed in 1920 within the **Russian Republic (RSFSR)**. In 1936 it became a constituent republic of the USSR. Kazakhstan occupies an area of 2,717,300 sq km, and is second in size only to the RSFSR among the Soviet republics. Its 1989 census population was 16,538,000 or 5.8 per cent of the USSR total. The Kazakhs themselves are a minority within the republic, accounting for just 36 per cent of the population in the 1979 census; Russians accounted for 41 per cent and Ukrainians for 6 per cent in the same year. Altogether the republic's population includes the representatives of more than 100 different national groups. Its capital is Alma-Ata. Kazakhstan is an enormously important agricultural producer, especially for grain, cotton and other industrial crops, and it has very large numbers of livestock, particularly sheep. Industrial production is based upon rich deposits of coal, tungsten, oil, copper, lead and zinc. In 1990 the republic was subdivided into 19 regions and 222 districts. In late 1986, and subsequently, the republic was affected by interethnic tensions. (*See also* **Nationality Question in the USSR**)

SLW

149

KHRUSHCHEV, NIKITA SERGEEVICH.
Soviet politician and party leader from 1953 to
1964. Born in 1894 of a peasant family, he
worked in the mines and plants of the Ukraine,
joining the **Communist Party of the Soviet
Union (CPSU)** in 1918. In 1929 he went to
Moscow for further study; he became a member
of the CPSU Central Committee in 1934, first
secretary of the important Moscow party organization in 1935, and then first secretary of the
Ukrainian party organization in 1938 and a full
member of the ruling Politburo after 1939. Back
in Moscow after 1949, he became CPSU First
Secretary after the death of **Stalin** and by the mid-
1950s he was clearly the dominant figure in the
nominally collective leadership. From 1958 onwards he was prime minister as well as party
leader; two posts it was decided to separate after
his fall in 1964 in order to avoid undue concentrations of power in the hands of a single person.
Khrushchev delivered his celebrated "secret
speech" to a closed session of the XX Congress
of the CPSU in 1956; it was an unexpected and
vigorous denunciation of the "grave violations of
revolutionary legality" of the Stalin era and
caused a sensation in the USSR, the world Communist movement and the wider world. Un-
published at the time, it became available from
Western sources and was finally published in the
USSR as late as 1989.

Under Khrushchev's leadership an attempt
(largely an unsuccessful one) was made to decen-
tralize economic management; the split with
China divided the world Communist movement;
and the Cuban missile crisis in 1962 led to a
humiliating Soviet backdown. Khrushchev, however, was also associated with a relatively moderate policy in the arts, and the "thaw" that took
place during his general secretaryship led to the
publication of works such as **Solzhenitsyn**'s
"One Day in the Life of Ivan Denisovich" (1962),
apparently as a result of Khrushchev's personal
intervention. Deposed in October 1964,
Khrushchev lived quietly as a "pensioner of all-
union significance" in Moscow, growing tomatoes, listening to the BBC, and dictating two
volumes of memoirs that were disowned at the
time but subsequently authenticated. He died in
1971.

The original "unperson' (that is, unmentionable in official sources) under **Brezhnev**,
Khrushchev came to be seen in increasingly
positive terms under the **Gorbachev** administration as a courageous reformer who had exposed
Stalin's crimes and raised popular living standards. A brief but complimentary reference in
Gorbachev's speech on the 70th anniversary of
the October revolution helped to initiate this

reconsideration. For political commentators such
as Fedor Burlatsky, writing in the late 1980s,
Khrushchev was a representative of the "New
Economic Policy" trend within the party, never
quite extinguished, which had supported democratization and was opposed to the use of force in
industry and agriculture, still more so in the cultural sphere. His fatal weakness, in Burlatsky's
view, was that he was unable to distinguish
between genuine supporters and flatterers, and
this had left him unprotected when his opponents
mobilized against him in 1964. Reflecting this
different and more positive view, extracts from
Khrushchev's memoirs began to be published in
the Soviet press in 1989, and there were calls
to rebury him with full honours in the Kremlin
wall.

SLW

KIRGHIZIA. Kirghizia, originally part of Soviet
Turkestan, became an autonomous republic within the **Russian Republic (RSFSR)** in 1926 and
then in 1936 a union republic within the USSR.
Its area is 198,500 sq km, and its capital is
Frunze. The 1989 census population was
4,291,000. The Kirghiz, who are of Turkic origin,
accounted for 48 per cent of the population in the
1979 census; a further 26 per cent were Russians,
and there are substantial Uzbek, Ukrainian and
Tatar minorities. The republic, much of which
is mountainous, is famous for its livestock breeding, and there are many light industries. The
republic is subdivided into four regions and 40
districts.

SLW

KISZCZAK, GEN. CZESŁAW. Born in Biel-
sko province, Poland, in October 1925 into a
peasant family. He took part in the resistance
movement and in 1945 joined the Polish Communist Party (PPR) and the Polish Army, passing
through the General Staff Academy and taking
the operational and strategic course of the
Voroshilov Academy of the USSR Armed Forces.
According to official records he served "for many
years" in military counter-intelligence organs.
Between 1972–79 he was concurrently head of
military intelligence and deputy chief of the
General Staff. In 1979 he was appointed head of
the internal service of the Ministry of Defence. In
1973 he was promoted to the rank of major general, in 1979 to lieutenant general and in 1983 to
that of defence general. With the onset of the
political crisis that began with the collapse of the
regime of Edward **Gierek**, Kiszczak's career took
a more clearly political turn. In July 1981 he was

appointed undersecretary of state in the Ministry of Internal Affairs, and became a minister in August.

At the VIII Congress of the **Polish United Workers' Party (PUWP)** in 1980 he became a candidate member of the Central Committee, and a full member the following year. Shortly after the proclamation of the **State of War** he became a candidate member of the Politburo and in 1986 a full member. He was also a member of the Military Council for National Salvation (WRON) that acted as the central ruling body under martial law (1981–83). He was elected to the *Sejm* in 1985. His public image underwent a certain change in 1988, when he was the first to float the idea publicly during the August strikes of a round-table meeting including representatives of various "workers' and social groups" (although not those who "rejected the constitutional order"). This occurred four days after the imposition of a curfew in key industrial centres and assumption of special powers to strengthen public order, and represented a change in approach on the part of the leadership and the adoption of a new conception of how the long-lasting Polish political crisis might be solved.

The round-table talks (*see* **Round-table agreement**), when they finally opened in February 1989, progressed smoothly and contributed to Kiszczak's presentation as a relatively liberal exponent of state power, sitting down with those for whose imprisonment he had been directly responsible a few years earlier. This did him little good in the subsequent elections and he was one of the leading politicians on the uncontested national list whose name was crossed off by a majority of voters and who were not elected to the *Sejm*. He also figured in later deliberations over the incumbency of the leading offices of state, and he was first suggested by **Jaruzelski** as a possible president and then prime minister, being endorsed in the latter post by a majority vote in the *Sejm*. He found it impossible to form a government, though, and was forced to resign as premier to be replaced by **Mazowiecki**, in whose government he went on to serve as Minister of the Interior.

PGL

KOSYGIN, ALEKSEI NIKOLAEVICH. Kosygin, born in 1904, was a Soviet politician and prime minister during the Brezhnev era. A member of the **Communist Party of the Soviet Union (CPSU)** from 1927, Kosygin joined the Central Committee in 1939 and from the 1940s onwards held a series of senior administrative posts in Soviet industrial management. In 1964 he succeeded Nikita **Khrushchev** as prime minster (strictly speaking, chairman of the USSR Council of Ministers), where he was particularly associated with the decentralizing "Kosygin reforms" of 1965. Together with Nikolai Podgorny, who was head of state, and Leonid **Brezhnev**, who was partly leader, Kosygin made up what was described as a "collective leadership" in the later 1960s; by the 1970s, however, it was clearly a Brezhnev leadership, and Kosygin's role within it became a steadily more marginal one. Kosygin, who died in 1980, is remembered for his personal modesty and willingness to sustain a dialogue with academics and intellectuals; but his direct influence on the Soviet policy process was in the end a very modest one and his economic reforms are today remembered as an instructive failure.

SLW

KRENZ, EGON. Former GDR statesman, born 1937. Egon Krenz was briefly the third leader of the GDR, succeeding Erich **Honecker** in October 1989, first as General Secretary of the **Socialist Unity Party of Germany (SED)** and then as head of state (Chairman of the State Council). Krenz had been, like Honecker, chairman of **Free German Youth (FDJ)** party youth organization (from 1974). He became a full member of the Politburo in 1983 and was made responsible for security and youth affairs. He was regarded as Honecker's designated successor, although he faded from prominence in the mid-1980s. He reappeared towards the end of the decade but made few friends when he supervised the fraudulent elections of May 1989 and visited Beijing to congratulate the Chinese leadership on its Tiananmen Square operation. During Honecker's illness in the summer of 1989, Krenz chafed at the lack of policy coming from stand-in Günter **Mittag** and began to plot with Günter **Schabowski** the removal of Honecker and Mittag. Although known as a hardliner, he initiated the *Wende* (turning point) in GDR politics and was responsible for the opening of the Berlin Wall on Nov. 9, 1989. His concessions were never enough, however, and he failed to establish either his own trustworthiness or the legitimacy of the SED. He resigned in December 1989 and was expelled from the party in January 1990. Thereafter he began to make a living writing for the West German popular press.

JO

KUČAN, MILAN. Born in 1942, Kučan graduated in Law from the University of Ljubljana,

151

where he served as a member of the University Committee of the **League of Communists of Yugoslavia (LCY)** and of the University Board of the Students' Union of Yugoslavia. In March 1968 he was elected President of the Central Committee of the Union of Youth of Slovenia. From April 1973 he served a five-year term of office as Secretary of the Socialist Union of Working People of Slovenia. From 1978 to 1982 he was President of the Slovene Assembly.

He joined the League of Communists of Slovenia (LCS) in 1958, and became a member of its Central Committee (CC LCS) in 1968. He was a member of the presidency of the CC LCS between 1974 and 1982 and of the presidency of the CC LCY during 1982–86. Since April 1986 he has been the President of the CC LCS.

PA

L

LATVIA. A Soviet regime was briefly established in Latvia in 1917–19, but Latvia's incorporation into the USSR as a union republic took place in 1940 following the Nazi–Soviet Pact of 1939 which had assigned the republic to the Soviet sphere of influence. Many Western governments have refused to recognize Latvia's incorporation into the USSR *de jure*, and the Latvian Supreme Soviet itself declared the incorporation an invalid and annexationist act in 1989. Latvia occupies an area of 63,700 sq km; its 1989 census population was 2,681,000 (just under 1 per cent of the Soviet total). According to the 1989 census just over half the population were ethnic Latvians; a very substantial minority — about a third of the total, and a still higher proportion in the capital city, Riga — are Russians. A prosperous commercial centre and port in the late pre-revolutionary period, Latvia is today an important centre of advanced engineering. Together with the other Baltic republics, Latvia experienced the rise of a strongly assertive nationalist movement in the late 1980s. (*see also* **Nationality Question in the USSR**)

SLW

LEAGUE OF COMMUNISTS OF YUGO-SLAVIA (LCY). At its sixth congress in 1982 the Communist Party changed its name to that of the League of Communists (*Savez Komunista*). This registered the intention of the Communist leaders to change the relationship between the party and the state. While under the system of administrative socialism, the machinery of government was completely merged with the party organization, under the new system the LCY presented itself in the role of arbiter without formal responsibility in the running of current affairs, and personnel changes in government were possible without engaging the authority of the League.

As early as January 1954 Milovan Djilas, who had advocated a second—albeit socialist—party, was discredited as a "deviationist". A real division of functions between the party and government could only be achieved if the League limited its role to that of ideological persuasion. This does not imply, however, that the League's functions have become fossilized: the fact that real power does now exist at the local republican and commune party levels illustrates that a degree of devolution from the centre has taken place over the past 30 years. Each republic and autonomous province has its own party organization, central committee and government.

The continued existence of the LCY and its monopoly of power have been a major constraint on the emergence and development of political pluralism. The extraordinary 14th Congress of the LCY set for January 1990 has expected to illustrate further the existing divisions between the liberal wing taken up by the Slovenes and Croats, who advocate various degrees of pluralism under the aegis of the LCY, and the more conservative and centralist tendencies espoused by the parties in Serbia and Montenegro. The Slovene party, under the leadership of Milan **Kučan**, advocates local autonomy, political pluralism and private enterprise, and has sanctioned the burgeoning of alternative political groupings, including the Democratic Alliance, the Peasant Party and the Greens.

Conservative elements within the LCY, particularly in Serbia, are increasingly concerned about the "challenge" which these alternative groupings pose to the League's authority.

Under Slobodan **Milošević**'s leadership, the Serbian party has revived dormant nationalist passions in the republic and campaigned for greater centralization and the strengthening of the federal government. This culminated in 1989 in the reimposition of Serbian control over the autonomous province of Kosovo.

It is now widely accepted that both schools of thought illustrate the declining relevance of the LCY. What remains unclear is the *dénouement* between two radically opposed programmes for change, upon which the political stability and economic recovery of Yugoslavia ultimately depend.

PA

LEIPZIG. Leipzig is the second city of the GDR, with a population of nearly 550,000. It lies in Saxony in the central south of the country and has for centuries been a cultural and economic centre. In the spring and autumn it stages the Leipzig trade fair, with wide international participation. It is also the centre for book publishing in the GDR and is the home of the Gewandhaus orchestra.

In 1989 Leipzig was crucial in the progress of the revolution in the GDR. From the late summer of that year weekly Monday demonstrations were held to protest at the abduracy of the **Honecker** regime in resisting reform. They were met with violence in October and were in imminent danger of being suppressed by Honecker in imitation of the Chinese in Tiananmen Square in June 1989. Once the regime had been overthrown there was no halt to the weekly marches, as calls for democratization became increasingly overshadowed by demands for German unity.

JO

LENIN, VLADIMIR IL'ICH. Russian Marxist and Soviet political leader. Born in Simbirsk in 1870 (now Ul'yanovsk in his honour), Lenin was the son of a school and civil service official. He gravitated towards the revolutionary movement at an early age, influenced by his brother Alexander who was executed in 1887 for a plot on the life of Alexander III. Lenin graduated with a law degree from Kazan University, but subsequently turned to revolutionary agitation among the St Petersburg working class. He was exiled to Siberia and on his release travelled to Western Europe, remaining active in the Social Democratic Labour Party, which split in 1903 into a moderate Menshevik and a more militant Bolshevik wing, led by Lenin. It was in exile that Lenin wrote some of his influential works, including *What is to be Done?* (1902) with its model of a centralized "vanguard" party, and *Imperialism* (1916) with its thesis that the advanced capitalist countries were interlinked and that a revolution in any one of them would precipitate a comparable change in the others.

After the outbreak of the Russian revolution in February 1917 the German government allowed Lenin to return there in a sealed train, judging (rightly) that his influence would be directed against Russia remaining in the war. Lenin, initially to some incomprehension but latterly with increasing support, took the view that the Provisional Government must be opposed and that the "imperialist war" must be turned into a "civil war". Having persuaded the Bolshevik leadership to take the same approach, Lenin led them to overthrow the Provisional Government in October 1917 and then to establish a Soviet government headed by a Council of People's Commissars. Lenin became chairman of their first Soviet government and was the dominant figure in the policies it adopted, from the civil war years to the mixed economy regime that was established in the early 1920s. Lenin's legacy was the subject of close scrutiny in later years, and particularly under **Gorbachev**; although defended by the leadership itself, it came increasingly to be argued that his legacy was on balance a harmful one with its emphasis upon the monopoly of a single party and his hostility to market mechanisms in economic life. Lenin died in 1924.

SLW

LENINGRAD. The Soviet Union's second-largest city and formerly capital of the Russian Empire and (briefly) of the USSR. Its census population (Jan. 1989) was 5,020,000; without suburbs 4,456,000. Originally called St Petersburg, the city was founded by Peter the Great as an outlet to the sea and a "window on Europe". A glittering and cultivated capital under the Tsars, the city (renamed Petrograd in 1914) became the spearhead of the Bolshevik seizure of power in 1917 and remained the country's capital until the following year. The city was renamed Leningrad in 1924. The city was beseiged by the Germans for more than two years during World War II and enormous damage to both people and property was suffered. An important port and centre of advanced engineering, Leningrad in more recent decades has become a base of hard-line members of the political leadership from Grigorii Romanov to Boris Gidaspov (elected the city party first secretary in 1989).

SLW

LIBERAL DEMOCRATIC PARTY OF GERMANY (LDPD — Liberal-Demokratische Partei Deutschlands). The LDPD was until the upheaval in the GDR in 1989–90 one of the National Front parties allied to the ruling **Socialist Unity Party of Germany (SED)**. It was founded in July 1945 as a liberal initiative with a middle-class constituency, but was rapidly pressured into subsuming itself into the orbit of the SED. After that it was little more than a means by which the SED could organize and discipline white-collar workers, craftsmen, businessmen and professionals. Its membership, at 199,000, was at its height in 1950 and then fell drastically to 67,000 in the early 1960s. From that point, like the other National Front parties (the **Christian Democratic Union of Germany — CDU**, the **National Democratic Party of Germany — NDPD**, and the **Democratic Peasants' Party of Germany—DBD**), the LDPD grew, as the SED encouraged organization of non-communists in order to bolster the system. In 1987 its membership was 104,000.

The LDPD managed to retain its leader during the revolution of 1989–90. Indeed, Professor Manfred Gerlach (born 1928, LDPD chairman since 1967) was the first leader of any of the subordinate parties to speak out in favour of reform. This contrasted with the rhetoric which he had been using for the previous 20-odd years. He came to be seen as a bridge between the SED and those demanding more thorough changes, and after the resignation of Egon **Krenz** as head of state in December 1989, Gerlach was elected to replace him in a provisional capacity. He declared his intention to retire from politics after the March 1990 elections.

The LDPD, like the other parties formerly allied to the SED, was grossly compromised by its past, and was struggling to hold its position against new groupings emerging with a liberal perspective. In the elections of March 1990, the Liberal grouping including the LDPD scored 5.3 per cent of the vote and 21 seats. Since then the Liberals moved rapidly towards becoming a sister party of the West German FDP. The NDPD also merged with them.

JO

LIGACHEV, YEGOR KUZ'MICH. A bluff, stocky Siberian who was widely seen as the leading conservative in the Soviet leadership, Ligachev was born in a village in the Novosibirsk region in 1920. He was educated locally and then attended the Moscow aviation institute where he graduated in 1943, completing his education at the Higher Party School in 1951. He has been a party member since 1944. Ligachev began his working life as an aviation engineer at a Novosibirsk factory, where he was elected first secretary of the Komsomol. From 1949 onwards he has been engaged in full-time party and state administration, first of all in Novosibirsk, and then from 1961 to 1965 as deputy head of the Agitation and Propaganda Department of the CPSU Central Committee in Moscow. In 1965 Ligachev returned to Siberia as first secretary of the Tomsk regional party committee, and then in 1983, during **Andropov**'s leadership, he moved back to Moscow as head of the Department of Organizational-Party Work of the Central Committee of the **Communist Party of the Soviet Union (CPSU)**, which is chiefly concerned with personnel matters. In December 1983 Ligachev became a member of the CPSU Secretariat, where from September 1988 he headed the Agricultural Commission of the Central Committee (the move was widely seen as a demotion). Ligachev was a candidate (from 1966) and then a full member of the Central Committee (from 1976), and he became a full member of the ruling Politburo in April 1985.

Ligachev acquired a reputation as the Politburo's leading hardliner during the late 1980s with a series of speeches which generally stressed the achievements of the Soviet party (including the **Stalin** and **Brezhnev** years), and

which took sharp exception to any capitalist methods of economic management. In an interview with a weekly paper at the end of 1989, for instance, Ligachev insisted that socialism could not be modernized by the adoption of capitalist principles. Socialist principles of economic management, he argued, were not inherently inefficient, whereas the introduction of private ownership would lead to unemployment, social tension and political instability. The Stalinist years, for Ligachev, were an "outrageous departure from socialist principles", in which his own family had suffered. There was nonetheless a need for unity and discipline, in society and in the CPSU particularly. The party, in Ligachev's view, was the only force capable of unifying a multiethnic society such as the USSR, and a society of that kind needed a single party system based upon a ruling CPSU. Although such views enjoyed support elsewhere within the leadership and in the wider society, Ligachev did not personally command a high level of personal popularity and (even before his 1990 retirement) he was not expected to represent a direct challenge to **Gorbachev**'s tenure of the general secretaryship.

SLW

LILOV, ALEKSANDUR VASILEV. Bulgarian Communist politician; Secretary of Central Committee (CC) of **Bulgarian Communist Party (BCP)** 1972–83; member of Politburo 1974–83; Director of Institute for Contemporary Social Theory 1983–89; Secretary and Politburo member again from December 1989 to February 1990; thereafter Chairman of Supreme Party Council.

After early work in the apparatus of Bulgaria's Komsomol, Aleksandur Lilov (born in 1933) studied at the Soviet Communist Party's Academy of Social Sciences before going on to propaganda and cultural posts in the BCP's central apparatus. As CC Secretary, he became identified with a relatively liberal line and is reported to have been closely allied with party leader Todor **Zhivkov**'s daughter Lyudmila. After the latter's death he seemed to be number two to Zhivkov in the pecking order and a possible successor to the ageing party leader. In 1983, he suffered the standard fate of "heirs apparent" to Zhivkov, being ousted from his leadership posts and relegated to academia. While this move was never officially explained, it probably had much to do with the fact that Lilov had been criticizing the "cult of personality" surrounding Zhivkov. A month after Zhivkov's removal as party leader, Lilov returned to his former posts and less than two months thereafter replaced Petur **Mladenov** as BCP leader. This was a move generally seen as substituting both a more progressive and a more effective figure for one unequal on both counts to the demands of the moment—and, at the same time, as preferring a more solid candidate to the apparent alternative, Stoyan **Mikhailov**.

RW

LITHUANIA. A Soviet regime was briefly established in Lithuania in 1918–19, but the present position of Lithuania within the USSR dates from 1940 when the republic applied for admission to the USSR following the 1939 Nazi-Soviet Pact, which allocated the republic to the Soviet sphere of influence. The capital, Vilnius, under Polish occupation from 1920, became part of Lithuania at the same time. Lithuania's incorporation into the USSR has not been recognized *de jure* by many Western governments and in March 1990 the Lithuanian Supreme Soviet, meeting after elections in which the nationalist *Sajudis* movement had been overwhelmingly successful, declared the incorporation invalid and the republic's independence fully restored. Lithuania has an area of 65,200 sq km and had a 1989 census population of 3,690,000. In the 1979 census 80 per cent of the population were ethnic Lithuanians; the remainder included Russian and Polish minorities. Lithuania is an important source of agricultural produce, particularly grain, potatoes and dairy produce; there is a substantial timber industry and engineering industries. Together with the other Baltic republics, Lithuania experienced the rise of a strongly assertive nationalist movement in the late 1980s. (*See also* **Nationality Question in the USSR**)

SLW

LIVING STANDARDS. The standard of living is one of the most difficult things to measure for the East European countries. This is partly due to the problem of concealed inflation (*see* **Inflation**). More fundamentally, it flows from the fundamental problems of quality and structure which affect supplies of consumer goods and services in Eastern Europe. A large proportion of the consumer goods supplied to home populations in Eastern Europe would be unsaleable on world markets at any price. To that extent, direct comparisons with living standards in the West are impossible. Beyond that, certain goods, particularly modern consumer electronics, are often simply unavailable from the legal retail network. Perhaps even more important, consumer services are very poorly developed. In the GDR, for instance, there is a two or three month waiting

period for shoe repairs. In the Soviet Union, housewives have to spend an extraordinarily high proportion of their time queueing. This reflects partly the pressure of repressed inflation, partly the inadequacy of retail facilities.

Repressed-inflationary pressures also find expression in unusually high levels of deposits in savings bank accounts. In the Soviet Union the aggregate volume of those nearly doubled between 1980 and 1988, to stand at Rb 297.5 billion—equivalent to nearly one half of national income—at the end of the latter year. These figures yield, however, but a conservative estimate of the volume of "excess" purchasing power in the economy. Cash hoards may also have increased very rapidly during the 1980s. Estimates of the current value of such hoards vary between Rb 70 billion and Rb 200 billion or more. Of course, a proportion of these savings is voluntary—against a rainy day, or towards a big purchase. But the greater part reflect simply the fact that supplies of goods in the Soviet Union do not match "planned" incomes, so that the level of those incomes is a fundamentally misleading indicator of real living standards. Another major complication in the assessment of living standards is the existence of the second economy. Accounting for 20–30 per cent of the "true" level of Soviet national income, and for a higher proportion of that of some of the other East European countries, the second economy provides a significant corrective to the consumer goods and services failings of the planned economics—but at much higher prices than those of the official economy.

The table presents the official figures on recent trends in living standards. The slow rate of growth they purport for the majority of the East European countries is misleading. When account is taken of the dimension of concealed inflation, slow growth boils down to stagnation. The substantial falls in living standards reported for Poland and Yugoslavia are real, and are largely due to the external debt-service difficulties which both countries ran into at the beginning of the 1980s. But while living standards have certainly fallen in Yugoslavia, *absolute* levels of consumer welfare remain high by the standards of the region. This is partly because Yugoslavia has operated a kind of market socialist system for so long, so that the characteristic East European problems of poor quality, shortages and inadequate services infrastructure are less serious, though certainly not absent. Beyond that, Yugoslavia's favoured location in the "sun belt" of Europe helps to keep welfare, and the perception of welfare, rather higher than monetary indicators might suggest. The same is true of

Real incomes and real wages, 1981– 88 (annual percentage change)

	Real income per head	*Real wage per worker*
Bulgaria		
1981– 85	3.7	2.2
1986	2.8	1.0
1987	4.0	3.9
1988	3.4	—
Czechoslovakia		
1981– 85	1.6	0.0
1986	2.5	1.1
1987	2.9	1.9
GDR		
1981– 85	4.2	—
1986	5.7	—
1987	4.6	—
1988	4.0	—
Hungary		
1981– 85	1.6	–0.8
1986	2.4	1.9
1987	0.7	–0.4
1988	–2.0	–6.7
Poland		
1981– 85	–1.7	–4.1
1986	1.7	2.6
1987	0.8	–3.5
1988	0.0	11.0
Romania		
1981– 85	3.5	1.5
Soviet Union		
1981– 85	2.1	—
1986	2.5	—
1987	2.0	—
1988	3.5	—
Yugoslavia		
1981– 85	–4.2	—
1986	10.0	—
1987	–6.8	—

Source: United Nations, Economic Commission for Europe, *Economic Survey of Europe in 1988 –1989*, p.153; *Statisticki Godisnjak Jugoslavije 1988*, p.106.

Bulgaria, and of some regions of the Soviet Union, particularly the Caucasus and Central Asia. The official figures may actually exaggerate the real drop in living standards in Yugoslavia since 1982, in that the debt-service crisis, and the ensuing crisis in the socialized sector of the economy, has provoked something of a flight into the second economy.

At a time of deep crisis in the East European economies, the immediate prospects for higher living standards do not look bright. Structural imbalances are so deeply ingrained in all the economies of the region that it is simply not pos-

sible to increase the output of consumer goods rapidly in the short term, particularly at the more sophisticated end of the market. Against a background of dangerously high levels of foreign debt the option of large-scale import of consumer goods from outside the region is not a practical one. In the Soviet Union the legalization in 1988 of private enterprise in services and small-scale manufacturing under the co-operative rubric brought some relief to consumers. It also generated sharp increases in prices which eventually forced the government, under some public pressure, to impose new restrictions on the co-operatives. The situation in the GDR is rather special, because of the scope for developing unique relationships with West Germany, even to the extent of some kind of German reunification. Elsewhere, the most optimistic scenario would see consumer supplies beginning to improve substantially in the mid-1990s, as restructuring gathers pace, and new legislation on joint ventures, special economic zones and so forth facilitates technology and design transfer from the West.

DAD

LUKANOV, ANDREI KARLOV. Bulgarian Communist politician; Deputy Prime Minister from 1976, candidate member of Politburo from 1979; first Deputy Prime Minister 1986–87; Minister of Foreign Economic Relations 1987–89; Secretary of the **Bulgarian Communist Party (BCP)** Central Committee and member of Politburo from November 1989 to February 1990; Prime Minister from February 1990.

Born in Moscow in 1938 of an exiled Bulgarian revolutionary family, Lukanov returned to Bulgaria as a boy, but received his higher education at Moscow's State Institute for International Relations. From 1963, he made his career in Bulgaria's foreign trade system. His background and talents won him swift advancement — a Deputy Premiership at 38, and Politburo candidacy at 41. His Moscow connections were strengthened by a spell as Bulgarian representative to the **Council for Mutual Economic Assistance (CMEA)** there, while his service as overseer of foreign trade from 1986 showed him to be pragmatic, flexible, and relatively receptive to Western ideas and methods. Rumoured to have been an important ally of Petur **Mladenov** in toppling party chief Todor **Zhivkov** in November 1989, he was rewarded by almost immediate — and probably overdue — promotion: his new position involved top-level responsibility for party personnel policy and for the economy, and made him number two in the BCP Secretariat. His appointment less than three months later to the premiership, where he replaced the Zhivkov holdover Atanasov, was widely perceived as a concession to reformist forces outside as well as inside the BCP, though he was unable to form the desired government of national unity. Generally,

his statements and actions since Zhivkov's fall bear out the impression that he is a progressive and bode well for the future of reform in Bulgaria.

RW

LUTHERANS IN THE USSR. There are at least one million Lutherans in the USSR today. They lack a central organization but have a legal existence. Their main base is among the Estonians and Latvians who were converted to Lutheranism by the Baltic German nobles. Additionally, Lutheranism is the largest denomination among the Volga Germans, who were deported by **Stalin** to Kazakhstan, where Lutheran congregations have re-emerged. Their position has been weakened in the late 1980s by the emigration to the FRG of pastors and the most active laity.

Lutheranism has not had the intensive link with national identity among the Estonians and Latvians such as the **Roman Catholic Church** has among the Lithuanians. Religion is a unifying force in Estonia, since Lutheranism is the traditional national denomination, but a divisive force in Latvia, since in the Latgale region the Latvians are predominantly Catholic. (Indeed there may now be more practising Catholics than Lutherans among Latvians.)

From 1987, however, representatives of the churches began to play a role in the emerging national movements in Estonia and Latvia (*see* **Nationality Question in the USSR**). In June 1987 an informal group, "Rebirth and Renewal", was formed by Modris Plate of the Lutheran Theological Seminary in order to defend religious rights in Latvia. This was critical of the leadership of the Latvian Lutheran Church for its submission to the state. In April 1989 "Rebirth and Renewal" swept the board at the elections for the General Synod of the Church. This coincided with the triumph of the nationalist Popular Fronts in Estonia and Latvia at the elections for the Congress of People's Deputies. The transformed political situation in the Baltic not only promised religious freedom for the churches but a position of enhanced influence, with priests taking up positions within the Popular Fronts.

PJSD

M

MARKOVIĆ, ANTE. A Croat by nationality, Marković was born in Konjic (Bosnia) in 1924. He joined the Communist Youth Movement of Yugoslavia in 1940, and the partisan movement in 1941. He became a member of the **League of Communists of Yugoslavia (LCY)** in 1943. He was educated in schools in Dubrovnik and Zagreb, and at the Technical High School in Zagreb.

He started his career in 1953 as electrical engineer at the Rade Končar engineering conglomerate in Zagreb, and became its Director in 1961 for the next 25 years. He began his political career in Zagreb in the 1960s as a member of the City Committee of the League of Communists of Croatia (LCC) and a member of the Presidium of the Economic Chamber of Croatia. From 1982 to 1986 he was a member of the Central Committee of the LCC and Prime Minister of Croatia, and has since 1986 been a member of the CC of the LCY.

He succeeded Branko Mikulić as Prime Minister of Yugoslavia in March 1989. As Prime Minister of Croatia he earned the reputation of a political liberal and an economic pragmatist. He has a thorough grounding in business and foreign trade and is an advocate of liberal foreign investment laws and closer economic ties with the West, especially the European Communities.

PA

MARXISM-LENINISM. The official ideology of the USSR and the other Communist-ruled states, based at least ostensibly upon the teachings of Karl Marx, Friedrich Engels and V. I. **Lenin**. (*See also* **Ideology**)

SLW

MASARYK, JAN. Born in 1886, Jan was the son of T.G. **Masaryk**. He was Czechoslovakia's Ambassador to the UK in the late 1930s and Foreign Minister in the Czechoslovak government-in-exile between 1940 and 1945, a post he also held in post-war Czechoslovakia until his death on March, 10, 1948. Through his war-time broadcasts to his homeland and his warmth and humour, he created a strong personal bond with his fellow-countrymen. Despite an official verdict that his death was suicide, a view shared by some close to him, many in Czechoslovakia have continued to believe he was the victim of a political assassination.

GW

MASARYK, TOMÁŠ GARRIGUE. Born in 1850, Masaryk was President of Czechoslovakia between its foundation in 1918 and 1935, two years before his death. Professor of Philosophy at Charles University in Prague, he was a prominent, if controversial, figure in Czech political life during the last years of the Austro-Hungarian Empire. Apart from a short period as a Deputy for the Young Czech Party in the early 1890s, he remained outside mainstream political movements, founding his own small Realist Party in 1900. His pre-eminence among Czech politicians was established following his departure from Austria in 1915 to launch a campaign for Czechoslovak independence. In his belief that the battle for a national state would be won in the capitals of Western Europe, where his own political sympathies lay, he differed from pan-Slav and pro-Tsarist Czech politicians who expected independence to be won with Russian help. Masaryk's war-time activities — his propagandist and diplomatic work in London, Paris and the USA, his efforts to organize a Czechoslovak army from prisoners-of-war in Russia which he unsuccessfully attempted to have transferred to the Western front — established his reputation at home and abroad and helped win support among the Allies for the creation of an independent Czechoslovakia. He was a natural choice as the new state's first President and his commitment to liberal democracy helped make Czechoslovakia the one parliamentary regime in Central Europe to survive intact for most of the inter-war period. Despite frequent denigration since 1948, his standing as a symbol of democracy remains high in Czechoslovakia.

GW

MAZOWIECKI, TADEUSZ. Born in Płock, Poland, in April 1927. He holds a degree from the University of Warsaw Law Faculty and started work in a publishing house, from which he was sacked at the age of 21 for "clericalism". He became an activist of the official Catholic organization PAX and edited a Catholic weekly in Wrocław. He was removed from this post following a move against the PAX leader, Bolesław

159

Piasecki, in 1954, and was excluded from PAX in 1955. In 1956 he helped organize the Warsaw Club of Catholic Intelligentsia and continued to play a leading part in its activities, acting as its vice-chairman until election as prime minister. He also helped found the influential Catholic journal *Wieź* (The Link), of which he was editor from 1958 to 1981. He was an activist in the independent Catholic group *Znak* and represented it as a deputy in the *Sejm* between 1961 and 1972. He was an author and signatory of the parliamentary interpellation concerning the events of March 1968, attempted in 1971 to convene a *Sejm* commission to investigate the response of the authorities to the workers' demonstration of December 1970 and in 1976 signed a protest against the proposed changes to be made in the constitution (*see* **Poland**—Constitution).

In May 1977 Mazowiecki acted as spokesman for the members of the **Committee for Workers' Defence (KOR)** who fasted in St Martin's Church in Warsaw to protest the continuing imprisonment of workers detained after the Radom demonstrations. The following year he signed the declaration of the Association for Scientific Courses (TKN or flying university) and acted as a member of its programme council. In August 1980 he initiated the appeal to intellectuals sympathizing with striking workers and became chairman of the group of experts attached to the Inter-enterprise Strike Committee in Gdańsk, acting as negotiator to achieve the agreement on union pluralism. He acted as adviser to **Solidarity** from 1980 and in 1981 became the editor of Solidarity's weekly paper. This activity was interrupted by the declaration of the **State of War**, during which he was interned until Dec. 23, 1982.

His collaboration with Solidarity continued and in 1987 became an adviser to the National Executive Committee (KKW). He was again present on the northern coast during the 1988 strikes and was one of the moving forces behind the organization of the round-table negotiations (*see* **Round-table agreement**), acting as chairman of the group concerned with trade union pluralism and co-ordinator for the opposition of the work of the negotiation teams. In 1989 he took up his work of editing the Solidarity weekly again when it was re-established and preferred to continue with journalistic work rather than participate in the elections, some reports suggesting that he was not satisfied with the manner in which Solidarity candidates were selected. The political situation in Poland following the elections, however, was quite different from that provided for in the round-table agreement and even from that foreseen when the Solidarity candidates were selected

by the Citizens' Committee (on which Mazowiecki had himself sat). When it became clear in August that a prime minister nominated by the **Polish United Workers' Party (PUWP)** was unlikely to be able to form a government, Mazowiecki's was one of the names that came forward as a likely candidate and he was soon confirmed in the position, becoming Poland's first non-Communist prime minister for over 40 years.

PGL

MEDIA. The mass media—press, radio and television—have always been central to achievement of political objectives in the USSR and Eastern Europe. At least until recently, state control was all-pervasive, and censorship strict and unchallengeable. In the USSR, until the changes of the **Gorbachev** era, even the existence of the censorship system was itself subject to censorship. There was certainly a spectrum: the Romanian media under **Ceauşescu** exceeded any others in the frequency with which the party leader and his wife were pictured and quoted on the front page; the Yugoslav press, at the other extreme, could cover a wide range of international news, included a certain amount of sex and sensation, and was responsible to the law and the courts rather than to a faceless bureaucracy. Nonetheless, in none of these countries was there a genuinely "free" press in the sense of a press that was wholly independent of government and powerful interests, and even the changes associated with *glasnost'* left some ambiguity about the extent to which newspapers and the media in general could safely criticize the leaderships of their countries and the policies they pursued. The picture varied considerably as between the USSR, with which we begin, and Eastern Europe.

The USSR. The Soviet leadership has consistently attached great importance to the development of the mass media—particularly so, perhaps, to newspapers, which played an important part in the Bolsheviks' seizure of power in 1917 and were for some time the only effective means of mass communication in the country. In 1913 just over a thousand newspapers were published with a daily print-run of 2.7 million copies; since then the number and circulation of newspapers, and of magazines and periodicals more generally, has grown enormously. Although the number of newspaper titles declined slightly during the early 1960s, the total circulation has increased steadily to a 1988 total of 217,407 copies per issue or more than seven for every 10 members of the population. (In the same year a total of 8,622 newspapers were published, and their annual print-run was 49,175 million copies.) These circulation levels are very high as compared, for instance, with the major Western countries. Periodical publications have expanded still more rapidly, attaining a total of 4,260.6 million copies in 1988, or an average of 263.8 million copies per issue (more than eight for every 10 members of the population).

"A newspaper", **Lenin** observed, "is not only a collective propagandist and collective agitator: it is also a collective organizer". Soviet newspapers and periodicals, accordingly, have somewhat different tasks to perform and are rather different in coverage and layout from their western counterparts. The Communist Party daily *Pravda*, for instance, founded in 1912, normally carries an "agitational" editorial on its front page drawing attention to what the party regards as the most important issues of the day in industry, agriculture, education or whatever. Its other five pages are usually devoted to party affairs (page 2), theory and culture (page 3), foreign news, supplied by the paper's own correspondents or by TASS, the official Soviet news agency (pages 4 and 5), and then finally sports reports, TV and radio programmes, a cartoon or two, and the weather (on the back page). *Pravda* comes out 365 days of the year and sells an average of 6.8 million copies per issue (this figure, for 1990, was down very considerably on those for earlier years). Its editor is always a figure of considerable political standing: the current editor, Ivan Frolov, is a member of the Central Committee Secretariat and a close adviser to General Secretary Gorbachev.

Other important daily papers in the USSR, which diverge somewhat from *Pravda* in their coverage and in some cases in their editorial philosophy, are *Izvestiya*, the governmment newspaper, founded in 1917 (9.6 million copies daily in 1990); *Komsomol'skaya Pravda*, the Komsomol paper, founded in 1925 (21.1 million copies daily); *Sel'skaya zhizn*, a party paper intended for a rural readership, published under various titles since 1929 (5.9 million copies daily); and *Trud*, the daily paper of the All-Union Trade Union Council, which was founded in 1921 and is currently among the best-selling Soviet daily papers (20 million copies daily, up from 12.3 million in 1980 and just four million 1970; its willingness to cover UFOs and other more unusual matters as well as labour issues is believed to be responsible). Also important is *Krasnaya zvezda* (Red Star), the daily organ of the USSR Ministry of Defence, which was founded in 1924. A daily paper called *Sovetskaya Rossiya* (Soviet Russia), intended for readers in the Russian Republic, was one of the most adventurous in extending the boundaries of discussion in the early Gorbachev years; it currently sells 3.1 million copies per issue. Some 4,696 of the USSR's newspapers appear in the Russian Republic; the others, with titles such as *Pravda Ukrainy* (Pravda of the Ukraine) or *Bakinskii rabochii* (Baku Worker), appear in the other 14 union republics.

The most popular journals in 1990 were *Zdorov'e* (Health), a popular scientific magazine (17.7 million copies daily), *Rabotnitsa* (Woman Worker), which sells 23.6 million copies daily, and *Krestyanka* (Peasant Woman), which sells 21.5 million copies every day. The most popular of all periodicals, a weekly newspaper known as *Argumenty i fakty* (Arguments and Facts), sold a massive 31.5 million copies in 1990, up by more than half on the year before. Some of the most important of the USSR's other periodicals are the party theoretical journal *Kommunist*, founded in 1924 and published 18 times a year; the literary monthly *Novy mir* (New World), founded in 1925 and traditionally the most "liberal" of the Soviet Union's journals (it published **Solzhenitsyn**'s *One Day in the Life of Ivan Denisovich* and in 1988 published Boris Pasternak's *Doctor Zhivago*); the illustrated weekly paper *Ogonek*, founded in 1923, and currently among the most lively and challenging of the magazines (it sells 4.5 million copies an issue); and the weekly paper *Literaturnaya gazeta* (Literary Gazette), which sells 4.2 million copies per issue and is very popular with intellectuals, particularly for its second (non-literary) part which deals with a wide range of controversial social issues. Among many humorous and mildly satirical publications the weekly paper *Krokodil*, founded in 1922, holds a special place (it sells 2.6 million copies an issue).

Sociological studies conducted within the USSR suggest that the majority of the adult population make considerable use of this substantial diet of newsprint. A study conducted in Leningrad, for instance, found that 75 per cent of those who were polled read a newspaper every day (a further 19 per cent did so three or four times as week), and even in relatively remote areas at least half the local population normally claim to read a newspaper daily, with the younger and better educated more likely to do so than the local population as a whole. Among the subjects treated in the papers, international affairs are almost always the most popular (74 and 69 per cent respectively of readers of *Pravda* and *Izvestiya* indicated that they consulted these columns the most frequently). Official communications were read by 81 per cent of *Pravda*'s readers, "surprising stories" were read by 71 per cent of *Izvestiya*'s readers, and moral themes (57 and 75 per cent respectively) and satirical articles (57 and 64 per cent respectively) were also popular. No more than 30 per cent of *Izvestiya*'s readers consulted its editorials, however; no more than 23 per cent read it articles on economics; and only 18 and 17 per cent respectively read its articles on propaganda themes and on the work of the soviets (supposedly the paper's main function).

One of the most important aspects of the work of Soviet newspapers is the correspondence they receive from their readers and other members of the public. Daily papers like *Pravda* and *Trud* receive half a million letters a year or even more; and the letters department is often the papers's largest (in *Pravda* it has a staff of about 100). Altogether an estimated 60–70 million letters are sent to the Soviet national dailies every year, an average of at least one letter a year from every third adult member of the population. Pensioners, it seems, are the most active correspondents, perhaps because they have more time than others, or perhaps because they have more problems. For reasons of space, only a small proportion (between 1 and 5 per cent) of letters can be published, but all must be acknowledged, and in addition statistical analyses are prepared in the newspaper offices of the kinds of problems that are raised in the letters that come in and of the kinds of correspondents from whom they have come. Analyses of this kind are regularly communicated to party and state offices and to bodies such as the Trade Union Council; and some letters are also taken up by the newspaper itself if the circumstances appear to justify it.

Experimental television transmissions began in the USSR in 1931, and regular programmes began to be broadcast from Moscow and Leningrad in 1939. A Third centre started to broadcast from Kiev in 1951, since when there had been a rapid expansion to the present total of 115 programme-making television centres, over 100 of which are able to operate in colour. The total daily output of Soviet TV is 500 hours on average, and programmes are made in 45 different Soviet languages. Central Television produced a total of 11 different channels in 1985, including rebroadcasts designed to allow for the different time zones of the USSR; the total daily output averaged 147 hours. All these and other television and radio activities come under the control of the State Committee for Television and Radio Broadcasting, which is represented on the USSR Council of Ministers and which provides the resources necessary from public funds (there is no licence fee and little advertising).

Central Television, which is based in Moscow, produces four main programmes. The first is the basic national network for informational, socio-political, cultural, educational, artistic and sporting programmes; it was broadcast for an average of 13.6 hours daily in 1985. The second programme, which is also intended for the USSR as whole, concentrates on cultural, educational and artistic matters and was also broadcast for an average of 13.6 hours daily in 1985. These are the two main national or "all-Union" programmes, and both are rebroadcast in five different reception areas at convenient times for viewers in other time zones. The third programme is intended for Moscow city, Moscow region and Ryazan region; it is informational and artistic in character, and is broadcast for 4.5 hours daily. The fourth programme, broadcast for 3.4 hours a day in Mosow, Moscow region and Kiev, is educational in character. Radio broadcasting, which began in 1919, is organized along broadly similar lines. The central radio offices in Moscow presently produce ten different programmes, the most important of which, the first programme, is broadcast 20 hours a day with four rebroadcasts for different time zones.

As of 1989 some 83.7 million radios were in service, and 89.9 million televisions (the great majority black and white, although all Central TV programmes are now broadcast in colour). This represented 99 TVs and 96 radios for every 100 families. The number of televisions available increased enormously during the 1960s and 1970s; in 1960 only 5 per cent of the Soviet population could watch television but by 1989 some 96 per cent could do so, and television signals could be received in more than 86 per cent of the territory of the USSR. The only households that still remain outside the reach of TV broadcasts are in sparsely settled areas, mostly in Siberia. Most urban residents watch television fairly regularly, and for many it is clearly an important source of news and information. According to surveys, of the events in the world abroad that are covered by the Soviet media 86 per cent are known to people through television, 77 per cent through the newspaper, and 62 per cent from the radio. The most important of all television programmes is the news, "Vremya", which is carried on all channels at 9 p.m. and is watched by an estimated 150 millon of the population. It is apparently compulsory viewing for members of the Soviet armed forces.

Since about the time of Gorbachev's accession, but in some cases even earlier, there has been more emphasis upon live audience reponse in TV programmes. An enterprising show called "12th floor" has been one of the most notable of these newer-style programmes: viewers can phone in during the show (staff are seen in the background answering the calls and the numbers to ring are displayed on the screen), and responsible officials are often asked to reply to criticisms on the spot.

There have been several "space bridges", linking up ordinary people (for instance in Leningrad and Seattle) for discussion of whatever most concerns them, including subjects like the war in Afghanistan. Television news has been improved by greater use of portable video equipment to allow for quicker responses to events and live interviews. Some lively thrillers have been presented, for instance "TASS is authorized to announce...", which was based on the work of Soviet counter-espionage and scripted by the Soviet John le Carré, Julian Semyenov. There have also been western imports, such as the British serial "The Boys from the Blackstuff", and there is even an early morning keep-fit session, presented by attractive young women. All this is some distance short of what Soviet viewers might ideally wish to see, but it is still a considerable change from the stodgy fare of the very recent past.

Eastern Europe. Communication with the masses, as already noted, was recognized at an early stage by **Lenin** to be a critical element in the revolutionary transformation of society. The ideological framework within which it was set suggested the line of development it might take and helped define the subject-matter of the communication that Communist mass media have primarily concerned themselves with. The subsequent transfer of the Soviet model to Eastern Europe had to take account of a more advanced level of social development both because of the later date at which the Communist transformation was beginning and because of the higher levels of social and economic development that prevailed in any case in the lands to the west of the Soviet Union. Levels of urbanization and economic development were higher, education more advanced and illiteracy levels lower that at the beginning of the Communist transformation in the Soviet Union. There was virtually no illiteracy from the outset in Hungary and East Germany, though levels were higher elsewhere. Twenty-four per cent were recorded as illiterate in Bulgaria in 1946, and a quarter still were in Yugoslavia in 1953.

Progress was made, though, and most concentrations of social backwardness were significantly reduced by the 1970s. The distribution of the technical facilities for mass communication also varied considerably. In 1949 there were only slightly more than 200,000 radios in countries like Bulgaria, Romania and Yugoslavia but over 2,200,000 in Czechoslovakia (Poland falling midway with 1,055,000). By 1968 Bulgaria had ten times as many with 2,245,000 and Romania, Yugoslavia and Czechoslovakia had over 3,000,000 (East Germany having more than

5,000,000 from the 1950s). Around 60 to 70 per cent of the region's population were estimated to listen to some kind of radio broadcast each day in the 1980s. The established listening patterns also produced a sizeable audience for foreign stations, particularly the BBC and Radio Free Europe — the significance of this practice being tacitly recognized by the East European regimes which continued to devote effort and expense (using considerable energy resources) to jamming western broadcasts.

Television coverage grew later. In 1960 there were 10 and 14 TV sets in Hungary and Poland respectively per 1,000 of the population, although already 58 and 60 in Czechoslovakia and the GDR. Ten years later there were 171 and 129 sets in Hungary and Poland, and already over 200 per 1,000 of the population in Czechoslovakia and the GDR. There was a similar lag behind Western Europe in other areas of technical provision although the lag has been progressively less, access to video-recorders rising dramatically through the 1980s in countries like Poland and Hungary with less constrained access to the West. Thus there have been well developed channels for mass communication in Eastern Europe and relatively favourable conditions for the dissemination of officially sanctioned information and ideas amongst the target populations. But East Europeans were, on the other hand, also more sophisticated that the Soviet peoples at the outset and less open to simple or relatively crude messages — particularly if (as was often the case) they were not very receptive to the message in the first place.

East European governments have therefore, especially in recent years, tended to supply considerable quantities of relatively acceptable entertainment on television as the leading medium of communication in preference to strong ideological messages which simply bore or anatagonize the viewers. News transmission and current affairs programmes, nevertheless, continued to carry a persistent ideological message while frequent history and drama series concerned with World War II tended to reinforce underlying anxieties about an external military and political threat. Some countries (Poland, Yugoslavia, Hungary) exerted less political control while others (Albania, Romania, East Germany and Czechoslovakia) remained more restrictive. But even a more conservative leadership like that in the GDR had given up trying to prevent the reception of West German TV, readily accessible in many parts of the country, and had even facilitated its reception elsewhere. Drawing their own conclusions from the observation that emigration applications from the Dresden area where West

German television programmes could not be received were particularly high, the authorities laid on cable reception to overcome the deficiency.

Television has certainly established itself in Eastern Europe and become an important leisure pastime for much of its population, probably no less (and, in view of lower incomes, restrictions on travel and independent social activities, possibly more) than for analogous groups in Western Europe. In facilitating socialization and the transmission of regime values it has played a particular role in rural areas and hastened the integration of peasants and the farming population into modern East European society. The lengthy periods of stability in countries like Hungary and Bulgaria may have been partly attributable to the thorough-going character of this process and the effective role played by the mass media. But recent developments certainly warn against overstating the socializing capacity of television and the integrative qualities of the mass media. The examples of the GDR and Romania are instructive in this respect. The reception of West Germany TV was certainly popular in the GDR and appreciated as a facility when access to the West and more direct experience of its values was restricted. In the short run it may well have helped sustain social stability.

But it clearly did not fully satisfy the aspirations of East Germans and may rather have kept them operating within tolerable bounds until fuller opportunities for their satisfaction presented themselves after the fall of **Honecker**. Romanian television broadcasts, on the other hand, were under tight political control during the period of Ceaușescu's leadership and transmission times themselves restricted because of energy shortages. The Bucharest television centre was nevertheless a major focus of activity during the revolution of December 1989 and the coalition of dissident workers and intellectuals made itself known as a public force in the confines of a TV studio in a matter of hours after the dictator's downfall. Generalization about the consequences of hard-line and permissive transmission policies, and the role of TV as a stabilizing or disruptive influence, is therefore not easy. What is clear is that the mass media, and television in particular, have played a key role in political and social processes in modern Eastern Europe and have been closely linked with leading aspects of change and stability.

As in Western Europe, the spread of television has reduced the entertainment role of the cinema (although it has remained an important means of access to Western and other cultures) and its importance as a medium of political communication. Lacking, in many areas, the background of widespread isolation and illiteracy that characterized the Soviet Union in the earlier decades of the century, film was never quite so important in Communist Eastern Europe as it was in the formative period of the Soviet state. The East European cinema has produced its own entertainment successes, although audiences have invariably preferred a Western product. Several countries have also developed a distinguished cinema industry whose films have had considerable international appeal for their intellectual and artistic qualities, although they have not generally been imbued with any strong socialist ethic. Countries like Poland and Hungary have sustained the production of high-quality films for a number of years while others, like Czechoslovakia, have tended to produce interesting films when political conditions (like those during the liberalization of 1968) permitted.

Television and, to a lesser extent, radio, in terms of their reach and social impact have also tended to overshadow the older media like newspapers and periodicals. The press, however, retained its prime role in acting as the official organ of the Communist party and most carefully modulated means of expressing leadership opinion. Like television and radio, all legally published material was subject to full ideological and government control and official censorship throughout the Communist period. Domestic TV and radio, however (apart from rare dissident initiatives), only offered a small number of channels while the press could offer a wide range of popular and specialist publications which provided for finer tuning in terms of the range of permitted opinion, the provision of more recondite information and the groups it was likely to reach. Some journals were permitted a wider range of discretion and it was notable in the development of events both in Hungary in 1956 and Czechoslovakia during 1968 that the publications of writers' unions (*Irodalmi Ujsag, Literarni Listy*) reflected the changing public mood and made a significant contribution to the process of change. Catholic publications in Poland (*Tygodnik Powszechny, Więź*) also provided important channels for the expression of independent opinion.

Apart from formal censorship the distribution of more sensitive material could also be restricted by placing limits on readership through the provision of paper. Official newspapers, particularly the formal Communist party organs, enjoyed the largest allocation of resources and highest print-run although they were far from being the most sought-after publications. Whether the bulk of them were ever read is a matter of some doubt, and many were distributed not to private individuals or purchasers but to official premises and public institutions (trade union offices, libraries, factory premises). A similar situation pertained with the availability of published books. Sought-after publications might be snapped up in minutes or never appear in the book-shops, while immense numbers of ideological volumes or contributions to the mountain of Leniniana took up significant proportions of the otherwise limited allocation of paper. Publishing houses linked with Communist parties and associated organizations also acted as important funding channels and contributed to the financing of a range of political activities.

But, despite these obstacles, the strong party monopoly and effective embargo, even during the post-**Stalin** period, an independent means of communication gradually began to emerge. Unofficial and self-produced (*samizdat*) periodicals and books increasingly became part of social life in several East European countries. The establishment of human rights and social self-defence organizations in the 1970s (**Charter 77** in Czechoslovakia, **Committee for Workers' Defence—KOR** in Poland) helped provide both content for independent publications and activists for their production and contribution. Press freedom became more firmly established and censorship more restricted in Poland during 1981, and the old controls were never reimposed with their earlier effect even following the imposition of a **State of War**. In 1989, initially in Poland and Hungary, the situation entered a period of radical change. An early step taken by the non-Communist prime minister in Poland was to replace the chairman of the government radio and television committee who, in turn, was quick to replace the former personnel director and appointed Stefan Truszczyński, who had directed **Solidarity**'s television activities during the election campaign, to head the Warsaw TV centre.

Much remained to be done and as the new radio and TV chairman, Andrzej Drawicz, pointed out major legislation had to be passed to put the activities of the mass media on a new basis. Change had also proceeded apace in Hungary and censorship was virtually suspended. Applications to set up commercial radio and television stations were already submitted in 1989, while newspapers could be started up without any official permission at all. Several opposition parties started their own publication, but the importance of the central direction of the media had not been eliminated and a survey carried out during the summer of 1989 showed that Communist politicians were given eight to ten times the coverage of the opposition. International communications organizations were also quick to perceive new opportunities and Axel Springer, Rupert Murdoch, Robert Maxwell as well as some French groups were already showing an interest in the growth of Hungarian commercial television. Murdoch, Maxwell and the American financier of Hungarian origin, George Soros, had already bought sizeable shares in some publications by the end of 1989.

SLW/PGL

MIKHAILOV, STOYAN. Bulgarian Communist politician; Secretary of the Central Committee (CC) of the **Bulgarian Communist Party (BCP)** 1978–88; Deputy Chairman of the Council of Ministers from November 1989 to February 1990.

A philosopher-sociologist by training and early career, Mikhailov (born in 1930) moved to ideological/propaganda work in the central party apparatus in 1973. As CC Secretary in the decade following 1978, he pursued a relatively liberal line, and was closely identified with the movement for *glasnost'* and democratization in 1987–88. For this he was removed from both Secretariat and CC in mid-1988 along with his ally Chudomir **Aleksandrov**—a victim of BCP leader Todor **Zhivkov**'s sharp turn towards hardline elements in the party. Banished to academia, Mikhailov returned to politics a week after Zhivkov's ousting, in the slightly more junior post of Deputy Premier for education and culture. Here, he lost no time in emphasizing that his radicalism was undiminished: his assertion in a December 1989 CC meeting that General Secretary Petur **Mladenov** and the post-Zhivkov leadership were little better than their predecessors provoked an offer from Mladenov to resign along with the entire Politburo—and comparisons with the maverick Soviet politician Boris **Yel'tsin**. He is reported to have been a contender for the post of party leader at the BCP's February 1990 Congress, when it was decided to remove Mladenov: his defeat by Aleksandur **Lilov** probably represented the choice of the safer and more substantial candidate—though Mikhailov had apparently moderated his line somewhat in the preceding weeks—and Mikhailov's weak position was demonstrated both by his failure to win a seat on the 131-strong Supreme Party Council elected by the Congress and soon afterwards when he lost his government post. A Mikhailov comeback seems improbable, though not impossible if circumstances should come to favour a BCP leader more radical than Lilov.

RW

MILOŠEVIĆ, SLOBODAN. Born in Pozarevac (Serbia) of mixed Serbian and Montenegrin parentage in 1941, Milošević studied Law at university, worked with Tehnogas and was then appointed Director of the Belgrade banking combine Beobanka. From there he was elected to the Belgrade city party committee and the Serbian party presidency. He was elected leader of the Serbian League of Communists in April 1987 by backing a resurgence of Serbian nationalism and advocating greater control by Serbia of its two provinces, Kosovo and the Vojvodina. He became President of Serbia in November 1989.

PA

MITTAG, GÜNTER. Former GDR politician and economic expert, born 1926. Günter Mittag rose through the party hierarchy from 1946, becoming a full Politburo member in 1966. His specialism was management of the command economy, and he was party secretary for the economy for most of the period 1962–89. Although from time to time he exposed failings in the system and demanded changes, he was responsible for the gross inadequacies of the planning structure, which he tried to disguise by ordering the manipulation of statistics. Despite health problems (diabetes and a partly amputated leg), he was a vigorous representative of the GDR in West German economic circles. When **Honecker** fell ill in the summer of 1989 Mittag deputised for him, but in his resolution to avoid reform he failed to grasp the depth of the crisis. He was dismissed in October 1989 along with Honecker and party propaganda secretary Joachim Herrmann. Mittag and Herrmann did not even receive the thanks accorded to Honecker. Mittag was later expelled from the **Socialist Unity Party of Germany (SED)** and charged with corruption and other offences.

JO

MLADENOV, PETUR TOSHEV. Bulgarian Communist politician; Secretary of Bulgarian Komsomol 1966–69; first Secretary of Vidin Province committee of the **Bulgarian Communist Party (BCP)** 1969–71; Minister of Foreign Affairs 1971–89; Politburo member from 1977; General Secretary of BCP from November 1989 to February 1990; Chairman of State Council (President) from November 1989.

Born in 1936 into a Bulgarian revolutionary family, Petur Mladenov was educated in philosophy at Sofia University before studying at Moscow's State Institute for International Relations. After some years of Komsomol and party work, he was reassigned to diplomacy, going straight to the top as Foreign Minister at the unusually early age of 35. Eighteen years in this post gave Mladenov considerable prestige and visibility but little obvious power base in the BCP apparatus, so it was something of a surprise when he emerged as General Secretary after the fall of Todor **Zhivkov**. As Foreign Minister, Mladenov had good reason for discontent with his erstwhile patron Zhivkov, whose policy towards ethnic **Turks in Bulgaria** had resulted in an international disrepute that had nullified Mladenov's careful diplomacy, and he seems to have played a key role in assembling the coalition of forces that toppled Zhivkov, perhaps precipitating the final crisis by a threat to resign — and, according to rumours, securing Soviet support during a stopover visit in Moscow. This role, rather than any reserve of personal power, explains Mladenov's emergence as party leader: in addition, he was one of the few acceptable members of the leadership in place in November 1989 — witness the fact that, of full Politburo members then in office, only Mladenov and Defence Minister Dobri Dzhurov found a place on the Politburo's successor body, the collective chairmanship of the Supreme Party Council, in February 1990.

Mladenov's months as General Secretary were marked by dramatic personnel change at the top; by substantial concessions on human rights and political freedoms; by increasingly vehement denunciation of Zhivkov and his economic legacy; by a reversal of Zhivkov's disastrous Turkish policy; by the formal abandonment of the constitutional provision for the BCP's "leading role" in Bulgarian society; by the promise of free elections; and by negotiations with the emerging opposition, and even the offer of a government of national unity. How far Mladenov was making the running rather than simply responding to pressure is another matter, and his replacement at the head of the BCP by the resurgent Aleksandur **Lilov** probably reflected the fact that Lilov was more of a man for the moment—a more authentic radical than Mladenov, with a party background that was simultaneously more solid than Mladenov's and less tainted by association with the final discreditable years of the Zhivkov regime. The reason officially given for Mladenov's resignation, however, was that of ill-health, and this may indeed have been a contributory factor, especially in such trying times: though only 53 at the time of his elevation, he had already undergone one major heart operation. Nevertheless, this change left Mladenov still President, and as such he will continue to enjoy considerably power and prominence in Bulgarian politics — unless and until he is swept aside by radicalism within the BCP or by a defeat for the party in the elections scheduled for May 1990.

RW

MLYNÁŘ, ZDENĚK. A leading proponent of political reform in Czechoslovakia throughout the 1960s, Mlynář, who was born in 1930, studied law at Moscow University in the early 1950s. In 1966, while employed in the Institute of State and Law of the Czechoslovak Academy of Sciences, he was appointed head of an academic team, set up with the approval of the then leader of the Communist Party and President, Antonín **Novotný**, to explore the issue of political reform. During the **Prague Spring**, he was one of the authors of the Communist Party's Action Programme and in May 1968 was appointed a Secretary of the Party Central Committee. After the **Warsaw Treaty Organization (Warsaw Pact)** invasion in August that year he was elected a full member of the Party Presidium, but resigned from all those posts in November. After signing **Charter 77**, he left Prague in 1977 for exile in Vienna where he began a programme of research on Communist systems.

GW

MODROW, HANS. GDR Prime Minister from November 1989, born 1928. Dr Hans Modrow was a key figure in the revolution which overtook the GDR regime in 1989–90, and he could be so because he had not been implicated in the abuses of the past. Although a loyal member of the **Socialist Unity Party of Germany (SED)** from the beginning of the GDR, he was for a long time distrusted by the party leadership and deliberately kept at a distance and out of high office.

Modrow was born at Jasenitz in what is now the north-east of the GDR. He joined **Free German Youth (FDJ)**, the **Free German Trade Union League (FDGB)** and the SED in 1949. From 1952 to 1961 he was active in the **Berlin** section of the FDJ, thereafter in the party organization in Berlin. His progress was at times unusually slow, indicating that his career was deliberately being restrained. He only become a full member of the Central Committee in 1967, and during his 16 years from 1973 as party secretary for the Dresden district was not admitted to even candidate Politburo status. By mid-1989 Modrow had developed a reputation, particularly in the Dresden area itself, as an honest and reform-minded man who spurned the luxuries enjoyed by other party leaders. He was viewed with distrust, however, by the Politburo and in mid-1989 a party commission was sent from Berlin to Dresden to deal with "political and economic shortcomings". In other words, Modrow was being investigated and disciplined. His main opponents were Günter **Mittag** and Joachim Herrmann.

When the crisis broke in the autumn of 1989 and Egon **Krenz** replaced Erich **Honecker** as party secretary, Modrow was increasingly mentioned as a necessary member of any reform government to give it credibility. Although not a close associate of Krenz, Modrow was elected to the Politburo in November and proposed as the new prime minister (Chairman of the Council of Ministers). He took office on Nov. 13, 1989 and appointed a coalition cabinet with many new faces. When Krenz was displaced as SED General Secretary and as Head of State, Modrow effectively became the leader of the GDR. He entered into the **Round Table** (Runder Tisch) discussions with opposition groups and parties, but had difficulty holding them and his coalition together. He had, for instance, to backtrack on his decision to retain a state security service. By late January 1990 Modrow was announcing clearly that the GDR was in deep crisis and that he needed the help of the opposition. It was agreed by most opposition groups and parties that they were willing to participate in a grand coalition government, provided that all ministers, including Modrow himself, temporarily laid aside their party positions. Modrow had already done this in all but name when he said that he was acting on behalf of his country rather than his party. At the beginning of February, Modrow took the step which no other SED politician had dared take before: he declared that the two German states should move towards one neutral federal fatherland with its capital in Berlin. The neutrality question remained the stumbling block with Bonn.

Modrow acquired a generally positive reputation at home and abroad, and this helped his party to more than survive the election of March 1990. The 66 seats and 16.4 per cent of the vote were not enough, however, to allow Modrow to continue, and his was a caretaker administration until Lothar **de Maizière** was charged with forming a new coalition government in April. Despite pressure from the **PDS**, Modrow failed to be elected president of the *Volkskammer* (parliament).

JO

MOLDAVIA. The Moldavian Soviet Socialist Republic was formed by the union of part of the former Moldavian Autonomous Soviet Socialist Republic (established in 1924), formerly included in the **Ukraine**, with areas of **Bessarabia** ceded to the USSR by Romania in 1940. Its area is 33,700 sq km, and its 1989 census population was 4,341,000 (about 1.5 per cent of the population of the USSR as a whole). According to the 1979 census 64 per cent of the population were ethnic Moldavians; there are also substantial Ukrainian and Russian minorities. The capital is Kishinev. Moldavia is an important agricultural producer in the USSR, particularly of wine, grain, sugar-beet and vegetables; there are also light industries. Communal tensions made themselves apparent in the late 1980s, particularly over the status of the national language, and the overthrow of **Ceauşescu** in December 1989 encouraged closer links with neighbouring Romania (for further discussion *see* **Nationality Question in the USSR**).

SLW

MOSCOW. The Soviet capital and its largest city; also the capital of the Russian Soviet Federal Socialist Republic (RSFSR), the Soviet Union's largest republic. Its population as recorded in the 1989 census was 8,967,000 (excluding suburbs, 8,769,000). Moscow rose to prominence as the centre of the principality which from the fifteenth century onwards gradually brought the Russian state into being; it became an important religious and commercial centre, and in the nineteenth century the main base of the important textile and metallugical industries. Seized by Napoleon in 1812, the city arrested the Nazi invaders just 30–40 km from the city centre in 1941 and suffered relatively little war damage. In Moscow the Kremlin (citadel) is the centre of government, incorporating government and parliamentary buildings; the party headquarters is at Staraya ploshchad' (Old Square), which is nearby. Apart from political, educational, manufacturing and other activities, Moscow has from 1987 housed the headquarters of the Russian Orthodox Church.

SLW

N

NAGY, IMRE. Communist leader in Hungary at the time of the 1956 Revolution. Nagy, born in 1896, came from a poor peasant family. He was taken prisoner by Russia during World War I and joined the Hungarian Section of the Russian Communist Party in 1918. He fought in the Civil War in Russia, then returned to Hungary in 1921. He was active in the Socialist Workers' Party of Hungary, a front for the then illegal Communist Party, between 1925 and 1927. In 1928, he fled to Vienna, then made his way to the Soviet Union, where he developed his interests in agricultural questions and economics. During World War II, he helped prepare Hungarian language programmes for Kossuth Radio, broadcast from the Soviet Union. At this time, he also became a close associate of the leading Soviet Communist, George Malenkov. He returned to Hungary with other exiled Hungarian Communist leaders in 1944, and took the post of Minister of Agriculture in the Debrecen coalition government, in which capacity he was responsible for the land reform which handed out land to the peasants. From November 1945 he held the post of Minister of the Interior, but he proved unsatisfactory, from the point of view of the Communist Party leadership, in using this post to secure Communist control over the administration, the police, citizenship matters, regulation of the press and social organizations. He was accordingly removed in February 1946, although he remained in the HCP Politburo.

Nagy was expelled from the Politburo in August 1949 after voicing misgivings about the policy of collectivization of agriculture, and retired to academic life, where he developed his connections with some radical populist thinkers. In 1951, he was brought back into the government as Minister of Food, later Minister for Collecting Agricultural Produce and Livestock. From 1952, he became one of five Deputy Prime Ministers, and in July 1953 he was promoted to Prime Minister. The latter appointment was clearly due to direct intervention by Moscow, in particular, by Malenkov, who at this time was Soviet Prime Minister; it seems very likely that Nagy was protected by the same connection during the peak of the period of Stalinist purges in Hungary. Nagy was appointed to restore some balance to the Hungarian economy after several years of **Rákosi**'s fanatical super-industrialization policies had brought about a state of near collapse which was a growing threat to political stability. The "New Course" which Nagy launched shifted investment resources away from heavy industry to agriculture, light and consumer goods industries with the aim of bringing about an immediate improvement in the population's standard of living and a more balanced pattern of growth.

Malenkov's position in Moscow, however, weakened in the course of the Kremlin power struggle of these years. He was removed from his post in February 1955, and Nagy was ousted by Rákosi in Hungary shortly after, in April. He then went into retirement, and wrote his famous personal manifesto, *In Defence of the New Course*, in which he elaborated a more or less systematic alternative Marxism, later dubbed "revisionism". The basic elements of his revisionism were: the repudiation of the rigid "dogmatism" of **Stalinism**, and the insistence that Marxism must be creatively developed to meet changing needs; the rejection of the Soviet model as unconditionally binding, and the assertion of the need to take specific national conditions into account; the insistence on the continuing validity of "national ideals" for Communists, and the need for relations between socialist states to respect the principles of national independence, sovereignty, equality, self-determination and territorial inviolability; and the affirmation of the role of ethical factors in politics, which required that Communists rule through persuasion, incentives and consent rather than coercion and terror.

After **Khrushchev**'s "secret speech" denouncing **Stalin** in February 1956, supporters of Nagy within the Hungarian Workers' Party began to press for his return, but they did not succeed in reinstalling him as Prime Minister until open mass revolt was already under way, by which time it was already too late for Nagy to restore the situation. He tried to win popular support for his government by securing the consent of Soviet representatives in Budapest for the establishment of a multi-party coalition government with the promise of free elections in future. But he was betrayed by the Soviets, who broke their promise to withdraw Soviet troops and instead sent in a massive new invasion force. Upon learning of this, Nagy felt he had no option but to announce Hungary's withdrawal from the **Warsaw Treaty Organization (Warsaw Pact)** and neutrality. As Soviet forces crushed the revolution, Nagy fled to the Yugoslav Embassy. He was given safe passage to leave for exile in Yugoslavia by **Kádár**, but when he tried to do so on 22 Nov., 1956 he was seized by Soviet troops and carried off to Romania. He was brought to trial in secret, but refused to admit any guilt. His execution was announced by the Hungarian authorities on 17 June, 1958.

The rehabilitation of Nagy not surprisingly became a great cause of democratic reformers in Hungary in the late 1980s as the political crisis gathered momentum. It was only possible after János Kádár was removed from the leadership in May 1988. The **Hungarian Socialist Worker's Party (HSWP)** Central Committee set up a committee of historians to re-examine the question of 1956, which concluded that it had not been a "counter-revolution" but a "popular uprising". The justification for Nagy's execution was thus undermined. The Hungarian Supreme Court annulled the verdict of treason passed on him on 6 June, 1989. Permission was given for the exhumation of his remains from the unmarked grave in a suburban Budapest cemetery, and he was reburied with much ceremony in June 16. The ceremony turned into a massive popular demonstration in favour of more rapid democratic reforms, and dealt a fatal blow to the HSWP's confidence in its moral authority.

JB

NATIONAL DEMOCRATIC PARTY OF GERMANY (NDPD — National-Demokratische Partei Deutschlands).

Along with the **Democratic Peasants' Party of Germany (DBD)**, the NDPD was founded in the Soviet Occupation Zone of Germany in April 1948 on the instigation of the **Socialist Unity Party of Germany (SED)**, in order to mobilize and to control a particular section of society. The NDPD, with its German nationalist aspect, was intended to attract former soldiers, particularly officers, and former members of the NSDAP (Nazi party) who were not implicated in serious crimes. It became part of the SED-dominated National Front (along with the **Christian Democratic Union of Germany—CDU**, the **Liberal Democratic Party of Germany—LDPD** and DBD) and thus little more than a mouthpiece for official ideology. Besides its original membership, however, it did develop a role as representative of small private or semi-private traders.

The NDPD increased its numbers from the mid-1970s to 110,000 in 1987, as part of an SED policy to build up the allied parties and draw more people into identification with the system. The events of 1989–90, however, threw the NDPD into confusion. Its long-serving chairman, Heinrich Homann (born 1911, member of the NSDAP—Nazi Party—in 1933, NDPD acting

chairman then chairman since 1967), resigned from his post. The next chairman, Günter Hartmann, lasted only until January 1990, when he was voted out in favour of Wolfgang Gläser. Gläser resigned shortly afterwards. The party was torn between its record of complicity in the old regime and its potential role as a mobiliser of the nationalist right. On this latter ground it competed with other groups emerging in the GDR (for instance, the **German Social Union (DSU)** and possibly with the West German *Republikaner*. In the March 1990 elections the NDPD performed abysmally (0.4 per cent of the vote and only two seats). Thereupon it decided to merge with the LDPD.

JO

NATIONAL FRONT OF THE CZECHO-SLOVAK SOCIALIST REPUBLIC.

Initially established in 1945 as a forum in which representatives of all permitted political parties could formulate a common policy, the National Front, expanded to include all major social and interest organizations as well as the political parties, became after February 1948 a mechanism by which the **Communist Party of Czechoslovakia** could ensure its control. Except during Alexander **Dubček**'s leadership, the Communist Party First or General Secretary has been Chairman of the National Front's Central Committee and his counterparts at lower levels of the administrative hierarchy (the party chiefs in Slovakia, the regions, districts, towns and villages) have chaired the Front's committees in those units. Nominally the National Front has been responsible for formulating election programmes and for organizing, through its electoral commissions, elections to the federal and republican parliaments and to regional, district and local national committees. Apart from the five legally recognized political parties (the Communist Party, the **Czechoslovak Socialist Party**, the **Czechoslovak People's Party**, the **Freedom Party** and the **Party of Slovak Renewal**), 29 other organizations ranging from the Revolutionary Trades Union Movement, the Czechoslovak Union of Women and the Socialist Youth Union, to the Union of Czechoslovak Philatelists and the Union of Beekeepers are reported to have been members in 1989.

GW

NATIONAL PEOPLE'S ARMY (GDR — NVA, Nationale Volksarmee).

The NVA is the army of the GDR. It was founded in 1955–56 from the ranks of the *Kasernierte Volkspolizei*

170

(KVP—People's Police in Barracks), as the GDR joined the **Warsaw Treaty Organization (Warsaw Pact)**. It was placed under the Ministry for National Defence. Military service was until the late 1980s 18 months for men (since reduced to 12 months), and conscientious objection was discouraged and rewarded with harassment. The NVA in the 1980s was 120,000 men strong, including 71,500 conscripts. In addition were a navy of 16,000 (8,000 conscripts serving 36 months), an airforce of 37,000 (15,000 conscripts), 390,000 reserves, and other armed forces under the authority of the ministries of National Defence, State Security (*see* **Stasi**) and the Interior. The defence budget (including internal and border security etc.) in 1988 was M 21.7 billion, nearly 8 per cent of Net Material Product.

The alleged militarization of society in the GDR was one of the main targets of opposition groups from the early 1980s. Church leaders were critical of military indoctrination of the young and the difficulties faced by those wishing to perform non-military national service.

Already before the cut in the period of compulsory national service, the GDR had announced a reduction of 10,000 men by the end of 1990, in line with defence cuts throughout the Warsaw Pact. In the aftermath of the revolution in the GDR, the NVA lost conscripts both to emigration and to desertion. By the spring of 1990 the army faced internal collapse, with a near halving in size.

JO

NATIONAL SALVATION FRONT (ROMANIA).

This took power from the **Ceauşescu** regime. At first declaring itself as solely an interim government, it later stated that it would stand as a political party in elections scheduled for May 1990. The NSF's first chairman was Ion **Iliescu**.

RH

NATIONAL TRADE UNION ACCORD (POLAND — OPZZ Ogólnopolskie Porozumienie Związków Zawodowych).

With the introduction in Poland of the **State of War** in December 1981 all existing trade-union organizations were suspended and then declared illegal in October 1982. Legislation was passed to permit the creation of unions on a new basis and care was taken not to reproduce the conditions that might give rise to another **Solidarity** or permit the rebirth of the original movement. They were to be organized separately, in the first instance, at enterprise level and then by industrial branch but not, like Solidarity, as a unified national structure organized by region. They were obviously designed to be more amenable to party–state control than the now outlawed union, and there was little enthusiasm amongst workers and employees to join them. While Solidarity had enrolled over seven million members within several weeks of its foundation, the new unions had mobilized only 4,299,000 by the end of 1984. Even party members required considerable encouragement before joining.

As part of the careful process of gradually building up a national organization the National Accord, the central trade union body, was finally established in November 1984. Its chairman, Alfred Miodowicz, was elected to the Politburo of the **Polish United Workers' Party (PUWP)** in 1986. The OPPZ was therefore clearly part of the political establishment and subject to central party control. On the other hand, particularly following the recent example of independent union activity in 1980 and 1981, it had to be given greater autonomy than the wholly discredited national organization of the **Gierek** period if it was to attract any support among the workers and perform any useful political or economic function. Criticism was heard of matters like food supplies, economic planning, housing provision and work safety, while at the X Congress of the PUWP, Miodowicz attacked the arrogance of economic administrators. Price reform and the government's counter-inflation policy were also major bones of contention, and the OPZZ took a highly critical view of Prime Minister Zbigniew Messner after the strikes of the summer of 1988 and certainly played a part in forcing his resignation on Sept. 19.

The relegalization of Solidarity in April 1989 by no means undermined the position of the OPZZ, which recorded a membership of 6,335,000 in 1988 while Solidarity was unable to claim even half that number at the end of 1989. The higher cost of Solidarity affiliation and continuing official subsidies for the OPZZ undoubtedly played a part in this, although the spiralling inflation rate, the strong emphasis placed by the OPZZ on wage indexation and the critical view it took of government economic policy (a position it could, of course, develop much more freely with the installation of the **Mazowiecki** government) were also significant. This particularly concerned the industrial unions within the OPZZ, which were most likely to be affected by the closure of outdated plant, and other unions were more disposed to take advantage of the changed political situation and sever links with the National Accord. The Teachers' Federation for

Higher Schools and Science thus left the OPZZ in November 1989.

PGL

NATIONALISM AND COMMUNISM IN EASTERN EUROPE.

For Marx and Engels, the international unity of the proletariat was a prerequisite for the success of the revolution, and Communism was incompatible with nationalism. In practice, Communist parties in power have more often than not incorporated elements of nationalism into their ideology, to increase their legitimacy. In Russia, the isolation of the revolution in a hostile world made it essential to appeal to patriotism for support, and the slogan of "Socialism in one country" took this a stage further (see **Nationality Question in the USSR**). The main problem with playing the nationalist card is that national minorities are often alienated from the state as a result.

For centuries, the Germans, Slavs, Hungarians and other ethnic groups have not lived in compact national territories but have formed a patchwork of communities throughout Eastern Europe and **Central Europe**. With the collapse of the multinational empires during and after World War I, new nation-states were formed. Several contained ethnic minorities who found themselves on the wrong side of the new borders and who might be suspected of being loyal to another state. Tensions over boundaries and over the treatment of fellow nationals in other states were a major disruptive factor in the international relations of the region between the wars. After World War II, boundaries were again adjusted and in some cases minority populations were expelled (particularly Germans from Poland and Czechoslovakia) in order to increase the correspondence between nationality (in the ethnic sense) and citizenship.

Nevertheless, the existence of national minorities remained a significant factor in the politics of several of the states of Central and Eastern Europe where the Communists took power after the war. The regimes applied widely differing approaches to the problem. The only state which right from the start attempted to follow the Soviet model of a federation of national republics was Yugoslavia.

The six "leading nations" of Yugoslavia—Serbs, Croats, ethnic Muslims, Slovenes, Macedonians and Montenegrins—have their own republic (the Muslims being the largest nationality in Bosnia-Herzegovina). In 1963 two autonomous provinces were established in Serbia: Kosovo, with an Albanian majority, and Vojvodina, where there is a Serb majority but a substantial Hungarian minority. Yugoslavia between the wars suffered from Serbian centralism, and the mutual massacres of Serbs and Croats during the war left a bitter legacy (see also **Religion and Communism**). The federal system was designed to overcome fears of Serb domination and to give power to the smaller nationalities in order to prevent the polarization of Yugoslavia between the two largest nations, Serbs and Croats. Yugoslavia was a more genuine federation than the USSR; not only the state but also the ruling party, the **League of Communists of Yugoslavia (LCY)**, was federalized (see also **Yugoslavia**—National Question).

Even while President Josip Broz **Tito** was alive, major differences arose over the path of economic development, with the more advanced northern and western republics, Croatia and Slovenia, objecting to being asked to subsidize the development of the southern republics, Serbia, Montenegro and Macedonia. In 1971 the League of Communists of Croatia placed itself at the head of the growing nationalist movement in their republic, linked with the **Roman Catholic Church**, in order not to be swept from power. Tito responded by threatening to use the Yugoslav army to bring the republic to heel, and the leadership was dismissed.

The army, dominated by Serbs and Montenegrins, has been a major force keeping Yugoslavia together. The LCY, after Tito's death in 1980, has been a confederation of eight quarrelling regional parties (and the military organization of Communists) rather than a disciplined body. Tito left a system where the leading bodies of the state and the LCY were composed of representatives of the republics and autonomous provinces (and in the case of the LCY, of the army as well). The post of president and LCY leader would rotate among the regions, preventing any individual or republic acquiring a dominant position. The effect of these arrangements was to encourage the fragmentation of Yugoslavia, as politicians became dependent for their careers on the regional League organizations and parliaments, rather than on all-Yugoslav bodies.

In March 1981 growing unrest among the Albanians in Kosovo, the poorest part of Yugoslavia, culminated in riots involving 10,000 to 20,000 people. The demand was for Kosovo to be upgraded to the status of a republic within Yugoslavia. With perhaps 40 dead and 1,000 wounded in clashes between the Muslim Albanians and the Orthodox Serbs, many Serbs emigrated from the province in fear of their lives. The Albanians' demand was resisted by the centre, partly because Serbia opposed the loss of territory which was of historic significance and on which Serbs continued to live, and partly because it seemed that the status of a republic might prove in the longer run to be a transition stage to the secession of Kosovo and its joining Albania. Order was restored by federal forces and the League leadership in Kosovo was purged.

An effect of the Croatian crisis of 1971 and the Kosovo crisis 10 years later was the growth of Serbian nationalism (*see also* **Serbian Orthodox Church**). This coincided with increasingly severe problems of inflation and unemployment in Yugoslavia, which called for some sort of economic reform. Divisions in the leadership on a nationalist basis made the achievement of consensus difficult. The more advanced republics favoured market reforms, whereas the Serbians were divided between reformers and conservatives. In the late 1980s, the Serbian leader Slobodan **Milošević** sought to manipulate the rising Serbian nationalism. He forced changes in the Serbian Constitution, reducing the power of the autonomous provinces, Kosovo and Vojvodina. In October 1988 the Vojvodina leadership resigned after a crowd of 100,000 in the capital demonstrated in favour of Milošević. In February–March 1989, in spite of strikes by Albanian workers in Kosovo involving up to 50,000 people, Milošević succeeded in forcing the local parliament to hand over their powers to Serbia. Part of the Kosovo leadership was arrested, and demonstrations by Albanians were brutally repressed by Serbian police.

These events led to a wave of hostility to Milošević among non-Serbs in Yugoslavia. Late in 1989, under the impact of events elsewhere in Eastern Europe, the republican assemblies of Slovenia and then Croatia abandoned the section of their constitutions guaranteeing the guiding role of the League of Communists. The way was prepared for a multi-party system. In January 1990 the League of Communists of Slovenia walked out of the LCY Congress and, following the example of the Communist Party of Lithuania, asserted its independence of its parent body. Serious doubts arose as to whether Yugoslavia would be able to survive. Further rioting in Kosovo in February 1990 exacerbated the crisis. At the same time, the army remained in place as a factor of national unity. The outside world was unwilling to see the collapse of Yugoslavia, and the central government appeared to be in a position to impose the economic package proposed by the IMF.

Discontent about Czech domination of Czechoslovakia led to the rise of Slovak nationalism in the late 1960s. The alliance of Czech reformers with Slovaks desiring more autonomy led to the overthrow of Antonin **Novotný** as First Secretary of the **Communist Party of Czechoslovakia** and the installation of Alexander **Dubček** in January 1968. After the Soviet invasion, the only survival of the **Prague Spring** was the federalization of the state: the formation of the Czech Socialist Republic and the Slovak Socialist Republic within the Czechoslovak Socialist Republic. The Communist Party remained unitary: the **Communist Party of Slovakia** remained as a regional component. Slovaks were over-represented in the new central leadership, headed by the Slovak Gustáv **Husák**, imposed in 1969 by the USSR. Slovak nationalism appears to have given the Husák leadership some basis of support. Very few Slovaks signed the **Charter 77** manifesto. In the late 1980s, however, the traditional link between Slovak nationalism and the Roman Catholic Church re-appeared, as the Church became more critical of the regime.

A wave of nationalism linked with anti-Semitism in Poland in the late 1960s led to the departure of the bulk of the most significant national minority, the Jews. Anti-Semitism was also a factor in politics in Hungary in the 1980s. (Jews played a prominent part in the cultural and unofficial political life of Budapest.) The principal manifestation of Hungarian nationalism in the 1970s and 1980s was a concern, found in the unofficial and sometimes the Communist Press, for the conditions of Hungarians living in Slovakia and particularly in Romania.

At the extreme of intolerance, Romania and Bulgaria pursued policies of trying to assimilate national minorities. Whereas Yugoslavia and Czechoslovakia were relatively new, multinational entities, Romania and Bulgaria could claim a history of several centuries. The **Ceauşescu** regime in Romania and the **Zhivkov** regime in Bulgaria both tried to increase their legitimacy by manipulating the nationalism of their indigenous people.

In Transylvania, Romania had jurisdication over a mixed Hungarian, Romanian and German population. Long part of Hungary, the region was of symbolic importance for both Hungary and Romania. Already in 1959 the Hungarian-language university at Cluj had lost its separate identity and the Hungarian Autonomous Region was reorganized in 1960. From 1959, the Hungarian minority suffered discrimination in jobs, housing, and cultural facilities, a situation which continued (with a break in 1967–71) to the end of the Ceauşescu regime. In 1967 the Hungarian Autonomous Region was abolished. The ill-treatment of the Hungarians in Transylvania accelerated in the 1980s. Nicolae Ceauşescu launched a plan to destroy the villages where both the Hungarians and Romanians lived, and rehouse them in "agro-industrial" blocks of flats where the language would be Romanian (*see* **Romania** —Village systematization).

As the USSR under **Gorbachev** allowed **human rights** issues to be legitimate subjects of international debate, the Hungarian government began to raise the treatment of Hungarians in Romania at international conferences and apparently within the **Warsaw Treaty Organization (Warsaw Pact or WTO)**. In 1988–89, with living standards falling seriously in Romania, the spectre of border conflict between Hungary and Romania loomed, with the USSR trying to reduce tension. Ceauşescu sought to turn Romanian opinion against the Hungarian minority, portraying them as agents of a hostile power. In May 1989 a Romanian military monthly, *Viata Militara*, called Hungary a "Trojan horse of imperialism".

The regime's attempt to appeal to nationalism finally failed. The attempt of the **Securitate** police in December 1989 to arrest the Hungarian Reformed Church pastor, László Tökés, in the Transylvanian city of **Timişoara**, brought a demonstration of the Hungarian community. They were joined by Romanians from the locality, and the resulting killings by the Securitate set in motion the chain of events that led to the fall of Ceauşescu. The **National Salvation Front**, which succeeded Ceauşescu, announced the reopening of the Hungarian university at Cluj, and promised to respect Hungarian rights (*see also* **Hungarian Minorities**).

Bulgaria under Todor Zhivkov carried out a policy of attempting to assimilate all the national minorities: the Macedonians in the 1960s, the Pomaks (Bulgarians who had adopted **Islam**) in the early 1970s and the Gypsies in the late 1970s. It was the attempt to forcibly assimilate the Turkish minority which attracted world attention in 1984. The resistance offered by those Turks who refused to adopt Bulgarian names led to violence and deaths. In summer 1989 around 300,000 Turks emigrated to Turkey, with little choice, at short notice and without most of their possessions. Only with the fall of Zhivkov were the Turks allowed to resume their old names, and then only after a chauvinist backlash manipulated by supporters of the former party leaders. (*see also* **Turks in Bulgaria**).

Nationalism was a two-edged sword in the GDR. The **Honecker** regime tried to present itself as the heir to the best traditions of German history and thought—Martin Luther, Frederick the Great, Marx, Engels and Rosa Luxemburg. Any development of German nationalism would be likely, however, to lead to demands for unification with the Federal Republic of Germany (FRG) in a single state. The leadership therefore tried to promote a policy of *Abgrenzung* (demarcation or limitation), emphasizing the distinctions between the two German states.

A discussion of nationalism in Eastern Europe should refer also to the relations of the governments with the USSR. Gradually, after Stalin's death, the regimes sought to expand their autonomy and resist Soviet control of their economies, through the **Council for Mutual Economic Assistance (CMEA)**, or of their armies through the WTO. The leading role was taken by Romania, which led the opposition to **Khrushchev**'s attempts to create a supranational planning body and established the principle of voluntary participation in CMEA projects. Romania also succeeded in securing the removal of Soviet forces and in refusing to allow WTO exercises on its territory. On occasion it raised claims to **Bessarabia** and Northern Bukovina, incorporated in the USSR after the Molotov-Ribbentrop Pact. This Romanian nationalism was the other side of the policy of Romanianizing the national minorities.

The Hungarian revolution of 1956 and the Czechoslovak reform movement of 1968 were not primarily motivated by nationalism but by the wish to democratize the political and economic institutions. The subsequent Soviet invasions of these countries naturally led to anti-Soviet feeling, but not to a rabid nationalist reaction. On the other hand, nationalism was an important component in the movement in Poland initiated in August 1980 by the independent trade union, **Solidarity**. The centuries-long link between Polish nationalism and Roman Catholicism was absorbed by Solidarity, and only the military crackdown of December 1981 could prevent the collapse of the official apparatus.

The fact that the transformation and collapse of the regimes in Eastern Europe in 1989 was made possible, and at least in the case of the GDR, promoted, by the new line coming from Moscow meant that nationalism was not a major factor in the immediate aftermath. The emphasis was on the rediscovery of the democratic traditions of the countries, however fragile those traditions might be. The mass desire for unification with the FRG which swept the GDR at the beginning of 1990 was not so much a wave of nationalism but rather a feeling of despair at the economic situation into which the Communists had brought the country, culminating in mass emigration to the FRG. The collapse of the Berlin Wall in November 1989 nevertheless gave an impetus to national feeling on both sides of the border.

It was the spectre rather than the fact of a revived German nationalism which prompted East Europeans to be concerned about the consequences of German unification. Already in November 1989 the visit of the German Federal Chancellor Helmut Kohl to Silesia in Poland had brought about a mass demonstration of Germans who were citizens of Poland, demanding rights for the German language. Ambiguities about the recognition by the West Germans of the post-war frontiers of Germany still remained in February 1990, despite the acceptance at the 1975 Helsinki Conference on Security and Co-operation in Europe (CSCE) that frontiers could only be changed peacefully and by agreement. It was no longer Soviet pressure but rather the fear of German nationalism which prompted the Catholic Prime Minister of Poland, Tadeusz **Mazowiecki**, to emphasize his country's commitment to the WTO in January 1990.

The projected withdrawal of the major part of the Soviet forces in Eastern and Central Europe, together with the likely unification of Germany, indicated the transformation of the security situation in the region. The danger of a revival of right-wing nationalism in Romania, Bulgaria, Poland or Hungary seemed real. Old enmities, hidden under the carpet for over 40 years, threatened to re-emerge. The most dangerous points of conflict seemed to be between Hungary and Romania over Transylvania; between Yugoslavia, Bulgaria and Greece over Macedonia; between Romania and the USSR over Moldavia and North Bukovina; between Poland and a future independent Lithuania over the Vilnius district; and over the German borders with Poland and Czechoslovakia. By February 1990 there was agreement between the major powers over the need for a new security system for Europe, maintaining NATO and the WTO, to be worked out by the participants in the CSCE process.

PJSD

NATIONALITY QUESTION IN THE USSR.
The "national question" in the Soviet Union arises from the success of the Bolsheviks after 1917 in establishing their power over most of the territory of the former Russian Empire, including members of nearly 200 nationalities and ethnic groups. These peoples represented a wide range of cultures, languages, religions and levels of development. Today, some of these groups have been assimilated by larger nationalities. Despite the processes of modernization and centralization over 70 years, most of the major Soviet nations, and especially those with their own Union Republics, have experienced a rise in their national awareness.

For most of the Soviet period (although not in the Stalinist purges) this national awareness typi-

cally expressed itself in a defence of the nation's language and culture against the spread of Russian. Depending on local conditions, it also sometimes took the form of resistance to the immigration of Slavs into the traditional homeland of the nation; an assertion of the nation's own history, as distinct from the imperial version emanating from Moscow; and calls for more resources for economic development. In the **Gorbachev** period, as *glasnost'* developed, it was expressed more strongly in calls for greater independence for the national republic, and in growing numbers of calls for secession of the republic from the USSR.

Before the revolution, **Lenin** argued that the way to counter nationalist demands for secession and at the same time to win the support of the non-Russians was to defend the right of the nations of the Russian Empire to self-determination. This right, however, was less important for Lenin than his belief in the need for the unity of the working class of all nations and his preference for large centralized states. After the Civil War, with the Bolshevik conquest of the Russian borderlands, he came round to advocate a compromise solution, federal in form. Thus in 1922 the **Russian Republic (RSFSR)** joined with the **Ukraine, Belorussia** and Transcaucasia to form the USSR. The situation was complicated by the fact that support for the Bolsheviks was strongest among the industrial workers, who tended to be ethnic Russians, and weak among the peasants, who belonged to the local nationalities. Lenin was alarmed at the danger of Russian chauvinism which he detected within party ranks. In particular he was concerned at the treatment by **Stalin**, then People's Commissar of Nationalities, of his native **Georgia** after it had been reconquered by the Red Army. To protect the non-Russians, Lenin insisted that the republics should have the right to secede from the USSR and that the the Russian language not be compulsory in the schools.

Over time, the number of republics grew by division and annexation, and new forms of national statehood were created for smaller nations. Under present arrangements, nations of over a million people living a compact area and with a foreign border are allowed the status of a Union Republic (15 of which made up the Soviet Union at the start of 1990). Other nations of over half a million may qualify for the status of Autonomous Republic within a Union Republic, and smaller nations may be given an autonomous *oblast'* (province) or national *okrug* (district). Until Gorbachev, however, the federalist form of the system was weakened by the fact that the constitution reserved most powers for the centre. Still more importantly, power in pratice was wielded by the highly centralized **Communist Party of the Soviet Union (CPSU)**, which always retained the option of removing local leaders who resisted the demands of Moscow.

In the 1920s, the republics were encouraged to promote the use of the local languages. Some received alphabets for the first time. The Communists tried to recruit members of the local nationalities for leading positions in the party and the state. They directed resources to the more backward parts of the country, to create a working class among the non-Russian nationalities. In the Ukraine, the largest republic after Russia itself, the Education Minister Mykola Skrypnik pursued a policy of "Ukrainianization"; Ukrainian was the language for the bulk of all business in the republic, from the Press to higher education. Not everyone in the Soviet Union was satisfied with these policies: in 1924 Georgia revolted against Bolshevik rule, while the Central Asian resistance continued until the beginning of the 1930s. Within the Communist Party itself, Moscow was confronted by a movement of 'Islamic Communists', led by Sultan-Galiev, who wished to create one large Muslim republic within the Soviet Union, from the Volga to Central Asia. The leadership's response was to purge Sultan-Galiev and create separate Union and Autonomous Republics for the most important Muslim nations, artificially exaggerating the differences between them (*see also* **Islam**).

The isolation of the revolution in Russia led to Stalin's adoption of the slogan "Socialism in one country" in 1924, appealing to Russian patriotism. From the late 1920s, local Communist leaders were regularly purged for "bourgeois nationalism" as Moscow sought to bring the republics under central control. The drive for the collectivization of agriculture decimated Russian and non-Russian peasants alike. Artificially-induced famine particularly hurt the nomadic Kirghiz and the Ukrainians. Indeed collectivization was seen by some in Moscow as having the aim of destroying the peasant base of Ukrainian nationalism. By the mid-1930s, Moscow was appealing to imperial Russian traditions in attempts to mobilize the country for industrialization and the approaching war. Whereas Lenin had described Tsarist Russia as the "prison-house of the peoples", from the 1930s the non-Russians were told that their absorption into the Empire had been voluntary and progressive. In 1938 the Russian language became a compulsory subject of study in all schools.

It would be wrong, however, simply to look for a re-assertion of pre-revolutionary values in the official political atmosphere of the 1930s. Rather, the decade saw the banning of much of the literary and cultural legacies of both the Russian and non-Russian peoples. The assault on religion from 1929 signified an attack on the national identities of the Russians, Armenians, Muslims and other Soviet peoples, given the close connection between religion and their national cultures (*see* **Religion and Communism; Russian Orthodox Church**).

The secret protocols of the Molotov-Ribbentrop Pact in 1939 provided for the Soviet Union to recover the Western Ukraine and Western Belorussia, which had been incorporated in Poland in 1921. The protocols also recognized a Soviet interest in the Baltic states of **Estonia**, **Latvia** and **Lithuania**, which had achieved independence from Russia after the revolution. In 1940 the USSR reoccupied the Baltic states, and their legislatures were forced to apply to join the Soviet Union. **Bessarabia** was detached from Romania and formed the Moldavian Soviet Socialist Republic, while Northern Bukovina was added to the Ukraine. The outbreak of the **Great Fatherland War** led to a Soviet withdrawal, but in 1944 Soviet forces returned and integrated the territorial gains resulting from the Pact into the USSR. The Sovietization of the Baltic and the Ukraine was accompanied by large-scale popular resistance and by mass deportations to Siberia (perhaps one third of the male population of Latvia). This led to a legacy of anti-Soviet feeling which was never far below the surface, until it emerged in the open under Gorbachev.

Stalin had responded to the Nazi attack in 1941 by appealing to the memory of Tsarist military leaders. His suspicion of non-Russian peoples and his ability to impose his paranoia on society led to the deportation to Central Asia of whole nationalities – Crimean Tatars, Volga Germans, Chechen, Ingush, Kalmyks, Kabardinians, Balkars, Karachais and Meskhetian Turks — on accusations that they had collaborated with the Nazis. He responded to the defeat of the Nazis by drinking the health of the "Great Russian people", the "leading people" of the Soviet Union. This developed into the Russian chauvinism of Stalin's last years. Official anti-Semitism increased: Soviet Jews were accused of "rootless cosmopolitanism". Many were purged and executed, and it seems that if Stalin had not died in 1953 a full-scale pogrom would have been officially organized.

After **Khrushchev**'s denunciation of Stalin in 1956, there was a revival among the non-Russian nationalities. More freedom was given to their writers and historians. The leading posts in the Communist parties and governments in the republics were as a rule thenceforth filled by representatives of the local nationalities. Often their deputies were Russians from outside the republic, sent in to watch over the locals. The deported nations were "rehabilitated", although not all were allowed back to their own territories. The republican leaders took measures, to defend their languages against the spread of Russian: **Azerbaidzhan** was the first republic to make the local language, Azeri, the state language of the republic. When Latvia and Azerbaidzhjan refused to enact a proposal from Moscow which seemed to favour the use of Russian, Khrushchev had to remove the local leaders.

Khrushchev's anti-religious campaign (1959–64) offended many nationally-minded people. Societies were established in the republics to protect cultural and historical monuments, which often meant churches and mosques. The rise of national feeling in the non-Russians was accompanied by its re-emergence among the Russians themselves, as the "village prose" writers such as Vladimir Soloukhin and Efim Dorosh praised Russian peasant morality and customs. Russians and non-Russians feared that Khrushchev's desire to build Communism by 1980 might involve an attempt to achieve the aim, which Lenin had set, of eradicating distinctions between nationalites, and bringing about their "fusion" in a Soviet melting-pot.

Under **Brezhnev** (1964–82) nationalism grew among both Russians and non-Russians. The native-language Press in most of the non-Russian republics rapidly increased its circulation until the mid-1970s, and the provision of television broadcasts in the native languages provided an added boost to the cultures of the republics. In Moscow, on the other hand, the central bodies of the party and state became dominated by ethnic Russians. The leadership was sympathetic to the use of Russian patriotic motifs and references to the "Great Russian people" abounded. At the same time Brezhnev was wary of offending the non-Russians by pushing this too far, and excessive adulation of **Stalinism** and the nineteenth-century Russian conservatives (which occurred in the Komsomol magazine *Molodaya gvardiya* — "Young Guard") was criticized and then prevented.

The nationalism of the non-Russians was much more harshly treated. In 1965–66 around one hundred Ukrainian intellectuals were arrested for their zeal in defending the Ukraine against Russification. Over the next few years leading Ukrainian writers such as Vyacheslav Chornovil and Valentyn Moroz were imprisoned for their support for the national movement. In 1972 the First Secretary of the Central Committee of the Communist Party of the Ukraine, Petro Shelest,

was removed for his covert and overt support for Ukrainian culture. At the same time Ivan Dzyuba, the author of *Internationalism or Russification?* (1967), which criticized Soviet nationality policy from a Leninist viewpoint, was arrested and sentenced.

The Crimean Tatars campaigned by demonstrations and petitions to be allowed to return to the Crimea. A single one of their petitions gathered the names of 60,000 representatives of their nation. Mustafa Jemilev and other leaders suffered imprisonment in labour camps as a result. Dissidents from the Baltic republics protested against Russification and the immigration of Slavs, which threatened to make the Latvians and Estonians minorities in their own republics.

The **human rights** movement in Moscow acted to unify the various nationalist movements, through the *samizdat Chronicle of Current Events*. An important role was played by Jewish activists. Following the six-day Arab-Israeli war in June 1967, part of the Soviet media began a campaign of anti-Semitism, thinly disguised as anti-Zionism. This was the main factor in the growth of the Jewish emigration movement, associated with a revival of interest in Judaism and the Hebrew language. The authorities fiercely resisted the movement at first, perhaps because the Soviet leaders feared that if the Jews were allowed to leave, then nationalities which had their own republics mighy follow their example and try to secede. The support of Western countries for the Jews was important in forcing Moscow to reverse its position in 1971, and allow 250,000 Jews to emigrate to Israel and the West over the following eight years.

From the mid-1970s, the authorities embarked on a major campaign to promote the teaching and use of the Russian language among the non-Russians. There were several reasons for this. Perhaps the most important was the result of the 1970 census, showing that the Russians were heading towards becoming a minority in the Soviet Union, while the Muslim nationalities were forging ahead. The Soviet army was concerned about the low level among conscripts of the understanding of Russian, the sole language of command. The army had long been praised as a "school of internationalism", and in practice served as the main instrument of Russification, but the growing proportion of conscripts unable to function in Russian threatened the efficiency of its operations. Furthermore, the prevailing economic development strategy would require Central Asians to work in Russian-speaking areas such as Siberia. At the same time, at least some of the proponents of Russian felt that the language could play the role of cementing the Soviet Union more closely together.

Proposals involved the compulsory expansion of the role of Russian in education, from theses for higher degrees down to the pre-school level. Despite rhetoric about the equality of languages, pupils in Russian-language schools outside the RSFSR were required to study the local language only to a nominal extent, while those in schools which were supposed to use the native language found that subjects other than the native language itself were increasingly taught in Russian. Provision of native-language teaching suffered, especially in the cities; Minsk, the capital of Belorussia, was reduced to one Belorussian-language primary school. The authorities proclaimed their aim to be not the elimination of the local languages — these were supposed to flourish, in official propaganda — but the achievement of "Russian-national bilingualism", the ability to function in both the native and the Russian tongues.

Without a return to the mass terror of the Stalin era, however, such policies could only provoke resistance. Writers, especially in Georgia and the Baltic republics, spoke out at official meetings and organized petitions. From 1977, small groups modelled on the Helsinki Monitoring Group in Moscow, compiling information on the violation of human rights by the authorities, appeared in the Ukraine, Lithuania **Armenia** and Georgia. The protection of people seeking to defend their national cultures was a major concern of their work. The groups were all broken up and their leaders themselves sent to the camps.

Probably stronger in Lithuania (*see* **Roman Catholic Church**) than anywhere else, the combination of religion and anti-Soviet nationalism presented a challenge to the Soviet authorities by the early 1980s. The mass arrests of dissidents kept the danger below the surface for the time being. The revolution in Iran, the war in Afghanistan and the rise of **Solidarity** in Poland were worrying developments for those concerned with keeping order in the non-Russian republics. The turn to religion and nationalism among representatives of Russians and non-Russians alike reflected the decline of belief in **Marxism-Leninism** and the spread of corruption and cynicism within the regime. Brezhev's policy of "stability of cadres" meant that many of the non-Russian republics were managed by local mafias, headed by the General Secretary's cronies, who saw corruption and nepotism as part of the spoils of office.

Even before Brezhnev's death, the KGB under **Andropov** had begun a campaign against corruption, and while the latter was General Secretary it pursued its investigations in Central Asia. Andropov and **Chernenko** were both still more intolerant of nationalism than Brezhnev had been. Gorbachev's policy of *glasnost'* allowed the accumulated and repressed grievances of past decades to be expressed. It is notable, however, that the first major ethnic disturbance of his period in office arose not from *glasnost'* but from his pursuit of the anti-corruption campaign, in the Republic of **Kazakhstan**. In December 1986, Gorbachev replaced the First Secretary of the Central Committee of the Communist Party of Kazakhstan, the Kazakh Dinmukhamed Kunaev, with a Russian, Gennady Kolbin. This led to demonstrations by Kazakhs in the capital, Alma-Ata, under slogans such as "Russians out of Kazakhstan!" and "Independence and a seat at the United Nations for Kazakhstan". The demonstration was brutally suppressed and further violence followed.

It was *glasnost'* which brought into the open the tensions between nationalities and concerns about the survival of the national cultures. At the congresses of the republican organizations of the Union of Writers leading up to the Congress of the Union of Writers of the USSR in June 1986, non-Russian writers articulated their fears about the future of their languages. The weekly newspapers of the Writers' Union in the republics began to carry such material regularly. Links developed between such different republics as Latvia and Uzbekistan as writers sought to pool their experience of promoting their native languages.

The catastrophe at the **Chernobyl** nuclear power station in April 1986 highlighted the importance of environmental issues in relation to the nationality question. It had been Moscow who had decided to site 40 per cent of the USSR's nuclear power capacity in the Ukraine, but it was the Ukrainians and Belorussians who suffered the consequences. For three years information was withheld about the radiation level. Not only was land rendered unusable, but deformities became widespread among animals and children.

Over the next few years environmental question attracted increasing concern in other republics, and Moscow was blamed.The pollution of the Baltic Sea evoked protests from the adjacent nations. Armenians protested about the construction of a potentially dangerous chemical plant. Kazakhs complained about the effects of nuclear weapons testing at Semipalatinsk. Central Asia were outraged at the drying up to the Aral Sea, caused by the diversion of water to irrigate the cotton fields. This resulted from Moscow's insistence in promoting a monoculture of cotton in Central Asia; moreover, the use of chemicals and pesticides in the production of the crop was affecting the quality of the air and the water, and was raising infant mortality to Third World levels.

A major conflict arose over a project to reverse part of the flow of two Siberian rivers, the Ob and the Yenisei, so as to provide irrigation to Central Asia and replenish the Aral Sea. Environmentalists and many Russians feared the consequences for the Russian North of a lowering of the water table, and even for the possible effect on the temperature level of the Arctic Ocean. Central Asians, with the support on this issue of certain Moscow ministries and technocrats predicted dire consequences if they did not get water for their expanding population. Although the Politburo decided in August 1986 to suspend the project, before long *glasnost'* allowed the Central Asians to renew their case.

From the beginning of 1987, *glasnost'* brought the release of most political prisoners, including nationalists, and it allowed greater tolerance of political activity. The latter developed gradually. It meant, first of all, permission to organize "informal associations" for cultural and political purposes; the tolerance of *samizdat* publications, which were previously considered illegal; and permission to hold demonstration.

Jewish groups demanding the right to emigrate were allowed to hold a series of demonstration in Moscow during 1987. Their example was followed by the Crimean Tatars, 500 of whom assembled in Red Square in July 1987 and were rewarded with an audience with President Andrei **Gromyko**. They were promised to be allowed to return gradually to the Crimea. The central authorities were clearly concerned about possible clashes between them and the present inhabitants of the Crimea if they were to be allowed to return *en masse*. In August, on the 48th anniversary of the Molotov-Ribbentrop Pact, thousands of demonstrators protested in the Baltic capitals, Riga, Tallinn and Vilnius.

The process of democratization in the party and the soviets led to the breakdown of " democratic centralism" in its traditional form within the party. Parallel with the loss of control at the centre came a series of breakdowns in law and order involving ethnic violence. The conflicts which occurred over 1988–89 could be divided into five categories as follows:

(i) Clashes between groups of different nationalities, without the (at least overt) involvement of the authorities (e.g. Novy Uzen, see below).

(ii) Disputes between union republican authorities and subordinate ethnically-based administrative units (e.g. Georgia–Abkhazia).

(iii) Conflicts between union republics (e.g. Azerbaidzhan–Armenia).

(iv) Disputes between the all-union authorities in Moscow and union republics (e.g. Estonia).

(v) Protests by nationalities seeking the return of their own territories (Crimean Tatars, Volga Germans).

Types (ii) and (iii) might appear to be less dangerous than type (iv) for the centre, but in the longer run this was an illusion. If Moscow backed one side, or failed to back either, then it was likely to alienate the nationality or nationalities which perceived that they had been let down.

The autonomous *oblast'* of Nagorno-Karabakh hit the world's headlines in February 1988, when its soviet voted to ask the Soviet government to allow the territory to leave the jurisdiction of Azerbaidzhan and join that of Armenia. Three-quarters of the population was Armenian, but in 1923 Moscow (with a view to its relations with Turkey) had separated the region from Armenia and placed it in Azerbaidzhan. The Azerbaidzhani authorities had neglected the social and cultural development of the enclave and hindered links with Armenia. In 1987, 75,000 people (nearly half the total population) petitioned the Central Committee in Moscow for a transfer to Armenia, but were refused. Following the decision of the regional soviet, the party and government leaders of Azerbaidzhan expressed opposition to the transfer, while the Armenian leaders gave support. The Gorbachev leadership indicated that it would not allow the borders to be changed without the agreement of both republics.

At the end of February, Azeri anger at the Armenians boiled up in the massacre of Armenians in the Azerbaidzhani city of Sumgait, near Baku. While the official death toll was 32 (26 Armenians and six Azeris), Armenians believed that many more of their own nationality had been killed in this pogrom. With memories of the 1915 Turkish genocide of the Armenians firmly rooted in the Armenian political culture, the Armenians looked to the Russians for protection. Religion played a role here since the Azeris are Muslims and the Armenians Christians. The result was a series of general strikes in Armenia, with demonstrations of up to one million people in the capital Erevan. Similar demonstrations occurred in Baku, where portraits of Ayatollah Khomeini appeared. Leading activists on both sides were arrested; the Armenian unofficial nationalist leader Paruir Airkyan was deported to Ethiopia.

Tension ran so high through the rest of 1988 that martial law was introduced in some districts. By December 148,000 Armenian refugees had fled from Azerbaidzhan to Armenia and 161,000 Azeris went in the opposite direction. The earthquake which devastated Leninakan and much of

Armenia in December 1988 did nothing to cool the developing nationalist passions, which were fostered by the television in both republics. Academician Andrei **Sakharov** headed a group of experts which visited the local leaders in December 1988, reportedly at the request of the CPSU Central Committee. At the same time the whole of the unofficial Karabakh Committee, the principal Armenian nationalist body, was arrested. In January 1989 Moscow established a form of "direct rule" in Nagorno-Karabakh. This was perceived as the first step towards giving the territory to Armenia. A Special Adminstration was established, headed by a Russian, Arkady Volsky, reponsible to Moscow.

The Armenian–Azerbaidzhani conflict provided a worrying backdrop to the 19th All-Union Party Conference, held in June/July 1988. The Conference passed a special resolution on inter-ethnic relations, promising more independence for the republics and a Central Committee plenum on the issue. Within the Department of Legal and State Affairs of the Central Committee, created after the conference, a sub-department on nationality issues was established.

Pressure for autonomy was greatest from the Baltic republics, and the Gorbachev leadership was sympathetic to granting them economic autonomy as part of the *perestroika* process. On the initiative of the Unions of Writers and other cultural organizations, Popular Fronts were established in all three republics with the official aim of assisting *perestroika*. In practice, these organizations wished to achieve the maximum possible degree of independence for the republics. Under conditions of *glasnost'* they attracted support from the media, and within the republican Communist Party organizations. In autumn 1988 the Party leaders of all three republics were replaced by men more sympathetic to the Popular Fronts. Each government passed legislation making the local language the official language of the republic, and reinstating the flag and anthem of the period of independence between the world wars. Vilnius Cathedral was restored to the Roman Catholic Church, and its first service was broadcast by Lithuanian television.

In November/December 1988, the USSR Supreme Soviet was due to pass amendments to the Soviet Constitution to allow the democratic reforms promised at the 19th Party Conference to be enacted. In the republics, there was concern that the provision allowing them the right to secede was being watered down. Demonstrations took place in the Baltic republic and Georgia, urging the rejection of the amendments. The Politburo sent three senior Central Committee Secretaries to the Baltic to urge moderation. The Estonian Supreme Soviet asserted its sovereignty, and resolved that if an All-Union law conflicted with an Estonian law, the latter would prevail.The Presidium of the USSR Supreme Soviet declared the resolution invalid, but sought to avoid a confrontation. It altered the proposed amendments, to meet the concerns of the republics.

These debates were affected by the approach of the elections for the new Congress of People's Deputies of the USSR, due in March 1989. The Popular Fronts in the Baltic republics were allowed to contest the elections. In other parts of the Soviet Union, but not in Central Asia or parts of the Ukraine, certain informal associations were also allowed to participate. The Lithuanian popular front, known as *Sajudis*, and the Estonian Popular Front won most of the seats in their republics, and the Latvian Popular Front also did well.

Before the Congress opened, however, events in Georgia provided an ominous warning of what might lie ahead. Conflict developed between the Abkhazian Autonomous Soviet Socialist Republic (ASSR) and the Georgian government over discrimination on the basis of nationality in admission to institutions of higher education. The Abkhazians, a Muslim people, began to demand that their republic be transferred to the RSFSR or given the status of a Union Republic. In Tbilisi, the Georgian capital, Georgians demonstrated outside the Government House against any change in the territory of their republic. Various Georgian nationalist informal groups such as the National Democratic Party and the Society of St Illiya the Just took part in the demonstrations and added demands on raising the status of the Georgian language and culture. On April 8, 1989 half a million people were on the streets; the Soviet flag was lowered and the Georgian flag raised. On the night of the following day, troops of the USSR Ministry of Internal Affairs broke up the demonstration with extreme brutality, using excessive concentrations of CS gas and other poisons, pursuing demonstrators with shovels and beating them to death. Foreign Minister Eduard **Shevardnadze**, the former First Secretary of the Central Committee of the Communist Party of Georgia, flew to Tbilisi and described the dispersal of the demonstration as "a shot fired at *perestroika*". The leadership of the Georgian Party and government was replaced. The incident demonstrated that despite the steps towards democracy, the old apparatus of repression was still intact and available to be used if there were threats to the security of the state.

At the Congress of People's Deputies, which met in May/June 1989, and at the sessions of the new Supreme Soviet which followed it, nationality questions played a prominent role. For the first time, deputies in a Soviet parliament questioned the legitimacy of the incorporation of their republics—the Baltic States and Georgia—in the USSR. Russian nationalist feelings were also expressed. Many Russians feel that the non-Russians live better than they do, and believe that the sacrifices made by the Russians to help the republics are not appreciated. Some Russian nationalists, such as the writer ,Valentin Rasputin, joined non-Russian nationalists in demanding that the USSR be made into a true federation. The RSFSR lacked a number of bodies which the other republics had: certain industrial ministries, an Academy of Sciences and above all a unified party organization. As a result, all-union bodies performed the functions intead of exclusively Russian ones. If the RSFSR had its own institutions, the all-union bodies could be pared down or disbanded, and all the republican bodies would have more independence. Other speakers advocated the use of market relations between republics to promote the integration of the Soviet Union on a voluntary basis, instead of the discredited central planning system. Representatives of the republics also made appeals to Lenin's views on national self-determination.

The summer of 1989 saw a series of violent ethnic clashes. In June around 100 people were killed when Uzbeks attacked Meskhetian Turks, who had been living in the Ferghana valley in **Uzbekistan** since Stalin deported them from Georgia. The rioters were equipped with firearms, including automatic weapons, and appeared to be well organized. It took over a week for Ministry of Internal Affairs troops to restore order. Moscow blamed "enemies of *perestroika*" for organizing the unrest. Sixteen thousand Meskhetian Turks had to be evacuated from Uzbekistan. In the same month, there was rioting in Novy Uzen, in Kazakhstan, between Kazakhs and member of Caucasian nationalities, including Chechens and Lezgins. Elsewhere in the republic armed Kazakh nationalists held meetings and attacked a police station. At the end of June clashes between Azeri settlers and Georgians in three districts of Georgia led to at least one death. In July clashes broke out in Abkhazia between armed detachments of Abkhazians and Georgians At least 32 people died, and armed groups attacked the offices of the Ministry of Internal Affairs in order to obtain more weapons. The same month there were armed clashes on the border of Tadzhikistan and **Kirghizia** over the use of the Matchoi canal. Tadzhik discontent over the inclusion of Bukhara in Uzbekistan continued.

The Armenia–Azerbaidzhan conflict escalated to the level of an undeclared civil war, with Azerbaidzhan blockading not only Nagorno-Karabakh but also Armenia itself. In retaliation, Armenians attempted to blockade the Nakhichevan ASSR, a part of Azerbaidzhan separated from the main territory of the republic by Armenia. In August the Popular Front of Azerbaidzhan organized meetings of half a million people in Baku, demanding the retention of Nagorno-Karabakh as well as democratic reform in Azerbaidzhan.

The absence of violence in other republics did not indicate a calm situation. In August, 1989 the Baltic Council, comprising the leaderships of the three Baltic Popular Fronts, organized a human chain through the three republics to mark the 50th anniversary of the Molotov-Ribbentrop Pact. Over a millon people took part. The Politburo in Moscow condemned the rise of nationalism and separatism in the Baltic and accused the local party leaders of succumbing to extremism. Not surprisingly, some of the Russian-speaking settler population in the Baltic republics became concerned as the governments took measures to strengthen the rights of the native cultures. "Internationalist" fronts were established— *Interdvizhenie* (Internationalist Movement) in Estonia, *Interfront* in Latvia and *Edinstvo* (Unity) in Lithuania—by executives and workers among the immigrants, in opposition to the Popular Fronts. *Interdvizhenie* organized strikes in Estonia in the late summer against a new electoral law which discriminated against immigrants. These did not gain widespread support, out the law was modified. In September, the Union of Writers of the RSFSR, led by conservative Russian nationalists, organized a "march of solidarity" with the "internationalist" fronts, from Moscow to the Baltic republics.

In **Moldavia**, the local Popular Front succeeded in winning support for a change in the law, to make Moldavian the state language of the republic. The Russian-speakers protested and many went on strike. A compromise was reached in the wording of the law allowing Russian to be the language of communication between nationalities in Moldavia. The ethnic situation in Moldavia is unique in the Soviet context in that Moldavins are ethnically Romanian, and the Moldavian language is practically the same as Romanian. Stalin had imposed the Cyrillic alphabet in order to turn the Moldavians away from Romania. The Popular Front campaigned for the restoration of the Latin alphabet, and this was achieved at the same time as Moldavian became the state language. There was as yet no demand for Moldavia to be allowed to unite with Romania, given the unattractiveness of the **Ceauşescu** regime.

It was not only the Russian speakers in

Moldavia who were concerned about the language law, but also the Gagauz, a small Muslim group living in Moldavia and speaking a Turkic language. Throughout the Soviet Union, there are cases where the nationalism of the dominant group in the Union Republic has to face not only the centre in Moscow but also minorities within the republic. For example, while the Moldavians were challenged by the Gagauz around Komrat and the Russians in Tiraspol, the Lithuanians were confronted by the demand for Polish rights, especially around Vilnius, the Estonians by demands for autonomy from Russian in the northeast, and the Georgians by the Abkhazians and South Ossetians. Since the small nationalities normally know Russian (as well as their native language) rather than the language of the Union Republic where they live, they tend to appeal the centre support againgst the Union Republic. Conversely the nationality dominant in the union republic tends to see the smaller nationalities as agents of Moscow.

Of all the Soviet nationalities, the Ukrainians and Belorussians have traditionally been the closest to the Russians in cultural terms. Russian, Ukrainian and Belorussian are all East Slavonic languages; the majority of the Ukrainians and Belorussians have traditionally been Orthodox, like the Russians; and the three nations all see themselves as descending from the Kievan Rus' state of the ninth to twelfth centuries. Because of this closeness, Belorussians and Ukrainians have been more susceptible than other major Soviet nations to replacing the use of their native tongue with Russian (without necessarily losing their national consciousness). Concern about the future of the native languages was one of the main factors in the formation of the Popular Fronts in Belorussia and the Ukraine in 1989, but their failure to achieve support on the scale of the Baltic Popular Fronts can be attributed to the lack of support for separatism among most of the population. Additionally the republican party organizations showed much hostility to the formation of the Popular Fronts. The Popular Movement for the Restructuring of the Ukraine, known as *Rukh*, could hold its organizing conference only in September 1989 when the Brezhnevite First Secretary of that republic, Volodymyr Shcherbytsky, was within weeks of being ousted from power.

The nationality question in the Ukraine is complicated by the different traditions of the West and the East. In the West, informal associations were able to organize demonstrations of tens of thousands of people on a regular basis. This was the traditional centre of Ukrainian nationalism, where the population adhered to the **Ukrainian**

Catholic (Uniate) Church. Outside the Western provinces (around Lvov and Ternopol) the population is traditionally Orthodox and has been part of the Russian State since 1654. In the East of the republic the population is partly ethnically Russian and partly ethnically Ukrainian, but the latter are very often Russian-speaking. The founding conference of *Rukh* in September 1989 showed deep divisions among the participants, reflecting the geographically-based traditions. Nevertheless *Rukh* was able to unite on questions of democratization, economic autonomy and religious freedom.

In September 1989 the long-awaited Central committee plenum on nationality policy took place. It failed to resolve any of the major problems that had arisen, but despite the ambiguous slogan "strong republics and a strong centre" it signalled that decentralization of power from Moscow to the republics would continue. The leadership promised economic autonomy for the republics (on the basis of *khozraschet*, or profit-and-loss accounting). As a first step, a substantial degree of autonomy was given to the Baltic republics, to take effect from the beginning of 1990. Russian conservatives resisted these moves, seeing them as steps towards political independence. Their fears seemed justified when the Estonian Supreme Soviet officially declared in November 1989 that its incorporation into the Soviet Union in 1940 had been illegal. Following this, the Georgian Supreme Soviet declares that the invasion of the republic in 1921 by the Bolsheviks had also been illegal. Georgia demanded the same degree of economic autonomy which had been given to the Baltic republics, and furthermore announced that it reserved the right to secede from the Soviet Union.

Also in November the USSR Supreme Soviet voted to end the "direct rule" in Nagorno-Karabakh and restore the region to Azerbaidzhani administration. This was after the Soviet of Nationalities, which through its Commission on Nationality Affairs was increasingly intervening in inter-ethnic conflict, had failed to negotiate a settlement between the Azerbaidzhani and Armenian governments, and after the Popular Front of Azerbaidzhan had organized a blockade of Armenia. The Soviet troops (who apparently were ordered to refrain from using armed force) were unable to restore order. The Supreme Soviet decision appeared to be a capitulation to the Azeris and perhaps to the other Soviet Muslim nations. The Armenians rejected the decision, and proceeded formally to annexe Nagorno-Karabakh and treat it as part of Armenia, and this infuriated the Azeris.

In 1988–89, the difficulty of holding the multinational Soviet state together under *perestroika* and *glasnost'* was cited by Gorbachev several times as a justification for maintaining a one-party system. Only the Communist Party, he said, could hold the USSR together. He resisted talk of extending the principle of federalism from the state to the CPSU. In practice, the nationality conflicts from 1988 showed how difficult it was for the central party bodies in Moscow to control the periphery. In December 1989 the Lithuanian Supreme Soviet removed from the Lithuanian Constitution the article concerning the "leading role" of the Communist Party, opening the way to a multi-party system. Latvia soon followed suit. Then in the same month the Communist Party of Lithuania voted to separate completely from the CPSU. This move evoked first hostility and then apparent reluctant acquiescence from Moscow, when it was explained that if the Lithuanian Communists did not leave the CPSU they would be severely defeated in the republican elections. Meanwhile the Second Congress of People's Deputies of the USSR in December 1989 voted to declare the Molotov-Ribbentrop Pact illegal. The threat of rising secessionist feeling in Lithuania brought Gorbachev himself to the republic in January 1990, but even his charisma failed to dispel the nationalist mood.

The 1989 census showed the proportion of Russians in the USSR to be down to 50.8 per cent while the share of the Muslims continued to grow. With over one sixth of the population, the Muslim peoples in 1989 had no representative in the Politburo. The Tatars, traditionally the most advanced of the Muslim nations, demanded that their Autonomous Republic, currently within the RSFSR, be given the status of a union republic. The Moscow leadership set itself against any changes in the borders of republics, but announced a concession to the non-Russian peoples living in the RSFSR: the Supreme Soviet of the republic would become bicameral, like that of the USSR, with a Soviet of Nationalities to give greater representation to the minorities. In general nationalist feeling does not yet seem to be as politically significant in Central Asia as in the Baltic or Transcaucasian republics, where there is a recent memory of independence, or Moldavia where there is a memory of being part of Romania. The national cultures in Central Asia are of more recent origin, while **Islam** remains a traditional unifying factor, separating the indigenous peoples from the European immigrants.

In response to the nationalism of the non-Russians, Russian nationalism seemed to be becoming more important during 1989. A backlash was occurring among Russians living both in the non-Russian republics and in the RSFSR, and this backlash seemed to be linked with conservative forces in the party and the armed forces. A concession to this pressure was the establishment of a Bureau for the RSFSR in the CPSU Central Committee. This was composed of regional party first secretaries and was headed by Gorbachev. It fell short of a fully-fledged party organization for Russia.

The Russian chauvinist and anti-Semitic group (or groups) *Pamyat'* (Memory) caused considerable alarm among Russian Jews and others. Leading figures in the RSFSR Writers' Union showed sympathy for this Russian chauvinism, and took an active part in establishing a network of cultural and political Russian nationalist organizations. These came together in the "Unified Council of Russia". Their desire to preserve the Russian Empire in whatever form joined with the fears of conservative Communist politicians at the possible consequences of *glasnost'* for the future of the USSR and the CPSU. Thus Russian nationalists and *apparatchiki* united behind a conservative programme for the RSFSR republican elections of March 1990.

The moves towards democracy in Eastern Europe in 1989 threatened to encourage still further the determination of the non-Russians to achieve more independence. The fall of the Ceauşescu regime gave a major boost to demands in Moldavia for reunion with Romania. Gorbachev's Politburo made clear its firm opposition to the secession of any republics from the USSR. The question remained, however, whether if a republic did try to leave the Soviet family the leadership would resort to force. Politburo members several times ruled out the use of force in such circumstances.

In January 1990, however, after a series of anti-Armenian pogroms in Azerbaidzhan and the apparent collapse of Communist Party rule in the republic, Soviet troops were sent in to restore order. Leaders of the Popular Front of Azerbaidzhan claimed that the reason for sending in the troops was to prevent the Popular Front's rise to power. The Baltic Popular Fronts had avoided the use of violence and sought to achieve compromises with Moscow, by working where possible with the local Communist Party organizations. Nevertheless, secessionist pressures were expected to increase in the Baltic, Transcaucasia and Moldavia after the republic elections in March 1990, and Lithuania, on March 11, the overwhelming success of *Sajudis* at the polls led to the formation of a nationalist administration and a declaration asserting the republic's wholly independent status. The resolution was declared invalid by the Soviet authorities; the Estonians, at the end of March, nonetheless resolved to proceed more gradually towards the same objective.

PJSD

NÉMETH, MIKLÓS. Hungarian Prime Minister from November 1988 to April 1990. Németh (born in 1948) comes from a peasant family, and joined the **Hungarian Socialist Workers' Party (HSWP)** in 1968. He studied economics at the Karl Marx University in Budapest, where he later taught. He held a scholarship for one year at Harvard University, where he studied economics. On his return to Hungary in 1977, he joined the National Planning Office as a deputy department head. In 1981 he moved into a party post in the Central Committee's Economic Policy Department. He was promoted to deputy head of this department in 1984, and later, in January 1987, became its head. In June of the same year he reached the top economic position of Central Committee Secretary responsible for economic affairs, and in May 1988, at the special party conference which removed **Kádár** and most of his closest associates from the leadership, Németh was elevated to the HSWP Politburo. Despite, or perhaps beacuse of, the meteoric progress of his career, Németh enjoyed little personal authority at this time, and was widely regarded as a protege of Károly **Grósz**, the new party leader whom he succeeded as Prime Minister in November 1988. But Németh rapidly moved to establish his independence from the party leader, who by the end of 1988 was losing support.

In March 1989, when he reorganized his government and reshuffled its personnel, he announced to the National Assembly that his proposals had not been cleared by the Politburo before being presented to the National Assembly. This signalled a major step in the dismantling of the *nomenklatura* system of party control over appointments. Nemeth's reputation as one of the leading reformists in the party thereafter grew rapidly. In October 1989, after the foundation of the Hungarian Socialist Party (HSP), Németh was drawn into its leadership. However, he resigned from his HSP position (while remaining a party member) in December 1989 after a particularly bruising and ultimately unsuccessful battle to win the support of the HSP's parliamentary faction of his IMF-backed austerity programme. He declared that he no longer felt it possible to combine leading posts in both the ruling party and the government. He has proved a courageous and effective Prime Minister in an extremely difficult period in Hungary's economic development. Opinion polls in late 1989 indicated that he had

eclipsed Imre **Pozsgay** as the most popular politician with the Hungarian public

JB

NEUES DEUTSCHLAND (ND—NEW GERMANY). This was the official party newspaper of the **Socialist Unity Party of Germany (SED)** from its foundation in 1946. It had a daily circulation of over a million in 1982. From 1978 to 1985 it was edited by Günter **Schabowski**, later the political associate of Egon **Krenz**. In the aftermath of the revolution of 1989, Schabowski complained that Erich **Honecker** had demanded to inspect each issue of *ND* before it appeared.

The revolution of 1989–90 meant the removal of current editor, Herbert Naumann, and his replacement by Wolfgang Spickermann and a new editorial team. It also meant *ND*'s redesignation in December 1989 first as "organ of the SED" (previously "Organ of the Central Committee of the SED") and then simply as "Socialist Daily Paper". *ND* retained its attachment to the **PDS** but its content was transformed from dogmatic propaganda into critical comment on current affairs.

JO

NEW FORUM (GDR—NF, Neues Forum). Founded in the autumn of 1989, New Forum came to be the first major opposition group to make an impact in the GDR. It was not conceived as a political party, but literally as a "forum" for open discussion. It began with an emphasis on socialist and humanitarian values and environmental concerns. It also concerned itself with the necessity for far-reaching economic reform in the GDR: in late November 1989 it held an international economics conference in East Berlin, where matters of currency reform, price subsidies, social ownership, and foreign trade were discussed fully. NF operated at this stage within the context of a GDR still independent in the future.

By January 1990 NF had reached a membership estimated at 150,000 and was publishing its own weekly newspaper, *Die Andere* ("The Other One"), but it was already falling behind in the political contest. A loose amalgamation, led informally by Professor Jens Reich of the Academy of Sciences, it found itself competing electorally with new parties linked explicitly with West German counterparts, and falling foul of internal disputes. The issue of German unity and the free market economy forced several of NF's leading figures to renounce the group's new policy. In the elections of March 1990 NF collaborated with other non-mainstream groups in the

Bündnis 90 (Alliance 90), but they only reached 2.9 per cent of the vote and 12 seats.

JO

NOMENKLATURA. *"Nomenklatura"* has often been used as a somewhat mysterious and even threatening term for the central governing groups in the USSR and Eastern Europe and the source of their power. The lack of clarity surrounding the phenomenon was encouraged by the fact that, while lying at the basis of Communist power and its exercise by ruling parties, public references to it were very rare and much secrecy surrounded its operation. The title, and even origins, of the modern practice derive from Roman schemes of social ranking and mediaeval records of properties and their tenants. In essence, *nomenklatura* consists of two sets of lists: one of all the important posts in the party and state bureaucracies and leading social organizations, and a second of all those regarded by the authorities as suitably qualified to fill them. The key decisions on who fills which posts have been reserved for the relevant Communist Party committees (the more important positions for the top party organs and those less critical for committees and secretaries further down the hierarchy) and this function was a major source of Communist Party power.

As Communist aspirations to control political, economic and social life have been virtually boundless, and as for much of the time hardly any organizations were allowed to operate autonomously, this aspect of Communist power was extremely wide-ranging and a central mechanism for the maintenance of control over the entire system. The process also operated internationally for much of the post-war period and Soviet control was exercised over major appointments within most areas of Eastern Europe, which served to reinforce Soviet influence over the region. As developed in the Soviet Union after the 1917 Revolution, the comprehensiveness of the system and the location of decision-making powers within the party organization made it an important aspect of the novel qualities of Communist Party rule and a practical expresion of the unprecedented attempt to establish a monolithic Communist authority. It also embraced elective positions, which accorded with **Lenin**'s idea of the party as a band of professional revolutionaries subject to a quasi-military (and thus centralized) form of discipline, but reduced the role of rank-and-file party members and their representatives who were supposed, even according to official party statutes, to elect party leaders and committee secretaries throughout the organization.

"Elections" were thereby reduced to a show of hands expressing the acceptance of decisions made on high and it was perhaps this blatant neglect of even inner-party democracy, combined with the growing secrecy surrounding all decision making as **Stalin** consolidated his personal rule, that led to the maintenance of a strict public silence about *nomenklatura* and the processes associated with it. Apart from the administrative resources that had to be assembled to operate a complex bureaucratic process in post-revolutionary Soviet Russia it was historically necessary, first, to subordinate government, economic and social organizations not just to the political leadership of the party but also to the administrative authority of its apparatus while, secondly, the party membership had also to be subjected to the power of the apparatus in order to eliminate any lingering attachment to effective democratic processes. All this took time and some of the conditions for its establishment grew slowly out of the post-revolutionary Russian situation. The essentials of the system were nevertheless confirmed in a resolution of June 1923 once Stalin had fully consolidated his control over the machine of the **Communist Party of the Soviet Union (CPSU)**. Before the end of the year key posts in a hundred or so central agencies had been scrutinized and over 5,500 officials had been entered into the *nomenklatura* of the CPSU Central Committee.

Over the years the system became greatly extended and, after World War II, was carried into Eastern Europe, where Soviet control over the occupation of many key positions plugged national networks into the central keyboard of Soviet power. As the Communist systems stabilized and evolved, the comprehensiveness of party rule and the extensive reach of *nomenklatura* processes meant that those on its lists were not just encompassed by a bureaucratic procedure but took on the character of a social category. By the 1970s, for example, it was possible to suggest that the *nomenklatura* of the CPSU Central Committee represented a reasonable definition of the Soviet ruling stratum. A dominant class within Soviet society could be identified which was composed of some 750,000 major *nomenklatura* appointees and their immediate dependents. Equivalent groups could be identified in other countries and the degree to which they became attached to their privileged positions and material benefits was the target of increasing criticism. In Poland the *nomenklatura*, numbering some 130,000 at the end of the 1970s, significantly strengthened its position under Edward **Gierek**. The role of *nomenklatura* was well recognized during the 1980 strikes (though direct calls for its abolition were regarded as too provocative) and its operation within the party was a focus of inner-party conflict throughout 1981.

Control over the Communist *nomenklatura* has proved to be remarkably difficult to impose, even when top leaders have publicly expressed the inclination to do this. Gen. **Jaruzelski** had clearly intended to tighten up on party procedures during the **State of War** in Poland and eliminate from the *nomenklatura* appointments over which political control was strictly unnecessary, it was nevertheless announced in 1989 that the formal extent of the Polish *nomenklatura* actually doubled in the early 1980s. With the ending of the Communist Party monopoly in most East European countries the process of *nomenklatura* appointment lost both its significance and basis, although those appointed under it often continued to exercise influence if not power. With the drive to introduce free market practices and privatize state-run enterprises there were, moreover, fears that *nomenklatura* appointees might maintain their dominance by transforming control over state property into private ownership and the acquisition of rights over private property. Contacts, specialist knowledge and uncertainties about the valuation of state property all made it easier for *nomenklatura* stalwarts to perpetuate their power on a new basis. On the other hand, it could be argued that this process of accommodation has weakened conservative resistance to the prospect of reform and ultimately increases the chances of overall change.

PGL

NOVOTNÝ, ANTONÍN. First Secretary of the **Communist Party of Czechoslovakia** from September 1953 until January 1968 and President of that country from November 1957 until March 1968, Novotný's reputation as a Stalinist was not unjustified during his first decade in power. Political show trials for which he must bear the responsibility continued in Czechoslovakia for two years after **Stalin**'s death in 1953 and even **Khrushchev**'s denunciation of Stalin in 1956 evoked little response in Prague. Eventually, in 1963, Novotný conceded that Czechoslovakia had suffered from Stalin's "personality cult" and during his last four years in office went some way to accept the case for economic and political reforms. Nevertheless, his commitment to reformism was always a hesitant one and, by the autumn of 1967, his attempts to obstruct changes he had sanctioned, the continuing arbitrary exercise of his personal power particularly against members of the cultural intelligentsia, and his disparaging attitude towards the Slovaks helped to

create a broadly-based coalition within the party Central Committee which was prepared to press for his removal. Born in 1904, Novotný died in 1975.

GW

NYERS, REZSÖ. The leading Hungarian politician associated with the economic reform of 1968 (the "New Economic Mechanism"), and, since 1989, leader of the **Hungarian Socialist Workers' Party (HSWP)**/Hungarian Socialist Party. Nyers (born in 1923) worked as a printer until 1945, when he became a leading figure in the **Hungarian Social-Democratic Party (HSDP)**, and a strong supporter of the HSDP's merger with the Hungarian Communist Party in 1948. He then became a member of the Central Committee of the newly formed Hungarian Workers' Party. He was closely associated with the co-operative movement in the 1950s, serving as Deputy President, then President, of the National Association of Co-operatives. For a brief period from 1956–57 he was Minister of the Food Industry. Nyers' political career really took off after 1960, when he was appointed Minister of Finance. In this capacity, he began to promote the idea of economic reform, which had been taken up then quickly discarded by the **Kádár** regime in 1957 in the first precarious months of its existense. By the early 1960s, Kádár had once more become interested in economic reform as a means of consolidating Communist rule, and Nyers was promoted in 1962 to the key position of HSWP Central Committee Secretary for Economic Affairs. In 1966, he was elected to the HSWP Politburo.

From this powerful vantage point, Nyers was able to direct the programme of detailed drafting of the economic reform throught an extensive network of committees of economic experts, who were given a relatively free rein elaborating the basic proposal, which was approved by the HSWP Central Committee in 1966 and implemented on Jan. 1, 1968. Nyers' concept of reform was never narrowly technocratic: he was aware of the need for change in both politics and ideology if the economic reform were to succeed. But after the Czechoslovak crisis of 1968 political reform was ruled out, and a political backlash against the economic reform itself gathered momentum from the early 1970s. From November 1972, the HSWP Central Committee began to introduce modifications to the economic reform which undermined it, and Nyers came under attack. At the end of 1973, he was removed from his post as Central Committee Secretary, and in 1975 he lost his seat on the Politburo. From 1974, he was

Director of the Hungarian Academy of Sciences Institute of Economics.

In the early 1980s, as the Hungarian economy slid into crisis. Nyers once more emerged as an authoritative spokesman for reform in the HSWP Central Committee and in his published articles and interviews. He was re-elected to the HSWP Politburo in May 1988 at the special Party conference which removed Kádár from the position of General Secretary. Károly **Grósz**, the new party leader, took Nyers on as a personal advisor on economic reform, and in November 1988 he was brought back into the government as Minister of State. As Grósz's own position weakened, Nyers came forward as the most suitable alternative party leader, and in June 1989 he was made party President and brought into the new four-man party Presidium. In the following months he came to represent a centrist force, trying to unite the party, now bitterly divided between radical reformers such as **Pozsgay** and the more conservative Grósz.

Nyers enthusiastically supported the HSWP's transformation into a democratic, Western style Socialist Party, but was unable to persuade the more conservative factions of the advantages of this change, and at the same time he alienated some of the more radical reformist groups by his willingness to compromise in order to prevent the party from splitting. He was elected President of the new party, and appealed to former HSWP members to sign up. The response to his appeal among the 720,000 former HSWP members was not enthusiastic: only about 10,000 signed up as members of the HSP by the first deadline of Oct. 31. Nyers then launched an energetic recruitment campaign, aiming to win about 100,000 members by the end of 1989.

JB

O

OLD BELIEVERS. The Old Believers (*starovery*; known also as *raskol'niki,* or Schismatics) were expelled from the **Russian Orthodox Church** in 1666 for opposing the reforms in ritual, introduced by Patriarch Nikon, which they saw as betraying Russian traditions. Originally severely persecuted, they subsequently became well represented in the Moscow merchant class. In the Soviet period they were initially seen as possible allies for the Bolsheviks, but after 1929 suffered alongside other religions (*see* **Religion and Communism**). They have perhaps a million adherents, a few of whom were able for a time to preserve their customs by living in remote communities.

In 1971 the Local Council of the Russian Orthodox Church lifted the excommunication imposed under Nikon and since then at least some of the Old Believers have moved closer towards Orthodoxy. There is as yet no national organization; indeed the Old Believers have always been divided between those who see a need for priests and the "priestless". The head of those with priests is the Old Believer Metropolitan of Moscow and All Rus, the Most Reverend Olimpy.

PJSD

P

PARTY OF SLOVAK RENEWAL (Strana slovenskej obrody). Founded on March 8, 1948, the Party of Slovak Renewal was one of two Slovak non-Communist parties within the **National Front of the Czechoslovak Socialist Republic**. It has been allocated four out of 350 seats in the Federal Assembly since that body's creation in 1969 and seven out of 150 in the Slovak National Council. An extraordinary congress of the party on 10 Dec. 1989 decided it would revert to the original name of the Democratic Party (*Demokratická strana*), used before 1948 and under which it had won 62 per cent of the Slovak vote in the May 1946 elections. Its programme, the congress declared, would be based on European Christian cultural and moral traditions.

GW

PDS (GDR). This is the new name carried by the previous ruling party of the GDR since Feb. 4, 1990. (*See* **Socialist Unity Party of Germany—SED**)

JO

PERESTROIKA ("reconstruction" or "restructuring"). The term that has been adopted by Mikhail **Gorbachev** in his attempt to establish a new model of socialism in the USSR. In its official interpretation, *perestroika* is the "strategic course worked out by the CPSU at the XXVII Party Congress [of 1986] and the following plenums of the Central Committee, and at the 19th Party Conference [in 1988]"; it is a "deep renewal of all aspects of Soviet society which is revolutionary in its character", involving the acquisition by socialism of the "most up-to-date forms of organization" and the "fullest disclosure of its merits in all respects: economic, sociopolitical and ideological" (this quote comes from the *Short Political Dictionary* published in Moscow in 1989). In respect of the economy *perestroika* involves "radical reform", including a transition from extensive to intensive forms of growth based on cost accounting and self financing. In politics *perestroika* involves the fullest development of democracy and self-management, and "new thinking" in Soviet foreign relations. In the social spheres *perestroika* involves a reorientation of production towards social needs, and observance of the principle of social justice. And in the moral and ideological sphere, *perestroika* involves the elimination of anti-social phenomena and the development of humane and undogmatic thinking. *Perestroika* became the most generally employed slogan to refer to the programmatic objectives of **Gorbachev**'s reform programme; the term itself was not, however, original to the Soviet leader (it had frequently been used by **Stalin** among others), and although in its general conception it aroused little opposition it also provided little in the way of practical guidance to party and state officials and to members of the wider society.

SLW

PIŁSUDSKI, MARSHAL JÓZEF. Born in December 1867 in Vilno, which now forms part of Soviet Lithuania. Piłsudski was central to the process of the restoration of Poland's statehood in 1918 and played a pivotal role in developments within the Second Republic, mounting a coup d'état in 1926 and prevailing over a semi-military dictatorship until his death in 1936. While the post-war Communist authorities attempted to minimize his national political role and associate him with pre-war fascism, the association with Polish independence assured him an important place in the national consciousness and the growing political role of Gen. **Jaruzelski** in the early 1980s could not fail to reinforce the contemporary relevance of his example. His early political career, however, was firmly bound up with the development of the Polish socialist movement and, following exile in Siberia from 1887, in 1893 Piłsudski was elected to the first central committee of the Polish Socialist Party (PPS). From an early stage he was instrumental in supporting the national tendency within the socialist movement.

He was arrested in 1900 but escaped in 1901 and later attempted to enlist the support of Japan in the struggle against the Russian authorities. Some support was forthcoming from its embassy and this helped Piłsudski build up the combat organization of the PPS and develop its terrorist activities, which eventually led to his expulsion from the main body of the PPS. The early years of World War I also saw considerable disagreement and dissension between the different nationalist Polish groups. Piłsudski's military activities continued with the submission of his Polish legion to Austrian command. He resigned the military position in 1916 and became increasingly disillusioned about the prospects for Polish independence under the Central Powers, being interned by the Germans in July 1917. He was released on the outbreak of revolution in Germany in November 1918 and appointed provisional head of state.

Piłsudski's post-war vision included an extensive Polish-led federation to the east and in May 1920 he launched a campaign into the Ukraine which was reversed by the Bolsheviks and only held at the battle of Warsaw in August. Unsatisfied with the new constitutional arrangements, he refused to stand for the office of president following the elections of November 1922 and resigned as chief of staff in 1923. He staged a coup in May 1926 but showed little inclination to rule directly, exerting strong influence behind the scenes and dominating through a key group of former legionaries. Nevertheless, he did act as prime minister between 1926 and 1928 and again in 1930. A loose network of support was organized within a Non-Party Bloc for Co-operation with the Government (BBWR) which in 1927 achieved a parliamentary majority in association with the left. Parliamentary support soon dwindled and Piłsudski's rule became increasingly authoritarian.

PGL

PODKREPA (BULGARIA). An independent Bulgarian trade union, founded in Plovdiv in late February 1989, *Podkrepa* ("Support") was subject to official harrassment during the first few month of its existence, but emerged as a force to be reckoned with after the fall of party chief Todor **Zhivkov**. It has been one of the two or three most important elements in the **Union of Democratic Forces**, the opposition umbrella organization, and has been active in organizing political strikes in support of opposition demands. At the end of 1989 it claimed a membership of 100,000 — an impressive advance on the mere handful of members it had just two months before. Possibly its growth will be checked somewhat by the greater independence being shown by the official trade union movement in the new conditions. There are signs that the post-Zhivkov BCP leadership regards it as one of the more dangerous opposition groups; at any rate, a circular from party headquarters to local organizations cited it as a prime example of groups raising "irresponsible" demands that could lead to the destruction of socialism — in contrast to "constructively" critical groups like **Ecoglasnost**, with which the party could work. *Podkrepa*'s ideas, at least as articulated by its leadership,

would seem to include an attachment to pluralist democracy and to market economics. Prominent among *Podkrepa*'s leaders are its chairman Konstantin Trenchev, and Nikola Kolev, one of its founder members.

RW

POLAND. *Population*: 37,769,000. *Area*: 312,683 sq km. *Top five trading partners*: USSR, Federal Republic of Germany, Czechoslovakia, German Democratic Republic, UK. *Urban population as percentage of total*: 61.2 per cent. *Birth rate*: 15.5 per thousand. *Life expectancy*: males 66.8; females 75.2.

Political background. Poland lies in the centre of the European continent and about two-thirds of its territory forms part of the North European Plain. To the west its border with the GDR lies along the Oder and Neisse Rivers and to the south, with Czechoslovakia, along the Sudeten and Carpathian mountains. The River Bug marks the border with the Soviet Union. Poland's history in modern times has been dominated by relations with its more powerful neighbours, Germany and Russia, and by the problems of national survival. Following the steady weakening of its position throughout the eighteenth century, Poland's neighbours intervened to forestall restoration of the country's fortunes and its territory was divided in a sequence of partitions between Austria, Prussia and Russia. The last of these, in 1795, spelt the end of the Polish state and it was only the collapse of the Central European empires at the end of World War I that permitted the re-establishment of an independent Polish state. The unification of an ethnically diverse population and accommodation of the different political forces that had developed under foreign rule provided the rulers of the Second Republic with a range of formidable problems, and in May 1926 Marshal **Piłsudski** staged a military coup to reinforce central control and impose a political order backed by military power.

The authoritarian element inherent in Piłsudski's action came to the fore as the years progressed and the rights of oposition parties were increasingly curtailed; the repressive character of the regime intensifying following his death in 1935. The problems of post-war economic recovery were exacerbated by the onset of international recession in the early 1930s, while Poland's international environment became more threatening with the resurgence of German power and the rise of Nazi forces. As the western powers had little capacity or inclination to tackle the growing threat to peace and stability in Central and

Eastern Europe, Poland's position became increasingly insecure as her unpredictable neighbours grew in economic strength and military might. Britain's formal guarantee in March 1939 of Polish independence, in agreement with France, did not alter the direction of developments in the East and the path to a German invasion of Poland on Sept.1, 1939, was smoothed by the Nazi-Soviet Pact of Aug. 23.

Poland suffered appalling human and physical destruction throughout the war, the loss of six million of her pre-war inhabitants (including most of the Jewish population) representing the highest proportion of deaths in any one of the countries involved in the conflict. The first to take up arms against Nazi forces, Poles also distinguished themselves by the tenancity, extent and organization of their resistance to the occupants. But the course taken by the war, with the entry of the Soviet Union into the Western alliance, later followed by the USA, meant that Soviet interests and demands for compensation for her losses had also to be taken account of, both on a regional and international basis. In view of Russia's traditional interests in East-Central Europe and her acute desire to secure once and for all the western border, the growing Allied tendency to meet Soviet demands could not fail to displease the Polish government-in-exile or the great majority of the domestic forces of resistance.

As World War II drew to a close it became clear that virtually all Soviet claims on Polish territory and the nature of her post-war order would be met. Extensive areas of the pre-war Republic which contained significant numbers of Belorussians and Ukrainians (as well as Poles) were assimilated by the Soviet Union, and Poland was awarded areas of pre-war Germany by way of compensation. As a result of the deaths during the war, agreed border changes and major population shifts, post-war Poland became a society marked by a much higher degree of ethnic homogeneity. In 1945 only 2 per cent of the population were identified as being ethnically non-Polish. It was also agreed that a democratic government friendly to the Soviet Union would be established. The decisions that made up this accommodation were summarized in the Yalta agreement reached between the Great Powers in February 1945 and have been interpreted either as a sell-out or as a realistic reflection of existing power relations ever since. The implications of the agreement were rather more complicated than that and it is significant both that they included provision for the holding of free and unfettered elections and that such elections were never held. A referendum held in 1946 did not allow the real issues surface and the elections of 1947 were far from

being free and unfettered. The Communist majority was achieved by extensive intimidation and ballot-rigging.

Poland thus passed into the Soviet Russian zone of influence and became firmly subject to the authority of its eastern neighbour as **Stalin** was reaffirming his dictatorship there after a certain measure of wartime relaxation in terms of domestic politics. In Poland this led to the adoption of a policy of accelerated industrialization, some (though relatively tentative) measures of argricultural collectivization and the imposition of one-party rule (exercised by the **Polish United Worker's Party — PUWP**) minimally qualified by the continued existence of two "auxiliary" parties (the **United Peasant Party** and **Democratic Party**). Despite the rigours of dictatorship and repression, Stalinist dictatorship was somewhat less bloodthirsty in Poland than it was in most other East European countries. Show-trials and executions of Communist leaders and officials were generally avoided and discredited leader Władysaw **Gomułka** (ousted for right-wing nationalist deviation in 1948) was not executed and survived to be reinstated amidst considerable popular acclaim in 1956. The political relaxation that suddenly became possible that year was, however, short-lived, and Gomułka's regime did not fulfil its early promise.

An authoritarian atmosphere began to re-emerge in 1957, although this did not become fully evident until the 1960s. Some recovery from the rigours and disfunctions of the command economy was also evident in the mid-fifties, but the respite and economic recovery was short-lived and gave way to tendencies of worsening economic stagnation in the sixties. The rise in living standards for Poles during that decade was lower than in all other East European countries. Developments after the 1967 Arab-Israeli war brought things to a head politically. Quiet sympathies for Israeli victories within the armed forces provoked official censure and led to a dangerous combination of official attacks on "cosmopolitanism" and "revisionism" involving strong elements of anti-semitism with attempts from groups within the Communist Party to compromise key members of the ruling elite and seize power. This led to an intensification of the authoritarianism of the Gomułka regime and further resistance to any ideas of democratic reform.

Price rises introduced just before Christmas 1970 sparked off strikes and worker demonstrations in the northern coastal towns, the repression of which, due to confusion and misjudgement (or, some claim, to cynical manipulation), turned into a massacre of workers who were in fact intending to return to work. Amidst the political crisis these developments had provoked at national level Gomułka fell ill and was replaced as party leader by Edward **Gierek**, an experienced party leader with a reputation for effective economic administration. This, it turned out, was something of a myth (or perhaps provincial experience was just not applicable to a national economy) and the strategy taken to accelerate the development of the Polish economy led to disaster. Large loans were accepted from foreign institutions (who were at the time only too happy to take advantage of the opportunities offered by the Eastern financial market) but the large quantities of exportable goods that were expected to be produced to pay for them never materialized.

The influx of foreign capital was followed by a sharp rise in output indices and the income of the workforce. The growth impetus soon petered out as national indebtedness grew without the capacity for repayment and the demand for retail goods dramatically outstripped the means of supply. A further attempt to raise food prices in 1976 was abandoned after worker protest in the town of Radom and the Ursus plant outside Warsaw. Government repression prompted the organization of a **Committee for Workers' Defence (KOR)** which proved to be a critical element within the growing underground opposition movement but which, partly due to the influence of his major foreign commitments, Gierek did not extirpate with the rigour and severity that earlier Communist leaders had shown. Foreign indebtedness continued to rise and the economy had entered a phase of severe crisis by the end of the decade. A massive strike wave again hit Polish industry in the summer of 1980.

This time the unrest was only settled following an agreement between the authorities and the strike leaders (advised by a group of experts and activists associated with KOR) which involved recognition of the free trade union **Solidarity**. The August agreement was followed by a 116-month period of freedom never previously seen in Communist Eastern Europe, although this occurred against a background of continuing economic crisis, declining production and falling living standards. Strikes organized in pursuit of Solidarity's demands were often blamed for this, but the causes of Poland's economic weakness lay far deeper. While the party leadership of Stanisław **Kania** and the governments of Józef Pińkowski and Gen. **Jaruzelski** expressed commitment to political and economic reform, progress in both these areas was painfully slow and there were clearly many at all levels of the political establishment and administration who were opposed to any recognition of Solidarity's demands.

Forces within Solidarity, too, were showing greater impatience and a desire to exert more pressure on the authorities. Although there was a growing public awareness that some new arrangement or political approach was likely to be needed , the declaration by Gen. Jaruzelski (now party leader as well as Prime Minister and Minister for Defence) of a **State of War** to safeguard national security was a considerable shock, and most of Solidarity's leadership and activists were swiftly rounded up and placed in internment camps. Some deaths occurred as police forces moved in to break strikes (seven died at Wujek colliery); but generally the repression was swiftly applied and relatively bloodless. The activities of trade unions and most social organizations were suspended and those which had taken an anti-regime stance were dissolved. The party was also purged of reformist elements as a result of which, combined with numerous resignations, the ranks of the PUWP were considerably thinned. The conditions of martial law were used by the authorities to put through some major price rises but, while some stabilization was achieved, no coherent programme for economic recovery was put into operation.

The State of War was suspended and finally lifted in July 1983, and an increasingly conciliatory stance was adopted by the authorities towards Polish society — although the return of Solidarity in anything like its orginal form was repeatedly ruled out. While the economic decline was halted, recovery was half-hearted and no real dynamic for growth or further development was set in motion. A "second stage" of reform was formulated and presented in 1987, but again had little impact on the economy — unlike the further wave of strikes which broke out in 1988. These brought the authorities into negotiation with strike leaders and eventually led to the agreement that permitted the relegalization of Solidarity and the organization of semi-free elections in June 1989. In them the Communist party received a humiliatingly low level of support and finally had to accept a minority role in a Solidarity-led government (see below).

Recent political developments. The period since the declaration of a State of War on 13, December, 1981 showed that force did not, any more than the hesistant and ambigous conciliatoriness shown by the major leaders after the strikes of August 1980, offer a viable solution to Poland's long-standing political and economic problems. At the root of these lay the fact that Communist rule was imposed on an unwilling Poland at the close of World War II and that Poles, with greater persistence than other East

European nations, have rejected Communist authority and those who embodied it in the political leadership. This was reflected in the recurrence of strikes and manifestations of political unrest that on several occasions led to changes of leadership, in the preservation of elements of the traditional structure of private agriculture and the influential role occupied by the Catholic Church in national affairs.

Whatever the problems of political instability and economic dislocation that accompanied the open conduct of Solidarity's activities in 1980 and 1981, there was no doubt that the imposition of martial law was profoundly unpopular and that a political order established by these means and retaining its essential characteristics had little chance of gaining public acceptance. While underground Solidarity and opposition activities did not offer much of a direct political threat to the authorities and many sectors of society came to acquiesce in the political stalemate, the semi-military Jaruzelski leadership made little headway in creating a more viable political solution or in securing the kind of material progress that might facilitate a longer-term stability. The approach taken by the authorities was to recognize the realities of the situation and their basic unpopularity, and thus to play down Communist ideology and avoid the crudities of traditional propaganda, and to set up a range of new organizations which, while lacking the capacity for indepedent decision making once possessed by Solidarity, were rather more than the transmission belts for Communist policy implementation that characterized more orthodox Soviet-type systems.

In the attempt to gather support reaching beyond the Communist party, Committees for National Rebirth were set up under martial law and, in the autumn of 1982, formed into a nation wide Patriotic Movement (PRON). By 1986, over 150 social organizations had affiliated themselves to it and 1.2 million individual members had joined. Legislation to permit the creation of new trade unions was also passed in 1982 and groups began to be formed at local level, a national co-ordinating organization (**National Trade Union Accord — OPZZ**) following only in 1984. Their growth, particularly in comparison with the rise of Solidarity, was slow and the new unions had only 4.3 million members by the end of 1984. A range of other organizations was also established.

The idea of establishing a "socialist pluralism" gained official support and proposals of a "coalition method" of exercising power came into prominence. Opinions in favour of the coalition method were first expressed in 1985 and intially evoked the criticism that it spelt abandonment of the leading role of the party. This was denied and, following assurances that the approach did not mean tolerance of anti-socialist forces, the coalition method was established as acceptable and realistic by the time the X Congress of the PUWP assembled in July 1986. Not coincidentally, this development accompanied the consolidation of **Gorbachev**'s leadership in the Soviet Union. Further signs of cue-taking from the Soviet Union followed with the announcement of the "second stage" of economic reform and the calling of a referendum in November 1987, supposedly to strengthen processes of social consultation, test popular opinion and establish social support for the processes involved.

This did not prove to be a great success. The government failed to get more than half the electorate to vote in favour of the programme for economic recovery, and only slightly more voted positively (46 per cent of the electorate) on a second question proposing political democratization, self-government and increased participation. The electorate were clearly not impressed by the exercise and their scepticism was largely validated by the government's decision to press forward with the programme anyway, one immediate result of which was the announcement of wide-ranging price rises in February 1988, which included a rise of around 40 per cent in the price of basic foodstuffs. Following particularly poor economic results in 1987 and the outcome of the referendum these rises were not received well by the mass of the population or by the Solidarity spokemen, while the official trade unions claimed some success in securing financial compensation for the effect of the rises on household budgets.

These developments marked the beginning of a year of the greatest political and industrial conflict since the rigours of martial law and the months preceding it. A wave of strikes broke out in May 1988 and a further round in August, which were only brought to an end with the promise of negotiations between the authorities and Solidarity representatives. Strikers' demands for the relegalization of Solidarity were taken on board with the agreement to discuss trade union pluralism, although the possibility of negotiation with those who rejected the "constitutional order" of the socialist state was ruled out. Continuing disagreement about who was to participate in the negotiations and resistance within the PUWP to the prospects of such developments meant that the round-table talks (*see* **Round-table Agreement**) did not finally open until February 1989. An agreement was signed in April which contained a number of significant proposals, amongst them being the agreement to legalize Solidarity (which occurred later that month).

The agreement also referred to major political changes. These provided for the right of Solidarity and other independent groups to propose candidates for 35 per cent of the 460 seats in elections to the Polish parliament (the *Sejm*), the remainder being reserved for candidates of the PUWP, its two allied parties and several official Catholic organizations. A new senate was to be established with 100 members, all of whom were to be freely elected and who would have the right to review and refer legislation back to the *Sejm* for further consideration. A new executive presidency was also to be introduced, whose occupancy would be determined by the vote of the National Assembly (a joint meeting of *Sejm* and Senate). The president would have powers to veto legislation, which the *Sejm* could only override by a two-thirds majority, and to introduce on his own authority a three month state of emergency, which could only be extended with the agreement of both chambers.

Arrangements were swiftly made for elections to *Sejm* and Senate and a first round was held in June. Solidarity-proposed candidates won 160 of the 161 seats available to them in the *Sejm* and 92 of the 100 Senate seats. A devastatingly low level of support for the ruling coalition thus emerged, a particular embarassment being the failure of all but two on the uncontested national list of prominent candidates. Although not having to face electoral competition, candidates on the national list did have to gain 50 per cent of the votes cast and this the great majority failed to do, many voters taking the opportunity to cross off the list the names of prominent politicians. No constitutional provision existed to fill these vacant seats, and it was agreed that run-off elections would be held between pairs of different candidates, each proposed by the ruling coalition.

Run-off elections were also held for the other unfilled seats. Solidarity-sponsored candidates won all 161 (35 per cent) of the *Sejm* seats open to them and 99 of the seats in the Senate. Independent opinion also had some influence on the occupation of seats by members of the party coalition, as Solidarity expressed its preferences and endorsed some candidates and had some effect both on the turnout in some constituencies and the candidates elected. In consequence, 25 of the "official" candidates could also be expected to side with Solidarity on most issues. This was to have an impact on the working of the arrangement made at the round-table to give the ruling coalition a built-in majority and on other aspects of the agreement reached earlier in the year. Clearly recognizing this, Gen. Jaruzelski originally showed reluctance to stand for the new presidency and, having decided to do so, received only one vote more than the bare majority needed to win. Similar difficulties were encountered in forming a government under PUWP leadership and efforts made by Gen. **Kiszczak**, the preferred candidate who had been Minister of the Interior and security chief through the 1980s, eventually had to be abandoned.

A coalition government was finally formed by Tadeusz **Mazowiecki**, former editor of the Solidarity weekly, and presented to the *Sejm* for approval in September 1989. It was composed of 23 ministers, 12 of whom were nominated by the Solidarity side and four of whom represented the PUWP. Each of the four parties (Peasant and Democratic Parties, as well as the PUWP and Solidarity) was also given the post of Deputy Chairman of the Council of Ministers, or Deputy Prime Minister. In the face of a worsening economic crisis and a rapidly accelerating inflation rate, the first task of the new government was to work out a programme of national economic recovery and proposals to this effect were put before the parliament in October 1989.

Constitution. The Constitution of the Polish People's Republic was proclaimed during the period of full **Stalinism** on July 22, 1952. Like the other constitutions already adopted in Eastern Europe it followed the Soviet model and declared Poland to be a country engaged in the construction of socialism. Major criticism followed proposals for revision made in 1975, which included an affirmation of the socialist character of the Polish state, the assertion of the leading role of the PUWP and an allusion to Poland's unshakeable fraternal ties with the Soviet Union. The outcry over the amendments to the Constitution was one of the first signs of Poland's capacity for organized political opposition that was to become increasingly evident as Gierek's regime ran out of steam. The proposals were finally amended to take some account of this resistance.

Further changes were made in 1980s as the special provisions of the State of War were transposed into the normal workings of the Polish state. The demise of Communist rule in Poland in 1989 led to an early reconsideration of the Constitution and the foundations it provided for the operation of the party state. Shortly after Christmas 1989 the Polish state was formally renamed the Polish Republic, the reference to the PUWP as a leading force removed and its first article reformulated to read: "The Polish Republic is a legal democratic state implementing principles of social justice".

Administrative structure. Administration in Poland since the war, as in other Communist countries, Has been characterized by a high degree of centralization, close surveillance by the PUWP (Communist Party) and overlapping responsibility for a wide range of activities. The central organ of government is the Council of Ministers (see below), or cabinet, which is proposed by the Prime Minister for appoval by the *Sejm*. The cabinet appointed in September 1989 contained 23 members in addition to the Prime Minister. In Poland there have tended to be a large number of economic ministries to cope with the exigencies of a centralized command (optimistically termed "planned") economy. The ministers represent the tip of a large central bureaucracy, which employed 49,466 people in 1986. Administrative processes passed through hierarchies which spanned 49 provinces (*województwa*) at the first tier and 822 towns and 2,121 rural communes at the second.

This structure was established in 1975 to replace one with three levels, comprising 22 provinces or conurbations, 317 counties and several thousand local communes. The post-1975 structure encountered persistent criticism for extending the reach of the provincial bureaucracy and reducing public access to the administration, and proposals for further reform have been made regularly. Much administration is supposed to form part of the process of self-government exercised through People's Councils. Under the pre-1975 system the presidium of the People's Council elected for each administrative unit was formally both an organ of self-government and an agency of the central authorities, although the latter role was plainly dominant. In 1975 executive powers were passed to a centrally appointed governor (*wojewod*, at province level) and the powers of the council, as the organ of formal self-government, supposedly strengthened by placing the local PUWP first secretary as their chairman. This practice was phased out in 1980, though no real improvement in the level of self-government was achieved in the following period.

One obstacle to the extension of effective self-government was the absence of local access to and control over funds, which remained subject to central or regional control. But neither were the People's Councils capable of any significant degree of self-government, as even their elected members were subject to the influence of the local authorities and party officials exercised over the electoral process through an umbrella organization known as the National Unity Front and then, in the 1980s, the Patriotic Movement for National Rebirth. The centralization of resources and political power was thus a prime characteristic of the adminstrative process, while further coordination and central control was achieved by

further supervision exercised through the party organization and the activities of individual party members within administrative and governmental institutions.

Council of Ministers. The Polish government, or Council of Ministers, is composed of members proposed to the *Sejm* (or Parliament) by the prime minister and accepted by them in a vote following parliamentary investigation of their credentials. The government endorsed by the *Sejm* in September 1989 was distinguished by the fact that it was the first composed of members nominated by a non-Communist prime minister since World War II. Miecysław **Rakowski** (elected in September 1988) stood down as Prime Minister in July 1989 and was succeeded in August by Gen. Kiszczak. Following consultations, Kiszczak discovered that he was unable to nominate a government that would be accepted by majority in the *Sejm* and was also obliged to resign. Proposals were made to find a premier from amongst the leading members of the parties formally allied to the PUWP, but that did not prove to be feasible either. It was necessary for President Jaruzelski, then, to invite a candidate sponsored by the Solidarity group to form a government, and this was proposed to Tadeusz Mazowiecki on Aug. 19, 1989.

The election of Mazowiecki meant also the formation of a government that would not be dominated by the PUWP and its allies, and the nature and extent of PUWP representation was for some days the object of some dispute. When finally proposed, four posts in the government were reserved for the PUMP and four and three respectively for the party's traditional (and carefully controlled) allies, the United Peasant Party and the Democratic Party. As they had virtually demanded, leading PUWP figures in the form of Generals Kiszczak and Siwicki became ministers for internal affairs and national defence respectively and the PUWP was also given responsibility for transport. One member from each of the traditional parties also became a deputy prime minister. Solidarity-sponsored members retained an overall majority with 12 members of the government, not including the prime minister. Leszek **Balcerowicz**, the Solidarity-nominated minister of finance, also became a deputy prime minister.

Of the 23 ministers approved in September 1989 eight were members of the current *Sejm* and two were senators. Two of the four deputy prime ministers were *Sejm* deputies. Seven ministers had some sort of academic background and another three practised economics in other areas. The Council of Ministers included two lawyers as well as the two Communist generals. Three ministers had some managerial experience, one was a medical doctor and another a theatre director. The Rural Solidarity member given responsibility for the co-ordination of rural affairs, A. Balazs, ran his own farm. The composition of the government therefore reflected a strong emphasis on economic expertise, in accordance with the nature of the critical problems facing the country in that area.

Economic background. The formation of modern Poland as a sovereign state after World War I had faced her with daunting economic tasks. The economy was basically an agricultural one and 64 per cent earned their livelihood from farming in 1921. Although some areas which had been under German control (like Poznan) had seen satisfactory levels of development and formerly Russian Territories (around Warsaw and Lodz, for example) had been the most prominent centres of industrial progress within the Tsarist Empire, the political authorities of the new Republic did not have an integrated economy at their disposal. There was no single currency, transport networks made little sense within the new borders and producers were often separated from their traditional markets. The construction of an effective national economy thus encountered several obstacles, while rampant inflation was a further problem in the early 1920s. The country had yet to achieve pre-war levels of industrial production before the onset of international recession in 1929. In the early 1930s national income and industrial output fell dramatically (by 25 per cent and 39 per cent respectively) and unemployment rose accordingly, increasing poverty levels and exacerbating existing problems of development.

In 1936 expansionist economic policies were finally adopted and output began to show a significant rise, a process that was already occurring to some extent in the international economy as a whole. While some degree of national economic progress was certainly evident by 1939, significant weaknesses and areas of major backwardness were still prominent. Further problems were caused by the extensive destruction suffered during the war. Apart from human losses there was great devastation of property and extensive loss of productive capacity. But, while the changes in Polish borders agreed by the major wartime allies meant a significant diminution of the state's area, important gains were derived from the acquisition of formerly German territory. The new Silesian areas were rich in minerals and brought extensive reserves of coal, copper and sulphur, as well as natural gas, while the lands bordering the River Oder represented a major addition to Poland's agricultural capacity.

The conditions for post-war recovery were advantageous.

A Three-Year Plan of Economic Reconstruction was adopted at the beginning of 1947 and declared completed in November 1949. National income, investment and consumption had broadly trebled since 1946 and wages had risen by a third. This programme of national recovery, however, was succeeded by a Six-Year Plan which incorporated Soviet-style objectives and placed priority on investment levels and heavy industrial development. Further, the 1948 version was superseded by a 1950 variant produced under the influence of the Cold War and the climate of full-blown Stalinism which then prevailed in Eastern Europe. This placed even greater emphasis on heavy industrial production and the military sector and incorporated quite unrealistic expectations of increased output. Stalinist planning in Poland was as ill-suited to domestic needs and unproductive in terms of national economic development as it was in other countries of Eastern Europe. Inflation increased (consumer prices rose by 80 per cent between 1950 and 1953), real wages fell (by around 8 per cent) and living standards began to decline with the neglect of agriculture, consumer industries and the provision of services.

But the balance was by no means all negative and the policies adopted made a significant impact on rural underemployment, with the rate of off-farm employment rising by 34 per cent between 1950 and 1955. General improvements also followed with the introduction of the New Course following Stalin's death in 1953. Wages began to rise again in 1954 and an annual increase of 5.1 per cent was recorded for the 1956–60 period. But the relaxation of the Stalinist model, the tolerance of the dissolution of most of the collective farms that had been established, and the reduction of the emphasis laid on heavy industry and the armaments industry were not followed by the adoption of a full-scale reform programme or a major qualification of the principles underlying the Stalinist system. Central planning, party control and ministerial administration remained dominant and no alternative framework for economic development was implemented.

The strengthening of central political control following the conflicts of 1956 were an important element in this and reformist ideas were generally not looked on favourably. An additional problem was the fundamental incompatibility within the East European economic model between the goals of high growth levels (which had been achieved in the early 1950s) and those of rising standards of living (which the policy changes under the New Course had favoured). The achievement of both together appeared to be impossible. For various reasons the living standards of the mass of the population were increasingly hit by the policies followed by Gomuɬka as his administration continued into the 1960s. Between 1966 and 1970 real wages rose by only 1.9 per cent each year, while those of most East European neighbours achieved a rate well over 3 per cent.

This sluggishness had direct political consequences, and the workers' demonstrations and protests in 1970 were a direct response to price increases. The accession of Edward Gierek to the leadership was linked in other ways to the underlying economic situation. For over a decade he had been the top party official in the industrial and mining province of Katowice (Upper Silesia) where wages had been high and Gierek's reputation for being a good leader and an efficient manager correspondingly elevated. His replacement of Gomuɬka at the top of the party hierarchy owed much to this public record and much was now expected of him with respect to the economy as a whole. Initial results seemed to substantiate these hopes and a rapid acceleration of economic growth was achieved. In 1971 and 1972 production topped plan targets and even faster growth occurred the following year, when national income rose faster than at any time between 1950 and 1972. As food prices remained at the same level there was a striking increase in real wages of 11 per cent.

Signs of future problems, however, could be seen in some of the forces that underlay these developments. In 1972 imports were considerably higher than exports and this underwrote both the high rate of investment increase (35 per cent in industry and 39 per cent in construction) and the sharp rise in national income recorded. Gierek saw considerable benefits to be derived from accepting foreign loans to raise investment levels, renovate plant and rapidly increase capacity to produce exportable goods. Increasing amounts of Western machinery were imported (from roughly $100 million per annum in the late 1960s to $1,900 million in 1974) and the balance of payments deficit rose accordingly, from a minimal $60 million in 1970 to $2,050 million in 1975. By the end of 1975 Poland's total foreign debt had risen to $6,352 million and reached $12,000 million by the spring of 1977. The policy of opening the door to foreign credits to remake Polish industry to produce the exports to pay off the debt was not a success.

The disappearance of cheap energy supplies during the 1970s and the subsequent inflation and economic dislocation this caused within the international system did not provide a favourable con-

text for Gierek to pursue his economic initiative. But it was not really the international environment that undermined his strategy. The rise in energy prices was not disadvantageous to Poland, which had plentiful supplies of coal and had an overall positive energy balance. The rapid intake of foreign credits occurred in the early 1970s, before the international recession took hold, and Poland's economy was in a precarious state already by 1974. The fundamental problem was that the resources were not put to effective use and that there was, in fact, little control exercised over a highly centralized economy. To this extent the critical weaknesses lay in the political sphere.

The spurt of growth ran out of impetus at an early stage and the consumer boom was clearly over by the middle of the decade. Cash might have been plentiful, but the goods were not available and further extensive imports were not longer possible. Gierek's attempts to gain control over economic processes and counteract the growing imbalance were also unsuccessful. The proposed rises in food prices ran into direct worker opposition in 1976 and efforts made to restrain investment and the continuing growth of heavy industry made little headway against vested interests and strong ministerial lobbies. Bad weather was a further brake on agricultural development, too, and the process of economic growth ground to a halt, eventually leading to a 2.3 per cent decline in national income in 1978. Worker incomes actually fell the following year. More concerted efforts were made under a new prime minister in 1980 to halt the economic collapse and some signs of progress could be seen. The situation was not amenable, as much for political as economic reasons, to the kind of solution the Gierek regime was inclined to seek and the situation escalated out of control following the attempt in July 1980 to raise prices by the back door, which was followed by a sustained wave of strikes and the eventual formation of the Solidarity trade union.

The period of Solidarity's legal existence, until December 1981, did not see any improvement in the economic situation although (despite what the leadership claimed) this was due not so much to the actions of the opposition and the activity of the free trade union but almost exclusively to the crisis of the command economy and its dependence on foreign inputs, which were increasingly difficult to obtain under the conditions of Poland's growing indebtedness. Polish national income continued to decline through the first year of official calculations, was 24 per cent lower than the level of 1978. Some stabilization was achieved in 1983, but even the level of partial recovery seen that year in terms of national income was not replicated in the years that followed, with the economy's showing in 1987 being particularly meagre. By 1988 per capita national income was still some way off the level reached 10 years earlier, while 1989 saw clear signs of further intensification of the economic crisis with declining production and galloping inflation.

Current economic developments. Much of this process of restricted economic development within the Communist framework and looming collapse had taken place against a background of discussion of reform and partial implementation of reform proposals, none of which had significantly altered the basic operational principles of the system. It essentially remained a centralized one where processes of production and distribution were administered rather than being determined by the market. Having initially spoken of reform Gierek fought shy of rocking the boat and opted for a credit-funded strategy of economic growth; Solidarity had been involved in working out a programme of economic reconstruction and reform for much of 1981 but its implementation had yet to begin by the time the State of War was declared; Jaruzelski nevertheless claimed to be pursuing an amended policy of economic reform from the beginning of 1982 and launched a "second stage" in 1987. Reform had been much talked of but little implemented, one of the major consequences of this being that the mass of the population were quite disillusioned with party–state initiatives in this area and increasingly pessimistic about the possiblility of any real improvement within the framework of anything like the existing system.

The failure to apply any successful solution to Poland 's longstanding economic problems meant that several symptoms of profound crisis dominated the situation during the 1980s. Foreign debt was a major sign of weakness which became progressively worse as the decade progressed. The level of hard-currency debt reached $39,000 million in 1987 (a figure somewhat inflated that year by the high level of the dollar then prevailing), with most of the increase since 1981 arising from Poland's inability to make interest repayments although hard-currency exports had exceeded imports every year from 1982 to 1987. A further symptom linked with this development was the progressive decapitalization of Polish industry, partly because of the difficulty experienced in obtaining spare parts for the equipment imported from the West in the 1970s and partly because of the diversion of available funds to the consumer sector to avoid further decline in living standards. Many investment projects begun under

Gierek were later frozen and there had been a tendency to resurrect these when resources were available, even though this promised to perpetuate inappropriate and outdated patterns of development.

A third symptom of crisis was the growing deterioration of Poland's infrastructure and continuing underinvestment in a range of notionally "unproductive" sectors like transport, energy, water services, housing, health and education. Housing had long been a major sourse of public concern and despair and the future only promised a lower level of provision, while medical services began to show critical signs of disintegration with many essential drugs and equipment disappearing from hospitals. Transport problems and power-cuts manifested themselves as consumer shortages as well as signficantly adding to the problems of maintaining production levels and providing the conditions for economic development. The neglect of infrastructure and continuing operation of industrial production by outdated methods was intimately connected with the rapid deterioration of enviromental conditions, which had further implications for health and medical services.

Issues of pollution and environmental deterioratior moved swiftly from being the consequences of carelessness or unpleasant byproducts of industrial growth to the status of critical factors in the prospects for economic and human survival. By the late 1980s enviromental damage was calculated to cost 10 per cent of the national income each year. Problems that were becoming evident in the 1970s reached critical proportions in the 1980s, and were not helped by the increasing use of brown coal in Czechoslovakia and the GDR as well as Poland which made a particular contribution to the atmospheric presence of sulphur dioxide. Unusually for Europe, in 1989 Poland still obtained 80 per cent of its energy from coal, of which 82 per cent went for industrial use. Half the country's water was so polluted it was not suitable for any use, and only 1 per cent was fit to be drunk. The consequences for people's health have become obvious. The incidence of child leukaemia in one part of Katowice doubled between 1977 and 1989. The chemical and metal pollution of land around Cracow was such that one quarter of the food grown there was not considered to be fit for consumption, a major problem for a country where agricultural production otherwise presented itself as a good sector from which to launch a rapid growth in exports.

The economic crisis of the 1980s thus derived from several areas of serious weakness within the socio-economic and political system which fed into one another and made the identification of a national solution even more difficult. By 1989 there were signs that the persistent crisis was once more leading to collapse of the economic system as a whole. From May 1989 production in the state sector went into decline and in the first nine months of the year production was 1.6 per cent lower than in the same period of 1988; exports were down by 1.8 per cent and imports rose by 3 per cent; average pay over the nine-month period was 177 per cent up on the previous year with retail prices for goods and services up by 120 per cent. A shift in gear in the rate of increase in prices and wages took place from the beginning of August as the Rakowski government took measures to create a more balanced market and decided to set prices more in line with the strength of supply and demand pressures. Prices of consumer goods and services thus rose by 44 per cent during the month of August and those of food products by 78 per cent, while wages increased by 67 per cent.

The motives of the Rakowski government in unleashing this degree of inflation and the strategy that underlay the measures were open to some doubt, particularly as Rakowski had failed to gain election to the *Sejm* in the June elections and declared his intention to resign from the government. The price rises were attacked as ill-prepared and unsuited to the enhancement of marketization and the achievement of greater balance between supply and demand. While food prices were raised and increased subsidies passed on to the farmers, the cost of agricultural inputs had risen even more (if they were obtainable at all), and in association with a situation of effective bankruptcy, industrial decline and economic disintegration, the incoming Solidarity-led government was now faced with a steeply rising rate of inflation. The dire economic situation was, indeed, a major factor in inducing Solidarity representatives to consider forming the new government, as it was clear that the ruling coalition did not have the credibility amongst the public to impose the measures that might be needed to restore economic equilibrium, nor was it in much of a condition to inspire the confidence of the international community.

Poland's international position was to the fore of the attention of the new government. Existing debts were a millstone around the neck of any government and the injection of new capital was needed to provide the basis for any coherent programme of economic recovery. Poland had received much encouragement to take the Western path (not least with the negative inducement of sanctions imposed after the imposition of martial law), which it had proceeded to do with

the holding of semi-free elections and then the abandonment of one-party rule. The installation of a Solidarity-led government thus provided Poland with favourable condition under which to approach the Western powers and international agencies for relief from the debt burden (Poland has been a member of the IMF from 1986), aid to stem the process of economic collapse and the means to construct a base for effective recovery. One of the first acts of the leading economic appointees in the new government was to attend the annual conference of the IMF and World Bank in September 1989.

Western powers and the international community did not respond to the formation of a Solidarity-led government with immediate offers of aid or significant measures of debt-relief. While the response was undoubtedly positive, it was also guarded and circumspect in economic terms, at least in the early stages and particularly on the part of the USA. Polish leaders expressed disappointment about this and some surprise — although whether an immediate large-scale economic response was really expected following the outcome of East–West economic links in the 1970s may be doubted. It was made clear by the IMF, not unexpectedly, that any eventual agreement or aid package would be dependent on the nature of the economic programme finally agreed on by the Polish government. The first full statements by Finance Minister Balcerowicz in October 1989 emphasized a strong commitment to far-reaching change, the structural transformation of the economy along market lines and the abolition of monopolies. Measures would be taken to curb inflation (forecast to reach 900 per cent or more by the end of 1989) and impose strict limits on the level of government subsidies, one consequence of which could well be the rise of unemployment to the level of 20 per cent. The introductory phase of the programme was planned to be completed by early 1990. The letter of intent on the Polish economic reforms was finalized in Warsaw on Dec. 19, 1989 and Poland's agreement with the IMF was signed on Dec. 23.

Foreign relations. Poland has occupied a particular place in post-World War II Europe. It was the first and one of the most critical bones of contention between the wartime allies and a major factor in the emergence of the Cold War. For the Soviet Union it had particular historical and strategic signficance and was regarded as especially important for future security. As a bridge to East Germany, with its large military garrison of 400,000 Soviet troops (ten times the number of those stationed in Poland for most of the

Communist period), Poland played through its links with the Soviet Union a major part in maintaining the division of Europe and was by some measure the most populous member of the European socialist community. At the same time, it had strong ties with the West of Europe and with the United States, where the Polish community is an important ethnic and political component within American society. Its strong Catholic commitment has encouraged it to maintain the orientation to the West and traditional anti-Russian sentiments were not weakened by post-war developments.

This dual orientation notwithstanding, Poland has remained firmly integrated with the two key institutions of the socialist community, the **Council for Mutual Economic Assistance** (CMEA — also called COMECON) and the **Warsaw Treaty Organization** (WTO — or Warsaw Pact). While Soviet military representatives were originally in positions of direct command over Polish forces this practice ceased in 1956, although the WTO (founded in 1955) remained under firm Soviet control and its forces subject to Soviet military command. With standard military forces of over 300,000 in the 1980s Poland had the largest army in Eastern Europe after the Soviet Union. From this strongly founded base within the Soviet camp Poland has on several occasions made overtures to the West in the security area. One of the first, in 1957, was the Rapacki plan, named after the foreign minister of the time, which proposed the banning of nuclear weapons from Poland, Czechoslovakia and the two Germanys. This was echoed by the more recent Jaruzelski plan, launched in 1987, which remained very much in the shadow of the **Gorbachev**–Reagan agreements in train at the time. The installation of a Solidarity-led government was accompanied by reassurances that it had no intention of withdrawing from the existing alliance structure.

Poland's trade with the West also tended to be relatively more developed than that of other Eastern countries. Through the 1950s and 1960s it stood at around 30 per cent of total turnover, while in the case of its neighbours the proportion fell between 10 and 20 per cent. By 1975 the amount of trade conducted with the West was nearing one half of the total. Soviet economic support for Poland also tended to be weaker and the level of subsidy was lower only for Romania, a less intimate ally of the Soviet Union. This situation changed with the onset of martial law and the imposition of Western sanctions, which encouraged stronger Soviet links.

The level of imports as a whole fell in the early eighties, standing in 1985 at 88 per cent of the 1980 figure and at only 6 per cent above that level in 1988. Imports from non-socialist countries bore the major part of this decline and in 1988 imports from these areas still stood at only 90 per cent of the 1980 total (those from the socialist community were already 16 per cent higher). Exports continued at a higher level and in 1988 Poland achieved 29 per cent more than in 1980. Most of this reflected, again, closer integration with socialist countries and exports to this area rose by 46 per cent between 1980 and 1988, against only 12 per cent to the rest of the world. The 1980s therefore saw an economic reorientation of Poland away from the West and the trend it had followed in the 1970s, a shift that was particularly marked in the first half of the decade. By 1985 the Soviet Union, by far Poland's greatest trading partner, accounted for 34 per cent of her imports and 28 per cent of exports.

But also striking was the low level of Poland's engagement overall in world trade and the fact that value traded per head of population was less than the world average, an equivalent for Poland of $369 in exports and $321 for imports in 1988. In terms of exports it fell even below the level of the Soviet Union (at $371) and Romania (at $692). Other socialist countries exported several times more and most West European countries achieved a level more than ten times higher. The important international role played by Poland in terms of political, security and military matters was not replicated in the area of trade and economic relations. This situation had clearly not improved as Poland's relative economic decline continued, both in relation to the developed countries of the West (and some of the rapidly advancing countries of the Pacific) and to partners within the socialist community who, whilst experiencing major economic problems, had not found themselves in a situation of such prolonged crisis.

With the removal of some of the major constraints that had been placed on government policy in the early 1980s, the Solidarity-led government therefore placed great emphasis on the economic aspect of Poland's foreign relations, on the reductions or rescheduling of the debt burden, and on the development of aid and economic co-operation programmes as a prerequisite for Polish recovery and fundamental condition for the enchancement of political democracy and state sovereignty. The apparent disappearance of the political controls formerly imposed by the Soviet Union and revision of the implications of CMEA and WTO membership left Poland freer to define its objectives and relations with both international organizations such as the IMF and World Bank and Western powers, like the United States and EC countries—dominant among which, from the Polish point of view, had to be the Federal Republic of Germany.

PGL

POLISH UNITED WORKERS' PARTY (PUWP — Polska Zjednoczona Partia Robotnicza).

The ruling Polish Communist party from 1948 to the installation of a government dominated by **Solidarity** sympathizers in 1989. The PUWP was formed in December 1948 by a merger of the existing Polish Socialist Party (PPS) and the Polish Workers' Party (PPR), which had been established in 1942 after the dissolution of the Polish Communist Party (KPP) in 1938. The two parties provided, respectively, 955,900 and 531,350 members and were united under the leadership as chairman of former **Communist International (Comintern)** official Bolesław Bierut. It operated according to the principles of the Soviet Communist party, dominating the structures of government and administration and maintaining strictly centralized control exercised through the Politburo and Central Committee. This situation did not change much after the death of **Stalin** in 1953 but was modified after the XX Congress of the Communist Party of Soviet Union in 1956, shortly after which Bierut died while still in Moscow.

Pressures for change and political liberalization led to the return to the leadership in October 1956 of Władysław **Gomułka**, who had been removed in 1948 as general secretary of the PPR three months before the unification of the parties and who had spent several years after that in detention. He led the Politburo to a confrontation with a visiting Soviet delegation led by **Khrushchev** and persuaded them to accept the validity of his version of a Polish road to socialism. This he successfully did and was regarded for some time by many Poles as an authentic national leader, receiving a substantial popular endorsement in the elections of January 1957. But he soon moved to clamp down on revisionism and reformist tendencies within the PUWP, which developed alternative sources of conflicts in the late 1960s from apparently nationalist and authoritarian groups around Mieczyslaw Moczar. Gomułka's departure from the leadership in December 1970 and his replacement by **Gierek** was received with some relief, and the more open style of Edward Gierek seemed to promise the establishment of a firmer base of popular support for the party.

That, too, soon evaporated and by 1976 Gierek was also relying on police measures to control the workers. Party membership continued to rise (to a high-point of 3,150,000 in mid-1980) but was weakened internally by bureaucratic pratices and extensive corruption. The PUWP experienced difficulties in developing a coherent response to the challenge posed by **Solidarity**, and major divisions existed within it and obstructed the implementation of the policy of moderate reform which party leader Stanisław **Kania** seemed to favour. At the Extraordinary IX Congress in July 1981, however, it finally opted for a programme of major reform. This did little to halt its declining public support and party ranks thinned further during the **State of War** introduced by Gen. **Jaruzelski** as party discipline was again strengthened. Young people and workers showed no inclination to sign up during the 1980s, and the paucity of public support for the PUWP (it claimed 2,132,000 members at the end of 1988) was finally made evident in the elections of 1989.

This shock was responsible for an eventual acceptance of the need for a radical review of the party's role and organization in a greatly changed political situation. At a specially convened Congress in January 1990 the PUWP dissolved itself and reformed as the Social Democracy of the Republic of Poland, electing as its leader the 36-year old Alexander Kwansniewski, formerly responsible for sport and youth affairs. Not all were content to stay within a single organization, and a Social Democratic Union was also set up under the leadership of Tadeusz Fiszbach. Fiszbach had been a popular party secretary in Gdańsk throughout the 1970s and had developed good relations with Lech **Wałęsa** and the Solidarity organization. Removed from the party apparatus during the State of War he was elected deputy speaker of the *Sejm* following the 1989 elections and maintained a more critical view of the PUWP's record than the majority of the party.

PGL

POZSGAY, IMRE.

Leading reform Communist in the **Hungarian Socialist Workers' Party** (HSWP — since October 1989 Hungarian Socialist Party). Pozsgay (born in 1955) joined the party in 1950, and began his career in the ideological and propaganda apparatus in the Bács County Committee of the HSWP, serving as its Ideological Secretary in 1965–70. He was promoted to Section Head of the HSWP Central Committee's Department of Agitation and Propaganda in 1970, and became Deputy Editor-in-Chief of a leading party social science publication, *Társadalmi Szemle*. In the early 1970s, his published articles showed clear signs of his commitment to the basic tenets of reform Communism, albeit expressed in the arcane terminology of ideological debate current in the period following the 1968 Czechoslovak crisis. Despite the anti-reform ideological backlash which occurred in Hungary in the mid-1970s, Pozsgay's career advanced steadily: in 1975, he became deputy Minister of Culture, and was promoted to Minister of Culture the following year. He retained this post until 1982. During this period, he developed extensive contacts with intellectuals in the fields of culture and the humanities, particularly among those of a "populist" persuasion. It was also under Pozsgay's patronage that the discipline of political science was allowed to establish itself in Hungary which introduced Western political and sociological concepts, and a more objective approach to the study of politics than the traditional Marxist-Leninist "Scientific Socialism".

Pozsgay's removal from the Ministry of Culture in 1982 was a clear indication that his reformism had begun to exceed the limits set by the **Kádár** regime, which had been seriously weakened by the critical economic situation in Hungary and alarmed by the political collapse in Poland. Poszgay was shifted sideways to become General Secretary of the Patriotic People's Front (PPF), hitherto an obscure and impotent body which Pozsgay nevertheless used as a legitimate basis from which to continue to skilfully promote his reformist ideas and, increasingly, to generate pressure for radical political reform. An important example of this was the programmatic document "Change and Reform", commissioned by Pozsgay's PPF from a group of leading reformist economists, which argued explicitly that consistent economic reform, and thus real improvement in economic performance, would not be possible without political reform including reform of the party and its position it the state and society. When the document was published in early 1987 it caused a furore and directly contributed to the mounting political crisis. Also, in 1987, Pozsgay used his position to support the foundation of a new political movement, the **Hungarian Democratic Forum**.

As the reformist tide gathered force, Pozsgay's personal authority grew, and he was brought into the new government of Károly **Grósz** as Minister of State with special responsibility for political reform. Far from being restrained by his incorporation in the leadership. Pozsgay continued to act as a catalyst for further change in 1989, most notably in promoting the reappraisal of the events of 1956. In winning the party's support for the introduction of a multi-party system, and in setting up the "Triangular Discussions" with the opposition at which basic constitutional reforms were negotiated. Pozsgay was elevated to membership of the four-man Presidium of the HSWP

set up in June 1989. By the summer of 1989, public opinion polls were revealing that Pozsgay was by far the most popular and widely trusted politician in Hungary, and at its founding Congress in October 1989, the Hungarian Socialist Party nominated him as their candidate for the forthcoming presidential election.

JB

PRAGUE (Praha). The capital and largest city of Czechoslovakia, Prague (in Czech Praha, in German Prag) constitutes one of the country's 12 administrative regions. Its area is 495 sq km and its 1986 population was 1,190,576. Prague is located on the Vltava (in German, Moldau) river. A hub for communications by river as well as road, rail and air, Prague is one of Europe's most important historic cities as well as a contemporary commercial and industrial centre. Its industries include engineering, printing and publishing, chemicals and consumer goods. Already a leading European city in medieval times, Prague came under Habsburg rule from 1526 and became the capital of the Czechoslovak state when it was established in 1918 following World War I. The city suffered extensive damage during World War II, when it was occupied by the Germans; it was liberated by Soviet troops in 1945. Prague was the city of Rilke, Kafka, Smetana and others and its historic and attractive centre has many other cultural associations. As well as governmental buildings, the city accommodates the Charles University (founded in 1348 and one of the oldest in Europe), the Czechoslovak Academy of Sciences and three archbishoprics.

SLW

PRAGUE SPRING. The popular name attached to the period of reform in Czechoslovakia which followed the election of Alexander **Dubček** as First Secretary of the **Communist Party of Czechoslovaka** on 5 Jan., 1968. Official policy, which sought to marry a socialist economy with Czechoslovakia's democratic traditions in what became known as "socialism with a human face", was set out in an Action Programme, published in April, which proposed democratization of the party and the political system, greater freedom of expression, a market-oriented economic reform and the introduction of a federal system to ensure greater equality between Czechs and Slovaks. As a result of the relaxation of political controls, public debate took on a life of its own, pressure grew for more radical changes, and new political groupings such as K231, a club of former political prisoners, and KAN (*Klub angažovaných* *nestraníků*), a club of committed non-party members, were formed as part of a broadening popular participation in political life. Concern on the part of the Soviet leadership (supported by their counterparts in East Germany and Poland) that the Czechoslovak Party had lost control, that pressure for reform would spread elsewhere in the Soviet bloc and that the Soviet Union's strategic defences might come under threat resulted in the **Warsaw Treaty Organization (Warsaw Pact)** invasion of Czechoslovakia on the night of August 20–21. Although Dubček remained in power until April 1969, the invasion effectively brought a halt to the reforms and, after Dubček's fall, a return to an authoritarian form of socialism based on the Soviet model.

GW

R

RAJK, LÁSZLÓ. Leading Hungarian Communist and most prominent victim of the Stalinist show trials in Hungary. Rajk (born in 1909) joined the illegal Communist Party of Hungary in 1931, and was expelled from university as a result. He fought in the Spanish Civil War in 1936–39, and was interned in Hungary during World War II from 1941 to September 1944. After his release, he was leader of the Communist Party in Budapest and played an active role in the organization of the underground resistance. After the liberation of Hungary he rose rapidly in the party to become a member of the Politburo and Central Committee. From 1946–48 he was Minister of the Interior, and, from August 1948, Minister of Foreign Affairs. Tensions between Rajk, as the leading figure in the party faction of "home" Communist (former resistance fighters), and the dominant "Muscovite" faction of **Rákosi**, became apparent in question of party policy and the subordination of the pace of change to Moscow's dictates. On May 30, 1949, Rajk was arrested on charges of "Titoism" and "Trotskyism", and in September he was tried, condemned to death, and was subsequently executed. In 1956, after the XX Congress of the Communist Party of The Soviet Union (CPSU), he was rehabilitated posthumously and his family secured permission for his reburial. The funeral, which took place on 6 Oct. 1956, turned into a massive public display of protest and had a devastating impact, precipitating the revolutionary events of the following weeks. Rajk's son, László Rajk Jnr., has been an activist in the democratic opposition since the 1970s.

JB

RÁKOSI, MÁTYÁS. The ruthless and fanatical Stalinist who led the Hungarian Communist Party (from 1948 Hungarian Workers' Party) from 1945 to 1956. Rákosi (born in 1892) began his political career as a prisoner-of-war in Russia in World War I, returning to Hungary in 1918 to play an active role in organizing the Hungarian Communist Party in the provinces. Subsequently he held a variety of posts in the short-lived Soviet Republic under Béla Kun. After a brief period of exile in the Soviet Union he returned to underground Communist activity in Hungary, but was arrested in 1925 and imprisoned until 1940 when he was permitted to leave for Moscow. He organized Hungarian émigrés and returned with them to Hungary after liberation by the Soviet Red Army to take over the government of the country as leader of the re-established Hungarian Communist Party. His period of rule is remembered for its total subservience to **Stalin**, the use of political terror against party and people alike, and serious economic mismanagement. After Stalin's death he successfully resisted pressures from Moscow to introduce a less severe form of rule, and ousted Imre **Nagy** from his post as Prime Minister. The tensions generated by this system of rule contributed directly to the crisis which erupted in 1956, when Rákosi's grip on power finally gave way. Despite the brutal restoration of Communist rule after 1956, Rákosi remained in disgrace. His party membership was suspended and he was eventually expelled from the party in 1962 on account of his unrepentent attitude. He died in Moscow in 1971.

JB

RAKOWSKI, MIECZYSŁAW FRANCISZEK. Born in December 1926 to a peasant family in Kowalewko, Bydgoszcz province, Poland, he was employed during the war in the Poznań railway rolling-stock plant. He volunteered for the Polish Army in 1945 and, having passed out from the Łódź political training school for officers, performed that function in the forces until 1949. Having joined the party in 1946, Rakowski proceeded to study journalism after leaving the army and took a post as a instructor in the Press and Publishing Department of the Central Committee of the **Polish United Workers' Party (PUWP)**. Between 1952 and 1955 he studied at the Warsaw Institute of Social Sciences, taking a doctorate in 1956, and in 1955–57 worked in the CC Propaganda Department. Amidst the political changes that accompanied **Gomułka**'s return to power Rakowski's public profile sharpened and he transferred to work on the new weekly paper *Polityka*, set up in 1957 by the authorities after the more outspoken reform-minded *Po prostu* had been closed down.

He became chief editor of the paper in May 1958 and in the same year chairman of the Polish Journalists' Association (serving in that capacity until 1962). He has written steadily and published a number of books on international relations and social and political topics. Rakowski retained editorial responsibility for *Polityka* until 1981 and built up its reputation as a relatively liberal and lively publication which nevertheless generally retained the confidence of the PUWP leadership and maintained close links with the political establishment. His ability to maintain both a liberal image and close relations with those in power made Rakowski a highly suspect figure for many people. One Polish journalist wrote a lengthy sardonic article on his changing hair-styles which, he suggested, changed as his career progressed along with his political views. In 1964 he became a deputy member of the PUWP Central Committee, in 1972 a deputy to the *Sejm*, and in 1975 a full member of the Central Committee. His political career took off in 1981, when Gen. **Jaruzelski** became Prime Minister and appointed Rakowski vice-premier with responsibility for relations with trade unions.

On the face of it this was intended to demonstrate the moderate stance of the Jaruzelski government, but Rakowski did not get on well with Lech **Wałęsa** and the **Solidarity** leadership and appeared to develop an increasingly antagonistic attitude to the independent union (possibly associated with the firming up of plans to introduce the **State of War**). He left the government with Jaruzelski in 1985 and became *Sejm* vice-marshall. He was elected to the PUWP Politburo in December 1987 and became a CC Secretary in June 1988. Following the August strikes and the growing prominence of Solidarity leaders, he was elected Prime Minister in September 1988. Along with many other prominent figures, he failed to gain election to the *Sejm* in June 1989 but was elected to replace Jaruzelski as PUWP first secretary on July 29. On Aug. 2 the *Sejm* voted to establish an extraordinary commission to examine the record of his government. In December 1989 the commission concluded that the decision to close the **Gdańsk** shipyard had been taken hastily and without consultation, and referred the matter to the Constitutional Tribunal for further deliberation. In January 1990 Rakowski presided over the dissolution of the PUWP at a special Congress but refused to stand for election to the leadership of the party that was formed in its place.

PGL

RELIGION AND COMMUNISM. Through the decades of Communist power in the USSR and Eastern Europe, before the regimes began to reform themselves or collapse, religion was the only form of dissent from the ideology which was offically tolerated. For the totalitarian system, religion was an anomaly, an exception to the rule that the state should control all forms of social activity. Where it was not suppressed, it was discouraged.

For Marx, religion was a feature of class society. It was a means both of comforting the oppressed masses with promises of a future heaven after this world, and persuading them to accept their exploitation. Religion was "the cry of the oppressed...the opium of the people". With the achievement of communism and the end of exploitation, it would wither away.

Lenin's approach can be characterized as "militant atheism"; religion was a fraud, and the party had a duty to struggle against any form of it. Religion would not disappear on its own. Atheism is a central and consistent element of **Marxism-Leninism**, and of all the varieties of Marxism-Leninism which have functioned as the official ideology of ruling Communist parties in the USSR, Eastern Europe and elsewhere. But this has by no means led to relentless religious persecution in all the Communist states at all times. Lenin's combination of unremitting hostility to religion and tactical flexibility has spawned what can be seen as two tendencies in the attitude of officials formulating and implementing policy towards religion — "fundamentalist" and "pragmatist".

The fundamentalists have been strongest in the ideological apparatuses and the youth organizations. The pragmatists are those who are more concerned with the smooth functioning of the economy, those less willing to risk political stability for the sake of ideological transformation, those concerned with integrating national minorities into multinational states and those concerned with the image of the state in the world outside. Both tendencies have periodically won the support of their party leaders.

In 1918, the revolutionary government passed a decree on religion, nationalizing all church property, separating the churches from the state and the schools from the churches. While in public disavowing any discrimination against believers, Lenin in practice set out to discredit and weaken, if not destroy, the **Russian Orthodox Church**. Lenin was flexible in tactics: he saw the Orthodox Church as the most dangerous religious body, because of its link with tsarism, and indeed its collaboration with the Whites in the early part of the Civil War. The struggle against other religions could be resumed later and the Bolsheviks in the meantime appealed to believers of other faiths, such as the **Old Believers** and the followers of **Islam**, to join with them. At the same time Jewish Bolsheviks were encouraged to campaign against Judaism.

After the Civil War, many bishops and nuns were killed or arrested for refusing to hand over to the government consecrated church valuables, which the government wished to sell to relieve famine. In 1922 Patriarch Tikhon was arrested, and the Bolsheviks attempted to place their own allies, the "Living Church" movement in the leading positions of the Church. The unwillingness of the believers to recognize the new Church leadership led the government to abandon them, and instead to put pressure on Tikhon and, after his death, the acting Patriarch, Sergii, to declare support for the Soviet authorities. Sergii's declaration of loyalty in 1927 was a victory for the government.

This declaration did little for the Orthodox Church in the short run. In 1929 the law on Religious Associations, much more restrictive than the 1918 decree, was passed. This law is the basis for all subsequent Soviet legislation on religion, and its principles were copied to a greater or lesser extent by other Communist countries. Religious worship could be undertaken only by a group of people in a locality after its registration had been accepted by the local authorities. A council of 20 (the *dvadtsatka*) was responsible for ensuring that the law was observed. Priests were not to have contact with people under18, and their activity was to be confined to the Church buildings leased from the state. Charitable work was forbidden. In practice, the churches were also handicapped by the shortage of Bibles and other religious literature.

At the same time, in 1929, the state launched an all-out physical attack on the Orthodox Church and all the other religious groups in the USSR. This was part of **Stalin**'s "left" turn, to force collectivization and industrialization. The party feared that the churches could provide a centre of peasant resistance to the new policies. The League of Militant Godless formed in 1925, was given free rein to fight the ideological struggle against believers, and organize the blowing-up of historic churches. The security police acted against the clergy. Bishops and priests were accused of espionage or treason, and executed or sent to the labour camps. The "Stalin" Constitution of 1936 supposedly guaranteed freedom of religious worship and anti-religious propaganda —clearly implying that attempts to spread religion were unconstitutional—although even worship was difficult with the absence of priests. Believers faced dismissal from work, while their children were victimized at school or taken away from their parents.

A change came with the Nazi invasion of the Western part of the Soviet Union. In 1941 the German occupiers allowed the churches to reopen and believers flooded throught the doors. Stalin saw the need to mobilize the religious for the war effort by making concessions to them. The League of Militant Godless was disbanded, the priests let out of prison and the churches reopened. Structures loyal to Stalin were created for the Muslims and for the **Baptists in the USSR**. The orthodox were allowed to elect Sergii

as Patriarch of Moscow, and received a relatively privileged position among Soviet denominations.

After the war, this relative detente with the "loyal" churches continued. The **Ukrainian Catholic (Uniate) Church**, seen by the authorites as a bastion of Ukrainian nationalism, was suppressed and forced into the Russian Orthodox Church. Here policy towards religion was subordinated to nationality policy (*see* **Nationality Question in the USSR** and **Nationalism and Communism in Eastern Europe**). Sects such as the "True Orthodox Church", the "True and Free Adventists" and the Jehovah's Witnesses, who were hostile to the regime, were driven underground. This policy of a differentiated approach to religions, according to their attitude to the state, was pursued by the Communist regimes in Eastern Europe as well.

The policy of the authorities was to try to bring the churches under state control, or where this was not possible to attempt to crush them. The **Roman Catholic Church** was regarded with particular suspicion, having its headquarters in the Vatican outside Communist control. It was the largest church in Poland, Hungary, Czechoslovakia, Lithuania, Croatia and Slovenia. The measures against the Catholic leaders paralleled those taken against the Russian Orthodox hierarchy after the revolution, with cardinals and archbishops being arrested. Only in Poland was the Catholic Church strong enough to withstand the pressure to adopt a loyalist attitude through the Stalinist years.

The Orthodox churches, on the other hand, had a tradition of subservience to, and dependence on, the state, and the patriarchates proved amenable to serving the national Communist leaders in Bulgaria, Romania, and Serbia. In Romania, 1.5 million Uniates were forced into the Romanian Orthodox Church in 1948. In Slovakia in 1950 580,000 Uniates were forced into the Russian Orthodox Church, receiving autocephaly in 1951. Only in 1968, with the **Prague Spring**, were they allowed to resume their Uniate status. In the GDR, special factors operated. Until the 1960s, the Catholic and Protestant churches were both united with their counterparts in the Federal Republic. Even at the height of Stalinism, no Church leader was removed from office. The Church leaders were anti-Nazi and possibly feelings of war guilt encouraged them to take a conciliatory (although not submissive) attitude to the **Socialist Unity Party of Germany (SED)**.

Yugoslavia's exit from the socialist camp led to the adoption, after a few years, of a more relaxed attitude to religion. The link between Serbian nationalism and the **Serbian Orthodox Church**, on the one hand, and between Croat and Slovene nationalism and the Roman Catholic Church, on the other, forced the federal authorities to rein in the expression of nationalism from the pulpits and the church newspapers at times of tension between nationalties. Alojzije Stepinac, a Croat who was made Cardinal of Zagreb in 1952, had been a supporter of Croatian independence during World War II. Serb suspicions of his Ustaša sympathies exacerbated relations between the two nationalities up to his death in 1960.

The other East European countries had to wait until Stalin's death for a loosening of discipline in the Soviet bloc and an improvement of the religious situation. In the USSR itself, **Khrushchev** launched an anti-religious campaign (1959–64) which ended Stalin's detente with the churches and seemed designed to prepare the way for the building of a religion-free Romanian communism by 1980. Beatings, rape and murder were employed against clergy and believers, and more churches were blown up.

Restrictions on the churches led to a split among the Baptists and dissent in the Russian Orthodox Church at the readiness of the Church leaders to co-operate with the atheist authorities and their refusal to speak out against persecution. The **Brezhnev** leadership ended the extremes of Khrushchev's campaign, but carried on persecuting priests who were over-zealous, and stepped up pressure on the Reform Baptists and Jews studying Hebrew.

By the 1970s, and into the 1980s, the different coutries had evolved their own approaches to the problem of religion. At the most extreme position was Albania, which had declared itself the world's first atheist state in 1967. Religion was, therefore, illegal. Religion had traditionally been a divisive factor in Albania's struggle for independence from the Ottoman Empire. It had been approximately 70 per cent Muslim, 20 Per cent Orthodox and 10 Per cent Roman Catholic. It has been said, however, that the religion of Albanians is Albanianism. The ultra-repressive, isolationist regime of Enver **Hoxha** and then Ramiz **Alia** has largely prevented any public expression of religious belief.

Next most repressive of religion were Romania and Bulgaria. The Orthodox churches in both countries were tightly controlled. In Romania, minorities such as the Protestants and Catholics among the Hungarians and Germans had difficulties while the Uniates were banned. In Bulgaria the Muslims were largely prevented from observing their worship. Marginally less repressive was the Czechoslovak regime, especially after it felt threatened by protest movements in the 1980s, and the Soviet Union before **Gorbachev**. There the secret legislation and secret instructions from the Soviet government's Council of Religious Affairs to the local authorities made a mockery of constitutional freedoms. Poland and Hungary were towards the tolerant end of the spectrum, because of the strength of the Roman Catholic Church in Poland and Janos **Kádár**'s policy of alliance with non-Communists in Hungary. The freest conditions were in Yugoslavia and the German Democratic Republic.

The situation of religion in the USSR changed with Gorbachev and *glasnost'*. The radical, pro-*perestroika* wing of the press began to campaign against the persecution of believers. Most religious prisoners were freed in 1987 and 1988. In April 1988 Gorbachev met the Russian Orthodox Patriarch of Moscow. He told the religious believers that they were regarded as loyal Soviet citizens, and appealed to them to work for *perestroika*. He promised a new law on freedom of conscience. Churches were given back to the Orthodox, and persecution of Baptists and the major Christian denominations was much reduced. In November 1989 Gorbachev visited Pope John Paul II in the Vatican, and it seemed that the problem of the Ukrainian Uniates was moving towards a solution.

The advent of *perestroika* in the USSR and the renunciation of Soviet intervention in Eastern Europe gave the green light to reform in the USSR's allies. The Catholic Church in Poland and Czechoslovakia played a significant role in promoting independent civic feeling in the late 1980s. Similarly the **Evangelical Church in the GDR** acted as an umbrella for political opposition. In 1988–89 in Poland and in late 1989–90 in the GDR and Czechoslovakia the churches were active participants in the round tables which brought the regimes and oppositions together to negotiate a transition towards free elections. In Romania, it was the persecution of the Hungarian Reformed Church pastor László Tőkés in **Timişoara** which proved the catalyst for the popular insurrection which brought down the **Ceauşescu** dictatorship in December 1989.

As Eastern Europe emerged from Communist rule, the churches faced two major challenges. Could they make a contribution to moderating the ethnic conflicts that threatened to emerge in the region, particularly in the Balkans? And could they resist the rising tide of secularization as the countries moved towards the acceptance of market economics and Westernization? (*See also* **Armenian Church**; **Bulgarian Orthodox Church**; **Czechoslovak Protestant Churches**; **Georgian Orthodox Church**; **Lutherans in the USSR**; **Romanian Orthodox Church**; **Ukrainian Autocephalous Orthodox Church**)

PJSD

ROMAN CATHOLIC CHURCH. Throughout the years of Communist rule in Eastern Europe, the Roman Catholic Church represented a challenge to those regimes ruling countries where it was well represented. It played a part in the transformation of some of the East European states in 1989.

Its strongest base is in Poland, where 95 per cent of the population are Catholics, and it is the denomination with the largest support in Hungary. In Czechoslovakia, it has approximate parity of nominal support with the **Czechoslovak Protestant Churches**, but it has the adherence of most Slovaks and much greater vitality among its Czech members than the Protestants are able to achieve. In Yugoslavia, it has the adherence of the Croats and Slovenes and minorities among other nationalities. It is in a minority position in the German Democratic Republic, Romania (mainly among the Hungarian and German minorities), Bulgaria and Albania.

In the USSR it has been important mainly due to its strength among the Lithuanians, and because of the growing support for the **Ukrainian Catholic (Uniate) Church**. There are also Roman Catholics among Soviet Belorussians, Poles, Ukrainians and other nationalities.

When the Communists came to power in Eastern Europe after the war, they were particularly suspicious of the Roman Catholic Church, because the centre of its power was located outside Communist control, in Italy. Large-scale arrests of archbishops, bishops and priests took place, and churches were closed, as the new rulers sought to crush to Church or bring its local leadership under control. Diplomatic relations with the Vatican were broken. The governments sponsored organizations to conduct pro-Communist propaganda among the priests, such as Pax in Poland.

Poland. The "Polish October" of 1956 led to an improvement in the situation there of the Church, which was allowed to conduct religious instruction inside state schools. It was allowed its own newspapers, albeit with limited circulation. "Clubs of Catholic Intellectuals" were established, with a handful of representatives in the *Sejm*, known as the Znak group.

Stefan, Cardinal Wyszyński, who headed the Church from 1948 to 1981, presided over a near-doubling in the number of priests (11,000 before the war to 20,000 in 1980) and a doubling in the number of churches (7,000 to 14,000). This reflected not an increase in religiosity, but a willingness to demonstrate Polish nationalism. Through the centuries the Catholic Church in Poland was the principal defender of Polish

nationality. With the Communists being seen as imposed by Soviet power, the Poles reaffirmed their nationhood by vesting authority in the Polish Church.

For its part, the Church provided an umbrella for the forces of opposition which developed in the 1970s and 1980s, while at the same time trying to demonstrate its usefulness to the regime by urging moderation on government and opposition alike. Thus while it expressed support for human rights, it avoided giving full support to workers' economic demands, and urged both sides against direct confrontation (which might, it was feared, lead to Soviet intervention). It could not go too far in the direction of mediation, however, because that would lead to the risk of losing the support of the people.

Under Pope John XXIII and Paul VI, the Vatican sought a *modus vivendi* with the regimes in Poland, the rest of Eastern Europe and the Soviet Union. Its *Ostpolitik* was partly linked with fears of the possible victory of a Communist-led government in Italy. More important was a belief that the political status quo in Eastern Europe was unlikely to change, and it would be necessary to negotiate with the authorities in order to ensure the supply of an adequate number of priests for the long term. In 1978, however, Karol, Cardinal Wojtya of Cracow became the first Polish Pope, as John Paul II. Critical of liberation theology in Latin America, and intolerant of independent thought within his own ranks, the new Pope adopted a more aggressive attitude to the regimes in Eastern Europe. Nevertheless he maintained Augustino, Cardinal Casaroli, as Secretary of State, in charge of foreign policy.

In 1979 the Polish Pope was invited to Poland. While the **Gierek** regime hoped to gain the Church's blessing, in fact it was both the Church and the opposition which gained from the visit. The Church organized the marshalling of the processions, and the boost to morale given by the Pope's presence was probably a major factor in the successful formation of the independent trade union **Solidarity** in August 1980. The left-wing intellectuals such as Adam Michnik and Jacek Kuron who became advisers to Solidarity were already reassessing the Church in a new light. The bulk of the working-class leadership of Solidarity, headed by Lech **Wałęsa**, were personally committed to the Church, and Wałęsa himself was believed to be close in his ideas to the Pope.

The episcopate opposed the declaration of martial law and the banning of Solidarity in December 1981. It urged both government and Solidarity to negotiate with each other. This was the message of Josef, Cardinal **Glemp**, who succeeded Wyszvński in 1981, and of the Pope when he returned again in 1983 and 1987. Many priests whose parishioners were Solidarity members would have preferred the Church to have taken a stronger line against the regime. Fr Jerzy Popiełuszko, who went further than the bishops would have liked in his attacks on the regime, was murdered by security police in 1984.

From 1987, as Poland's economic difficulties worsened, reformist elements who were prepared to make concessions to the Church came to the fore in the party. The Church insisted on the recognition of Solidarity. During 1988 and into 1989 discussions for the **Round-Table Agreement** took place from time to time between representatives of the government, the Church and Solidarity. When the latter showed its industrial strength in spring 1988, the Church mediated between the union and the authorities. Faced with hardliners in the regime attempting to block the relegalization of Solidarity, the Church swung found more firmly in support of the opposition, from the time of the strikes of August 1988. In Spring 1989 Church representatives helped to push through the arrangements for free elections. Even before these, in May 1989, the *Sejm* passed legislation giving full legality to the Roman Catholic Church and its activities.

In the election campaign, bishops and clergy gave support to Solidarity-backed candidates. The Solidarity victory in June led to the formation of a coalition government of Communists and non-Communists, with a non-Communist and Catholic majority. Much of the Communist power structure for the time being remained intact. The government was headed by Tadeusz **Mazowiecki**, a journalist on a Church newspaper. Mazowiecki is believed to have been recommended for the post by Wałęsa. Like its Communist predecessor, the government needed to carry through a programme of economic restructuring which would cause unemployment and severely reduce the living standards of part of the population. It hoped that the Catholic Church would support this programme and use its influence within the Solidarity trade union to assist its implementation. In July 1989 it restored diplomatic relations with the Vatican.

Hungary. The suppression of the Hungarian revolution of 1956 forced the Primate, Jozsef, Cardinal Mindszenty, to take refuge in the American Embassy, where he remained for 15 years, in spite of the efforts of the Vatican to persuade him to leave. The situation of the Roman Catholic Church began to improve when the **Kádár** regime began to seek alliances with non-Communist forces in the early 1960s. Relations between the state and the Vatican improved with the signing of an agreement in 1964.

László, Cardinal Lékai, Primate of Hungary from 1976 to 1986, pursued policy of collaborating with the government in political matters while obtaining the maximum freedom to pursue the re-Christianization of Hungary. After John Paul II became Pope, the Vatican began to urge Lékai to play a more aggressive role. Lékai's conciliatory policies led him into conflict with clergy who were more hostile to the government, and in particular with the "basis communities" of rank-and file clergy and laity. Some of these, such as that headed by Fr György Bulányi, opposed military service, and provided a framework for the emerging independent peace movement in Hungary.

In 1987, László Paskai became Primate. In 1988 he took part in a meeting of religious leaders with Prime Minister Károly **Grósz**. He and other bishops pressed for Catholics to be allowed conscientious objection to military service and for new laws on religion, allowing the Church to operate outside church buildings. The government promised a new law for 1990. In May 1989, as the ruling party was in the process of transforming Hungary into a multi-party system, it gave permission for the formation of Christian political parties. In February 1990 Prime Minister Miklós **Neméth** visited the Vatican, and the two sides announced the resumption of diplomatic relations.

Czechoslovakia. Repression of the Catholic Church increased after the Soviet invasion in 1968. The government organized a pro-regime group of priests within the Church, called *Pacem in Terris*. František, Cardinal Tomášek, his position weak because of the conciliatory policy pursued by the Vatican at the time, distanced the Church from the human rights document **Charter 77**. The Church suffered a severe shortage of bishops and the Cardinal needed state approval to fill the vacancies. Nevertheless some priests openly supported the document. John Paul II, after becoming Pope, encouraged Tomášek to speak out against the government, and both he and the Vatican condemned the *Pacem in Terris* group. In the early 1980s the **Husák** leadership responded to the increased militancy of the Catholic Church with arrests and imprisonments.

This repression seems to have raised the standing of the Church in Czechoslovakia. A commemoration of St Methodius in 1985 attracted hundreds of thousands of participants. In 1987–88 a petition in support of religious freedom was signed by half-a-million people, including the Cardinal. This attracted more support than any other dissident document in Czechoslovakia.

During 1988 and 1989 a series of demonstrations also took place, protesting against religious persecution, with young people playing an important part. Tomášek moved into open opposition, as Catholics played an increasing role in Charter 77 and the movements for religious and political rights began to coalesce together into a plausible opposition.

The transformation of the regime in November/December 1989 under popular pressure left the Roman Catholic Church in a strong position. It had helped to bring down the Communist power structure. After Václav **Havel** was sworn in as President, the television transmitted a celebratory mass by Tomásek in the main Prague cathedral.

Yugoslavia. In the 1950s the Catholic Church in Yugoslavia achieved more freedom than in any other Communist state, with its own relatively free newspapers. In 1970 Yugoslavia established full diplomatic relations with the Vatican. The position of the Catholic Church in Yugoslavia is complicated by its links with Croat and Slovene nationalism. In 1971 *Matica Hrvatska* (Croatian Motherland), a cultural-nationalist movement with support from Croation bishops, became so influential in Croatia that the Croatian Communists felt that compelled to join the nationalist bandwagon for fear of being swept aside. This created a crisis in relations between the Yugoslav republics. Again in the 1980s, as economic problems worsened in Yugoslavia and tensions grew between Serbs and Albanians over Kosovo (*see* **Yugoslavia** — National Question; **Nationalism and Communism in Eastern Europe**), the Catholic Church was an important centre of Croat nationalism. As Slovenia adopted a multi-party system in 1989, a Christian Democratic movement appeared.

GDR. In the GDR, the Catholic Church claims less than 10 per cent of the population. After Joachim Meisner became Cardinal in 1983, it began to give support to the independent peace movement, and in 1985 Meisner attacked the division of Germany. By the time of the fall of the **Honecker** regime the Church was playing a role, albeit subordinate to the **Evangelical Church in the GDR**, of seeking to manage a peaceful transition to democracy in East Germany.

USSR. All the Soviet leaders before Mikhail **Gorbachev** were especially hostile to Catholicism. Not only was the Vatican outside their control but Catholicism was clearly linked with Lithuanian nationalism, and through the Ukrainian Catholic (Uniate) Church with Ukrainian nationalism (*see* **Nationality Question in the USSR**).

Persecution of Lithuanian Catholics continued through the **Khrushchev** and **Brezhnev** eras, with the official Church structure lacking any legal recognition. In response, Lithuania created the only opposition in the Soviet Union in the 1970s which could claim a mass base. A network of *samizdat* publications, such as the *Chronicle of the Lithuanian Catholic Church*, founded in 1972, and organizations such as the Catholic Committee for the Defence of Believers' Rights, founded in 1978, had the support of much of the local clergy. The network fostered the creation of a formidable movement, in which religious feeling was fortified by Lithuanian nationalism. In 1979 a petition for the return of the church at Klaipeda attracted 150,000 signatures — 5 per cent of all Lithuanians. Many priests were accusing the Vatican of abandoning them in the interests of *Ostpolitik*.

After 1978, these fears disappeared, as John Paul II began to put pressure on Moscow to allow the Church hierarchy to be restored and improve the religious conditions in Lithuania. In 1979 he met Foreign Minister Andrei **Gromyko**. The Soviet leaders responded by allowing the Pope to make new appointments within the Soviet Union but cracking down on dissident activity. In 1983 Frs Alfonsas Svarinskas and Sigitas Tamkevičius were sent to a labour camp for their defence of religious rights. Gorbachev's *perestroika* led to their release in 1988 and the creation of a new political environment in Lithuania. The Klaipeda church was returned in 1988; in 1989 the main cathedral in Vilnius, the capital, was returned to the Church, and the first mass from it was broadcast by Lithuanian television.

In November 1989, Gorbachev became the first Soviet Communist Party leader to visit the Vatican. He invited John Paul II to become the first Pope to visit the USSR. Previously the main obstacle to a papal visit had been the question of the legalization of the Uniates. This had kept the Pope away from the celebrations of the Orthodox millennium in 1988. The changes in Soviet society made the propects for a visit more promising. At the same time, Gobachev and the Pope agreed in principle to establish diplomatic relations.

PJSD

ROMANIA. *Population*: 23 million (1989). *Area*: 237,500 sq km. *Main trading partners*: USSR, USA, Italy, Federal Republic of Germany, German Democratic Republic, Poland (1985). *Urban population as percentage of total*: 53 (as reported November 1989). *Birth rate*: 14 per thousand. *Life expectancy*: "about 70 years".

In the Romanian language, Romania is România; previously in English called Rumania, the "o" deliberately replacing the "u" to emphasize the country's Roman connections.

Geography. Romania has experienced numerous changes in her boundaries. At present, the country comprises as main provinces (not administrative divisions) Wallachia, Moldavia, Transylvania, the Dobrogea, the Banat and Maramures. **Bessarabia**, which belonged to Romania between 1918 and 1940, is now within the USSR. Romania is bounded by the USSR, Hungary, Yugoslavia, Bulgaria and the Black Sea. The country's area is divided about equally into plains (less than 200 m elevation), upland (200 to 300 m) and mountains (averaging 800 m). The Carpathian Mountains form a roughly circular redoubt enclosing Transylvania and there is another mountainous region to the south-west. Romania has a rather extreme continental climate but is generally well watered.

Demographic trends. The population has been growing, but at a declining rate (currently the rate is about 0.5 per cent annually), due to the declining birth rate. The migration from country to town must be partly responsible, but is the more remarkable given the usual non-availability of contraceptives, harsher penalties for abortion, monthly gynaecological tests (at least in theory) of women seeking state payment or certification, and higher taxation of childless couples. It therefore perhaps reflects as well problems with accommodation, food or other needed supplies and/or black market activities, Romanians' abilities to get round the letter of the law, or lack of confidence in the future. It is also very possible that infant mortality has risen. (Age-specific death rates are not published and other mortality data are patchy.) By contrast to the national average the birth rate of the gypsies is very high and other ethnic differences apparently exist (see below). Under **Ceauşescu**, state policy was intrusively and oppressively pro-natalist, evidently for political rather than economic reasons; however, it seemed to attain its purpose as regards Romanians only in areas (such as Băcău, in central Moldavia) where there was already a tradition of large families. Following the overthrow of the Ceauşescu regime (see below), the discomforts of women in particular resulting from the lack of contraceptives received much publicity in the Western media and advice was proferred on setting up birth-control centres.

Minorities. According to the 1977 census the total population was 21,559,416 including 19,001,721 Romanians; thus non-Romanians amounted to 2,557,695. The Romanian proportion, 88.1 per cent was higher than in previous censuses: in 1966 this proportion had been 87.7 per cent; in 1956, 86.2 per cent; in 1930 (within wider frontiers) only 71.9 per cent. In 1977 the largest minority was Hungarians, stated to number 1,705,810; jointly with Albanians in Yugoslavia (also 1.7 million) this was the largest minority in Europe not counting the USSR. (The Hungarian view is that this total is really two million, not 1.7 million.) The Hungarians as a proportion of the total have declined (in 1977, 7.9 per cent; in 1966, 8.5 per cent). The second largest minority is the Saxons (or Germans), in 1977 358,732 or 1.7 per cent; in 1956 they had been 2.2 per cent . The third largest minority is gypsies, who unlike those already mentioned are increasing in numbers probably quite rapidly although the reported rise from 64,197 in 1966 to 229,986 is unbelievable. Jews, in 1930 comprising about 3 per cent of the population, comprised in 1977 only 0.1 per cent. Many smaller groups are also present including Szeklers, Turks, Ukrainians and Russian-speaking Lipovans.

Officially, all nationalities are treated equally with Romanians but the secretary of each county has to be a Romanian and a certain proportion of its committee members. The chief discrimination against Hungarians is linguistic—public notices being almost exclusively in Romanian—and educational. Thus, Tîrgu Mureş, although about 50 per cent Hungarian in population, appears on a cursory glance entirely Romanian (although the civic theatre is divided among Hungarian and Romanian performances 50:50). Hungarians may not emigrate, but about 25,000 have fled as refugees to Hungary which does not now send them back. Saxons may leave, and a large proportion of young people in particular have left for West Germany, which is reported to pay emigration charges. Their applications to emigrate are, however, subject to long delays. The departure of émigrés can be a bonus for gypsies who take over vacated dwellings. Economically, Romania's minorities might be an asset resulting from different national aptitudes; this is exploited to a certain extent. Politically, the minorities weaken the state (as they are more willing or able to emigrate than Romanians); on the other hand the fragmentation strengthened the Ceauşescu government, as long as the different national groups did not combine forces against it. An alliance, at least temporary, between ethnic groups seems in fact to have been the essential basis for the overthrow of the Ceauşescu regime, which was triggered by moves by the **Securitate** against an ethnic Hungarian priest.

State structure. Romania consists of 40 counties plus **Bucharest** municipality, which are divided into about 3,900 communes (these latter forming part of the postal address). The counties (*judeţ*) are of approximately equal area but are rather different in population. As regards city size, while no other city rivals Bucharest, a number are around the 300,000 mark and several of these (**Braşov**, **Timişoara**, Cluj) contain substantial non-Romanian minorities.

Constitution. This is in flux; the previous constitution was approved in 1965. The "Grand National Assembly", elected every five years, was in theory the supreme body, but as in other Soviet bloc countries until reformed was a rubber-stamp body. It elected the Council of State, whose chairman since 1974 bore the title of President. The latest elections for the Grand National Assembly were held in March 1985. All candidates were nominees of the Socialist-Democratic Unity Front. Romania was a classic police state, with exit being controlled (the frontiers being studded by watchtowers and patrolled by border guards), the secret police (Securitate) spied on everyone, and there was a high level of secrecy. Since the overthrow of the Ceauşescu regime a more libertarian situation prevails but the total structure has not been determined.

History. Apart from a few months in 1600 Romania has existed within approximately its present frontiers only since 1918, though Romanians also trace ancestry from Dacia and from the Roman province of that name, about the start of our era. Except at these times, Romanian history is the history of the different territories of which Romania is made up, although the two principalities of Wallachia and Moldavia shared many characteristics and were eventually united (1859). Transylvania was for about 900 years under Hungarian rule, while almost all the rest remained under Turkish suzerainty between about 1400 (or later) and 1878; this territory was not, however, divided into *pashaliks* but was ruled indirectly, which differentiates Romanian experience from elsewhere in south-east Europe. Although indirect rule preserved local laws and a nobility it contributed towards making Romania a more corrupt country, a feature which can be traced today. During the Turkish-dominated period, Wallachia and Moldavia were in general treated the same, Transylvania rather less unfavourably. Ruling by native princes came to an end with the execution (1711) at Instanbul of the Wallachian prince

Constantin Brâncoveanu and his two sons and son-in law. Thereafter Wallachia and Moldavia were ruled by Phanariot Greeks appointed from Istanbul. The modern history of Romania begins with the merging of Wallachia and Moldavia (which was supported by Napoleon III), the coronation of King Carol I (a Hohenzollern) in 1866 and the gaining of independence by these principalities (1878), as a result of the Russo-Turkish war of 1877 in which Romanians took part. This was followed by a considerable growth of Bucharest. Romania reached her biggest territorial extension in 1918, thanks to her wartime participation and the simultaneous defeat of both Russia and Austria-Hungary.

Romania entered both world wars, in 1916 on the side of the Allies, in 1941 on the side of the Axis; in either case the course of events was not what her rulers anticipated (although large Romanian forces were involved and fought bravely); yet ultimately she emerged in each case on the winning side (though not in World War II gaining the status of an Allied belligerent), due mainly to others' victories and in 1944 (Aug. 23, now the national day) to a lightning switch to the winning side. However, both wars resulted in great destruction and heavy casualties, and as a result of the later one a Communist regime gained power and stayed in power until December 1989. Although during that time sharing most other typical features of Soviet bloc states such as absence of political democracy, censorship, secrecy, adherence to the **Warsaw Treaty Organization (Warsaw Pact)**, central planning, state or cooperative ownership of means of production, Romania to some extent (within limits) followed a more independent policy in foreign relations (see below).

Romania's constitutional history since 1859 has been largely royalist (1866 to 1947), partly a hardline (but nationalist) Communist regime. The country has shown no aptitude for parliamentary democracy, the fascist Iron Guard having been the Communists' rivals between the two world wars. Middle and working classes have not allied despite common adherence to the **Romanian Orthodox Church** (the largest Patriarchate apart from the Russian one), which for centuries was the chief repository of Romanian culture and nationalism. Peasant revolts have taken place, notably in 1514, 1774 and 1907, but never achieved success, being always brutally suppressed. Cruelty was also the trademark of Vlad the Impaler. Romanian history includes no female rulers or heroines, probably due to oriental (Turkish) influence. Temporally, as well as territorially, Romania's history is fragmented: little can be found to praise between the brief brilliance of Michael the Brave (1600) and Alexandru Ioan Cuza (1859). Yet the Romanian people view unification as a success, and can also celebrate some achievements in economics, science and sport.

Economy. Romania's economic development, like her constitutional history, has been handicapped by a late start, except in oil extraction and refining. Up to 1945 Romania was thought of primarily as an agrarian country and a food exporter. Both Nazi Germany and the Soviet Union (up to **Khrushchev**) saw the Romanian economy in that light. At least since **Gheoghiu-Dej** nationalism has been to the fore in official economic priorities and this has been expressed in strivings towards self-sufficiency in terms understood at that time, that is in the direction of emphasizing ferrous metallurgy, machine-building and other industry. Furthermore, the hardline Ceauşescu regime showed a preference for extremist policies, emphasizing growth in statistical terms and self-reliance at the expense of present satisfactions and to some extent even despite absence or shortage of basic necessities.

Under Ceauşescu the economy was planned, in the Stalinist way: there were one-year and five-year plans and a comprehensive system of ministries, including even a Ministry of Tourism. The intermediate body was called a *Central*. Similarly, the banking system was centralized. On the other hand, during the previous decade self-reliance had been promoted. Regions in effect traded what they had in surplus for what they were lacking. For instance, Transylvania exchanged natural gas for petrol.

Draft, revised and approved versions of five-year plan targets were published. The plan for 1986–90, for instance, approved the following percentage growth rates on average per annum: national income 9.9–10.6, net industrial production 13.3–14.2, gross agricultural production 6.1–6.7. It is highly probable that these targets are very over-optimistic. Planning irrationalities are obvious, notably the severe shortages of food and electricity or the completion outside Suceava (Moldavia) in 1986 of a huge ultra-modern ball-bearings factory which by June 1989, if not later, had still yielded no output.

The main factor in Romania's present economic difficulties nevertheless has not been inefficient planning but the priorities chosen by the Ceauşescu regime: to undertake gandiose projects, demolish and replace dwellings and other structures, and to repay foreign debts as quickly as possible, despite the resulting impact on living standards and in particular on food supplies. The fact that in recent years economic statistics appear to have become unreliable may have contributed towards this mistaken ordering, if sycophants failed to present the situation to the top leadership. In April 1989 Ceauşescu announced that all foreign debts had been repaid.

Agriculture. Romania is generally favoured for agricultural production, although the climate is continental with hot summers and cold winters. Rainfall is adequate, and Romania has much bigger water resources than Bulgaria, though drought can have adverse effects and the most fertile soils have low and unreliable rainfall. Arable comprises 42 per cent of Romania's territory. A good balance of plains, hills and mountains provides a range of microclimates.

As elsewhere in Eastern Europe, land is farmed partly by co-operatives, partly by state farms and partly by individual peasants. The shares farmed in these ways are respectively about 61 per cent, 30 per cent and 9 per cent; thus private land ownership (especially of hills, mountain tops, irregularly shaped plots and in general in broken ground) remains substantial. In more open ground there are large massifs of land belonging to state or co-operative farms and privately owned animals have to graze along the verges.

The range of crops grown is very wide, comprising grains (wheat especially in Wallachia, maize almost everywhere, oats, rice between northwards-flowing parallel channels of the Danube), industrial crops (hemp and sugar beet in the south-west, sunflower), vines (on southward-facing slopes of the Carpathians and in the Dobrogea), hops (mainly in Transylvania, where most breweries are), potatoes and vegetables, fruit, flowers (in hothouses), reeds (in the Danube delta). Home-made wine is made from elderflower. Since 1961–65 the potato yield has risen about threefold. Livestock (cattle, sheep, pigs) are numerous. Meat comes especially from private peasant production (possibly over 45 per cent of the total) whereas eggs and chickens come mainly from henhouses within the State Farm sector. Fish comes chiefly from the Danube delta. Since 1981, the harvests of maize and potatoes show a tendency to increase, but of wheat to remain static. Outputs of meat and milk show little tendency to rise but of hens' eggs and wool rather more.

Irrigation is on quite a big scale and is supported by appropriate equipment such as large-dimension sprinklers. Since 1974–76 the area of irrigated land has doubled. More surprisingly, given the favourable land-to-people ratio, the government has shown concern for reducing the areas taken up by villages. Major land amelioration schemes have been effected, for instance Sculeni-Gorban, completed in 1987, created over

200,000 hectares of ameliorated fields. Mechanization is uneven.

Over the past 40 years the labour force employed in agriculture has fallen from 75 per cent to under 30 per cent, a trend which is obviously relevant to village systematization. Still more relevant is the fact that the proportion *living in* the countryside has not declined proportionately, which appears to indicate that country-dwellers commute to work in towns, and yet this is not visibly taking place and indeed it seems to be precluded by transport limitations. A partial explanation may be that mainly younger and more able-bodied people commute while older people, especially women (grandparents etc.) remain behind to work on the co-operative farm or on a private plot. This, however, implies a fall in the quality of agricultural labour, and labour insufficiency in agriculture has been officially cited. On the other hand, those left behind may retain links to urban migrants and provide something to supplement their skimpy rations. Those lacking such support have a much harder time. However, the private sector has by no means been left to its own devices. In January 1984 compulsory deliveries of livestock products were introduced, while plots not cultivated to the best effect may be confiscated.

Mining. Romania's mineral resources include oil, coal and natural gas. Oil production (centred around Ploieşti and Piteşti) was in the past sufficient to allow Romania to export oil but the country is now a net importer. Natural gas output is declining due to exhaustion of reserves which may be entirely gone by 1995 unless extraction is restricted (as the 1990–95 plan envisages). Hard coal is mined, but is less than one fifth of the total output; the rest is lignite and brown coal of much lower calorie content. Other minerals include small quantities of iron ore, bauxite, copper, lead and zinc as well as gold, silver and uranium.

Labour force. The economically active population comprises about 10.5 million people (1985: 10,568,000) or 46 per cent of the population, which is about normal in the Balkans (Bulgaria too has 46 per cent). Unemployment is not officially recognized; usually where this happens there is extensive underemployment, which is probably the case mainly in the countryside. Phenomena of overemployment (the temporary or partial participation of schoolchildren, soldiers or prisoners — building by whom is popularly reckoned to be of the highest quality) are also visible. About 72 per cent of economically active persons work in the state sector. Including also the co-operative and private sectors, about 29 per cent work in agriculture and 37 per cent in industry, which signifies proportionately fewer employed in other sectors in Romania than in Bulgaria. The proportions employed in building, transport and communications, and trade have recently been tending to fall. During the 1980s the growth of total employment has slowed down.

Living standards and national income. Romanian currency is the leu (plural lei). The national income (net material product by Western definitions) was officially given as 772 billon in 1986 in current prices and as 794.7 billion in 1988; retail sales as 308 billion in 1988; and the average net remuneration of working people (monthly) in 1988 as 2,946–3,135 (the latter being for end-1988). Whatever official statistics state, suppressed inflation is clearly present and the leu commands in practice, relative to foreign currencies, nothing like its official value. Black market exchange rates go up to seven times the official rate. The leu is in practice devalued by non-availability or shortages of goods. Living standards in Romania are currently among the lowest in Europe: possibly on average they are lower in Albania where, however, egalitarianism is more marked which is an offsetting factor. The official ratio in Romania between highest and lowest incomes is 4.5 to 1.

Foreign trade. Romania is a full member of the **Council for Mutual Economic Assistance (CMEA)**, since 1972 of the International Monetary Fund, and also of the World Bank and GATT. This gives her an unusually wide footing in both Eastern and Western economic institutions. (Bulgaria, for example, is not a member of GATT, though she has applied to join.) Romania's trade is correspondingly more diversified as regards countries than that of Bulgaria. In 1985, 39.3 per cent of her exports went to "socialist" countries while 47.7 per cent of her exports came from them. Trade with the USSR comprises less than 20 per cent of her total trade whereas the Bulgarian proportion exceeds 55 per cent. After the USSR, Poland and East Germany are her biggest trading partners in the Eastern bloc, while Italy, the United States, West Germany and France are important Western partners. Britain rates somewhat lower. Among Third World countries, both Iran and Iraq are important. Unlike other Soviet bloc countries, Romania co-operates economically and technically with Israel. Session XI of the two countries' joint commission was held in November 1988.

Among commodity groups, Romania exports especially machinery and equipment, secondly fuels, minerals and metals, and thirdly industrial consumer goods, while she imports primarily fuels, minerals and metals and secondly machinery and equipment.

Joint ventures with Western firms have been allowed since 1971; the Western share must not exceed 49 per cent. The legislation is rather restrictive and not many ventures have been started, though some collaborations, for example with Citroen to produce the Oltcit car, are important.

Since 1981, Romania has followed a unique trade policy of seeking to repay her foreign debt as quickly as possible. At the end of 1981 this was at a peak level of $10.2 billion. By end-1986 this had been reduced to $6.4 billion and on April 12, 1989, President Ceauşescu announced that the debt had been entirely repaid. This has been achieved through a positive balance approaching, and occasionally exceeding, an annual figure of $2 billion. This extremely high rate of repayment has been the central fact in the Romanian economic situation through out the 1980s. It has been achieved predominantly by cutting imports while maintaining a high rate of exports. At the same time, foreign exchange and gold reserves have been run down. The fact that exports have been kept up, but imports not, has explained the discrepancy between what can be seen in the fields and what is — or rather, is not — in the shops. According to IMF statistics, in 1980–85 Romania was a net importer of foodstuffs and agricultural raw materials but a net exporter in all the other years, on average to the tune of about $250 million yearly. Between 1981 and 1984, imports of these commodities were almost halved. However, cuts in imports did not affect foodstuffs alone. Modernization too has been neglected, which must impair Romania's competitiveness during the 1990s and beyond. The same result would follow from Romania's loss of MFN status *vis-à-vis* the United States and from her relegation to less favourable status by the EC countries as well.

However, in consequence of debt repayment Romania can expect to have available annually about the sum previously earned as surplus. This might be used to save on exports, to expand imports, or some combination of these two. During the final months of the Ceauşescu regime it seemed probable that some alleviation of day-to-day supplies would be allowed to occur, but that continuation of large unfinished prestige projects, including the rebuilding of central Bucharest, would go on swallowing up large sums. The new government in fact immediately released supplies for the shops and probably will either halt or greatly scale down prestige construction.

Foreign relations and foreign policy. Bordering entirely on Communist countries and on the Black Sea, decisively weaker in strength than one of these (the USSR) and unable for economic reasons to spend much on defence, Romania has appeared at first sight to have little capacity to conduct an independent foreign policy. However, Romania is too big for her subjugation to be viewed as a minor adventure. Any incursion from outside would evoke a strong nationalism, while the weakness of her armed forces is in some degree compensated by physical barriers — the Carpathians and the Danube—which also restrict the usefulness of occupying Romania, from the angle of accomplishing any further military advance. Not being bordered by any NATO country, Romania (unlike Czechoslovakia) offers no corridor of access from the West. This combination of strength, weakness and strategic unimportance has brought the result that Romania has been enabled to pursue a more independent policy in foreign relations than any other country in the Soviet bloc. She did not take part in the invasion of Czechoslovakia (indeed she appeared to be herself threatened), maintained relations with China when these had been broken off by the Soviet Union, kept up relations with Israel, and took part in the 1984 Olympic Games, unlike any of the other Soviet bloc countries. Only in Romania were large-scale demonstrations seen in favour of nuclear disarmament although these were, of course, officially sanctioned.

During the period of the **Brezhnev** government the Romanians made it clear that they did not agree that Warsaw Treaty Organization (Warsaw Pact) defence expenditure needed to be further increased. As regards international economic relations, Romania rejected Soviet suggestions that she should not build up her heavy industry and ensured that no planning organ covering the whole Eastern bloc was set up. On the other hand, she did not transgress certain limits. Within Romania, party control and censorship stayed in force. Romania has not withdrawn from the Warsaw Pact; though objecting, she ultimately agreed to its renewal for a further period of 20 years (though the President's brother stated in 1989 that he did not believe the USSR would defend any other Pact country against capitalist attack). Much the same propagandist shibboleths continued to be proclaimed in Romania as, until not long before, in other Soviet bloc countries. No irredentist claim was made concerning Bessarabia though most Romanians consider it to be in the USSR unjustly. The immobility of frontiers in Eastern Europe is at this point disadvantageous to Romania, but it is advantageous in that she (not Hungary) possesses Transylvania. Thus by standing pat Romania defended her interests within the prevailing correlation of forces.

This at least was how matters stood until the advent of **Gorbachev** and the fundamental, if non-violent, reforms which have since taken place almost throughout Eastern Europe. However, these changes affect the situation profoundly. That the Soviet Union should start to adopt more liberal policies than other countries within the bloc was fundamentally unsettling to them. This was never the case before, and the reversal of roles has been startling to all of them, but Romania has not adapted to the situation. The role that Ceauşescu previously envisaged, of Romania as an intermediary between East and West, proved now irrelevant. Romania's show of relative independene was no longer needed by the West, while Gorbachev observed with growing irritation policies which conflicted with his own. In turn Ceauşescu, rejecting both *glasnost'* and *perestroika*, moved from a position of disagreement, yet ultimate compliance, with Soviet policies to one of direct confrontation.

Armed forces. Romania belongs to the Warsaw Treaty Organization (Warsaw Pact), but since 1958 there have been no Soviet forces in Romania, whose participation in Pact manoeuvres has been only at staff level. The armed forces comprise about 250,000 men, including 17,000 border guards and security troops numbering about 20,000 who are better equipped and trained than the army, and some 12,000 patriotic guards (the last having been a party-directed force). Under Ceauşescu, and presumably in future if this category is retained, the security troops were volunteers, the bodyguard of the former President being reputedly composed of orphans brought up in his service. The larger part of the army consists of conscripts who would work part-time on building projects, agriculture etc. The conscription period is two years for army and air force, two-and-a-half years for the navy. Total defence spending is apparently not large.

The navy, which includes even frigates, has bought Chinese gunboats, whereas the army and air force have mainly Soviet-made equipment. Much of the equipment in any case is obsolescent. A nominally civil air lifting capacity is positioned at Bucharest airport (Otopeni), which is defended by anti-aircraft guns. The deployment of land and security forces under Ceauşescu showed that internal order was envisaged more than frontier defence (although some projects connected with water may have had a subsidiary defensive purpose). Bucharest and Constanţa were strongly garrisoned, and there was an army base at Braşov. Helicopters were stationed near the centre of the country, probably for intervention across a wide radius. The principal base for

gunboats on the Danube River is Tulcea while Giurgiu is a subsidiary base.

Village systematization. This was the intention, stated by President Ceauşescu, to demolish up to 8,000 of Romania's 13,000 villages and to resettle their populations in towns which would be appropriately developed and called "agro-industrial centres". Although systematization had been mooted before, interest in it was intensified after the appointment in 1965 of the new party leader. The scheme was outlined more definitely in March 1988. The "agro-industrial centres" would include both industrial plants and social amenities. People would be housed in three- and four-storey blocks of flats. Unusually for Romania, this programme has been given widespread publicity in the West, and has evoked protests from a number of governments and from certain prominent figures. It has aroused particular hostility in Hungary where it is seen as a threat to the Hungarian villages and therefore to their national culture. This Hungarian approach, expressed in print and on television, undoubtedly coloured Western impressions.

Very few travellers in Romania have seen any actual evidence that the process has been carried out. Where it has been, this has been in predominantly Romanian areas near to Bucharest. The scheme seems to be going ahead at a very slow pace. By a law approved on April 18, 1989, 28 villages were redesignated as towns. Almost all of these apparently could claim both industrial and agricultural potential, and had been improved through economic and cultural development.

The motives for the scheme seem to have been ideological, political and economic. It is a Marxist aim to reduce differences between town and country. In Romania — as elsewhere in southeastern Europe—another official aim is to reduce or eliminate minority differences. The emphasis on use of the Romanian language is an example. To blur specifically Hungarian village features (for example) would probably be welcomed. Even now, these ethnographic features receive no emphasis in tourism. Potentially not less sinister, elimination or contraction of private plots makes people more dependent on official sources of supply and consequently reduces their independence *vis-à-vis* the state. Moreover, flat-dwellers are probably more readily supervised by the **Securitate** (security police) than are inhabitants of scatered cottages.

There were also economic motives. Official statements pointed out that to bring modern facilities to great numbers of villages, many of which are also widely spread out, would be irrational and extremely expensive. Such facilities can be more easily and cheaply provided for more concentrated settlements. The desire was also expressed to enlarge the area of cultivated land through curtailment of the areas occupied by villages. Romania today experiences a problem of transportation, in particular of commuting. This problem might be eased if more people lived closer to their work, as could be achieved in the agro-industrial centres.

On the other hand, to demolish vast number of villages and to rebuild accordingly would be hugely expensive and probably aesthetically damaging (though the assumption apparently made by some, that *all* Romanian villages are worth preserving for aesthetic reasons, is scarcely true). Romania civilization has prevalently been one of villages; to destroy them, thus means destroying characteristically Romanian things, of which prototypes are preserved in the Village Museum in Bucharest. The attachment of individuals to their native localities is obviously assigned minimal weight in official thinking, but some local resistance to systematization has been reported.

Given the many obstacles — economic, social and international — to implementing the scheme on any large scale, such implementation even under Ceauşescu was probably unlikely. The post-Ceauşescu government has announced that the scheme has been abandoned. A parallel may be drawn with the rather similar *agrogorod* scheme proposed for the USSR by Khrushchev in 1957, which was never put into effect.

Overthrow of the Ceauşescu regime. During the final months of 1989 the Ceauşescu regime entered a terminal stage. Although the country's foreign debts were stated to have been extinguished no improvement in living standards was visible, and the onset of winter without any significant alleviation of the heating situation created forebodings. Visitors' reports spoke of increasing readiness to criticize the country' ruler. Weatern media reports became uniformly hostile. The crumbling of the Soviet bloc in Hungary, East Germany and Czechoslovakia one after another evoked expectations that Romania would not stand aside from the same process. On the other hand, the iron grip of the Ceauşescus in conjunction with Romania's historical differences, in particular the absence of any tradition of successful popular revolt and the lack of solidarity among the different classes and nationalities, suggested that some time would elapse before Romania followed suit. The President seemed not to anticipate fatal trouble as he visited Iran on Dec. 18–20.

It was therefore with expectation not unmixed with surprise that the world learned that at Timişoara an operation to arrest a dissident ethnic Hungarian priest, László Tökés, had triggered off an uprising against the regime itself. A massacre of protesters by the Securitate took place on Dec. 17 in front of the city's opera house. Presumably Ceauşescu himself had given the order to fire; if so, he — as indeed had been forecast — did not lose his nerve, being determined to hold on to power to the last. Though over 100 people were killed in Timişoara (this number being vastly magnified in contemporary Western reports) the action boomeranged against the regime since the Romanian army in this neighbourhood took the side of the uprising. However Timişoara, though an important city, could not by itself overthrow the government; everything depended on whether the revolt would spread. The President, who theoretically should have been the best informed person in the country, proved to have fatally overestimated his own popularity. A rally on Dec. 21 of those he believed to be his supporters in front of the headquarters of the **Romanian Communist Party (PCR)** in Bucharest suddenly escaped from control as some of those present demanded to be told what had happened in Timişoara; Ceauşescu, annoyed, broke off his address and television coverage was immediately cut. Security forces tried but failed to disperse the crowd using tear gas. Earlier, Brigadier-Gen. Vasile Milea, the Defence Minister, had refused to give the order to fire on the crowd and was either himself shot or forced to commit suicide. The crowd then stormed into the building, and the President with Elena **Ceauşescu** and Emil **Bobu** found themselves obliged to flee by helicopter from the building's rooftop.

It is unclear what their intended final destination was — presumably somewhere abroad. The group transferred to a car which soon fell into the hands of their enemies. At Trigovişte the President and his wife were put on trial. The trial was held in secret and only an edited version of what happened has been released. As far as can be judged, the Ceauşescus remained defiant to the end, with the President refusing to answer questions except from the Grand National Assembly. The pair were sentenced to death, and expressed a wish to die together; the sentences were carried out on Dec. 25 1989. The **National Salvation Front** had now supplanted the Ceauşescu government. To justify the precipitate and secretive procedure and immediate execution, the Fromt pointed out that the conflict was still raging, and that the Ceauşescus would have become the focus for a rescue attempt; it was therefore necessary to decapitate the regime without delay.

The subsequent course of events can be understood as showing that this was indeed necessary. The Securitate fought desperately for a week against the Romanian army, which had now gone over wholly to the new regime. Fewer in number than the army, the Securitate proved to be better armed and individually determined. Moreover, they knew the layout of an underground labyrinth of tunnels which the army did not. The struggle centred round the television station (from which the success of the overthrow had been announced) and the international airport at Otopeni, as well as in the centre of Bucharest. While the numbers of casualties continued to be exaggerated in contemporary reports, some hundreds of people were killed in these battles. Major damage resulted in the capital's centre and some damage elsewhere.

Other important scenes of regional conflict were Sibiu, where Nicu Ceauşescu was party boss, and Braşov. Bucharest airport reopened on Dec. 27. The following day was fixed as the deadline for Securitate members to surrender, but passed with little result. However, on Jan. 3 the army claimed to be in full control.

Popular reactions comprised a mixture of jubilation at the Ceauşescus' overthrow and grief that so many people had died to bring that about. The extent to which the uprising was spontaneous remains, however, not completely clear. For at least two years rumours had circulated in Romania that the USSR intended to take a hand in choosing Ceauşescu's successor, and Gorbachev's refusal to intervene in his favour and call to other socialist countries to support the "Romanian people" may have been pre-arranged. At any rate, the National Salvation Front quickly assumed power, although being inexperienced in exercising it they showed some vacillation as to what to do next. This did not jeopardize the success of the uprising because support for their former regime outside the Securitate proved to be minimal.

Ion **Illiescu** was announced to be President, and Dumitru Mazilu Vice President (the latter, however, was subsequently dismissed); Petre Roman Prime Minister; General Nicolae Militaru as Defence Minister. The new government announced a number of measures, which included: abolition of the death penalty; reduction of the working week to five days; lifting of the ban on contraception; the use of "Comrade" in official speeches and publications would be discontinued; removal of the red star and other Communist symbols, and dropping of "Socialist" from the country's title; abolition of the State Planning Committee; an end to village systematization. It was stated that Romania would maintain all its alliances, and particularly its loyalty to the Warsaw Pact. Romania would, however, seek full diplomatic relations with the EC. It was announced that national elections would be held; at first April 1990 was named, later these were scheduled for May 1990. Among the political parties which began to reconstitute themselves following decades when they had been illegal were: the National Christian Peasant Party; the Liberal Party; the Group of Social Dialogue; the Democratic Party; and the Democratic Union of Hungarians in Romania. Student and environmental groups also emerged. The voices of protesters against the Ceauşescu regime, such as Silviu **Brucan** and Doina **Cornea**, were heard now more clearly.

Reports from outside Bucharest are fragmentary, but tempering to the wind was apparent in the reactions to Ceauşescu's overthrow in some outlying authorities. One Communist council on hearing the news is reported to have immediately voted itself out of office, then back into office three hours later as non-Communists. At Baia Mare (Maramureş) the former managers, party chiefs etc. put on tricolour armbands but local workers insisted on vetting and only two out of 45 kept their positions.

Other members of the Ceauşescu family, including Nicu, had been arrested. Trials started of Securitate men and former Politburo members, who were charged with genocide and invariably convicted, and sentenced to long terms or to life imprisonment.

In January 1990 the number killed, which had reportedly been as high as 60,000, was reduced to a maximum of 10,000 and it was claimed that 50,000 people were executed during Ceauşescu's rule. Later, the number killed in the uprising was officially stated to have been 689, just over 1 per cent of the maximum figure at one time claimed. Nevertheless, the loss of life in Romania contrasted with the bloodless retreat from Communist power elsewhere in Eastern Europe.

Representatives of the Western powers began to converge on Bucharest, including the French prime minister and the German foreign minister. Demostrations by crowds in front of the headquarters of the National Salvation Front continued; the demands included replacement of officials regarded as compromised by their association with the Ceauşescu regime and work to enable to be more self-supporting. Student demonstrations called for sacking of old guard personnel. The volatile situation, in which mobs realized their power while the new government was inexperienced in maintaining a particular line of conduct, resulted in disorder and U-turns.

Although much about Romania's political future remains unsettled, its citizens had gained more liberty and Romania, in turning away from Communism, had rejoined the mainstream of evolution in Eastern Europe.

RH

ROMANIAN COMMUNIST PARTY (PCR— Partidul Comunist Roman).

The PCR was founded in 1921, but was banned in April 1924 and then operated underground; party congresses were held abroad. The party had some successes in organizing strikes but its competitor, the fascist Iron Guard gained more support. During wartime its members were imprisoned; there was no resistance such as in Yugoslavia. The PCR supported the coup on Aug. 23, 1944 but was not one of its main organizers. It then joined in successive electoral alliances, first of all in a National Democratic bloc and later in a People's Democratic Front. In November 1946 the PCR obtained 73 seats in the National Assembly out of a total of 414. The PCR merged with the Social Democratic Party early in 1948 to form the Romanian Workers' Party. Gheorghe **Gheorghiu-Dej** became the first secretary of this in 1955. After his death in 1965, Nicolae **Ceauşescu** was elected its first secretary and, in July 1965, its general secretary; the same congress changed the name back to the PCR. In 1968 the party denounced the Gheorghiu-Dej regime, and in the same year it condemned the Soviet military intervention in Czechoslovakia. At a congress in November 1979 and a conference in December 1982 the PCR endorsed programmes to update the country's economic structure and to intensify economic development. The party's 13th Congress in November 1984 endorsed guidelines for development between 1986 and 1990 and its long-term development up to 2000. These complacent programmes were interrupted by the severe energy crisis of 1984–85, which since then has been only marginally alleviated. In 1986 foreign trade fell, contrary to expectation. Following riots at **Braşov** in November 1987 an extraordinary conference in December 1987 criticized violations of party rules etc., but insisted on repayment of foreign debts as speedily as possible. The PCR's latest (14th) Congress was held in November 1989 and re-elected Nicolae Ceauşescu as its general secretary for a further five years.

In 1983 the PCR had 3,370,043 members; in Dec. 1986, 3,639,344; as announced on Nov. 20, 1989, 3,831,000. Relative to their population numbers Romanians were slightly over-represented, Hungarians slightly under-represented, Saxons substantially under-represented. The Party had representation in almost all organizations and most territorial units: in 1989 it had 59,554 basic organizations, 6,603 party committees in enterprises, institutions and agricultural units etc. The total membership amounted to about one in six of the entire population, a most unusually high ratio in Communist states (one in 20 being more normal). It was unclear at the time whether this very high ratio indicated genuinely higher support than elsewhere or simply enhanced opportunism.

The truth became clear at the time of the overthrow of the Ceauşescu regime: the vast majority of members belonged because this was obligatory for their careers; the party's role was not to lead, but chiefly to applaud and to obey. Conviction of any verities of **Marxism-Leninism** seemed nowhere to be found. No doubt, the semblance of things at this time was not completely truthful, much more than it had been before. At the start of 1990 the complaint was being strongly voiced that the members of the interim government included too many former Communists; the problem is that virtually everyone of any distinction was in fact a party member. Objectively, it can be said that the party as such played no role in the uprising, either in favour of the regime or against it: major actors in the scene were citizens, students, workers, dissidents, the **National Salvation Front**, the Army and the **Securitate**. The party seemed to dissolve spontaneously. In response to pressure from demonstrators, the new President announced its abolition; this was quickly rescinded as not being democratic, but the party's "enormous wealth" was to be appropriated by the state. Because of its identification with the Ceauşescu regime, the Romanian Communist Party will evidently not play any active role in the near future; whether it may do so later cannot be foreseen, but appeared in early 1990 to be unlikely.

RH

ROMANIAN ORTHODOX CHURCH.

The Romanian Orthodox Church is the principal church in Romania, with 17 million baptized members, 9,000 priests and 11,000 churches. Since the Communists came to power the Church has been under firm political control. In the 1970s and 1980s, the hierarchy were forced to give full support to Nicolae **Ceauşescu**'s personality cult. In comparison with other religions, such as the Uniates, who were banned, the Catholics and the Protestants, the Orthodox Church had a privileged position (*see* **Religion and Communism**).

Both Ceauşescu's parents received grandiose Orthodox funerals, broadcast on television. At the same time the totalitarian regime campaigned against religion, razing historic churches in the city centres and forcing the clerics to give such measures their support. The Romanian Patriarch Justin (Moişescu) was succeeded in 1986 by Teoctist (Arapasu). In March 1989 the Holy Synod thanked the "deeply respected" Ceauşescu for "the unending rise in the people's material and intellectual living standards", and called him "the greatest and most brilliant hero" in struggle for "the victory of mankind's ideals of freedom and progress".

Dissent from the pro-government position of the Church among priests and laity developed from about 1977. Indeed the all-pervasive presence of the **Securitate** police meant that it was difficult for any opposition to Ceauşescu to develop anywhere else. The Lord's Army, a ginger group within the Church founded back in 1923, re-emerged as a focus of rank-and-file opposition.

After the fall of Ceauşescu in December 1989, the hierarchy denounced the former leader, expressed support for the **National Salvation Front** and held a celebratory mass in Bucharest Cathedral. It appeared that the Patriarchate might find it hard to establish its credibility in the post-Ceauşescu Romania.

PJSD

ROUND TABLE (GDR—Runder Tisch). The Round Table discussions which took place in the GDR on an irregular but increasingly frequent basis from Dec. 7, 1989 were the forum for the elaboration of the political future of the GDR. For the first time on a formal basis the government of the GDR was exposed to opposition criticism and proposals.

The Round Table was in fact rectangular, chaired at one end by church representatives and addressed by government spokespersons. At the end of January 1990 the 39 participants were as follows: the **Liberal Democratic Party of Germany (LPDP)** (3); the **National Democratic Party of Germany (NDPD)** (3); the **Democratic Peasants' Party of Germany (DBD)** (3); the **Christian Democratic Union of Germany (CDU)** (3); the Association of Mutual Peasant Aid (*Vereinigung der gegenseitigen Bauernhilfe*) (2); the Sorbian Round Table (1); the **SED-PDS** (3); **Democratic Departure (DA)** (2); the Independent Women's Association (*Unabhängiger Frauenverband*) (2); the Green Party (*Grüne Partei*) (2); Initiative for Peace and Human Rights (*Initiative Frieden und Menschenrechte*) (2); the Green League (*Grüne Liga*) (2); **New Forum (NF)** (3); Democracy Now (*Demokratie Jetzt*) (2); the **Social Democratic Party of Germany (SPD)** (2); the United Left (*Vereinigte Linke*) (2); and the **Free German Trade Union League (FDGB)** (2). Other organizations were permitted observer status.

Meeting first in the Dietrich-Bonhoeffer-Haus and later in the conference building in the grounds of Schloss Niederschönhausen in East Berlin, the Round Table had no official parliamentary or governmental function. Its plenary sessions and its numerous working parties soon, however, became crucial in the direction of GDR policy. The sessions were earnest and purposeful, but had many chaotic, angry moments. On occasions the **Modrow** government had to back down on policy (on the **Stasi**, for instance), and by February 1990 several of the new groups represented at the Round Table joined the governmental coalition. As the elections of March 18, 1990 approached, competition between the parties increased and the Round Table was closed down.

JO

ROUND-TABLE AGREEMENT (POLAND). The idea of round-table talks that gave rise to the agreement emerged after a wave of industrial unrest and strikes in Poland in August 1988, when **Solidarity** chairman Lech **Wałęsa** negotiated with Communist leaders (for the first time since 1981) and agreed to organize the talks as a condition for quelling the strikes. They were to examine questions of trade-union pluralism, the legal recognition of Solidarity and a range of social, economic and political issues. Originally announced for mid-October, the talks were repeatedly postponed. Objections were raised by the authorities to the inclusion of opposition figures like Jacek Kuroń and Adam Michnik, while it proved necessary also to secure major changes in policy and leadership of the **Polish United Workers' Party (PUWP)**. The round-table meeting finally opened in early February 1989 with numerous representatives of the authorities and opposition groups discussing in a range of specialist and plenary meetings.

An initial agreement on issues of political reform was reached on March 9 and, while by no means all outstanding issues were settled, a comprehensive agreement was signed on April 5. This provided for the relegalization of Solidarity and a number of political reforms. Thirty-five per cent of seats in the next *Sejm* were to be reserved for opposition candidates and they would be able to compete for these in elections to be held in the immediate future. A new Senate was to be established and in which all seats would be open to electoral competition, and a new presidency with extensive powers would be established the incumbent of which would be elected by a joint meeting of *Sejm* and Senate.

PGL

RUSSIAN ORTHODOX CHURCH. The Russian Orthodox Church was the established church in Tsarist Russia and remains the principal denomination of the Russian people. Orthodoxy is the largest denomination among the Ukrainians and Belorussians also, and has adherents among many other nationalities of the USSR. At present the Moscow Patriarchate of the Russian Orthodox Church holds jurisdiction throughout the Soviet Union, except in Georgia where the **Georgian Orthodox Church** has autocephaly. The Russian Orthodox Church claimed 50,000,000 adherents in the late 1980s.

In 1917, the Bolsheviks were especially hostile to the Orthodox Church because of its previous subordination to the Tsarist state (*see* **Religion and Communism**). After much persecution and pressure, the Patriarchal *locum tenens* Metropolitan Sergii (Stragorodsky) issued a declaration of loyalty to the Soviet state in 1927. This led to the splitting away of the "True Orthodox Church", who rejected Sergii's declaration and maintained an underground existence. The official Church itself suffered intense persecution during the 1930s, but during the **Great Fatherland War**, **Stalin** turned to it for support against the Nazis. In 1943 Stalin met Sergii and soon afterwards the latter was made Moscow Patriarch. Thousands of churches were re-opened. After Sergii's death in 1944, he was succeeded as Patriarch by Aleksii (Simansky), from 1945 to 1970, who in turn was followed by Pimen (Izvekov) in 1971.

Throughout this time, the Church hierarchy remained subject to the control of the state, exerted primarily through the Council for Religious Affairs. This body had control over appointments within the Church, and over the life of all its parts, from the hierarchy to the parishes. In public and international forums, the hierarchy defended all aspects of official Soviet policy and denied that there was any persecution of the faith in the USSR. Leading clergy played a particularly important part in promoting Soviet foreign policy within ecumenical bodies such as the World Council of Churches, especially where peace and disarmament initiatives were concerned. It played a particular role in helping to consolidate the Soviet position in Eastern Europe after World War II, by developing links with Orthodox sister churches there. Although the Russian Orthodox Church is in communion with the Ecumenical Patriarch of Constantinople and the other Ortho-

dox patriarchs, it does not recognize the primacy of Constantinople, and has tried to build for itself a "leading role" among the Orthodox Churches of Eastern Europe.

Internally, the Church was conscripted by Stalin to play its part in his nationality policy. In 1946, following the annexation of the Western Ukraine by the USSR, the **Ukrainian Catholic (Uniate) Church**, which was seen as a bulwark of Ukrainian nationalism, was forced into the Russian Orthodox Church. At the same time, the Orthodox Church was given especially favourable conditions to work in the Ukraine. In the 1970s, there were serious concerns among official party circles about demographic changes in the USSR, favouring the Muslims at the expense of the Slavs (*see* **Nationality Question in the USSR**). Some ideologists emphasized the common historical roots of the Russians, Ukrainians and Belorussians, in an attempt to consolidate an East Slav bloc around which the Soviet Union could be cemented. The Church and its intellectual sympathizers argued that orthodoxy was a factor helping to integrate Soviet society. In 1988, Metropolitan Vladimir of Rostov and Novocherkassk, the Chancellor of the Patriarchate, stated that 6,893 parishes were functioning. Of these over 4,000 were reportedly in the Ukraine. The growing demands articulated under **Gorbachev** in the Ukraine for the restoration of the Uniate Church, and for the re-establishment of the **Ukrainian Autocephalous Orthodox Church**, are therefore most unwelcome to the Patriarchate, which would lose over half its parishes.

The Patriarchate produces a monthly *Journal of the Moscow Patriarchate* and twice-yearly theological collection *Bogoslovskie trudy*. These publications, with a circulation of 25,000 and 3,000 respectively, are virtually inaccessible to the ordinary Soviet believer, as indeed is religious literature in general. In these words, the ideologists of the Patriarchate have emphasized the contribution to Russian history and culture made by the Orthodox Church, especially when it helped to preserve Russian consciousness during the Tatar yoke. They highlight the loyalty of the Church to the Soviet state, especially its wartime role.

This loyalty has been seen by dissidents within the Church as subservience to an atheist state. From 1965, a parish priest, Fr Gleb Yakunin, participated in appeals to the Patriarchate to stand up to official persecution of believers and the closure of churches. He appealed for world pressure on the Soviet government to grant religious freedom. In 1976 he established the Christian Committee for the Defence of Believers' Rights in the USSR.

This was composed of Orthodox clergy and laity and it monitored the abuse of the rights of members of all religions in the Soviet Union. In the 1970s a flourishing Orthodox *samizdat* literature developed. Perhaps the most influential of these publications was the Russian nationalist journal *Veche* (1971–74), founded by Vladimir Osipov. Fr Dimitry Dudko attracted many young people to his Moscow church for his question-and-answer sessions. Unofficial Orthodox circles and societies appeared in Moscow and Leningrad in the mid-1970s, involving young intellectuals. In the late 1970s and early 1980s, the KGB cracked down on this activity, sending the main participants to labour camps.

There was a growing intellectual curiosity about, and attraction to, orthodoxy, which in the 1970s was reflected in films (e.g. those of Andrei Tarkovky), art (Ilya Glazunov), and officially-published literature (the village prose school). This was linked with the growing national consciousness and nationalism of the Russian, itself a response to the growth of nationalism in the republics and among the Jews. The introduction of *glasnost'* into the media allowed these religious and nationalist strivings to be carried further. Not only creative writers but respected philologists such as Academicians Dmitri Likhachev and Sergei Averintsev were allowed to express their appreciation of Orthodoxy.

The development of *glasnost'* both coincided with, and was itself promoted by, the commemoration of the millennium of Russian Orthodoxy in June 1988. Already in 1983, under **Andropov**, the Monastery of St Daniil in Moscow had been handed back to the Patriarchate, so that its headquarters could return (from Zagorsk) to the capital in time for the millennium. The logic of *perestroika* was to make legal concessions to all denominations and believers. During 1987 most of those imprisoned for religious and political reasons were released from the camps. In April 1988 Gorbachev bestowed a particular favour on the Orthodox Church by meeting Patriarch Pimen and other senior hierarchs. He promised a new law on freedom of conscience, praised the patriotism of believers and urged them to support *perestroika*. To the horror of party conservatives, the Communist struggle against religion was effectively abandoned at the highest level.

The Soviet media, and particularly the radical pro-*perestroika* wing, gave substantial coverage to the millennium. Articles criticized the negative treatment given to believers in the past. The event was made international, with senior representatives of foreign churches invited and with the presence of the world Press. Soviet television had broadcast the Orthodox Easter service in 1988, and although the attention it gave to the Church diminished after the millennium celebrations, in 1989 it broadcast further services and sermons. In January 1990, for the first time, it broadcast an Orthodox service on Christmas Day.

In other respects, the situation of the Church also improved. Churches which had been confiscated were returned to the believers or built anew (totalling 2,000 in 1988 alone, it was claimed). The monasteries at Optina Pustyn and the Kiev-Pechera Lavra were handed back to the Church. More Bibles were produced, new seminaries were opened and the number of priests accepted for training was increased, with the permission of the government. The ban on the charitable functions of the churches was lifted; here the authorities hoped to use the dedication of the believers to perform social work, such as assisting in hospitals.

In general, the Orthodox Church took a higher political profile. It was represented on the USSR Cultural Foundation, the Lenin Children's Fund, the Peace Fund and various other cultural organizations, including some of a Russian nationalist tendency. In 1989 four members of the Orthodox clergy were elected to the Congress of People's Deputies. In that forum, they were able to call for a re-assessment of the role of religion as well as for the opening of new churches. With the new political tolerance, independent Orthodox thinkers became active in informal associations. In 1989 Osipov formed the Christian Patriotic Union; the same year Aleksandr Ogorodnikov, a founder of the Moscow Christian Seminar in 1974, helped to found the Christian Democratic Union of Russia, which was accepted as a member of the international organization of Christian Democratic parties.

The main problem facing the Russian Orthodox Church as it entered the 1990s was that it was still headed by a Brezhnevite leadership, who were accustomed to state control and who were ill-prepared for the political struggle for religious freedom which *perestroika* made possible. Already at the Local Council of the Russian Church, held during the millennium celebrations, there were signs of unrest among the clergy and the laity. A new statute was adopted, making the leadership more responsive to the believers. In April 1989 the Holy Synod established a commission to investigate the repression of Orthodox Church members "in Soviet times".

The new political environment permitted a form of spiritual revival in the Russian Orthodox Church, sometimes linked with Russian nationalism. If the Church leadership passed into the hands of people committed to establishing their independence of the state, its influence might considerably increase over time, with unpre-dictable consequences. A further problem was that there seemed to be a growing contradiction between the Church's theoretical role as the national church of the Russian people and its actual imperial role as the church of Russians, Ukrainians, Belorussians and other nationalities of the USSR.

PJSD

RUSSIAN REPUBLIC (RSFSR). By far the largest of the USSR's 15 republics, the Russian Republic occupies 17,075,000 sq km (about 76 per cent of the country's total area) stretching from the Far North to the Black Sea in the south and from Kalingrad in the west to Vladivistok in the Far East. Its 1989 census population was 147,386,000, 51.4 per cent of that of the USSR as a whole; its capital, as well as that of the USSR as a whole, is **Moscow**. Some 82 per cent of the republic's population is Russian, and there are significant numbers of at least 38 other national groups. The Russian Republic has enormous min-eral resources, including iron ore, timber, coal and oil as well as gold, platinum, zinc and other metals. It produces about 70 per cent of the total agricultural and industrial production of the USSR. Constituted as such in 1917 following the October revolution, the RSFSR joined with three other republics in 1922 to establish the USSR. In 1990 the RSFSR contained 16 autonomous republics, subordinate to it in authority, as well as five autonomous regions, 10 autonomous areas, 55 territories and regions and 1,034 districts.

SLW

RYZHKOV, NIKOLAI IVANOVICH. Promi-nent Soviet politician; Chairman of the USSR Council of Ministers since 1985. Ryzhkov, a Russian by nationality, was born in a village in the Donetsk region on Sept. 28, 1929. In 1950 he graduated from the Kramatorsk engineering col-lege, and in 1959 he completed his education at the Urals Polytechnical Institute. He has been a member of the **Communist Party of the Soviet Union (CPSU)** since 1950. Ryzhkov began his

working life at the massive "Uralmash" engineer-ing works, where he rose steadily through the ranks until he became (in 1965) chief engineer. In 1970 he moved to become director of the Urals heavy engineering factory, and then the following year returned to "Uralmash" where he was employed as general director until 1975. Since 1975 Ryzhkov has held a succession of party and (more often) governmental posts, becoming a first deputy minister of heavy and transport engineer-ing in 1975, and then in 1979 first deputy chair-man of the State Planning Committee (Gosplan). In 1982 Ryzhkov became a member of the Central Committee Secretariat, where (until 1985) he headed its economic department. In September 1985 he became Chairman of the USSR Council of Ministers (or in effect prime minister), securing nomination to that post again in 1989. He has been a member of the CPSU Central Committee since 1981, and in April 1985 became a full member of the ruling Politburo without passing through the customary candidate stage.

Ryzhkov has become an increasingly promi-nent member of the **Gorbachev** administration, consistent with the attempts that have been made to shift executive authority from party to state institutions. He enjoyed a position of particular prominence during the Armenian earthquake of December 1988, when he took responsibility for relief operations on behalf of the Politburo, and he has headed party or state missions on other occasions, for instance in Uzbekistan during the communal disturbances in 1989. Reflecting in part this greater prominence, and in part his repu-tation as an honest and effective administrator, Ryzhkov was generally placed in third position, behind Gorbachev and **Yel'tsin**, in Soviet opinion polls in the late 1980s; some even saw him as a widely acceptable successor to Gorbachev in the event of a sudden change of leadership. Ryzhkov was described as a "diligent and hard-working executive" but "no strategist" in Boris Yel'tsin's perhaps somewhat partial memoirs; whatever his faults, he had clearly emerged by the early 1990s as the second most important figure in the Soviet leadership.

SLW

S

SAKHAROV, ANDREI DMITRIEVICH. The Soviet Union's best-known dissident during the **Brezhnev** years, Andrei Sakharov (born 1921) combined several different careers. His first, for which he received a number of high state decorations, was as an outstanding nuclear physicist and one of the fathers of the Soviet atom bomb. His second, from the late 1960s, was as an increasingly prominent and uncompromising dissident, the author of a memorandum entitled *Progress, Coexistence and Intellectual Freedom* (1968) which called for US–Soviet co-operation in limiting the proliferation of nuclear arms and in dealing with the problems of the Third World, Sakharov became more generally concerned with problems of freedom of speech and thought and the circulation of information, and he became an increasingly outspoken critic of the censorship and political trials that were taking place in the USSR in the 1960s and 1970s. Sakharov (who was awarded the Nobel Peace Prize in 1975) was dismissed from his post at the Lebedev Physics Institute for these activities, although he remained a member of the USSR Academy of Sciences. In 1980, after a series of warnings, he was stripped of his state honours and expelled to the city of Gorky, which is normally out of bounds to foreigners; he continued with his scientific work but was repeatedly subject to police and other forms of harassment. The position of dissidents changed radically with the accession of **Gorbachev** to the general secretaryship, and at the end of 1986, quite without warning, the Soviet leader telephoned Sakharov in Gorky and invited him to resume his valuable work. A few days later he was one of the star participants at an international forum, "For a Nuclear Free World, for the Survival of Humanity", which was held in the Kremlin and addressed personally by Gorbachev. Sakharov, it emerged, had made no concessions as the price of his release, and while he spoke strongly in support of Soviet arms control and other foreign policy initiatives he criticized several other developments, in particular the increasing powers that had accumulated in the hands of the new leader. Sakharov, after some difficulties had been surmounted (*see* **Elections and Electoral System in the USSR**), became a candidate from the Academy of Sciences to the Congress of People's Deputies in 1989, and after his election he became an increasingly prominent and outspoken parliamentarian, with (opinion polls established) a large public following. Sakharov differed publicly with Gorbachev on a number of issues, particularly (in late 1989) the removal of the leading role of the **Communist Party of the Soviet Union (CPSU)** from the Soviet constitution. Gorbachev, nonetheless, was among the signatories to the official obituary that appeared in the press on Sakharov's death shortly afterwards, and in March 1990 the figure widely regarded as the "conscience of the nation" was vindicated when the CPSU itself proposed the removal of its guaranteed monopoly.

SLW

SCHABOWSKI, GÜNTER. Former GDR politician, born 1929. Günter Schabowski was editor of the **Socialist Unity Party of Germany (SED)** party newspaper *Neues Deutschland* ("New Germany"), before becoming SED First Secretary for **Berlin** and a full Politburo member in 1985. In 1989 he assisted **Krenz** in the ousting of **Honecker** and for a short time was the public spokesman of the new regime. It was Schabowski who gave the laconic announcement on Nov. 9, 1989 that GDR citizens were to be allowed to travel freely. Like Krenz he failed to master the rapidly changing situation and in the winter of 1989–90 was deprived of office and of his party membership.

JO

SECOND ECONOMY. The "second economy" is the term which has come to be used by economists to cover the various types of private economic activity which are a vital component of Soviet-type economic systems. Sometimes the terms "shadow economy" or "informal economy" are also used. There are various definitions available: the leading American expert on this subject, Gregory Grossman, has defined it as including all economic activities which are (a) carried out for direct private gain, and (b) in some significant respect in knowing contravention of existing law. It thus covers the black market in currency and goods, various forms of bribery and corruption of officialdom, under-the-counter payments to, among others, doctors, shop assistants, and other state employees for the provision of goods or services in short supply, thefts of state property, the use of equipment and time belonging to the state sector for private production activity, as well as independent private entrepreneurial activity in the field of goods production and services. The Hungarian economists I. Gabor and P. Galasi, on the other hand, employ a significantly broader definition which includes legal as well as illegal activities, that is, the important small-scale private sector in agriculture, licensed private artisans, and also the new forms of private and cooperative small-scale firms legalized in Hungary in 1982 (see below).

Inevitably it is extremely difficult to estimate the size of this "second" or "shadow" economy. However, detailed survey data collected from recent Soviet émigrés by V. Treml of Duke University suggest that in the late 1970s, earnings from illegal second economy sources accounted on average for around 30 per cent of total per capita annual incomes of inhabitants in Russia and the Baltic Republics, while in Armenia, this proportion appears to have been as high as 64 per cent. Data for Hungary are rather more extensive due to the more relaxed attitude of the regime on this question. Reszö **Nyers** estimated in the early 1980s that about 18 to 20 per cent of the Hungarian GNP was accounted for by the second economy. Sociological research in Hungary has shown that 75 per cent of households were engaged in secondary earning activity of some kind, and it has been estimated that net incomes equivalent to one third of total official earnings were derived from the second economy. The phenomenon appears to be endemic to all Soviet-type economies, and has always been present to some degree albeit in different forms; but there is some reason to believe that the scope of secondary economic activity increased rapidly in the Soviet Union in the **Brezhnev** period, when consumer expectations began to rise rapidly and the corruption of the state and party bureaucracy accelerated. In **Kádár**'s Hungary, with its more reformist orientation in economic policy and rather relaxed political climate in general, a greater toleration of informal private activities was characteristic. This was also true of Poland in the 1970s and 1980s; the manifold forms of the second economy were certainly more visible in these countries, and probably somewhat more extensive than in the more hardline regimes. Nevertheless, its importance should not be underestimated in any country.

Various sources confirm the major role of the second economy in the provision of foodstuffs, particularly fresh fruit and vegetables, eggs and poultry (about 50 to 60 per cent of total consumption of these goods in most countries); consumer services such as car maintenance, house repairs and construction. It thus performs a vital complementary role to the "first" economy, supplementing the deficiencies of its massive, unwieldy and inflexible enterprises, in meeting consumer requirements, and to this extent, supports the whole economic system as well as providing the basis of political stability. But many secondary activities are parasitic on the state sector and tend to undermine it. For example, the use of the state firm's time and equipment for the production of items which are then sold or exchanged illegally severely affects the productivity of the state sector, but this type of activity is widely tolerated by managers, ever anxious to retain labour in the context of chronic, systemic labour shortage. Moreover, the returns to labour expended in the second economy are estimated to be possibly five to ten times higher per hour than official earnings; the state sector is either unable to compete with this level of wages due to its low productivity, or it responds by granting inflationary wage payments. A key element of this problem is due to the fact that the vast proportion of secondary economic activity is part-time: individuals understandably prefer the security net provided by official employment in the state sector, with all its attendant welfare benefits, pension rights and holiday entitlements, to the highly insecure, politically vulnerable and punitively taxed status of a legal private entrepreneur. For many too, the official job itself is the source of additional illegal income from bribes, or is the means of obtaining materials and equipment unavailable legally to small-scale private purchasers.

The second economy also has the effect of redistributing incomes independently of the intentions of the central authorities. In some respects, it may serve to supplement some relatively low official incomes: for example, doctors may rationalize their acceptance of "gifts" from their patients for the provision of nominally free services by referring to the generally low salaries they receive by comparison with the relative position of their Western counterparts. On the other hand, successful entrepreneurs on the second economy may derive very high incomes due to the chronic shortages of consumer goods and the distorted nature of the market in which they are operating. Hungarian economists have pointed to the tendency of private entrepreneurs to indulge in socially divisive "conspicuous consumption", on account of legal restrictions and political disincentives to investment of high incomes.

An obvious solution to many of the negative aspects of the functioning of the second economy is to legalize it, and thus, it is hoped, to integrate it effectively into the first economy, and also to derive some taxation revenue from it. This has taken place in Hungary to a rather limited extent with the introduction of new forms of private economic activity in 1982. These included the GMK

(Business Partnership), a form of small co-operative of up to 30 participants; the VGMK (Enterprise Business Partnership), comprising a group of employees of a given firm who sub-contract work from their enterprise; and various forms of specialized teams. On the whole, these did not attract an enormous amount of interest, with the exception of the VGMK, which turned out to be in practice merely a new form of "work brigade" permitting managers to evade central wage restrictions and thus to keep skilled workers. A major problem was the level of taxation, which remained too high to offer real incentives to draw illegal entrepreneurs out of the shadows. The second economy as a whole played a vital role in the 1980s: economists estimate it was the sole source of real growth in the Hungarian economy. In the most recent period since 1988, the economic reforms, which now include wholesale privatization of large parts of the state sector itself, will eventually eliminate the division between "first" and "second" economies.

In the Soviet Union, the process of *perestroika* is gradually moving round to the question of private ownership and entrepreneurship, but the ideological and political barriers to reform of this type remain formidable. A very restrictive Law on Individual Labour Activity was introduced in 1986, and a more encouraging Law on Co-operatives for agriculture and construction work was brought in in 1987. These have made some impression, but continue to be restricted in their real economic effect by high levels of taxation and the resistance of local officials who are responsible for licensing and supervision. In any case, given the acute shortages now endemic in the Soviet economy, legal entrepreneurs still have to resort to less than wholly legal means to obtain materials and parts. The illegal private sector remains entrenched as before, and may even be a source of resistance to economic reform, which would certainly threaten high incomes derived from certain types and aspects of second economy activity.

JB

SECURITATE (ROMANIA). Under **Ceauş-escu**, the well-armed and much feared secret police. Their numbers are unknown, though probably exaggerated by popular opinion; following the overthrow of the Ceauşescu regime, a figure of 70,000 was quoted. Some wore uniforms (with blue shoulder-flashes) while others were in plain clothes, though sometimes recognizable by where they were or through their behaviour. Even foreign tourists were not entirely exempt from their attentions. When the uprising against Ceauşescu

occurred the Securitate upheld their oath to him personally by opening fire on the populace and by their determined resistance against regular forces. A number have since been brought to trial and sentenced to long terms of imprisonment. It is claimed that the Securitate has been broken up and its structure destroyed, but by no means all Romanians believe this.

RH

SED-PDS (GDR). SED-PDS (Socialist Unity Party of Germany — Party of Democratic Socialism) was the new name carried by the previous ruling party of the GDR from Dec. 17, 1989 to Feb. 4, 1990. (*See also* **Socialist Unity Party of Germany—SED**)

JO

SEJM (POLISH DIET). The *Sejm*, or Polish parliament, is the highest organ of state power in Poland and exercises formal control over the government (embodied in the Council of Ministers) and other major state bodies. For most of the post-war period it passed or confirmed all legislation and appointed from amongst its members the Council of State, which acted as a collective presidency. In practice, the Communist system of rule gave more power to the **Polish United Workers' Party (PUWP)**, and the prime minister, as head of the government, was subordinate in power to the leader of the ruling party. The *Sejm* only met in plenary session for about 10 days a year and its major function was ritualistic and legitimizing, although some more practical tasks were performed by its specialist committees. Most of its 460 members were elected in multi-member constituences which, despite some variation over time, presented the electorate with little effective choice and gave the PUWP a built-in majority.

Both the practice and formal status of the *Sejm* changed considerably in 1989. As part of the round-table agreement 35 per cent of the seats were allocated to the opposition and the proportion of seats reserved for the PUWP was reduced from 53 to 38 per cent, although the overall Communist majority was planned to be maintained through the association of the PUWP with its coalition partners (the **United Peasant Party** and **Democratic Party**) and official Catholic groups. While the *Sejm* would retain legislative powers within the political system, it was agreed to establish a 100-member Senate which would be freely elected and have the right to discuss legislation and refer proposals back to the *Sejm* for further consideration. The *Sejm* and Senate together constitute the National Assembly (*Zgro-*

madzenie Narodowe) which gathers to elect a president who would stay in office for six years and whose powers would include those of the existing Council of State and the right of veto over legislation, which the *Sejm* could only overturn with a two-thirds majority.

In terms of the allocation of seats the election of June 1989 proceeded according to plan, although 33 of 35 candidates on an uncontested national list failed to gain the required 50 per cent of the vote and special arrangements had to be made to fill the vacant seats. Candidates sponsored by **Solidarit**y won all 35 per cent of the seats (a total of 161) they were permitted to contest. But it soon became evident that the majority arranged for the PUWP-dominated coalition would not be operative and that the Communist party's major partners, the United Peasant Party and the Democratic Party, did not see it in their interests to continue with the earlier arrangement. The PUWP candidate for prime minister, Gen. **Kiszczak**, was endorsed by the *Sejm* but found it impossible to form a government. A new coalition of the Citizens' Parliamentary Club (OKP) of Solidarity deputies with the UPP and DP was proposed and agreed under the leadership of Solidarity candidate Tadeusz **Mazowiecki**, who became prime minister in September 1989.

PGL

SERBIAN ORTHODOX CHURCH. The Serbian Orthodox Church enjoys wide support as the national Church of the Serbs, the most numerous of the peoples of Yugoslavia. The Church has about 10 million believers, 2,000 priests and 3,000 churches. Since 1958 the head has been Patriarch German (Djorić).

Seeing itself as the traditional principal defender of the Serb nation, it has been brought by its nationalism into conflict with the authorities, especially at the all-Yugoslav level. (*See also* **Yugoslavia** — National Question; **Nationalism and Communism in Eastern Europe**.) The relatively tolerant attitude of the **League of Communists of Yugoslavia** (in comparison with other ruling Communist parties) meant that the more usual relationship between state and Orthodox Church found in other Communist systems, in which the state controlled the church, was not reproduced to the same extent in Yugoslavia. A major dispute with the state came over the creation of the Macedonian Orthodox Church, supported by the Yugoslav federal authorities to promote Macedonian national consciousness in a region traditionally regarded by the Serbian Church as its own.

The Serbian Church tried to re-assert itself as the defender of the Serbs in the crises which developed from 1981 over Kosovo. In this autonomous province of Serbia, the numerically-dominant Albanians began to agitate for raising the status of Kosovo to that of a republic within Yugoslavia. Ethnic clashes between Serbs and Albanians broke out on several occasions. This led to a flood of Serbs out of Kosovo, which contains sites important in Serbian history, such as the Pec monastery. The Church's appeals in defence of the Serbs coincided with, and gave backing to, a growing Serbian nationalism within the League of Communists of Serbia. This centred on Slobodan **Milošević**, who became President of Serbia in 1989. The federal authorities were alarmed at the growth of Serb nationalism, but the moves towards political pluralism and the support of public opinion made it difficult to impose restrictions on the Church.

PJSD

SHEVARDNADZE, EDUARD AMVROSIE-VICH. A former Georgian party first secretary, Shevardnadze became better known internationally as **Gorbachev**'s foreign secretary. A Georgian by nationality, Shevardnadze was born in that republic on Jan. 25, 1928. He graduated from the Kutaisi pedagogical institute in 1959, having already graduated (in 1951) from the Higher Party School of the Georgian party. He has been a member of the **Communist Party of the Soviet Union (CPSU)** since 1948. From 1948 onwards Shevardnadze was engaged in Komsomol work, eventually (in 1957) becoming first secretary of the republican Komsomol organization and a member of the bureau of the national Komsomol. From 1961 onwards Shevardnadze was engaged in party and state work, first as the head of two district party committees, and then from 1964 as a deputy minister and then (from 1965) minister for the preservation of public order and (from 1968) minister of the interior in the Georgian republic. In 1972 he returned to party work, becoming first secretary of the party organization in the Georgian capital Tbilisi and then (later the same year) first secretary of the Georgian Communist party organization. He became a member of the CPSU Central Committee in 1976, and in 1978 became a candidate member of the ruling Politburo. In July 1985 he was promoted to full membership of that body.

Shevardnadze's nomination to succeed the veteran foreign minister Andrei **Gromyko** in July 1985 was something of a surprise. Gromyko, over a period of nearly 30 years, had made the post his own; Shevardnadze had virtually no experience of work of this kind, and was little known abroad.

He was, however, personally committed to the policies that Gorbachev was pursuing, and had promoted them while party leader in Georgia; and as foreign minister he took a large part of the responsibility for restructuring the Ministry of Foreign Affairs and promoting "new thinking" in Soviet foreign policy (*see* **USSR**—foreign policy). Interviewed in the government paper *Izvestiya* in the spring of 1989, Shevardnadze laid particular emphasis upon extending the principles of *glasnost'* to the making of foreign policy. He had not himself been involved, he explained later in the year, in the decision to send Soviet troops into Afghanistan; and this and other misjudgements were much more likely to occur, in his view, if the decisions concerned were taken out of reach of public scrutiny. Shevardnadze accordingly insisted on the accountability of foreign policy-making to the Soviet parliament, and he established a group for the study of public opinion within the Ministry in order to relate its decisions more closely to the society on whose behalf they were made. Perhaps best seen as the means by which Gorbachev was able to extend his influence into the sphere of Soviet foreign policy-making, Shevardnadze nonetheless was independently committed to the same principles and his more open and good-humoured manner of promoting them made a considerable contribution to their success.

SLW

ŠIK, OTA. Born in 1919, Šik, then Director of the Economic Institute of the Czechoslovak Academy of Sciences, headed the team which prepared the economic reform programme approved by the **Communist Party of Czechoslovakia** Central Committee in January 1965. Although he was known as the "father of the Czechoslovak economic reform" and appointed a Deputy Prime Minister in April 1968 to oversee its implementation, he was also an outspoken advocate of democratic political reform. He was forced to resign his government post after the **Warsaw Treaty Organization (Warsaw Pact)** invasion of Czechoslovakia in August 1968 and thereafter pursued an academic career in exile in Switzerland.

GW

SOCIAL DEMOCRATIC PARTY OF GERMANY (SPD — Sozialdemokratische Partei Deutschlands). The original SPD was the social democratic party which was founded in Gotha in 1875 and adopted a Marxist programme in Erfurt in 1891. By the eve of World War I it was the largest party and had the largest parliamentary party in Germany. It survived various splits, only to be banned by the Nazis in 1933. It was refounded in the Soviet Occupation Zone in 1945, but was forced to merge with the KPD (Communist Party of Germany) in 1946 to form the **Socialist Unity Party of Germany (SED)**. In the Federal Republic of Germany the SPD continued, to become one of the major parties of West German politics.

The new form of the SPD in the GDR was founded (originally as the SDP) at Schwante, north-west of Berlin, on Oct. 7, 1989. At this stage it was an illegal organization. The 43 people originally involved had by the end of January 1990 become a membership of 45–50,000. At the party's first national delegates' conference in January 1990 it was decided to change the name from SDP to SPD in order to recognize its commitment to German unity and to facilitate links with the SPD in the Federal Republic. Willy Brandt, honorary chairman of the West German SPD, was asked to assume the same position in the GDR party. He attended an emotional meeting in Gotha early in 1990.

The SPD represents a revitalization of social democratic ideals in the GDR, and has rejected collaboration with the **SED-PDS**. The latter dismantled its party symbol of two hands when the SPD demanded that it be "given its hand back" in recognition of its rejection of the union of 1946.

The leader (secretary) of the SPD was Ibrahim Böhme (born 1948), who was a member of the SED until he resigned in 1976 in protest at the expulsion of the singer, Wolf Biermann. He afterwards spent a total of more than 15 months in detention. He was offered a minor post in the **Modrow** government but turned it down. He took the SPD into the March 1990 elections in the confident expectation of it emerging as the largest party, only to be badly disappointed with 21.9 per cent of the vote and 88 seats. Later in March Böhme himself fell victim to accusations of collaboration with the **Stasi.** He denied these, but then resigned on grounds of ill health, with the announced intent of clearing his name. He was succeeded by Markus Meckel.

JO

SOCIALIST UNITY PARTY OF GERMANY (SED — Sozialistische Einheitspartei Deutschlands). The SED was the Marxist-Leninist political party which ruled the GDR from its inception until the revolutionary changes of 1989–90. It was founded in April 1946 in the Soviet sector of Berlin as an amalgamation of the KPD (Communist Party of Germany) and the **Social**

Democratic Party of Germany (SPD). The latter had in fact a larger membership in the Soviet Occupation Zone, but was pressurized into unity and then submission by the Moscow-supported Communists. Many Social Democrats, who had entered the unified party in the hope of new and genuine co-operation on the left, found themselves hounded out of office or out of the party altogether. The party came under the control of its General Secretary, Walter **Ulbricht**, who pursued a hardline pro-Soviet line from 1950 until his dismissal in 1971. The SED organized other political tendencies into subservient National Front parties (the **Christian Democratic Union of Germany — CDU**, the **Liberal Democratic Party of Germany — LDPD**, the **National Democratic Party of Germany — NDPD**, the **Democratic Peasants' Party — DBD**) developed its youth movement, **Free German Youth (FDJ)**, and followed economic policies of nationalization, collectivization and central planning.

Ulbricht was followed at the summit by his protégé, Erich **Honecker**, who was First (then General) Secretary from 1971 to 1989. As Ulbricht gave way reluctantly to his own chosen successor, so Honecker was eventually forced to yield to the man he had marked out to follow him Egon **Krenz**.

The SED was organized on the principle of "democratic centralism", which meant in fact that the direction of power was entirely from the top downwards rather than the reverse.

Constitutionally, the highest organ of the party was the five-yearly party congress, which elected the central committee. This in turn elected the Politburo and the Secretariat. In practice, all decisions were taken in a small, highly secretive circle of top party functionaries.

The presence of the SED permeated all facets of life in the GDR, either directly or indirectly. Whether it be in the FDJ youth organization, the **Free German Trade Union League (FDGB)** trade union organization, the agrarian *Vereinigung der gegenseitigen Bauernhilfe* (VdgB — Association of Mutual Peasant Aid), the Academy of Social Sciences, or any number of other associations, the party controlled and supervised.

Party adherence became a prerequisite for career advancement in many fields, but the SED was not a party which allowed membership on a casual basis. Only in the initial years was entry encouraged on a wide basis, in order to weaken the original Social Democrat presence. Subsequently, strict criteria were adopted, with the aim of producing ideologically and socially reliable party cadres. With time the party grew to a maximum membership (including candidate members) of 2.3 million.

The leading role of the party was enshrined in the constitution of the GDR, and in practice the SED was the decisive organ of government in the state. The Council of State (*Staatsrat*) was chaired in latter years by Erich Honecker, General Secretary of the party and also Chairman of the National Defence Council. He was thus head of state. Similarly, Willi **Stoph** was Chairman of the Council of Ministers (*Ministerrat*) and the equivalent of prime minister.

After 44 years of dominance, the SED in the early 1990s was in terminal decline. The leadership endeavoured to stem the tide of the reforming process emanating from Moscow under Mikhail **Gorbachev** and already put into practice in Warsaw and Budapest. The attempt failed utterly in the summer and autumn of 1989, and even with major concessions the new leadership of Krenz was unable to halt the challenge to the party. The political suppression, personal corruption and evidence of complete economic mismanagement made it impossible for the party to continue as before. Krenz was abandoned in December 1989, and the upper echelons of the old party were almost completely swept aside.

The new chairman, Gregor **Gysi**, made it his purpose to regenerate the party as the "Party of Democratic Socialism" (**SED-PDS**, then **PDS**), but meanwhile the membership base had halved and the sole remaining SED figure with power, prime minister Hans **Modrow**, was being moved further and further into coalition agreements and the necessity of looking to German unity. Proposals have been made on several occasions to dissolve the party entirely, so far without success, but the PDS faced a daunting challenge in the elections of March 1990. The SPD has already re-emerged, and significantly perhaps, on Jan. 31, 1990 the KPD was refounded in Berlin, with the aims of humanism, peace and social justice.

In the event, Gysi and Modrow managed to salvage something for their party in the March elections. With 16.4 per cent of the vote and 66 seats, the PDS emerged as the third largest party after the CDU and the SPD. It did so presumably on the votes of those loyal to a separate GDR and fearful of a sell-out of perceived social and socialist achievements. Its stronghold was the capital, East Berlin, where it came second to the SPD.

JO

SOFIA (Sofiya). The Bulgarian capital and its chief industrial, transportation and commercial centre. The city itself had a population in 1987 of 1,128,859; it constitutes one of Bulgaria's nine regions, and stands in the centre of the Sofia region. Originally a Thracian and Roman foundation, the city passed to the Ottomans in 1382 and was then taken by the Russians in the Russo-Turkish war of 1877–78, becoming (1879) the capital of a newly independent Bulgaria. Among the chief manufactures are engineering and metal products, machinery, textiles, rubber and leather goods, furniture, footwear, chemicals, and bricks and tiles. Apart from party and governmental headquarters, Sofia houses a university (founded in 1889) and two ecclesiastical sees.

SLW

SOLIDARITY (POLAND — Solidarność). Solidarity, or the "Independent Self-Governing Trade Union Solidarity" (*Niezależny Samorządny Związek Zawodowy "Solidarność"*) grew out of the strike movement of August 1980 in **Gdańsk** and the agreement signed there on Aug. 31 by the authorities with the Inter-enterprise Strike Committee (MKS). Strike committees elsewhere turned themselves into the founding bodies of an independent self-governing union, with leaders of regional unions (representing three million members from 3,500 plants) meeting in Gdańsk on Sept. 17 to affiliate themselves with the intention of registering as a national union. The regional basis of the union was meant to maintain strong local links with rank-and-file members and forestall the incorporation of a dominant national leadership by party and government. Integration was to be achieved through a National Co-ordinating Commission (from which 11 members were selected to form a Presidium) headed by Lech **Wałęsa**. Following some obstruction from the authorities the union was registered by the Supreme Court on Nov. 10, 1980.

Its membership level rose rapidly and by the end of November 7.5 million, representing 54 per cent of employees in the socialist sector, were estimated to have joined. It had 9,486,000 members by the end of June 1981, compared with 13,626,000 registered by the official union in 1979. Conflict between Solidarity and the authorities continued and there were numerous local strikes in early 1981, frequently associated with specific local abuses and the reluctance of officials to implement reforms. A major crisis occurred on March 19 in Bydgoszcz when a meeting was broken up by police and some Solidarity officials apparently beaten up on purpose. After a warning strike on March 27 a threatened general strike was avoided, although Wałęsa was criticized for being too conciliatory in dealings with the government. Solidarity held its first Congress in two stages, in September and October 1981, and approved union statutes and a full programme.

It did not provide a basis for the development of better relations with party and government authorities, and the union was suspended on Dec. 13 as a **State of War** was declared throughout the country. Most Solidarity leaders were interned, although some went underground and remained at large. The union was officially dissolved in October 1982. Political restrictions were progressively relaxed so that, after the amnesty granted in September 1986, virtually all politicial prisoners were released and, while Solidarity kept an underground organization, it was also able openly to establish a Provisional Co-ordinating Commission (TKK). But it was only after the strikes of 1988 and the initiation of the round-table negotiations in February 1989 (*see* **Round-table Agreement**) that the relegalization of Solidarity really came on to the agenda. Final ratification of its status came in April and Solidarity exerted a major influence on the elections in June. Following the collapse of the ruling coalition led by the **Polish United Workers' Party (PUWP)** in August, a new coalition was formed around the group of Solidarity-sponsored deputies and their favoured candidate, Tadeusz **Mazowiecki**, appointed prime minister. The union was reported to have 2,200,000 members in October 1989 and a Congress was planned to be held in April 1990.

PGL

SOLZHENITSYN, ALEXANDER ISAEVICH. Russian writer and the outstanding living representative of Soviet literature. Solzhenitsyn was born in Kislovodsk in 1918 and grew up in Rostov, where he studied mathematics at university. During World War II he served in the Red Army, rising to the rank of artillery captain, and was decorated for bravery. In 1945, while still serving on the German front, he was arrested for criticizing **Stalin** in letters to a friend and spent some years in prison, later being exiled to Kazakhstan. After Stalin's death in 1953 his position improved, and he was restored to Soviet citizenship in 1956. Solzhenitsyn first became prominent with the publication of his short novel based on his prison camp experience, *One Day in the life of Ivan Denisovich*, in the literary journal *Novy mir* in 1962. **Khrushchev**, it is believed, intervened personally to secure the publication of this book; Khrushchev's successors were less favourably disposed towards literature of this kind and prevented the publication in the USSR of *The First Circle* (1964), *Cancer Ward* (1966) and *August 1914* (1972). Solzhenitsyn was expelled from the Union of Soviet Writers and prohibited from living in Moscow; in 1970 he was awarded the Nobel Prize for Literature, but chose not to accept it personally in case he was unble to return to the USSR. In 1974 Solzhenitsyn was arrested, formally accused of treason, and forced to emigrate; he lived first in Switzerland and then latterly in Vermont, USA, where he continued his writing, commentating occasionally on Soviet affairs. The accession of **Gorbachev** led to a series of changes in Soviet literature, which affected the position of émigré authors among others. Despite some continued official hostility a number of minor works (including some that had not previously been published in the USSR) appeared in Soviet journals in 1989, and then in the latter part of the year his three-volume documentary of political repression from 1918 to 1956, *Gulag Archipelago*, began to appear in *Novy mir* (its full publication in book form was to follow). Solzhenitsyn was readmitted to the Writers' Union, and efforts were made to have his Soviet citizenship restored; Solzhenitsyn himself remained an uncompromising critic of Soviet socialism, but by the early 1990s he was on his way to being fully restored to his central position in modern Russian literature.

SLW

SOVIET RELATIONS WITH THE COMMUNIST WORLD.

Relations between the Communist states had for some time before **Gorbachev**'s accession been less amicable than a common dedication to working-class interests might have suggested. The first split occurred as early as 1948 when Yugoslavia was denounced by the Soviet Union and its allies for supposedly giving too much favour to peasants at the expense of the working class and for exercising party authority in an insufficiently decisive manner. In fact there appears to be no doubt that **Stalin** simply resented the independence that the Yugoslav leaders were displaying and believed they could be brought to heel as easily as Communist leaders in other parts of Eastern Europe. If so, he miscalculated badly: the Yugoslavs arrested Soviet supporters within the Communist party and weathered the storm with a largely united people behind them. In 1955 **Khrushchev** and Bulganin made a visit to Belgrade in an attempt to secure a reconciliation, and the following year a Soviet—Yugoslav communiqué was signed in Moscow which brought the dispute to an end. A dispute in Hungary at about the same time was not resolved so amicably, at least in part becuse Hungary occupied a far more important strategic position in terms of Soviet security than did Yugoslavia. An attempt to establish a "liberal Communist" re-

gime under Imre **Nagy** which appeared likely to take Hungary out of the **Warsaw Treaty Organization**, (**WTO** or Warsaw Pact) was brutally crushed by Soviet tanks in October 1956, and a new leadership under János **Kádár** was installed which took a long time to establish any measure of domestic support.

The next crisis in inter-Communist relations was a result of the attempt by the **Dubček** leadership in Czechoslovakia to establish an alternative model of socialism, one that accorded more closely with the humanistic and democratic traditions of their country. There was apparently no Soviet objection in January 1968 when, following economic and other difficulties, Antonín **Novotný** was replaced as party first secretary by Alexander Dubček, a Slovak who had received part of his education in the USSR. With the publication of the party's "Action Programme" in April 1968, however, it became clear that relatively far-reaching changes were envisaged, among them the abolition of censorship, restrictions on the power of the secret police, a genuinely independent judiciary and freedom of travel. After direct negotiations with the Czech party leadership proved of no avail the USSR and four other Warsaw Pact allies intervened militarily in August 1968 and re-established Communist orthodoxy. An authoritative article in *Pravda* entitled "The defence of socialism is the highest international duty" set out what later became known as the "**Brezhnev doctrine**": this insisted that the interests of the Communist countries as a whole took priority over over the wishes of any individual Communist country and that no defection from the Communist camp could be permitted. **Brezhnev** himself, addressing the Polish party congress in November 1968, made it clear that any threat to the socialist order in a given country would be considered "not only a problem of the people of the country in question, but a general problem and concern of all the socialist countries.

Difficulties in Soviet relations with its East European neighbours continued into the 1970s and 1980s, particularly in Romania (which had not taken part in the invasion of Czechoslovakia and refused to allow any Soviet troops to be stationed on its territory) and above all in Poland. **Stalin** is reported to have remarked at the end of the war that to establish Communist rule in Poland would be like "trying to saddle a cow" and Soviet relations with that country (the largest and most populous in Eastern Europe have borne out these apprehensions. Perhaps the most important single explanation was that Polish political values and practices were rather closer to those of Western Europe than to those of the more authoritarian East. Poland, for instance, unlike Russia, was a participant in the great movements in early modern European history such as the Renaissance and the scientific revolution, and the country's legal system, literary forms and religious faith aligned it firmly with the liberal West rather than the statist East. An estimated 90 per cent of the population adhered to the Roman Catholic faith, and the Church had a massive presence in Polish society, including its own university, large numbers of priests, newspapers and periodicals, and representatives in the armed forces and the Polish parliament, the *Sejm*. The election of Cardinal Wojtyla of Krakow as Pope John Paul II in 1978 and his visits to Poland in 1979 and subsequently emphasized these attachments and strengthened the historic association between the Catholic faith and Polish nationhood.

The Polish leadership, headed by Edward **Gierek**, had been experiencing increasing economic difficulties during the 1970s as an over-ambitious expansion programme began to founder and foreign debts began to mount (*see* **Poland** — Current economic developments). Efforts to improve matters by raising prices and reducing subsidies led to open resistance and had to be rescinded. The regime became increasingly authoritarian in its attempts to deal with the problems it was confronting; the society, in turn, began to establish public associations of all kinds, most notably the **Committee for Workers' Defence (KOR)**, which were independent of party and state control. In July 1980 a dispute at the Lenin shipyards in the Baltic port of Gdańsk led to the formation of an inter-strike committee and shortly afterwards to the establishment of **Solidarity**, the first (and so far the last) genuinely self-governing trade union that has ever existed in a communist-ruled country. Solidarity, at its peak, embraced more than nine million of Poland's 13 million workers; it prompted the formation of a country counterpart, Rural Solidarity, and profoundly affected the ruling **Polish United Workers' Party**, about a third of whose members are estimated to have joined Solidarity at this time. The regime (headed by Stanislaw **Kania** after Gierek's resignation in 1980, and then from 1981 by Wojciech **Jaruzelski**) committed itself to a programme of "renewal" (*odnowa*), but the economic situation continued to deteriorate, while Solidarity for its part became increasingly powerful, radical and politicized in its objectives (*see* **Poland**—Recent political developments).

Developments of this kind were obviously worrying to the Soviet leadership, which began to speak openly of the dangers of "internal counter-revolution". This had normally been sufficient pretext for direct military intervention, and some

action of this kind appears to have been under consideration in December 1980 and again in March 1981. The **Communist Party of the Soviet Union (CPSU)** also expressed its concern in a letter of June 1981 to the Central Committee of the Polish party. The letter expressed the CPSU's "deep anxiety for the fate of socialism in Poland", regretted that the necessary measures had not been taken against domestic anti-Soviet and anti-socialist forces, and called upon the Polish party to "reverse the course of events and channel them in the right direction". In the end the situation was not restored (from the Soviet point of view) until December 1981, when Jaruzelski declared a state of martial law, suspending Solidarity and interning some of its most prominent members. The Polish – Soviet alliance, he promised in a public broadcast, would remain the "cornerstone" of Polish foreign policy; Poland would also remain an "indestructible part of the Warsaw Treaty and a reliable member of the socialist community of nations". Jaruzelski's action may have pre-empted Soviet military intervention, but it did not, in the long run, resolve the problem of political order, nor indeed the problem of economic reform. It was not in fact until a newly legalized Solidarity had been successful at the polls and formed a majority administration in 1989 that the making of public policy began again to command at least a minimum of public acceptability. The Soviet response, this time round, was to accept the election of a Solidarity prime minister with relatively good grace (Jaruzelski, after all, had become president); more generally, Soviet theorists began to accept that socialist countries could have legitimate differences of interest and that these could be resolved only through discussion, not by the imposition of a Soviet *diktat*.

Soviet relations with the largest of its neighbours, the People's Republic of China, have also been difficult and at times have broken down altogether. The Chinese leaders appear to have been dissatisfied with a number of aspects of the Sino-Soviet treaty of 1950, been and at the XX Congress of the CPSU in 1956 they were reportedly unhappy about the manner in which Khrushchev had denounced the actions of Stalin. The Chinese, as late as 1957, still accepted Soviet leadership of the international Communist movement: "in the socialist camp there must be a head", Mao explained to students at Moscow University, "and that head is the Soviet Union. Among the Communist and workers' parties of all countries there must be a head, and that head is the CPSU". Soviet support for the Chinese atomic programme, nonetheless, was withdrawn the following year, the USSR was neutral during the

Sino-Indian war of 1959, and in 1960 the dispute between the two Communist giants came into the open. Khrushchev, speaking at the **Romanian Communist Party** Congress in June of that year, attacked the Chinese leadership by name. All Soviet technicians were withdrawn; trade between the two countries dropped off sharply; and a series of hostile open letters was exchanged, the Chinese accusing the Russians of "revisionism" while the Russians accused the Chinese of "dogmatism" and "splittism" (or of attempting to break up the world Communist movement).

Relations deteriorated still further during the late 1960s. In 1966 both sides recalled their ambassadors, and in 1969 open military hostilities broke out along the Ussuri river, which marks the Sino-Soviet border in Siberia. Since then relations have slowly normalized. Negotiations on matters in dispute were opened in 1969; in 1970 the ambassadors returned to their posts; and trade began to increase substantially. The two sides, however, were still separated by traditional rivalries extending over several centuries as well as by differing interpretations of Marxism, disputed borders and rivalry in their relations with other countries; indeed it was perhaps surprising that their earlier association had lasted as long as it did. So far as the Chinese were concerned, in the late 1970s, there were "three great obstacles" to the restoration of closer relations: Soviet troops in Afghanistan, the Soviet military presence along their long common border, and Soviet support for the Vietnamese-sponsored regime in Kampuchea. The Soviet leadership, for its part, deplored Chinese policy on many international issues but called for the normalization of relations "on the basis of peaceful coexistence". By 1981, however, in Brezhnev's view "unfortunately", there was still no sign of an improvement in the relationship.

Gorbachev, in his accession speech, called specifically for closer relations between the USSR and China, and added that this was "entirely feasible" if there was some reciprocity on the Chinese side. The Chinese deputy premier (and later premier) Li Peng, who was in Moscow for the occasion, publicly agreed that an improvement in relations was desirable; an agreement on educational exchanges and a trade pact followed later in the year. Gorbachev, addressing the XXVII CPSU Congress in 1986, was able to welcome the improvement that had already taken place in relations with "socialist China". Differences remained; but it was also clear that in many cases the two countries could work together, on an equal and principled basis, without prejudice to the interests of other countries. In a speech at

Vladivostok the following July he expanded these remarks to a broad conception of an Asian security zone. The Pacific region, Gorbachev observed, had not been militarized to the same extent as Europe. There was however some danger of developments of this kind given the resources of the powers that were active in the region. The two biggest wars since 1945, the Korean and Vietnamese, had taken place in Asia; and there was no counterpart to the Helsinki Final Act and the framework of dialogue it had established. In these circumstances, Gorbachev explained, the Soviet Union would expand its bilateral ties with all the states, socialist and non-socialist, in the region. He indicated, on a point of particular importance to the Chinese, that the withdrawal of a substantial number of the Soviet troops stationed in Mongolia was under active consideration: and he announced that six Soviet regiments were being withdrawn from Afghanistan. The Soviet Union and China, Gorbachev observed, had the same priority—to accelerate social and economic development; and he suggested specific forms of co-operation in cross-border trade, railways and space exploration. Gorbachev welcomed the broader ideas that were in circulation concerning Pacific economic co-operation and the possibility of a Pacific "Helsinki". More significantly, he supported proposals to establish a Pacific nuclear-free zone and to lower levels of troops and armaments to that of "reasonable sufficiency".

Proposals such as these went a long way to alleviate Chinese concerns and brought closer the possibility of a summit meeting between the two leaderships for which Soviet spokesmen had for some time been calling. The final obstacles were removed when the Chinese foreign minister visited Moscow in December 1988 and **Shevardnadze** visited Peking early in the following year; both sides agreed on the desirability of "Chinese-Soviet relations of a new type". Gorbachev, finally, was able to visit Peking in May 1989, the first Soviet leader to do so for 30 years. The talks, inevitably, were overshadowed by public demonstrations of support for the Soviet leader which in turn contributed to a wave of public resistance to the policies of the Chinese government itself. There was some substance, nonetheless, to Gorbachev's claim that relations between the two countries were entering a "qualitatively new stage", and he suggested several ways in which such relations could be carried further, including a new "liquid coal" pipeline, a new "silk way" from China to Europe, and various forms of inter-regional co-operation. The joint communiqué with which the visit concluded welcomed the normalization of relations between the two countries, and between their two ruling parties. Although there were differences on the form of government that should be established in Kampuchea, both sides welcomed the Vietnamese commitment to withdraw its troops by the end of September 1989. The level of armed forces along the Sino-Soviet border would be reduced to a minimum, and any remaining territorial differences would be resolved on the basis of international law. The Chinese leaders, finally, were invited to make an official visit to the USSR so that the discussions could be continued.

SLW

SOVIET RELATIONS WITH THE DEVEL-OPING WORLD. Soviet policy-makers in the **Stalin** years had generally taken little interest in the colonial or newly independent world. Under **Khrushchev**, however, there was a reassessment, and Soviet policy has from this time onwards sought to further links of all kinds with the developing nations both at the political level and through trade, investment, arms sales, the training of students and so forth. A particularly close interest has been taken in states of "socialist orientation" in the developing world, particularly in Africa. States of "socialist orientation", in the Soviet view, are those that are carrying out major social transformations such as the nationalization of foreign monopolies, redistribution of land and industrialization, and which are taking steps to further public education and to reduce poverty and unemployment. Of particular importance from the Soviet point of view, states of this kind are held to be "objectively anti-imperialist" in that they generally seek to oppose the substantial control over their domestic affairs that has traditionally been exercised by the major capitalist powers.

Some countries of "socialist orientation", such as Afghanistan, became very close allies of the USSR in the **Brezhnev** years and indeed all but members of the socialist state system. Soviet intervention in Afghanistan in December 1979 followed a coup in that country in April 1978 which brought a pro-Soviet Marxist government to power headed by Hafizullah Amin. The coup was apparently neither instigated nor expected by the Soviet authorities, and it brought a regime to power which was bitterly divided by factional differences. The new government provoked widespread rebellion by instituting a series of far-reaching reforms in a brutal and disorganized manner. Before December 1979 there were already 7,000 Soviet military and civilian advisers in Afghanistan, but the government called for further Soviet support to suppress the domestic resistance. On Dec. 24 the Soviet authorities, fearing a further change of government and perhaps of political orientation, began to airlift troops into Kabul; it was claimed that they were responding to an appeal from the Afghan government to suppress a counter-revolution which was being fomented from outside the country, and that their action was justified by the Soviet–Afghan friendship treaty. On Dec. 27 Babrak Karmal, who had been a member of the post-coup government but who had subsequently been exiled to the USSR, announced that the former president had been deposed and that he had taken power; the following day it was announced that Hafizullah Amin had been executed for "crimes against the noble people of Afghanistan".

The months and years that followed saw the establishment of a much more substantial Soviet presence in Afghanistan than any that had previously existed, including political and economic links as well as a growing military commitment. For at least some Western observers Soviet action was not simply a violation of international agreements but an attempt to establish a greater degree of influence in the Persian Gulf, an area of enormous significance for Western oil supplies and one in which the Western position had aleady been weakened by the overthrow of the Shah of Iran. Others saw the action in a more defensive light: as Brezhnev explained at the XXVI Party Congress in 1981, the situation in Afghanistan posed a "direct threat to the security of [the Soviet] southern frontier", and it was certainly true that an unstable, possibly militant Islamic government in a state immediately adjoining the USSR's southern borders might have quite serious implications for public order in the traditionally Muslim republics of Central Asia. Whatever the Soviet objectives might have been, it soon became apparent that it would be very difficult to achieve them.

Babrak Karmal, for a start, proved unable to unite the warring Khalq (Masses) and Parcham (Banner) factions of the People's Democratic Party, the organization upon which his authority depended. Karmal was subsequently replaced as party leader and president by Najibullah, but there was little progress in establishing the broadly based "government of national reconciliation" which was his declared objective. There was considerable destruction in Afghanistan itself: between a quarter and a fifth of the population became refugees, perhaps a million Afghans died, and a series of civil and military objects including roads, bridges and airfields were destroyed. Soviet forces were able to employ enormous firepower, including helicopter gunships and SU-25 attack aircraft, but they established firm control only in the major cities and along the major highways, and much of the countryside remained in the hands of the *mujahaddin* guerrillas, particularly during the hours of darkness. The war was an unsatisfactory one for the USSR in several other respects. It alienated world opinion, particularly in the Third World; it was very expensive (according to figures made public in 1989, the cost was about five billion rubles annually); and it was very costly in terms of human life (according to figures again made public in 1989, nearly 14,000 Soviet servicemen lost their lives in the course of the war, more than 11,000 of them in combat). The war became a most unpopular one domestically as the toll of dead and injured steadily mounted. Despite attempts to glamourize those who died fulfilling their "internationalist duty" in Afghanistan, there were many letters in the Soviet press complaining of the one-sided treatment of the war that had been provided in the Soviet media and of the failure to make proper provision for the wounded on their return to the USSR. There were even suggestions, in published letters, that senior officials had used their influence to prevent their own sons being sent to the front line.

Influenced by considerations such as these, successive leaderships had attempted since almost the beginning of the war to extricate their forces from the conflict. Soviet forces were not, at least in the first instance, to be withdrawn unconditionally. Rather, in negotiations that had proceeded under United Nations auspices since 1981, they were to withdraw upon a number of specific conditions. As Brezhnev told the XXVI Party Congress in 1981, "the sovereignty of Afghanistan must be fully protected, as must its non-aligned status". This meant in practice that all foreign intervention, by the United States and Pakistan as well as the USSR, must come to an end; secure guarantees must be provided that there would be no further intervention in Afghan affairs; and the People's Democratic Party (which remained strongly Soviet-aligned) was to be accorded a dominant position in any future Afghan government. Further negotiations led finally to a series of agreements. Signed in Geneva in April 1988, providing for the withdrawal of Soviet forces. The agreements—comparable, in *Pravda*'s view, to the INF treaty—included bilateral accords between Afghanistan and Pakistan on non-interference and non-intervention, and on the voluntary return of refugees; a Soviet–US declaration in support of these agreements; and a joint agreement on the settlement of the Afghan situation which provided for the "phased withdrawal" of Soviet troops, half of them between May and August 1988 and the

remainder within the following nine months. Soviet troop withdrawals began on May 15 and were completed on schedule on Feb. 15 1989; **Shevardnadze**, addressing the Supreme Soviet in October 1989, described the whole espisode as a violation of "general human values" and of party and state procedures.

Developments in Afghanistan assumed a greater significance for Western governments than they would otherwise have had because of the place they appeared to occupy in an "Arc of Crisis" that extended from the Middle East to South-Eastern Asia. The formation of an anti-Western government in Iran after the fall of the Shah, the increasingly explicit Marxist-Leninist orientation of the People's Democratic Republic of Yemen and Soviet involvement in the Horn of Africa, together with the build-up of the Soviet fleet in the Indian Ocean, seemed to offer convincing evidence of a wide-ranging and effective Soviet strategy directed against vital Western interests, not least the supply of oil and the security of major shipping routes. The intervention of Cuban troops in Angola in 1975 and in the Ogaden war between Ethiopia and Somalia in 1977–78—in both cases, it was assumed, acting as Soviet proxies—appeared to provide further evidence of a new global interventionism. It was in these circumstances that Western governments began to consider initiatives such as a rapid deployment force in the Gulf area and other measures designed to protect their essential interests.

Soviet strategy had in fact been much more reactive and rather less successful than this picture tended to suggest. This was clearly the case in Soviet relations with Egypt, which became the USSR's most important ally in the Middle East after the mid-1950s when Western governments refused to finance the Aswan Dam. The USSR had been one of the first governments to recognize the state of Israel in 1948, but Soviet support was thereafter thrown behind the Arab cause and behind the Egyptian war effort in particular. Soviet–Egyptian relations remained close even after the death of Nasser in 1970, and the following year, under his successor Anwar Sadat, the two states concluded a 15-year friendship treaty, the first of its kind to be made between the USSR and an Arab government. Its 12 articles covered military as well as economic collaboration, and the Soviet presence in Egypt in the early 1970s became the largest anywhere outside the Communist bloc at this time. In 1972, however, following a number of disagreements, 20,000 Soviet military advisers were ordered to leave the country. In 1976 the friendship treaty was abrogated, Soviet debts (some $11 billion) were repudiated, and the Egyptians moved closer to the

USA, which had played a central role in the Camp David and other peace negotiations in the area. In 1984, under Sadat's successor Mubarak, the two countries again exchanged ambassadors, but there seemed little likelihood that Soviet–Egyptian relations would ever regain their former intimacy.

Rather closer relations were maintained, in the late 1980s, with the People's Democratic Republic of Yemen (South Yemen), which signed a friendship treaty with the USSR in 1979 but remained a very minor power in terms of size and influence. Military co-operation also led to the conclusion of a friendship treaty with North Yemen in 1984. Iraq, with whom a friendship treaty was concluded in 1972, has remained a much more important Soviet ally in the region, but relations have sometimes been difficult, particularly following the outbreak of the Iran – Iraq war in 1980. The war was an "absolutely senseless" one, according to Brezhnev at this time, and the USSR initially took a broadly neutral position, hoping to retain the alliance with Iraq but at the same time not to alienate the new and anti-Western Khomeini government in Iran. Latterly the USSR appeared to have reverted to its traditional support for Iraq, while calling for a negotiated settlement at the earliest opportunity. The August 1988 ceasefire was warmly welcomed. Close relations were also maintained with Syria (which concluded a friendship treaty with the USSR in 1980), and with India, which signed a friendship treaty as early as 1971 and which has remained one of the closest of the USSR's non-Communist allies under Indira Gandhi and her successor Rajiv. The USSR became India's main external source of weaponry and rendered extensive economic aid; Soviet support was in part a response to the support that Pakistan received from the Chinese, with whom the Indians had an unresolved border dispute. **Gorbachev** made an official visit to India in November 1986, concluding with the signature of a "Delhi Declaration" in which both sides pledged themselves to the peaceful resolution of international disputes. A further official visit took place in November 1988, in the course of which both sides reaffirmed their commitment to the Declaration and to the elaboration of a long-term programme for economic, trade, cultural, scientific and co-operation to the year 2000.

Relations with the largest non-Arab country in the Middle East, Iran, were rather more complex both before and after the fall of the Shah. Soviet agreements with the Shah included credits for arms purchases and the construction of an oil pipeline. Iran, in fact, was the Soviet Union's largest trading partner in the Middle East during this period. After the overthrow of the Shah in 1979 the USSR ordered the local Communist party (Tudeh) to support the Ayatollah Khomeini, and even began to supply the new regime with weapons. As Brezhnev explained to the XXVI Party Congress in 1981, developments in Iran were "complex and contradictory" but what had taken place was nonetheless an "anti-imperialist revolution". Relations were not disturbed even when the Khomeini government arrested Tudeh leaders and dissolved their movement in 1983. Latterly, however, the Khomeini regime began to describe the USSR as the "greater Satan"; cultural exchanges were ended, the size of the Soviet mission was restricted, Soviet journalists were refused entry visas, and in March 1988 there was an attack upon the Soviet embassy in Tehran. Both Soviet and American leaders, by the late 1980s, had a common interest in a negotiated end to the Iran–Iraq war and in an international agreement guaranteeing freedom of movement in the Gulf, but neither could necessarily manipulate events in the region to its advantage and neither, perhaps, quite understood the nature of a popular movement so far removed from its own cultural assumptions.

This varied picture of successes and reverses suggested that the USSR was not, in the "Arc of Crisis" or anywhere else, pursuing a long-term strategy based on Marxist-Leninist doctrine. The evidence suggested rather that the USSR was a defensive and sometimes opportunist power, responding to changing circumstances in much the same way that any other government (or its tsarist predecessor) might have done. Nor was it a particularly successful strategy, despite some apparently spectacular advances in Africa and Afghanistan. The Soviet Union, for instance, sometimes backed the wrong horse (such as Nkomo rather than Mugabe in Zimbabwe). The main instruments of Soviet influence were arms sales and direct subsidies, both expensive to maintain; and neither necessarily secured a permanent commitment (Egypt and Somalia, for instance, abrogated their friendship treaties with the USSR in the 1970s, and the USSR was unable to prevent the replacement of a friendly regime in Grenada by American military action in 1983). Local allies, it turned out, were often reluctant to accept guidance from the USSR; some of them (Egypt, Iraq, the Sudan and Ethiopia) persecuted and even executed large numbers of their domestic Communist party members, and others took different views on international issues (Iraq, for instance, openly supported Somalia in the Ogaden war). Soviet allies sometimes found themselves opposed to each other (such as the Baathist governments of Syria and Iraq, or

Ethiopia and Somalia), and others entered into agreements with Soviet adversaries (both Angola and Mozambique, for instance, signed non-aggression agreements with South Africa in 1984, and Soviet clients generally found it difficult to resist the powerful influence of Western governments and corporations, or in the case of Ethiopia, relief agencies).

It was perhaps above all because of this disenchanting experience that the USSR, under Gorbachev's leadership, began to take a more distanced view of the future development of Third World states. Gorbachev's report to the XXVII Party Congress in 1986 was the first in modern times to make no reference to the need to assist "national liberation" movements in the developing countries; rather, the Soviet leader appeared to favour a "comprehensive system of international security" involving "the use for the welfare of the world community, above all of the developing countries, of part of the funds that [would] be released as a result of the reduction in military budgets". The Party Programme, adopted at the same congress, promised only that the Soviet Union would "do what it could" to assist socialist-oriented states in the developing world; and authoritative commentaries made it clear that the USSR preferred the peaceful settlement of regional conflicts rather than the "export of revolution". The USSR, as before, remained ready to further its own interests wherever it could, and those interests were not always in agreement with those of Western governments – nor had they been under the tsarist government. There was, however, a greater awareness of the need to develop a framework of rules which could operate in the interests of the world community as a whole — against terrorism or narcotics, for instance — and a greater readiness to establish relations with traditionally conservative states — including South Africa and the Arab monarchies — as well as with those that claimed to adhere to **Marxism-Leninism**. How far this reorientation extended was likely to depend at least as much upon the responses of Western governments and the behaviour of the other states concerned as it did upon the Soviet authorities themselves.

SLW

SOVIET RELATIONS WITH THE WEST.
The central issue in global terms, for any Soviet General Secretary, is the relationship with the other superpower. The state of those relations, on **Gorbachev**'s accession, was not an encouraging one. The wartime alliance had been followed by an occasionally hot "cold war" and then, from the 1950s onwards, by a cautious search for a limited *modus vivendi*. The first major step towards what became known as "detente" was probably the Partial Test Ban Treaty, signed by Britain, the USA, the USSR and eventually 103 other nations (but not China or France) in 1963 (for the background to these issues *see* **Arms Control**). There appears to have been some resistance within the Soviet military to **Khrushchev**'s doctrine of "minimum deterrence"—the USSR, he had complained in 1963, could not produce "nothing but rockets"—and the Cuban missile crisis and later the Vietnam war delayed the signature of further agreements. But then in 1968 a Nuclear Non-proliferation Treaty was signed, in 1971 a treaty was signed prohibiting the testing or use of nuclear weapons on the sea bed and in 1972 three related treaties were signed in Moscow by Leonid **Brezhnev** and Richard Nixon. These were SALT I (Intermediate Agreement on the Limitation of Strategic Offensive Arms), a Treaty on the Limitation of Anti-Ballistic Missile Systems (the ABM treaty) and a set of Basic Principles for the conduct of US–Soviet relations. SALT I, the most important of these, placed limits on the further construction of intercontinental nuclear weapon systems by both sides; it was intended to remain in force for five years or until superseded by a more comprehensive agreement, and it was the first real fruit of negotiations that had been proceeding since the late 1960s.

In June 1979 a further agreement, SALT II (Treaty on the Limitation of Strategic Offensive Arms), was signed by American and Soviet representatives in Vienna, based upon the provisional agreements reached in Vladivostok and earlier. The treaty limited each side to no more than 2,400 intercontinental launching vehicles and heavy bombers until 1981, and to 2,250 thereafter until the treaty expired in 1985. The treaty, however, was not presented to the US Senate for ratification, following Soviet military intervention in Afghanistan in December 1979. The deepening crisis in Poland during 1980 and 1981, and what was believed to be a Soviet role in the imposition of martial law in December 1981, made matters worse; so too did Cuban intervention in Angola, and US support for the Contra guerrillas in Nicaragua. "Detente" quickly became a pejorative term, and President Reagan, elected in 1980, referred to the USSR in a celebrated phrase as an "evil empire". The Russians, he declared at his first press conference, would "lie and cheat and pursue their ends of world domination". Economic, cultural and other relations between the superpowers also deteriorated; the Olympic games of 1980 were a notable casualty.

"Detente" had also involved a series of parallel

negotiations and agreements on territorial, economic and other matters. An agreement on the first of these had always been an objective of the Soviet leadership, in order to stabilize the situation in Europe and thus secure formal Western acceptance of the post-war settlement in Eastern Europe. Towards this end they advanced the idea of a European security conference from the mid-1960s onwards. After some detailed negotiation about the composition and scope of such a gathering, the Conference on Security and Co-operation in Europe (CSCE) finally opened in 1973 in Helsinki, and in August 1975 the 33 participating nations signed a Final Act—an agreement rather than a formal treaty—which recognized existing boundaries in Europe, in effect legitimizing the division of the continent into Soviet and Western spheres of influence which had existed since the end of the war. The Soviet and East European participants, however, were obliged in return to give their agreement to the so-called "Basket 3", which concerned the movement of people and ideas between East and West in areas such as tourism, the reunification of families and access to printed and other media.

With the deterioration in East–West relations more generally in the late 1970s, other sets of negotiations made less progress. MBFR (Mutual and Balanced Force Reduction) talks began at Vienna in 1973 but became deadlocked around questions such as the way in which the forces deployed on both sides should be counted and whether absolute or relative reductions should be made: the first of these suited the East, which had larger totals, but the second was pressed by Western negotiators. INF (Intermediate-Range Nuclear Force) talks began at Geneva in November 1981 but broke down two years later. Geneva was also the location for the START (Strategic Arms Reduction) talks, which began in June 1982 but made no more progress. Although negotiations on arms reductions were about to resume in Geneva when Gorbachev assumed the general secretaryship, cruise and Pershing-II weapons had already been deployed in Western Europe following the NATO "dual track" decision of 1979 (this was itself represented as a response to the Soviet decision to replace its ageing SS-4 and -5 missiles in eastern Europe with more modern SS-20s). Weapons such as the Pershing-II, launched from western Europe, could reach Soviet territory in about 10 minutes and were seen as strategic rather than intermediate in character by Soviet negotiators. For the USA, on the other hand, strategic weapons were those that were launched from the USSR (or from nuclear submarines) and which in turn gave greater opportunities for defensive action.

Chemical weapons, and the whole question of verification, raised additional difficulties.

Perhaps most fundamental of all, however, was the climate of hostility and mistrust that existed between East and West during the "new cold war" of the late 1970s and early 1980s; and it was the dissipation of this climate, above all through a series of face-to-face meetings between the Soviet and American leaders, that contributed most directly to the resumption of progress in arms control and other matters. The first of these summit meetings took place at Geneva in November 1985; it provided an opportunity for an exchange of views on the progress made at the arms talks and on regional issues. The importance of the summit was, above all, that it had taken place, and that the two leaders had been pictured together in amicable fireside discussion. The communiqué that was issued after the meeting noted that the talks had been "frank and useful" and did not disguise the fact that there were still "major differences" on a series of key issues; but the two leaders had achieved a better understanding of their respective positions and had agreed on the importance of maintaining a "constant dialogue". The Soviet Politburo, reviewing the talks, described them as a "major political event" and thought particularly significant the two leaders' declaration that a nuclear war could not be won and must never be fought; this was at odds with the views of some influential US (and Soviet) strategists.

The joint statement that had been issued by the two leaders at Geneva also addressed some of the issues that had arisen in the arms control negotiations. The statement called for a 50 per cent reduction, "appropriately applied", in their strategic arsenals, an interim INF agreement and appropriate measures to "prevent an arms race in space". This was an allusion to the Strategic Defense or "Star Wars" Initiative that the American President had unveiled in March 1983. Reagan himself claimed that the SDI was defensive in character, since it was designed to dispose of nuclear weapons before they reached their target, and that it was in any event a programme of research in the first instance. Critics of the programme, who were numerous in the USA as well as in the Soviet Union, maintained that it would violate the ABM treaty and therefore undermine the whole concept of deterrence by allowing a first strike to be delivered from behind a space "shield" which would prevent or at least reduce the risk of retaliation. There were additional concerns in Europe, given that the SDI programme was designed to ensure immunity for the United States and that it might prejudice the US commitment to European security in the event of nuclear war. Gorbachev, both at Geneva and his subsequent address to the Supreme Soviet, argued that SDI was in effect a new type of armament, a "space-strike weapon" which could be used against missiles, satellites or land-based targets. It would certainly give a new twist to the arms race; indeed some of Reagan's advisers appeared to be recommending SDI precisely because they thought the Soviet economy would collapse under the strain of attempting to match it. At a conference in Stockholm in late September 1986, nonetheless, a last-minute agreement was reached that each side should give the other advance warning of troop movements, and that on-site verification should be permitted on a limited basis for the first time. It was in these difficult but not unhopeful circumstances that the two leaders met again, at a reputedly haunted house in Reykjavik on Oct. 11–12, 1986.

The Soviet negotiators arrived, as Gorbachev claimed subsequently, with a package of arms reduction proposals that would if accepted have marked a "new era in the history of humanity". In the discussions Gorbachev proposed a cut of at least 50 per cent in US and Soviet strategic arms, leading to their total elimination by the end of the century. The whole "triad" of strategic arms was to be involved, including land-based missiles, sea-launched missiles and heavy bombers. Both US and Soviet intermediate-range missiles in Europe were to be eliminated entirely, without reference to the British and French deterrents (this was a concession as compared with the Soviet position at Geneva); and discussions should start immediately on the elimination of such missiles from Asia, and on shorter-range or tactical missiles. The ABM treaty was to be respected by both sides for at least a further 10 years (it was of indefinite duration but both sides had the right to withdraw after due notice). Laboratory research on SDI could continue; but it could not, Gorbachev insisted, be tested, let alone deployed, in space. And it was on this point that the discussions broke down, as Gorbachev was unwilling to allow any element in his package of proposals to be agreed without agreement on all the others.

The third summit between the two leaders, which took place in Washington in December 1987, was undoubtedly the most significant. Indeed it was historic, in that it provided for the first time for the elimination of an entire class of nuclear arms—land-based missiles of intermediate and shorter range. Although this represented no more than 4 to 5 per cent of their combined nuclear arsenals, it was nonetheless the first significant agreement of this kind between the two powers since the ABM treaty of 1972, and

was held by both sides to presage the conclusion of an agreement the following year which would make cuts of up to 50 per cent in strategic nuclear arms. The agreement, which was of unlimited duration, made no direct reference to SDI; nor did it involve conventional or chemical weapons, although both sides expressed a wish to reach an agreement on such matters at the earliest opportunity. The two sides, however, did instruct their negotiators at Geneva to "work out an agreement that would commit the sides to observe the ABM treaty, as signed in 1972", and to devise measures which would help to "ensure predictability in the development of the US–Soviet strategic relationship". Further measures were agreed to improve Soviet-American bilateral relations; and President Reagan accepted Gorbachev's invitation to visit the USSR the following year.

In his television address to the Soviet people on the results of the summit Gorbachev described the INF treaty as a "major event in world politics" and a "victory for the new political thinking", which represented a "first step towards the actual liquidation of the nuclear arsenal". Although only a small number of weapons had been eliminated, scientists had calculated that just 5 per cent of the weapons that existed were sufficient to destroy the world. The agreement, moreover, had shown that it was possible to restrain and even reverse the arms race. There were still powerful forces in the West, however, that were opposed to ratification of the treaty and anxious to "compensate" for it by the modernization of existing arsenals and the rapid development of SDI. Such "dangerous tendencies" could undermine the achievement of the summit in helping to bring about the demilitarization of international relations. The Politburo, meeting on Dec. 17, welcomed the agreement as "historic", and Soviet public opinion, according at least to some rapidly-conducted opinion polls, appeared to take the same view.

The fourth and final summit between the two leaders took place in Moscow in May–June 1988; it was the first visit by a US President to the Soviet capital for 14 years. During the summit talks were held on arms control, human rights, and regional and bilateral issues, with both sides reportedly obtaining a "better understanding of each other's positions" on all such matters. The INF treaty, agreed at Washington the previous December, was formally signed by the two leaders on June 1, following its ratification a few days earlier by the US Senate and by the USSR Supreme Soviet (the first Soviet rockets were destroyed, to some publicity, in early August). A joint statement issued by the two leaders described the meeting as an "important step in the process of putting US–Soviet relations on a more productive and sustainable basis"; in particular, a draft treaty on the reduction and limitation of strategic nuclear arms had been discussed and a series of agreements had been made on the contentious question of the verification of nuclear testing. Nevertheless, "serious differences" remained on important issues. Gorbachev, at a press conference on June 1, expressed the view that more could have been achieved, including a joint statement of political principle and some advance in the discussions on conventional arms; but politics, in the end, was the "art of the possible". The Politburo, at its meeting a few days later, described the summit as a "major event in international life" whose main result had been the "deepening of the political dialogue between the Soviet Union and the USA".

The dialogue did, indeed, continue under Reagan's successor George Bush. The two leaders held their first meeting in December 1989 on two storm-tossed vessels off the coast of Malta; it was dubbed the "seasick summit". The meeting was not intended to lead to a formal outcome but it concluded, symbolically in Gorbachev's view, with the first joint press conference held by leaders of the two nations. Their discussions, Gorbachev indicated, had been conducted in a "good atmosphere", although there were clear differences of opinion on disarmament and chemical weapons, and there had been a "constructive" (code for sharply polarized) discussion on regional issues. There was, nonetheless, a broad measure of agreement that the next step in bilateral relations should be a 50 per cent reduction in strategic offensive weapons, and an agreement to this effect was expected in 1990. There was also agreement that the "Helsinki process" that had been initiated in 1975 should be taken further, reflecting the rapid and far-reaching nature of changes in the European continent; Gorbachev, in this connection, pointed out that the existence of two German states had been "decided by history" and warned against an "artificial acceleration" of their increasingly close relationship. Soviet–Western relations, throughout the period as a whole, had developed rapidly in commercial, scientific and other terms, and rested upon an increasingly widespread perception that the Cold War had been succeeded by a period in which differing interests would be resolved without the use of force. (*See also* **Arms Control**)

SLW

SOVIET WOMEN'S COMMITTEE. This organization was established after World War II and grew out of the Soviet Women's Anti-Fascist Committee which had been set up in 1941. Its official brief is to develop co-operation with women's organizations abroad in order to promote peace, friendship and mutual understanding. Since 1985 its role has expanded and it has been placed at the apex of the hierarchy of the *zhensovety*, or women's councils. The Committee has its headquarters in Moscow. It meets in plenary session once a year and directs its daily work from a smaller Presidium. The current chairperson is Zoya Pukhova who has extensive experience in the textile industry. She worked her way up from a weaver to factory director. From 1968 to 1987 Valentina Tereshkova, pilot and astronaut, held this post.

The East European states have similar committees: the Committee of Bulgarian Women, the Democratic Women's Federation of Germany, the National Council of Hungarian Women, the Czechoslovak Women's Union, the Polish Women's League, the National Women's Council (Romania), the Conference for Social Activities of Yugoslav Women and the Women's Union of Albania. In common, they all aim to involve women in society and politics. All except the Women's Union of Albania are officially committed to promoting peace and to enhancing the mutual understanding of women of the world.

MB

SPORT. An interesting aspect of both *perestroika* in the Soviet Union and the turbulent events in Eastern Europe in the late 1980s has been the intensive debate on sport. In East Germany, some sports stars have been physically assaulted and their conspicuous sports reward symbols — cars and city apartments — vandalised. In Romania, Czechoslovakia, Hungary and Poland, a number of prominent sports clubs have changed their name, dropping the security police tag ("Dinamo" in East Germany, Romania and Yugoslavia).

Such events demonstrated that far from being on the periphery of politics, sport in Eastern Europe had been at the centre of state policies, identified in the popular consciousness with the old regime, privilege, distorted priorities and, in the case of the non-Soviet Communist states, a Soviet-imposed institution.

In fact, throughout the 1980s radical changes began to appear in Communist sport, breaking the mould of its functionalized and bureaucratic (plan-fulfilment) structure. Until then, not only had the Soviet-pioneered, state-controlled system hampered a true appraisal of realities that lay beneath the "universal" statistics and "idealized" veneer, it had prevented concessions to particular groups in the population — the "we know what's best for you" syndrome, whereby men tell women what sports they should play; the fit tell the disabled that sport is not for them; the old tell the young they can play on their (old) terms, in their clubs, using their facilities; and political leadership, mindful of the nation's and ideology's international reputation, decide that competitive Olympic (i.e European) sports are the only civilized forms of culture.

It has to be said that this system has not only helped to make several Communist states (the USSR, East Germany, Hungary, Cuba) forces to be reckoned with in world sport, its orientation on social change through sport (for purposes of improving defence, health and hygiene, integration, productivity and international prestige) has found ready imitators in many developing states.

Since it was the Soviet system of sport that was imposed upon or slavishly imitated in all Communist states after World War II, including China and the German Democratic Republic, despite their own long sports traditions, it will be instructive to review the evolution of Soviet sport since 1917.

Soviet sports history. After the Russian Revolution of 1917, several political leaders wondered whether sport should exist at all in a workers' state. After all, as they pointed out, sports as we know them today, disciplined and competitive, were largely developed in the early years of Western industrialization by the "middle classes" or bourgeoisie and imbued with their values as a means of preparing them for future careers in *laissez faire* capitalism or as agents of colonial development. If it were ideology alone which determined the story of Soviet sport, we might well be looking at an entirely different pattern of recreation than that which presently exists in the USSR. But there have been many factors that have shaped Soviet sport over the last 70-odd years—Russian historical traditions, climate, the twin processes of urbanization and industrialization, international status, military considerations, and so on.

It has to be remembered that the USSR has progressed unevenly from a way of life which quite recently was largely traditionalist in a comparatively brief historical span. The rapid process of modernization and the high rates of change in socio-demographic indices (e.g. changing from an 80 per cent peasant, illiterate society to a totally literate, 35 per cent peasant society in the Soviet period) have ineluctably put their imprint on Soviet sport. In practical policy, at least from the early 1930s until the mid-1980s, Soviet leaders would seem to have opted for the following:

(i) the organization of working people in their free time to the maximum possible extent within the framework of a tidy hierarchical and functional structure;

(ii) the cultivation of competitive sport (a leisure-time analogue of competition between people at work designed to raise work tempos) with—again, as at work—material rewards for victors, the more efficiently to improve people's readiness for work and to pre-train soldiers for the Soviet nation-state;

(iii) using sport, specifically as a means of obtaining the fit, obedient and disciplined workforce needed for achieving economic and military strength and efficiency—in particular, in order to: (a) raise physical and social health standards; (b) develop general physical dexterity, motor skills and other physical qualities needed in "labour and defence"; (c) socialize the population into the new system of values; character training advanced (so the Soviet leaders seem to have believed) by sport, in such values as loyalty, conformity, team-spirit, co-operation and discipline, which may well have encouraged compliance and co-operation in both work and politics, including an uncynical attitude towards political leaders; (d) encourage a population, in rapid transition from a rural to an urban way of life, to identify themselves with wider communities — all-embracing social units such as the workplace, the neighbourhood, the town, the region, the republic and, ultimately, the whole country. By associating sport (like other amenities) organizationally with the workplace, the party leadership and its agencies could, moreover, better supervise, control and "rationalize" the leisure time activities of employees;

(iv) linking sport ideologically and even organizationally with military preparedness. In a vast country with problems of communication, lukewarm popular attitudes towards physical exercise and few sports facilities for most of the Soviet period, military organization of sport was actually an efficient method of deploying scarce resources in the most economical way and using methods of direction which were, perhaps, more effective coming from paramilitary than from civilian organizations.

Three features of this Soviet sports system that have been copied in Eastern Europe and that distinguish it from that of Western nations need to be explained.

First, sport is a political institution in the USSR run by the state. The USSR National Olympic Committee (NOC) is therefore a government body appointed by the USSR Sports Committee (which is, in Western terms, a government ministry) and run by a member of the ruling political party in the USSR — the **Communist Party of the Soviet Union**. The policy of both the Sports Committee and the NOC is always determined by the party and government. For example, any decision of Olympic or other sporting boycotts is made by the party Politburo without consultation with the NOC or Sports Committee; the decision is simply passed down for implementation (as happened in regard to the Soviet boycott of the 1984 Summer Olympics in Los Angeles). In the past this Soviet party Politburo decision had been passed down also to other members of the **Warsaw Treaty Organization (Warsaw Pact)**.

Second, all athletes of Master of Sport ranking and above (International Class Master of Sport and Merited Master of Sport) have always been full-time professionals or "state amateurs" whose job of work, as inscribed in their work record, is sport, and whose remuneration is from sport in accordance with their qualifications, ranking and attainments. It has to be said in parenthesis that the Soviet leadership only introduced 'state amateur' status into Soviet sport in the late 1940s, under International Olympic Committee pressure, as a ploy to join the Olympic movement (the USSR and other East European states were admitted in 1951). From that time the appearance had to be given that performers received no remuneration from their sports performance, nor did they devote themselves full time to sport. In fact, they either received officer sinecures (if men) in the armed forces or the state security services (the Dinamo Club which, throughout Eastern Europe, has been sponsored and financed by the security police) or they received payment for fictitious work at factories, or they remained students for as long as their active career in sport lasted.

Third, at least until the *glasnost'* period of openness was inaugurated by **Gorbachev**, no autonomous body or articulated interest group was capable of exerting any appreciable influence on state policies in sport, particularly those that affected international relations — let alone counteracting or modifying them. It follows, therefore, that Soviet external sports relations have always kept in step with the evolution and sometimes erratic course of Soviet foreign policy, at one time involving the boycott of the Olympic Games (before World War II and in 1984), at another their passionate defence.

Changes since 1985. With the mood of *glasnost'*, the sudden spate of honesty after 1985 and the broaching of previously censored subjects have revealed the dark side of Soviet sport and stirred up considerable debate. Journalists now talk

frankly of match fixing in the major spectator sports (soccer, ice hockey, basketball and volleyball), bribery of referees, drug-taking and other nefarious activities hitherto mentioned only in the context of capitalist sport.

The following would seem to be the major trends in Soviet sport in the late 1980s and early 1990s.

(i) *Sport for all.* The Soviet leadership has always maintained in public that *massovost'* (mass enrolment) takes precedence over *masterstvo* (mastery), and down the years it has produced regiments of statistics to prove the case: that millions are regular, active participants in sport; that the vast majority of school- and college-students gain a *GTO* (*Gotov k trudu i oborone* — "Prepared for Labour and Defence", initially based on Baden-Powell's Boy Scout athletics and marksman's badges) national fitness programme; that rising millions (a third of the population) take part in the quadrennial spartakiads; and that the bulk of workers do their daily dozen — "production gymnastics" — at the workplace.

We now learn in this "honesty is the best policy" era that these figures were fraudulent and a show to impress people above and below and to meet preset targets (each school, region, factory and farm received a sports quota and incurred penalties if they fell short). It is now admitted that only 8 per cent of men and 2 per cent of women engage in sport regularly, that only 0.5 per cent of Moscow's 11-year-olds meet the *GTO* standards, and some two-thirds of workers never take any physical exercise.

A first step to involve more people in sport was to depart from the previously hallowed principle of free sport by introducing charges for use of pool, gym, court and stadium. Further, a number of co-operative (i.e. private) health, fitness and sports clubs have been permitted to open. The *GTO* system has been quietly dropped, as have the spartakiads. The trade unions have declared their intention of reducing top-level leagues and competitions, to close down some of the elite sports schools they had been financing, so as to divert more funds to sport for all and to cater for a diversity of interest groups and health clubs.

(ii) *Independent clubs.* Young people have not sat around awaiting government resolutions. In fact, a major cause of official action is that young people have been turning their backs on official organizations, like the Young Pioneers and Young Communist League (Komsomol — *see* **Youth** — The Komsomol in Soviet history), as well as officially-recommended and sponsored activities, and have been forming their own groups and clubs. In the field of sport, the clubs range from soccer fan clubs to groups for sports in which the authorities have been slow to provide facilities— aerobics, yoga, body building, jogging, karate and other combat sports. The forced acceptance of such independent clubs is a radical departure for the authorities; after all, no youth groups free of party tutelage had been tolerated since the 1920s.

Young women, in particular, have long ignored the strictures of male leaders about their participation in "harmful" sports. As recently as 1973, the Sports Committee issued a resolution discouraging women from taking part in sports, like soccer, that were allegedly harmful to the female organism and encouraged male voyeurism. Within the space of a few years, however, Soviet women have held four national judo and a world judo championships. The first women's national soccer championships were held in August 1987 and by 1989 some 50 clubs contested the championships from almost every part of the country. Moscow State University formed its first women's water polo team in 1982, and today the sport has spread to several other cities. Weightlifting and bodybuilding are developing apace, and women's ice hockey has reappeared for the first time since the 1920s. Women are also doing the marathon, pole vault, triple jump and hammer throwing.

These changes have all come about by a few women defying official sanction, ridicule and even persecution to establish their right to pursue the sport of their choice.

(iii) *Changing the image of Soviet sport*. With the disclosure of the many unsavoury aspects of Soviet sport that had previously been hidden from public gaze, many people have raised questions about the very fundamentals of Communist sport: its ethics and ethos.

A jounalist from the weekly magazine *Ogonek* has derided the "win at all costs" mentality and the privileges for the elite. He and several others broke the silence on extensive drug-taking in Soviet sport. The one-time weightlifting Olympic champion (and now Deputy to the Congress of People's Deputies) Yuri Vlasov, was the first to accuse Soviet athletes of using anabolic steroids for "several decades". In mid-1989, the Moscow newspaper *Leninskoe znamya* admitted that some 290 athletes and coaches had been punished for using forbidden drugs in the three years prior to the Seoul 1988 Olympic. No other country in the world has had anything like that number of positive drug tests registered. In December 1989, the one-time swimming coach Sergei Vaichekovsky, who was in charge of Soviet swimming from 1973 to 1982, claimed that from 1974 "all Soviet swimmers were using banned substances". He

indicated that while the East German method was to give drugs only during periods of intensive training, Soviet swimmers took drugs to within a month of major meetings. What this seems to show is that drug taking in Soviet and East European sport has gone on for years with the knowledge and active collaboration of the authorities.

Under pressure, the sports establishment has talked of taking steps to make all sports, particularly soccer, clubs self-financing and officially to give all players of Master of Sport ranking and over what they have always had unofficially: professional status. Indeed, a number of top soccer teams have become openly professional; in cycling, a 14-strong team signed a contract in late 1988 with a San Marino firm to form the first-ever professional Soviet cycling team. Perhaps the greatest *volte face* in sporting principles is the entry of Soviet boxers and wrestlers into the professional ranks.

Fears are being voiced, nonetheless, that the encouragement of open professionalism might spoil the "stars" even more than at present. It is nostalgically recalled that once upon a time Soviet athletes would go through fire to gain medals and glory for their country: "That was before good mother Adidas fed them from her bountiful bosom, spoiled them with life on the foreign circuit or even overseas training. Today's athletes, however, are scientifically programmed, rigged out in the latest fashions and packed full of home-produced vitamins; as a result, we've produced capricious idols and we don't know what to do with them."

(iv) *Convergence in sport*. Yet another consequence of the "new thinking" is the bringing closer of some facets of Soviet sport to those in the commercial West; it is nonetheless a contradictory process that may have popular acclaim, yet at the same time lead Soviet sport further away from the new morality it seeks.

For a start, commercial sports like golf, baseball, Grand Prix motor racing, American football, even Spanish bull-fighting, have all arrived in the USSR. They accompany the resurgence of dog (borzoi) racing, snooker and billiards, bodybuilding and various combat sports, including the Chinese wushu.

Sponsorship, both domestic and foreign, has become a common feature in a range of sports, and leading Soviet soccer, basketball and ice hockey players are being "sold" to top Western teams. At home, top players have demanded their own trade unions and a larger proportion of foreign currency earned on the overseas circuit, for example in tennis.

Not everyone is happy at what they see as a

race for irrational glory, as the cultivation of irrational loyalties, as unreasonable prominence given to the winning of sports victories, the setting of records and the collection of trophies—a fetishization of sport. In fact a feature of popular antipathy to the pre-Gorbachev "stagnation" period is precisely reaction against the tub-thumping, flag-waving obsession with international sports success. It is this popular mood that is so prominent in East Germany and Romania.

Conclusions. As we have seen, the turbulent events in the USSR and Eastern Europe since 1985, particularly in 1989, have radically affected attitudes towards sport. While there have been those in the West who have looked with envy at the successful talent spotting and nurturing system developed in the Communist states, bringing several of them considerable success in world sport and the Olympic Games—with the USSR and the German Democratic Republic dominating the summer and winter Olympics of recent years—popular attitudes within the Communist states themselves have been quite different, as recent reactions against elite sport have shown.

First, the sports system, with its concentration of functional ends, including the demonstrating of "Communist" superiority in world sporting arenas and forums, is perceived by ordinary people to be associated with the old regime. The sports "stars" are seen to have done well out of the old system, and acquired an unfair distribution of perquisites.

Second, the sports system has been dominated by the clubs of the security police and the armed forces—Dinamo (Dinamo Kiev, Tbilisi or Moscow; Dinamo Tirana, Bucharest, Zagreb, Berlin) and the Central army clubs (Dukla Prague, Red Star Belgrade, Steava Bucharest, Honved in Hungary, Leigia in Poland). With the welling up of hostility and revenge in regard to the paramilitary forces that have shored up the old regimes, it is natural that their sponsored sports clubs have suffered by association.

Third, *glasnost'* clearly favours sport for all and sport for fun rather than elite sport. That is the popular demand of the times. Such a change in priorities is not coming about as a gift from above. While the coming of a new leader in the Soviet Union and new governments elsewhere has accelerated the process of change, it is opposition to the old regime and mounting disaffection from official institutions and values that have initiated and carried it forward. In sport this has meant the people of the USSR and Eastern Europe fighting to win the right to their own physical culture and personality.

JWR

STALIN, JOSEPH VISSARIONOVICH. Soviet politician and party leader; associated particularly with **Stalinism** as a form of rule and social system. Born in the town of Gori in Soviet Georgia in 1879, Stalin (whose real name was Djugashvili) was the son of a shoemaker and for some time a student for the priesthood at the theological seminary in Tiflis (now Tbilisi), the Georgian capital. Expelled from the seminary, he became a convert to Marxism and joined the Social Democratic party in the Caucasus, siding with the harder-line Bolsheviks after the split in the party in 1903. Stalin attended party congresses abroad, but unlike **Lenin** and **Trotsky** did not spend prolonged periods in other European countries; possessed of a shrewd intelligence, he was nonetheless no match for the cultured figures that dominated Russian socialism at this time and appears to have resented their theoretical attainments. Stalin was arrested in 1913 and exiled to Siberia, where he remained until an amnesty was granted after the February revolution of 1917. Back in St Petersburg (by then renamed Petrograd), he became associated with the Bolshevik paper *Pravda* where he initially took a position of qualified support for the Provisional Government that had been formed after the abdication of the Tsar.

After the October revolution Stalin entered the new Soviet government as commissar for nationalities, where his authoritarian instincts were noted disapprovingly by Lenin. In 1922 Stalin became general secretary of the party, a position to which little importance was attached at the time but which allowed him to build up a network of supporters through his use of patronage. After Lenin's death Stalin successfully allied himself with Grigorii Zinoviev and Lev Kamenev against Trotsky, and then with Nikolai Bukharin against Zinoviev and Kamenev. Stalin subsequently turned on Bukharin and secured his removal from power. The central question at issue during these years was, at least ostensibly, the future of the Soviet economy and more generally of the revolution itself. Trotsky was more sceptical of the ability of the Russian revolution to survive by itself without a revolution elsewhere in Europe; Stalin and his supporters argued by contrast that there could, at least for an extended period, be "socialism in one country". Stalin initially supported the continuation of the New Economic Policy, a mixed economy with a substantial private sector which had been instituted as a temporary measure in 1921. In the late 1920s, however, influenced by tactical as well as other considerations, he brought about a change of course involving the adoption of the first Five-Year Plan in 1928, and over the 1930s the collectivization of the countryside. This period is what became known to Soviet historians as the "great transformation" (*velikii perelom*); it was accompanied by extensive purges at all levels of the Soviet system whose demographic as well as psychological impact is still a force in contemporary Soviet life.

The nonaggression treaty with Germany of 1939 had been designed to keep Soviet Russia out of World War II. Stalin, who took over the premiership from Molotov in 1940, appears to have been reluctant to believe the evidence that began to reach him that the Nazis, despite the treaty, intended to invade. The Soviet Union was certainly ill prepared when Nazi forces struck without a formal declaration of war on June 22, 1941, and advanced rapidly on **Leningrad** and **Moscow**. Stalin initially panicked, but later emerged to take a central part in the Soviet wartime leadership and in the strategy that led to the defeat of the Nazis and the conclusion of a peace settlement. He had meanwhile become marshal of the Soviet Union (1943) and generalissimo (1945). At the Yalta and other conferences at the end of the war Stalin proved an astute diplomat, securing the recognition of a Soviet sphere of influence in Eastern Europe around which an "iron curtain" soon descended.

Despite these impressive victories, Stalin became increasingly suspicious of those around him and the last years of his rule saw renewed repression, in some cases (such as the "doctors' plot") with anti-Semitic overtones. He died on March 5, 1953 of a cerebral haemorrhage; his funeral was marked by genuine popular grief as well as by concern about the kind of regime that would succeed him.

SLW

STALINISM. A form of dictatorial, centralized and frequently repressive rule, characteristic of Soviet politics during the **Stalin** era but encountered in other Communist-ruled systems at other times. The question of Stalinism, its definition and explanation, has been a central one in the USSR and Eastern Europe, and it has been particularly relevant during periods of transition from authoritarian to more pluralistic forms of government. In the USSR the question of Stalinism was first publicly raised by Nikita **Khrushchev**, most dramatically at the Congress of the **Communist Party of the Soviet Union (CPSU)** in 1956. Stalinism was identified at this time as a form of rule characterized by the "cult of personality"; it was, in other words, a distortion of socialism and of Leninist principles, and under Khrushchev a determined effort was made to return to those healthy Leninist foundations in order to eliminate the harmful consequences of the "cult of personality" from Soviet life. The legal system was reconstituted on a basis of "socialist legality", attempts were made to revive inner-party democracy (for instance, by compulsory turnover rules), and Stalin himself was removed from the Lenin Mausoleum in 1961 and from the towns, streets and other geographical features to which he had given his name (the most conspicuous of these changes was when Stalingrad, site of one of the most celebrated battles of World War II, reverted to the name of Volgograd).

Khrushchev's immediate successors, and in particular Leonid **Brezhnev**, slowed down the pace of change, but it has been resumed again with new energy under the **Gorbachev** leadership since 1985. Gorbachev, to begin with, was reluctant even to concede the terms of the question. "Stalinism", he told an interviewer from the French Communist paper *L'Humanité* in February 1986, was a "notion made up by opponents of Communism and used on a large scale to smear the Soviet Union and socialism as a whole". The "personality cult" had been condemned by the Congress of the CPSU in 1956, and the appropriate conclusions had been drawn. That, it appeared, was that. By the following February, however, Gorbachev was insisting that there must be "no forgotten names [or] blank spots" in Soviet history or literature, and in July 1987 he told a group of media workers that they could "never forgive or justify what happened in 1937–38. Never". By November 1987, when he came to give his address on the 70th anniversary of the revolution, the terms of the debate had advanced still further. Trotskyism remained a "leftist pseudorevolutionary rhetoric" which was hostile to the very nature of Leninism; Bukharin and other Politburo moderates, equally, had underestimated the need for urgency in the construction of socialism at that time. The path that had been chosen, industrialization based on heavy industry and collectivization of the countryside, had been the only possible way forward in the circumstances that then prevailed. The command-administrative system that had been established for the management of the economy, however, had been allowed to extend into sociopolitical life, choking off its democratic potential, and this had led to the "wanton repressive measures" of the 1930s—"real crimes" in which "many thousands of people inside and outside the party [had been] subjected to wholesale repression". This was a lesson that subsequent generations must not forget.

Gorbachev was able to announce that the Politburo had established a special commission to investigate the crimes of the period, and that a new textbook on the history of the CPSU would be prepared. The textbook, by early 1990, had still to appear; but the Politburo commission, chaired initially by Mikhail Solomentsev, set to work immediately and had cleared more than 600 purge victims by the following August. The most notable victim of the purges, Nikolai Bukharin, was one of the first to be rehabilitated through this process. In February 1988, 50 years after his show trial and 100 years after his birth, Bukharin and 18 other members of the "anti-Soviet right-Trotskyist bloc" were officially cleared of the charges against them by the USSR Supreme Court. In July Bukharin was posthumously restored to party membership, and in October he was reinstated as a member of the Academy of Sciences. The same month a Bukharin exhibition opened in the Museum of the Revolution in Moscow, and in the Lenin Library; a film of his life was reportedly in preparation. Bukharin's articles and books also began to reappear: his eulogy on the fifth anniversary of Lenin's death appeared in the party theoretical journal *Kommunist* in January 1988, and his collected works were issued later in the year in several editions.

The rehabilitation of Bukharin was followed by the judicial and political rehabilitation of those involved in the "Leningrad affair" of 1950, and in July 1988 by the rehabilitation of Lev Kamenev. Grigory Zinoviev, Karl Radek and other old Bolsheviks who had been sentenced to death in 1937. In October the "Workers' Opposition" group was cleared of all charges, followed in December by the "Jewish Anti-Fascist Committee". **Trotsky**'s son Sergei Sedov, another victim of the purges, was rehabilitated in November 1988, and Trotsky's own contribution to the revolutionary cause began to receive a more balanced historical assessment (some of his works were even republished) although there was little indication that he would—or perhaps ever could—be restored to full political respectability. The Politburo, immediately after the 19th Party Conference in 1988 had concluded, decided that a monument to the victims of the purges should be constructed (a decision to this effect had been taken in 1961 but not implemented); a more general decision, in early 1989, moved beyond the consideration of individual cases and provided for the rehabilitation of all who had been unjustly treated or imprisoned during the 1930s, 1940s and early 1950s, with the exception of war criminals and those who had falsified evidence. At least 25,000 victims of the infamous "special boards" were affected by this decision, and over 47,000 altogether had been rehabilitated by March 1989.

Just as the victims of Stalinism were to be rehabilitated, so too the instruments or beneficiaries of Stalinism were exposed and dishonoured. One of the first to be denounced was Pavlik Morozov, the 14-year-old schoolboy who had informed on his parents for expressing anti-Soviet views in the early 1930s. He had then been killed by a group of *kulaks*, one of them his uncle. Pavlik Morozov was not a symbol of dedication and class consciousness, an article in the youth magazine *Yunost'* explained, but a "symbol of legalized and romanticized treachery". A much more important figure, Stalin's chief prosecutor Andrei Vyshinsky, was denounced in January 1988 in a full-page article in *Literaturnaya gazeta* as a "monster whose claws still defile our criminal procedure and legal system". Vyshinsky, whose prosecution speeches had typically ended with the words, "Shoot the mad dogs!", had been "hand-picked by Stalin to be the blood-soaked director of the purge trials". Vyshinsky, it emerged, not originally a member the Bolshevik party, had actually signed an order for the arrest of Lenin as a German spy while acting for the Provisional Government during 1917; this made a mockery of his claim 20 years later that Lenin's closest allies, the victims of the purge trials, had been plotting to do away with Lenin himself. Stalin's cultural commissar, Andrei Zhdanov, was stripped of his posthumous honours in early 1989; Leningrad University, which had been given his name, was one of the principal beneficiaries. Beria's shortcomings, including his sadism and depraved sexual appetites, were also exposed to public censure.

An adequate account of Stalinism and the Soviet past had necessarily to involve the historical record itself, and not just judgements about it. In this respect also the Gorbachev years made some significant contributions. The Nazi-Soviet Pact of 1939 with its secret protocols providing for the annexation of the Baltic republics was one such document: for many years unmentionable in Soviet writings, what purported to be an authentic text was published on the Baltic press in the summer of 1988 and in 1989 its existence was acknowledged by the Kremlin leadership. An extended discussion took place about the numbers that Stalin had killed: for some it was about a million by the end of the 1930s, while for others such as the historian and commentator Roy Medvedev the total was at least 12 million, with a further 38 million repressed in other ways (the archives, it emerged, were in a state of some disorder and unlikely ever to yield a definitive total). Perhaps still more significant, a number of mass graves of the victims of Stalinist repression began to be discovered and reported in the local press. One of the most important of these was in the Kuropaty forest near Minsk, where what was described as a "human slaughter-house" was discovered in 1988. Both archaeological and eye-witness evidence indicated that the victims had been shot during the period 1937–41; most were peasants, but latterly some had been members of the NKVD itself. The total number of victims was estimated at 30,000 or even more. More victims of the purges were found buried in a mass grave near **Kiev**, near Donetsk in the Ukrainian coalfields, and just outside Leningrad. There was an "Altai Kuropaty", and still further graves were found near Tomsk, outside Chelyabinsk and in Moscow itself. This grisly record, still expanding in the early 1990s, was in itself a critique of Stalinism more powerful than anything historians could muster; it made it unlikely that a revival of Stalinism could ever convincingly be mounted.

SLW

STASI (GDR). "Stasi" is the nickname for the office and personnel of the *Ministerium fur Staatssicherheit* — MfS (Ministry for State Security) in the GDR, founded in 1950 and abolished during the revolution of 1989. Led since 1957 by Minister Erich Mielke (born 1907), it expanded into a vast network of internal and external espionage. By the end it had 86,000 full-time employees, 109,000 informers, 2,000 buildings, and an immense arsenal. The Stasi involved itself in surveillance of multifarious kinds and overt suppression of dissent. Its high command structure remained unclear, since Egon **Krenz**, the former party secretary for security, claimed that **Honecker** and Mielke took all decisions between them. The internal security budget in 1989 was M 3.6 billion, about 1.3 per cent of total government spending.

So feared and hated was the Stasi that it was one of the first institutions to be reformed at the end of 1989. It became first of all the Office of State Security, as Mielke was dismissed and arrested, and then **Modrow**'s proposal to revive a Ministry was defeated by opposition objections. In January 1990, in one of the few violent incidents of the revolution in the GDR, tens of thousands of East Berliners stormed and ransacked the headquarters of the organization in the Normannenstrasse in Lichtenberg, East Berlin.

At this point the apparatus of the Stasi had not yet been fully dismantled. A government spokesman announced that 30,000 employees had been dismissed, 22,500 were being found other jobs, and 20,000 more were due to leave soon. This still left around 13,500 unaccounted for, and

some operations—particularly in West Germany—were still continuing. It has also reported that former Stasi agents had been finding employment not only in the GDR but also in the West German police.

The damage which the Stasi did in the GDR continues to be felt, as accusations have been made of emergent politicians' murky pasts in its service. Wolfgang Schnur of **Democratic Departure (DA)** had to resign after admitting involvement; Ibrahim Böhme of the **Social Democratic Party of Germany (SPD)** did so while denying it. An investigation has been requested into the possible Stasi pasts of all new *Volkskammer* deputies.

JO

STATE OF WAR (POLAND). A State of War was declared in Poland by Gen. **Jaruzelski** in the early hours of Dec. 13, 1981 after 14 months of qualified Communist rule and free trade union activity in Poland. A Military Council of National Salvation, it was declared, would rule for an unspecified length of time to protect the legal order and restore social discipline. The official reason for its introduction was the defence of the Polish state against the counter-revolutionary intentions of **Solidarity** and/or the threat of a Soviet invasion to maintain Communist rule. Neither reason was particularly convincing, as Solidarity in general terms had no inclination or plans to make an assault on the state while the Soviet authorities appeared to have played a part in the preparation of Jaruzelski's action and constituted a fabricated rather than real threat as an invasion force.

Under the State of War thousands of Solidarity activists were interned, civil rights and the activities of most social associations suspended, and a curfew and rigorous political discipline imposed. Reformist activities within the **Polish United Workers' Party (PUWP)** were also curtailed and the names of nearly 100,000 members taken off party lists in a matter of weeks. The full rigours of the State of War began to be lifted after a few weeks and it was suspended on Dec. 31, 1982, being fully revoked in July 1983. Political order, in the sense of the crushing of opposition, was restored but little support gained by the regime following the elimination of the popular Solidarity movement. Strikes were banned, price rises pushed through and the pace of economic decline slowed down during the year which followed the proclamation of the State of War, but it did not provide the conditions for sustained economic recovery.

PGL

STOPH, WILLI. Former GDR statesman, born 1914. Willi Stoph joined the KPD (Communist Party of Germany) in 1931, and served in the German army during World War II. Subsequently he had a long career in the **Socialist Unity Party of Germany (SED)**, filling numerous functions and joining the Politburo in 1953. For most of the period 1964–89 he was the equivalent of prime minister (Chairman of the Council of Ministers). On **Ulbricht**'s death he became head of state (Chairman of the Council of State) from 1973 to 1976, but in this position as in his other he was subordinate to the General Secretary of the party.

For all his long years near the top of GDR politics, Stoph failed to make a strong public impact. Only in March 1970, when he received West German Chancellor Willy Brandt at a pioneering encounter in Erfurt, did he have a high profile. Even then the crowds were more appreciative of the West German "Willy" than the East German "Willi". Stoph showed every outward sign of loyalty to **Honecker**, even when the latter notoriously poked fun at him in public. The two never seemed particularly close associates, but Stoph fulfilled a useful role as a dependable undemonstrative anchorman. In the autumn of 1989 Stoph did not immediately share Honecker's demise, but his government resigned on Nov. 7, 1989 and he was replaced on Nov. 13 by Hans **Modrow**.

JO

STOYANOV, DIMITUR IVANOV. Bulgarian Communist politician: Minister of Internal Affairs 1973–88; candidate Politburo member 1984–88; Central Committee Secretary and full Politburo member from December 1988 to November 1989; retired thereafter.

As Interior Minister, Stoyanov (born in 1923) was the key figure in the implementation of party leader Todor **Zhivkov**'s policy of forced assimilation of ethnic **Turks in Bulgaria**. In the aftermath of the fall of the prominent reformist Chudomir **Aleksandrov**, Stoyanov was rewarded by Zhivkov with promotion to Aleksandrov's old post as CC Secretary responsible for personnel, with full Politburo status — a position which, given time and more conventional conditions, Stoyanov might have used to construct a political machine that would have given him a good chance of succeeding Zhivkov. In summer 1989, he enjoyed a conspicuously high profile and made surprisingly democratic-sounding speeches — presumably trying to soften his hardline image and broaden his appeal. But events moved too fast for him: the increasing discredit of Zhivkov combined with fear of Stoyanov to produce the toppling of the former followed within a week by the removal of the latter along with two other close associates of Zhivkov.

RW

SVOBODA, LUDVÍK. President of Czechoslovakia from 1968 until 1975, General Svoboda had a chequered political career. He served as Minister of Defence, ostensibly without party affiliation, in the coalition governments between 1945 and 1948, and was to continue in that post after the establishment of effective one-party rule in February 1948 until his dismissal in April 1950. During World War II, he had served as commander of the Czechoslovak Division in the Soviet Union and it was **Khrushchev**'s interest in Svoboda's whereabouts during a visit to Czechoslovakia that brought about his transfer from the collective farm to which he had been "exiled" after his resignation from the government to a post in the Military History Institute in Prague. His high reputation in Moscow at a time when the Soviet leadership was growing anxious about developments in Czechoslovakia made him an astute choice for the post of President during the 1968 **Prague Spring**. Svoboda's refusal to accept a "workers' and peasants' government" chosen by Moscow immediately following the **Warsaw Treaty Organization (Warsaw Pact)** invasion in August 1968 ensured the survival of the **Dubček** leadership for another eight months. Despite his support for the reformers at that point, he regarded resistance to Soviet demands as futile and supported accommodation with Moscow as the only practical policy. Born in 1895, Svoboda died in 1979, four years after his resignation from the presidency.

GW

SZÜRÖS, MÁTYÁS. Hungarian diplomat and **Hungarian Socialist Workers' Party (HSWP)** specialist in foreign affairs. Szürös (born in 1933) studied in Moscow at the Institute of International Relations, then returned to Budapest to work in the Ministry of Foreign Affairs from 1958–62. From 1962 to 1965, he worked in the Hungarian Embassy in East Berlin, then returned to Budapest to work in the HSWP Central Committee's Department for Foreign Affairs, becoming Deputy Head of that Department in 1974–75. He then returned to the East Berlin Embassy as Hungarian Ambassador until 1978, and from 1978 to 1982, he held the key post of Hungarian Ambassador in Moscow. This latter promotion was accompanied by his election to membership of the Central Committee of the HSWP. He was brought back to Budapest in 1982 to become

Head of the HSWP Central Committee Department for Foreign Affairs, and the following year was appointed to the post of Central Committee Secretary. It was in this capacity that he became known for introducing a new line in Hungarian foreign policy, hitherto marked by complete obedience to Moscow. Szürös published a controversial series of articles in 1984 and after, in which he defended the right of each socialist country to pursue its national interest, and in particular to continue to develop its links with the West at a time of heightened tension between the superpowers. This had much in common with the line also being advocated by **Honecker** in East Germany at the same time.

A new idea emerged of the special role of small nations as mediators between East and West. This idea was virulently attacked by Prague and Moscow, but after **Brezhnev**'s death it gained increasing currency, particularly once **Gorbachev** came to power. Mátyás Szürös can thus clearly be counted among the leading reformists in the HSWP. In the most recent period his career has turned towards domestic politics (to what extent this reflects his own choice is not clear). In spring 1989 he was persuaded to take over the post of Speaker of the National Assembly, which was hardly a promotion. But in October 1989 the job of acting President was also thrust upon him, pending the presidential election. His role has been the not unimportant one of steering the major constitutional reforms through the National Assembly, and it fell to him to proclaim, on Oct. 23, 1989, that Hungary was no longer a "People's Republic" but simply a "Republic" — "an independent, democratic legal state".

JB

T

TADZHIKISTAN. The Tadzhik Soviet Socialist Republic became a constituent member of the USSR in the 1929. Its area is 143,100 sq km, and its capital is Dushanbe. The 1989 census population was 5,112,000 (the republic had the highest rate of increase of all Soviet republics since the previous census 10 years earlier). According to the 1979 census, 59 per cent of the population were ethnic Tadzhiks, who speak an Iranian dialect; of the remainder, 23 per cent were Uzbeks, and there were substantial Russian and Ukrainian minorities. The republic includes some of the Soviet Union's highest mountains and hydroelectricity is important; the population is principally engaged in farming, horticulture and cattle breeding. The republic is subdivided into one autonomous region, three regions and 45 districts.

SLW

TIMIŞOARA. Romania's fourth largest city, population 261,000. Capital of the Banat (part of which is in Yugoslavia), an ethnically varied area which has belonged to Romania since 1918. In 1987 the city was the scene of a demonstration in sympathy with that in **Braşov**. In December 1989 events in the city sparked off the overthrow of the **Ceauşescu** regime. The first confrontations between pro- and anti-Ceauşescu forces took place here. Early reports spoke of extremely heavy casualties, with 3,000 or even 4,000 killed, but this figure was later scaled down to just over 100.

RH

TIRANA. Capital of Albania (since 1920) and of Tirana district, with a population in 1989 of around 220,000. The city has grown only slowly in recent years as migration within Albania is discouraged. Tirana is Albania's only city of substantial size and is the governmental, administrative, commercial, cultural and scientific capital. It is approximately in the geographical centre of the country and being partly surrounded by mountains is the terminus of a railway spur line (providing a direct link with Durrës). Previously a town with oriental characteristics and smaller than Shkoder or Durrës, Tirana now far surpasses both. Its architecture is a mixture of old houses lining narrow streets and new, mainly stereotyped blocks along wider roads, with the latter gradually gaining ground. Among the world's capitals. Tirana is noted for its extremely light motor traffic, commuting being mainly on foot or by bicycle, in part by bus. Rinas Airport, about 20 km to the north, links Tirana with a number of European cities.

RH

TITO, JOSIP BROZ. Former President of Yugoslavia; born in Kumrovec (Croatia) in 1892. Trained as a locksmith. In World War I he served as a private in the Austro-Hungarian army and was captured in 1915 by the Russians. He spent some years in Russia during the revolution. He returned to Yugoslavia in 1920 and became a founder member of the Communist Party of Yugoslavia (CPY). In 1928 he became Secretary of the Party committee in Zagreb. He was sentenced to five years imprisonment for political and trade union activities and was released in 1934. He attended the Seventh Congress of the **Communist International (Comintern)** in Moscow in 1935 as a member of the Yugoslav delegation. He returned illegally to Yugoslavia in 1936 and was appointed the following year Secretary General of the CPY on Comintern orders. He worked underground until he left Belgrade in 1941 to lead the popular resistance against the occupying Axis forces. At the Anti-Fascist Council for the National Liberation of Yugoslavia (AVNOJ) meeting in Jajce in 1943 he was nominated leader of the provisional government. From 1945 to 1953, when he became President of Yugoslavia, he served as Prime Minister and Minister of Defence. In 1948 he rejected **Stalin**'s orders and took Yugoslavia away from rigid socialist lines by developing a system of worker participation and self-management. He became Life President of the republic in 1971 and Life President of the renamed **League of Communists of Yugoslavia** until his death in 1980.

PA

TOURISM. Throughout Eastern Europe and the USSR foreign tourism is on a small scale by comparison with Western Europe or the Mediterranean. However, it results in important transfers and earnings of foreign exchange, especially for countries such as Yugoslavia and Bulgaria, and its political impact tends to be far greater. It was because East German tourists (this at any rate is what they had claimed to be) visiting liberated Hungary and Poland, and even Czechoslovakia, could then cross into the West that the GDR government found itself obliged to concede freedom of movement and the breaking down of the Berlin Wall. Less spectacularly, tourism by East Europeans within the region has for years been punching holes in those countries' foreign trade monopolies, by virtue of the bringing across frontiers for private sale of transportable items that are in short supply in the places visited—here Poles importing unofficially into Romania small electronics, medicines and cosmetics are a notorious case—or through the personal export of items which are relatively cheap and abundant. Reacting to these infringements, visited countries have imposed restrictions recently on the personal export of a number of types of goods which are in short supply on their home markets. Tourism is also a two-way spreader of information through means distinct from official channels, thus enabling a broader and probably truer picture to be collected. The extent of foreign tourism within an East European country tends therefore to be roughly in inverse proportion to the intensity of national secrecy.

East Europeans have travelled (and do travel) relatively more than West Europeans within Eastern Europe owing to propinquity, but also owing to political/ideological prohibitions or restrictions on travel to "capitalist" countries which have been enforced by the Soviet bloc countries. These restrictions in turn made it harder for the authorities to prohibit travel *within* Eastern Europe. This was what made it impossible for the **Honecker** regime to ban East German travel to Czechoslovakia. One result of unlimited travel to the West must therefore be a drop in East European travel within Eastern Europe. During the period (about four decades for most East Europeans) when travel restrictions were enforced, tourists visiting a given country were not permitted to travel onwards. This applied also to Finland, which consequently was visited by substantial numbers of Soviet citizens. Although the East German example may prove infectious, these restrictions still apply to Soviet citizens. A visa is required for visiting the USSR as well as the other countries and nowadays is granted as a rule but not quite without exceptions. Visitors with Soviet or US passports are not allowed into Albania.

Everywhere in Eastern Europe and the USSR, albeit in greater or less degree, foreign tourism is nationally organized. This reaches a pinnacle in Albania, where with the exception of foreign VIPs (such as Josef Strauss) all foreign tourists must be included within organized parties and except when on foot have to go about in groups. Similarly, in the more open countries (such as Hungary and Yugoslavia) accommodation in private lodgings is allowed, whereas in Romania it is not. A national network of mountain routes may be marked (for example, in Bulgaria). A Ministry of Tourism or some other national body (for instance in Bulgaria "Balkanturist") normally exists and publishes brochures, supplies guides etc. It is not unknown for ministerial representatives to intercept a tour and to make recommendations, for instance about where it would be best to stay. Certain hotels may also be reserved for foreigners (either permanently or at certain times of year) or foreigners are given priority in them. The hotel network is also an important outlet for goods which are sold only for foreign exchange. Numbers of tourists are also nationally regulated, by bilateral agreement: for instance in 1989, 210,000 Soviet tourists were to visit Bulgaria and 53,000 Bulgarians the USSR. Western tourism into these countries except for Yugoslavia, and apart from business visits, is handled mainly by established but not mass agencies, with tourism via individual arrangements much less common than to other European destinations. Many nationalities are represented among Western tourists in Eastern Europe, but West Germans tend to comprise the numerous nationality: thus in 1985, 189,000 West Germans visited Bulgaria. (The totals considered here do not include *gastarbeiter* in transit.)

The comparative importance as reception points of the various countries is about the same for tourists from Eastern Europe as for tourists from elsewhere. For both groups, the southern tier — Hungary, Yugoslavia, Romania and Bulgaria — is more important than the northern one (Poland, East Germany, Czechoslovakia). The reasons — the southern group has more attractive scenery, more sunshine and (except Hungary) warmer seacoasts — are in part the same, but also the northern tier tends to have more currency to spend. For reasons such as these, East German tourists in, for example, Bulgaria, have been numerous. Albania is a special case because of lacking diplomatic relations with the USSR. West or North European tourists plus Greek family visitors number some 30,000 annually, whereas hardly any tourists come from Eastern Europe and no Albanians tour abroad.

The different East European countries have something in common as regards their touristic attractions but also exhibit significant differences. The most advanced and Western-seeming is Hungary, which offers sophisticated Budapest (less expensive than Vienna), lakeshore holidays on Lake Balaton, Art Nouveau and Tokay wine, but few scenic attractions apart from the Danube bend. Yugoslavia, much bigger in area and more varied, offers the Dalmatian coast with Roman and Venetian remains, the Ruritanian former capital of Montenegro, Cetinje, Marshal Tito's tomb in Belgrade, Danubian castles, the ethnic variety of both Christian and Muslim areas as well as both Latin and Cyrillic alphabets etc. Galloping inflation is a complication. Bulgaria has set out to organize tourism on a big way and its offerings include splendid beaches with well-arranged facilities and picturesque monasteries. Danube cruises are available too. Romania as well has a chain of Black Sea resorts but tourism in the country as a whole is not on a commensurate scale. Recent restrictions, especially on electricity consumption — which severely curb evening entertainment — as well as mediocre food, have discouraged visitors. Romania does offer three unique attractions: painted monasteries, the Danube delta (for bird-watchers especially) and Dracula (a fictitious figure but developed from a spectacularly cruel ruler in the fifteenth century, Vlad the Impaler). Romania has folklore and charming wooden villages (by no means all demolished, indeed some are being embellished). Romania can also be a Mecca for those with something to sell or a talent for currency deals. Albania delights through its strangeness, folklore and scenery and the scantiness of motor traffic but facilities are few. Poland and East Germany are mainly important as countries from which tourists come, though here as elsewhere the political events of 1989-90 may attract the more intellectual sort of tourism. Czechoslovakia too receives substantial numbers, partly owing to being adjacent to the countries just mentioned and partly to excellent beer and the unimpaired charms of medieval Prague. On the other hand, its officialdom has been regarded as formidable. It has spas and mountains but (pace Shakespeare) no seacoast.

The Soviet Union is a special case because of its huge size: a tour encompassing any substantial fraction of it is impossible, and most internal journeys have to be by air. Tours are arranged through Intourist, though individual motoring is permitted along a good many routes. Package tours usually focus on specific regions, for instance Moscow and Leningrad (although these cities are 640 km apart), or Central Asia. For obvious reasons Moscow especially is a natural magnet. The Black Sea coast is eagerly sought by Soviet citizens, but less justifiably from abroad. Artistic and literary tours are popular, while for Russian-speakers the current political ferment is an interesting time. The climatic range is very

wide and with severe winter temperatures; this is not always realized by foreign visitors. Tours within the USSR tend to be good value but do involve long-distance travelling with interesting scenery few and far between. A substantial fraction of the country remains out of bounds or is inaccessible due to lack of communications or facilities. Owing to these features the potentialities for developing tourism within the USSR, except to specific kinds of destinations, appear rather limited. Nevertheless, considerable numbers of East Europeans visit the Soviet Union, while larger numbers of Soviet citizens visit as tourists Eastern Europe.

RH

TRADE UNIONISM. Trade unions never developed in Eastern Europe in the pre-communist period in the way they did in the West. With the obvious exception of East Germany in the pre-Nazi period and also of Czechoslovakia, a combination of political oppression and lack of industrialization meant that the scope for trade union activity was sharply limited. With the consolidation of the Bolshevik dictatorship in the Soviet Union after 1921, any prospects for a wholly independent trade union movement in that country were dashed. But during the period of the New Economic Policy the official trade unions, under the distinguished leadership of Politburo member M. Tomsky, later murdered by **Stalin**, did do something to defend the shop-floor interests of the workers. In addition, enterprise trade union secretaries were important managerial figures in their own right, forming a *troika* with the director and the secretary of the party committee.

The uneasy compromise between communist monolithism and sectional interest could not survive the impact of crash industrialization and Stalinist terror in the 1930s. In the early years of the first Five-Year Plan factory trade union committees were still notably resisting the raising of piece-work norms in the interests of rapid increases in production. By the middle 1930s, however, the trade unions had been reduced to the status of a government department. The enterprise trade union secretary was still an important figure — but he was just another *apparatchik*, concerned only with plan fulfilment, whatever that cost the workers.

After the death of Stalin the Soviet trade unions managed, like other public institutions, to reassert a degree of independence. Union officials began to concern themselves again with working conditions, safety etc. Determination of wage rates remained the prerogative of the government, though union secretaries may have come to wield a degree of influence over actual wage payments in a period of substantial wage drift. Strike action, official or unofficial, remained absolutely proscribed, and isolated outbreaks of labour unrest were put down with considerable brutality during the **Khrushchev** and **Brezhev** periods.

The situation has changed dramatically in the **Gorbachev** period. But it is not the official trade union movement which has blossomed under *perestroika*. The first hint of things to come came in 1988, with the formation of an independent bus drivers' union in the town of Lipetsk. In the middle of 1989 Soviet independent trade unionism hit the headlines as newly-born organizations organized strikes throughout the coal-fields of the Soviet Union. The authorities agreed to negotiate with the strikers, and conceded most of their demands. Most dramatically of all, 1989 witnessed the inception of an independent army officers' union. At the end of 1989 the Soviet government sought to limit this growth in independent labour activism through the imposition of a 15-month ban on strikes throughout industry. The Supreme Soviet rejected the proposal, but accepted a compromise which outlawed strikes in "key" industries — energy, transport, metallurgy and chemicals.

The trade union structures imposed by Stalin on the six East European **Council for Mutual Economic Assistance (CMEA)** members were carbon copies of the Soviet structure as it gelled in the 1930s. In consequence unions played absolutely no role in the public lives of these countries for some three decades. A dramatic change occurred in the aftermath of the first great crisis of East European communism — the Polish crisis of 1979–80. The **Gierek** government of the 1970s managed to compile a catalogue of colossal economic mismanagement and corruption which left Poland with an enormous balance-of-payments deficit, a massive external debt, and downward spiralling production levels. When meat prices were raised in June 1980 in an effort to restore macro-economic balance the Polish workers revolted, as they had done in similar circumstances in 1970. But this time the revolt took an organized form and resulted in the birth of the **Solidarity** trade union, the first independent union in Communist Eastern Europe. Within a few months it had 10 million members. Right from the start Solidarity was committed to a direct challenge to Communist rule, and it came as no surprise when the new Communist strongman, Gen. Wojciech **Jaruzelski**, moved against the trade union. After the declaration of martial law in December 1981, Solidarity was banned in 1982. It continued to operate underground, but Jaruzelski had considerable success in stabilizing

the Polish political situation, and in creating new "official" unions, which counted a membership of 3.5 million by the beginning of 1984. Jaruzelski failed, however, to breathe new life into the prostrate Polish economy, and with new political pressures now emanating from further east was unable to stem a new Solidarity offensive. Jaruzelski conceded free elections in 1989, which Solidarity, now operating openly as a political party, won by a landslide. In 1989 a Solidarity government under Tadeusz **Mazowiecki** was formed *(see* **Poland** — Recent political developments).

The history of labour organization in Yugoslavia has been quite different from that in the **Warsaw Treaty Organization (Warsaw Pact)** countries. The official trade union structure has, indeed, played the same role as it does in other communist dictatorships, serving as a vehicle for the implementation of party policy at shop-floor level. But the creation of a system of workers' councils in 1950, followed by the abandonment of central planning in favour of market socialism, gave Yugoslav workers a unique platform from which to articulate their interests. Elected on the basis of manhood suffrage (though with a party veto on candidates), the workers' council is supposed to exercise general supervision over the general business strategy of the enterprise, policy on profit ploughbacks, distributions, wage scales etc. In practice, strategic matters tend to be decided on by local politicians. But the workers' council did give the Yugoslav proletariat a degree of influence over wages and working conditions, even as Yugoslavia was going through the process of initial industrialization, without parallel in any other East European country. Workers' councils are, of course, by definition limited to single enterprises. Yugoslav workers have enjoyed no more extensive rights of combination on industrial or craft basis than any other East European workers.

The workers' council system has tended to break down under the pressure of the economic and political crisis of the 1980s in Yugoslavia. As the prestige of the **League of Communists of Yugoslavia** has declined, overt interference by politicians in enterprise affairs has if anything increased. Legislation aimed at controlling inflationary pressures has emasculated workers' councils' rights to fix their own wages. More generally, it has become painfully clear that the problems of the Yugoslav economy are too vast to be tackled by any single workers' council. The formation of an independent Peasants' Union in Slovenia in 1988 may mark the beginning of a new phase in workers' organization in Yugoslavia. And as Slovenia prepared for free elections in 1990, it looked as if the Peasants' Union might follow the lead of Solidarity in reconstituting itself into a political party.

The year 1989 was a watershed for trade unionism in Eastern Europe, as for every other dimension of East European public life. But the pattern of "new unionism" is a very uneven one. Trade unions played very little role in the peaceful and predominantly middle-class revolutions in East Germany, Czechoslovakia and Bulgaria, or in the bloody upheaval in Romania. In Poland, trade unionism has inherited the revolution it started, and in the Soviet Union the new unionism is one of the most dynamic elements in the emerging socio-political pluralism of that country. But in both countries a number of foundamental questions are being posed which only the future can answer. In Poland, can a Solidarity government, in concert with the IMF, impose the very kinds of unpopular austerity measures whose imposition in 1980 gave birth to Solidarity in the first place? How will a Solidarity government committed to liberalization and privatization cope with the impact of these measures on the pattern of employment and unemployment amongs its supporters? These are all problems with which Western Labour and Social Democratic governments have had to grapple— with varying degrees of success—in the past. But the restructuring problem faced by the Polish government is so vast that there must be considerable doubt as to whether Solidarity-in-power can retain the support of its working-class grass roots.

Gorbachev's problem in the Soviet Union is a rather different one. The unofficial mineworkers' unions of 1989 showed some tendency to follow the Solidarity pattern in making political demands going far beyond what is normally associated with trade unionism in the West. For a leader still committed to the political leadership of the Soviet Communist Party this must be very disturbing. But some of those miners' organizations also demanded financial autonomy, with the implication of a degree of self-management *and* an end to subsidization from Moscow. In his drive to implement the principle of self-financing at regional and enterprise level, Gorbachev must find the prospect of self-financing coal mines an attractive one. Even if Soviet miners are not asking for the blank cheques normally demanded by British coal-miners, however, the political price of such self-management may be too high for Gorbachev to pay.

DAD

in the **Communist Party of the Soviet Union**. Born in 1879 of Jewish parents in the southern Ukraine, Trotsky (whose real name was Leon Davidovich Bronshtein) gravitated towards revolutionary politics at an early age. He was arrested in 1898 for the first time, and exiled to Siberia in 1900. He escaped, went abroad and became active in the Russian Social Democratic Labour Party, taking an initially Menshevik and then intermediate position between the two factions after the party split at its congress in 1903. Returning to Russia in 1905, he became for a short time the chairman of the St Petersburg Soviet; arrested and banished to Siberia, he again escaped and went to Vienna, where he worked as a journalist. Expelled from France during World War I, he went to New York and from there (in May 1917) he returned to Russia, now under the control of the Provisional Government. He was one of the chief organizers of the Military-Revolutionary Committee which guided the Bolshevik seizure of power in October 1917, and thereafter became people's commissar for foreign relations in the new Soviet government and then commissar for war, where his leadership was an important factor in ensuring the Bolshevik victory in the civil war.

After **Lenin**'s death Trotsky was outmanoeuvred by Stalin, who had secured control of the party machine; he was dismissed as commissar of war in 1925, left the Politburo in 1926 and the party in 1927, and in 1928, was sent into internal exile in Kazakhstan. He was forced to leave the USSR itself in 1929, living in Turkey, France and Norway before taking up residence in Mexico, where he gave general guidance to the "Left Opposition" that opposed Stalin and **Stalinism** both inside the USSR and in the world Communist movement. In 1940 he was assassinated by Ramon Mercader, who was acting as a Soviet agent. Trotsky's writings as well as his personal example have been enormously influential, more perhaps outside the USSR than within it. Under **Gorbachev**, however, he began to be treated more objectively in Soviet historiography and political drama; his son Sergei Sedov was rehabilitated in 1988 (Trotsky himself had not been sentenced by a Soviet court and could not therefore be restored to public favour in the same way), and in 1989 his writings began to reappear in a wide variety of periodicals at the same time as public attacks upon the USSR's Stalinist legacy became increasingly sharp and uncompromising.

SLW

TROTSKY, LEON. Soviet Marxist and political leader, and the principal opponent to **Stalin** with-

TURKMENIA. The Turkmen Soviet Socialist Republic was formed in 1924 and entered the

USSR as a constituent republic in 1925. Its area is 488,100 sq km, and its 1989 census population was 3,534,000. The capital is Ashkhabad. According to the 1979 census, 68 per cent of the population were ethnic Turkmenians; 13 per cent were Russians living mainly in urban areas, and 9 per cent were Uzbeks. The chief occupation is agriculture, based upon irrigation; the area is important for cotton, wool, Astrakhan fur, carpets and maize, and there are significant mineral resources. The republic is divided into five regions and 44 districts.

SLW

TURKS IN BULGARIA. Turks constitute Bulgaria's largest ethnic minority: estimates of their numbers (as of January 1989) range between 800,000 and 1.5 million. They are concentrated in the country's eastern regions, around Shumen, Khaskovo, and Kurdzhali. Turkish-speaking and Islamic by religious tradition, they have been a natural target for the attentions of a periodically nationalistic and assimilationist Bulgarian government: apart from offending the tidy-minded desire for homogeneity, they are an unwelcome reminder of the country's five centuries of Turkish rule.

Early in the period of Communist rule, around 150,000 were allowed to emigrate to Turkey. A further 80,000–90,000 left in the decade after 1969, when an agreement was reached with Turkey. In 1984–85, the **Zhivkov** regime started to pursue a policy of forced assimilation ("**Bulgarisation**") — e.g., compulsory changing of Islamic-sounding names to Christian/Bulgarian equivalents, and a ban on the public or educational use of the Turkish language — underpinned by a simple denial that the Turks existed as a separate minority, as opposed to a special type of ethnic Bulgarian. This policy met with a good deal of resistance, some of it violent, and was enforced with much brutality, resulting in not a few deaths. Internationally, this brought Bulgaria into some disrepute. After an outbreak of concerted Turkish protests in May 1989, it was decided to allow any who wished to emigrate to Turkey. An estimated 300,000 took this option, despite the economic hardships involved, before an overwhelmed Turkey closed the border to them that August. The economic disruption and labour shortages entailed, combined with the diplomatic repercussions, contributed to the weakening of the position of Bulgarian leader Todor Zhivkov, who had all along been closely identified with the repressive policy.

After mass demonstrations by ethnic Turks in Sofia at the end of December 1989, the successor regime of Petur **Mladenov** publicly reversed the Bulgarisation policy — thus provoking counter-demonstrations from the enraged ethnic Bulgarian inhabitants of the Turkish areas. Whatever policy is chosen, therefore, this seems likely to be a sensitive issue for some time to come, and it remains to be seen what proportion of the Turks who left in 1989 will choose to return.

RW

U

UKRAINE. The Ukrainian Soviet Socialist Republic is the second largest and second most important of the 15 constituent republics of the USSR. First proclaimed in December 1917, it was finally established in December 1919 and in 1922 became one of the original members of the USSR. Its 1989 census population was 51,704,000, 18 per cent of the USSR total; about three-quarters of the population are Ukrainian, and most of the remainder are Russian. Its capital is Kiev (1989 population 2,587,000); its area is 603,700 sq km. The Ukraine contains some of the richest land in the USSR and produces nearly half of the total value of agricultural produce in the USSR, and about a quarter of its industrial output; its coal and iron resources are particularly important. In 1990 it was subdivided into 25 regions and 480 districts. A nationalist movement, intermittently active, became particularly strong in the late 1980s. (*See also* **Nationality Question in the USSR**)

SLW

UKRAINIAN AUTOCEPHALOUS ORTHODOX CHURCH. The Ukrainian Autocephalous Orthodox Church was established in the Soviet Ukraine in 1921. This was a reaction to the long-standing domination of both the central bodies of the **Russian Orthodox Church** and ethnic Russians in the Ukraine over the Russian Orthodox Church in the Ukraine. The new church was tolerated by the Bolsheviks in Moscow since it weakened the structure of the Russian Orthodox Church (*see* **Religion and Communism**), and by the Ukrainian Bolsheviks as a manifestation of "Ukrainianization" (*see* **Nationality Question in the USSR**). It drew strength during the 1920s from the growing national feeling in the Ukraine, but was suppressed in 1930 when Moscow began to crack down on Ukrainian nationalism. It was forcibly reincorporated into the Russian Orthodox Church.

As *glasnost'* developed under **Gorbachev**, demands began to appear in the Eastern Ukraine for the re-legalization of the Ukrainian Autocephalous Orthodox Church. These did not seem to have the same breadth of support as the demands for the legalization of the **Ukrainian Catholic (Uniate) Church** had in the Western Ukraine; after all, Ukrainian autocephaly did not have the same chance to strike roots in the population as the Uniate Church.

The growth in Ukrainian national sentiment in 1988–89, and particularly the concern with the Ukrainian language, gave reason to expect a growth in support for the revival of the Ukrainian Autocephalous Orthodox Church. The Moscow Patriarchate sought to counter this by importing 100,000 Ukrainian-language Bibles and raising the status of the Metropolitan of Kiev and Galicia, the Patriarchal Exarch to the Ukraine, Filaret. In October 1989 Archbishop Ioann of the Russian Orthodox Church came out of retirement in order to seek to lead the newly-emerging Autocephalous Church, and was excommunicated by Patriarch Pimen of Moscow and all Russia.

PJSD

UKRAINIAN CATHOLIC (UNIATE) CHURCH. The Ukrainian Uniate Church, now also know as the Ukrainian Catholic Church, was created by the 1596 Union of Brest. By this act, the Polish rulers of the Ukraine pressed most of the bishops of the **Russian Orthodox Church** in the Ukraine into a structure where they maintained the Eastern rites but recognized the supremacy of the Pope. The Uniate Church became associated with Ukrainian nationalism. During World War II **Stalin** incorporated the Western Ukraine, where the Uniates were strongest, into the USSR. In order to combat Ukrainian nationalism (*see* **Nationality Question in the USSR**), Stalin ordered the Soviet security police to enforce the incorporation of the Uniate Church into the Russian Orthodox Church. This was achieved at the "Lvov Sobor" of 1946, dissenting bishops having been arrested (*see also* **Religion and Communism**).

Over subsequent decades, the Western Ukrainian parishes were often Orthodox in name only, as priests and laity preserved their Uniate traditions. The Uniates faced a propaganda campaign from the state and the Moscow Patriarchate, accusing them of such crimes as collaboration with the Nazis. As far as the state was concerned, the Church was illegal; activity in it was considered to be Ukrainian nationalist and counter-revolutionary, to be dealt with by labour camp sentences. The Uniate leader, Yosyf Cardinal Slipyj, was imprisoned from 1945 to 1963, when he emigrated to Rome. There he campaigned for the **Roman Catholic Church** to take a stronger line in defence of the Uniates. After his death in 1984, Pope John Paul II replaced him with Archbishop Myroslav Lubachivsky.

In 1982 an Initiative Group for the Defence of the Rights of Believers and the Church in the Ukraine was established by Uniates in the Ukraine, led by Yosyf Terelya. The leaders were arrested, but with the coming of *glasnost'* and the release of prisoners in 1987 Uniate political activity began again. During 1988 and 1989 there were large demonstrations in the Western Ukraine, especially in Lvov, where demands for political change were linked with calls for freedom for the Ukrainian Catholic Church. These demonstrations were called by informal associations such as the human rights organization, the Ukrainian Helsinki Union, and the religio-nationalist Ukrainian Culturological Club. The millennium of the baptism of Kievan Rus in June 1988, lavishly celebrated by the Russian Orthodox Church, provided a focus for Uniate services and demonstrations for religious freedom. Foreign dignitaries, meeting political and official Church leaders, began to raise the question of the legalization of the Uniates. By 1989 it was clear that the religious situation in the Ukraine was worse than anywhere else in the Soviet Union.

While the **Gorbachev** leadership favoured increased religious freedom, there seemed to be two main obstacles for the Uniates: the conservative nature of the party leadership under Volodymyr Shcherbytsky, who survived in office until September 1989, and the resistance of the Russian Church hierarchy to the loss of the Ukraine, where over half its churches were located. With the Eastern Ukraine being traditionally Orthodox and the West traditionally Uniate, religion has always been a divisive issue in the Ukraine. The growth of nationalist feeling in the Ukraine in the 1980s led to a renewed demand inside the Russian Orthodox Church, articulated under *perestroika*, for the re-establishment of the **Ukrainian Autocephalous Orthodox Church**.

This coincidence of demands for religious freedom for Uniates and Orthodox found expression in the programme adopted in September 1989 by the Rukh, the Popular Movement for the Restructuring of the Ukraine. In November 1989 Gorbachev visited Pope John Paul II in the Vatican. It appears that around the time of this meeting the Soviet authorities gave assurances to the Vatican that the difficulties faced by the Ukrainian Catholics would be removed. In the meantime, however, Uniate believers took matters in their own hands by physically taking over several of the most important church buildings in the Western Ukraine, ignoring the protests of the Moscow Patriarchate and gaining the apparent acquiescence of the authorities.

PJSD

ULBRICHT, WALTER. GDR statesman, born 1893, died 1973. Walter Ulbricht was the first political leader of the GDR, dominating its development until his dismissal as First Secretary of the **Socialist Unity Party of Germany (SED)** in 1971.

Born in Leipzig, Ulbricht joined the SPD before World War II and the KPD (Communist Party of Germany) afterwards. He led an active political career in the Weimar Republic, becoming a member of the *Reichstag* in 1928. On Hitler's assumption of power, Ulbricht fled first to Paris and then to Moscow. There he helped to found the National Committee for a Free Germany in 1943. He was heavily engaged in the early work of the SED and became its General Secretary in July 1950. His domination of the party saw the purging of its Social Democratic component and the imposition of Stalinist practice. Ulbricht oversaw the almost complete nationalization or collectivization of GDR industry and agriculture in the 1950s; he co-operated with the USSR in the suppression of the uprising of June 1953 and the invasion of Czechoslovakia in 1968; and he ordered the building of the Berlin Wall in 1961.

When President Pieck died in 1960, Ulbricht became head of state (Chairman of the Council of State). He retained this position even when ousted by Erich **Honecker** in 1971 as First Secretary of the party. He had proved difficult with the Soviet leadership, which wanted to foster relations between the GDR and the Federal Republic. After his death Ulbricht's name was increasingly blotted out from official depictions of the GDR's history. He had not been popular and association with him was not regarded as an advantage by his successors. By the 1980s, however, his reputation was somewhat rehabilitated by a leadership almost as strongly orthodox Stalinist as he had been.

JO

UNEMPLOYMENT. The notion of unemployment as we understand it in the West has not been directly relevant to the East European countries in the post-war period, with the exception of Yugoslavia. Indeed for the smaller East European countries the war, and the imposition of Communism, represented a major watershed in this respect. In the inter-war period Eastern Europe had been buffeted by the same volatile trends which saw dramatic increase in unemployment in the early 1920s, and again after 1929, in the West. In the more urbanized countries of north-eastern Europe unemployment remained very high throughout the 1930s. In the Soviet Union the rate of unemployment remained relatively high throughout the New Economic Policy (NEP) period 1921–29. **Stalin** "abolished" unemployment, and with it unemployment benefit, in 1930. Registered unemployment fell from 1.37 million on Oct. 1, 1928 to 335,000 on Oct. 1, 1930, though 230,000 of the total reduction was accounted for by changes in definition. In truth, the very nature of Soviet-style industrialization, with its obsessive emphasis on the fulfilment of centrally-determined output targets, tended to create a uniquely Soviet-style pattern of full employment. Production goals for priority industrial sectors were often breathlessly ambitious. Enterprise managers freqently found themselves in a situation where targets could only be met on the basis of hiring large numbers of extra workers, over and above the numbers prescribed in plans. Significantly total non-agricultural employment in the Soviet Union reached 22,804,000 by the end of the first Five-Year Plan in 1932, compared to a plan figure of 15,764,000, as the new industrial enterprises mopped up existing unemployment and pulled in underemployed people from the countryside. Managers tended to take on extra workers for two main reasons: firstly, in order to have plenty of manpower to throw into the fray as deadlines approached, and "storming" became necessary; secondly, in order to set up semi-handicraft "dwarf-workshops" to make modest but essential industrial supplies — nails, nuts and bolts, castings — on an in-house basis. In a world dominated by quantitative production targets there was little incentive for any organization to make such "fiddly little things" for any except their own use.

A significant degree of over-manning is, therefore, built in to Soviet industrial structures, and this pattern of over-manning was exported to the rest of Eastern Europe after 1945 — to the serious detriment of economies like the Hungarian which lacked the Soviet Union's vast labour reserves. Superimposed on this was a more purely political factor. Leonid **Brezhnev**, Soviet party leader 1964–82, followed a policy of maintaining political stability by giving security of tenure to almost everyone — politicians and factory workers alike. It had always been difficult for a Soviet director to sack a worker, but under Brezhnev it became very difficult even to get rid, for example, of employees who turned up for work drunk. From the late 1960s, under the rubric of the "Shchekino experiment", some Soviet directors were given

greater freedom to make surplus workers redundant. But the experiment was never generalized during Brezhnev's lifetime. The importance of the political factor is strikingly illustrated by the Hungarian case, where transition to market socialism in 1968 removed the strictly economic incentive to over-manning, but where extreme reluctance to countenance redundancy survived to the mid-1980s. The pattern throughout the area of the **Council for Mutual Economic Assistance (CMEA)** up to the early 1980s was, then, one of very low levels of open unemployment. What unemployment there was was largely of the short-term frictional variety, as people changed jobs, though there were a few regional pockets of worklessness, sometimes restricted to one sex. This apparently favourable picture did, however, conceal a great deal of underemployment at shop-floor level.

The pattern in the Soviet Union changed dramatically after the death of Brezhnev. **Andropov** initially sought to strengthen directors' powers to fire as a dimension of the discipline and anti-drunkenness campaign. But as the slogan of *perestroika* came to dominate policy-articulation under **Gorbachev**, the notion of redundancy came to take on a much deeper meaning. It became clear that industrial restructuring would mean the contraction or closing-down of many obsolescent plants and sub-sectors, and that this would involve redeployment of labour on a massive scale. Falling birth rates and the exhaustion of rural labour supplies from the 1960s onwards had already highlighted the essential link between labour productivity and economic growth in a period of faltering performance, and the central importance of cutting back on over-manning in all sectors of the economy.

Since Gorbachev took over the Soviet leadership in 1985 the right to make workers redundant has been extended to all enterprise directors in the Soviet Union. Many of them remain reluctant to use it, partly because they are disinclined to risk upsetting their workforce, partly because the Soviet planning system still operates mainly on the basis of output targets. Still, much has changed, and more than one million jobs were lost in the state sector of the Soviet economy in the course of 1988. Over the same period unemployment seems to have increased by about the same amount. The plan fulfilment report for the first half of 1989 gave us, for the first time since NEP, an official figure for the number of "those who could be brought into social production activity if the appropriate conditions were created". The figure given was six million — 3.5 per cent of the active population. About 1.5 million of these are housewives, the majority of whom are probably not actively seeking work. As many as 3.5 million may be accounted for by tramps and the frictionally unemployed. This confirms the picture of the emergence of around one million "genuine" structurally unemployed in the late 1980s. In aggregate, that represents no great problem. But about half the six million total relates to Central Asia, Kazakhstan and the Caucasus. It is officially admitted that there is massive unemployment—in some cases over 20 per cent—among young people in rural Central Asia, and this may have been a major factor in outbreaks of ethnic sectarian violence in Central Asia in 1989.

On the longer-term perspective, official projections taking the Soviet economy up to the year 2000 envisage that by that date some 20 million manual jobs will have disappeared as compared with the 1985 situation. The government line is that those made redundant in this way will all be retrained, and new retraining programmes are already being set up. But the experience of the West suggests that it will be difficult for the Soviet Union to go through such a fundamental process of restructuring without creating a good deal of unemployment. Some radical economists, like Nikolai Shmelev, also a member of the Congress of People's Deputies, argue that such an increase is both inevitable and desirable from the point of view of overall economic efficiency.

Elsewhere in the CMEA region the pattern is very mixed. The GDR has had no open unemployment problem, partly because of the slow pace of economic reform, partly because it can "export" all its unemployment to West Germany, In Bulgaria, too, a cautious stance on *perestroika* has combined with the wholly politically induced flight of Muslims from Bulgaria (the country lost 3 per cent of its population in this way between May and August 1989) to maintain the traditional pattern of "full employment". The momentous political events of late 1989 are bound to affect all of these factors, though open unemployment will probably not rise dramatically in either country. In Poland, employment in the state sector is falling rapidly, but many of the people leaving are either moving into the private sector or simply retiring. In Hungary, a country which has always suffered from severe labour shortage problems, 20,000 people—about 0.5 per cent of the active population—were registered as unemployed in 1989. As of the same year unemployment in Czechoslovakia appeared to be negligible. no figures are available for Romania.

In Yugoslavia the early transition to a form of market socialism ensured that employment and unemployment patterns would develop rather differently than in the CMEA area. In contrast to the built-in over-manning which the Soviet-type economic system tends to induce, the principle of profit-sharing which forms part of the Yugoslav self-management system gives workers a *ceteris paribus* incentive to minimize the number of workers in their enterprise, in order to maximise the per capita pay-out. In practice, Yugoslav economic development in the 1950s followed a fairly typically East European "extensive development" pattern with large-scale transfers of labour from the countryside resourcing much of the rapid economic growth achieved in that period. From the early 1960s, however, labour shortages began to appear, and these shortages represented one of the factors behind the movement in the 1960s towards a more full-blooded version of market socialism. But the degree of regional variation in the situation was extreme. In 1970 Slovenia, the most developed part of Yugoslavia, faced the prospect of 30,000 unfilled vacancies, and the situation had eased little by the mid-1970s. Meanwhile aggregate unemployment in Yugoslavia as a whole increased from under 300,000 in 1971 to nearly 500,000 some 5.5 per cent of the total active population, by 1974. By 1981 it had reached 833,000, with unemployment in Kosovo, the poorest area of Yugoslavia and the scene of extreme ethnic tension between Albanians and Serbs, standing at around 27 per cent of total active population. Unemployment in Yugoslavia grew substantially again after the breaking of the foreign debt crisis in 1983, though the level remains very low in Slovenia, and comparatively low in the other north-western parts of Yugoslavia.

Even with comparatively high average levels of open unemployment, the Yugoslav economy is by no means free of the characteristic East Europe pattern of under-employment. Studies of manning levels in industry present a clear picture of typically inflated workforce numbers, in relation to given technologies, across the country. Even Slovenia is no exception. It is estimated that in 1985 there were still some 100,000 surplus workers out of a total number of 841,000 employed outside private agriculture in that republic. For Yugoslavia as a whole it has been suggested that two million out of the 6.7 million people employed in the socialized sector are in "non-jobs". As it seeks a new growth path consistent with the maintenance of external financial balance, Yugoslavia faces a restructuring problem only marginally less great than the Soviet. As in the Soviet Union, it is difficult to see how this restructuring can be achieved without increasing unemployment, certainly in the short run. But the **League of Communists of Yugoslavia**, like the **Communist Party of the Soviet Union**, remains reluctant to abandon the option of the "political factory", and local politicians are particularly reluctant to sanction the liquidation of plants and jobs in "their" areas.

Future trends in policy on unemployment in Eastern Europe may, then, be as much a function of developments in relation to the position of Communist parties as of more specifically economic considerations. We can expect post-Communist governments in Poland, Hungary and elsewhere to take a tougher line on budget support for loss-making enterprises. Whether in the long run that will make for more or less unemployment is another question.

DAD

UNION OF DEMOCRATIC FORCES (BULGARIA—UDF).

This was set up as an umbrella organization in early December 1989 to co-ordinate the activities of the various Bulgarian opposition groups flourishing in the aftermath of Todor **Zhivkov**'s removal as leader of the **Bulgarian Communist Party** (and was successor, in this role, to the looser grouping "Citizens' Initiative"). Its most important elements are the independent trade union movement *Podkrepa*; the ecological pressure group *Ecoglasnost*; the **Club for the Support of Glasnost' and Democracy**; the Committee for Religious Rights and Freedoms; and the Independent Society for Human Rights. Other groups include the Club of Persons Illegally Repressed After 1945; the Independent Student Society; the Bulgarian Workers' Social Democratic Party; and the "Nikola Petkov" breakaway group of the **Bulgarian Agrarian National Union**. To date, the UDF has been quite successful in mobilizing popular pressure on the post-Zhivkov Communist leadership, entering into negotiations with the government in January 1990, and rejecting several Communist offers of seats in a government of national unity before the general election planned for May. 1990. Whether so heterogeneous a grouping can maintain its political cohesion indefinitely is another matter; for instance, there were already signs in December 1989 that the Communist leadership was intending to exacerbate and exploit the differences between "constructive" *Ecoglasnost* and "destructive" *Podkrepa*, and some elements within the UDF were reported to have been tempted by the offer of participation in government. Prominent among the UDF's leaders are its chairman Zhelyu Zhelev (of the Club for Glasnost' and Democracy), and its secretary Petur Beron (an *Ecoglasnost* member).

RW

UNION OF SOVIET SOCIALIST REPUBLICS (USSR).

Population: 288.8 million (1990). *Area*: 22.4 million sq km (8.65 million sq miles). *Top five trading partners*: GDR, Poland, Bulgaria, Czechoslovakia, Hungary. *Urban population as percentage of total*: 65.8 per cent (1989). *Birth rate*: 18.8 per thousand (1988). *Life expectancy*: 69.6 years in 1988 (males 64.8; females 73.6).

Land and people. The Soviet Union is the world's largest state. Its total area accounts for about one sixth of the world's land surface; it is nearly three times as large as the United States of America, and nearly 100 times as large as the United Kingdom. Such is the natural and human variety of the Soviet Union that it is perhaps better described as a continent rather than a country. It is inhabited by over 100 different national groups; its land area stretches over 6,000 miles across Europe and Asia, embracing 11 different time zones; it has the world's longest land frontier, and the world's longest (mostly frozen) coastline. The great extent and variety of the Soviet land-mass has always made it difficult for central governments to impose the degree of control that they have wished over outlying areas; but it has also meant that this is a country almost impossible to conquer, as a series of invaders from east and west have discovered to their cost.

The Soviet climate is also a varied one, both from place to place and from season to season, given that few parts of the USSR are close to the moderating influence of the sea. The whole of the country, in fact, lies in relatively northerly latitudes compared with the world's other major countries. The northernmost point of the USSR is just a few hundred miles south of the North Pole, and some 40 per cent of the country consists of permafrost. The southernmost parts of the USSR, at the other extreme, are predominantly desert and border on Turkey, Iran and Afghanistan. **Moscow**, the capital, is about as far north as Edinburgh, but it is much colder in January (when the average temperature is minus 9°C) and rather warmer in summer (the average in July is 18°C). **Leningrad**, the former capital, is as far north as the Shetland Islands and nearly as far north as Anchorage in Alaska; the average temperature here is minus 8°C in January and 17°C in July.

Elsewhere in the country the range of climatic variation is far greater. Yakutsk, for instance, in eastern Siberia, has an average temperature in January of minus 44°C; temperatures here are as low as any that occur in the inhabited world, but in summer (an average of 19°C in July)they are as high as in most parts of the British Isles. This wide range of climatic variation makes agriculture difficult in all but the most temperate parts of the country; it hinders transport; and it makes construction very difficult (at such low temperatures metal becomes brittle and oil rapidly solidifies). Some have even speculated that it may help to explain the Russian character, with its characteristic swings between sorrow and joy, apathy and enthusiasm, and sobriety and drunkenness.

Geographically, the USSR can be divided into three major zones. The north and north-east, including most of Siberia, is generally too cold for successful agriculture, with the exception of some livestock farming, and human settlement is generally sparse. Air temperatures are not high enough to evaporate the relatively low levels of rainfall or other forms of precipitation, and large areas become flooded or boggy in the summer months. Although very rich in natural resources, including oil and coal (the Kuznetsk basin, near Kemerovo, is the most important mining area in the USSR after the Donets basin in the Ukraine), the adverse climatic conditions and limited transport infrastructure mean that the costs of extraction are disproportionately high. A major new railway line, the Baikal-Amur main line, was constructed between 1974 and 1984 in an attempt to improve communications between the Baikal area and the Pacific coast. Siberia contains the Soviet Union's "science city". Akademgorodok near Novosibirsk, which houses the Siberian branch of the Academy of Sciences, and part of the shore of Lake Baikal, in eastern Siberia, has been developed as a "Siberian Riviera". Labour turnover and outmigration nonetheless remain high, despite higher wages and other benefits, and this whole area (about 57 per cent of the whole country) accounts for no more than 10 per cent of the total Soviet population.

The second main geographic zone is that which covers most of Soviet Central Asia. This is an area of high summer temperatures but very low levels of precipitation, and substantial parts are desert or otherwise unsuitable for cultivation. A plan to divert the USSR's north-flowing rivers southwards towards the Caspian, which would have extended the area suitable for cultivation but with enormous and upredictable consequences for the ecological balance elsewhere in the USSR and abroad, was officially abandoned in 1986. Large drainage and soil improvement schemes have however been undertaken, and attempts have been made (with only limited success) to develop more hardy crop species. There is substantial mining (coal and many other minerals are found in Kazakhstan) but for the most part this is an agricultural area, particularly important for its grain and cotton crops. The area also contains the

Soviet "cosmodrome", at Baikonur in central Kazakhstan.

The third main geographical zone, and by far the most important in terms of economic activity and human habitation, consists of central and southern European Russia. This area contains the fertile soils of the central black-earth region, together with the very rich iron and coal deposits of the Donbas in the southern Ukraine, still the most important in the USRR. Towards the south of this area lies the very rich sub-tropical region near the Black Sea in the Caucasus, famous for its fruit and wine and for its agreeable climate, which has encouraged inward migration from other parts of the USSR. Most of the USSR's major cities and industries are located within this region, which accounts for a relatively small proportion of the country's total land area (one sixth of the total land area, west of the Volga and south of Leningrad, contains no less than two-thirds of the country's total population). European Russia is equally predominant in science, education and government, and is generally the most "advanced" part of the USSR in its social and cultural development.

The total Soviet population, according to the census of January 1989, was 286.7 million; this makes the USSR the third most populous state in the world. Population growth, after some years of stagnation, began to rise in the early 1970s and this trend accelerated in the 1980s. The highest rate of increase during the 10 years since the previous census was in Central Asia (22–34 per cent); there was a more moderate rate of growth (13 and 17 per cent respectively) in Kazakhstan and Azerbaidzhan; and there was a much lower rate of 10 per cent or less in the other republics, with the lowest rates of all in the Baltic. Some 23 cities had a population of a million or more at the time of the census; Volgograd, in May 1989, became the 24th. The rate of growth of population has been particularly large in the largest cities, with a 29 per cent increase in the population of the "millionaire cities" between the last two censuses. The urban population as a whole increased by 25.2 million over the same period, 14.6 million of which represented natural growth and 10.6 million of which represented migration into the cities and the transformation of rural communites into towns. The Soviet population has become steadily larger since the revolution, although there were many deaths during the years immediately after the revolution and an enormous loss during World War II, when as many as 20 million died—far more than any country has ever lost in any war. Direct military losses during the four years of hostilities are estimated at 7.5 million, and civilian deaths at between six and eight million. In addition to these, labour camps continued to operate during the war, carrying out military tasks as well as others and with a higher than average rate of losses, bringing the total of direct or indirect war deaths between 1941 and 1945 up to 20 or even 25 million. Losses were concentrated disproportionately among men of military age, and the normal male–female balance within the population has still not been restored more than a generation later. As of January 1989, there were 151.2 million females but only 135.5 million males; the relative predominance of females is particularly marked in urban areas (1,126 women for every 1,000 men).

There have been considerable changes in the social structure of the USSR over the same period, as government policies and other developments have affected the way in which people earn their living. The gradual industrialization of the country, particularly rapid during the late 1920s and 1930s, has led to a steady increase in the proportion of the population classified as workers (in industry or in state-owned agriculture). The number of white-collar employees, including managers and administrators as well as teachers, doctors, actors and others who engage in predominantly non-manual work, has increased at a comparable rate over the same period. The proportion of collective farmers has however fallen quite sharply as substantial numbers—as in other countries—have left the countryside for the bright city lights. Illiteracy, which was a serious social problem before the war, has meanwhile been almost totally eliminated, and the USSR has now (at least in formal terms) one of the best-educated populations in the world. One illustration of this is that the USSR publishes about a quarter of the world's books; another, that it employs about a quarter of the world's scientific staff (how effectively is another matter).

Like many other urbanizing and developing countries, the number of births in the USSR has tended to fall over the years, although the 1980s have seen a stabilization and even a slight reversal of this trend. The birth rate is lowest (down to 15 per thousand births) in the Ukraine, Russia proper and the Baltic; it is very much higher in the traditionally Muslim Central Asian republics (up to 42 per thousand in Tadzhikistan, for example), and it is generally rather higher in rural as compared with urban areas. The marriage rate has varied relatively little over the 1970s and 1980s; the divorce rate, however, has continued to increase, and now accounts for more than one marriage in three. Life expectancy increased steadily from pre-revolutionary times (when it was just 32 years) up to the early 1970s, when it was 69.5 years; it then fell to 67.7 years in 1984

before improving somewhat to 69.8 years in 1986 (65.1 years for men and 73.8 for women). Reflecting official embarrassment, this information was simply not published after 1972, but it reappeared, reflecting **Gorbachev**'s policy of *glasnost'*, in the 1985 statistical yearbook. So too did the figure for infant mortality, 26 per thousand births (in 1988, 24.7), which is significantly above the figure for the developed capitalist countries (in Britain, for instance, the figure was 9.3 in 1985). Allowance must however be made for the increasing proportion of births that are occurring in the less developed Central Asian republics of the USSR, where infant mortality rates are very much above those for the rest of the country.

State structure. The USSR is officially a federation consisting of a voluntary union of 15 sovereign union republics (the RSFSR or **Russian Republic**, the **Ukraine**, **Belorussia**, **Latvia**, **Lithuania**, **Estonia**, **Moldavia**, **Georgia**, **Armenia**, **Azerbaidzhan**, **Kirghizia**, **Kazakhstan**, **Uzbekistan**, **Turkmenia** and **Tadzhikistan**). The RSFSR is by far the largest of these republics, accounting for about 76 per cent of the total area and for about 51 per cent of the total Soviet population. All of the other republics are far smaller and most of them have a population of just a few million. The union republics are described in the present constitution, adopted in 1977, as "sovereign Soviet socialist states", and they have a considerable range of formal powers, including the right to secede and to establish diplomatic relations with foreign powers. Two of them, the Ukraine and Belorussia, have in fact been members of the United Nations since its foundation. The laws of the USSR as a whole, however, take precedence over those of the union republics, the decisions of the central government are binding throughout the USSR, and the state as well as the party is officially committed to the doctrine of democratic centralism under which the decisions of higher bodies are binding upon those below them. The union republics, accordingly, are rather less than sovereign states, nor is the USSR a proper federation; but they do provide a formal expression of the multinational character of the state (in each of them a particular nationality is supposed to be predominant), and they exercise a substantial number of devolved powers of government. One of the objectives of the national movements in the late 1980s and early 1990s has been to extend those powers further; in Lithuania, in March 1990, this took the form of a declaration of full independence.

The principle of democratic centralism applies not simply to relations between the federal government and the union republics, but also to relations between the union republics and the lower levels of government that are responsible to them. The most important of these sub-divisions are the regions (*oblasti*) into which the eight largest republics are divided, and the districts (*raiony*) into which the regions, larger cities and the other union republics are divided. A number of nationalities that are not sufficiently numerous to have their own union republics exercise a more limited range of powers within autonomous Soviet socialist republics (ASSRs), autonomous regions or autonomous areas. There were 114 regions in the USSR in 1990, which together with the 20 ASSRs, eight autonomous regions, ten autonomous areas and six territories (*kraya*) form the "provincial" level of government in the USSR. Below them come the urban and rural districts (628 and 3,193 respectively in 1990), and then the, towns, urban settlements and villages which constitute the lowest level of government, or local government proper. At all levels of this system soviets or councils are elected, since 1989 for five years, at a time. In 1990 more than 2.3 million citizens were serving on elected bodies of this kind at various levels, and more than 30 million citizens were associated with their work, usually by unpaid duties on a voluntary commission of some sort. The soviets in turn elect executive committees or (at the union or autonomous republican level) councils of ministers to carry on the day-to-day work of government.

From 1937 until 1988 the representative system was headed by the Supreme Soviet of the USSR, which was elected every five years and met twice a year for a couple of days to approve government proposals. It was among the world's least influential legislatures, although its committee system did begin to develop increasingly effective powers of scrutiny of government performance and the budget. Following an extended discussion the constitution was amended in December 1988 so as to provide for an entirely new representative body, the USSR Congress of People's Deputies. The Congress was to meet in regular session once a year and would elect a standing parliament, the Supreme Soviet, from among its members. The Congress is exclusively empowered to adopt and amend the constitution and to determine the national and state structure of the USSR; it also establishes the "guidelines of the domestic and foreign policies of the USSR", including long-term state plans and programmes. The Congress consists of 2,250 deputies, 750 of whom are elected by territorial electoral districts with equal numbers of voters, and 750 of whom are elected by national–territorial electoral districts (32 from each union republic, 11 from each

autonomous republic, five from each autonomous region and one from each autonomous area). A further 750 deputies are elected by public organizations including the **Communist Party of the Soviet Union (CPSU)** and the trade unions, which were allocated 100 seats each.

The first Congress of People's Deputies, which met in Moscow from May 25 to June 9, 1989, soon emerged as a Soviet representative institution of a rather different character from those that had preceded it. Gorbachev, as expected, was elected to the newly-established post of Chairman of the USSR Supreme Soviet, or president. What could not have been expected, however, was that two candidates were nominated to stand against him, and that he secured election, after a series of searching questions from the deputies, by a less than unanimous vote (2,123 in favour but 87 against). Anatolii Luk'yanov, who was elected First Vice-Chairman of the Supreme Soviet four days later, faced a still more extended inquisition from deputies, including questions about his responsibility, while working in the central party apparatus, for the increase in reported crime that had taken place over the same period. Gorbachev addressed the Congress on May 30, and prime minister Nikolai **Ryzhkov** on June 7; most of the remainder of the session was given over to speeches from deputies, initially on procedural matters, but latterly on all aspects of party and state policy and often of a sharply critical character.

The head of the **Soviet Women's Committee**, for instance, Zoya Pukhova, complained that the USSR was lagging behind many developing, not to speak of developed countries in its attention to women's rights, and called for "more profundity" in the speeches of Gorbachev and other leaders on these matters. The former Moscow party secretary, Boris **Yel'tsin**, complained that power was still monopolized by the party and state apparatus and warned that the head of state had accumulated so much authority that a "new dictatorship" was possible. Another target was the Committee of State Security (KGB). Yuri Vlasov, a former Olympic weightlifter, in an astonishing speech, listed the sites in which the KGB had buried its victims and accused it of crimes "unknown in the history of humanity". He went on to describe the contemporary KGB as an "underground empire", all-powerful and largely uncontrolled, and called for its headquarters to be moved from central Moscow and for its activities to be directly supervised by the Congress and Supreme Soviet. Andrei **Sakharov**, the physicist and former dissident who became the country's most popular parliamentarian before his death in December 1989, read out an alternative programme which included the removal of the Communist Party and its leading role from the constitution. All these developments were followed on Soviet television, so avidly indeed that there was a fall of about 20 per cent in labour productivity over the same period. Later sessions of the Congress were transmitted, in shortened form, after working hours.

One of the first acts of Congress was to set up the new-style Supreme Soviet, a much smaller body of 542 deputies which was expected to remain in session for most of the year (the constitution suggested it would normally have two three- or four-month sessions every year). The Supreme Soviet, according to the constitution, is the "permanent legislative, administrative and control body of state authority of the USSR". It consists of two chambers, the Council of the Union and the Council of Nationalities, each of which has an equal numbers of deputies and equal powers. The Council of the Union is elected from among deputies representing territorial districts and public organizations; the Council of Nationalities is elected by deputies representing national–territorial districts and public organizations. The Supreme Soviet, under the constitution, appoints the chairman of the USSR Council of Ministers (or prime minister) and, on his recommendation, the other members of the government. More generally, it deals with national-level policy on economic, financial, social and cultural questions; it approves the state plan and budget, regulates the conduct of foreign policy and determines the use of Soviet armed forces domestically and internationally.

Despite the charge of an outspoken historian, Yuri Afanasyev, that it was a "Stalinist-Brezhnevite" body with an "aggressively obedient majority", the new Supreme Soviet, when it met for the first time on June 3, 1989, soon showed that it was a very different institution from its docile predecessors. One sign of this was the elaborate committee system that was set up, including committees of the Supreme Soviet as a whole as well as commissions attached to each of its two chambers. One of the Supreme Soviet's new committees dealt with defence and state security; another dealt with *glasnost'* and the rights of citizens. Some 928 deputies, about half of whom were members of the Supreme Soviet itself, were elected to serve on the new committees and commissions, and about two-thirds of the work of the new parliament was expected to take place under their auspices. Another promising sign was the establishment of an organizational base for the Supreme Soviet in central Moscow, with a library and electronic services. Yet another, potentially more significant difference was the

formation of an inter-regional deputies' group, in effect a radical caucus, under the leadership of Boris Yel'tsin and others. The group, which had its own funds and a newspaper, represented at least the embryo of a form of parliamentary opposition that had no obvious precedent in the Soviet period.

Much of the business of the first session of the new Supreme Soviet was concerned with the consideration of prime minister Nikolai Ryzhkov's nominations to the new Council of Ministers. It was a very different team, at least in terms of personnel. Only 10 of Ryzhkov's nominees had served in the Soviet government elected in 1984, and fewer than half had served in the outgoing administration. Nearly a third were entirely new to government service, six were members or candidate members of the Academy of Sciences, and the average age was a modest 55 (the final list included the Soviet Union's first non-party minister, a biology professor who became head of the Committee on Nature Conservation).The structure of the new government was also a different one.There were no more than 57 ministries and state committees altogether; some 25 ministries were to be wound up, and those that remained were to be "ministries of a new type", exercising general rather than detailed supervision within the area of competence. What was certainly new was the attention with which Ryzhkov's proposals were received: all the candidates were closely questioned both in committee and later in the Supreme Soviet itself, and at least six of the original nominations were rejected. This "parliamentary marathon" took about three weeks; Ryzhkov later suggested it had been the most unusual process of government formation in Soviet history.

Formally speaking the Council of Ministers is responsible both to the Congress of People's Deputies and to the Supreme Soviet, and it must report to the Supreme Soviet on its work at least once a year. The Council of Ministers is empowered to deal with all matters of state administration which do not fall within the competence of other bodies; in practice this includes the conduct of a wide variety of government business, including economic management, foreign relations, defence and social welfare. Under legislation approved in June 1989 the Council of Ministers contained 26 "all-union" ministries, based in Moscow and for the most part responsible for heavy industry, and 11 "union-republican ministries, based in Moscow and also in the republics, and including foreign affairs, finance, justice, culture and internal affairs. There were four all-union state committees, including science and technology, and 15 union-republican committees, including the State Planning Committee

(*Gosplan*), the State Committee on Material-Technical Supply (*Gossnab*), the State Committee on Labour and Social Questions, the State Prices Committee, the State Education Committee and the Committee of State Security (KGB). Some other minor state functions, including utilities and inland water transport, are wholly regulated at the republican level.

A further body, the Presidium, is formed on an *ex officio* basis and is also accountable to the Supreme Soviet. Broadly equivalent to a collective presidency, it consists of a chairman, a first vice-chairman, 15 vice-chairmen (one from each of the union republics) and the chairmen of the two chambers of the Supreme Soviet, the chairman of the Committee of Public Inspection (a supervisory agency) and the chairmen of the committees and commissions of the Supreme Soviet. The Presidium, according to the constitution, is responsible for convening sessions of the Supreme Soviet, co-ordinating the activities of its committees and commissions, conferring titles and distinctions, and other largely ceremonial functions. The chairman of the USSR Supreme Soviet, who is separately elected by the Congress of People's Deputies and who is responsible both to the Congress and to the Supreme Soviet, was in effect the Soviet president until the formal institution of that office in March 1990. The chairman (from 1989 to 1990, Mikhail Gorbachev) is empowered to exercise "general guidance" over the work of the Congress and Supreme Soviet, and is required to report periodically to both of these bodies on "important issues of Soviet domestic and foreign policy".

These provisions were modified somewhat by the decision of the third Congress of People's Deputies, meeting in March 1990, to establish the entirely new position of President of the USSR. The new post, it was explained in official commentaries, was intended to make a reality of the stream of legislation that had issued from the Congress and Supreme Soviet, but often to no very obvious effect. The presidency was also intended to make possible a swift executive response to rapidly changing local situations, including ethnic disturbances. The new presidency — to which Gorbachev was elected on March 15 — certainly disposed of impressive powers. He could nominate the prime minister and leading government officials, veto legislation, propose the resignation of the government and rule by decree. He enjoyed the usual ceremonial powers of state, and also headed a Presidential Council which took overall responsibility for Soviet foreign and domestic affairs, and a Federal Council which was concerned with the affairs of the USSR as a national–territorial state. There was

some concern, about Soviet liberals, that these extensive powers could open the way to a new dictatorship; in reply, it was pointed out that the President, elected in the first instance by the Congress of People's Deputies, would in future be elected by a national competitive ballot, and for maximum of two five-year terms. Based for 70 years or more on the authority of a single ruling party, these changes at least potentially represented a shift towards a system with much more in common wih the USA or France than with the principles of Leninism.

Political background. Soviet rule in the USSR was established on Nov. 7, 1917 (Oct. 25 by the calendar that was being used at the time in Russia) when a Military-Revolutionary Committee under the control of the Bolshevik party arrested the provisional government which had ruled since earlier in the year and transferred power to the second all-Russian Congress of Soviets. This in turn elected a new Soviet government, headed by **Lenin**; power in fact belonged to the Bolshevik party, the more radical wing of the Russian Social Democratic Labour Party, within which Lenin had earlier established his ascendancy. In July 1918 a constitution was adopted for the Russian Soviet Federal Socialist Republic (RSFSR), which was the first of its kind to be established. In the course of the civil war other Soviet Republics were established in the Ukraine, Belorussia and Transcaucasia; these formally combined in December 1922 to form the Union of Soviet Socialist Republics. In 1924 the Uzbek and Turkmen republics and in 1929 the Tadzhik republic became constituent members of the USSR, with the status of union republics. At the VIII Congress of Soviets in December 1936 a new constitution was adopted, at which the Transcaucasian republic was separated into Georgian, Armenian and Azerbaidzhani union republics, which also became constituent members of the USSR. The Kazakh and Kirghiz republics, previously autonomous republics within the RSFSR, became full union republics at the same time. The changes that took place during World War II led to the incorporation under a secret protocol to the Nazi-Soviet Pact of 1939, of the three Baltic republics. Moldavia became a Soviet Republic at the same time.

After an acknowledged retreat into a mixed economy — the New Economic Policy — during the 1920s, a decision was taken at the end of the 1920s to industrialize on the basis of centralized state planning. The first Five-Year Plan was introduced in 1928 and pronounced achieved, "ahead of time", at the end of 1932. It is probably fair to say that there has been no more significant development in the post-revolutionary period, and this pattern of centralized state direction of the economy has persisted, with minor variations, up to the present period. At the same time agriculture was collectivized, "voluntarily" but in fact with great loss of life, and all other spheres of Soviet life, from the family to sport and recreation, were placed under the detailed direction of the state. Initially very successful (even the most "revisionist" recalculations of economic growth after 1928 show Soviet rates exceeding those of the developed capitalist nations), this system became steadily less effective as a means of directing social and economic development, and the post-**Stalin** period has essentially consisted of an attempt to devise a substitute for what has come to be known as a "command-administrative system" developed during these years. **Stalinism** had a still greater direct bearing upon political liberties and the development of democracy based upon the elected soviets; by the 1930s, if not earlier, any elements of democracy that still remained within the party and the state had been eliminated, and large numbers of political opponents had been arrested and in many cases shot on groundless charges.

With all its faults it was widely believed that this was a system that had "won the war" with Nazi Germany, although the coats of doing so were horrendous, and for an older generation of Soviet leaders there is still much to be said for this centralized, state-directed form of social direction, modified in various respects but not abandoned in principle. The post-Stalin years have nonetheless seen a continuous search for an alternative, socialist (in the sense of being based on public ownership) but also democratic, in a way that (it was argued) the Soviet system had been during its nearly Leninist years. The first Soviet leader to make a determined effort to cleanse the Soviet system of its Stalinist deformations while yet retaining its healthy Leninist essence was Nikita **Khrushchev**, particularly through his "secret speech" to the XX Congress of the CPSU in 1956. There followed an attempt to develop a new legal system based on " socialist legality", and a more responsive political system based upon "Leninist norms of party life" such as collectivism and rank-and-file initiative. Many of these reforms, however, were ill-considered and hastily implemented, and when Khrushchev was compelled to resign in October 1964 there was a widespread wish (and certainly in the party and state leadership) to avoid any more of the "harebrained schemes" with which he was associated. The **Brezhnev** years developed, in part, as a reaction to the hectic pace of change under Khrushchev; they in turn became years of immo-

bilism and "stagnation", and the task that Gorbachev inherited on becoming party leader in 1985 was to resume the reformist programme, defined once again as an attempt to eliminate the bureaucracy, corruption and inertia of the Brezhnev and Stalin years and to return to healthy Leninist foundations. The Brezhnev legacy, and then the resumption of reform under **Andropov, Chernenko** and Gorbachev, is considered in the next section.

Recent political development. The Brezhnev era, at the time, had seemed to be something of a success story. The expansion of Soviet authority internationally, and of Brezhnev's own position domestically, advanced side by side. After years of privation and then (under Khrushchev) administrative reorganization, the Brezhnev era was one of stability both of structure and of personnel. "Stability of cadres" (or officials) was indeed one of its principal slogans. One of the ways in which the new regime made its priorities apparent was by reversing the well-meaning but often ill-considered reorganizations of the Khrushchev era (faults of this kind came to be known, under Brezhnev, as "subjectivism" and "voluntarism", in contrast to the deliberation and use of purportedly scientific techniques of the new General Secretary). One of Khrushchev's principal innovations, the *sovnarkhozy* (regional economic councils), introduced in the late 1950s with a view to reversing the concentration of powers into Moscow-based ministries, was brought to an end in 1965. Plans to democratize the Communist Party by requiring a high level of turnover among its committees and elected officials, introduced into the Party Rules in 1961, were reversed at the next party congress in 1966. The rehabilitation of the victims of the Stalin era, a process that began soon after the XX Congress of the CPSU in 1956, was discontinued. "De-Stalinisation" itself came to an end, and in the late 1960s it appeared possible that the former leader might even be restored to public favour; his books began to reappear in public libraries, there were approving references to him in official speeches, the term, "cult of personality" dropped out of use, and in 1970 a bust — slightly larger than all the others — appeared above his grave immediately behind the Lenin Mausoleum.

A modest "thaw"in the arts, symbolised by the publication of Alexander **Solzhenitsyn**'s *One day in the Life of Ivan Denisovich* in 1962, came to an end at the same time, and the later 1960s and 1970s saw a series of determined attempts to marginalize dissidents or "other-thinkers" as they were known in official circles. The first dissidents to become widely known in the West were the literary critic, Andrei Sinyavsky, and the translator, Yuli Daniel, who were put on trial in 1966 and sentenced to seven and five years' imprisonment respectively for having published works abroad that were held to have "defamed the Soviet system". Both Sinyavsky and Daniel denied the charges and had taken no steps to transmit their works abroad, hardly evidence of an intention to circulate slandrous falsifications which was the crime of which they were accused. The court, nonetheless, found them guilty and sentenced them accordingly. The arrest of Sinyavsky and Daniel was soon followed by similar action against other dissidents. In 1968 Alexander Ginzburg and Yury Galanskov were found guilty of circulating materials on the Sinyavsky-Daniel trial, and others were arrested on Red Square for demonstrating against the Warsaw Pact intervention in Czechoslovakia. In 1970 the historian Andrei Amalrik was put on trial and convicted; in 1974 Solzhenitsyn was arrested and then deported; and in 1976 Amalrik, Vladimir Bukovsky and others were encouraged or compelled to follow him into emigration. In 1978 Anatoly Shcharansky was found guilty of treason and Yuri Orlov of anti-Soviet agitation and propaganda (in 1986 both of them were permitted to emigrate); and finally in 1980 Academician Sakharov, one of the few prominent dissidents who had remained in the USSR and at liberty, was sent into internal exile in the city of Gorky, 250 miles east of Moscow and out of bounds for foreigners. Efforts were made at the same time to prevent the publication of unofficial or *samizdat* books and periodicals, and action was taken against unauthorised civil rights organizations such as the Helsinki Monitoring Group which had tried to keep a record of Soviet violations of the 1975 Final Act of the Helsinki Conference on Peace and Cooperation in Europe.

The Brezhnev period, at the same time, saw a sustained improvement in living standards and some attempt to develop mechanisms of "participation" at all levels of the society. Gross social product doubled between 1960 and 1970, and more than trebled between 1960 and 1980. Industrial production more than quadrupled over the same period. Agricultural production increased much more irregularly (in 1981 and 1982 the harvests were so poor that the figures were simply suppressed, and a much-publicized "food programme" was introduced in order to convey at least the appearance of decisive action). Despite these difficulties, the real incomes of ordinary citizens more than doubled over the two decades and the wages paid to collective farmers increased more than four times. This was not simply a matter of figures, which were based on

sometimes arbitrary definitions and often (it later became clear) falsified to a major degree. Educational levels, for instance, rose sharply (there were about three times as many members of the society with a higher education in 1980, for instance, as there had been on Brezhnev's accession). There were more hospital beds, more doctors, more houses, more refrigerators, and very many more TVs. And despite the disappointments in agriculture, for which climatic conditions were at least partly to blame, there were considerable improvements in the Soviet diet, in social security programmes, and in clothing (as any visitor could testify).

By the early 1980s, in parallel with these domestic changes, the USSR had begun to acquire an international influence that accorded more closely with the country's enormous territory, population and natural resources. Forced to back down in humiliating circumstances in the Cuban missile crisis of 1962, the USSR had since acquired a strategic capability which gave it an approximate parity with the USA by the end of that decade. The Soviet Union had one of the world's largest armies and one of its largest navies, and it stood at the head of one of the world's two major military alliances (*see* **Warsaw Treaty Organisation**). It was the centre of one of the world's major trading blocs, the **Council for Mutual Economic Assistance (CMEA)** or Comecon, and was an influential member of the United Nations. Its status as a superpower had been enhanced by a series of negotiations and agreements with its major capitalist adversary, particularly SALT 1 in 1972 and its unratified successor, SALT 2, in 1979. The USSR was represented much more widely in international affairs than ever before, and it stood at the head of a steadily increasing number of Communist-ruled states, the most recently of which to be established were in south-east Asia. Andrei **Gromyko**, foreign minister throughout the Brezhnev era, was able to tell a party cogress with, only a hint of exaggeration that the USSR was an international power of such importance that without its participation not a single global issue could be resolved; Brezhnev himself was able to claim that the "correlation of forces" throughout the world was moving steadily in favour of the USSR and socialism.

Brezhnev himself occupied an increasingly prominent place within the political system domestically (for Brezhnev's personal biography see the entry for Leonid **Brezhnev**). Originally a collective leadership, it became a leadership "headed by comrade L. I. Brezhnev" in the early 1970s. By the mid-1970s Brezhnev had became *vozhd'* or boss, a term previously used to describe

Stalin. He became a Marshal of the Soviet Union, and in 1977, after a new constitution had been adopted, he assumed the presidency or chairmanship of the Presidium of the USSR Supreme Soviet. The combination of posts was intended to allow him to represent the USSR with full authority internationally, rather than as "just" the leader of the Communist Party. A signatory already to the Helsinki Final Act of 1975, he travelled abroad with increasing frequency, and received foreign visitors both in Moscow and (in the case of the East European leaders) at regular sessions at the Politburo summer complex in the Crimea. Brezhnev's health, however, became increasingly uncertain and his retirement, from the general secretaryship if not from the presidency, was under active discussion when he died on Nov. 10, 1982, just three days after the anniversary parade in Red Square.

The following day it was announced that Yuri Andropov, the former KGB head who had became a member of the Central Committee Secretariat earlier in the year, was to be the chairman of the committee making arrangements for Brezhnev's funeral, and on Nov. 12 it was announced that an emergency meeting of the Central Committee had elected him to the vacant general secretaryship. Brezhnev was buried on Nov. 15, Andropov making the funeral oration, and a week later the new general secretary made his first speech as party leader to the Central Committee, a brief but effective review of Soviet foreign and domestic policy. In May 1983 it became known that Andropov had succeeded Brezhnev as chairman of the Defence Council of the USSR, and on June 16, 1983, he was elected to the vacant state presidency. Andropov's own health, however, was far from certain, and his period of effective authority in fact lasted for no more than a few months. He made significant contributions to the reform of Soviet **ideology**, and took the lead in encouraging a campaign against corruption and indiscipline in industry and the wider society. Nonetheless, it was not entirely unexpected when on Feb. 11, 1984, the central press reported that Andropov had died two days earlier after a "long illness". Once again the party leadership was plunged into the search for a successor.

As before there were two principal contenders: Konstantin **Chernenko**, whose political fortunes had revived with Andropov's illness, and Gorbachev, who was evidently Andropov's own favoured candidate for the succession. Chernenko was the one who was chosen, on Feb. 13, 1984, partly because of his seniority and experience and partly because it seemed too soon to elect the Politburo's youngest member to its supreme executive position. The presidency and chairmanship of the Defence Council, as well as the party leadership, had become vacant with Andropov's death; Chernenko, in February 1984, was identified as head of the Defence Council (in practice, commander in chief), and in April 1984, on Gorbachev's nomination, the first session of the newly-elected Supreme Soviet elected him to the vacant presidency. Chernenko was nevertheless, at 72, the oldest general secretary ever to have assumed this office, and he had a history of lung disease which caused difficulty in breathing. Perhaps inevitably, it was regarded as a transitional general secretaryship from the outset and led to no significant changes in personnel or policy. He died on March 10, 1985; the next day, with unprecedented speed, an extraordinary session of the Central Committee elected Mikhail **Gorbachev** as its third general secretary in three and a half years.

The advent of a new general secretary has normally meant a significant change in the direction of Soviet public policy, although any change of course has usually taken some time to establish itself as the new leader gradually marginalizes his opponents and co-opts his supporters on to the Politburo and Secretariat. At the outset of his administration Gorbachev's objectives, and indeed his personal background, were still fairly obscure even at leading levels of the party. Andrei Gromyko, proposing Gorbachev's candidacy to the Central Committee, explained what had convinced him personally that Gorbachev would be a suitable general secretary: Gorbachev, he indicated, had chaired meetings of the Politburo in Chernenko's absence and had done so "brilliantly, without any exaggeration". Gorbachev himself, in his acceptance speech, paid tribute to the late general secretary and then pledged himself to continue the policy of his two predecessors, which he defined as "acceleration of socio-economic development and the perfection of all aspects of social life". There were, however, some elements in the new general secretary's biography which suggested this new administration would be more than a continuation of its immediate precursors.

One of those elements was Gorbachev's own background, particularly his education and more youthful generation. Gorbachev was born, according to his official biography, on March 2, 1931 to a peasant family in the Stavropol territory in southern Russia. Not exceptionally young, by the standards of previous general secretaries, on his appointment, he was nonetheless the first party leader since Lenin not to have served in the ranks during World War II, and he was the first (also since Lenin) to have acquired a university law degree (for a more detailed account of his personal background *see* the entry for Mikhail **Gorbachev**). Gorbachev worked first as a mechanic at a machine-tractor station, and then in 1950, with the help of his local party organization, enrolled in the Law Faculty at Moscow State University, where he was active in the Komsomol and where he met his future wife (*see* Raisa **Gorbachev**). After graduation Gorbachev returned to Stavropol where he worked in the Komsomol and party apparatus, becoming first secretary of the city party committee in 1966, territorial party first secretary in 1970, and a Central Committee member at the XXIV Party Congress in 1971. In 1978 he became a member of the Secretariat, in 1979 he joined the Politburo, and in 1980 he became one of its full voting members.

Apart from Gorbachev's personal characteristics, such as his relative youth and education, there were also clues in speeches before his assumption of the general secretaryship as to the direction of policy he was likely to pursue. Perhaps the clearest indication of this kind was a speech Gorbachev delivered to an all-union conference on ideology in December 1984. The speech contained positive references to self-management, which Lenin had "never counterposed to Soviet state power". It acknowledged the various interests of the different groups in Soviet society, and the need for a greater measure of social justice (which had become a coded form of attack upon the Brezhnev legacy). There was enormous scope, Gorbachev went on, for the further development of the Soviet political system, and of socialist democracy. This was partly a matter of developing all aspects of the work of the elected soviets, and of involving workers more fully in the affairs of their own workplace. It was also a matter of securing a greater degree of *glasnost'* or openness in party and state life. Speeches of this kind, in effect an election manifesto to the Central Committee "selectorate", made it clear that Gorbachev would continue Andropov's emphasis upon efficiency and discipline but also that they would be placed within a broader framework involving democratic reform and a reassertion of the moral values that were, for Gorbachev, implicit in socialism.

The direction of reform became still clearer at the April 1985 Central Committee plenum, the first that Gorbachev addressed as party leader. There had been significant achievements in all spheres of Soviet life, Gorbachev told the plenum. The USSR had a powerful, developed economy, a highly skilled workforce and an advanced scientific base. Everyone had the right to work, to social security, to cultural resources of all kinds, and to participation in management. But

further changes were needed in order to achieve a "qualitatively new state of society" including modernization of the economy and the extension of socialist democracy and popular self-government. The key issue was the acceleration of economic growth. This was quite feasible if the "human factor" was called more fully into play, and if the reserves that existed throughout the economy were properly utilized. This in turn required a greater degree of decentralization of economic management, including cost accounting at enterprise level and a closer connection between the work that people did and the payment they received. The months and years that followed saw the gradual assembly of a leadership team to direct these changes and the further extension of what was already a challenging reform agenda.

Of all the policies that were promoted by this new and Gorbachevian leadership, *glasnost'* was perhaps the most distinctive and the one that had been pressed furthest by the early 1990s. *Glasnost'*, usually translated as openness or publicity, was not the same as freedom of the press or the right to information; nor was it original to Gorbachev. It did, however, reflect the new general secretary's belief that without a greater awareness of the real state of affairs and of the considerations that had led to particular decisions there would be no willingness on the part of the Soviet people to commit themselves to his programme of *perestroika*. "The better people are informed", Gorbachev told the Central Committee meeting that elected him, "the more consciously they act, the more actively they support the party, its plans and programmatic objectives".

As a result of such convictions, the Gorbachev leadership made steady and sometimes dramatic progress in removing taboos from the discussion of public affairs and exposing both the Soviet past and the Soviet present to critical scrutiny. The Brezhnev era was one of the earliest targets. It had been a time, Gorbachev told the XXVII Party Congress in 1986, when a "curious psychology—how to change things without really changing anything"—had been dominant. A number of its leading representatives had been openly corrupt, and some (such as Brezhnev's son-in-law, Yuri Churbanov) were brought to trial and imprisoned. More generally, it had been a period of "stagnation", of wasted opportunities, when party and government leaders had lagged behind the needs of the times. The Stalin question, however, was clearly the most critical one, as it had been for all Soviet reformers. Gorbachev, to begin with, was reluctant even to concede there was a question. Stalinism , he told the French press in 1986, was a "notion made up by enemies of Communism";

the XX Party Congress in 1956 had condemned Stalin's "cult of personality" and drawn the necessary conclusions. By early 1987, however, Gorbachev was insisting that there must be "no forgotten names, no blank spots" in Soviet literature and history, and by November of that year, when he came to give his address on the seventieth anniversary of the revolution, he was ready to condemn the "wanton repressive measures" of the 1930s, "real crimes" in which "many thousands of people inside and outside the party" had suffered.

In the course of his speech Gorbachev announced that a Politburo commission had been set up to investigate the political repression of the Stalinist years, and this led to the rehabilitation of many prominent figures from the party's past (and thousands of others) during 1988 and 1989. The most important figure to be restored to full respectability in this way was the former *Pravda* editor Nikolai Bukharin, whose sentence was posthumously quashed in February 1988 (later in the year his expulsions from the party and the Academy of Sciences were both reversed). Two other old Bolsheviks, Grigorii Zinoviev and Lev Kamenev, were rehabilitated in July 1988. **Trotsky** had not been sentenced by a Soviet court and there was therefore no judgement to be quashed; but his personal qualities began to receive some recognition in the Soviet press, and in 1989 some of his writings began to appear in mass-circulation as well as scholarly journals. An extended discussion took place about the numbers that Stalin had condemned to death: for some it was about a million by the end of the 1930s, but for others (such as the historian and commentator Roy Medvedev) it was at least 12 million, with a further 38 million repressed in other ways. Perhaps still more significant, a number of mass graves of victims of the Stalin period began to be uncovered, the most extensive of which were in the Kuropaty forest near Minsk. The victims, as many as 100,000 or more, had been shot between 1937 and 1941; this, and the other mass graves that began to be discovered in the late 1980s, was an indictment of Stalinism still more powerful than anything the historians and writers could muster.

Glasnost' led to further changes in the quality of Soviet public life, from literature and the arts to statistics and a wideranging discussion on the future of Soviet socialism. Public information began to improve, with the publication of statistics on crime, abortions, suicides and infant mortality. Subjects that had been taboo during the Brezhnev years, such as violent crime, drugs and prostitution, began to receive extensive treatment. Many events of the past, such as the devastating

earthquake in Ashkhabad in 1948 and the nuclear accident in the Urals in 1957, were belatedly acknowledged. Figures for defence spending and foreign debt were revealed for the first time to the Congress of People's Deputies in 1989. The Congress itself was televised in full and followed avidly throughout the USSR, so too were Central Committee meetings, Supreme Soviet committee hearings and other public occasions. Still more remarkably, the Soviet **media** were opened up to foreign journalists and politicians, and even (in a few cases) to émigrés and unapologetic opponents of Soviet socialism; and the first "space-bridges" were instituted, linking together studio audiences in the USSR and many Western nations. Opinion polls suggested that *glasnost'*, for all its limitations, was the change in Soviet life that was most apparent to ordinary people and the one they most valued.

The "democratization" of Soviet political life, of which *glasnost'* was a part, was also intended to release the human energies that, for Gorbachev, had been choked off by the bureaucratic centralism of the recent past. The Soviet Union, he told the 19th Party Conference in the summer of 1988, had pioneered the idea of a workers' state and of workers' control, the right to work and equality of rights for women and all national groups. The political system established by the October revolution, however, had undergone "serious deformations", leading to the development of a "command-administrative system" which had extinguished the democratic potential of the elected soviets. The role of party and state officialdom had increased out of all proportion, and this "bloated administrative apparatus" had begun to dictate its will in political and economic matters. Nearly a third of the adult population were regularly elected to the soviets and other bodies, but most of them had little influence over the conduct of state and public affairs. Social life as a whole had become unduly "governmentalized", and ordinary working people had become "alienated" from the system that was supposed to represent their interests. It was this "ossified system of government, with its command-and-pressure mechanism", that was now the main obstacle to *perestroika*.

The Conference duly approved the notion of a "radical reform" of the political system, and this led to a series of constitutional and other changes in 1988 and 1989. An entirely new electoral law, for instance, approved in December 1988, broke new ground in providing for (though not specifically requiring) a choice of candidate at elections to local and national-level authorities. A new state structure was established, incorporating a relatively small working parliament for the first time in modern Soviet political history and (from March 1990) a powerful executive presidency (see above). A constitutional review committee, similar to a constitutional court, was set up as part of a move to what Gorbachev called a "socialist system of checks and balances". Judges were to be elected for longer periods of time, and given greater guarantees of independence in their work. And the CPSU itself was to be 'democratized', although in practice the changes were less dramatic than in other parts of the political system. Leading officials, it was agreed, should be elected by competitive ballot for a maximum of two consecutive terms; members of the Central Committee should be involved much more directly in the work of the leadership; and there should be much more information about all aspects of the party's work, from its finances to the operation of its decision-making bodies.

Together with these changes, for Gorbachev, there must be a "radical reform" of the Soviet economy (for a full discussion see below). Levels of growth had been declining since at least the 1950s. In the late 1970s they reached the lowest levels in Soviet peace-time history; growth, in the view of Soviet as well as Western commentators, may in fact have ceased altogether during these years, at least per head of population. Indeed, as Gorbachev explained in early 1988, if the sale of alcoholic drink and of Soviet oil on foreign markets was excluded, there had been no real growth in the USSR for at least the previous 15 years. Growth, at least for many reforming economists, could not be an end in itself; what was important was the satisfaction of real social needs. But it was equally apparent that without some improvement in living standards there would be no popular commitment to *perestroika*, and no prospect that socialism would recover its appeal to other nations as a means by which ordinary working people could live their lives in dignity and prosperity. There was indeed a real danger, in the view of economists like Nikolai Shmelev, that without radical reform the USSR would enter the twenty-first century a "backward, stagnating state and an example to the rest of the world how not to conduct its economic affairs".

Radical reform, as Gorbachev explained to the XXVII Party Congress and to an important Central Committee meeting in the summer of 1987, involved a set of related measures. One of the most important was a greater degree of decentralization of economic decision making, leaving the broad guidance of the economy in the hands of the State Planning Committee (Gosplan) but allowing factories and farms throughout the USSR much more freedom to determine their own priorities. They should be guided in making such decisions by a wide range of "market" indicators, including the orders they received from other enterprises and the profits they made on their production. Retail and wholesale prices would have to reflect the costs of production much more closely so that enterprises could be guided by "economic" rather than "administrative" regulators and so that the massive subsidies that held down the cost of basic foodstuffs could be reduced. Under the Law on the State Enterprise, adopted in 1987, enterprises that persistently failed to pay their way under these conditions could be liquidated; some economists were willing to argue that a modest degree of unemployment was not simply a logical but even a desirable feature of changes of this kind. The state sector, more generally, should be gradually reduced in size and co-operative and even private economic activity should be expanded in its place. Gorbachev described these changes, which were gradually brought into effect during 1987 and 1988, as the most radical to have taken place in Soviet economic life since the adoption of the New Economic Policy in the early 1920s.

The "Gorbachev revolution", by the early 1990s, had attracted unprecedented international attention, and yet its objectives and likely consequences were far from clear five years after its inception. What, for instance, was the "socialism" to which such a system was supposed to be committed as part of a transition to a fully Communist society? Khrushchev had promised that the USSR would construct a society of this kind by 1980 in the Party Programme that was adopted under his leadership in 1961. His successors swiftly dropped that commitment and began to describe the USSR, from the early 1970s, as a "developed socialist society", whose evolution into a fully Communist society was a matter for an unspecified point in the fairly distant future. Brezhnev's successors in turn made it clear that the USSR was at the very beginning of the stage of developed socialism, whose proper development would require a "whole historical epoch". Gorbachev, for his part, has avoided the term "developed socialism" and opted instead for "developing socialism", in effect a postponement into the still more distant future of the attainment of a fully Communist society (*see* **Ideology**).

It remained unclear, these generalities apart, how a "developing socialist society" was to be conceived and how its further development was to be assured. It certainly excluded some of the utopian emphases of Khrushchev's Party Programme of 1961: Gorbachev's revised Programme of 1986 avoided any mention of dates or stages by which full Communism was to be reached, and there was no longer any commitment to the increasing provision of public services to all who needed them without charge. It was not, evidently, a society that would be based upon state ownership and control—there would certainly be a substantial private and co-operative sector, and foreign as well as domestic ownership —and it was not a society in which it was assumed that all its members had a basic identity of interests. Gorbachev set out a vision of the "qualitatively new state of society" that he hoped to achieve at the 19th Party Conference in 1988, but it was clearer in its denunciation of the "deformed" socialism of the 1930s than in its depiction of the society that he hoped to construct in its place. Addressing a Central Committee meeting in July 1989, Gorbachev could offer only the "broad outline" of the socialist society of the future. It would, he explained, be a "society of free people ... built on the principles of humanism, socialist democracy and social justice"; it would be a society in which the people had "absolute power and all human rights"; and there would be a "rich inner life and a high level of culture and morality". Statements of such a kind, whatever their merits, could hardly hope to offer practical guidance to party members and the broader public in their daily life; nor did they necessarily carry conviction at a time of manifest economic difficulty, nationalist discontent and the open acknowledgement of all kinds of mistakes and shortcomings by those who exercised political authority.

An obscurity about objectives was compounded by some uncertainty on the part of the instrument that was supposed to realize those aims, the **Communist Party of the Soviet Union (CPSU)**. Traditionally, a centralized Marxist-Leninist party exercising a "leading role" in the society had been taken as perhaps the single most important defining characteristic of a Communist system. The role of a party of this kind, however, became more difficult to sustain in a society in which a wide range of political forces had taken advantage of the opportunities of "socialist pluralism"; in March 1990, indeed, the party itself proposed the removal of its guaranteed monopoly position from the Soviet Constitution. Perhaps the most serious challenge to the party's political leadership came from the process of electoral reform which allowed the return of deputies armed for the first time with a genuine popular mandate. The March 1989 elections, which were the first exercise of this kind, saw a series of senior party officials defeated at the ballot box in a manner that clearly called into question the party's claim to rule (*see* **Elections and Electoral System in the USSR**). The experience was repeated at local elections in the various republics

in late 1989 and 1990. How, in these circumstances, could the party insist on its own ministerial candidates if "the people's representatives" decided otherwise? How could it satisfy the claims for resources that those representatives made of it? And how could it resist even a demand for outright independence if the voters returned a majority of nationalists at a subsequent election, particularly if local Communists sided with nationalist opinion rather than with Moscow?

Gorbachev had hoped, in his speech on political reform to the Central Committee in January 1987, to combine control "from below" with the continued maintenance of political leadership "from above" by the Communist Party. His assumption appears to have been that the Soviet people were basically committed to collectivist values, and that they would respond to his call for a more open, pluralist socialism in which human rights would be respected and a diversity of interests could express themselves. His emphasis upon leadership change equally reflected the view that the Soviet system was fundamentally sound and that it had been "subjective" causes, above all the failures of party officials at national and local level, that had led it into a pre-crisis or even crisis situation. The experience of his first five years was that the appointment of his own management team made relatively little difference (within two or three years he was being forced to sack the people he had himself appointed). The opportunities that were provided for "socialist democracy" led to no obvious improvement in economic performance but rather to the open articulation of national and other differences (and indeed to substantial loss of life). The Communist Party itself, confronted by such challenges, began to experience what was frequently described as a "crisis of confidence" and found itself increasingly divided and at odds with a resentful society. By the early 1990s it was this question of political authority, or more generally of the managability of the processes of change he had encouraged, that was perhaps the most fundamental of all those the Soviet leader still confronted.

Economic background. The Soviet Union presents the classic case of crash, or "forced draft " industrialization, pushed through on the basis of a highly centralized and quasi-military system of economic planning. Under Stalin this system developed as a highly effective instrument of rapid *resource mobilization*, as the Soviet planners sought to marshal the productive potential of the tens of millions of under-employed peasants and housewives of the traditional economy, and the vast energy and mineral resources of the country. Early Soviet industrialization was in many ways a very wasteful process. Plan implementation was based on obligatory output targets, backed up by material and status incentives for fulfilment, and disincentives for under-fulfilment which ran from purely material losses through to a fate worse than death. This one-sided emphasis on output, which mirrored the inflexible industrial production priorities of Stalin himself, inevitably tended to induce insensitivity towards other economic considerations — costs, productivity, new technology etc. Fuel was utilized with extreme diseconomy, and the transport patterns induced by an obsession with large plants ("gigantomania") compounded technical inefficiency with grossly excessive haulage of heavy products like cement. In their desperate quest for high output, Soviet directors often engaged new labour greatly in excess of technically normal requirements, as they sought to build in a "safety factor". Thus over the period of the first Five-Year Plan, 1928–32, the aggregate plan for absorption of new labour into urban activities was overshot by seven million — nearly 50 per cent. By the same token, management showed inevitable hostility to technological changes which forced them to stop production of tried and trusted lines for re-tooling, and thereby threatened fulfilment of the monthly plan. Early Soviet economic growth was, then, very much *extensive growth* — based on a high rate of mobilization of new inputs, rather than a high rate of increase in the efficiency with which those inputs were used. But that is not, *per se*, a reason for dismissing it. The Soviet growth record, however calculated or recalculated, stands testimony to the success of the strategy. Under difficult international conditions, despite a devastating war from 1941 to 1945, and in the face of the cruelly self-inflicted wounds of high Stalinism, the Soviet economy was able to report growth rates of national income of 5 per cent or more throughout the period 1928 –1960. Industrial growth rates were even higher.

But by the early 1960s a downward trend in growth rates was detectable. The trend was briefly reversed by the partial planning reforms of the **Kosygin**/Brezhnev government (see below), but re-emerged with a vengeance in the 1970s. By 1980 the Soviet economy was hardly growing at all in real terms. Now growth rates fell away in the West too, after the first oil shock of 1974, and even more so after the second oil shock of 1979. But the Soviet Union, as a major energy exporter, actually benefited from the oil shocks, so that we can hardly blame international trading patterns for the slow-down. What peculiarly Soviet factors can we adduce?

Most obviously, domestic factor supply conditions were worsening dramatically from the 1960s onwards. As the process of transfer of surplus able-bodied labour from the countryside came to its logical end, as the female participation rate rose to a level which brought rates of natural increase in the European parts of the USSR down to near-zero, so labour abundance turned into labour shortage. It was in the mid-1960s that exploitation of Siberian hydrocarbons began, as the readily accessible Caucasian and Volga reserves approached exhaustion. From the early 1970s the capital costs of establishing new oil and gas wells in ever more inhospitable parts of Siberia maintained a sharply upwards trend. There is little reason to doubt that through the 1970s extraction costs of energy materials in the Soviet Union grew as fast as international oil and gas prices.

Against this background, the peculiarities of centralized planning turned into fatal weaknesses. With labour now in short supply, only increasing productivity could provide a sound basis for further growth. But the pattern of universal overmanning at enterprise level, forced on managers by the nature of central planning, condemned the Soviet economy to systematically low-productivity production patterns. Again, in-built resistance to technical change meant that the new wave of electronics-based innovation which swept the world economy in the 1970s and provided the basis for a new take-off into rapid growth, particularly in Japan and the United States, simply passed the Soviet Union by. On the energy side, Soviet planners found themselves faced with a startling dilemma. Oil had become so expensive, and so costly to produce, that an optimal Soviet energy policy would have devoted the great bulk of Soviet oil output to export for hard currency. In practice, the inherent wastefulness of domestic energy utilization meant that a large proportion of it continued to be burned in inefficient thermal power stations, producing power to be used in energy-inefficient industrial enterprises. The decade of the 1970s witnessed no effective reduction in the coefficient of energy utilization to national income in the Soviet Union. Over the same period it fell by some 30 per cent in the seven leading industrial countries of the world.

There was also a purely organizational dimension. By very dint of the success of the Stalinist model in fostering quantitative growth, the Soviet economy became rapidly a much more complex organism to administer. The central planning apparatus, always over-worked, came increasingly to find the burden of planning simply unbearable. By the 1970s Gosplan (the State Planning Commission) was having to tell enterprises to organize component production on a local basis

273

or do without. Thus operational decentralization was already being forced on the Soviet authorities at a time when the philosophy of the system was still staunchly centralist. But this kind of ad hoc decentralization sometimes did more harm than good. In the investment sphere, for instance, the Soviet economy has always suffered from a problem of overheating, or, as the Russians call it, "excessive spread". Because the great bulk of investment finance came traditionally from non-returnable budgetary grants, there was every reason for ministries and enterprises to try to maximize the volume of funds coming their way, irrespective of considerations of optimal allocation — in much the same way that competing bureaucracies do in the West. And the surest way of guaranteeing a vigorous flow of funds in the future was to start as many projects as possible in the present. So there were always too many projects on the go, and as a result completion periods tended to be grossly excessive—normally around three times as long as in the West. Khrushchev's attempts in the late 1950s to solve the problem by giving regional authorities more control over investment simply made the problem worse. The policies of the Brezhnev/Kosygin government, which sought to combine maintenance of the traditional system for priority projects with decentralization to enterprise level for small-scale projects, made it worse still, because it simply generated mutually destructive competition between centralized and decentralized investment sectors for scarce investment supplies.

We can see the same pattern if we review the Kosygin industrial planning reform of 1965 as a whole. In terms of its basic elements, it seemed a very sensible reform. The old gross-output success indicator was replaced by sales and profit was introduced as a key indicator for the first time, all this reflecting an obvious concern to improve resource allocation procedures. The price system was reformed, a capital charge introduced, and a new incentive system established which made enterprise profits, rather than ministerial funds, the main source of bonus payments. In practice, however, this rationalization of the system of planning parameters, with its elements of selective decentralization, was never backed up by any general decentralization. The Planning Commission continued to grapple with an impossible work load, and enterprises continued to produce and deliver in accordance with instructions from superiors, rather than on the basis of market signals. In that context, profit was simply not permitted to play the resource allocation role it plays in market economies. With fixed prices and contracts, legitimate profit-maximization turned too easily into profiteering. And as the conservatives

gained the upper hand again at the political level in the early 1970s, this kind of malfunction provided a convenient excuse to abandon what limited steps forward the reform had achieved. By the mid-1970s the planning system was again as unrepentantly centralist and command-based as it had ever been under Stalin.

We can extend the analysis on the socio-political dimension. As long as Stalin was alive, Soviet citizens performed their duties out of fear of the stick as much as out of expectation of the carrot. This tended to induce an uncreative approach to work, but it did impose an effective discipline. Under Brezhnev, everything became much more easy-going. At the level of the political elites, life-time security of tenure became an almost universal principle, and the same rule operated for the majority of ordinary working people. A tenured and feather-bedded working class in the present provided, no doubt, a crucial political bulwark for a Communist regime that was already losing its credibility as the deliverer of some kind of materialist paradise in the future. But losses from absenteeism, drunkenness and sheer sloth mounted, and by the late 1970s experienced workers were bragging that they could get away with anything.

The Stalinist profile of economic development was unbalanced development *par excellence*. High rates of growth of national income derived mainly from high rates of growth of industrial production, and these in turn reflected principally the achievements of the heavy industrial sectors — steel, energy and machinery. The sector which came worst out of all this was agriculture. Stalin's collectivization of the early 1930s had imposed a socialist form of organization on the Soviet peasant by brutal force, in the face of widespread opposition. Policies towards agriculture throughout the period of Stalin's rule were fiercely oppressive, and rural living standards remained lower than they had ever been in the pre-collectivization period. Investment flows into agriculture were also restricted. Not surprisingly, then, the new socialist agriculture performed poorly, and when Stalin died in 1953 aggregate levels of agricultural production were not much higher than they had been in 1928.

Khrushchev initiated a major policy change in the mid-1950s, raising agricultural procurement prices sharply, and thus making it possible for farms to make substantial increases in wages and investment outlays. These policies bore fruit in a 50 per cent increase in aggregate agricultural output from 1953 to 1958. They faltered rather during Khrushchev's last years in power, but the new Brezhnev/Kosygin leadership which took over in 1964 revived the main features of Khrushchev's early agricultural strategy. Prices were improved again, and wages and investment levels rose accordingly. By 1975 the total income of the average collective farmer, taking into account income from the private plot which every peasant was allowed, approached some 80 per cent of the average industrial wage, while state farm workers were by that year as well off as their industrial compatriots. In the early 1970s a gigantic programme of land improvement measures was initiated in the non-Black Earth region of European Russia.

After initial successes in the late 1960s, however, the agricultural policies of the post-Khrushchev government collapsed in ruins. Aggregate agricultural output was no higher in 1980 than it had been in 1972, despite the commitment of well over 20 per cent of total Soviet investment to the sector, year after year. What went wrong with such apparently sensible policies? We can list the main factors as follows:

(i) The land-improvement drive soon turned into an exercise in highly politicized gigantomania such as might have taken even Stalin's breath away. Many of the drainage and irrigation systems installed simply did not work, and enormous environmental damage was done. On balance, the return to this massive investment outlay was zero, or even negative.

(ii) After initial movements towards a more flexible system of organization within collective and state farms, which would have permitted a partial return to individual farming, a reaction set in in the early 1970s, paralleling the general political reaction of the time. This reimposed the traditional pattern of command and hierarchy on farm labour forces, and thereby largely neutralized the incentive effects of better pay.

(iii) The wage increases were in any case to a great extent fictitious, since consumer supplies to rural retail networks remained at a totally inadequate level. With vodka often the only consumer good in abundant supply, it is hardly surprising that the demoralization of the countryside inherited from Stalin seemed if anything to deepen during the late Brezhnev period.

But while it was most striking in the countryside, the gap between increases in money wages and increases in consumer supplies was a general problem throughout the late Brezhnev period. The early Stalin era had witnessed rampant inflation, as the Soviet government printed money to conceal the sharp drop in living standards which nearly all sections of the population suffered. After the war, however, the inflationary gap was closed, and it was not until the 1970s that it began to emerge again as a serious problem. But the aggregate price level was kept largely under control by Brezhnev, and macro-economic imbalance developed mainly in the form a growing *repressed inflationary gap*, manifesting itself in growing queues, an increasing overhang of involuntary savings (total savings bank deposits grew from 46.6 billion rubles in 1970 to 156.5 billion in 1980) and an intensification of second-economy activity.

The economic crisis of the late Brezhnev era was, therefore, not just a crisis of growth. It was also a crisis of balance and structure, as the Soviet authorities sought in vain to correct the imbalances which Stalin had quite deliberately introduced into the system. In agriculture, indeed, attempted correction tended simply to generate new imbalances. Improved prices for farmers had to be paid from somewhere, and Brezhnev's reluctance to change the traditional "cheap food for the workers" policy meant that that somewhere could only be the budget. By around 1980 total food subsidies were running at an annual level of some 8 per cent of national income. In the fuel industries too, the level of subsidization was rising, as marginal extraction costs continued to increase sharply. The combined pressure of inflationary increases and an increasingly disorganized investment front produced similar trends in manufacturing. These trends inevitably imposed unbearable pressure on the state budget. By the time Brezhnev died, the annual budget deficit was running at some 10 billion rubles, and on a sharply rising trend. There is a very real sense, then, in which the Soviet economy of about 1980 was simply running at a loss, and this picture is confirmed if we look at production function data. These reveal that by the 1970s total factor productivity in the Soviet Union was stagnating, or even falling. In other words, aggregate outputs were at best simply reproducing aggregate inputs. This forms the immediate background to the emergence of the *perestroika* movement.

Current economic developments. With the death of Brezhnev in November 1982, a process of reappraisal began which has continued to the present time, and which has been marked by a deepening radicality, both in the diagnosis of the ailment, and in the prescription for recovery. Yuri Andropov wasted no time in proclaiming a drive against indiscipline and alcohol abuse, and with Mikhail Gorbachev already in charge of overall economic policy-making a new set of planning reform measures was introduced in 1983. These were reminiscent of **Kosygin**'s reform of 1965— marked by renewed emphasis on profitability and effective incentives, but also by a familiar failure to grapple with the basic issue of general over-centralization. It was not, indeed, until Gorbachev succeeded to the General Secretaryship in 1985 that the new reform movement entered uncharted territory. The essential elements of the *perestroika* programme are, certainly, familiar enough. What has changed is that this time the issue of over-centralization has been attacked directly. Here are the main elements in Gorbachev's programme:

(i) Profit should be confirmed as the key success-indicator for all enterprises in the state sector.

(ii) The principle of "100 per cent self-financing" should be generally introduced. This means that enterprises should as a rule finance all their own expansion and modernization plans out of profit ploughbacks and/or bank credit. It also means that directors should have the power to manoeuvre their wage fund within wide limits, and to take on new workers, or create redundancies, as they see fit.

(iii) The centre should continue to fix prices of key commodities, but leave the bulk of transaction prices to be settled between buyer and seller.

(iv) The consumer goods industries and the retail network should plan their activities on the basis of consumer demand.

(v) "Wholesale trade in the means of production", i.e. market allocation of industrial inputs, should be introduced gradually, with the proviso that a significant quota of strategic and staple commodities would remain subject to direct allocation by the central authorities for the foreseeable future.

(vi) The system of state and collective farms should be replaced by a network of medium-sized family farms, operating on a lease hold basis.

(vii) There should be a significant degree of privatization (under the *alias* of the co-operative movement) of the production and distribution of some consumer goods lines, and of many service sectors.

(viii) The banking system, whose role under the old system was essentially a passive accounting one, should be transformed into a Western-style, active banking sector, capable of playing a key role in the allocation of investible funds.

(ix) Foreign trade, previously the monopoly of a bureaucratically organized Ministry of Foreign Trade, should be opened up to the producers and consumers of tradeable goods. In principle all Soviet enterprises now have the right to export and import, and to retain pre-determined proportions of their hard-currency earnings form exports, though trade in a number of strategic commodities, including energy materials and grain, remains under the direct control of the central authorities.

This seems an eminently sensible, if still slightly cautious package. Yet its impact on Soviet economic performance has been, at best, equivocal. The year 1989 witnessed a new fall in the real rate of growth of national income to around zero, and an escalation in the rate of open inflation to 10 per cent or more. In popular perception at least, living standards are falling. With a growing strike movement and universal unrest in the non-Russian periphery of the Soviet Union, Gorbachev's political position is coming under increasing threat, raising serious questions as to whether he will be able to maintain impetus in the economic reform programme. Now many of the root causes of these difficulties are essentially political. But they do also serve to highlight crucial dilemmas at the purely economic level.

At the most general level, the problem is that Gorbachev is faced with a mask for which there is no precedent—the task of *reinventing* the market. This is not a problem which has ever been faced by a Western economy, except to a limited extent after World War II; it is a problem which is not addressed by economic theory. Like Stalin, then, but in a very different way, Gorbachev is breaking new ground. Ironically, however, the distortions which have built up over the period of centralized planning and Stalinist development strategy make painless transition to a market economy impossible. To put flesh on this statement, let us examine the key issue in current Soviet economic policy-making — the budget deficit.

The Soviet budget was already substantially in the red in the late Brezhnev years, but the deficit has grown dramatically over the late 1980s, as shown in the table below.

Soviet budget deficits, actual and projected (billion rubles)					
1984	*1985*	*1986*	*1987*	*1988*	*1989*
11.0	17.0	49.8	64.4	68.8	120

The estimated figure for 1989 would bring the deficit up to some 20 per cent of national income. The main immediate causes of this trend are two fold — he impact of the anti-alcohol campaign and that of the collapse in world oil prices on budget revenue. According to the official budget figures, which may well understate, net annual budget revenue from foreign trade operations fell by around 20 billion rubles in 1985–88. But the key question is less that of the proximate sources of the Soviet Union's "bad luck" than of the inability of the Soviet government to adjust other parts of the budget — most obviously on the expenditure side—in order to bring the deficit under control. And here we find budgetary inflexibilities reflecting structural blockages in the economy itself. Food subsidies accounted for some 16 per cent of budget expenditures in 1986–87 or 10 per cent of national income. The Soviet President has said many times that he is determined to cut back on these. But here political complications impinge heavily, for food prices are one of the biggest inputs into popular Soviet assessments of material welfare—perhaps even bigger than food supplies themselves. To date little has been achieved, despite the new, tougher line on liquidating loss-making farms, and food subsidies in 1989 were projected at 88 billion rubles—nearly 14 per cent of the likely level of national income. The picture is the same with respect to defence expenditure. We need not doubt the Soviet leader's sincerity in seeking arms reduction. But Soviet and Western sources are agreed that for the time being defence expenditure continues to grow as a proportion of Soviet national income. This is, no doubt, largely because of the continued impact of past decisions.

Subsidies to production sectors outside agriculture are officially projected at 11 billion rubles for 1989—a suspiciously low figure, if we compare it with the "qualitative" evidence of repeated attacks in speeches and in the press on industrial loss-makers. The fact is, however, that the most important financial flows running from budget down to ministry and enterprise come under the capital, rather than the current account. Thus in 1987 "grants to the economy"—on paper at least exclusively for investment purposes—represented 57 per cent of total budget expenditure. As we have seen, one of the main policy aims of Gorbachev's industrial planning reform has been to shift investment over on to a more profit-financed basis, with the dual purpose of improving the quality of project choice and taking some of the pressure off the budget. Indeed by the first half of 1989 nearly 47 per cent of total state investment was being financed from enterprise development funds. But the excessive ambition of the investment components in the 1986–90 Five-Year Plan (which were in any case over-fulfilled in quantitative terms over the three-year period 1986–88), coupled with the failure to create a proper market for investment supplies, conspired to produce trends reminiscent of the late Khrushchev era, or indeed of the early 1970s, as the Kosygin/Brezhnev reforms became bogged down in half-measures. Over 1988 taken by itself, total investment expenditures grew nearly 5 per cent, while commissionings of new capacities increased by less than 1 per cent. During the first half of 1989 gross investment expenditures grew

by 3 per cent while commissionings fell by 0.8 per cent, against a planned increase of 13 per cent. Thus contemporary investment patterns are simply tying up more and more resources in unfinished projects. Underlying these trends there exists an essential problem in Soviet investment planning which has remained unchanged since the days of Stalin. It is too easy to obtain investment finance, whether from the budget, or from profits which are inflated by excessively high prices and monopoly advantage in many sectors. It is too difficult to obtain investment supplies. In periods when enterprises are allowed more financial autonomy in relation to investment, they compete more fiercely with centralized investment fund-holders for available investment supplies. The situation towards the end of the 1980s was further exacerbated by laudable attempts to grapple with the housing crisis. As the supply situation accordingly worsened, all investors tried to start more and more new projects, because this helped to bolster the case for future investment supply requests. In 1988 the number of new construction starts increased by 41 per cent, and it was planned to increase by another 6 per cent in 1989. The result is a vicious circle which pushes up the volume of unfinished construction and stretches out construction times. It is reported that it currently takes on average four to five times as long to build an industrial enterprise in the Soviet Union as it does in the West. If that is so, then the situation has got much worse since the Brezhnev days, when it was, indeed, bad enough.

There are, certainly, short-term plans to reverse the explosion of ill-directed investment expenditure. Total centralized investment spending is scheduled to be cut by 7.5 billion rubles and 9 billion rubles respectively for 1989 and 1990 against the targets originally embodied in the Five-Year Plan. Perhaps more significant, a number of big projects, notably the multi-billion dollar complex of petro- and gas-chemical plants scheduled for Western Siberia, are likely to be shelved. But there are absolutely no signs that the schedule will be met, and the reasons for this are not far to seek. As long as the planning bureaucracy remains essentially unreformed, cuts are likely simply to intensify bureaucratic squabbling over funds, with each organization trying to show that its projects should not be cut, or at least to ensure that it will still have some projects left at the end of the day—and of course the best way to do that is still to get as many projects as possible going in the first place. Thus while the state investment component seems in principle to offer the clearest prospect for a substantial cut in Soviet budget expenditure, the odds are stacked against any immediate improvement.

The link between the budgetary problem and the inflation problem in the Soviet Union is a very clear and simple one. In the absence of a bond market, and against a background of caution on foreign borrowing, deficits can only be met through the emission of cash. So budget deficits have a direct and immediate impact in terms of creating cash holdings amongst the population in excess of available supplies of goods. From 1988, as the progress of *perestroika* set in motion a wave of co-operative development which effectively re-established a free-market private sector in services, and conceded to enterprise directors increased powers to determine their own prices, the repressed-inflationary gap inherited from Brezhnev began to emerge into the open. The short-term reaction of the Soviet government to this inflationary leakage was — predictably enough — to slap on emergency price controls and impose new restrictions on the co-operatives. But this amounts to sabotage of the marketizing rationale of the entire *perestroika* package. We are unlikely to find a better illustration of a common enough economic policy problem — the incompatibility of short-term and long-term aims — or of the terrible burden that inherited structural distortions place on the shoulders of the fledgling *perestroika*.

If expenditure patterns are stubborn, could anything be done to attack the problem on the revenue side? Could, for instance, the issue of bonds be used as a means of funding the deficit? One idea was that the deficit should be covered through the issue of state loans by the State Bank. These loans would then serve as the basis for credit creation by commercial banks, thus effectively setting up a Western-style National Debt, which could then be manipulated as a tool of monetary control. The State Bank could keep control over the total money supply through varying the rate of obligatory minimum reserves with the State Bank. These ideas were interesting, in that they attacked the problems of budget deficit and excess liquidity amongst the population simultaneously. Inevitably, however, they raised as many problems as they solved. Presumably loan-backed currency issues would be embodied in a new currency unit. But this sounded like currency reform, and indeed that highly sensitive issue received a good deal of explicit public attention in its own right. Such a reform offered a number of attractions, quite apart from the question of the specific form it might take. Above all, it would serve as a signal for, and a symbol of, a "fresh start". If the old currency were phased out altogether, the exchange of currency notes would give the authorities a chance to flush out **second economy** money, and get a grip on the growing

Soviet commercial crime industry. But if currency reform were to be used as a basis for attacking directly the overhang of "involuntary" savings which has built up over decades of inadequate consumer supplies, it would have to involve some degree of non-equivalent exchange, some confiscatory dimension, in relation to existing savings account and cash holdings. Stalin did it after the war. Was that a good, or a bad precedent for Gorbachev? All the indications were that the Soviet government would take a very cautious line on currency reform.

The battle for *perestroika* was, therefore, anything but won by the early 1990s. For all the genuine radicality of Gorbachev's approach, the old problem of partial and uneven decentralization producing perverse results was still present, particularly in the investment sphere. The reform was not moving fast enough, and the signs from 1989 were that short-term difficulties were tending to slow the pace to a critical degree. But even if Gorbachev managed to restructure the economic system once and for all over the early 1990s, he would be left with the problem of restructuring the economy itself. The structure of the Soviet capital stock has been grossly distorted by decades of obsession with heavy industry and the sinews of war. It will take decades to correct these distortions, and it would be naive to believe that they can be corrected simply by marketizing the economy overnight — that would simply produce massive inflation or massive unemployment, or possibly both. Even on the best assumptions, *perestroika* was going to be a very long haul, and no dramatic upturn in Soviet economic performance should be expected before the twenty-first century.

Foreign policy. Gorbachev's early policy pronouncements gave little indication that one of the central features of his administration would be its emphasis on "new thinking" in international affairs. His address to an ideology conference in December 1984, shortly before taking office, stressed the "necessity of a fundamental change through accelerated economic development" and pointed to *glasnost'* as a means of promoting this process. The section on foreign policy, however, was couched in much more orthodox terms, accusing capitalism of resorting to "wars and terror" in order to further its objectives and of constantly seeking "social revenge" on a global scale. A policy of nothing less than "state terrorism" had been adopted in central America, the Middle East, Afghanistan and southern Africa. The military-industrial complex had strengthened its influence on US foreign policy, and so too had the multinational corporations; together they had declared a "crusade" against Communism, which was threatening the future of the world community as a whole. In relations between the two "opposing systems", conflict clearly took precedence over competition.

A somewhat different tone began to emerge relatively quickly, particularly in an address that Gorbachev gave to British members of parliament later the same month. In the speech Gorbachev expressed a wish for renewed dialogue and co-operation, above all in relation to the threat of a nuclear war in which there could be "no winners". This, however, was only an example of the kind of issue that required the concerted action of states with different social systems. Another was the need to resolve regional issues peacefully; others were the fight against famine and disease, protection of the environment and the global supply of energy and natural resources. The atomic age, Gorbachev suggested, required a "new way of political thinking", above all the recognition that all the peoples of the world lived in a "vulnerable, rather fragile but interconnected world". Whatever divided them, they had to share the same planet; and this dictated a "constructive dialogue, a search for solutions to key international problems, for areas of agreement". A country's foreign policy, Gorbachev noted, could not be separated from its "internal life, its economic and social goals and needs"; the Soviet Union, for its part, needed peace so as to be able to achieve its "truly breathtaking creative plans". In his electoral address of February 1985 Gorbachev returned to the European theme, regretting the loss of impetus that had occurred since the signature of the Helsinki Final Act 10 years earlier and expressing the hope that West Europeans would not allow "our common home" to be converted into a testing-ground for American doctrines of "limited" nuclear war.

Gorbachev's speech on his election as party leader laid proper emphasis on domestic priorities, but also called for better relations with the "great socialist community", particularly China, and for the continuation of "peaceful, mutually advantageous co-operation" with the capitalist world, leading if possible to an agreement that would provide for the complete elimination of nuclear arms and with them the threat of nuclear war. His address to the Central Committee in April 1985, his first full statement as party leader, called for "stable, proper and, if you like, civilized inter-state relations based on a genuine respect for international law". The unity of the socialist states and their military-strategic parity with the NATO countries must at all costs be preserved, as the only secure guarantee against the "aggressive appetites of imperialism". But there

was no "fatal inevitability of confrontation" between the USSR and its major capitalist adversaries. On the contrary, none of the nations wanted war, and "ever new progressive and democratic forces" had appeared in the capitalist countries which were strengthening the common struggle for peace. In his speech to French parliamentarians the following October Gorbachev laid particular emphasis upon the ever-growing "interdependence between countries and continents" in ecological as well as military and economic terms. His address a few days later to the Central Committee in Moscow balanced these remarks with more familiar declarations about the "further strengthening of the positions of existing socialism" and growing opposition to the "reactionary, aggressive forces of imperialism".

Gorbachev's address to the XXVII Party Congress in February 1986 was relatively short of surprises in terms of foreign policy; there was nothing, at any rate, to compare with the unilateral moratorium on nuclear testing which had been announced just a few weeks earlier (see below). It did, however, make clear the extent to which the Soviet approach to international affairs had changed as compared with the relatively simple priorities of the Brezhnev era. Gorbachev pointed out that the contemporary world was "complicated, diverse, dynamic, permeated with contending tendencies, and full of contradictions". The gradual development of societies from capitalism to socialism, he insisted, was still a necessary, law-governed and irreversible process. Capitalism was a system plagued by problems and crises, and one that was aggressive and interventionist by its very nature. It contained its own "internal antagonistic contradictions", based on the exploitation of labour, and also contradictions as between the various capitalist countries. Relations were worsening, moreover, between the major capitalist nations and the developing countries, which were being robbed of the fruits of their labour and forced to suffer poverty, illiteracy and famine.

Beyond these differences, however, lay a further group of contradictions relating to the pollution of the environment, the air and the oceans, and the depletion of the world's natural resources. These were problems that no single group of states could resolve by itself; and there were many others. No single group of states, for instance, could deal with the problem of "corruption and vandalisation" in the cultural sphere (Soviet spokesmen at this time generally cited the "Rambo" films and other examples of "warnography"). Nor could capitalist or socialist states deal by themselves with the threat of a nuclear catastrophe, or the difficulties that were facing the developing countries. Gorbachev invited the major capitalist countries to undertake a "sober, constructive assessment" of problems of this kind, based if nothing else on their common need for self-preservation. They lived, he declared, in an "interdependent, in many ways integral world" in which they must co-operate for their common benefit; and he appealed for co-operation on this basis with social democrats, and even religious organizations. But what was most distinctive about the speech was its central proposition, that global problems demanded global solutions and that socialism as such provided no solution to them.

This "new thinking" in Soviet foreign policy was set out more fully over the months that followed. The "Delhi declaration" of November 1986, for instance, committed the Soviet leader to a "non-violent" as well as nuclear-free world. An extraordinary gathering, the "International Forum for a Nuclear-Free World, for the Survival of Humankind", brought West German Greens, clerics, Academician Sakharov and Western film stars like Gregory Peck and Claudia Cardinale together in Moscow in February 1987. Gorbachev's address emphasized that the USSR and its people were "part of a world community" and that their goal was the "humanisation of international relations". A new defence doctrine began to take shape at the same time: it was intended to be non-offensive in character and to give other states no reason to fear for their security, notwithstanding the immense size of Soviet armed forces and the perceptions of those forces that were entertained particularly in Europe.

The Soviet leader had already taken several unilateral initiatives towards this end. The first was the decision, in April 1985, to freeze the deployment of SS-20 missiles in Europe; the second was the moratorium on all underground nuclear testing which began on Aug. 6, 1985, the anniversary of Hiroshima, and was eventually extended until February 1987. Gorbachev added a more elaborate proposal in January 1986, calling for the elimination of all nuclear weapons by the year 2000; a commitment to this objective was written into the new Party Programme, which was adopted shortly afterwards. A new military doctrine, "reasonable sufficiency", was adopted by Gorbachev at the XXVII Party Congress and subsequently by the Warsaw Treaty Organization. Nor were these simply doctrinal changes: there were substantial cuts in Soviet military spending and troop numbers from 1989 onwards, and much more information was made available on the structure and size of the military budget and on troop and weapons deployments (see below).

The Central Committee's Theses, adopted shortly before the 19th Party Conference in 1988, contained the first official criticism of Soviet foreign policy in the Brezhnev and Gromyko years, suggesting that there had been too much "dogmatism" and "subjectivism" at this time and that Soviet policy had lagged behind the important changes that were taking place in world affairs. Too much emphasis had been placed upon the strengthening of security by military rather than political means, and this had placed on undue burden on the domestic economy. The party's "new political thinking", by contrast, recognized the existence of a complex and contradictory world in which there were threats to the survival of humanity as such but also great opportunities for coexistence and co-operation. The main elements in this "new political thinking" included the gradual liquidation of nuclear arms by the year 2000, the establishment of a system of comprehensive security, a doctrine of military sufficiency and non-aggression, and improvements in the world economy. This, the Theses made clear, was the "foreign policy credo" of the Gorbachev administration. Other commentaries went further in their criticism of the Brezhnev-Gromyko legacy, and the new foreign minister Eduard **Shevardnadze** was among those who was clearest in his call for a proper mechanism of democratic control so that the mistakes and violations of international law of these years did not recur.

A still more important statement of the "new political thinking" in Soviet foreign policy came in the Soviet leader's address to the General Assembly of the United Nations in December 1988. In the speech Gorbachev expressed his personal support for the United Nations, which had "increasingly manifested its ability to act as a unique international centre in the service of peace and security", and repeated his belief that the most important issues that faced the world community were global rather than regional in character. This had been made clear by the development of nuclear weapons, by new popular movements and ideologies, and by scientific and technical developments. Improvements in communications had brought the world more closely together; the world economy was increasingly a "single organism". The French and Russian revolutions had made an enormous contribution in their time to human progress, but they lived today in a different world in which universal human values must have priority. This meant a common search for a new quality of international interaction, less dependent on military force and free of ideological prejudice.

In more practical terms Gorbachev pointed to the need for a greater measure of agreement on the reduction of all forms of armaments and on the elimination of regional conflicts. There should be a "more intense and open dialogue" between political leaders and their societies (he himself had already had more than more 200 meetings with foreign governmental and political representatives). The United Nations should itself play a greater role, especially in issues such as Third World development, environmental assistance and the peaceful use of outer space. The UN could also play a greater part in regulating regional conflicts, such as Afghanistan. More work needed to be done to clarify and strengthen international law, particularly in relation to **human rights**. Most spectacularly of all, the Soviet leader announced a reduction of 500,000 in the size of Soviet armed forces over the following two years, including reductions in the number of divisions in both Europe and Asia and changes in the structure of the forces that remained (including the withdrawal of a large number of tanks) so that their purposes became more clearly peaceful. Corresponding moves were suggested on an international scale to "convert the armaments economy into a disarmament economy". Helpful though such measures were likely to be in domestic terms, the simultaneous resignation of the Soviet Chief of Staff suggested that not all powerful institutional interests had been persuaded of their necessity. (For the structure and organization of Soviet forces, see below. For Soviet foreign relations with particular regions of the world, *see* **Soviet Relations with the Communist World**; **Soviet Relations with the Developing World**; and **Soviet Relations with the West**.)

Defence and security. Soviet relations with the rest of the world are a product of a number of factors, among them the degree of influence that the Soviet economy and Soviet-oriented political movements can exert upon the course of global developments. Probably no single factor exerts so direct an influence upon the place of the USSR in the international community, however, as Soviet military power. The popular jibe, "a third-world country with strategic arms", is hardly adequate, and yet the USSR's status as one of the world's two superpowers is founded ultimately on her possession of a formidable military might which is roughly equivalent to that of the United States. The USSR is also the world's second biggest arms exporter (about half of the USSR's trade with the third world is in arms), and the Soviet Union stands at the centre of one of the world's two major alliance systems, the Warsaw Treaty Organization. Soviet armed forces have a considerable influence upon domestic developments as well: conscription into the army, for instance,

helps to bring together the various national groups of the USSR; military spending and production account for a considerable proportion (the best estimates suggest about 15 per cent) of the national economy; and questions of East–West arms control are among the most important concerns of the Politburo at its weekly meetings, if press reports are any guide.

There is certainly no doubt that Soviet military might in its various forms is very considerable. There are five main branches of the armed forces —army, navy, air force, air defence and strategic rocket forces — all of which come under the administrative control of the USSR Ministry of Defence, headed by the Minister of Defence (since May 1987, General Dmitri Yazov). The Minister of Defence is normally a member of the party Politburo, which exercizes supreme command over the armed forces, and the General Secretary of the CPSU (from March 1990, the USSR President) is automatically Commander in Chief. It is believed that supervision of military and strategic questions is in practice devolved upon the Defence Council of the USSR, which is appointed by the President, and which plays a role similar to that of the National Security Council in the USA. The President also appoints the members of the Soviet high command, and formally speaking decides all questions of war and peace (in practice all of these decisions will be taken by the ruling Politburo). Day-to-day operational matters come under the control of the Main Political Administration of the Ministry of Defence, which is jointly subordinated to the Council of Ministers and to the party Central Committee.

The total strength of the Soviet armed forces in 1989 was about 4.3 million (including an estimated 2.7 million conscripts), with an estimated 55 million reservists and a further 570,000 in paramilitary forces. Soviet armed forces are based upon conscription, which begins at the age of 19 (or 18 for graduates of secondary schools). Active service lasts for two years in the army or air force and for three years for sea-going naval personnel. Service in the reserves lasts up to the ages of 35–50 depending upon fitness, family status and other considerations. Conscientious objection is treated as a criminal offence; as Article 63 of the Constitution states, "military service in the ranks of the USSR Armed Forces is the honourable duty of Soviet citizens". The current strength of the Soviet army is estimated to be about 1.6 million, including 1.2 million conscripts. The Soviet navy, which advanced rapidly in size and global reach under its former head Admiral Gorshkov, was estimated in 1989 to have 437,000 men enrolled within its ranks. The Soviet air force was believed to have a further 448,000 men serving within its ranks. About 90 per cent of all officers are members of the CPSU or the Komsomol, and 50 per cent have had an engineering or technical education.

The balance of military advantage between East and West is a function not simply, or even primarily, of numbers of men under arms; the decisive factor, in the nuclear age, is the number and capacity of the weapons systems that are available for use by either side. Perhaps the most important change in this respect was the attainment by the USSR of strategic parity in the later 1960s (for a more detailed discussion, *see* **Arms Control**). The decisive moment so far as the Soviet authorities were concerned appears to have been the Cuban Missile Crisis of 1962, when Soviet military inferiority was made painfully apparent and the USSR had to back down in a humiliating fashion when challenged by President Kennedy's blockade. The changes that have taken place since then in the strategic weaponry of both sides are very considerable. The USSR's armoury of strategic weapons has moved from a position of inferiority to approximate parity by 1969/70 and to a position of numerical superiority in many respects by the later 1970s and 1980s. The USA retained a position of superiority in terms of warheads for rather longer, but an approximate parity in this respect as well was established in about 1982. In 1989, American strategic nuclear arms carried a total of 14,530 warheads, mounted for the most part on submarines (SLBMs) or bombers; Soviet strategic nuclear forces carried a total of 12,403 warheads (both counted under SALT conventions), most of which were mounted on ICBMs. Considerable improvements have however been made in submarine-based ballistic missiles in recent years, and in both countries newer generations of missiles have been introduced which are much more accurate than those they are replacing.

Both sides also maintained formidable numbers of air- and sea-launched theatre or intermediate and battlefield or short-range nuclear weapons, based for the most part in Europe. The increase in the number of missiles that were deployed in this way (forward deployment) introduced a greater element of instability into the strategic balance, given that some of these weapons could reach major Soviet cities in a matter of minutes. The build-up of nuclear missiles in Europe followed the NATO "two-track" decision of 1979, which led to the deployment of Lance and Pershing II missiles in some western European countries, and the replacement of ageing Soviet SS-4 and -5 missiles in eastern Europe by more modern SS-20s. According to data made

available by the Stockholm Peace Research Institute (SIPRI), the USA maintained a total of 9,957 warheads in its theatre nuclear forces in 1987. The USSR maintained a total of not less than 9,351 warheads in the same year, although differences in reliability, targeting, explosive force (kilotonnage) and so forth made comparisons difficult. In Europe, nuclear weapons were also deployed by the UK and (outside the NATO framework) by France.

Underpinning all of this on both sides is military spending, the level of which in the USSR is particularly difficult to estimate precisely. The official figure for Soviet military spending, at least until recently, was the one that was approved every year by the USSR Supreme Soviet as a part of the state budget. This figure, the only Soviet declared military expenditure until 1989, increased quite rapidly between 1965 and 1970 and then remained at the same or even a lower level throughout the 1970s. A significant increase took place in the budget for 1985, caused, the Minister of Finance explained, by a sharp deterioration in the global situation brought about by the "reactionary imperialist circles of the US and its allies in the NATO militarist bloc", which had been "whipping up international tension" and increasing military spending on an "unprecedented scale". The defence vote, accordingly, went up from 17,054 million rubles in 1984 to 19,063 million rubles in 1985; the 1986 budget increased it still further to 20.2 billion rubles—about 4.6 per cent of total budgetary spending. Gorbachev, speaking to the Congress of People's Deputies in May 1989, offered what he described as the "real figure for military spending" — 77.3 billion rubles, or nearly four times as much as had previously been admitted. Military expenditure had however been frozen over the two previous years, and it was proposed to reduce it by 14 per cent over 1990 and 1991.

These totals are however of little value in attempting to compute the share of state spending and of GNP that is accounted for by defence. The declared Soviet total is supposed to include "the cost of weapons, ammunition, technical equipment, fuel, food and other equipment supplied to the Soviet armed forces", plus military schools, hospitals, sanatoria, sports, the pay of those employed, "the financing of capital construction" and so forth, according to Soviet textbooks on budgetary procedures. Although this seemed to exclude research and development and did not mention pensions, this covered the bulk of what would normally be considered to be military expenditure. The budgetary figure, however, remained very low until Gorbachev's statement to the Congress of People's Deputies, and it fell slightly between 1970 and 1984 at a time when the USSR was, on its own admission, achieving nuclear parity with the USA. It has often been suggested that additional military expenditure is concealed within the total for "education and science", where spending doubled between 1970 and 1986 and by the latter date was more than double the reported figure for defence. It is clear, however, that additional military expenditure must be concealed elsewhere within the budgetary totals, and that total Soviet defence spending must be considerably greater than even the "real figures" reported by Gorbachev in 1989.

Western experts have employed a number of techniques to obtain an alternative and more realistic figure for defence spending. One of these methods uses residuals: that is to say, the difference that remains when known and identifiable civil expenditure has been excluded. This approach, however, encounters serious difficulties based upon the West's relatively limited knowledge of Soviet budgetary procedures. An alternative approach is employed by the CIA, which uses a hybrid estimate based partly on its knowledge of Soviet prices and partly on its knowledge of the production of weapons themselves as obtained by satellite and other intelligence sources. It has proved very difficult, however, to cost Soviet military output; prices must either be estimated in ruble terms, or else based upon what it would cost an American contractor to produce them—a method that dramatically inflates the costs involved.

Based on these methods, the CIA estimated Soviet defence expenditure in 1984 to be about 75 billion rubles in 1970 prices, or about $200 billion. The Pentagon's Defence Intelligence Agency offers ruble and dollar estimates which are considerably higher. A number of academic estimates are also available which diverge still more widely. There was however fairly general agreement that the USSR spent about 15 per cent of its national income on defence in the late 1980s (the USA spends about 7 per cent); there was also substantial agreement that the USSR increased its defence spending by 4 or 5 per cent until the late 1970s, when, according to the CIA, the rate of growth of military expenditure fell back to about 2 per cent. This slowdown in Soviet military expenditure reflected the more general slowdown in the Soviet economy as a whole, and suggested that defence could not be wholly isolated from the performance of the economy as a whole as some had argued. The Stockholm International Peace Research Institute, which produces independent data on matters of this kind based on published sources, estimated that Soviet defence expenditure was about $142 billion in 1984. In its 1987 yearbook, however, it concluded that no satisfactory figure for Soviet defence spending could be computed and offered no figures of the kind it had reported in earlier years.

Whatever figures are employed, it is clear that defence represents a very heavy burden on the Soviet economy. There is broad consensus, for instance, that the Soviet Union spends about twice as high a proportion of its GNP on defence than does the USA; with a rather smaller economy, this is relatively speaking a much heavier commitment. The defence sector also deprives the civil economy of large amounts of investment goods, as well as substantial research and development assets and qualified manpower. According to Western estimates, about a third of the output of the metalworking and machine tool industries is allocated to military purposes, together with a fifth of metallurgy output and about a sixth of all chemical and energy supplies. In addition, the defence sector attracts the highest priority for personnel, materials and equipment, and is protected from the shortages and bureaucratic delays that afflict other parts of the economy. The high level of secrecy that is observed in the USSR about these matters also limits the transferability of research that has been carried out in the military sector to civil purposes. The USSR has, then, a number of compelling domestic reasons for proposing the limitation and reduction of nuclear arms internationally, and Soviet–Western negotiations on the reduction of nuclear and other arms have been the central focus of international relations since at least the 1960s.

SLW/DAD

UNITED PEASANT PARTY (POLAND — UPP, Zjednoczone Stronnictwo Ludowe).

For 40 years after its formation in 1949 in Poland the UPP acted, with the **Democratic Party**, as one of the two auxiliary political organizations which served to buttress the rule of the **Polish United Workers' Party (PUWP)**. After World War II the Polish Peasant Party (PSL) emerged as the major focus of political opposition to the extension of communist influence and its leader, Stanisław Mikołajczyk, acted as deputy prime minister in the government agreed on by the allies after the Potsdam conference of 1945. Intensifying Communist pressure weakened the position of the party and its leader, who was forced to leave Poland in October 1947. Its organization was taken over by those willing to serve Communist interests and what was left of it was merged with the pro-Communist Peasant Party (SL) to form the politically subservient UPP in November 1949. This permitted the authorities to claim some peasant support for the collectivization of agriculture, formally spelt out as PUWP policy in July 1948.

Collectivization in fact made slow progress in Poland (only 9 per cent of arable land was collectivized in 1955), but this was due rather to the resistance of peasant farmers and the caution of the authorities than to any defence of peasant interests mounted by the UPP. The Peasant Party leadership only moved to press for change and embrace the reform process after the PUWP Central Committee meeting that saw the return to power of Władysław **Gomułka**. As Gomułka's removal from the leadership in 1948 had been closely linked with his resistance to forced collectivization, his return meant the improvement of conditions for agricultural production and some respite for the farming population. In December 1956 a Declaration of Principles of PUWP/UPP Co-operation was signed and the Peasant Party promised a larger political role, the number of its deputies in the *Sejm* rising from 90 to 118 following the elections of January 1957.

This did not spell any real change in power relations although, unlike the situation in the PUWP (where the number of peasant members fell from 175,000 to 117,000 between 1955 and 1959), peasant membership of UPP rose from 156,000 to 174,000 over this period. Some over-eager to press farming interests were purged in 1957 and 1958 but the Peasant Party probably continued to exercise a stronger influence over policy, at least until 1962 when the price paid for agricultural produce was cut following a particularly good harvest and the chairman, Stefan Ignar, was replaced by Czesław Wycech. From then on the UPP remained politically compliant and in 1980, as in 1956, the Peasant Party only increased its level of activity once change was under way in the PUWP. At the end of 1988 it had 526,200 members. In 1989 the leader of its group of *Sejm* deputies, A. Bentkowski, was quick to perceive the critical position of the PUWP leadership and to form an alliance with the **Solidarity** deputies. In November 1989 the UPP reconstituted itself as the Polish Peasant Party — Rebirth (PSL "Odrodzenie").

PGL

URBÁNEK, KAREL. Elected General Secretary of the **Communist Party of Czechoslovakia**

following the resignation of the party leadership on Nov. 24, 1989, Urbánek, who was born in 1941, was one member of a younger generation brought into the Czechoslovak Party Presidium under Miloš **Jakeš**. A railway worker by original occupation, he joined the apparatus of the party's South Moravian Regional Committee in 1973. His fairly rapid rise to the top began with his appointment first as party chief in Brno in 1984 and then, in March 1988, as Head of the Political and Organizational Department of the party Central Committee in Prague. In October that year, he was made a full member of the Communist Party Presidium and appointed chairman of the newly created Committee for Party Work in the Czech Socialist Republic. Although he was ready to adapt to the new political environment of a multi-party system, competitive elections and coalition government that emerged in Czechoslovakia at the end of 1989, his period as party leader was short-lived. He was replaced at an extraordinary party congress on Dec. 20, 1989 by Vasil Mohorita, the former Chairman of the Socialist Youth Union, and elected chairman of the party's Central Control and Auditing Commission.

GW

UZBEKISTAN. Soviet rule was established in Uzbekistan in 1917, and a Soviet Socialist Republic was formed in 1924. In 1925 the republic became a constituent member of the USSR. Uzbekistan occupies an area of 447,400 sq km; its 1989 census population was 19,906,000, or about 7 per cent of the USSR total (it is the third most populous republic after the **Russian Republic** and the **Ukraine**). The Uzbeks themselves constitute 69 per cent of the total population, according to the 1979 census; there are also substantial Russian, Tadzhik and Tatar minorities. Uzbekistan, in economic terms, is famous above all for its cotton crop, the largest in the USSR and the third largest in the world; there are also important mineral deposits. Output figures for many forms of production, particularly of cotton, were inflated during the **Brezhnev** years when corruption became rampant under the late party first secretary Rashidov, who was subsequently disgraced. The republic includes 12 regions and 155 districts.

SLW

W

WAŁĘSA, LECH. Born in September 1943 in a village near Dobrzyn, Poland (Włocławek province) to a peasant family whose ancestors had apparently known better days. His father died in 1945 after release from a German camp, and Wałęsa's mother later married the brother of her first husband — a solution to family difficulties that caused some resentment on the part of the children. School attendance was accompanied by agricultural work-duties and off-farm labour. In 1959 he began a course in agricultural mechanization at the district vocational school in Lipno and began working as an electrician for a State Machinery Centre (POM) serving the local collective farms. Between 1963 and 1965 Wałęsa performed his national service but did not settle down for long on his return, leaving for Gdańsk in 1967 where he got a job at the shipyard. Following the worker demonstrations in 1970 he was elected chairman of the workshop strike committee and spent several days in detention.

Conditions in the shipyard worsened in the mid-1970s and Wałęsa spoke out incautiously during 1976 at a trade union meeting, receiving a dismissal notice from the shipyard soon afterwards. He found new employment in a machine repair plant and was elected to the official Conference of Workers' Self-Government (KSR) there. After criticizing its operation his job was abolished and employment suspended, while during 1978 he became increasingly active and committed to the free trade union movement. After attempts to celebrate the ninth anniversary of the 1970 events he was detained by the police and again dismissed. When the Lenin shipyard came out on strike in August 1980 Wałęsa joined and was instrumental in extending it beyond the plant through the Inter-enterprise Strike Committee (MKS), of which he became chairman. On Aug. 31 he signed with deputy premier Jagielski the agreement that was to be the basis for the registration of the free trade union **Solidarity**.

A National Co-ordinating Commission of Solidarity was set up in September by representatives of the regional organizations that had recently come into being and Wałęsa was elected chairman, final legal recognition of Solidarity as a national union being granted in November 1980. At the end of August 1980 Wałęsa effectively became a leading national politician and, increasingly, emerged as an international figure, too, meeting the Pope in January 1981 and visiting Sweden and Japan soon after. Tensions within the union became particularly evident at the time of the Bydgoszcz crisis in March 1981, while relations with the party/state authorities became markedly more difficult from July. With the installation of the **State of War** he was interned and released 11 months later in November 1982. He took up employment at the shipyard in the spring of 1983 and in October of that year was awarded the Nobel Peace prize. He maintained cautious contact with underground Solidarity and participated in the strikes of 1988, emerging as an officially recognized public figure again towards the end of the year. He did not stand as a candidate in the parliamentary elections of 1989, but played a major part in the direction of the Citizens' Committees that organized the campaigns of Solidarity-sponsored candidates and the formation of the Solidarity-led coalition that signalled the end of Communist rule in Poland.

PGL

WARSAW (Warszawa). The capital city of Poland with a population of 1,651,200, lying on Poland's main river, the Vistula (Wisla). Remains of a settlement dating back to the tenth century have been found in the area and development centring on a village called Warszowa grew from the end of the thirteenth century. It became the capital of the province of Mazovia in the fifteenth century and became incorporated into the crown lands of the Jagiellonian state in 1526, the *Sejm* beginning to meet there in 1569 and the election of Polish kings occurring from 1573. The court moved to Warsaw from Cracow (Kraków) in 1611, at which point it became the state capital. It grew extensively in the seventeenth century, although suffering devastation during the Swedish invasion (1655–56). Manufacturing developed in the eighteenth century and it became the centre of the Polish Enlightenment under Stanislaw August Poniatowski (1764–95).

Following the Warsaw insurrection of 1794 and the Third Partition, which saw the final dismemberment of the traditional state, the city came under Prussian occupation. Napoleon's creation of the Duchy of Warsaw was followed by the establishment of the Congress Kingdom of Poland (1815–30) which, with the capital Warsaw, was incorporated into the Russian Empire after the November uprising. Industrial development was strong in the late nineteenth century and by 1903 its population had reached

756,000. After World War I it again became the capital of a Polish state, population rising to over one million in 1925. Much devastation and plunder occurred following the Nazi occupation in 1939, with the city's Jewish population (400,000 in 1939) being particularly ravaged. After extensive deportations those surviving in the ghetto rose in 1943, 60,000 dying in the action. In 1944 the rest of the population mounted a further uprising which, after early reverses, the Nazi forces crushed at the cost of nearly 200,000 Polish lives during the fighting. Warsaw was the only Allied city to be a war-time battleground. Remaining inhabitants were deported after the uprising and the bulk of the city was destroyed.

Warsaw again became the Polish capital on Feb. 1, 1945 and extensive work was undertaken to rebuild the city, including the reconstruction of the Old Town and (on the initiative of **Gierek**) the Royal Palace. Major industrial growth also took place with the development of engineering, metallurgy, machine production, chemicals, printing and textiles. This produced a working class which again played an important role at critical political junctures involving, for example, employees of the Żeran car works in the leadership changes of 1956 and the Ursus steel workers in the 1976 demonstrations. Leading political and governmental bodies, including the *Sejm* and the Central Committee of the **Polish United Workers' Party (PUWP)**, are located in the city, as are major cultural, scientific and educational bodies. Construction of an underground railway was begun in the 1980s, an initiative later criticized by international economic agencies for extravagance in view of Poland's persistent economic difficulties.

PGL

WARSAW TREATY ORGANIZATION (WTO—Warsaw Pact).

Origins. The Warsaw Treaty organization (WTO) was established by the Treaty of Friendship, Cooperation and Mutual Assistance signed in the Polish capital on May 14, 1955. The signatory states were the Soviet Union, Bulgaria, Czechoslovakia, the German Democratic Republic (GDR), Hungary, Romania and Albania. The Treaty contained a collective defence obligation by which, according to Article 4, the parties would individually or collectively come to the assistance of a member-state subject to armed attack in Europe by any state or group of states. Article 5 provided for the establishment of a Joint Command of the members' armed forces. Article 6 established a Political Consultative Committee (PCC), which would meet twice a year, as the

main formal organ for political consultations within the alliance. Article 3 provided for consultation on international questions affecting the member-states' common interests. It was also indicated in Article 5 that the alliance was seen as contributing to the maintenance of Marxist-Leninist political systems in Eastern Europe, referring to the protection of the "peaceful labour of their peoples" in addition to defence against agression and a guarantee of the territorial status quo.

The WTO as a military alliance. The formal basis of Soviet–East European security relations had been established earlier through a network of bilateral mutual assistance treaties signed in 1948. The USSR's occupation and Sovietization of Eastern Europe had allowed the creation of a geographical buffer zone between the USSR and Western Europe. This forward defensive zone was covered by an integrated air defence network from 1948 and provided a staging area from which Soviet armed forces stationed in Eastern Europe might be able to launch an invasion of Western Europe. As East European armed forces began in 1949 to receive Soviet equipment and were enlarged and restructured on Soviet organizational lines they assumed a titular role in Soviet military strategy in Europe.

The military Joint Command was set up in Moscow in early 1956, while in the same year the PCC created a Secretariat and Permanent Commission which was intended to facilitate common stances on foreign policy issues. The new alliance appears to have played only a very minor military role in the first half-decade of its existence, despite the post-Stalin Soviet leadership's desire to place greater stress on formal institutional channels in Soviet–East European relations in the economic and military spheres.

The USSR's relative neglect of the WTO as a military organization in its first few years of existence suggested that operational military factors were not the primary Soviet motives in establishing the WTO in 1955. The prospect of such an alliance had been raised by the USSR in the East–West diplomatic exchanges of 1954–55 over the Paris Agreements which provided for the entry of a re-armed Federal German Republic into the Western European Union and the North Atlantic Treaty Organization (NATO). The Warsaw Treaty was described as a response to West Germany's entry into NATO. At the July 1955 Geneva Conference the East proposed a non-aggression treaty between the two blocs and the creation of a pan-European collective security system: the WTO would be dissolved in the event that NATO were also dismantled, a position that was to be publicly reiterated on many future occasions. The WTO may thus have been conceived initially as a bargaining counter in the mid-1950s exchanges over European security and the role of Western Germany in the Western alliance system.

The only immediate military advantage accruing to Moscow from the Warsaw Treaty lay in the new basis provided for the continued presence of Soviet troops in Hungary and Romania after the Soviet military withdrawal from Austria pursuant to the Austrian State Treaty of May 15, 1955. In the aftermath of the Soviet military suppression of the October 1956 Hungarian uprising, the USSR signed new status-of-forces agreements governing the stationing of Soviet troops in Poland, Hungary, the GDR and Romania and in 1958 withdrew its forces — as a result of host government pressure — from Romania. The East European forces were relieved of their Soviet commanders as a concession to national feelings. Despite the existence of the Joint Command of the WTO, the USSR seemed to attach little importance to the contribution of its East European allies to Soviet military strategy, as the Non-Soviet Warsaw Pact (NSWP) forces had first to undergo reorganization and re-equipment in order to serve a useful military role in an East–West conflict.

Changes in Soviet military doctrine in the early 1960s, including large cuts in Soviet ground forces and preparation for rapid offensive nuclear operations in a European war, led the USSR to accord greater significance to the potential wartime roles of NSWP forces and to seek to integrate them more effectively into Soviet military planning. The WTO consequently acquired military functions of its own. In 1961, with the erection of the Berlin Wall and stabilization of the GDR, it became possible to institute large-scale multinational exercises involving most member-states and their number increased dramatically in the rest of the decade. These were part of a broader effort at military integration including modernization of the NSWP forces and weapons standardization.

In 1969 the military institutions of the WTO were reformed and expanded. The membership of the Joint Command was altered so as to remove the East European Ministers of Defence from a status of formal subordination within this organ to the WTO Commander-in-Chief, a position which has always been occupied by a Soviet officer and Deputy Defence Minister. The Joint Staff of the Joint Armed Forces was created with, again, a Soviet Chief-of-Staff, Soviet First Deputies and East European Deputies. A Military Council was set up, together with a Technical Council. Finally, the irregular meetings of Defence Ministers

occurring in the 1960s were institutionalized in the form of a Committee of Defence Ministers as the highest consultative body in the WTO for discussion of military matters.

The reconstitution of the Joint Command and establishment of a Joint Staff suggested that the alliance had become a distinct entity in its own right for the wartime command of the armed forces of its member-states. However, available evidence suggests that the WTO has not had a wartime operational command structure of its own nor its own mobilization and logistic support arrangements. It seems that in wartime NSWP forces would come under the command of the Soviet General Staff and would be organized in Soviet-designated fronts. Yet the bulk of East European forces would have been delegated to rear security roles ensuring the passage of Soviet divisions from the USSR to the Central Front. To ensure the capacity for surprise attack through initially un-reinforced offensive operations employing forces already in place near the NATO–WTO line of contact, the USSR evidently planned to rely primarily on its own resources at the outset of an East–West War.

The 1969 reforms did, however, underline the value Moscow attached to select East European elements of the WTO Joint Armed Forces in its offensive military strategy, particularly from the armed forces of the Northern Tier states of Poland, the GDR and, to a lesser extent, Czechoslovakia. Available evidence suggests that all of the six East German divisions, three or four Polish divisions, two or three Czech divisions and a very small proportion of Hungarian and Bulgarian forces were assigned to the WTO Joint Command in the late 1970s/early 1980s. The majority of WTO joint exercises have involved the Northern Tier armies and modernization has been concentrated in the elements of Polish and East German forces apparently assigned for service in joint battle groups integrated with the Soviet formations that would form the bulk of the forces of the wartime joint fronts. The armed forces of Bulgaria and Hungary participated in multilateral exercises much less frequently and their modernization lagged behind that of the Northern Tier states.

Despite planning to rely largely on its own forces in the conduct of a major military offensive against Western Europe, the USSR has had to concern itself with the political *reliability* of East European armed forces. The **Prague Spring** of 1968 and the purging of, and mass resignations from, the Czech officer corps following the Soviet-led invasion of Czechoslovakia cast a long shadow over what had been one of the largest and best East European military establishments. Five

Soviet divisions were stationed "temporarily" on Czech territory in the aftermath of the Czech crisis to deter further political turmoil. Despite doubts as to Czech willingness to fight in any conflict with the West, the structure of the WTO was relied upon to ensure that some Czech formations would participate in joint force groupings closely integrated under Soviet command.

Poland has had the largest and one of the best equipped military establishments in Eastern Europe and the Polish authorities seemed to accept the assignment of some of their formations to integrated offensive roles. As with the GDR, the national interest lay in a rapid military thrust into West Germany that would bring victory before Polish territory became a target for NATO nuclear strikes. Thus, the USSR could count on the Polish military to fight for a reasonable period of time in an East–West war. However, the 1980–81 Polish crisis strengthened Soviet concern for the security of rail links through Poland to the Group of Soviet Forces in Germany. The imposition of martial law in December 1981 did little to enhance the reliability of Polish conscripts in the event of war with the West and the continuing tensions in Poland probably caused Moscow to view its Polish ally as more of a liability than an asset.

Military integration was taken farthest in the GDR where, despite their small number, East German army divisions were well equipped to take part in a rapid offensive against West Germany. They come under the direct authority of the WTO Joint Command even in peacetime. The Romanian armed forces in effect were withdrawn from the WTO military structure in the late 1960s as **Ceauşescu**, concerned to assert his independence from Moscow, reoriented them exclusively toward the defence of Romanian national territory against external aggression from any quarter. Among the East European members of the WTO the forces of the three Northern Tier states were the most relevant to Soviet war planning and the WTO framework was designed to ensure that select elements of GDR, Polish and Czech forces would be available at the outset of a war in Europe to contribute to Soviet offensive operations. Yet the USSR's "coalition warfare" doctrine probably placed little faith in the reliability of its key allies in a protracted and increasingly destructive military conflict with NATO.

In the mid-to-late 1960s the **Brezhnev** leadership in the USSR sought to employ the WTO as an institution through which to strengthen the political cohesion of the socialist bloc and to enhance its role in foreign policy co-ordination. East European responses showed a desire for more genuine consultation within the alliance and

an enhanced role for the non-Soviet allies in the making of WTO military policy. The 1969 reforms of the military institutions of the WTO appeared to accord a greater degree of formal equality to the East Europeans. Yet the Soviet effort to deepen integration in the WTO prompted a protracted debate in East European politico-military circles. Many of the issues raised by the East Europeans in the late 1960s' debate stemmed from the USSR's domination of policy-making in the alliance—a characteristic of the WTO that the 1969 reforms did little to alter—and some of the bones of contention subsequently resurfaced.

The lack of any effective East European voice in the higher military bodies of the WTO was criticized most vociferously by Romania. Bucharest argued that the post of WTO Commander-in-Chief should be rotated among the member-states rather than always being filled by a Soviet general. The USSR's allies should also be consulted through the WTO on Soviet planning and doctrine for the use of nuclear weapons. Most significantly, the allies should be allowed to develop their own national military doctrines. Similar military–political concerns were echoed by Polish and Czech military officers, the latter explicitly formulating and openly airing their professional and national grievances during the 1968 Prague Spring.

In the mid-1960s, issues of *burden-sharing* were first raised in the WTO. There were complaints about the unfair offset costs of Soviet forces in Eastern Europe and the constraints on modernization of the NSWP armed forces posed by the large size of their ground forces. Moscow's export of some of its most modern weapons systems to major Third World clients before their introduction into the allied armies caused resentment in the East European military establishments. However imperfect, the standardization of weapons and equipment in the WTO tended to benefit the USSR disproportionately as it dominated the development of all major weapons systems. Soviet predominance in collective decisions on weapons programmes ensured that military research and development benefited the Soviet defence industry.

On the other hand, the USSR has consistently shouldered the lion's share of the economic burden of the WTO's collective defence effort. This has been estimated in the West to be about 80 per cent of defence spending in the alliance. Reflecting its wider superpower concerns, the USSR was estimated to spend 11–13 per cent of GNP on defence in 1979, while the equivalent estimates for its WTO allies were: the GDR 6.3 per cent, Czechoslovakia 2.8 per cent, Poland 2.4 per cent, Bulgaria and Hungary 2.1 per cent and Romania

1.4 per cent. At the November 1978 meeting of the PCC the USSR urged its allies to increase their defence spending by 5 per cent annum as a response to NATO's recent adoption of its Long Term Defence Programme requiring 3 per cent per annum increases in defence budgets in real terms. East European responses varied considerably but the inherent tensions over burden-sharing continued into the 1980s. Ceauşescu made the 1978 Soviet proposal public and denounced it, announcing a symbolic reduction in the Romanian defence budget. Though this move was coldly received in Eastern Europe, Hungary and Poland discreetly signalled their own unease with Soviet demands for increased defence spending.

There is some evidence that defence spending in the WTO has been subject to intra-alliance bargaining. Romania, for example, was able in the 1970s to reduce the ratio of defence spending to GNP while the GDR increased the ratio by more than the rate of GNP growth and responded more positively than any other ally to the 1978 Soviet request. In the first half of the 1980s the GDR increased its annual defence expenditure by 6 per cent while Poland, Hungary and Romania showed significant reductions in real term. While the maintenance of its image as a loyal supporter of Soviet policies and therefore of its value to the USSR may partly explain the GDR's response, Polish special pleading, on the other hand, allowed Warsaw to turn chronic economic weakness into a strong bargaining position.

The WTO and the defence of socialism from within. The East European regional system has been the principal ideological extension of Soviet Marxism-Leninism, buttressing internal regime security in the USSR. The maintenance of this ideological as well as military buffer zone was the core objective of Soviet post-war policy in Europe. Party, state and military links with the East European Communist Party regimes were designed to sustain the cohesion of the "socialist community". **Stalin**'s death in 1953 led to the search for more refined channels of Soviet influence and control in the region and the establishment or revival of a network of multilateral organizations to replace some of the Stalin-era levers of control and in order to diffuse growing nationalist feeling in Eastern Europe.

Within 18 months of its inception the Warsaw Treaty was used by Moscow to justify, after the event, the Soviet military suppression in November 1956 of the Hungarian move toward a multi-party political system and a security policy of neutrality. **Khrushchev** thereby made explicit the WTO's role in the defence of socialism against internal threats and indicated that no rul-

ing Communist Party could renounce its state's membership of the alliance without the concurrence of all its allies (especially the USSR). The USSR had not formally consulted the WTO in advance of the Soviet action, nor were the allies involved in the invasion itself. In the summer of 1968 the WTO provided the pretext for Soviet – East European manoeuvres in and around Czechoslovakia designed to increase the psychological pressure on the reformist **Dubček** leadership and to prepare the ground for implementation of the eventual Soviet decision — encouraged by East German and Polish calls for decisive action — to intervene in that country in August. The WTO exercises preceding the invasion were organized by the WTO Commander-in-Chief but command of the actual invasion was passed to the Commander-in-Chief of the Soviet Ground Forces.

Through symbolic participation by East German, Polish, Hungarian and Bulgarian military units, what was in effect a military intervention against an allied Communist Party leadership organized and led by the USSR gained the appearance of a collective act undertaken by the majority of the socialist community. During the 1968 Czech crisis and the crisis in Poland in late 1981 meetings of the WTO's PCC were employed in tandem with bilateral contacts to put pressure on the recalcitrant or ineffective national party leaderships. Multinational WTO manoeuvres were held around Poland in late 1981 on similar lines to the Czech-related actions in 1968.

The crushing of the Prague Spring was retrospectively rationalized in terms of the precepts of "socialist internationalism", given a sharper and more restricting interpretation under what became known in the West as the **Brezhnev doctrine**. This stressed the limited nature of the sovereignty of the states in the USSR's ideological sphere of domination. Each Communist party had a responsibility to the other Communist parties as well as to its own people. A threat to socialism in one socialist state was considered to be of common concern to all the members of the socialist community. Fraternal states were not obliged to respect the sovereignty of a state in which the socialist order was under serious threat from within, as state sovereignty could not be approached in an abstract, non-class manner. This doctrine afforded Moscow the right to intervene in allied countries in defence of or to restore the exercise of a "leading and guiding role" by the Communist Party operating on strictly democratic–centralist lines. After the invasion of Czechoslovakia five Soviet divisions were "temporarily" stationed in that country by an agreement in October 1968 and a May 1970 Soviet-

Czech Treaty included the common international-ist duty to defend the gains of socialism and strictly to observe obligations under the Warsaw Treaty.

The military structures of the WTO seem to have been shaped by the USSR in such a way as to prevent the emergence in Eastern Europe of any national military establishment that would be capable of operating independently of, and therefore in opposition to, Soviet armed forces. Moscow's allied would thus be incapable of mounting effective resistance to a Soviet-led mil-itary intervention in their internal affairs. The sys-tem of joint WTO military exercises since 1961 facilitating the integration of allied forces into Soviet offensive nuclear doctrine minimized the ability of non-Soviet regular armies to conduct large-scale operations alone. Under the pretext of joint exercises Soviet troops were able to enter the territory of allied states in which no Soviet garrison existed and to increase their numbers in proximity to states in internal crisis.

The establishment of a unified alliance military doctrine of offensive coalition warfare deliberate-ly precluded the adoption by the NSWP forces of the national defence of the homeland as their pri-mary mission. Indeed, Soviet calls in the mid-1960s for greater military integration in the WTO prompted Polish, Czech and Romanian com-plaints about the absence of national military doc-trines. Albania refused to participate in any WTO exercises, eventually leaving the alliance in 1968. After 1964, Romania refused to permit WTO exercises on its territory or to allow its troops to take part in exercises abroad. Romania did not take part in the intervention in Czechoslovakia and, alarmed by the possibility of Soviet pressure against itself, asserted the principle of exclusive national control of Romanian armed forces and moved to introduce an independent national doc-trine of territorial defence.

In peacetime the East European forces assigned to the WTO Joint Armed Forces remain under national control, as confirmed by the 1969 reform of the alliance's military institutions which ignored earlier Soviet desires for suprana-tional control of the WTO forced in peacetime. The 1969 changes improved the formal status of the non-Soviet military leaders. In addition to the reconstitution of the Joint Command, the new Committee of Defence Ministers would now meet annually. East European officers gained somewhat broader opportunities to contribute to military decision making in the alliance through the new Military and Technical Councils and Joint Staff of the Joint Armed Forces.

Despite the concessions made to allied de-mands for increased alliance consultation, the reforms did not alter the practice whereby all top positions in the Joint Command and its Staff are held by Soviet officers. The Joint Command is directly subordinate to the WTO Commander-in-Chief and is composed of East European deputy commanders and Soviet officers charged with co-ordinating the interaction of allied service branches and special services. The Soviet WTO C-in-C also has liaison officers in the allied defence ministries. The Joint Staff operates to some degree outside the aegis of the CDM and PCC, under the direct control of the WTO C-in-C. It plays the key role in integrating NSWP forces assigned to the Joint Command with the Groups of Soviet Forces in Eastern Europe and Soviet formations in the USSR's Western military dis-tricts and assigning joint missions. The C-in-C also appears to have other un-named agencies working under him to co-ordinate military doc-trine, political work in the armed forces and officer education.

All these organs and agencies serve to weaken the NSWP states' control over their national armed forces. This pattern of activity, ultimately leading to the dispersal in wartime of selected NSWP units into larger Soviet-dominated forma-tions, reflected the priority Moscow gave to com-mon regime security in Eastern Europe as the main purpose of the WTO. With the exception of Romania, which successfully detached itself from these arrangements, the East European Party leaderships largely supported this Soviet policy. Soviet intervention capability, enhanced by WTO arrangements, helped to deter challenges to the existing monopoly of political power enjoyed by the ruling East European Communist parties.

The WTO as an international diplomatic actor. One of the major reasons for the establishment of the WTO in May 1955 may have been to serve as a bargaining counter in the mid-1950s East–West dialogue over European security arrangements. The likelihood of its dissolution declined, howev-er, as the Warsaw Treaty acquired greater significance in legitimizing Soviet hegemony in Eastern Europe in the wake of the Soviet suppres-sion of the **Nagy** regime in Hungary in November 1956. Despite the interlocking network of bilater-al mutual assistance treaties that would continue to exist in its absence, the dissolution of the mul-tilateral alliance would have been seen as evi-dence of a reduced Soviet commitment to enforce political orthodoxy and alignment with Moscow in the region.

In the mid-1960s Moscow attached greater importance to the WTO as a multilateral platform from which to launch Soviet proposals on East–West arms control and co-operation. The WTO's multilateral image was improved somewhat by the 1969 reform of its organs and the institution-alization of foreign policy consultations by the creation of a Committee of Foreign Ministers in 1976. This proved useful in the multilateral conference diplomacy that began in the 1970s on European arms control and in the Conference on Security and Co-operation in Europe. The USSR also tried to achieve common alliance declaratory stances on aspects of Soviet foreign policy outside Europe, with mixed results, reflecting the tension between the increasingly global involvements of Moscow and the more limited regional preoccupations of its allies. In 1969 and on several occasions in the 1970s, the USSR tried unsuccessfully to get a symbolic East European military presence on the Sino-Soviet border. The allies were highly reluctant to accept any formal extension of WTO obligations to extra-European areas.

Moscow's concern with foreign policy co-ordination provided its allies with the opportunity to press their own interests through WTO channels. In the late 1960s the East German leader **Ulbricht** sought alliance cohesion in the face of West German efforts to establish relations with East European states before intra-German relations had been normalized. In 1969–71 he used WTO meetings to urge Soviet caution in concessions to the West over Berlin and intra-German ties. His successor **Honecker** came to play the role of model ally in the 1970s, aware that the fullest possible integration in the socialist bloc offered the most reliable guarantee of the GDR's policy of demarcation toward West Germany.

The deterioration of superpower relations following the Soviet abandonment of the Geneva Nuclear and Space Talks in late 1983 was accompanied by Soviet attempts to rein back East–West dialogue in Europe. The GDR and Hungary were keen to limit the damage to European detente caused by the breakdown of the superpower arms control process, with Budapest stressing the important role of small states in preserving European detente. There followed a debate among WTO members on the role of alliance obligations and national initiatives in East – West relations in which the GDR — wary of Soviet willingness to manipulate improvements in intra-German relations as a way of punishing West Germany for its support of US/NATO positions — took the side of Hungary against the more orthodox Czech leadership. By the end of the **Chernenko** era, it had become clear that certain WTO allies, in addition to the longstanding maverick Ceauşescu, were increasingly reluctant to sacrifice their own national interests in East–

West detente for the sake of foreign policy unity in the bloc.

In April 1985, with little fanfare, the Warsaw Treaty was renewed for 20 years, with provision for a further 10-year automatic extension. The Treaty's text went unaltered and there were no changes in the structure or processes of the organization. Less then five years later the continued existence of the WTO seemed in some doubt as the organization had lost some of its original rationale and it looked for new roles in the "Post-Cold War Era" (*see also* **Arms Control**).

The reduced utility of military power in Europe. At the end of 1988 the USSR had 29 divisions stationed on the territory of four of its WTO allies. In the Southern Tier, only Hungary hosted Soviet forces, of which there were 65,000, forming the Southern Group of Forces with their HQ in Budapest. In peacetime these forces are linked to the USSR's Southwestern Strategic Direction or Theatre of Military Operations. In the Northern Tier countries, Soviet forces are linked to the Western Strategic Direction. The Central Group of (Soviet) Forces "temporarily" stationed in Czechoslovakia since 1968 was comprised of 70,000 troops, headquartered in Milovice. The HQ for the Western Strategic Direction is at Legnica in Poland, which also hosts the HQ of the Northern Group of Forces, containing 40,000 Soviet troops. By far the largest Soviet military contingent abroad since World War II has been in East Germany. The Western Group of Forces (until recently known as the Group of Soviet Forces in Germany), with its HQ at Zossen-Wunsdorf, contained 380,000 troops in 1988.

In 1989 the members of the WTO were estimated to have the following total armed forces personnel: USSR — 4,258,000; Poland — 412,000; Czechoslovakia — 199,700; GDR — 173,000; Romania — 171,000; Bulgaria — 117,500; Hungary—91,000.

In February 1986 **Gorbachev** announced the concept of "reasonable sufficiency" as a central component of Soviet military doctrine. In May 1987 the concept was extended to the WTO in an alliance statement "On the Military Doctrine of the Warsaw Treaty Member States". The WTO declared its desire to reduce its military potential to a level sufficient for defence and repelling aggression. It sought to negotiate with the West the reduction of armed forces and conventional armaments to "a level at which neither side, while maintaining its defensive capacity, would have the means to stage a surprise attack against the other side or engage in offensive operations in general". The WTO claim to have shifted to a defensive doctrine cast doubt on its earlier assertions that its doctrine was defensive in nature. What the 1987 declaration did indicate, however, was that the technical or operational side of military doctrine would now be brought into greater conformity with its political side.

In the Conventional Forces in Europe (CFE) negotiations that began in March 1989 the USSR indicated its willingness to accept very large asymmetrical reductions in its forces in Eastern Europe and west of the Urals. Should the CFE talks produce a treaty in 1990, as expected, then the USSR's military capabilities in Europe will be radically reduced in the 1990s, making an offensive military strategy against the West impractical and severely constricting the political utility of Soviet military power in Eastern Europe. Such "New Thinking" in Soviet conventional arms control policy supported the impression that the Gorbachev leadership had indeed fundamentally revised its definition of its security interests in Europe and the ways of achieving them.

At the United Nations in December 1988 Gorbachev announced that the Soviet armed forces were to be unilaterally reduced by 500,000 men by the end of 1990. This would include the withdrawal of 240,000 personnel from Eastern Europe and the USSR west of the Urals. Of these, 50,000 would come from six Soviet divisions to be withdrawn from the GDR, Czechoslovakia and Hungary and disbanded by 1991. At the outset of the CFE talks in March 1989 it was stated that total cuts in WTO military personnel would amount to 300,000 by 1991. The first phase of Soviet withdrawals from the GDR and Hungary was to involve 20,000 troops by the end of August 1989. The second phase would run from May to August 1990.

The withdrawals from Hungary were planned to embrace approximately 25 per cent of the 62,000 Soviet troops stationed there, including a tank division and tank training regiment, an assault landing battalion and a fighter aircraft regiment. Withdrawals from the GDR would include two tank divisions, two tank training regiments and eight independent battalions in 1989, and two more tank divisions and other units in 1990. Reductions of Soviet forces in Czechoslovakia would start in May 1990, involving 6.6 per cent of Soviet troops, including a tank division. Several Soviet units in Poland would also be withdrawn.

Gorbachev also announced the withdrawal of 10,000 Soviet tanks from Eastern Europe and the western USSR. Half of these would be taken from Soviet tank and motorized rifle divisions based in Eastern Europe, including six of the 14 Soviet armoured divisions then based in the GDR, Czechoslovakia and Hungary. Four tank divisions

would be withdrawn from the GDR and one each from Czechoslovakia and Hungary. The removal of 5,000 Soviet tanks from Eastern Europe — about half of which would be the most modern types — would amount to a reduction of more than 50 per cent in Soviet tank strength there. Around 8,500 Soviet artillery pieces would be withdrawn from Eastern Europe and the western USSR, a cut of about 26 per cent, and 800 Soviet combat aircraft would be withdrawn, of which almost 300 were expected to be taken from Eastern Europe. Soviet divisons remaining in the GDR, Poland, Czechoslovakia and Hungary were to be reorganized in such a way as to enhance their anti-tank and anti-air defensive capacity and reduce somewhat their ability to fight offensively. Soviet assault landing and assault river-crossing units and equipment — associated most clearly in NATO perceptions with offensive Soviet intentions — forward deployed in Eastern Europe were to be reduced. When completed, these reductions would almost completely remove any Soviet-WTO ability to launch a short-warning or surprise attack on the Central Front.

In early 1989 cuts in the armed forces personnel of all the non-Soviet allies, except Romania, were announced. These amounted to 5.7 per cent in the GDR by the end of 1990, 8.8 per cent in Hungary, 8 per cent in Czechoslovakia and 7.4 per cent in Bulgaria. The GDR would cut about 20 per cent of its tanks and there would be significant reductions in the tank strengths of Czechoslovakia, Bulgaria, Hungary and Poland. According to the Soviet Foreign Minister **Shevardnadze**, the total WTO tank reductions by 1991 would be 12,000 and a total of 930 combat aircraft would be cut. The USSR also stated that its defence budget was to be reduced by 14.2 per cent. Defence spending cuts were then announced for 1989 by Hungary (17 per cent), Poland (4 per cent), the GDR (10 per cent), Bulgaria (12 per cent) and Czechoslovakia (15 per cent by 1991).

In mid-February, 1990, the USSR accepted the US proposal in the CFE talks that Soviet forces stationed outside the USSR in Central Europe should be limited to 195,000 men. If implemented, this would represent a reduction of 355,000 in the personnel levels pertaining at the beginning of 1989.

The end of the Brezhnev Doctrine. The new Soviet leadership under Gorbachev proved much more tolerant of domestic diversity in Eastern Europe, especially as the pace of economic and political reform in the USSR itself increased in 1987. The September 1986 Stockholm Agreement on confidence- and security-building measures in Europe repudiated the use or threat of force in relations between states, including those between states in the same alliance. In his November 1987 speech on the anniversary of the October Revolution, Gorbachev indicated that relations between Marxist-Leninist parties were to be subordinated to inter-state relations based upon peaceful coexistence. The joint Soviet-Yugoslav declaration of March 1988 declared that states were entitled to complete independence in internal affairs regardless of their socio-political system, "the forms and nature of their international alliances, or their geographic position".

By the time of Gorbachev's speech to the Council of Europe's Parliamentary Assembly in July 1989 plans for a multi-party system in Hungary were far advanced and the **Polish United Workers' Party** had been humiliated in the Polish elections in June. Eastern Europe was polarized with the Romanian and Czech leaderships being the most critical of developments in Hungary and Poland. Ceauşescu allegedly sought WTO action to defend socialism in Poland and prevent the rise of a Polish government dominated by **Solidarity**. The Soviet leaders, while responding positively to developments in Poland, were reluctant overtly to apply pressure for reform on the orthodox leaders of the GDR and Czechoslovakia.

In his Strasbourg address, Gorbachev reaffirmed that the Soviet concept of a "Common European Home" precluded the use or threat of force not only between but also within alliances. The subsequent WTO Summit meeting in Bucharest on 7–8 July collectively reiterated the Strasbourg line that the WTO members had the right to determine their domestic policies "without outside interference". Even before the East European upheavals of autumn 1989 it thus appeared that, in the words of the Hungarian delegation to the Bucharest PCC meeting, "the period of enforcing the so-called Brezhnev Doctrine is over once and for all".

The Soviet leadership refrained from an explicit condemnation of the 1968 suppression of the Prague Spring — the inevitable consequence of denouncing the Brezhnev Doctrine — until such an act would no longer, ironically, constitute interference in the internal affairs of the orthodox Czech Party leadership. Although the Polish and Hungarian parliaments denounced the invasion of Czechoslovakia in August and September 1989 respectively, Moscow argued that an official re-evaluation of the events of 1968 had to await the Czech regime's own reassessment. With the resignation of those Czech Party leaders associated with the post-1968 normalization, the new Czech Party leadership announced its own negative verdict on the invasion on Dec. 2, while, the follow-

ing day, the new coalition government called for talks on the complete withdrawal of Soviet troops from Czechoslovakia. On Dec. 4 at the Moscow WTO Summit the alliance issued a collective denunciation of the violation of Czech sovereignty signed by the five states which had participated in the August 1968 invasion.

A new political environment. The official rejection of the Brezhnev Doctrine confirmed the earlier signs that Gorbachev had abandoned the USSR's ideologically oriented concept of its security interests in Eastern Europe: it no longer viewed the survival of Marxist-Leninist regimes in Eastern Europe as indispensable. The speed with which the Communist parties of Czechoslovakia, Bulgaria and East Germany moved to surrender their monopoly on political power in late 1989 took the USSR and the West equally by surprise. The bloody downfall of the Ceauşescu regime in Romania in the "Christmas Revolution" of 1989 was followed by the sudden imminence at the turn of the decade of German unification and the Soviet Communist Party Central Committee's decision in February 1990 to retreat from its political monopoly in the USSR itself. These events confirmed the change in status of Eastern Europe from that of a Soviet sphere of domination toward the role of an uncertain and potentially unstable sphere of security.

The inauguration fo the Solidarity-led Polish government of Tadeusz **Mazowiecki** in September 1989 was accompanied by assurances that Poland would not withdraw from its alliance obligations to the WTO. Prior to a very successful visit to Warsaw by Shevardnadze in late October, the Polish government newspaper stated that Poland "respected the right of our Eastern neighbour to a security cordon and regarded it as the principal guarantee of our own security". In Moscow in November, Mazowiecki expressed his satisfaction that the WTO was ceasing to be an "instrument subordinate to ideology" and had begun to reflect the mutual interests of the member-states. He welcomed the emphatic recognition of complete national sovereignty contained in the Oct. 27 Communique of the WTO Committee of Foreign Ministers. On Feb. 11, 1990, Moscow signalled its acceptance of bilateral talks on withdrawal of the Soviet forces stationed in Poland.

With general elections due in March 1990, the Hungarian government continued to call for the WTO to adapt to changing East–West relations, while being careful to reaffirm Hungary's membership of the alliance and fulfilment of its obligations for as long as the WTO existed. Yet it was also made clear that Hungary aspired to eventual neutrality. Bowing to growing public pressure, Prime Minister **Németh** announced in January 1990 that the departure of all Soviet troops from Hungary as soon as possible was to be discussed with Moscow. By mid-February it was officially predicted that an accord would be reached within weeks.

On Dec. 8, 1989, Moscow agreed to talks with the new Czech interim government on withdrawal of Soviet troops from Czechoslovakia. By the end of February the USSR had agreed to remove a substantial part of its forces before the Czech elections in June 1990, although an accord on their complete withdrawal by the end of the year, as demanded by Prague, had yet to be reached.

The USSR began to reduce its forces in Eastern Europe as part of the unilateral Soviet armed forces cuts announced by Gorbachev in December 1988. The future levels of NATO and WTO forces and equipment from the Atlantic to the Urals were under negotiation in the CFE. Moscow was therefore reluctant to reach bilateral accords with its allies on complete withdrawal of Soviet forces from their soil before a CFE agreement was reached with NATO.

The virtual collapse of the GDR in late 1989 brought the issue of German unification to the fore, raising sensitive questions about the future boundary between NATO and the WTO and German acceptance of the post-war western frontier of Poland along the Oder and Neisse rivers. While relieved at the fall of Honecker in October 1989, the USSR initially spoke strongly in favour of the continuing existence of a separate East German state as an inalienable part of the WTO and Soviet ally. However, by late January 1990, Moscow bowed to the strength of the unification tide and concentrated on managing its implications for the existing pattern of security arrangements in Europe. After the softening of the Soviet stance, the GDR interim Prime Minister **Modrow** on Feb. 1 unveiled a four-stage plan for German unity. This envisaged military neutrality for the two Germanys on the way to federation. After also meeting Gorbachev, Gregor **Gysi** the leader of the renamed **Socialist Unity Party of Germany (SED)**, insisted that a unified Germany would have to be not only neutral but also demilitarized. This was reminiscent of the 1952 Soviet proposal for neutrality and demilitarization as the price for German unification.

Subsequent developments indicated that the USSR might not ultimately insist on the withdrawal of West Germany from NATO as a condition of German unification. The Bonn government was resolutely opposed to this and Gorbachev did not demand German neutralization or demilitarization when Chancellor Kohl

and Foreign Minister Genscher explained their plan to him on Feb. 10. Bonn argued that a united Germany should remain in NATO. Measures would, however, be agreed to prevent a NATO Germany becoming a threat to Soviet security interests in Europe. East German territory would have "special military status"; no West German or NATO forces would be deployed on the territory of the East and Soviet troops would be able to remain there for a transitional period. Shevardnadze accepted a few days later that German neutrality might be unattainable, thus presenting a much softer line on this issue than the Polish and GDR governments or even Gorbachev himself who, just over a week after Kohl's visit, seemed to reject anything less than neutrality.

Soviet anxieties over the pace and shape of the German unification process were to some extent shared by the other three victorious wartime allies. In mid-February NATO and WTO foreign ministers agreed in Ottawa on a formula for "Two-Plus-Four" negotiations to be held after the March 1990 East German elections. This forum would deal with the external implications of German unification, including the security of neighbouring states. It would approve the resolution of military issues and the confirmation of the borders of neighbouring states. It would also agree on an end to the four-power regime in Berlin and the ceding of those powers' residual rights in Germany.

Moscow found pressing common interests with the Polish Solidarity government in preserving the post-war territorial status quo in Europe in the process of German unification. Polish fears for their Western border with Germany were rekindled by the rapid pace of events there and the reluctance of the West German Chancellor either to agree that the 1970 Polish–West German Treaty had settled the border issue or to give an unambiguous commitment in advance that a unified Germany would respect the current borders of Poland. The Czech interim government also supported the Polish stance on the need for categorical guarantees for its western border. Poland's demand to be included in the "Two-Plus-Four" Talks were rejected by Bonn but were received sympathetically by the Modrow government in East Berlin. Gorbachev called for special consideration to be given to Poland's concerns. The longer that uncertainty over German border revisions was allowed to linger, the greater the potential challenge might be to the USSR's own western borders.

By the end of January 1990 the USSR had in effect accepted that it would soon lose the military advantages it had enjoyed through the garrisoning of 19 Soviet divisions in the Eastern sector of Germany. Moscow would be deprived of the ability to mount a large-scale offensive against West Germany at very short notice. Depending on the future military situation in its former sector, the USSR could also see its *cordon sanitaire* in Eastern Europe rolled back to the borders of Poland. At the very least, the WTO faced the prospect of losing one of its strategically most important members.

Towards a new type of alliance? In mid-1989 Soviet leaders began to indicate that the nature of the WTO would soon have to be changed and its institutions reformed to reflect the shifts that had occurred in Soviet policy towards Eastern Europe and radical improvements in East–West relations. Gorbachev stated in Strasbourg that as the military confrontation in Europe was reduced so the WTO would be transformed from a "military-political" to a "politico-military" alliance. In Warsaw in late October, Shevardnadze talked of a gradual shift to a more political defence arrangement in which problems of internal security within the alliance would be resolved by political means. He had recently stated that although all alliance obligations remained in force, co-operation in the WTO would have to be placed on a new basis. Gorbachev's military adviser Akhromeyev raised the possibility of disbanding the military aspects of both Cold War alliances.

Exactly what form the re-vamped WTO would take remained a matter for speculation in early 1990. The outcome of general elections in East Germany and Hungary (March 1990), Bulgaria and Romania (May 1990) and Czechoslovakia (June 1990) and the attitudes toward Moscow of the new governments were bound to have a major influence on the alliance's future evolution. Moscow would no longer be able to shape the reform debate to its own preferences. Military officials from several WTO states hinted in late 1989 early 1990 that changes in both the political and military structures of the alliance were being discussed. Soviet General Chervov stated that the Political Consultative Committee would probably be replaced by a new supreme political organ that better reflected the political diversity of the member governments and the absence of ruling Communist parties; the WTO command and control structure would have to be modified to accommodate the more nationally-oriented military doctrines being developed by Czechoslovakia, Hungary and the GDR.

In October 1989, two leading Soviet commentators provided a further insight into possible Soviet thinking on how to adapt the WTO to the end of Soviet hegemony in Eastern Europe. A "mature political alliance" was needed to institutionalize "mature alliance relations" between politically diverse and genuinely sovereign member-states. The WTO would function purely as an intergovernmental organization. Political co-operation on internal alliance issues would have equal priority with East–West co-operation in building a "Common European Home". Its institutions would focus on co-ordination of the foreign policy aspects of East–West security issues (in relations with NATO and the EC) and on developing a mechanism for resolving conflicts between WTO member-states themselves that might arise due to territorial disputes and ideological differences. They proposed the setting up of a new international secretariat on NATO lines with a Secretary General, to be sited in Eastern Europe. Each member-state would have a permanent diplomatic delegation to the WTO headquarters and permanent representatives to the alliance would meet regularly. Permanent and temporary committees would be established to examine a broad range of common military, technical, economic and social issues. There would also be a parliamentary body similar to NATO's North Atlantic Assembly.

In early 1990 the future survival of even a radically reformed Warsaw Treaty Organization seemed far from assured. Changes in its methods of operation, institutions and military relationships would have to be considerable in order to transform the alliance into one which would be genuinely attractive to the populations of Eastern Europe and their freely elected, mostly non-Communist governments. The image of the WTO as an arrangement that institutionalized Soviet political hegemony and the Communist monopoly of power in Eastern Europe would be difficult to dispel, despite the popularity in the region of Gorbachev's *perestroika* and New Political Thinking in foreign and security policy. Growing popular pressure for the unilateral withdrawal of all Soviet forces from Eastern Europe, regardless of progress on multilaterally agreed conventional force cuts in Europe and the continued presence of some US forces in Western Europe, threatened to obscure the measure of common interest shared by Moscow and its allies. One of the major justifications for the perpetuation of the Warsaw Treaty in the 1990s could well prove to be its role as a partner in the negotiation of a new European security order within the framework of the Conference on Security and Co-operation in Europe.

DS

WOMEN'S ISSUES. The new Bolshevik state in 1917 was officially committed to the emancipation of women and to equality of the sexes, as were the People's Democracies of Eastern Europe 30 years later. Their leaders' support for Marxism and for the eventual construction of communism meant that the ideas of Marx, Engels and Lenin on women were incorporated into ideology and, where appropriate, enshrined in law.

The history of these states, however, suggests that cultural resistance to the liberation of women was strong, especially in rural areas. Economic priorities and scarce resources also constrained the implementation of many policies that were necessary pre-requisites for emancipation, such as the widespread provision of kindergartens and public restaurants. In a context of rapid industrialization planned "from above", women came to be viewed foremost by policy makers as a labour resource, necessary for the fulfilment of economic plans. In the countryside they were essential participants in the collectivization of agriculture.

The numerous problems faced by women, such as an arduous "double burden" or "double shift", queues for food, the low mechanization of housework, lack of contraceptives, an inhumane abortion system, and chauvinist male attitudes at work and at home, were not discussed openly so long as ideologists loudly proclaimed that the "woman question" had been solved. Not until 50 years after the Russian Revolution was the woman question realistically proclaimed "unsolved", allowing space for discussion of "non-antagonistic contradictions", or problems, under socialism. The female double burden was finally recognized as one such problem. Underpinned by economic and demographic problems, a heated debate took place under **Brezhnev** about women's contribution to production and reproduction. More extensive discussions about female roles have been spurred by *glasnost'*. Women's issues, once taboo, came onto the agenda in the late 1980s. These included prostitution, abortion, contraception, rape and the self-immolation of Muslim women.

The Marxist heritage. Friedrich Engels, Karl Marx and August Bebel lay the foundation of Marxist ideas on women. Extensions to their thoughts were later made by Lenin, Trotsky, Aleksandra Kollontai and Inessa Armand.

According to the Marxist theory of historical materialism, women were doubly oppressed under capitalism. Firstly, capitalists exploited women workers, alongside men, because they extracted surplus value from all labour power in order to make profits. This meant that workers were paid less than the price of the product which they had produced, and they were thus "alienated" from the fruits of their labour. Engels held

that the bourgeois family was particularly oppressive because marriage was a form of business deal in which women were expected to produce male heirs for their husband's property. For a man to be sure of the paternity of his children, he had to constrain his wife's sexual behaviour and ensure that she remain monogamous.

Engels argued that the basis of honest and affectionate relationships was missing from the bourgeois family since monogamy was marred by the ownership of property, and women by extension were viewed as property by their husbands. By contrast, Engels believed that working-class men had "no stimulus whatever" to oppress women because they owned no property. This idealization of working-class families bore little resemblance to nineteenth-century life.

The overthrow of capitalism was seen as the key to women's liberation. If a capitalist economic base were replaced by a socialist one, male and female workers would not be exploited by bosses. If private property were abolished, control of the means of production would fall to the majority of the people, to the working class. The bourgeois family would be shattered because the economic foundation upon which it was built would be demolished.

The Marxist solution to women's subordination was an economic one. A change in property relations would free working men and women from the exploitation of private capital, and end women's slave status in the family. Thereafter socialist society would draw women into social production, ensure their financial independence from men, and pull them out of what what Lenin saw as the demoralising confines of "domestic drudgery".

Marx, Engels and Lenin did not reflect in detail upon how the personal could be political. They did not focus on socialization processes which perpetuate gender stereotypes, nor on the psychological results of being treated as inferior. Although August Bebel was sensitive to women's personal dilemmas, it was Armand and Kollontai who devoted more attention to male/female relations, the significance of motherhood, and why women were less politically active than men.

Inessa Armand and Aleksandra Kollontai. Armand and Kollontai maintained that women could only be liberated under socialism, yet recognized that a change in economic system alone would not transform women's lives. They supported equal rights in law, but like Lenin and Trotsky were aware that this did not entail immediate equality in life. Socialist revolution and equal rights were just necessary starting points, as were nurseries, kindergartens, public restaurants and laundries. The entire fabric of family life and social patterns had to be radically altered too, resulting in what Armand called "new household forms" and "new ways of upbringing".

Kollontai went further and advocated a radical transformation of the psyche. She argued that revolution both demanded and gave rise to "a new basis for psychological experience". She criticized conservatives for wanting to re-establish traditional family patterns and socialists for "putting off the problem until tomorrow". Although Kollontai did not offer a systematic analysis of gender roles and patterns of domination, she did attempt to incorporate interpersonal relations, including sexuality, into Marxism. Her writings on the significance of "wingless eros" (sex without love) and "winged eros" (sex with love) were not welcomed into Bolshevik thought.

Armand and Kollontai held that changes in domestic life were specific to women's liberation and integral to building socialism. Moreover, the success of socialism depended upon the success of women's liberation. Armand argued that without transforming the family "it is impossible to create a new person, impossible to construct socialism". She was aware of the enormity of the task and cautioned that it would "take time". Trotsky also warned that traditional attitudes died hard and the scarcity of material resources would mean slow progress.

Women's organizations in the 1920s. Armand and Kollontai also favoured policies to mobilize women into the workforce and to draw them into politics. Women were less politically active than men, and thus they needed to be reached, enlightened and politicized through special approaches. The women's department of the Central Committee of the party, the *Zhenotdel* (*Otdel po rabote sredi zhenshchin*), was set up in 1919. Armand and Kollontai were its first two directors. The official goals of the *Zhenotdel* were to expand the influence of the party over women, thereby winning women's support for revolution; to draw women into the party, trade unions and soviets; and to liaise with other organizations, such as trade unions, to promote the construction of nurseries and canteens. The broad tasks of the *Zhenotdel* were administratively subdivided into; organizational-instructional work; agitation-propaganda; the press; work among women of the East. Agitation and propaganda necessitated the development of an array of social organizations which targeted women at work, at home, and in regular meeting places. These included delegates' meetings, women's clubs, women's shops and red tea houses. Rural women and nomads were reached by Houses of Dekhanki and red tents.

The success of women's organizations in the 1920s was mixed. Thousands of women were encouraged to join the labour force and lead varied lives. However, many party committees opposed work among women and failed to give them unqualified support. Popular culture, especially in rural areas, viewed them with suspicion. Political agitators found their work slow and controversial; in traditional Muslim areas, they suffered especially violent abuse, and some were murdered. When in 1930 the "woman question" was declared "solved" and the *Zhenotdel* disbanded, women made up 13.5 per cent of party members.

Women and socialist construction. Central planning began in 1928. In the first 12 years of rapid industrialization the female workforce increased fourfold, from nearly three million to over 13 million by 1940. The **Great Fatherland War** (1941–45) escalated the demand for female workers, and in 1945 women comprised 56 per cent of workers and employees. Then labour shortages in the 1960s required efforts to draw the remaining housewives out of the home. The number of women staying at home fell to six million in 1970 from 18 million in 1959. The demand for female labour was heightened by a deficit of males in the population. In 1946 women of working age outnumbered men by an enormous 20 million. This severe population imbalance according to sex was mainly due to war losses of the 1940s and, in part, the cumulative effect of male deaths during the Civil War, collectivization and the purges. Although Marxist ideology proclaimed the importance of female participation in the workforce for their own liberation, economic and demographic imperatives demanded it.

Female labour became concentrated in traditional sectors of light industry, such as textiles, food and clothing, or at the bottom of job hierarchies in new fields, such as engineering, Although the Soviet state expanded job opportunities for women, access to new possibilities did not result in equal pay or equal promotion. On average, women earned two-thirds of male salaries, due to job segregation. Moreover, job segregation intensified in the early 1930s. Women were also less likely to be promoted than men. They enjoyed some upward mobility during the Great Fatherland War, but when the men returned from the front women tended to be demoted, or willingly stood down. Traditional notions of "men's work" and "women's work" reinforce these patterns.

By the 1960s, 1970s and 1980s, the segregated patterns of male and female labour familiar to capitalist economies were firmly entrenched in state socialism. Although variations were evident, such as a much higher percentage of women doctors in the USSR, they did not always mean a signficantly different result for gender. Medicine was a low-status profession, without high salaries; and even though most doctors were women, most doctors in top positions were men. The same applied to the teaching profession.

The pattern of women's participation in politics has also differed from that of men. Throughout Soviet history there has been an inverse relationship between power and gender. Women have been largely absent from top decision-making jobs on the Politburo, Secretariat, Council of Ministers and Departments of the Central Committee. In fact, there have only been two women on the Politburo—Ekaterina Furtseva from 1957 to 1960 and Alexandra Biryukova from 1988. By the 1980s, the female percentage on the Central Committee was as low as 4 per cent. Since women make up 53 per cent of the population, the gap between female responsibility in top decision making and female presence in society is huge. Moreover, the 29 per cent of party members who are female tend to be active at the local level, where they make up one third of the secretaries of primary party organizations. Moving up the hierarchy, just 7 per cent of party secretaries at regional (*oblast'*) and territorial (*krai*) levels are women.

The female profile on the soviets before they were reformed under **Gorbachev** was much higher. This, however, reflected their weakness as institutions and was in keeping with fixed quotas of female representation defined "from above". Women made up 49 per cent of the deputies to the local soviets after the elections of 1987. Consistent with the past, their presence fell below this at republic and All-Union levels. After the 1985 elections, women composed 36 per cent of the deputies to the Supreme Soviets of the republics, and 40 per cent in autonomous republics. At the apex of the system, women made up 33 per cent of deputies to the All-Union Supreme Soviet after elections in 1984. Their higher presence on the soviets, however, did not indicate an equality with male deputies. Study of the composition of the soviets shows a division of deputies into females "by hand" and males "by brain". Whereas women deputies tended to be drawn from the ranks of workers and farmers, men were much more likely to hold top party and state posts. The continuity of male deputies on the soviets was also higher than the continuity of women because men were more likely to be re-selected. A higher turnover of female deputies meant shorter political experience and fewer opportunities for affecting the legislative process.

Women in Eastern Europe. Before the East European states became People's Democracies after World War II, they differed greatly according to culture, religion, birth rates, literacy rates, social structure and level of economic development. Countries with low level of economic development and large rural populations tended to have higher illiteracy rates among women. In the late 1940s and early 1950s, between 30 and 35 per cent of women in Bulgaria, Romania and Yugoslavia were illiterate and over two-thirds of females over nine years of age in Albania. In sharp contrast, by 1921 most women in Czechoslovakia were literate.

State socialism brought equality of the sexes in law (the right to vote had already been won in Czechoslovakia and Poland in 1918 and in Bulgaria in 1938). As in the USSR, economic plans drew women into the workforce. By 1970, women made up 54.2 per cent of the labour force in Romania, 51.9 per cent in Poland, 51.9 per cent in Bulgaria, 51 per cent in the USSR, 49.1 per cent in the GDR, 48.7 per cent in Czechoslovakia, 48.3 per cent in Hungary, 47.9 per cent in Yugoslavia and 44.9 per cent in Albania. Patterns of employment, however, varied. In more rural societies, most women were employed in agriculture. Seventy-five per cent of working women in Romania worked in the fields and 50 per cent in Bulgaria and Yugoslavia. Moreover, a process of feminization of the fields took place in Czechoslovakia, Poland and Romania. For example, when the number of workers in agriculture began to decline in Romania after 1960, the percentage of women among farm workers increased from 55 per cent to 59 per cent. When men moved to towns for higher pay, women were left to work the land.

After 50 years of socialist rule, despite differences in level of economic development and urbanization, the position of women in the East European states is in three main respects similar to that in the USSR. First, women are concentrated in relatively low-skilled, low-paid jobs at the bottom of job hierarchies. Second, they are underrepresented in positions of power relative to their percentage in the population. Third, they endure a "double burden" or "double shift" of paid work topped with unpaid housework. Thus "formal equality" in law has not resulted in what ideologists refer to as "factual equality", or equality in life.

In these respects too, the lives of women in Eastern Europe are similar to those of women in Western Europe and North America. But what distinguishes them is the degree of strain generated by the double burden, which is seriously aggravated by queues, food shortages and a lack of household appliances. Inadequate housing stock and overcrowded living conditions, especially in Poland, add to domestic tensions. Daily life, however, has been made easier in the GDR, Czechoslovakia and Hungary, because consumer goods are relatively more plentiful than in other East European states. But the lack of contraceptives in some East European states injects more stress into women's lives.

A strict pronatalist policy was applied in Romania under **Ceauşescu** and this resulted in extremely restricted supplies of condoms. Other contraceptives were not available and it was illegal to import contraceptive pills (more liberal policies are however being followed by the post-Ceauşescu administration in that country). While not as officially opposed to contraception as Romania was, Bulgaria, Poland and the USSR do not produce adequate supplies. By contrast, contraceptives are more easily obtained in Hungary and Czechoslovakia and widely available in Yugoslavia. In the GDR the pill is the most available method and is free of charge.

Pronatalism can also affect abortion policy. In Romania abortion was legal from 1957 to 1966, then banned except in cases of rape, incest, congenital disease and threats to the life and health of the mother. A slight easing in the law in 1972 extended legal abortion in the first trimester of pregnancy to women over 40 and to those with four or more children. However, all other abortions (until December 1989) were illegal. By contrast, abortion in the GDR is legal and free during the first trimester. It is also easily granted in Yugoslavia. From 1956 abortion in Hungary was available on request, but due to anxiety about low birth rates, legislation in 1973 restricted abortion to pregnant teenagers, single women, married women over 35 and those with two or more children. Pronatalism in Czechoslovakia does not affect abortion policy in the same way; abortion rights were granted in 1957 on social grounds and in 1987 all restrictions were lifted. First trimester abortions are easily obtained in Poland, Bulgaria and the USSR, but in poor conditions. Abortion rates in Poland and Yugoslavia tend to be lower than in other states due to Catholicism in the former and a healthy supply of contraceptives in the latter.

Socialist policies to ease motherhood, combined with pronatalism in some states, have resulted in state support for maternity leave throughout Eastern Europe and extensive kindergarten provision. While details vary, Hungary is illustrative of the trend. Here women enjoy maternity leave on full pay for up to 20 weeks. If mothers choose to stay at home after this period, they receive a child-care allowance for a further 31 months. Working mothers have the right to two 45-minute nursing breaks a day and 60 days paid leave per year to look after a sick child under the age of three. Networks of kindergartens back up working women. However, the supply of childcare facilities varies across states, and frequently does not meet demand in rural areas. Overcrowding and the quality of care are heavily criticized.

Other variations in the way in which leaderships have approached aspects of the "women question" can be traced to differences in political regimes. At a time of enmity with the USSR and friendship with the People's Republic of China, Stalinist Albania in 1966 launched a cultural revolution "from above". A "revolutionary" attack on the superstructure of society (ideas and institutions) attempted to emancipate women, draw them into the labour force and undermine "backward customs" and religion. A very different example was provided by Romania, where the personality cult of Nicolae Ceauşescu in a highly authoritarian and nepotistic system extended to his wife, Elena **Ceauşescu**. She became a full member of the Central Committee in 1972, a full member of the CC Executive Committee in 1973 and in 1979 won ministerial status and became a vice president of the Council of Ministers. The media habitually referred to her as "comrade academician doctor engineer Elena Ceauşescu".

Despite the occasional prominence of women at the apex of party hierarchies, Politburos have generally lacked female members, or enjoyed one, at best two. In the 1980s, Yugoslavia and the GDR stood out for each having two females simultaneously on the Federal Executive Council and Politburo respectively. As in the USSR, the political involvement of women increases towards the bottom of political hierarchies.

Opposition politics has offered women different sorts of political opportunities. Before Martial Law was imposed in Poland in 1981, women made up 50 per cent of **Solidarity**'s members. But the female profile was low at the top of the Solidarity hierarchy. In 1981, 7.8 per cent of the 881 delegates to Solidarity's Congress were women. Nor did women take a leading role in the **Committee for Workers' Defence (KOR)** or in the new Solidarity government of 1989. Women, may however, play a more active role in the 1990s in a reforming Czechoslovakia. Women have already been active in **Charter 77**, and Charter policy gave women, such as singer Marta Kubisova, representation at high levels.

Party policy under Gorbachev. In 1985 the CPSU's four stated policy priorities for women were similar to those of the past: first, support for the combination of motherhood and work in the economy; second, increased opportunities for part-time work; third, more promotions of women to senior jobs; and fourth, the revival of the *zhensovety* (*zhenskie sovety*), or women's councils. Stalin, **Khrushchev** and **Brezhnev** had stressed commitment to the first priory. The second came onto the agenda during Brezhnev's leadership, largely because women wanted more flexible working arrangements. The need to promote more women had been mentioned by both Khrushchev and Brezhev, but results had lagged behind statements. And the *zhensovety* had been set up by Khrushchev to encourage more women into the workforce and into political activity.

Official documents, such as the 1986 Party Programme, included a section on women. Speeches delivered at the XXVII Party Congress in 1986 and the 19th All-Union Party Conference in 1988 also mentioned women's roles. Thus, women's issues retained a modest visibility in conventional political arenas. At the Party Conference in 1988 Gorbachev announced that the woman question was one of "state importance" and regretted that "there are still daily cares largely preventing women from enjoying their rights fully". He suggested that "this situation could exist for years" because "women's opinions were not duly reckoned with". Gorbachev declared that "we must work to change the situation essentially, so that the door should be open wide for them to governing bodies at all levels". He also noted that "questions directly concerning women's interests would not be solved without their participation and without their decisive judgement".

Three months later, in September 1988, Alexandra Biryukova was promoted to a candidate (non-voting) member of the Politburo. The general pattern of women's involvement in politics, however, remains as before, with few women in top posts. For this reason, some criticize Biryukova's promotion as tokenism and view her as a "yes-woman" of the past, more likely to raise her hand in agreement than to raise her voice in dissent.

Critics also point out that the revived *zhensovety* are weak social organizations, primarily "helpers of the party" which will not tackle many problems central to women's lives. Alternative women's groups, however, have not been among the numerous informal groups that have mushroomed since 1987, apart from a small women's groups in Leningrad which puts out *Zhenskoe Chtenie* ("Women Reading"), organized by Ol'ga Lipovskaya. The democratization of civil society has not yet given rise to a women's movement. Moreover, changes in the electoral system have resulted in fewer women being returned in 1989 to the Congress of People's Deputies.

A move away from set quotas of female representation on the soviets has meant a fall in the female composition on the USSR Supreme Soviet from 33 to 17 per cent. It seems that women candidates are less likely to be nominated to stand for election, as has been the case in Western liberal democracies. It may also be true that voters are less likely to vote for women candidates, although this awaits thorough research. However, of the 750 seats to the Congress of People's Deputies reserved for social organizations, the *zhensovety* were guaranteed 75. There has, however, been widespread criticism of these saved seats as undemocratic. With their aboliton in future elections, the percentage of female deputies is likely to plummet. Nevertheless, those women who do win seats will become deputies in their own right, not because they have been selected "from above". But there is fear that women will be discriminated against in nomination procedures and that without the protection of saved seats, democratization will mean a lower presence of women in conventional political arenas. In November 1989 a worried **Soviet Women's Committee** issued a statement calling for support for the nomination of female candidates in all forthcoming elections.

Some fear that *perestroika* in the economy will also mean a reduction in the size of the female labour force. New technology, efficiency, streamlining and rationalization mean unemployment. Since women are concentrated in unskilled work in need of mechanization, they may suffer a higher unemployment rate than men. Some policy makers and demographers believe that female unemployment could usefully cushion the impact of job losses and also contribute to higher birth rates among Slavs and Baltic peoples.

Critics of this view point out that a majority of women do not wish to leave the labour force. In her speech to the 19th party Conference in 1988, Zoya Pukhova, Chair of the Soviet Women's Committee, asked whether it was just to advocate that women should stay at home since this would deprive them of the opportunity of attaining "factual equality". She noted that research indicated that 80 per cent of women workers would not voluntarily leave their jobs.

"New" women's issues. What became different for women during the Gorbachev years was the extent of debate about their lives. By 1987 the strength of *glasnost'* was growing rapidly. It meant more detailed discussions of "old" issues, such as working conditions, the strains of the

double burden, part-time shifts, and the quality of care in kindergartens. But it also heralded an openness about "new" issues, previously taboo, which broadened the scope of the "women question". However, unbounded discussions did not take place immediately and many questions remained unasked. There was, nevertheless, a significant break with silences of the past.

At last, for example, prostitution was acknowledged to exist, whereas previously it had been declared a blight of capitalism, unknown to socialism. Although accurate statistics have not been compiled, in 1987 it was reported that the files of one Moscow police chief provided a record of 3,500 prostitutes, aged between 14 and 70. Sociological research suggests that young women become prostitutes often because their low salaries prevent them from obtaining goods that they need, such as boots at 120 rubles a pair. The money earned from prostitution frequently begins as supplementary.

Official silence has also been broken about the enormous number of abortions endured by women, even though they were legal. Soviet statistics indicate that in 1985 there were 100.3 abortions for every 1,000 women between the ages of 15 and 49, totalling 7,034,000 abortions. This average is exceeded in the Russian republic, reaching 123.6 abortions per 1,000 women. Evidence suggests that only 15 to 18 per cent of women in the Russian republic have never had an abortion. Many Soviet women endure six or more abortions in a lifetime. Lower figures in Uzbekistan, Azerbaidzhan, Tadzhikistan, Armenia and Turkmenia of 46.9, 30.8, 38.4 and 40.9 abortions per 1,000 women respectively, can be accounted for by larger family size among Muslim populations and by the inclination to reproduce rather than abort. Lithuania stands out among the Baltic states for its low abortion rate of 46.3 abortions per 1,000 women between 15 and 49. This can be explained by the strength of Catholicism among Lithuanians, who make up 80 per cent of the republic's population. Offical statistics, however, do not capture the extent of the problem. In some parts of the country illegal abortions account for 80 per cent of all abortions. Women seek illegal abortions either because they do not wish those in official channels to be aware of their plight, or because pregnancy has gone beyond the legal termination date, extended in 1989 to 28 weeks.

According to women's reports, the legal abortion system is harsh. Patients must queue for treatment, bed linen is often dirty, and medical workers show disrespect. The procedure is performed without anaesthetic; little understanding is shown for the pain and ill-health which follow. Illegal abortions result in at least 600 deaths each year from botched work and many women suffer infertility and disability.

Glasnost' has enabled the link to be made between large numbers of abortions and a lack of contraception. The spread of AIDS to the USSR has also led worried men to ask why so few condoms are available. According to the Soviet press, condoms are produced in two factories, resulting in only 220 million a year for a population of over 280 million. One critic describes the supply as "laughable" because each male citizen is able to "count on four condoms a year". Letters to the press complain that "it has been a year since the chemists in Lvov stocked condoms" and "they cannot be bought at all in Belorussia". A black market has developed and prices have apparently rocketed one hundredfold. *Glasnost'* has helped the extent of the problem to be identified. However, citizens await concerted efforts to remedy it.

Topics which edged onto the agenda with greater hesitancy include self-immolation of Muslim women and rape. One form of suicide known to exist for some time, but cloaked in silence, was death by fire. *Glasnost'* allowed journalists to report that in 1984 in Tadzhikistan there were 30 known cases, increasing to 40 in 1986. According to the press: "One girl's father would not allow her to go to school, and she could not bear it. Another lived with relatives who tried to marry her off against her will. Still another was beaten by her husband, ridiculed by his relatives, and saw no other way out." Apparently, nearly all self-immolations occur at home in front of relatives. Traditional customs which confine women clash with modern Soviet notions of emancipated women and put Muslim women under tense emotional strain. Some see suicide as the only salvation from disciplined and restricted lives.

Least attention has been given to rape. The occasional article argues that "it is time that we talked frankly about so-called sex-crimes" and regrets that the "head-in-the-sand-attitude" of pretending rape does not exist "verges on connivance with the criminals". Systematic statistics are lacking. Figures released in Belorussia suggested that in 1987 the number of rapes increased by more than 50 per cent. Reported crimes had been committed by over 200 men, of whom 43 per cent were teenagers. More than 70 per cent of the victims were minors. Several gang rapes were reported in technical schools. Due to the extent of unreported rape, these figures are likely to be highly unreliable.

Glasnost' has meant a range of social problems has been identified, and debates, some more open than others, are currently being conducted about how best to tackle them. The most important contemporary debate for women's daily lives, however, concerns the "old" issue of how to combine production with reproduction. Those who oppose female unemployment, such as Zoya Pukhova, criticize the custom of linking home, family and childcare "solely with women" and argue that it is necessary "to increase the prestige of fatherhood". In a similar spirit, delegates at the All-Union Conference of Women held in Moscow in January 1987 called for a *perestroika* of men and declared that they should share equally in housework and childrearing. The journalist Larissa Kuznetsova and philosopher Ol'ga Voronina have called for an end to men's patriarchal habits, arguing that the spiritual life of the USSR depends upon an improvement in male/female relations. In March 1989 the journal *Kommunist* carried a particularly cutting article on current inadequacies in the study of women's lives, and called for the development of disciplines of "social feminology" and "applied feminology".

As the Soviet state moves into the 1990s, it seems that many of the ideas which logically follow on from the writings of Armand and Kollontai are about to develop. Many of them are likely to be opposed.

MB

Y

YEL'TSIN, BORIS NIKOLAEVICH. Radical Soviet politician. Yel'tsin was born on Feb. 1, 1931, in the village of Butko in the Talitsky district of Sverdlovsk region. According to his autobiography, published abroad in 1990, Yel'tsin had a hard upbringing. Local harvests were bad, there were always shortages of food, and they would not have survived the war but for the milk and sometimes warmth of the family nanny-goat. Yel'tsin lost two fingers in an accident during his schooldays, and contracted typhoid fever; his father was a harsh disciplinarian. He did well at school, however, and went on to study as an engineer at the Urals Polytechnical Institute, where he met his future wife and perfected his volleyball technique.

After some years spent in the building trade, Yel'tsin began to make his way up the political ladder. He joined the **Communist Party of the Soviet Union (CPSU)** in 1961 and from 1968 onwards became first a department head, then a secretary, and from 1976 first secretary of the Sverdlovsk regional party committee. In 1985, according to his autobiography with some reluctance, he was persuaded to move to Moscow to take up a position as head of the construction department of the central party apparatus. From 1985 to 1986 he was a member of the CPSU Secretariat, becoming Moscow party secretary in December 1985. His outspoken criticism of the central leadership, particularly at a Central Committee meeting called to celebrate the 70th anniversary of the revolution in November 1987, led to his removal from the Moscow party secretaryship shortly afterwards, and from the Politburo (where he had become a candidate member in 1986) in February 1988.

Yel'tsin became first deputy chairman of the State Construction Committee at the end of 1987 and his political career appeared to be in eclipse. In March 1989, unprecedentedly in recent years, the Central Committee decided to investigate his increasingly outspoken views and determine if they were compatible with party membership. Yel'tsin, however, began to enjoy an increasingly large public following (in opinion polls in 1989 he was placed second, after **Gorbachev**, in order of esteem), and at the much more open elections to the Congress of People's Deputies in March 1989 he won over 89 per cent of the vote in the Moscow national-territorial seat in a contest with the officially-favoured candidate, the director of an automobile plant. Yel'tsin in turn became a member of the new Supreme Soviet (after one of the deputies originally chosen had stood down) and the chairman of one of its committees; he relinquished his ministerial position in order to take up his deputy's mandate, the two having become incompatible under constitutional amendments of 1988. In further elections in March 1990 he was overwhelmingly elected in Sverdlovsk to the RSFSR Supreme Soviet, and in May 1990 he was elected to the republican presidency.

Yel'tsin had by this time become joint chairman of the radical Inter-Regional Group of Soviet Deputies, and an increasingly outspoken critic of official privilege and inequality. His programme, as he set it out in his autobiography and to the Central Committee in February 1990, involved the private ownership of property (including productive resources), independence for the republics, financial autonomy for factories and farms, freedom of political association and freedom of conscience. Part of this programme, particularly its attack on privilege, enjoyed widespread support; logically, however, it entailed substantially higher prices and possibly unemployment, and this left Yel'tsin with a substantially larger following as an anti-establishment figure than as a political alternative to the Gorbachev administration.

SLW

YOUTH. The year 1989 marked a watershed in East European history. In one country after another the ruling regime succumbed in the face of mass popular protest; Hungary, Poland, the German Democratic Republic, Bulgaria, Czechoslovakia and, most dramatically of all, Romania all saw their Communist party leaders ousted, a new government installed and contested elections promised. It was likely that not one of those countries would have a Communist regime by the end of 1990. **Stalinism** was dead, and Leninism in its death throes.

In each of those East European societies it has been young people who have pioneered change: they led the strike movement in Poland, demanded reforms in Hungary, marched and demonstrated in East Germany and Czechoslovakia, and led the armed rebellion in Romania. Their collective pressure brought down governments, introduced democracy, gained the right to free speech, travel and elections. Such youth-inspired insurrections were not achieved everywhere without bloodshed, as events in Romania and China witnessed. Yet, perhaps for the first time in history, virtually the entire world, East and West, reacted in shock and revulsion at the oppression, condemning the oppressors and condoning change. The very murder of hundreds of Chinese young people by their own government acted as a spur to successful insurrection in the Communist countries of Eastern Europe, as if distancing themselves from their own history (the abortive uprisings in Poland and East Germany in 1953 and 1954, Hungary in 1956 and Czechoslovakia in 1968). Enough of lies, hypocrisy, police surveillance and outside *diktat*!

This was "revolution" from below, a unique moment in history when young people have acted successfully to change history, evoking memories of the events of 1968 in the West when youthful rebels made the qualitative leap from particular grievances to universal transformation, challenging hierarchy, institutional totems of bourgeois culture, gender, racial oppression and the colonization of everyday life by the state and militarism.

The popular "revolutions" in Eastern Europe throughout 1989 were evidently triggered by the policies of *perestroika*, *glasnost'* and democratization launched since 1985 in the USSR after Mikhail **Gorbachev** came to power (*see* **USSR**— Current political development). The apparent difference between events in the USSR and in the rest of Eastern Europe, according to many scholars in East and West, is that whereas the "revolution" is *from below* in Romania, Czechoslovakia, Poland, etc., it is *from above* in the USSR in the time-honoured fashion of Peter the Great, Catherine the Great, **Lenin** and **Stalin**, dragging a resisting, conservative population forward. **Gorbachev** himself claimed that democracy, a multi-party system and free elections were fine for the rest of Eastern Europe, but not for the USSR with its multi-ethnic community unfamiliar with democratic processes; they would lead, he asserted, to anarchy, internecine warfare and the break-up of the Soviet Union (although the constitutionally guaranteed leading role in the **Communist Party of the Soviet Union**—**CPSU** —could be relinquished). Yet while much of the change in the USSR may be attributed to wise leaders, their achievement, as J.K. Galbraith has pointed out, "is in bowing to and not resisting the deeper, more important if less visible forces that were actually in control".

Soviet youth initiative, it must be stated categorically, is by no means a response to an appeal from on high. Independently of the will of the leadership in the USSR, as elsewhere in Eastern Europe, a new youth movement began to take coherent shape in the early 1980s, well before the advent of Mikhail Gorbachev to high office in March 1985. Youth disaffection from official organizations (like the Soviet Young Communist League—Komsomol—which lost some 10 million members by the end of the 1980s) and values has been a widespread and mounting problem for the authorities. Despite the ferment and diversity in Soviet youth ranks over the years, almost all Soviet youth history has been written of in East and West in terms of the Komsomol, as if the history of Western youth was identical to that of the Boy Scouts and Girl Guides. In so far as the Komsomol became the prototype of all the monopolistic youth organizations in Eastern Europe, despite the strong traditions of the Boy Scouts, Sokol and YMCA, it will be instructive to examine its development within the Soviet Union.

The Komsomol in Soviet history. The Bolsheviks had no youth organization before October 1917. Nor had any other Russian political party. But the Bolsheviks were well aware of the potency of youth in and after revolution. As Lenin put it, "young people . . . will determine the outcome of the entire struggle". Although youth "factions" had been attached to the first workers' councils (soviets) in 1905, the birth of the Komsomol is officially set as the autumn of 1918. Between Oct. 29 and Nov. 4, 1918, 194 delegates representing as many as 120 different youth groups met in Moscow at the first Komsomol Congress. While the Congress expressed "solidarity with the Russian Communist Party (Bolsheviks)", it also declared the Komsomol an "independent organization". Its first rules reiterated that it was a "fully independent organization" whose activities were based on the "principle of complete freedom of action". Lenin had insisted that "we have to be unreservedly in favour of the youth league's *organizational independence*, and not just because the opportunists are scared of that independence. Without complete independence young people will not be able either to make good socialists or to prepare themselves for taking socialism forward". After Lenin's death in 1924 this statement was to be suppressed for over 60 years. In any case, autonomy was not to last long under Civil War conditions. In 1919 the word "independent" was erased from the Komsomol rules, and at the III Congress, held in October 1920, and at which Lenin spoke, the "freedom of action" principle also disappeared.

Similarly, initial relative freedom to elect people to top posts soon gave way to party control of nomination. Up to 1920, members elected the

Central Committee by voting for nominees individually; and since there were more nominees than posts, an element of choice obtained. In 1920 the choice was removed: delegates to the III Congress were presented with a single list of nominees drawn up in advance by the party, with only one nominee for each vacancy. Delegates had to vote on the list as a whole.

From then on up to the late 1980s, no real elections took place, not only to the Komsomol Central Committee, but to secretaryships of local committees as well. In fact, from its Central Committee down to its smallest branch, the Komsomol has functioned under direct party tutelage; and since the leading Komsomol officials were (and are) themselves party members, they have always been subject to party discipline and removable on party command. One Komsomol leader, Alexander Kosarev, was even a member of the party Politburo. All first secretaries (the *de facto* leaders) of the Komsomol have been automatically co-opted on to the party Central Committee, and all ideology secretaries to candidate membership of the party Central Committee. Serving one's time as a Komsomol leader has always been a natural step up the ladder to party leadership, as is the case with Mikhail Gorbachev.

If that were not enough to ensure party control, the party has over the years arbitrarily removed Komsomol officials and leaders whenever it has wished; and that includes the mass arrest and execution of virtually the entire Komsomol leadership during the Stalin purge years of the 1920s and 1930s. Of the first seven Komsomol leaders between 1918 and 1938, six were shot and one spent 18 years in a Magadan labour camp.

Although the principle of Komsomol organization, "democratic centralism", was from the outset far more centralist than democratic, and has remained so right up to the present in the USSR, early Komsomol meetings gave vent to dissension and the initial congresses produced many divided votes. Even during the early 1920s the Komsomol in its activities was still relatively independent, as Ralph Fisher attests in his history of Komsomol congresses: "Komsolites were still able to disagree openly on moderately consequential issues; they could still register dissenting votes; and their sharp criticism of arbitrary rule within the League could still be spread in the published record."

Even this limited freedom to demur vanished by the mid-1920s. The Komsomol could not dare question in the slightest degree the supreme authority of the party; voting on all issues became mechanical and any dissenters (or even supposed dissenters) were removed. The Komsomol was the first important organization to be purged (for its alleged "Trotskyist leanings"). Not even abstentions from voting were recorded at congresses after 1926—right up to the XX Congress in 1987 (when two opposing votes and four abstentions were recorded, though this went unmentioned in the Komsomol press and the official stenographic publication).

Initially the Komsomol was very small, the largest membership during the founding period being some 400,000— that is, under 2 per cent of those within the eligible age group, and two-thirds the then size of the party. Like the party, it aimed to recruit only "outstanding representatives" and had no pretensions at embracing all young people, even if that were possible. Although favoured by the ruling party, it had to vie for members and attention with surviving pre-revolutionary youth organizations like the Boy Scouts, the YMCA, the Jewish Maccabee and various religious youth groups. It was not until 1922 that such rivals were proscribed, although the VII Congress in 1926 still mentioned the existence of "leagues of Christian youth" and other non-Communist youth associations. From 1926 up to the *perestroika* period, however, the Komsomol had the field to itself.

The tasks of the Komsomol were set by the party as early as March 1919. It was to be a "source of trained reserves for the party" and to help the party implement its policies. It was "to organize and train young people in a Communist manner, to build a Communist society and to defend the Soviet Republic".

In the years to follow, the Komsomol retained many of the characteristics it had acquired under Civil War conditions — its organizational structure based on democratic centralism, its role of replenishing the party with young recruits, of political socialization of young people and helping the party to carry out its policies, as well as its political control by the party. On the other hand, from being a tiny "vanguard" of youth, it became a mass organization; it shifted its organizational base from home to school and workplace. And since the mid-1920s it had no formal rivals, nor had dissent, independent initiative or free elections been permitted.

Under Gorbachev, however, the situation changed rapidly. Since its peak in 1985 of nearly 42 million members—65 per cent of the eligible age group—the Komsomol had lost 10 million members by the end of the decade and is still rapidly declining, with every perceived ethnic offence — in Georgia, Armenia, Azerbaidzhan, Moldavia, the Baltic Republics — often precipitating a mass walk-out or, as in the case of the Baltic area, the severing of ties with Moscow.

In the current debate on the "youth problem" in the USSR, reconsideration of the past is constantly providing food for thought on exactly how the Komsomol evolved as it has and what are the lessons to learn. That has had implications that go far beyond the Soviet Union, for it was precisely the Komsomol monopoly of youth organizations that provided a blueprint for party control of young people throughout Eastern Europe after World War II—and the eventual revolt by young people.

The "Informals". The opting out of the official youth organization was reflected in the USSR during the latter part of the 1980s by the rapidly growing establishment of informal youth groups and clubs. While interest groups, urban gangs, religious and other unofficial and often illegal associations of young people had existed for a long time, the real "take-off" came after youth groups forced official recognition in May 1986; henceforth they were able to register and have somewhere to meet. Within a year there were said to be over 30,000, and most young people belonged to one or other informal group.

It is not easy to categorize them: some last for a few weeks; some are local, some nationwide, some are pro-, some anti-Soviet; some are a purely domestic phenomenon, some are Western-influenced. It would be wrong completely to identify Soviet "Westernized" groups, however, with their Western originals. They may take the Western name (like rocker, punk, hippy, heavy metal) and the external trappings, even experience an "affinity of spirit", yet their aspirations, lifestyles and roots are often markedly different from the Western standard-bearer. On the whole, their desire seems not to live in a Soviet version of Western society; they want, as young Westerners were demanding in the 1960s, a right to take part in the formation of policy and society, to play a meaningful and constructive role. *Glasnost'* has made this a more tangible and realizable goal than ever before. For convenience here, these groups are divided into five categories: personal interest, public pressure, Western-oriented, ultra-patriotic and illegal groups.

(i) *Personal interest groups*. The youth culture of earlier years tended to develop on domestic roots; the influence of Western youth culture was relatively weak, mainly because of the country's isolation. The unofficial youth culture of the 1960s, during the first period of "thaw" under Nikita **Khrushchev**, was primarily constructive, idealistic and socialist-oriented. The disillusionment among young people after 1964, when Khrushchev was ousted by **Brezhnev**, therefore, has to be seen in the context of the deteriorating political climate under Brezhnev. During the Brezhnev years, 1964–82, most of the institutions for official youth culture (especially the Komsomol) became exceedingly formal and bureaucratic, acting merely as "conveyor belts" for party policies. Steadily, the younger generation turned away from them, and the gap between official and unofficial youth culture, between the bland optimism of official reports and the social apathy, disillusion and distrust of authority among young people, grew wider all the time. It was in this period that the ever-growing vacuum tended to be filled by Western youth culture, with its rock music, trends and fashions, and its consumerist, hedonistic ideology.

Today, personal interest groups have expanded from clubs for lovers of jazz, folk and rock music to include young people eager to build their own housing and cultural amenities, to exchange videos and computer games. They involve women's lib groups, including those in sport—young women who have long ignored the pontification of male leaders about their participation in "harmful" sports like soccer, ice hockey, judo, weightlifting, bodybuilding and long-distance running. The interest groups, however, are no longer the dominant form of association for young people they once were. The gap between their relatively socially-beneficial activity, on the one hand, and the relatively asocial actions of modern youth appears to be widening.

(ii) *Public pressure groups*. Pressure groups are not confined to young people, though it is youth that has often inspired them and provided the bulk of their membership, as in the Green movement in the West. Such groups cover areas ignored or treated inadequately by the state, such as the environment, the disabled, orphans, one-parent families, animal protection and the preservation of monuments. It is such pressure groups that have brought into being in recent years a variety of charitable organizations, often involving the churches, such as the Soviet Culture Fund (to rehabilitate Soviet writers and artists), the Children's Fund (for orphans and underprivileged children), the Animal Protection Society launched by the poet Yevgeny Yevtushenko in early 1988, the Paraplegic Sports Federation set up in 1987 (and which sent the first-ever Soviet disabled—blind—athletes to compete in a Paralympics—in Seoul 1988), the Charity Society (for the aged, handicapped, orphans, underprivileged children and one-parent families), even a Gulliver Club for 190 cm plus tall people (with its own café, shop and marriage guidance bureau).

Some young people have taken the law into their own hands to try to safeguard the national heritage. For example, when the Moscow City

Council decided to pull down the seventeenth century Shcherbakov Palace complex, a group of students occupied the buildings and held them for two months. Not only was the complex saved, it remained in the hands of the "invaders" who set about restoring it. Politicization of parts of the youth movement has also led to the emergence of expressly political groups impatient with the distortion of socialist ideals, Marxism, Leninism and Russian and Soviet history. The formation of such pressure groups is a radical departure from past youthful activity, with potentially serious implications for Soviet society.

(iii) *Western-oriented groups*. It was with the relaxation of tension with the West during the late 1970s that various Western youth subcultures, like that of mods and rockers, hippies and punks, bikers and skinheads (known in Russian as *Britanskii uzhas*—"British horrors"), soccer and ice hockey fans, found their eager imitators among Soviet youngsters, with all the gear and artefacts, even sometimes the macho, racist and hooligan ideology. Many young people developed a defiant attitude to Soviet ideology and the older generation, giving themselves foreign names, like Charlie, Sex, Foreigner and Stalker, renaming their districts Hollywood, California, and Pentagon, even using a Russian-English patois—such as *shoesy, flat, gerl, police, high-life, parentsy, night-life, childrenyata* — and meeting in "bunkers", the central heating basements of blocks of flats.

Until 1985 the official Soviet response to such Western "infiltrations" was generally to expose bourgeois propaganda, denigrate rock, inculcate a faith in Soviet patriotism and Communism, reinforce the monopoly powers of Soviet youth organizations, do whatever possible to suppress alien culture and harass its imitators. A few, less "extreme" foreign stars, like Cliff Richard, Abba and Elton John, were invited for tours, and a list was compiled of Western and Soviet groups whose records were not to be played publicly in the USSR.

The results, we now learn from the Soviet media, have been widespread disaffection from and contempt for official organizations and Communist ideology, and an alarming increase in a wide range of deviant activity, particularly drug taking, gang warfare and soccer hooliganism. The interest in all new strains of Western pop music— from heavy metal and punk to break dancing and reggae—has burgeoned, forcing official attitudes to change and abandoning the jamming of foreign radio stations.

(iv) *Ultra-patriotic groups*. If the new liberalization has created legal opportunities for liberals and Western-oriented youngsters, it has also pro-

duced an ultra-patriotic, conservative backlash from some, especially Russian, young people determined to combat liberalization itself. In recent years a motley assortment of youths in and around urban conurbations have been forming their own clandestine vigilante groups to fight what they perceive as anti-social and, therefore (to them, axiomatically), anti-Soviet behaviour. The Rambo-style youth cult known as the *Lyubery* (named after the Moscow industrial suburb of Lyubertsy), for example, espouses violence in pursuit of the *Lyubery* mission, victims being mainly Westernized youth (punks, hippies, heavy metal fans). These "muscular socialists" are self-appointed guardians of what they see as genuine Soviet values and way of life.

The emergence of such unofficial conservative groups as the *Lyubery* partly has its source in the confusion felt by the many thousands of young men who have returned after their harrowing experience in Afghanistan (between 15,000 and 20,000 young men were sent to Afghanistan each year between 1980 and 1988). Battle-hardened and prematurely aged by their service, some "*Afgantsy*", as they call themselves, find it hard to settle back into civilian life and to accept with equanimity the Western youth culture they see around them. Because they find the authorities dragging their feet in tackling social ills, many *Afgantsy* are setting up their own veterans' associations — the "Green Hats", "Blue Berets", "Reservists", "Paratroopers" and "International-Soldier Councils", which all engage in what their members call "military-patriotic education of young people". This sometimes means meting out rough justice to those who do not share their patriotic ardour and perception of morality.

(v) *Illegal groups*. During the period of disorientation exacerbated by *perestroika*, a range of "isms" and faith has attracted youthful support, though none have so far filled the vacuum left by the once all-pervasive, and now discredited, Communist monolith. The one that is most shocking to the older generation (who lost 20 million people in World War II) is fascism. There can be no doubt the mounting popularity of fascism among both adults and young people. Naturally, as with Western rebellious rock groups like the Sex Pistols, Iron Maiden and Black Sabbath, the intention is sometimes more to shock and draw attention than actively to propagate fascist ideology.

But several reports in recent years talk of clear cut young people dressed in Nazi-imitation uniform. Some go on weekend "archaeological" expeditions for Nazi weapons, medals and uniforms to old wartime battle sites. The letters "NF" (from the British National Front) are a relatively

common sight on city walls. Press reports talk of
the murder of a mushroom picker in the woods
near Leningrad by a man dressed in SS uniform,
and the rape by two young fascists, calling themselves "Paul" and "Bormann", of two schoolgirls
on whose backs a swastika was carved with a
knife and razor. Many letters have been published
in periodicals from young "*fashiki*". And in 1987,
the paper *Leningradskaya pravda* described a
Nazi group of 39 technical college students, who
wore Nazi uniforms, home-made medals and
orders; they had their own "Führer" as well as SS
and SA sections, and had as their stated objective
the establishment of National Socialism in the
USSR.

The extreme right has reared its ugly head in a
number of nationwide organizations, such as
Pamyat', which claim as many as 20,000 members in Moscow alone and branches in 30 cities.
Its policies are blatantly anti-semitic and fascist,
yet they seem to gain sympathy with a substantial
section of particularly Russian people, especially
in the police and KGB (prosecutions, nonethe-
lees, were instituted in 1990).

Conclusions. Many of the processes described
above are mirrored throughout Eastern Europe.
Many of the problems patently originate in the
leadership's past policies. The all-embracing
youth organization and the party have clearly
estranged many young people through execessive
bureaucracy, sermonizing, hypocrisy and invasions of personal life styles. This has resulted in
indifference, on the one hand, and defiance on the
other.

Like Western youthful rebels in the 1960s,
Soviet youth opposition does not present a coherent alternative possessing public support. In neither period (whether the West in the 1960s or the
USSR in the 1980s) did a pre-revolutionary situation exist; yet by force of circumstances it was
and is young people who emerged as pioneers of
change. This cannot be said of the young people
of other parts of Eastern Europe where a revolutionary situation came to a head in 1989, and it
was young people who mainly stormed the ram-
parts and brought about political change.

The Soviet and East European youth movement, disparate as it may be, is by no means based
solely on the privileged youth (of, say, the LSE,
Nanterre, Berkeley or Moscow University), the
transient student hierarchy who, in the West, have
an uncomfortable habit of "growing up" into conservative stockbrokers or college lecturers. That
at least gives the youth of Eastern Europe a
broader base and much greater hope for the
future.

JWR

YUGOSLAVIA. *Population*: 23.8 million (est.
1988). *Area*: 225,804 sq km, of which 36 per cent
forests, 28 per cent arable, 25 per cent pasture, 3
per cent permanent crops. *Main languages*:
Serbo-Croat, Slovene, Macedonian, Albanian,
Hungarian. *Gross Social Product* (equivalent to
95 per cent of GDP on standardized Western
accounting procedures) at 1972 prices: 397 billion dinars; growth rate of GSP 1984–88: 0.7 per
cent per annum; growth rate of GSP per head
1984–88: –0.1 per cent per annum. *Foreign debt*
1988 (repayable in convertible currencies) $18.7
billion. *Trade* (1988): exports $12.7 billion, of
which 75.3 per cent to convertible currency area;
imports $13.3 billion, of which 76.6 per cent from
convertible currency area. *Main trade partners*:
EC (mainly Italy, Federal Republic of Germany);
Comecon; Less Developed Countries. *Urban
population as percentage of total*: 47 (1981).
Birth rate: 15.3 per thousand (1987). *Life expectancy*: 71 years (1981).

Political background. The Kingdom of Serbs,
Croats and Slovenes was created at the end of
World War I on the ruins of the Austro-Hungarian
Empire and surrounding territories. It included
the states of Serbia and Montenegro which were
granted independence from the Ottoman Empire
under the 1878 Treaty of Berlin; Croatia-
Slavonia, formerly under Hungarian rule within
the Austro-Hungarian monarchy; the Vojvodina,
formerly an integral part of Hungary; Slovenia,
previously an Austrian province; the Dalmatian
coast; and Bosnia-Hercegovina, formerly jointly
administered by Austria and Hungary. Macedonia, which came under Serbian control in 1913,
was granted the status of republic in the Yugoslav
state after World War II.

The unification of the South Slav territories
into a common state brought together under one
political roof a diversity of Slav and non-Slav
nations, whose linguistic and cultural background, religion and economic development were
extremely varied. These differences were intensified by the polarization of economic and political power in different parts of the newly created
state. Whereas economic power was concentrated
in the more developed regions of Slovenia and
Croatia, political power became a quasi-
monopoly of Serbia, which gradually imposed its
own political institutions on the kingdom's other
nations.

Largely because of the failure to ensure a more
even distribution of political power among its
constituent elements, the Kingdom proved incapable of maintaining popular support and political unity. In response to increasingly frequent
political clashes, King Alexander suspended the

constitution in 1929 and announced the formation of the Kingdom of Yugoslavia, which persisted until the German invasion of 1941. The subsequent national uprising against the occupying forces of Germany and Italy was fought alongside a bitter civil war between the partisans, Cetnik royalists and Croat Ustashi. The Communist-led partisan movement under the leadership of **Tito** emerged as the most decisive anti-German force, which put the party in a commanding position to take power after the war. A constituent assembly which met in November 1945 declared Yugoslavia a republic, and most of the economy was nationalized the following year.

The evolution of Yugoslavia's post-war administrative and political structure has been shaped by three main sets of factors: first, the creation of a new socialist social order on the foundations of a largely undeveloped inherited economic structure; second, a desire among the Titoist leadership to experiment with new ideas and institutions, often regardless of financial costs; finally, exogenous pressures to depart from the initial Stalinist model: Tito's rejection of Soviet hegemony in 1948 had a disastrous impact on post-war economic reconstruction, but in the longer term served as an ideological platform for the birth and development of self-management and non-alignment.

The first of a number of post-war constitutions was adopted in January 1946 and was modelled on the 1936 Soviet constitution. It formally institutionalized the six republics within a federal structure (Slovenia, Croatia, Serbia, Bosnia-Hercegovina, Macedonia and Montenegro) and two autonomous regions attached to Serbia (Vojvodina and Kosovo-Metohija). These sub-units acknowledged the mixed population and preponderance of a Hungarian and an Albanian minority respectively. Although formally endorsing the federal principle that conferred on each republic the right to secede, both state and party remained highly centralized and hierarchical. Although one Chamber in the bicameral Federal Assembly — the Council of Nationalities — was chosen by the parliaments of the six republics and two autonomous regions, the legislative and executive powers were effectively vested in the Presidium of the Assembly and the Government. In the party, the ruling principle was that of "democratic centralism" base on the "dictatorship of the proletariat" and exercised by the party in the name of the workers.

The first Five-Year Plan (1947–52) signalled the introduction of a centralized planning system and laid down an ambitious industrialization programme: high rates of investment in the economic sector combined with the modernization of the industrial infrastructure and the rapid growth of the industrial labour force resulted in growth rates of just under 15 per cent between 1946 and 1949. The break with the **Cominform** in 1949, however, abruptly severed Yugoslavia of its major source of capital and material supplies, and the economic dislocation that ensued forced the Tito leadership to reappraise the country's institutions and ideology. Thus, in the first instance, Yugoslavia's road to socialism was born of necessity, not of conviction.

In June 1950 the first law on workers' self-management was passed, handing over the control of economic enterprises to the workers and proclaiming the birth of "self-management". In practice, however, the economy was still managed from the centre.

Many of the features of self-management were incorporated in the 1953 and 1963 constitutions. The former strengthened the system of self-management in industry and added a chamber of producers to the federal and republican assemblies. The latter extended the rights of self-management to educational, cultural, health, social welfare and administrative institutions. The process of decentralization was carried a step further in 1965 with the introduction of economic reforms aimed at creating a freer market economy. Although the reforms signalled a decisive movememt towards greater autonomy for the republics and communes, they also severely weakened macro-economic management and co-ordination. With the benefit of hindsight, the economic problems that emerged in the mid-1970s and whose acuteness has been threatening the foundations of Yugoslavia's socio-political structure in the 1980s can be dated back to the mismanagement of the 1965 reforms. The implementation of over-ambitious reform policies was already in those days inhibited by the restraints imposed on decision-makers by the harsh realities of the economic and financial situation. Although firms were free to invest their own funds, this was greatly curtailed by their frequent inability to accumulate sufficient resources to make this freedom effective.

Official intervention was reduced further in the early 1970s when the introduction of "market socialism" increased the independence of managers. Under the 1971 constitutional amendments, major economic responsibilities (particularly in the fiscal area) were delegated to the republics and provinces. A system of "social compacts" and "self-management agreements" was created for co-ordinating the economic behaviour of enterprises. This involved "social agreements" between the state, the trade unions and the enterprises, and "self-management agreements" among enterprises in the same industry. As enterprises were given the right to invest in other enterprises, the longer-term objective was to enhance the mobility of capital and the formation of mergers or Joint Ventures between domestic enterprises. The constitutional amendments relied on consensus, and by implication gave each republic and province the right of veto, which was used throughout the 1980s as a powerful brake on decision making, particularly in the field of economic reform.

The 1974 constitution instituted the concept of "delegated democracy", which ensured that the delegates to the republican and provincial legislatures would be elected by secret ballot from the Basic Organizations of Associated Labour (BOALs) and other local authorities. Within the BOALs the constitution forbade the election of managerial and technical staff to the Workers' Councils in an attempt to separate policy-making from technical administration. In practice, the Workers' Councils have ceased to be the key figures in major political decisions, but have become subordinated to the enterprise directors and technical experts whose expertise has made them dominant figures in the decision making of enterprises.

National Question. "The National Question" in Yugoslavia has been foremost among the list of priorities of the post-war administration. Whilst in the 1950s and early 1960s a degree of credibility existed in Tito's claim that the National Question was on its way to a peaceful solution, most observers in the early 1990s would agree that the resurgence of overtly nationalist behaviour involving conflicting national and regional interests exacerbated the general malaise which gripped Yugoslavia in the 1980s. Judging from recent speeches by leading politicians at federal and regional levels of the **League of Communists of Yugoslavia (LCY)**, the intensity of nationalist prejudice and inter-nationality mistrust is currently at its highest since 1971, when Tito defused Yugoslavia's most serious post-war political crisis in Croatia.

Arguably the role played historically by Croat-Serb relations in the national question has in the 1980s been overshadowed by the dispute between Serbs and Albanians in Kosovo and the growing rift between Serbia and Slovenia (both issues are discussed below). Since 1971 when Tito purged the Croatian leadership of both "nationalists" and liberals", the "Croatian factor" has been conspicuously absent from the discussion of current nationality questions. Croatia has instead played a careful balancing act between the diverging interests of Serbia and Slovenia.

The introduction of economic reforms in 1965 enhanced the power of self-managed enterprises and reduced the economic powers of the federation to a minimum of macro-economic instruments. In the political sphere, a plethora of constitutional amendments in the 1960s combined with a new constitution in 1974 extended the republics' legislative autonomy and granted wider powers to government institutions at the commune level. As a result, social and political values became increasingly differentiated along regional and ethnic lines; this was sharpened by differences in growth rates and per capita incomes between republics and nationalities.

The growth of republican autonomy in the 1970s prompted a surge of nationalist feeling throughout the federation with the tendency to interpret every issue in national terms. In Kosovo, an autonomous province within the republic of Serbia, a series of Albanian nationalist demonstrations culminated in 1981 in armed clashes between students and the police, with resulting deaths and injuries. The disturbances took on overt symptoms of Albanian nationalism and irredentism, in the form of demands for the elevation of the province to the constitutional status of a republic, and in some extreme cases, for the unification of the Albanian population in Yugoslavia with neighbouring Albania. This was exacerbated in the late 1980s by the growing rift between Albanians and Serbs in Kosovo: recurring acts of Albanian intimidation directed at the province's minority Serbian population led to a growing exodus of Serbs from Kosovo and a backlash of Serbian nationalism in other regions. Although the Kosovo problem appears to be containable, the revival of Serbian nationalism which it provoked at the turn of the decade whipped up popular separatism in other republics.

Slovenia, for instance, became increasingly resentful of the inefficiency with which a significant proportion of its hard currency income was channelled into the less developed regions. This dissatisfaction manifested itself in public snubs at the power elite in Belgrade, the publication of interviews with political prisoners and the leading dissident Milovan Djilas, as well as demonstrations and strikes by factory workers against low pay and falling living standards. In Bosnia-Hercegovina, which is home to most of the country's 5.5 million Muslims, periodic trials since 1983 of Islamic fundamentalists have resulted in jail sentences of up to five years for the advocates of an "Independent Muslim State".

The ascendancy of Slobodan **Milošević**, the Serbian leader, who was brought to power by backing a renaissance of Serbian nationalism, has succeeded in exploiting Serbia's grievances against the Albanians in Kosovo. Milošević was instrumental in pushing through the constitutional amendments of March 1989 which curtailed the province's autonomy: Serbia regained control of Kosovo's police, courts and civil defence, and will in future only require two-thirds of the votes in the republican parliament to amend the Serbian constitution. As the Serbs account for about 60 per cent of the population of Serbia, and the Albanians only 20 per cent, any future referendum on Kosovo will automatically reflect the Serbian position.

A major factor that has fuelled nationalist tensions has been the failure to equalize differentials in per capita income throughout the federation. Over a 30-year period (1954–85) differences in per capita incomes have widened. This trend has persisted in spite of the fact that during some periods the growth rate in the social product of the less developed republics has either matched or even exceeded that of the more developed regions. The benefits of economic growth in the poorer regions have been negated by high rates of population growth: between the mid-1950s and the mid-1980s the natural growth rate of the less developed south has been two to three times higher than that of the more advanced north; birth and fertility rates have followed a similar pattern.

By the mid-1960s, after two decades of concentrated investment in the less developed south, the more developed northern republics began to question the usefulness of their contributions to the various development funds, on the grounds that income differentials had failed to narrow between north and south. Thus, the regional development problem was no longer solely the result of economic stagnation in the south, but one of increasing inter-regional differences.

A plethora of administrative measures over the past 25 years has failed to narrow the North–South divide, and the future of Yugoslavia's regional policy seems to hinge on the federal government's ability to break down protectionist barriers between the various republics to facilitate the flow of capital and labour. The 1986–90 Social Plan did not suggest any radical departure from the current policy of transferring investment resources from the more developed to the less developed regions. As capital-output and capital-labour ratios have shown a conspicuously high degree of inefficiency among the dominant industrial sectors of the less developed regions, the implication of widespread wastage in investment continues to be a disincentive for new investments in those regions.

Recent political developments. The Collective Presidency which took effect after Tito's death in 1980 consists of nine members: one representative from each of the six republics and two autonomous provinces, and the president of the Central Committee of the League of Communists. The members from the republics and provinces are elected to their posts every four years by deputies at the League's Congress. The Collective Presidency elects annually from its own ranks and by rotation the President of the Federal Republic, whose role is largely ceremonial. The Collective Presidency also proposes the Prime Minister of the federation whose appointment needs to be confirmed by the National Assembly.

Tito instituted the principle of "collective state leadership", which set a one-to four-year term for all executive positions, from the leaders of local communities to the Prime Minister (who has a four-year term). The main objective was to accommodate the divergent interests of Yugoslavia's nations and nationalities and thus minimize internecine conflicts. During the first year after Tito's death the country went through a remarkably smooth political transition. The collective leadership passed resolutions calling for the increase of exports to the hard currency area and the rationalization of imports, and the dinar was devalued. What the new leadership needed most was time to legitimize the succession process by cultivating the Tito myth.

However, as early as the spring of 1981, the leadership was still unprepared for the outburst of nationalist unrest in the Albanian-dominated province of Kosovo. The initially hesitant reaction to the disturbances was followed by excessively repressive measures which resulted in deaths, signalling the emergence of the first post-Tito political crisis. Although some attempts were made to apportion the blame for the unrest to outside influences (such as provocation and interference from neighbouring Albania and the activities of extreme political factions within Kosovo), the increased frequency of press reports documenting the rapidly deteriorating economic situation gradually shifted the cause of the nationalist disturbances away from political to economic factors.

Throughout the 1980s, growing unemployment, hyperinflation and the soaring hard currency foreign debt became symbols of a deepening economic crisis, which could no longer be overlooked by the politicians. Yugoslav institutions have been experiencing a "crisis of confidence", the root of which lies in a set of political and social institutions which have failed to respond adequately to changing economic pressures. The post-Tito leadership has had to preside over a period of stagnation and inflation which a plethora of stabilization measures has failed to reverse. The popular optimism of previous decades has in the 1980s given way to apathy and cynicism.

Among the attempts to explain the current political malaise in Yugoslavia, two schools of thought have emerged. One identifies shortcomings in the present system of decentralization which it suggests has not gone far enough, and argues for the transfer of decision making from the republican and regional bureaucracies to the industrial and financial enterprises themselves. According to this "liberal school", greater financial responsibility at enterprise level would help make the current crisis a more manageable task. This view contrasts markedly with the more conservative approach of those seeking to preserve a more undiluted version of Tito's legacy: this rests on a recentralization of the state and party as well as on more government control over the economy.

Internal reform attempts in the 1980s have by and large been ill-fated because of the government's failure under the premierships of both Milka Planinc and Branko Mikulić to achieve a national consensus on the solution to the country's overwhelming problems. The exercise of the power of veto by the constituent republics and provinces has become a *modus operandi* for important decisions and has been the cause of the breakdown between decision making and implementation. In the absence of such a consensus the authority of the central government has been shown to be very weak. A further deterioration of the economic situation could result in the government losing all credibility *vis-à-vis* the population and by implication strengthen the case of the nationalists, who forecast that the country is on the brink of becoming ungovernable.

The economy in the 1980s has affected different regions in different ways, sharpening internal conflicts and making the search for a workable compromise much more difficult. The depth of the conflict is illustrated in the struggle within the party itself between the liberal wing taken up by the Slovenes and Croats, who advocate various degrees of pluralism under the aegis of the LCY, and the more conservative and centralist tendencies espoused by the parties in Serbia, Montenegro and Macedonia.

The Slovene leader, Milan **Kučan**, is an exponent of local autonomy, political pluralism and private enterprise. Under his leadership the Slovene party has tolerated the burgeoning of "radical" bodies including peace movements, environmental organizations, movements for religious freedom, an independent peasants' union (with its own programme) and the influential youth movement, which vents its criticism of the LCY and the army in the bi-monthly newspaper *Mladina* ("Youth"). The Slovene argument for reform is set against the backdrop of the 1988 federal constitutional changes. The draft constitution produced in 1989 deletes all reference to the League of Communists as a constitutionally recognized vanguard party, thus reducing it to the same status as other political organizations. Other sets of proposals address the issues of economic deregulation and political (re)centralization. The Slovenes and some circles in Croatia have been campaigning for greater freedom for the enterprise in which outsiders are allowed to hold equity stakes, and where bankruptcies and takeovers would act as genuine incentives for greater efficiency.

Since the accession in September 1987 of Slobodan Milošević to the leadership of the Serbian League of Communists, the "war of words" between Serbia and Slovenia has intensified. The ascendancy of Milošević marked the end of a period of liberal experimentation under his predecessor, Dragiša Pavlović, who was forced to resign for advocating a "democratic dialogue" with the Kosovo leaders and closer economic, political and cultural ties in this ethnically troubled province. Milošević's strong populist appeal has revived dormant nationalist passions in Serbia and given him a degree of popular legitimacy in his campaign for a stronger federal centre and greater control over the two autonomous provinces of Vojvodina and Kosovo. Milošević's popularity in Serbia is matched by passionate hostility in other non-Serb parts of the federation, where it has stirred fears of a revival of Greater Serbian nationalism, and does not augur well for future political consensus.

The worsening economic situation, growing industrial unrest and political discontent in the late 1980s have revived the debate over the Yugoslav army, namely whether a further slide in the economic or political crisis would "tempt" the army to intervene to "restore order". The likelihood of military intervention seems to hinge on the army's "threshold of maximum tolerance". Some generals (for example Maj. Gen. Tomislav Perumičić argued as long ago as 1986 that "the forces of counter-revolution" had already exceeded that threshold. On the other hand, more recent pronouncements in the wake of the Ljubljana military trial in 1988 seemed to suggest that the army's high command did not favour repression as a means of strengthening national unity. Thus, although the danger of a military coup may have receded, it is still not clear where the army stands on the most important economic and political questions. The military leadership is divided among officers from Yugoslavia's various republics, and it can only be assumed that differences of opinion do exist. Thus the outcome of the debate on Yugoslavia's future within the military will be significant in the medium term, because it may either create a precedent of "openness" which may benefit other spheres of society, or alternatively strengthen the links between Serbia and the army.

In one scenario the country could be divided between Slovene politicians calling for more accountability and the Serbian party's endorsement of the army as the most effective instrument in preserving the unity of the federation. Since Tito's death, the army's influence has increased significantly. Although it has previously been essentially concerned with protecting Yugoslavia from external dangers (whether from the West or the East), the relaxation of international tensions in the **Gorbachev** era may turn its attention more towards internal conflicts.

There is broad agreement in Yugoslavia that the existing constitution of 1974 has been a powerful brake on decision making, particularly in the field of economic reform. It was against this background that the Federal Assembly gave final approval in November 1988 to 39 amendments to the constitution, with the objective of removing institutional obstacles to economic reforms. However, the amendments must first be translated into federal laws, and the process of consultation is slow as changes must be agreed unanimously by the republics and provinces.

The ideological vacuum which existed in Yugoslavia at the start of the 1990s has prompted the argument that the country's troubles are beyond the capacity of the present system, raising questions on the continued relevance of the official ideology of self-management and the monopoly of power vested in the LCY. The Slovene experiment with liberalization of the late 1980s has given rise to a system where public opinion is increasingly allowed an independent voice, and where serious moves are being made towards a multi-party system, but where the LCY has so far retained firm control of all major aspects of decision making. By tolerating the criticism of alternative movements, the Slovene leadership has succeeded in reducing the credibility gap between itself and society by encouraging an element of consultation. It intended to put its credibility to the test in 1990 in genuinely free elections. Further constitutional changes in the early 1990s appeared likely, which might usher in a multi-party system for the whole federation. (See below for further details on Slovene and the 1989 Slovene constitution.)

Economic background. Yugoslavia displays many of the features of an economy at the "middle stage" of development: on the one hand, the transformation of the economy from a predominantly agricultural to an industrial one proceeded rapidly in the post-war period. Urbanization and industrialization, combined with a low population growth, resulted in marked improvements in living standards. Between 1965 and the early 1980s, the growth in gross social product (GSP) averaged 6 per cent per annum, while the ratio of investment to GSP at 28 per cent per annum was higher than that of any OECD country with the exception of Japan. On the other hand, there was still a per capita GSP much below that of most OECD countries, high unemployment and severe regional disparities.

The high growth rates of the 1970s were followed by a slowdown in economic activity in the 1980s. This was attributable to the policies pursued in the boom years, when much of the growth was financed by foreign capital and borrowing, which was frequently channelled into unco-ordinated and prestige investments. Furthermore, the economy did not adjust to changing world economic conditions in the mid-1970s; the failure to switch over to alternative sources of energy in the wake of the upsurge in oil prices played a major part in the resulting inflation, current account deficits and growing levels of foreign indebtedness.

In response to IMF adjustment programmes (the latest of which was agreed in 1988), the government tackled the country's economic problems with mixed success. On the external front, restrictive economic policies, combined with successive depreciations of the dinar, helped to reduce the trade deficit and turn the balance of payments current account in convertible currency from a record $3.3 billion deficit in 1979 to a record surplus of $2.2 billion in 1988. By contrast, anti-inflationary policies were relatively unsuccessful, with retail price inflation averaging over 1,000 per cent in 1989. Fragmentation of the domestic market and the lack of competition have also been major difficulties.

Yugoslavia's agriculture is characterized by the "coexistence" of state (and co-operative) and private sectors. The state sector evolved in the immediate post-war period, when the government nationalized large private farms, church land and medium sized farms in excess of 10 ha. In 1986 agriculture employed 2.4 million people (25 per cent of the domestic labour force), of which 2.1 million were in the private sector, which occupies 83 per cent of agricultural land. This represented a fall of 1.4 million since 1971, when agriculture made up 47 per cent of the total domestic labour force. The declining labour force is attributed to income differentials between agriculture and industry, and employment opportunities abroad.

Although throughout the 1980s Yugoslavia has been a consistent net exporter of food, it also imports many food products which could be grown locally. A more worrying trend is the decreasing value of those exports. This is due to a number of factors: the general fall in world agricultural prices in the first half of the 1980s; the growth in protectionism for agricultural produce, particularly in the EC; the lack of a strong marketing strategy for food exports; and the low ceilings on the size of private plots which, although profitable, do not lend themselves to rational farming.

Economic efficiency criteria have been underused in investment allocation between the state and private sectors. Notwithstanding the latter's higher productivity in livestock farming, the social sector continues to be regarded as the "growth pole" and to enjoy the preponderant share of investment resources. The relative contribution of agriculture to the social product has been declining throughout the 1970s and 1980s.

The 1986–90 Social Plan makes proposals for a more rational utilization of the land and for increased output and exports. Investment plans give priority to drainage and irrigation projects, and to the food processing and packaging industry, which is seen as a major growth area for agricultural exports in the 1990s. Material incentives are available to mitigate the worst effects of agricultural protectionism on world markets, and special incentives are envisaged to step up agricultural development in the highlands. The programme for agricultural production up to the turn of the century envisages an annual increase in output of between 4 to 5 per cent, and over the period 1986–90 planned export growth is set at 5 per cent annum. These targets, however, are over-optimistic and unlikely to be fulfilled.

Industry has been the leading sector in Yugoslavia's post-war economic development: by the mid-1970s manufacturing and mining made up 45 per cent of the Gross Social Product. The manufacturing sector grew rapidly in the 1960s and 1970s, with the volume of output doubling between 1970 and 1980; this resulted in the development of a well diversified industrial sector producing a wide range of capital and consumer goods. Yugoslavia also developed important processing and extractive industries based on a sizeable domestic supply of mineral and energy sources.

The fastest growth has been in the capital goods sector at the expense of the energy and intermediate goods producing sectors. The rapid growth in industrial production in the 1970s slackened in the early 1980s, as restrictive stabilization measures depressed domestic demand for industrial goods; this was compounded by a shortage of foreign currency which reduced the level of imported raw materials and intermediate inputs. In the 1980s the main industrial sectors in output terms included metal working, electrical machinery and equipment, food processing, textiles, non-electrical machinery and equipment and chemicals.

The main force in Yugoslavia's economy is its industry, which needed to raise its level of hard currency earnings through increased exports, particularly to the hard currency area, if the foreign debt was to be contained. Much hope was pinned on the engineering sector, where domestic research and development assisted by external technology transfers resulted in the production of a diversified range of sophisticated products. Mining and quarrying also make an important contribution to the economy. Yugoslavia is one of Europe's leading producers of copper, silver, mercury and bauxite. Other mineral resources include coal (mostly lignite), non-ferrous metal ores (lead, zinc, chrome, nickel, manganese), building stone (marble), oil and natural gas, gold, platinum and uranium.

Coal is the main source of energy and this is likely to remain the position until the end of the century. A nuclear power station at Krsko in Slovenia became operational in 1981, but plans to build another one were abandoned in the wake of the **Chernobyl** accident. Consequently, coal production is set to expand from around 70 million tonnes in 1986 to 93 million tonnes in 1990 and 150 million tonnes by the turn of the century. Most of this growth will come from the exploitation of lignite, reserves of which are put at 200 years. Domestic oil reserves are small and at present rates of consumption they are not expected to last for more than another decade. Yugoslavia's energy problem was exacerbated in the 1970s when little was done to adapt to changing world market conditions: the share of oil in energy consumption actually rose in the aftermath of the 1973 oil crisis.

Faced with the need to increase hard currency earnings, since the early 1980s Yugoslavia has increasingly looked at invisible earnings as a major contributor to its balance of payments: this means mainly tourism, shipping and remittances from Yugoslavs working abroad. Although Yuogslavia is well placed with regard to both its location and climate to exploit its tourist potential, the tourist industry has been growing relatively slowly, mainly because of the lack of an adequate infrastructure (particularly in terms of shortages of both accommodation and trained personnel), but also because it has been highly sensitive to exogenous factors, such as economic recessions in the countries from which the visitors come, changes in holiday fashions and stiff competition from destination countries.

After disappointing years in 1982 and 1983, earnings from tourism recovered during the following two years to the tune of $1 billion per annum. By 1988 tourist earnings exceeded $2 billion when some nine million foreign tourists spent 52.4 million nights in Yugoslavia. However, income from tourism may be much higher, as almost 50 per cent of hard currency earnings disappears in the black economy. With this in mind, the authorities have since early 1989 encouraged individual Yugoslavs to invest in tourist facilities in the private sector, including boarding houses, restaurants and holiday resorts.

Net remittances in the Yugoslav context are made up of remittances from Yugoslavs abroad minus withdrawals from the private hard currency savings accounts held by Yugoslavs and used for such purposes as foreign travel. Workers' remittances constitute the second largest source of Yugoslavia's invisible earnings after tourism. However, the decline in remittances since 1983 represented a worrying development from the point of view of the balance of payments, and more so after 1985, since the bulk of remittances were in West European currencies, which appreciated against the dollar. This was exacerbated by the continuing rise in withdrawals from the hard currency private accounts in Yugoslavia, reflecting growing uncertainty about domestic inflation.

Throughout the post-war period the transportation and communications system in Yugoslavia has been the main bottleneck in the economy. It has proved incapable of meeting the growing demand for its services by both local users and foreign tourists and businessmen. The share of transport costs in total production costs, which is two to four times higher than in West European countries, has undermined the competitiveness of Yugoslav goods on the world market. The railway system is the main bottleneck, with 9,400 km of standard and narrow gauge track, of which only one third is electrified. Lack of investment is the main defect and stems from the failure to charge economic fares and from the diversion of funds into industrialization.

At the end of 1986 the road network consisted of 71,315 km of modern roads. The backbone of the system, the motorway between Austria, Greece and Bulgaria, is unfinished: so far only 46 per cent has been built and the target date of 1992 for completion seems highly unrealistic. Air transport would benefit from greater competition.

The national airline, JAT, uses most of its hard currency income to subsidize internal flights. New aircraft when bought from Boeing and McDonnell Douglas should enable it to compete on a limited number of routes in the newly deregulated European market. Two other companies, Adria Airways from Ljubljana and Aviogenex, a member company of the Belgrade based Genex group, are expanding rapidly and are starting to compete with JAT on some routes.

The post-war period has been characterized by housing shortages, and although considerable progress has been made in alleviating this, the quality of accommodation remains less than satisfactory. The cost of housing has increased, particularly in the more recent high inflation years, and levels of activity in real terms have been falling as investment has been curtailed by restrictive stabilization policies.

At its peak in 1980 the construction industry employed over 400,000 workers at home and over 200,000 workers abroad, but numbers fell thereafter. Housing completions fell from 52,000 in 1983 to 38,000 in 1988. The sectors' contribution to GSP has been falling steadily, but more rapidly since the early 1980s, plummeting from 9.6 per cent in 1982 to 7.3 per cent in 1987. Construction work has been hit by the international recession: the value of work abroad fell from a peak of $2.6 billion in 1983 to $1.3 billion in 1988.

Although Yugoslavia has some considerable experience of overseas construction work, competition has recently become much higher, particularly in the favoured Middle East market. Some firms have moved towards the EC, but the less developed world remains the largest market, accounting for 90 per cent of overseas construction work.

Current economic developments. High inflation in the second half of the 1980s has been eroding the social fabric of Yugoslav society, particularly within the regional context. Slovenia, for example, the richest republic, whose average income is six times higher than that of Kosovo, the poorest, has been better able to weather the inflation storm. Price rises in 1986 and 1987 were steepest in Slovenia, where relatively more efficient enterprises had enough of a market hold in certain sectors to dictate prices to the other republics, with the consequence that richer republics became price makers, while poorer ones became price takers. The rate of inflation had been accelerating throughout the 1980s, but spiralled dramatically in the last four years of the decade. Retail prices rose on average by 88 per cent in 1986, 117 per cent in 1987 and 180 per cent in 1988. The estimated annualized rate of inflation for 1989 was in excess of 1,000 per cent.

Various incomes policies have failed to contain real wage increases because of the absence of stringent monetary policies and financial discipline over enterprises. The control of the money supply has proved largely ineffective in reducing inflation for two major reasons. First, because of the growing number of foreign exchange deposits which have enabled Yugoslav deposit holders to operate outside dinar restrictions. Secondly, there has been an upsurge in the number of inter-enterprise credits which have emerged in reaction to tight monetary policy. Periodic upward revisions of credit and monetary targets throughout 1987 and 1988 have meant that this policy offered little resistance to inflation. The combination of credit ceilings on banks and low interest rates created instability in the relationship between money and income, thus undermining monetary control. There were, however, some indications in 1987 and 1988 that improvements in the methods of monetary control were put into effect. Credits extended by the national banks of the republics are now included under the credit ceiling, and the investment lending criteria used by banks, particularly to loss-making enterprises, were tightened, with some progress recorded towards achieving real positive interest rates on bank loans.

Arguably the most significant development was the introduction in early 1988 of interest rates on bank deposits, linked to inflation in the previous month. As long as inflation was going up, this still meant that the real rates were negative, but it was a move in the right direction. The bankruptcy law, which became effective in July 1987, gave firms, which have been in deficit for two consecutive years, six months to solve their liquidity problem. Failing to do so should automatically send them into receivership. The objective was to stop local banks from pumping subsidies into loss-making enterprises, which are often kept afloat as prestige industries by local politicians.

In the 1980s the Yugoslav economy became very dependent upon foreign trade as exports proved to be the major engine of economic growth. With domestic demand under severe restraint for most of the decade, the country's economic development and ability to continue with debt repayments came to depend on export performance. The share of exports (of both goods and services) in GSP increased from 10.6 per cent in 1979 to 26.1 per cent in 1985 and remained at about this level in 1988. Overall this reflects the transfer of resources to the external sector, growth in the world economy and the promotion of exports. The structure of exports changed over the 1980s, with manufactures increasing at the expense of agricultural products and raw materials. Industrial products accounted for over 84 per cent of exports in 1988, including machinery and transport equipment (31 per cent), manufactures (29 per cent), of which clothing and footwear are the most important, and chemicals (9 per cent). Given the importance of the manufacturing sector to Yugoslavia in terms both of employment and value added to GSP, the export performance of this sector was likely to be of crucial significance to its future prospects.

Export growth depends upon the strength of Yugoslavia's major trading partners, particularly the Federal Republic of Germany, Italy and the USA. In 1988 the EC took 38.4 per cent of Yugoslav exports, the USA 5.8 per cent and socialist countries 34.4 per cent, of which the USSR made up 18.7 per cent; whilst developing countries accounted for about 14 per cent. In Western Europe, the largest sources of imports were West Germany (17.2 per cent), Italy (14.3 per cent), Austria (4.6 per cent) and France 4.2 per cent).

The share of imports in GSP fell from 26.1 per cent in 1985 to 20.9 per cent in 1987 with constant pressure to limit imports through administrative controls. Figures for 1988 show an increase in this proportion but with the rate of inflation so high the GSP estimate may be distorting the final import/GSP ratio. In 1988 the major imports were machinery and transport equipment, manufactures (excluding machinery), fuels and chemicals.

The balance of payments in convertible currencies shows that the improvement since 1983 originated from a sharp reduction in the trade deficit rather than from an increased surplus in invisibles. The declining surplus in invisibles up to 1984 was due to a sharp rise in net interest payments and the relative stagnation of net income from tourism and net workers' remittances. Overall, the hard currency current account has been in surplus since 1983, falling from $779 million in 1984 to $245 million in 1986 before rising again to $1.1 billion in 1987 and soaring to $2.2 billion in 1988.

Invisible exports make a substantial contribution to the economy: the major sectors include tourism, emigrants' remittances, transport and construction earnings. Together, these earnings turn a trade deficit into a balance of payments surplus, although more recently the fall in the trade deficit itself has become significant as a result of export growth and import restrictions. With regard to tourist receipts, the country's dependence on Western Europe, and the FRG in particular, is clear; 66 per cent of tourists come from

Western Europe and of these 50 per cent are West German, with Italians accounting for a further 20 per cent. Earnings from this sector reached $2 billion in 1988. Emigrants' remittances once again show the importance of the West German economy, since 49 per cent of Yugoslav workers abroad are located there. Despite the fact that 15,000–20,000 return home each year, in 1987 a similar number left for work abroad and of these, 90 per cent found employment in the high wage Swiss economy.

One of the most severe constraints on Yugoslavia's economic development has been the level of the country's hard currency indebtedness. At the end of 1988 the gross value of that debt was $18.7 billion; $17.6 billion of this was medium- and long-term credits. Yugoslavia's external debt is untenable in the long term as it is imposing servicing strains prejudicial to growth and the proper management of the economy.

The convertible currency foreign debt rose rapidly in the 1970s and the early 1980s to $18.6 billion (excluding $1.8 billion of short-term debt) in 1982, illustrating the external borrowing required to finance the current account deficits during this period. The elimination of the current account deficits since 1983 has helped to stabilize the convertible currency foreign debt, which has stayed at approximately the same level since 1982, in spite of the adverse effects of the weakening dollar. However, the debt service burden continued to rise until 1987: debt servicing costs (including short-term debt) reached $5.7 billion in 1987 and still stood at $5.2 billion in 1988, compared with only $4.3 billion in 1982. However, as a proportion of foreign exchange receipts, debt servicing fell from a peak of 45 per cent in 1986 to 36 per cent in 1988.

External borrowing throughout the 1960s and 1970s allowed Yugoslavia to maintain levels of domestic investment well in excess of domestic saving, and to enjoy relatively high economic growth. It was not until the early 1980s when the external debt servicing became unbearable that the growth rate of GSP in real terms slackened, and became negative in 1983. The growth of Yugoslavia's debt is typical of a developing non-oil exporting country which experienced a growing external debt burden throughout the post-war period. This was largely the result of changes in the debt structure from soft government loans to high-interest private loans.

From 1981 Western creditors began to restrict new lending to Yugoslavia as obvious consequences of economic mismanagement emerged; these included a growing debt-servicing burden, large current account deficits and dwindling hard currency reserves. Given the magnitude of the external debt and of payments falling due at the time, rescheduling became imperative in 1982 and again in 1983. Since the mid-1980s Yugoslavia's creditors—the banks, governments and international institutions — have become increasingly critical of the structural economic and political weaknesses which they hold responsible for the country's faltering growth and soaring inflation.

The lack of macroeconomic planning power at the federal level has resulted in contradictory initiatives in the implementation and speed of economic reforms. As a result, Yugoslavia's economic credibility abroad has dwindled to an all-time low: a survey of the creditworthiness of East European countries based on bankers' perceptions worldwide conducted by *The Institutional Investor* in March 1989 ranked Yugoslavia second lowest after Poland.

Foreign investment. Foreign investment in Yugoslavia is just over 20 years old. Legislation was introduced in 1967 allowing foreign investors to invest directly through Joint Ventures. The underlying motive was for private foreign investment to contribute not only capital and hard currency, but, more significantly, modern technology, managerial knowhow and easier access to Western markets. The 1967 law had to be consistent with the essence of the Yugoslav system of self-management, which ruled out joint stock companies as well as the fully controlled subsidiaries of multinationals. Foreign investment was liberalized further in 1984, with a new Joint Venture law designed to bring the Yugoslav investment climate rather closer to that prevailing in Western countries, and notably permitting Foreign Direct Investment (FDI) in services, in particular the tourist industry.

The new legislation introduced in 1988 focuses on free trade zones, services and small enterprises both in the socialist and privately run sectors. Western investors are now allowed to set up wholly owned companies with limited liability, and the partners to a Joint Venture will have the right to choose the management, set the salaries and hire the workforce, implying a collective contract between the companies and the trade unions. Although foreign investment never "flocked" to Yugoslavia, in the first 10 years of the Joint Venture legislation (1968–77) 164 Joint Ventures with Western participation were set up, and in the next four years 63 Ventures were established. The largest amount of capital came from the USA, with many large multinationals (General Motors, Honeywell, Goodrich, Texaco and Chevron) setting up projects in the country. West Germans have also been active, and important investors include Bayer, Hoechst and Volkswagen. Overall, $758 million in foreign capital was invested in 252 Joint Ventures in the period 1968–84. Between 1984 and 1988 another 116 contracts brought in some $250 millon in foreign capital. By far the largest amount of capital came from French businessmen, who invested $143.2 million, $120 million of which was placed in one large tourism project.

Available data show a concentration of foreign investment in the production of ferrous and non-ferrous metals, chemicals and transport. Throughout the 1980s foreign investors have concentrated on large-scale projects in the basic industries (for example metal production), while investment in the wood and rubber industries has fallen significantly.

Recently-released figures from Yugoslavia (1989) indicate that the number of Joint Ventures has increased at a surprising rate since the new legislation took effect at the beginning of 1989. A truly remarkable 302 contracts were registered with the Federal Secretariat for External Relations in the first nine months of 1989. Just under 200 were set up as Joint Ventures and 60 as fully owned subsidiaries of foreign firms. At least one third of newly registered contracts involves West German partners, and 98 have been signed by Italian investors.

Prospective foreign investment in the 1990s will remain subject to tremendous uncertainty. As Yugoslavia's balance of payments is likely to remain fragile, existing restrictions on the use of imports and foreign exchange are unlikely to be removed completely. Although the latest foreign investment regulations go some way towards meeting foreign investors' criticisms, foreign firms are unlikely to search for Yugoslav partners on a truly large scale until they regain confidence in the economic system. On balance, the growth of Joint Ventures in 1989 reflected the end of a period of uncertainty for foreign firms, which had withheld investment funds whilst the new legislation was being drafted in 1988; it also suggests that some Western firms have decided that the new contractual arrangements provide a convenient means of maintaining a foothold in the Yugoslav market during a period of economic and political transition.

Foreign relations. Politically and militarily Yugoslavia pursues a policy of non-alignment. The first conference of the non-aligned movement was held in Belgrade in 1961 when Tito expounded the goals of non-aligned developing nations and their compatibility with Yugoslavia's foreign policy. Edvard **Kardelj**, Yugoslavia's main ideologist, developed the theme of peaceful co-existence between states belonging to different social systems. Tito attacked the Soviet intervention in the Hungarian revolution of 1956 and the Soviet-led invasion and occupation of Czechoslovakia in 1968. He rejected the **"Brezhnev Doctrine"**, whereby the Soviet Union granted itself the right on behalf of international Communism to intervene in the internal affairs of other socialist states. As a result, Yugoslavia was singled out for criticism by the socialist bloc for deviating from the path of socialism: the Yugoslav system of self-management became associated with "revisionism".

In the 1970s Yugoslavia's anti-bloc diplomacy came under renewed pressure as economically it was looking westward for loans and investments, yet ideologically it remained closer to the East. It was also during this period that Yugoslavia started to normalize relations with neighbouring Albania. Both countries converged in their perception of the threat posed by the Soviet invasion of Czechoslovakia and sought to co-ordinate their foreign policy in an effort to strengthen their internal security. Throughout the 1970s Yugoslav-Albanian relations witnessed a gradual rapprochement, which was paralleled by Belgrade's devolution of powers to the Albanian-dominated province of Kosovo.

In the post-Tito era (after 1980) Yugoslavia's influence in world politics declined, as the collective leadership in Belgrade realized that it could not muster Tito's international charisma to sustain Yugoslavia's centrestage performance in foreign policy. The leadership has instead focused on domestic economic and political issues. The constant rotation of officials has also not facilitated consistency in the planning and execution of foreign policy.

President Gorbachev's official visit to Yugoslavia in March 1988 and his endorsement of Yugoslavia's own road to socialism have eliminated much of the tension which pervaded the previous 40 years of Yugoslav-Soviet relations. This rapprochement could also lead to a radical change in the two countries' trade relations, particularly as the Soviet economy switches from defence expenditure to consumer and non-defence investment. If this is combined with the growing demand for better quality products on the Soviet market, Yugoslav industry stands to gain by deriving further competitive momentum.

The future of Yugoslavia's relations with the EC seems to hinge on two major sets of factors: first, the full convertibility of the dinar, which would be a precondition for Yugoslavia's application for membership, remains a very distant prospect. Second, in the shorter term, Yugoslav exports to the EC will continue to be restricted by

EC protectionism, which has worsened since Spain and Portugal's entry.

Republics and provinces. The six republics and two autonomous provinces which make up the Yugoslav federation are outlined below.

SLOVENIA. With a per capita income of $4,500 in 1981, twice the national average and some six times that of the poorest region (Kosovo), Slovenia's population of just under two million is the richest in Yugoslavia. In 1986, 841,000 people were employed in Slovenia, or 43 per cent of its population. Slovenia's unemployment in mid-1988 was only 1.4 per cent of the working population; the republic is the source of employment for some 80,000 workers from other Yugoslav regions, and its export record (at 20 per cent of total Yugoslav exports) compares favourably with its relative size (with only 10 per cent of the country's population). The high levels of economic growth in the post-war period brought the Slovene economy close to the levels of development of middle industrialized countries.

Thirty-two of Yugoslavia's 140 largest enterprises are based in Slovenia. Iskra (electronics) has been the flagship of Slovene industry with a bias for high technology and exports. Smaller enterprises such as Elan, the ski manufacturers, have also developed strong foreign interests. In just 20 years Elan has captured 10 per cent of the world ski market to become the world's second largest ski manufacturer.

CROATIA. Croatia is, in terms of population, the second largest republic after Serbia with 4.5 million inhabitants, or 20 per cent of the federation. Croatia makes up, with Slovenia and northern Serbia, the core of the industrial heartland of Yugoslavia. It accounts for over 20 per cent of total exports and 25 per cent of the social product. In 1985, 1.5 million people were employed in Croatia, or 33 per cent of the republic's population.

The tourist industry, which is Croatia's major source of hard currency (over 80 per cent of foreign tourists spend their holidays in the republic), is one of the most recent areas of the Yugoslav economy to be opened to foreign investment. Most foreign interest is concentrated along Croatia's Dalmatian coast, where several major projects including new hotels and marinas are being negotiated.

In spite of being better off than most other republics, Croatia also has pockets of underdevelopment for which it receives aid from the Regional Fund.

Croatia's "success story" lies in the development of its Dalmatian coast, where a combination of tourism and industrial growth has turned a once impoverished coastline into a flourishing tourist industry. Forty-eight of Yugoslavia's 200 largest enterprises are based in the republic, including the giant petrochemicals complex INA, Rade Končar (electronics) and the shipping company Jugolinija.

THE VOJVODINA. The Vojvodina is an autonomous province within Serbia. A multi-ethnic province which borders Hungary and Romania, its population of two million is made up of 54 per cent Serbs, 18.9 per cent Hungarians, 5.3 per cent Croats, 3.4 per cent Slovaks, 2.3 per cent Romanians, 2.1 per cent Montenegrins, 8.2 per cent who identify themselves as Yugoslavs and 5.8 per cent others. The economy is dependent on agriculture, chemicals and petrochemicals: 60 per

Yugoslavia—Regional distribution of social product 1954–1985						
Regions	*Social Product per capita (Yugoslavia=100)*					
	1954	*1964*	*1970*	*1975*	*1981*	*1985*
More developed regions						
Slovenia	188	187	193	201	199	201
Croatia	119	119	125	124	126	123
Vojvodina	88	116	110	121	—	—
Serbia	84	95	97	92	91	90
Less developed regions						
Montenegro	53	72	78	70	76	80
Bosnia-Hercegovina	82	69	67	69	67	70
Macedonia	69	73	64	69	69	65
Kosovo	48	37	34	33	—	—
YUGOSLAVIA	100	100	100	100	100	100

Sources: World Bank and OECD.

cent of the land is arable and produces some 5mn tonnes of maize and 1.8 million tonnes of wheat a year. Oil production, to the tune of 1.2 million tonnes per annum, and gas exploitation (one billion m^3) save Yugoslavia about $1 billion a year in import substitution. Concentration on oil and gas for consumption within Yugoslavia has constrained the province's export drive, with the result that it has accumulated a sizeable share of the country's hard currency debt (estimated at 7 per cent by the Vojvodjanska Bank in 1985).

SERBIA. Serbia is Yugoslavia's most populous republic with 9.3 million inhabitants, of whom 5.7 million are in Serbia proper (i.e. excluding the Vojvodina and Kosovo), and 6.2 million are Serbian orthodox. Serbia's capital Belgrade is also the federation's seat of government. Income and employment patterns vary enormously within the republic, with the more industrialized and urbanized north enjoying higher living standards and lower unemployment than the less developed south, where pockets of underdevelopment are on a par with some of the less developed regions of Montenegro, Macedonia and Kosovo.

Just under 50 of Yugoslavia's 200 largest enterprises are based in Serbia. Generalexport, a successful conglomerate with diversified operations in domestic and foreign trade, tourism, catering, aviation, industrial and agricultural products and finance, accounts for 12.5 per cent of total Yugoslav exports and maintains a large network of subsidiaries and representative offices in Western Europe and the USA.

Serbia is home to Yugoslavia's largest automobile factory, Cvrena, Zastava, which started to produce passenger cars in 1954 under licence from Fiat. The Zastava cars have been built with Fiat licences ever since, including the latest Yugo model, which forms part of an ambitious export development programme.

MONTENEGRO. Montenegro, the smallest republic, with an area of 3,812 km^2 or 5.4 per cent of the territory of the federation, and a population of 584,000 out of a total of 23 million, is also one of the least developed regions. In terms of per capita income, however, Montenegro ranks above the other less developed republics, and lags only just behind Serbia, thanks to recent improvements in infrastructure and the development of tourism.

Up to World War II Montenegro had virtually no industry. The mountainous terrain acted as a barrier to development. In the post-war period the development strategy focused on the exploitation of metallurgical resources. Between the mid-1940s and the mid-1970s the republic's annual growth rate averaged 6 per cent, whilst industrial growth averaged 14 per cent. Therefore, industry, which represented only 5.8 per cent of the social

product in 1947, climbed to 33 per cent in 1975 and to 40 per cent in 1986, employing 30.5 per cent of the working population.

These impressive results, however, have failed to reduce the economy's dependence on the energy intensive basic industries, which make up 70 per cent of industrial activity. Economic development remains oriented towards mineral exploitation.

Montenegro's industrial flagship is the Aluminium Combine of Titograd (KAT) which produces over 100,000 tonne of aluminium per annum, half of which is destined for the export market.

MACEDONIA. Macedonia's population at the last census (1981) was 1.9 million, including 1.3 million ethnic Macedonians, 380,000 Albanians and 90,000 Turks. Economic indicators point to widespread levels of underdevelopment: the second lowest per capita income after Kosovo, low labour efficiency, few manufacturing industries, relatively high unemployment (22.9 registered unemployed for every vacancy offered in 1987), a high birth rate (one-and-a-half times the national average) and large households. Macedonia recorded some of its highest economic growth rates in the mid-1970s, but this could not be sustained in the 1980s. Of all the less developed regions, Macedonia derives the greatest percentage of its income from light industry. The other major employers include textiles, metallurgy and the tobacco industry. The difficulties experienced by Macedonia's tobacco industry in the 1970s were exacerbated in the early 1980s when world prices fell. This resulted in reductions in the quantities of tobacco sown with some areas switching over to food production.

Macedonia has failed to attract any significant amounts of foreign investment and is only represented by a handful of companies among Yugoslavia's 200 largest firms.

BOSNIA-HERCEGOVINA. Bosnia-Hercegovina is a multi-ethnic republic with a population of 4.1 million. Muslims make up the largest group (1.6 million), Serbs total 1.3 million and Croats 750,000. In the immediate post-war period 77 per cent of the population was engaged in agriculture and a mere 14 per cent in industry. By the mid-1980s agriculture still remained a major employer with 40 per cent of the working population. After decades of low economic growth, there was an upsurge of economic activity in the 1970s when growth exceeded for the first time the Yugoslav average. Mineral resources and other raw materials abound but have not been exploited to their full potential due to shortages of investment and extractive equipment.

The 1984 Sarajevo winter Olympics gave a

boost to various public works of renovation and development in the city; this, however, did little to alleviate the widespread pockets of underdevelopment, which continue to depress the republic's average per capita income.

KOSOVO. Kosovo is without doubt the least developed region in Yugoslavia. In 1981 the income per capita was a mere $800 or 30 per cent of the national average and approximately one seventh of that of the richest republic, Slovenia. Other economic indicators confirm this discrepancy: the Kosovar population owns only 2.5 per cent of all automobiles in the country, 2.5 per cent of radios and television sets and 1.8 per cent of tractors. The province has the highest rate of unemployment (in 1987 there were 80 registered unemployed for every vacancy offered), the highest birth rate (27 per 1,000), the least developed infrastructure and the largest households. The weak infrastructure, contrasting with the province's socio-economic potential, is exemplified by a growing trade dependency on the other republics and failure to attract foreign investment in spite of an abundant wealth of energy and mineral resources.

The 1989 Slovene constitution. On Sept. 27,1989 the Slovene Parliament approved a set of amendments to the republic's constitution: these guarantee the republic's right to secede from the federation and to develop a multi-party system. The principle of Slovene sovereignty and the right to secession will form the basis for defining the republic's political and economic system within the Yugoslav federation. The changes, prompted by a desire to resist centralization, delete all reference to the League of Communists of Slovenia as a constitutionally recognized vanguard party, thus reducing it to the same status as other political organizations.

The constitutional amendments were drawn up after 18 months of discussion by the Slovene parliament's constitutional commission, made up of representatives from different political groups. For the first time in Yugoslav post-war history, there was a likelihood that the League of Communists would no longer be in a commanding position when elections were held in the spring of 1990. Of equal significance was the decision by the Congress of the League of Communists of Croatia on Dec. 13, 1989 to endorse a multi-party system and free elections, thus opening the way for a non-Communist government in Yugoslavia's second largest republic.

The Slovene and Croat "experiments" appear to have opened the way for the introduction of a multi-party system and free elections throughout Yugoslavia. A draft LCY declaration published on Dec 15, 1989 stressed the League's readiness to forgo its monopoly of power and seek Yugoslavia's "full participation in integration processes in Europe and membership of the European Communities and the Council of Europe". The document also called for radical market-oriented economic reforms and an independent judiciary to be guaranteed by a new Yugoslav constitution.

PA

Z

ZÁPOTOCKÝ, ANTONÍN. A founding member of the **Communist Party of Czechoslovakia**, whose father had been a leading figure in the Social Democratic Party before World War I , Zápotocký joined the party leadership in 1922. He helped establish the unified Revolutionary Trades Union Movement (ROH) after World War II. He succeeded Klement **Gottwald** as Prime Minister in June 1948 and became President of Czechoslovakia following Gottwald's death in March 1953. Born in 1884, Zápotocký died in November 1957.

GW

ZHENSOVETY (USSR — Zhenskie Sovety). *Zhensovety* (women's councils) were promoted by Nikita **Khrushchev** after 1958. They were set up in factories, offices and on farms and at *oblast'*, *krai* and *raion* levels of administration. Their aims were several: to involve women in social activity and politics; to draw housewives into the workforce; to promote Marxism-Leninism; to defend women's interests. The *zhensovety* did not share a uniform pattern of work; some were subordinate to the party, others to the soviets and still others worked closely with the trade unions.

Although they formally existed under **Brezhnev**, the *zhensovety* were more active in some parts of the Union than in others. In 1986, at the XXVII Party Congress, **Gorbachev** announced that they should be revived. By April 1988 there were 236,000 *zhensovety* involving 2.3 million female activists. As before, their work is tailored to local conditions. It is common for the *zhensovet* to be organized into sections, such as "production", "daily life and social problems", "children" and "culture". A particularly popular demand from women workers to the *zhensovet* is that is organizes shopping facilities in the workplace to ease the burden of queueing after work. By 1989 not all factories had formed their own *zhensovet*, especially those with active trade unions. Distinct from the past, the *zhensovety* are now hierarchically organized and come under the umbrella of the **Soviet Women's Committee**. In the elections to the Congress of People's Deputies in 1989, the *zhensovety* enjoyed 75 of the 750 seats reserved for social organizations.

MB

ZHIVKOV, TODOR KHRISTOV. Leader of Bulgaria for most of the post-war period. First/General Secretary of the **Bulgarian Communist Party (BCP)** 1954–89, simultaneously Chairman of the Council of Ministers (Prime Minister) 1962–71 and Chairman of the State Council (President) 1971–89; "retired" November 1989, thereafter disgraced.

Born in 1911 into a peasant family. Todor Zhivkov moved to Sofia as a youth and worked as a printer. He joined the BCP in 1931 and held various minor offices in it during the 1930s while continuing his printing work. He rose to greater prominence as a partisan fighter during the latter part of World War II, and was entrusted by the party with organizing the September 1944 coup in Sofia. Post-war, he served as, *inter alia*, party boss in the capital, until he was promoted to the Secretariat in 1950.

In 1954 he was appointed to what then appeared to be the subordinate post of First Secretary of the BCP through the influence of the previous incumbent, his patron Vulko Chervenkov, who remained Prime Minister and apparent "number one". Through a combination of the patronage powers of the First Secretaryship, astute exploitation of the destalinization issue, and the support of Nikita **Khrushchev** — the chief destalinizer in Moscow—Zhivkov emerged as the dominant leader marginalizing Chervenkov. After some years of consolidation and manoeuvring, Zhivkov enhanced his position further in 1962 by taking over the premiership, thus achieving the combination of offices which his patron Khrushchev now enjoyed in Moscow.

The fall of Khrushchev in 1964 does not appear to have weakened Zhivkov unduly: he survived a coup attempt by military and party elements in the following year, apparently with Soviet help, and enjoyed good relations with Khrushchev's successor Leonid **Brezhnev**. And he showed himself a master in the art of maintaining power in the succeeding two decades, playing factions off against each other and eliminating possible rivals whom he had himself elevated (Mitko Grigorov in 1966, Boris Velchev in 1974, Aleksandur **Lilov** in 1983). The fact that Zhivkov exchanged the premiership for the presidency in 1971 signalled no weakening of his position, since it was in the context of a new constitution that enhanced the presidency's status. In the late 1970s Zhivkov even managed to manoeuvre his gifted daughter Lyudmila into a position of sufficient prominence to prompt speculation about a possible dynastic succession at the head of the Bulgarian party and state, but any such designs were cut short by her early death in 1981.

In the second half of the 1980s, Zhivkov's position began to deteriorate for various reasons. Economic performance faltered; relations between Zhivkov and Soviet leader Mikhail **Gorbachev** were reportedly bad; and Zhivkov was faced with pressure from both inside and outside Bulgaria to emulate Soviet economic reform, democratization, and *glasnost'*. On the economic front, Zhivkov responded with conspicuous activity that had some genuine reformist substance but in the end amounted more to a combination of formalistic renamings and disruptive reorganizations, and achieved little. Politically, he allowed a brief period of *glasnost'*, but imposed a clampdown when it seemed to be getting out of hand and leading to a challenge by Chudomir **Aleksandrov**, mooted at the time as a possible "Bulgarian Gorbachev". Aleksandrov was decisively purged from the leadership in mid-1988, but Zhivkov's reprieve was temporary only. Party opinion was alienated further by the disastrous economic and diplomatic effects of Zhivkov's policy towards ethnic **Turks in Bulgaria**; by the worsening economic situation and Bulgaria's burgeoning foreign debt; by the offensive nepotism that elevated Zhivkov's drunkard son Vladimir to an undeserved Central Committee post in mid-1989; and by the alarming advancement of erstwhile police chief Dimitur **Stoyanov** to the post of party personnel chief and thus to a strong position in an eventual contest to succeed Zhivkov — a reliance on the police that was the corollary of Zhivkov's move against the liberal wing of the party represented by Aleksandrov.

In a characteristic change of tack, Zhivkov began to sound more progressive in his speeches in autumn 1989 — as did Stoyanov. In this, both were no doubt acknowledging the underlying strength of the forces for change, and trying to reach some accommodation with them. But this last-minute conversion came too late, and a coalition against Zhivkov was assembled by Foreign Minister Petur **Mladenov**, toppling him at a CC Plenum on Nov. 10, 1989. Zhivkov's departure was presented at the time as relatively graceful: he retired "with thanks" and "at his own request". But within a month, the Central Committee's thanks had been publicly withdrawn, and Zhivkov found himself under house arrest.

RW

ZOG, KING. King Zog reigned in Albania from Sept. 1, 1928 to April 7, 1939. Before crowning himself he had been Minister of the Interior and then President. During his earlier period he called himself Zogu, previously Zogolli. Zog's initial power base was in Mat (north-central Albania). In 1924 he overthrew the government of Bishop Fan Noli with Yugoslav military aid. As King, he pursued a policy partly of resistance towards but mainly of accommodation with the Italians, but fled the country when the Italians invaded in 1939. Zog survived numerous assassination attempts; in Vienna he even fired back at his assailant. Although a Muslim, he married (in 1938) a Hungarian Roman Catholic. During his reign efforts were made in education and towards emancipation of women. Economic progress was vitiated by the Great Depression, which hit Albania severely, but included some road building and the introduction of a national currency (the lek). Above all, suppression of the blood-feud brought economic gain as well as the strengthening of national unity.

RH

INDEX OF ENTRIES

This index records all individual entries in the Encyclopaedia. In addition, and to supplement the numerous cross references given in bold in the text, country-specific entries are grouped below under the name of the country to which they refer.